PriceWaterhouseCoopers

Manual of Accounting
Management Reports and Governance – 2011

UK Accounting Consulting Services
PricewaterhouseCoopers LLP, Chartered Accountants

Published by

 CCH
a Wolters Kluwer business

Wolters Kluwer
145 London Road
Kingston upon Thames
KT2 6SR
Telephone: 0844 561 8166
Facsimile: +44 (0) 208 547 2638
E-mail: cch@wolterskluwer.co.uk
Website: www.cch.co.uk

ISBN 978–1–84798–345–9

Printed and bound in Italy by Legoprint
Typeset by YHT Limited, London

British Library Cataloguing-in-Publication Data.
A catalogue record for this book is available from the British Library.

Authors

PricewaterhouseCoopers' Manual of Accounting – Management Reports and Governance is written by the PricewaterhouseCoopers LLP's UK Accounting Consulting Services team.

Writing team led by
Barry Johnson
Peter Holgate

Authors, contributors and reviewers

Michelle Amjad	Joanna Malvern
Hayley Bartlett	Avni Mashru
Suzanne Baughen	Helen McCann
Erin Bennett	Malcolm Millar
Elizabeth Buckley	Janet Milligan
Daniel Blight	John Patterson
Gillian Burrows	Monica Peters
Dasa Brynjolffssen	Jennifer Peterson
Lisa Dang	Tom Quinn
Kate Elsdon	Marian Lovelace
Ilaria Evans	Iain Selfridge
Michael Gaull	Laura Taylor
Jyoti Ghosh	Sandra Thompson
Jonathan Gibson	Sarah Troughton
Imre Guba	Gail Tucker
Rodney Hamill	Dewald T van-den-Berg
Margaret Heneghan	Eleonora Van den Haute
Mike Higgs	Mike P Vickery
Peter Hogarth	Simon Whitehead
Claire L Howells	Barbara Willis
Wendy Jessup	Michelle Winarto
Hannah King	Katie Woods
Sabine Koch	

Preface

PricewaterhouseCoopers' Manual of Accounting – Management reports and governance is a practical guide to the legal and other regulatory requirements that impact elements of financial statements that are common to users of both IFRS and UK GAAP, often referred to as the 'front half' of the financial statements, together with other legal issues. The Manual includes practical advice based on our work in the PricewaterhouseCoopers LLP's UK Accounting Consulting Services team in advising the firm's clients, partners and staff.

The Manual deals with the requirements of the new Combined Code on corporate governance and looks at the rules for the business review and guidance for the operating and financial review. Also explained are the directors' report and their remuneration report, together with the legality of directors' loans. The legal aspects concerning areas such as company reporting periods and purchase of own shares, together with their accounting implications, are fully explored. This book supplements our three books which deal with the latter half of the financial statements: 'PricewaterhouseCoopers' Manual of Accounting – IFRS for the UK', 'PricewaterhouseCoopers' Manual of Accounting – UK GAAP' and PricewaterhouseCoopers' Manual of Accounting – Financial instruments'.

Even in a work of this size it is not possible to cover every aspect of company reporting.

We hope that finance directors, accountants, legal practitioners, company administrators, financial advisers and auditors will find this manual useful.

Barry Johnson, Peter Holgate
PricewaterhouseCoopers LLP
London
October 2010

Contents

Abbreviations and terms used

AAPA	Association of Authorised Public Accountants
ABI	Association of British Insurers
AC	Appeal Cases, law reports
Accounts	financial statements
ADR	american depositary receipts
AESOP	all employee share ownership plan
the 1985 Act	the Companies Act 1985 (as amended by the Companies Act 1989)
the 1989 Act	the Companies Act 1989
the 2006 Act	the Companies Act 2006
ACCA	Association of Chartered Certified Accountants
ACT	advance corporation tax
AFS	available-for-sale
AG	Application Guidance
AGM	Annual General Meeting
AIM	Alternative Investment Market
AIMR	Alternative Investment Market Rules
AITC	Association of Investment Trust Companies
All ER	All England Law Reports
AMPS	auction market preferred shares
APB	Auditing Practices Board
APC	Auditing Practices Committee
App	Application note of a Financial Reporting Standard
App	Appendix
ARC	Accounting Regulatory Committee
ARSs	auction rate securities
ASB	Accounting Standards Board
ASC	Accounting Standards Committee
BBA	British Bankers' Association
BC	Basis for Conclusions (to an accounting standard)
BCLC	Butterworths Company Law Cases
BERR	Department for Business, Enterprise and Regulatory Reform (formerly the DTI and now BIS)
BIS	Department for Business, Innovation and Skills (formerly BERR before that DTI)
BNA 1985	Business Names Act 1985
C	currency unit
CA85	the Companies Act 1985
CA06	the Companies Act 2006
CCA	current cost accounting

CCAB	Consultative Committee of Accountancy Bodies Limited
CC	The Combined Code – Principles of good governance and code of best practice
CC(CP)	Companies Consolidation (Consequential Provisions) Act 1985
CEO	chief executive officer
CESR	Committee of European Securities Regulators
CGAA	Co-ordinating Group on Audit and Accounting Issues
CGU	cash-generating unit
Ch	Chancery Division, law reports
Chp	Chapter
chapter (1)	'PricewaterhouseCoopers' Manual of accounting' – chapter (1)
CIF	cost, insurance, freight
CIMA	Chartered Institute of Management Accountants
CIPFA	Chartered Institute of Public Finance and Accountancy
CISCO	The City Group for Smaller Companies
Cmnd	Command Paper
CBO	collateralised bond obligation
CDO	collateralised debt obligation
CLO	collateralised loan obligation
CMO	collateralised mortgage obligation
COSO	Committee of Sponsoring Organisations of the Treadway Commission
CPP	current purchasing power
CR	Report of the committee on The Financial Aspects of Corporate Governance (the 'Cadbury Report')
CSR	corporate social responsibility
CTD	cumulative translation difference
CUV	continuing use value
DG XV	Directorate General XV
the 7th Directive	EC 7th Directive on Company Law
DP	discussion paper
DRC	depreciated replacement cost
DTI	Department of Trade and Industry
DTR	double taxation relief
EASDAQ	European Association of Securities Dealers Automated Quotation
EBIT	earnings before interest and tax
EBITDA	earnings before interest, tax, depreciation and amortisation
EC	European Community
ECU	european currency unit
ED	exposure draft
EEE	electrical and electronic equipment
EFRAG	European Financial Reporting Advisory Group
EGM	extraordinary general meeting
EITF	Emerging Issues Task Force (US)
EPS	earnings per share
ESOP	employee share ownership plan
ESOT	employee share ownership trust
EU	European Union

EU 2005 Regulation	Regulation (EC) No 1606/2002 on the application of International Accounting Standards
EUV	existing use value
FASB	Financial Accounting Standards Board (US)
FEE	The European Federation of Accountants
FIFO	first-in, first-out
financial statements	Accounts
FLA	Finance and Leasing Association
FM	facilities management
FOB	free on board
FPI	foreign private investors (US-listed)
FRAG	Financial Reporting and Auditing Group of the ICAEW
Framework	Framework for the preparation and presentation of financial statements
FRED	Financial Reporting Exposure Draft
FRA	forward rate agreement
FRC	Financial Reporting Council
FRN	floating rate note
FRRP	Financial Reporting Review Panel
FRS	Financial Reporting Standard
FRSSE	Financial Reporting Standard for Smaller Entities
FSA	Financial Services Authority
FVTPL	at fair value through profit or loss
GAAP	generally accepted accounting principles (and practices)
GAAS	generally accepted auditing standards
GB	Great Britain
GCFR	Going Concern and Financial Reporting - published by the joint working group of the Hundred Group of finance directors, ICAEW and ICAS
GRI guidelines	Global Reporting Initiative guidelines
HMSO	Her Majesty's Stationery Office
HP	hire purchase
HMRC	HM Revenue & Customs
IAASB	International Auditing and Assurance Standards Board
IAS	International Accounting Standard (see also IFRS)
IASB	International Accounting Standards Board
IASC	International Accounting Standards Committee
IBF	Irish Bankers' Federation
IBNR	incurred but not reported
ICAEW	Institute of Chartered Accountants in England and Wales
ICAI	Institute of Chartered Accountants in Ireland
ICAS	Institute of Chartered Accountants of Scotland
ICFR	Internal Control and Financial Reporting - published by the joint working group of the Hundred Group of finance directors, ICAEW and ICAS
ICR	Industrial Cases Reports
ICSA	Institute of Chartered Secretaries and Administrators
IFAC	International Federation of Accountants

IFRIC	International Financial Reporting Interpretations Committee
IFRS	International Financial Reporting Standard (see also IAS)
IG	Implementation Guidance (to an accounting standard)
IGU	income-generating unit
IIMR	Institute of Investment Management and Research (see SIP)
IoD	Institute of Directors
IOSCO	International Organisation of Securities Commissions
IPO	initial public offering
IPR&D	in-process research and development
IR	Statement on interim reporting issued by ASB
ISA	International Standard on Auditing
ISA (UK & Ire)	International Standard on Auditing (UK and Ireland)
ISDA	International Swap Dealers Association
ISP	internet service provider
IVSC	International Valuation Standards Committee
JWG	Joint Working Group
LIBID	London inter-bank bid rate
LIBOR	London inter-bank offered rate
LIFFE	the London International Financial Futures and Options Exchange
LIFO	last-in, first-out
LR	UK Listing Authority's Listing Rules
MBO	management buy-out
MD&A	management's discussion and analysis
MR	Master of the Rolls
NASDAQ	National Association of Securities Dealers Automated Quotations
NCU	national currency unit
NIC	national insurance contributions
OFR	operating and financial review
OEICs	open-ended investment companies
OIAC	Oil Industry Accounting Committee
OTC	over-the-counter market
PA	preliminary announcement
para(s)	paragraph(s) of Schedules to the Companies Acts, or IFRSs or IASs or FRSs, or SSAPs, or FREDs, or EDs, or DPs, or text
PCAOB	Public Company Accounting Oversight Board (US)
PE	price-earnings
PFI	Private Finance Initiative
PLUSR	Plus Rules for Issuers (for PLUS-quoted entities)
PPE	property, plant and equipment
PPERA	Political Parties, Elections and Referendums Act 2000
PPF	Pension Protection Fund
PRAG	Pensions Research Accountants Group
PS	Practice Statements

QC	Queen's Counsel
QUEST	qualifying employee share ownership trust
R&D	research and development
RDG	regional development grant
Reg	regulation of a statutory instrument (for example, SI 1995/ 2092 Reg 5 = regulation 5 of The Companies (Summary Financial Statements) Regulations 1995)
RICS	Royal Institution of Chartered Surveyors
RS	Reporting Standard
SAC	the Standards Advisory Council
SAS	Statement of Auditing Standards
SC	Session Cases
Sch	Schedule to the Companies Act 1985 (eg CA85 4A Sch 85 = Schedule 4A, paragraph 85)
SDC	Standards Development Committee
SEC	Securities and Exchange Commission (US)
Sec(s)	Section(s) of the 1985 Act/Sections(s) of the 2006 Act
SEE	social, environmental and ethical
SERPS	State earnings related pension scheme
SFAC	Statement of Financial Accounting Concepts issued in the US
SFAS	Statement of Financial Accounting Standards issued in the US
SI	Statutory Instrument
SIC	Standing Interpretation Committee of the IASC (see IFRIC)
SIP	Society of Investment Professionals (formerly IIMR)
SIPs	share incentive plans
SMEs	small and medium-sized entities
SOI	Statement of Intent
SoP	Statement of principles
SORIE	statement of recognised income and expense
SORP	Statement of Recommended Practice
SPE	special purpose entity
SPV	special purpose vehicle
SSAP	Statement of Standard Accounting Practice
Stock Exchange (or LSE)	the London Stock Exchange
STRGL	statement of total recognised gains and losses
TR	Technical Release of the ICAEW
TUPE	Transfer of Undertakings (Protection of Employment) Regulations
UITF	Urgent Issues Task Force
UK	United Kingdom
US	United States of America
VAT	value added tax
VIE	variable interest entity
WACC	weighted average cost of capital
WEEE	Waste electrical and electronic equipment
WLR	Weekly Law Reports

Chapter 1

Introduction

Introduction

Corporate reporting today

1.1   Recent years have seen major changes in financial reporting worldwide. It would be difficult to argue with the assertion that the biggest single change has been the process of global harmonisation around international financial reporting standards (IFRS), including their adoption for the consolidated financial statements of listed companies in the UK and the rest of the EU. But an important further trend has been the increasing importance and role of the various constituents of what is often called the 'front half' of the annual report, that is: management's commentary on how the business has fared since the last report; governance reports; reports on directors' remuneration; and indeed the statutory directors' report. This second trend is the subject of this book.

1.2   While the directors' report has long been a legal requirement for UK companies, the other parts of the front half are more recent. They are part of a trend that recognises that pure accounting numbers, however good the accounting policies and however extensive the footnote disclosure, are only part of the story. To be really useful to investors and other users, they need to be supplemented by additional disclosure – often in narrative form – that seeks to give a sense of context, an explanation of what is going on and a sense of what might happen in the future. This, taken in aggregate, can be described as 'corporate reporting', as opposed to financial reporting.

1.3   The emphasis on a broader notion of corporate reporting is to some extent a social and political trend. There has been much debate in the last years leading up to the company law reform, culminating in the enactment of the Companies Act 2006 about whether directors should have as their, and their companies', objectives a narrow focus on the shareholders or a wider focus on a range of stakeholders. However, what is clear is that both the government and a wide range of opinion believe, as a general principle, that narrative reporting is increasingly important.

1.4   The Companies Act 206 requires management to provide a fair review of the company's business along with a description of its principal risks and uncertainties, in other words a business review. The requirement to present a business review is noteworthy in two respects. First, it applies to all companies, except those that are 'small' according to the definitions in the Companies Act. Thus many medium-sized private companies, including wholly-owned subsidiaries of groups, have to produce business reviews. Secondly, the requirements are flexible and tailored to the circumstances. For example, the review should be *"a balanced and comprehensive analysis of the development and performance of the business of the company during the financial year, and the position of the company at the end of that year, consistent with the size and complexity of the business".* Also, key performance indicators need to be disclosed *"to the extent necessary for an understanding of the development, performance or position of the business of the company".* This is sensible, in that it expects more when there is more to tell and where, in practice, there is a significant public interest to satisfy.

1.5   Little guidance is available on the practical aspects of preparing a business review, which, for a large diverse company, could be detailed and complex. In fact, most UK listed and public interest entities provide the business review information in the form of an operating and financial review (OFR) and consider it a key mechanism for communicating with investors. The ASB has issued non-mandatory guidance to assist companies preparing OFRs, which although not written with the business review specifically in mind, does deal with a number of its required disclosures. The guidance is principles based, that is, information should be presented through the eyes of management focussing on matters relevant to members in a way that is comprehensive, understandable and forward looking as well as being balanced, neutral and comparable over time.

1.6   The Financial Reporting Council, primarily the Financial Reporting Review Panel (FRRP), has an increasing interest in the 'front half' of companies' annual reports, reflecting the importance of elements such as the operating and financial review, the business review, and reports on governance and remuneration. In particular, the FRRP now has responsibility for reviewing directors' reports (including business reviews) to ensure compliance with the Companies Act.

1.7   Some aspects of the front half owe more to politics than to financial reporting. Politics, rather than accounting as such, lies behind the extensive disclosures required in the UK of directors' remuneration. Politics, in a broad sense, is already taking narrative reporting into more fields. Corporate reporting is starting to encompass environmental reporting and social reporting of various kinds, some of which are new requirements of the Companies Act 2006.

International developments

1.8   The developments in narrative reporting are to a degree domestic matters, some resulting from UK legal requirements.

1.9   Although it is seen in the UK as part of the directors' report, the requirement for a business review has an EU origin, namely a 2003 amendment to the earlier 4th and 7th accounting directives. The recitals to the 2003 directive say: *"The annual report and consolidated annual report are important elements of financial reporting. Enhancement, in line with current best practice, of the existing requirement for these to present a fair review of the development of the business and of its position, in a manner consistent with the size and complexity of the business, is necessary to promote greater consistency and give additional guidance concerning the information a "fair review" is expected to contain. The information should not be restricted to the financial aspects of the company's business ......".* In the UK, this type of thinking is reasonably well established. This appears to be less the case in some other EU member states, so it is reasonable to assume that the business review will be implemented with a variety of speeds and degrees of enthusiasm.

1.10   There are also further international comparisons that can be made. For example, both Australia and Canada have similar guidance and principles to those used by the ASB in its OFR guidance. The US SEC requires a Management Discussion and Analysis (MD&A), which while differing in detail, is largely based on the same objectives and principles as used by the ASB.

1.11   The IASB is also involved in the debate on the basis that management commentary lies within the boundaries of financial reporting and, therefore, is within the scope of the conceptual framework for financial reporting. An exposure draft of the IASB's proposals, 'Management commentary', was published in June 2009. It is consistent with the ASB's guidance having as one of its main principles that any narrative should seek to explain an entity's financial statements through the eyes of management. The Chairmen of the FASB and IASB appear to agree, with Rober Herz (Chairman of the FASB) stating:

> *"Businesses are complex and numbers on their own are never going to tell the full story. Narrative reporting is a vital complement to the figures."*

In addition, Sir David Tweedie (Chairman of the IASB) has said:

> *"The narrative statement is not an adjunct. It is a key component."*

Corporate governance

1.13   The UK has a well established corporate governance regime, that stems from the early 1990s when the Cadbury Committee reported in response to a series of scandals, fuelled by the then recession. Some governance issues have attracted significant political and public interest because they strike at the root of the objectives of companies – none more so than the accountability of boards to shareholders in relation to executive pay. The regime in the UK is set out in a corporate governance code – the Combined Code – which uses a 'comply or explain' principle, whereby if a company has not complied with the Combined Code's provisions during the year it provides an explanation for those provisions with which it did not comply.

1.14   The Combined Code has continually been updated and improved since it was first published. On 28 May 2010 the FRC published the further revision; the UK Corporate Governance Code, which replaces the 2008 Combined Code. The new edition of the Code applies to all Premium listed companies for financial years beginning on or after 29 June 2010, including overseas companies. The 2008 Combined Code (renamed the UK Corporate Governance Code) continues to apply for December 2010 calendar year end reporters. The new 2010 Code includes amongst other changes annual re-election of all directors and external facilitation of board performance reviews at least every three years (both these provision apply for FTSE 350 companies only).

The approach in this Manual

1.12   Considerations relating to the front half apply to all UK companies at least to some extent. Even the smallest company has to prepare a directors' report. Other requirements come into play once a company achieves a certain size, becomes listed or pays its directors above a certain amount. For these various reports, we give our views on what the requirements or recommendations mean and on what is good disclosure in the areas in which there are no rules or guidance. As part of that approach, this Manual contains many examples and extracts from financial reports.

1.13   This Manual can be viewed as a supplement to two other works. One is the 'PricewaterhouseCoopers' Manual of Accounting – UK GAAP', which gives guidance to the many UK companies that still follow UK GAAP. The second is the 'PricewaterhouseCoopers' Manual of Accounting – IFRS for the UK', which applies to those UK listed groups that have to follow IFRS and other entities that have opted to apply IFRS. The issues described in this Manual relating to the 'front half' apply to some extent to both categories of company, though the requirements and expectations for listed companies are greater than for others.

Chapter 2

Business review

Business review

Introduction

2.1   This chapter takes its name from the statutory business review, a disclosure required within the directors' report by the Companies Act 2006. (See further chapter 3 for guidance relating to other parts of the directors' report).

2.2   However, the chapter deals not only with the statutory business review, but also with the voluntary and good practice corporate reporting often set out in the front section (front half) of an entity's annual report. Such information is often referred to as 'narrative reporting'. Expanding on the business review, it should also complement and supplement the financial statements.

2.3   In the UK, this information has historically formed an operating and financial review (OFR). While there is no UK requirement for an entity to prepare an operating and financial review, many UK listed and public interest entities produce one voluntarily and consider it a key mechanism for communicating with investors.

2.4   To assist directors in preparing OFRs, the ASB issued a non-mandatory reporting statement, 'Operating and financial review' (referred to in this chapter as RS (OFR) or the reporting statement). Although non-mandatory, it is recommended for quoted companies and any other companies that purport to prepare an OFR and it is generally accepted that directors of a company preparing an OFR will give due regard to it.

2.5   There is variety in the way companies structure the front half of their annual reports. The 2006 Act gives directors safe harbour from civil liability for statements or omissions in the directors' report (and also the directors' remuneration report prepared by quoted entities) and as a result many identify the entire front half as the directors' report. Others name the majority of the front half 'business review', or alternatively have separate sections for an operating, financial and/or business review, directors' report, corporate governance statement and directors' remuneration report.

2.6   Safe harbour will also cover separate voluntary OFRs or narrative reporting outside the directors' report provided that there is a specific cross-reference from the directors' report to the OFR. Where it is not included within the directors' report, the business review should be incorporated into the directors' report by specific cross-reference.

2.7 The first part of this chapter sets out the business review requirements. Following this, the chapter covers the ASB's RS (OFR). Little guidance is available on the practical aspects of preparing a business review, which, for a large diverse company, could be detailed and complex. Although not written with the business review specifically in mind, RS (OFR) does deal with a number of its required disclosures. Thus, it is common for those preparing an OFR, which incorporates a statutory business review, or those simply preparing a business review as part of the directors' report, to comply with RS (OFR), to ensure that investors receive the most appropriate information. As such, the example disclosures within the OFR section of this chapter may also be considered when preparing a business review.

2.8 Finally, there is a short section detailing international developments in front half reporting.

2.9 Further information, including details of the latest developments in corporate reporting and guidance on and examples of good practice disclosure can be found on PwC's corporate reporting web site, www.corporate reporting.com.

Business review

2.10 The directors should include in their report a review of the business of the company and its subsidiaries. [CA06 Sec 417(1)]. Where a company is entitled to the small companies exemption (see further chapter 31 of the Manual of Accounting – UK GAAP), the directors' report need not contain a business review.

2.11 The purpose of the business review is to inform the company's members and help them assess how the directors have performed their duty to promote the company's success. [CA06 Sec 417(2)].

2.12 In promoting the company's success, directors must, in particular, have regard to:

- The likely consequences of any decision in the long-term.

- The interests of the company's employees.

- The need to foster the company's business relationships with suppliers, customers and others.

- The impact of the company's operations on the community and the environment.

- The desirability for the company maintaining a reputation for high standards of business conduct.

- The need to act fairly as between the company's members.

[CA06 Sec 172].

2.13   The business review must contain, at a minimum:

■   A fair review of the entity's business.

■   A description of the principal risks and uncertainties facing the entity.

[CA06 Sec 417(3)].

2.14   The review should be consistent with the business' size and complexity and provide a balanced and comprehensive analysis of:

■   The development and performance of the entity's business during the financial year.

■   The entity's position at the end of the year.

[CA06 Sec 417(4)].

2.15   The review should also include the following, to the extent necessary for an understanding of the development, performance or position of the entity's business:

■   Analysis using financial key performance indicators (KPIs).

■   Where appropriate, analysis using other KPIs, including information on environmental and employee matters.

[CA06 Sec 417(6)].

2.16   The review must contain, where appropriate, references to and additional explanation of amounts included in the financial statements. [CA06 Secs 415(1), 417(1), 418(2), 417(8)].

2.17   Where a company qualifies as medium-sized in relation to a financial year (see chapter 31 of the Manual of Accounting – UK GAAP), the directors' report for the year need not comply with the KPI requirements of section 417(6) of the 2006 Act (see para 2.15), so far as they relate to non-financial information.

2.18   Where an entity is a parent company and prepares consolidated financial statements, the business review should be a consolidated review covering the company and its subsidiary undertakings included in the consolidation. [CA06 Sec 417(9)]. There is no requirement for the parent company to prepare a separate review for the company alone.

Lack of objective assessment criteria

2.19   The legislation requiring a business review is not supported by any reporting statement or other formal guidance. Accordingly, the interpretation of what is meant by, for example, 'a fair review' is open to interpretation. We can, however, look to statements made by appropriate bodies, such as the Department for Business, Innovation and Skills (BIS) (formerly BERR) and the ASB, in order to formulate some assessment criteria against which minimum compliance with the business review can be assessed.

2.20 For example, BIS, in the 'Invitation for comments on the business review', stated that a company would *"…include information on the objectives, strategies… where necessary to provide a fair review of the company…"*.

Applying the requirements to different sizes of company

2.21 As mentioned above, all companies must prepare a business review, other than those entitled to the small companies exemption (see para 2.10). The ASB's reporting statement on the OFR offers some guidance on practically implementing the various business review requirements, although this is of more relevance to listed companies (see further from para 2.38). Guidance to assist directors in preparing a business review is limited for private entities.

2.22 Many of the requirements of the business review are preceded with the words *"to the extent necessary for an understanding of the development, performance or position of the company's business"*, thus giving directors some discretion over the level of detail that should be presented in the business review.

2.23 Bearing in mind that the overriding purpose of the business review is as a tool for communicating with members (see para 2.11), we believe that the type and extent of disclosure required depends on the extent to which an entity's share ownership structure is dispersed and how close/involved the owners are to the business' management. This distinction can be summarised as follows:

■ For owner-managed companies, members already have a good understanding of the company's development, performance and position. Consequently, the minimum information to comply with the legislation is all that is needed to present a clear picture to members.

■ The position for wholly-owned subsidiaries of a parent company that actively monitors the business performance on an ongoing basis is similar to that for owner-managed companies. Often both the management and reporting of risk and key performance indicators for wholly-owned subsidiaries are undertaken at the group level. In such circumstances, it is appropriate to clarify this position and also state that the company's directors believe that analysis using key performance indicators is not necessary or appropriate to understand of the business' development, performance or position. The statement should usefully refer to further information available in the group annual report, making clear that it does not form part of the company's report. The cross-reference should be to a specific paragraph, heading, or page in the group annual report. See further paragraph 2.25 below.

■ For public interest companies, AIM-listed (or PLUS-quoted) companies and private companies (including wholly-owned subsidiaries) where ownership is distinct from those who manage the entity on members' behalf, the amount of information disclosed should reflect the explicit requirements implied by BIS in its pronouncements and guidance (for example, *"the business review would include information on objectives, strategies and resources where necessary to provide a fair review of the company"*). The minimum disclosures described for owner-managed entities should be supplemented by additional contextual information around risk and key performance indicators, as well as a description of the entity's strategy and business environment.

- Fuller disclosure is necessary for quoted companies, to assist members in understanding the entity's development, performance and position. The most appropriate guidance is in the recommendations of the ASB's RS (OFR). (See from para 2.38 below).

2.24   Given the broad nature of the categories set out above, and particularly public interest entities with dispersed ownership, there needs to be a degree of flexibility in the approach chosen by companies depending on their circumstances.

2.25   As mentioned in the second bullet point in paragraph 2.23, a pragmatic approach to the disclosure of principal risks and KPIs for a wholly-owned subsidiary of a UK parent company may be taken, where the subsidiary is managed as part of a wider unit, on a group basis rather than a statutory basis. Suggested wording is provided below:

*"**Principal risks and uncertainties***

From the perspective of the company, the principal risks and uncertainties are integrated with the principal risks of the group and are not managed separately. Accordingly, the principal risks and uncertainties of R Group Ltd, which include those of the company, are discussed on page x of the group's annual report which does not form part of this report.

Key performance indicators (KPIs)

The directors of R Group Ltd manage the group's operations on a divisional basis. For this reason, the company's directors believe that analysis using key performance indicators for the company is not necessary or appropriate for an understanding of the development, performance or position of the business of R Ltd. The development, performance and position of the retail division of R Group Ltd, which includes the company, is discussed on page y of the group's annual report, which does not form part of this report."

2.26   Illustrative examples of business reviews for each category of company can be found in full at www.corporatereporting.com/practical-guides.html. These include some information already required in the directors' report; disclosure on future developments and research and development. [SI 2008/410 7 Sch 7(1)(b), (c)]. We believe these disclosures, and others such as details of post balance sheet dividends, are best placed alongside the business review disclosures in order to provide a more complete picture of corporate performance. Examples of good disclosure by listed companies are available on www.pwcinform.com.

2.27 The table below provides a guide to the type of information that should be included in a business review for private entities with dispersed ownership and public interest entities (other than those for whom compliance with the ASB's reporting statement is more relevant).

Heading	Suggested type of content
Principal activities	Nature of the business, extent of operations. Results in terms of revenues and profits. Net debt position and net cash inflow.
Business environment	Description of the market and competitive environment – market factors and dynamics that can affect the business environment, for example, competitors and market outlook.
	Regulatory environment – legal, agency or other regulatory factors that impose requirements on the conduct of business activities; for example, deregulation and privatisation.
	Macro environment – factors that could have a material impact on corporate performance, for example; interest rates, demographics and economic outlook.
Strategy	Overriding objectives of the company and, where relevant, the group.
	The company's and, where relevant, the group's strategy for achieving these objectives and an explanation of each strategy, as well as how successful implementation of the strategy is measured.
Research and development (R&D)	Actions taken in the area of R&D and how these link into the group's strategy.
Future outlook	Expected development of the business environment and any planned actions to address these developments.
Principal risks and uncertainties	The principal risks and uncertainties that have the focus of the directors' attention – not simply a list of all risk factors that the group faces – as well as the approach taken by management to these risks.
Key performance indicators	The measures used to assess progress against objectives and strategies – including quantifying of these measures, trend data, definition, method of calculation and any relevant narrative.

2.28 In January 2007 the ASB issued 'A review of narrative reporting by UK listed companies in 2006' with the aim of keeping the spotlight on narrative reporting and encouraging continuing improvement in this area. The report assessed 23 companies' annual reports with a year end of 31 March 2006 against both:

■   the ASB's OFR reporting statement; and

■   minimum compliance with the business review.

2.29 The ASB's assessment of minimum compliance provides some 'indicators' for the FRRP, which has the business review within its scope. For example, the document notes that:

> "While the requirements to disclose KPIs is a matter of judgement for the directors, the lack of inclusion of any KPIs in a Business Review in the future will provide the Financial Reporting Review Panel (FRRP) with a possible indicator that the Review may not be compliant with the law."

2.30 The ASB's views relating to the business review requirements are summarised below:

Business review [CA06 Sec 417].	ASB interpretation
"a fair review of the company's business"	Description of the business and the external environment in which it operates. Discussion on the objectives of the business and the strategies to achieve those objectives.
"a description of the principal risks and uncertainties facing the company."	Description of principal risks rather than simply providing a list of all the possible risks they may face.
"The review must, to the extent necessary for an understanding of the development, performance or position of the business of the company, include: (a) analysis using financial key performance indicators, and (b) where appropriate, analysis using other key performance indicators, including information relating to environmental matters and employee matters."	Explicit identification of financial and non-financial key performance indicators.
"The review must, where appropriate, include references to, and additional explanations of, amounts included in the company's annual accounts."	Resources available to the business, particularly those items not reflected in the balance sheet. Financial position.

2.31 In summary, a significant number of key disclosure recommendations of RS (OFR) are consistent with the requirements of the Companies Act relating to the business review. See from paragraph 2.38 for guidance on RS (OFR).

[The next paragraph is 2.34.]

Key performance indicators

2.34 Key performance indicators (KPIs) are defined as *"factors by reference to which the development, performance or position of the business of the company can be measured effectively"*. [CA06 Sec 417(6)]. The ASB's reporting statement on the OFR provides a more detailed definition, describing KPIs as *"...quantified measurements that reflect the critical success factors of an entity and disclose progress towards achieving a particular objective or objectives"*. [RS (OFR) para 3].

2.35 The 2006 Act does not prescribe specific KPIs that entities should disclose. Entities use a variety of different KPIs and the relevance of a particular KPI varies from industry to industry and even from one entity to another within an industry. In addition, methods of calculating particular KPIs may vary from one entity to another. Directors will, therefore, need to decide which KPIs and how many best reflect their judgement of what is needed for an understanding of the business. This approach will reflect the view that KPIs are principally of use in measuring an entity's performance and the entity's position, rather than measuring the entity's performance against other entities.

2.36 Directors may look to RS (OFR) for further guidance on disclosure of KPIs. The reporting statement sets out the recommendations for disclosure for each KPI. In addition, RS (OFR)'s implementation guidance contains examples of disclosure of KPIs. Further guidance on KPIs, including example disclosures, is provided in the OFR section of this chapter from paragraph 2.192. At the other end of the scale, reduced disclosure may be appropriate for wholly-owned subsidiaries of a UK parent company, where the business is managed on a group basis rather than a statutory basis (see para 2.25 above).

Interaction between the directors' report, business review and OFR

2.37 If companies that prepare an OFR in accordance with RS (OFR) were also required to give information to meet the business review requirements in their directors' report, there would be considerable duplication.

2.37.1 BIS' 'Guidance on changes to the directors' report requirements in the Companies Act 1985 – April and December 2005' clarified that where the directors' report and a voluntary OFR are published together, it is acceptable to cross-refer from the directors' report to a business review in the OFR. This guidance is considered to be relevant to similar provisions of the 2006 Act. The cross-reference must clearly refer (by page numbers, paragraph numbers or headings) to the specific section in the OFR. The guidance provides example wording for such a cross-reference as follows:

> *"The information that fulfils the requirements of the business review can be found in the OFR on pages x to y, which are incorporated in this report by reference."*

Additional matters for quoted companies

2.37.2 Sometimes referred to as the enhanced business review, the 2006 Act requires the directors of quoted companies to disclose the following in their directors' report:

- The main trends and factors likely to affect the future development, performance and position of the company's business (see from para 2.37.6 below).

- Information about persons with whom the company has contractual or other arrangements that are essential to the company's business (but see para 2.37.19 and also from para 2.37.16).

- Information about:

  - environmental matters (including the impact of the company's business on the environment) (further guidance is provided from para 2.106.1);

  - the company's employees (further guidance is provided from para 2.146); and

  - social and community issues (further guidance is provided from para 2.106.1);

including information about any policies of the company in relation to those matters and the effectiveness of those policies. [CA06 Sec 417(5)].

2.37.3 The review must also contain, where appropriate, references to and additional explanation of amounts included in the financial statements. [CA06 Sec 417(8)].

2.37.4 The disclosures are required *"to the extent necessary for an understanding of the development, performance or position of the company's business"*. If the review does not contain information on the items listed in the second and third bullet points above, it must state so. [CA06 Sec 417(5)].

2.37.5 The government expressed the view that the additional disclosures would add value to the quality of reporting without imposing unnecessary costs.

Likely future developments

2.37.6 As noted in paragraph 2.37.2, section 417(5)(a) of the 2006 Act requires the directors' report of a quoted company to contain an indication of the main trends and factors likely to affect the future development, performance and position of the company's business.

2.37.7 As with the provisions relating to a review of the company's business during the year, the 2006 Act contains no amplification as to the extent and the scope of this commentary. In practice, directors tend to interpret this requirement by providing information that will have a significant impact on future earnings and profitability of the company or the group. For example, information on such matters as development of new products or services, business expansion or rationalisation plans, capital expenditure plans and proposed disposals and acquisitions, is fairly common.

2.37.8 Quoted companies can refer to RS (OFR) for further guidance in this area (see from para 2.131).

2.37.9 Companies traded on a regulated market in the UK (for example, the main market of the LSE or the Plus Market's PLUS-listed market) are required to comply with the requirements of the UKLA's Listing Rules.

2.37.10 For listed companies, the wording for the note on future developments will have to be chosen very carefully. Otherwise, there is the danger that the note could, at some later stage, be construed as a profit forecast. Appendix 1 of the UKLA's Listing Rules defines 'profit forecast' as follows:

> "A form of words which expressly states or by implication indicates a figure or a minimum or maximum figure for the likely level of profits or losses for the current financial period and/or financial periods subsequent to that period, or contains data from which a calculation of such a figure for future profits or losses may be made, even if no particular figure is mentioned and the word 'profit' is not used."

It defines a profit estimate as:

> "a profit forecast for a financial period which has expired and for which results have not yet been published."

2.37.11 The requirement that a business review should incorporate forward-looking information and KPIs has led many companies to believe, erroneously, that they will be expected to report profit forecasts. The business community's overriding concern with the business review, that it will expose directors to the rigorous policing of published prospective financial information (PFI), is misplaced. Forward-looking information, properly presented, can be used to provide investors with a broad-based view of corporate performance without having to disclose sensitive PFI. The real issue is not whether forward-looking statements turn out to be accurate, but whether they were made in good faith and with due care and attention. The 2006 Act introduced 'safe harbour' for directors from civil liability for statements in the directors' report (see from para 2.37.21).

2.37.12 The City Code on Takeovers and Mergers states that if a company has issued any statement that constitutes a profit forecast and that forecast relates to a period during which a takeover bid arises, then that forecast must be repeated in any offer or defence document and accountants must report on it. [City Code rule 28.3(d)].

2.37.13 The UKLA's Listing Rules state that, if a listed company has published a forecast or estimate for a financial period for which the results have not yet been published and subsequently it is required to produce a Class 1 acquisition circular or any circular, then the issuer must either repeat or update the forecast in the listing particulars or the relevant circular or include an explanation of why the profit forecast is no longer valid. The same rules apply if a company is the subject of a Class 1 acquisition by a listed company. [LR 13.5.33R].

2.37.14 CESR's recommendations for the consistent implementation of the Prospectus Regulation, which have been adopted by the FSA through the Prospectus Rules, state that there is a presumption that an outstanding forecast will be material in the case of share issues. Accordingly, the issuer of a prospectus would either have to include a profit forecast in the prospectus or a statement that it is no longer valid. [CESR recommendations para 44].

2.37.15 In the circumstances described in paragraphs 2.37.12 and 2.37.13, if the directors' report of a listed company is construed as including a profit forecast or an estimate, it would have the following consequence:

■ Accountants would be required to report that the forecast or estimate has been properly compiled on the basis stated and that it is presented on a basis consistent with the accounting policies of the company or group in question. [City Code rule 28.3(b); PR Annex 1 item 13.2].

■ The directors would have to state in the circular that any profit forecast or estimate had been properly compiled on the basis stated and presented on a basis consistent with the company's accounting policies. [LR 13.5.32R (2)].

■ Whenever a listed company has published a profit forecast or estimate, whether in a City Code, Listing Rules or Prospectus Rules document, the following year's financial statements have to explain any differences if the actual results for the period reported in those financial statements differ by ten per cent or more from any published forecast or estimate made by the company for that period. [LR 9.2.18R (2)(c)].

Contractual arrangements

2.37.16 As noted in paragraph 2.37.2, information about persons with whom the company has contractual or other arrangements that are essential to the company's business should be disclosed (but see para 2.37.19).

2.37.17 An example disclosure of contractual arrangements is given in Table 2.1.

2011

Table 2.1 – Contractual and other arrangements essential to the business

Lonmin plc – Report and accounts – 30 September 2009

Directors' Report – Governance (extract)

4. The Company's business and statutory disclosures (extract)

4.11 Essential contractual arrangements

Certain Group companies are party to contracts and other arrangements which the Board judges are essential to the business of the Company.

For any mining company, its mineral rights and mining licences are of crucial importance and therefore the New Order Mining Licence granted by the South African government's Department of Minerals and Energy to certain Group companies in respect of the Marikana operations falls into this category, as do the old order mining rights in respect of the Limpopo operations and the various prospecting rights held by Group companies.

The remaining essential contractual arrangements can be summarised as follows:

- Contracts for the purchase of inputs – while most of the supplies needed to operate the Group's mines and refining facilities are secured through competitive tendering in the open market, the Group is heavily dependent on Eskom for the supply of electricity, and Rand Water in respect of the supply of water. The Company does not believe that it has any debt facilities which could not be replaced in the open market.

- Contracts relating to labour and services – the principal arrangements essential to our business are collective agreements with trade unions representing the majority of the Group's employees, most notably with the National Union of Mineworkers in South Africa.

- Contracts for the sale of goods – certain Group companies are party to separate contracts with BASF and Mitsubishi, under which substantially the whole of the Group's production of finished metal for the period under review was sold.

2.37.18   The ASB's reporting statement provides further guidance on disclosure around relationships. See from paragraph 2.146.

Seriously prejudicial

2.37.19   A limited exemption has been provided under the Companies Act 2006 such that disclosure of information is not required regarding *"information about impending developments or matters in the course of negotiation if the disclosure would, in the opinion of the directors, be seriously prejudicial to the interests of the company"*. [CA06 Sec 417(10)].

2.37.20   In addition, quoted companies need not disclose information about essential contractual or other arrangements if such disclosure would, in the directors' opinion, be seriously prejudicial to the counterparty of those arrangements or contrary to the public interest. [CA06 Sec 417(11)].

Disclosure of business model for listed entities — UK Corporate Governance Code (2010)

2.37.20.1 For financial years beginning on or after 29 June 2010, the UK Corporate Governance Code (2010) introduces a recommendation for listed companies that the annual report should include an explanation of the basis on which the company generates or preserves value over the longer term (the business model) and the strategy for delivering the objectives of the company. [UK CGC C.1.2]. The recommendation goes further than the statutory requirement for an enhanced business review for quoted companies described from paragraph 2.37.2 above.

2.37.20.2 The FRC introduced the recommendation for listed companies to disclose the business model, setting out the strategy for generating long term value, in order to address a gap in reporting. In addition, the FRC believes that the new recommendation will help to illustrate how the directors have applied the following new principle on risk:

> "The board is responsible for determining the nature and extent of the significant risks it is willing to take in achieving its strategic objectives..." [UK CGC C.2].

2.37.20.3 The footnote accompanying the recommendation to disclose the business model states that it would be desirable if the explanation were located in the same part of the annual report as the business review. It goes on to say that guidance on what should be considered in an explanation of the business model is provided in paragraphs 30 to 32 of the ASB's reporting statement on the OFR – see further from paragraph 2.101 below. The FRC considers that companies that are properly applying the ASB's reporting statement will already be meeting the new recommendation.

Directors' liability: safe harbour

2.37.21 A further amendment provided by the Companies Act 2006 arising from the consultation on narrative reporting is for directors to be given safe harbour from civil liability for statements or omissions in the directors' report and the directors' remuneration report (including any summary financial statements derived from those reports). The safe harbour provision is considered further in chapter 8.

2.37.22 Historically, many listed companies presented an OFR as a separate statement within the annual report. The business review is required to be included within the directors' report, although BIS has indicated that a cross-reference to information contained elsewhere in the annual report (for example, in the OFR) is acceptable (see from para 2.37). Safe harbour will, therefore, also cover separate voluntary OFRs or narrative reporting outside the directors' report provided that cross-referencing from the directors' report to the OFR is explicitly provided.

2.37.23 Under the 2006 Act, the directors are liable to the company, and not to third parties. They are liable if statements are untrue or misleading and are made in bad faith or recklessly. They are liable for deliberate and dishonest concealment of material facts.

2.37.24 A similar safe harbour also exists for issuers of securities traded on a regulated market in respect of disclosures under the implementation of the Disclosure and Transparency Rules.

Auditor responsibilities

2.37.25 The auditor is required to state in their report whether in their opinion the information given in the directors' report is consistent with the financial statements. See further chapter 3.

Operating and financial review

2.37.26 As mentioned in paragraph 2.3 above, there is no UK requirement for an entity to prepare an operating and financial review (OFR). Many UK listed and public interest entities produce one voluntarily and consider it a key mechanism for communicating with investors.

2.37.27 To assist directors in preparing OFRs, the ASB has issued a non-mandatory reporting statement, 'Operating and financial review' (RS (OFR)). Although non-mandatory, it is generally accepted that directors of a company preparing an OFR will give due regard to it (see further para 2.40).

2.37.28 Further publications that may provide additional guidance to companies in preparing an OFR include:

Title of publication	Description
Guide to forward-looking information – Don't fear the future: communicating with confidence	This guide provides practical guidance on how the reporting of forward-looking information can be achieved, together with examples from progressive companies, both in the UK and elsewhere, who are already adopting a forward-looking orientation in their narrative reporting.
Guide to key performance indicators – Communicating the measures that matter	A practical publication that has been developed to highlight the increasing demand for reporting of key performance indicators (KPIs). It addresses many of the questions posed by these demands and demonstrates what good reporting of KPIs looks like with a collection of examples drawn from the UK and elsewhere.
Report Leadership: Tomorrow's reporting today	Provides a framework, strategic thinking and practical ideas for improving the content of annual reports, including the narrative section.

These publications are equally relevant to companies preparing a business review to form part of a directors' report (see from para 2.10). All of these publications can be found at www.corporatereporting.com, which also provides further examples of good narrative reporting. The publications are located under the 'Toolkit' tab, followed by 'Practical Guides'. Many illustrative examples of OFR reporting can be found on www.pwcinform.com.

Location of the OFR within the annual report

2.37.29 Historically, many listed companies have presented an OFR as a separate statement within the annual report. As explained in paragraph 2.37.22, the business review is required to be included within the directors' report, although BIS has indicated that cross-referencing to information contained elsewhere in the annual report (for example, in the OFR) is acceptable (see from para 2.37).

2.37.30 However, the Companies Act 2006 introduced provisions that give directors a 'safe harbour' in respect of civil liability arising out of the content of the directors' report (see further chapter 8). Thus, companies may wish to include the OFR within the directors' report in order to benefit from the 'safe harbour' provisions.

Good practice reporting

2.37.31 Entities, in particular quoted companies, should look to the recommendations of the ASB's RS (OFR) as the most appropriate guidance for front half reporting. The rest of this chapter focuses on the reporting statement.

ASB's reporting statement: operating and financial review

Scope and definitions

2.38 The ASB's reporting statement has been written with quoted companies in mind, but applies to any entity that purports to prepare an OFR.

2.39 The term 'quoted company' is defined in the Companies Act as a company whose equity share capital:

- has been included in the official list in accordance with the provisions of Part VI of the Financial Services and Markets Act 2000;
- is officially listed in an EEA State; or
- is admitted to dealing on either the New York Stock Exchange or the exchange known as NASDAQ.

[CA06 Sec 474].

2.40 This means, for instance, that companies traded on AIM and other public companies, that are not 'quoted' as defined in the Act, are not specifically covered by the reporting statement's scope. Nor are large private companies. However, many such companies may voluntarily prepare an OFR. The reporting statement applies to them if they 'purport' to prepare an OFR. [RS (OFR) para 2]. 'Purporting' to prepare an OFR would normally mean that the entity uses the words 'operating and financial review'.

2.41 An OFR is defined as *"a narrative explanation, provided in or accompanying the annual report, of the main trends and factors underlying the development, performance and position of an entity during the financial year covered by the financial statements, and those which are likely to affect the entity's future development, performance and position"*. [RS (OFR) para 3].

Approach adopted by the ASB

2.42 The ASB sets out in its OFR reporting statement a number of principles that directors should follow in developing an OFR and the key elements of a disclosure framework that directors should address.

Objective

2.43 The objective of an OFR is to provide a balanced and comprehensive analysis, consistent with the business' size and complexity, of:

- The development and performance of the entity's business during the year.

- The position of the entity at the end of the year.

- The main trends and factors underlying the development, performance and position of the entity's business during the year.

- The main trends and factors that are likely to affect the entity's future development, performance and position.

The analysis should be prepared so as to assist members to assess the strategies adopted by the entity and the potential for those strategies to succeed. [RS (OFR) para 1].

Principles

2.44 The ASB's reporting statement 'Operating and financial review' adopts a principles-based approach.

2.45 Seven principles are set out in bold in the reporting statement. These are:

- The OFR should set out an analysis of the business through the eyes of the board of directors (see further from para 2.46).

- The OFR should focus on matters that are relevant to the interests of members (see further from para 2.48).

- The OFR should have a forward-looking orientation, identifying those trends and factors relevant to the members' assessment of the current and future performance of the business and the progress towards the achievement of long-term business objectives (see further from para 2.53).

- The OFR should complement as well as supplement the financial statements, in order to enhance the overall corporate disclosure (see further from para 2.64).

- The OFR should be comprehensive and understandable (see further from para 2.79).

- The OFR should be balanced and neutral, dealing even-handedly with both good and bad aspects (see further from para 2.92).

- The OFR should be comparable over time (see further from para 2.93).

Principle 1 — Business analysis through the board's eyes

2.46   This principle states that *"The OFR should set out an analysis of the business through the eyes of the board of directors"*. [RS (OFR) para 4]. It ensures that the matters that are reported to the company's members are those of most interest to the board; for example, the strategies the board will implement to achieve the company's objectives, specific performance measures they regularly review and significant risks.

2.47   The reporting statement notes that the directors should disclose appropriate elements of information used in managing the entity and its subsidiaries. More emphasis is given in a group situation to matters that are significant to the group as a whole. [RS (OFR) para 5]. Significant matters may include matters relating to a specific business segment where this is relevant to understanding the business as a whole; for example, particular emphasis on a geographical segment where developments in a new market are significant to the entity as a whole, because expansion in that area is a major part of the strategy.

Principle 2 — Focus on matters relevant to members

2.48   Principle 2 states that *"The OFR should focus on matters that are relevant to the interests of members"*. [RS (OFR) para 6]. This is consistent with directors' and auditors' reporting on the financial statements.

2.49   The priority of the OFR is to report to members, however, it will also be of interest to other users, such as other investors, potential investors, creditors, customers, suppliers and society more widely. The directors should consider the extent to which they should report on issues relevant to these other users where they are also of importance to members because those issues influence the business' performance and its value. The OFR should not, however, be used as a replacement for other forms of reporting addressed to a wider stakeholder group. [RS (OFR) paras 7, 27, 28].

2.50 The interests of other OFR users may significantly affect the directors' perspective, because they also affect the members' assessment. Factors that may contribute to the relative importance include relationships with key resources (for example, reliance on skilled employees, dependence on a few large customers or suppliers) and the power of other users to affect the entity's business (for example, actions of regulators and unions).

2.51 These issues should be covered by the OFR where they are significant, because the actions of the other users may affect the business and thus the interests of members.

2.52 The example in Table 2.2 indicates that while the company limits its OFR audience to shareholders, it acknowledges that further tailoring can be made to enhance the usefulness of the report to all readers.

Table 2.2 – Reporting to members

Stagecoach Group plc – Annual Report and Financial Statements – 30 April 2007

3. Operating and financial review (extract)

3.1 Introduction (extract)
The Operating and Financial Review that follows is intended largely to reflect the recommendations of the Accounting Standards Board's 2006 reporting statement of best practice on the Operating and Financial Review. We continue to monitor developments in best practice with a view to further tailoring our Operating and Financial Review to enhance its usefulness to readers of the Annual Report.

3.2 Cautionary statement (extract)
The Operating and Financial Review has been prepared for the shareholders of the Company, as a body, and no other persons. Its purpose is to assist shareholders of the Company to assess the strategies adopted by the Company and the potential for those strategies to succeed and for no other purpose.

Principle 3 — Forward looking

2.53 Principle 3 states that *"The OFR should have a forward-looking orientation, identifying those trends and factors relevant to the members' assessment of the current and future performance of the business and the progress towards the achievement of long-term business objectives"*. [RS (OFR) para 8].

2.54 Issues that should be addressed are those that have affected development, performance and position during the year and those that are likely to affect the entity's future development, performance and position. [RS (OFR) para 9].

2.55   There are no rules dictating what information a company must provide in its OFR. Directors must decide which information to include on the basis of their own business dynamics and those of the industry sectors in which they operate.

2.56   Issues might include:

■   An explanation of the resources, principal risks and uncertainties and relationships that may affect the entities long-term value, for example development of new products or services.

■   An analysis of the trends and factors the directors believe are likely to impact future prospects, for example introduction of new technology.

■   Information on future targets, for example, for key performance indicators.

2.57   The reporting statement acknowledges directors' concerns regarding the disclosure of forward-looking information. It notes that some forward-looking information cannot be objectively verified, even though it has been given in good faith. It states that directors may want to include a statement in the OFR that such information should be treated with caution and explain the uncertainties inherent in such information. [RS (OFR) para 10].

2.58   As noted from paragraph 2.37.21, directors may wish to include forward looking information in the directors' report, rather than a separate OFR in order to benefit from the 'safe harbour' provisions contained within the Companies Act 2006, protecting them from civil liability for forward-looking statements made in the directors' report.

2.59   An example of a cautionary statement used by a UK company that conveys a warning similar to that suggested by the reporting statement is given in Table 2.3.

Table 2.3 – Cautionary statement

Smiths Group plc – Annual Report and Accounts – 31 July 2009

Operating and financial review — extract

The purpose of this Report is to provide information to the members of the Company. The Annual Report contains certain forward-looking statements with respect to the operations, performance and financial condition of the Group. By their nature, these statements involve uncertainty since future events and circumstances can cause results and developments to differ materially from those anticipated. The forward-looking statements reflect knowledge and information available at the date of preparation of this Annual Report and the Company undertakes no obligation to update these forward-looking statements. Nothing in this Annual Report should be construed as a profit forecast.

2.60   The reporting statement also recommends commentary on the impact on future performance of significant events after the balance sheet date. [RS (OFR) para 11]. An example is provided in Table 2.3A.

Table 2.3A – Significant events after the balance sheet date

Marconi Corporation plc – Report and Accounts – 31 March 2005

Key Customer Overview (extract)

In the year ended 31 March 2005, our ten largest customers were (in alphabetical order): BT, Deutsche Telekom, E-Plus, Metro City Carriers (Germany), O2, Telecom Italia, Telkom South Africa, Telstra, US Federal Government and Vodafone. In aggregate, these customers accounted for 57 per cent of sales from Continuing Operations. The ten largest customers accounted for 55 per cent of sales from Continuing Operations in the year ended 31 March 2004.

Sales to BT

BT was our largest customer and accounted for 25 per cent of sales from Continuing Operations for the year ended 31 March 2005 (year ended 31 March 2004 was 25 per cent).

The breakdown of our revenues from BT is as follows:

Sales to BT, Year ended 31 March 2005
£ million

Services of which:		173
Cable Services	*101*	
IC&M and Support	*72*	
Optical		88
Legacy Access		48
Broadband Access		13
Total Sales		**322**

Of our total sales revenues of £322 million with BT, £173 million were services revenues. The largest element of our services revenues for the year ended 31 March 2005 was the £101 million earned under our four-year frame services contract with BT Cable Services. The contract, which runs to 2008, involves the installation of fibre and copper services to residential and business users and is not directly associated with the BT 21CN network transformation project.

The balance of our services revenues (£72 million) was for the installation and commissioning and support of optical, access and switching equipment.

Our optical sales to BT are under a three-year frame contract, which guarantees Marconi a minimum of 70 per cent of BT's transmission requirements until March 2006. Optical sales to BT in the year ended 31 March 2005 were £88 million.

Broadband access rollout, which is also covered under our three-year frame contract with BT, accounted for £13 million of product sales in the current financial year, having increased to £7 million in the final quarter of the year. The contract with BT runs until August 2006.

Legacy access products made up the balance of sales to BT (£48 million).

While it has recently been announced that Marconi has not been selected as a preferred supplier for BT's next-generation 21st Century Network, we expect to continue to supply products and services to BT under existing contracts.

OUTLOOK (extract)

Following BT's announcement on preferred suppliers for its 21CN project, we currently expect a reduction in BT revenues from equipment sales and associated services in the order of £50 million in FY06 compared to FY05.

2.61 OFRs should discuss forward-looking comments, both positive and negative, made in previous years' reviews, whether or not these have been borne out by events. [RS (OFR) para 12]. The discussion would usefully include the reasons why any previous predictions have not been fulfilled.

2.62 Such comments might include previous discussions around likely trends and factors impacting the business – for example whether 'gross domestic product' (GDP) growth rates have matched forecasts. They may also include goals or targets set by the company and an explanation comparing actual performance with those goals.

2.63 The example in Table 2.4 explains the financial goals set in previous years and how performance over a period of time compares with those goals, including high level commentary. Further detailed explanations of performance are given in subsequent pages of the annual report.

Table 2.4 – Forward-looking comments made previously

Cadbury Schweppes plc – Annual Report and Accounts – 31 December 2006

Transforming our performance

We set five goals to focus our energy and measure our performance, both internally and externally. Since 2003, we've made good progress against these goals. We delivered above average returns to our shareowners and improved our structure, culture and capabilities. We now have much stronger confectionery and beverages businesses and enhanced capabilities to support them.

We also set three financial goals in 2003, for sales, margin and cash flow. We delivered much improved revenue growth in line with the goals we set and improved cash flow generation.

Although we improved our margins, our margin performance was below the goal we set ourselves, because of significant increases in raw material costs in each of the last three years, events in the UK and Nigeria, and our continued investment behind revenue growth.

How we've performed against our financial goals:

	2003 Financial goal	2004-2006
Revenue growth	3-5% p.a.	5.1% average p.a[1]
Margin growth	50-75bps p.a.	27bps average p.a.
Free Cash Flow generation[2]	£1.5bn in 2004-2007	£1.0bn in 2004-2006

Principle 4 — Complement and supplement the financial statements

2.64 Principle 4 states that *"The OFR should complement as well as supplement the financial statements, in order to enhance the overall corporate disclosure"*. [RS (OFR) para 13].

Supplementing the financial statements

2.65 Supplementing the financial statements means:

■ providing additional explanations of amounts recorded in the financial statements; and

■ explaining the conditions and events that shaped the information contained in the financial statements.

[RS (OFR) para 15].

2.66 The information recorded in financial statements is increasingly complex. For example, pension liabilities are significant for many companies — an understanding of these is essential for investors. The OFR (and the financial statements themselves) can be used to provide additional information to aid that understanding. Events and conditions also shape amounts recorded in the financial statements.

2.67 Taking the example of pensions, it is difficult to truly understand the risks inherent in a scheme and the chances of increased cash contributions or other action being needed in the future.

2.68 One company that supplements its financial statement information on pensions in this way is shown in the example in Table 2.5.

Table 2.5 – Supplementing financial statements

Tomkins plc – Annual Report – 30 December 2006

Actuarial assumptions

Actuarial assumptions are reviewed on a regular basis and updated where appropriate. Tomkins believes that all defined benefit pension plans reflect appropriate mortality assumptions.

Of our total defined benefit pension plan liabilities of £648.9 million, £489.8 million relates to benefits that are deferred or currently being drawn, £20.5 million relates to benefits for active participants that have been frozen in respect of future service or pay-related accruals, and a further £22.9 million relates to plans with benefits based on length of service rather than changes in salary scale. Therefore, £533.2 million of liabilities are not sensitive to changes in salary scale. The majority of defined benefit pension plans are closed to new entrants and therefore the impact of changes in salary scale is limited. £115.7 million, or 17.8%, of the total defined benefit pension plans liabilities are sensitive to salary scale. The table below shows the estimated sensitivity of the liabilities of the defined benefit pension plans to changes in the mortality and salary scale. The impact of changes in the discount rate and expected return on assets is shown in note 33 to the financial statements.

Assumption	Assumption change	Impact on	Estimated impact
Life expectancy	Increase by 1 year	Liabilities	Increase by 2.6%
		Service cost	Increase by 2.4%
		Interest cost	Increase by 2.7%
Salary scale	Increase by 0.5%	Liabilities	Increase by 1.3%

[The next paragraph is 2.70].

Complementing the financial statements

2.70 Complementing the financial statements means providing useful financial and non-financial information about the business and its performance that is not reported in the financial statements, but which is judged by the directors to be relevant to the members in evaluating past results and assessing future prospects. [RS (OFR) para 14].

2.71 Our ongoing research programme with investors over the past decade has clearly shown that, as investors model the future, they typically have insufficient contextual and non-financial information to underpin their cash flow projections. Traditional reporting focuses on past financial performance, which is not the only guide to future returns. The OFR's requirement to complement the financial statements addresses that need.

2.72 Contextual information can be defined broadly and will be unique to each company and its industry sector. It may include information about the markets in which the company operates and expectation for growth. How the company plans to achieve its objectives and the resource and relationships it will need to manage to do, so are key pieces of information to allow investors to evaluate the company. The disclosure framework included in the reporting statement (discussed from para 2.96) provides guidance on the type of information to be reported, much of it contextual in nature.

2.72.1 Similarly, an entity might use the OFR to disclose non-financial information that is relevant to business performance. Examples might include health and safety statistics, such as accident rates, environmental information such as total carbon dioxide emissions and community and social issues. Such factors may have major impacts on the business and, where they are significant, disclosure may be necessary for an assessment of the business' development, performance and position. The impacts are potentially limitless and can include regulatory penalties for underperformance, litigation, employee loyalty, reputation and customer confidence.

Providing non-statutory financial information

2.73 One specific area of financial reporting that is increasingly being considered by companies is the reporting of non-GAAP information – financial figures that differ from those reported on a statutory basis.

2.74 Where amounts from the financial statements have been adjusted for inclusion in the OFR, that fact should be highlighted and a reconciliation provided. [RS (OFR) para 15].

2.75 This is an important recommendation and mirrors guidance issued by the Committee of European Securities Regulators (CESR) in November 2005, 'Recommendations on alternative performance measures'. This contained a number of recommendations relating to alternative measures produced by companies that have adopted IFRS. More information can be found at www.cesr.eu.

2.76   These recommendations include:

- The principles for financial reporting contained in the IASB Framework and the qualitative characteristics of understandability, relevance, reliability and comparability in the Framework should be followed when reporting alternative measures.

- Alternative performance measures should be defined (both the terminology and the basis of calculation).

- Alternative performance measures should only be presented with defined measures and should be reconciled to the defined measures.

- Comparatives should be given and alternative measures should be presented consistently over time.

- Defined measures should be presented with greater prominence than alternative measures.

- An explanation should be provided to explain why alternative measures are presented and how they are used internally.

2.77   We consider that the recommendations above set out by CESR on the use of alternative performance measures should be adopted in OFRs. These recommendations extend to the 'highlights' sections, press releases and commentary sections related to both preliminary and interim announcements, interim management statements and reports and elsewhere in annual reports. See chapter 4 of the Manual of Accounting – IFRS for the UK and chapter 31 of the Manual of Accounting – UK GAAP for further information.

2.77.1   Some companies present an analysis that uses widely accepted measures, such as profitability measured in terms of constant exchange rates, or accepted industry-specific measures, such as replacement cost profit (as used in the oil and gas industry) or the achieved profits method (used in the insurance industry). Despite being widely understood, any such measures should be defined in the annual report and the use of consistent measures across an industry will aid comparison by users.

2.78   An example of a company providing alternative performance measures in accordance with the CESR guidelines is shown in Table 2.6. As well as discussing such measures in the OFR, this company includes non-GAAP information on the face of its primary financial statements, a practice that is acceptable under IFRS and UK company law, where the CESR guidance has been followed.

Table 2.6 – Alternative performance measures

Diploma PLC – Annual Report – 30 September 2006

Operating and Financial Review (extract)

ALTERNATIVE PERFORMANCE MEASURES
The Directors consider that there are alternative measures which are helpful in assessing the underlying operating performance of the Group. For internal management reporting purposes, the Board uses a number of financial measures (which are not defined within IFRS) to assess the underlying operational performance of the Group and its businesses. As such the Board believes these measures are important and should be considered alongside the IFRS measures. The alternative performance measures, which have been used in this Annual Report, are described in note 2 to the consolidated financial statements.

ALTERNATIVE PERFORMANCE MEASURES (note 2)

	Note	2006 £m	2005 £m
Profit before tax		31.2	17.2
Less: Profit on sale of property		(11.1)	–
Add: Amortisation of acquisition intangible assets		0.3	–
ADJUSTED PROFIT BEFORE TAX		20.4	17.2
ADJUSTED EARNINGS PER SHARE	10	62.8p	53.7p

Notes to the Consolidated Financial Statements (extract)

2. ALTERNATIVE PERFORMANCE MEASURES
The Group uses a number of alternative (non-Generally Accepted Accounting Practice ("non-GAAP")) financial measures which are not defined within IFRS. The Directors use these measures in order to assess the underlying operational performance of the Group and as such, these measures are important and should be considered alongside the IFRS measures. The following non-GAAP measures are referred to in this Annual Report.

2.1 Adjusted profit before tax
On the face of the consolidated income statement, "adjusted profit before tax" is separately disclosed, being defined as profit before tax and before the costs of restructuring or rationalisation of operations, the profit or loss relating to the sale of property and the amortisation and impairment of acquisition intangible assets. The Directors believe that adjusted profit before tax is an important measure of the underlying performance of the Group.

2.2 Adjusted earnings per share
"Adjusted earnings per share" is calculated as the total of adjusted profit, less income tax costs, but excluding the tax impact on the items included in the calculation of adjusted profit and the tax effects of goodwill in overseas jurisdictions, less profit attributable to minority interests, divided by the weighted average number of ordinary shares in issue during the year. The Directors believe that adjusted earnings per share provides an important measure of the underlying earning capacity of the Group.

2.3 Free cash flow
On the face of the consolidated cash flow statement, "free cash flow" is reported, being defined as net cash flow from operating activities, after net capital expenditure on fixed assets (excluding business combinations), but before expenditure on business combinations and dividends paid to both minority shareholders and the Company's shareholders. The Directors believe that free cash flow gives an important measure of the cash flow of the Group, available for future investment.

2.4 Trading capital employed

In the segment analysis in note 5 to the consolidated financial statements, "trading capital employed" is reported, being defined as net assets less cash and cash equivalents and deferred tax assets, and after adding back retirement benefit obligations. Return on trading capital employed is defined as being adjusted profit before finance income and tax, divided by trading capital employed plus all historic goodwill and as adjusted for the timing effect of major acquisitions and disposals. Return on trading capital employed at the sector level does not include historic goodwill. The Directors believe that return on trading capital employed is an important measure of the underlying performance of the Group.

Principle 5 — Comprehensive and understandable

2.79 This principle states that *"The OFR should be comprehensive and understandable"*. [RS (OFR) para 16]. The reporting statement adds to this principle by stating that directors should consider whether the omission of information might reasonably be expected to influence significantly the assessment by members. [RS (OFR) para 17]. This is similar wording to that used in defining materiality in IAS 1, 'Presentation of financial statements', and the Statement of Principles in the UK (see further chapter 4 of the Manual of Accounting – IFRS for the UK and chapter 2 of the Manual of Accounting – UK GAAP) and is, perhaps another way of saying that all material information should be included.

2.80 The reporting statement notes that the recommendation for the OFR to be comprehensive does not mean that it should cover all possible matters. The objective is quality not quantity. It is not possible for a reporting statement to list all of the elements that might need to be included, as these will vary depending on the nature and circumstances of the particular business and how it is run. [RS (OFR) para 18].

2.81 A simple example of what types of information might be relevant to one entity's OFR, but not to another's might be:

	Company A	Company B (Operates solely in the UK, sourcing its product and making sales in the UK)
	(Operates internationally)	
Exchange rates	Relevant	Less relevant
Political disturbances	Relevant	Less relevant
Cross border tax rules	Relevant	Less relevant
Hyperinflation	Possibly relevant	Less relevant
Global market trends	Relevant	Less relevant

2.81.1 The question of whether information is comprehensive may be particularly difficult to assess when dealing with the future and forward-looking statements. This is a natural consequence of the increased uncertainty inherent in predicting the future.

2.82 The reporting statement notes that, where relevant, directors should explain the source of information and the degree to which the information is objectively supportable, so that members can assess the reliability of the information for themselves. [RS (OFR) para 19]. Table 2.8 shows an example of disclosure of sources and provides both trend data and a forward-looking orientation to the information.

2.83 It is likely that directors, as well as making the 'cautionary statement' referred to above in paragraph 2.58, may, in particular, wish to explain fully the basis for predictive (forward-looking) statements and the degree of objective evidence supporting the statements. This is not to say that objective evidence does not exist for predictive statements or that uncertainty should, in itself, restrict directors' predictive statements, but rather that appropriate caveats may need to be given.

2.84 One type of forward-looking statement for which objective evidence should exist, is the expected growth rate for a particular country in which the entity may wish to expand its business. Such growth rates or rates of consumer spending may be based on estimates made by governments or by international organisations such as the World Bank. Another example is forecast growth rates for an industry sector where a recognised and reputable organisation provides industry specific data. An example of the latter is provided in Table 2.8, explaining the source and its objectivity.

Table 2.8 – Objective evidence for forecasts

Emap plc – Annual Report and Accounts – 31 March 2007

Business review (extract)

UK advertising
Advertising accounted for 45% of Continuing Group revenue in 2007, showing that the state of the UK advertising market has an effect on our performance. However, over the last five years the proportion of our revenue derived from advertising has declined from 50% to 45% and we would expect this trend to continue in the future as we reshape the Group.

In the UK, the Advertising Association (AA) is recognised as a reputable, independent source of information and estimates of growth for the advertising market. The Internet Advertising Bureau (IAB) is an independent source of information and estimates for the internet advertising market. According to the latest available AA estimates (Mar 07), in 2006 the total advertising market in the UK was broadly flat, with consumer magazine, radio, B2B magazine and TV advertising all showing declines. In this environment, our ability to grow the amount of advertising across our traditional media platforms has been challenging and the state of the advertising market will continue to affect our prospects going forward.

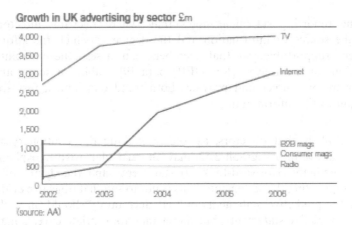

Growth in UK advertising by sector £m

(source: AA)

The internet continues to be the fastest growing medium for advertising, up 41% in 2006, driven by increasing broadband penetration and internet usage. Internet advertising accounted for 12% of total UK advertising spending in 2006, up from 8% in 2005 (source: AA).

2.85 The directors should consider the key issues to be included in the OFR. The inclusion of too much information may obscure judgements and will not promote understanding. Where additional information is included elsewhere in the annual report or other reports, cross-referencing to those sources will assist members. [RS (OFR) para 20].

2.86 However, where information, such as environmental or employee information, is included in a separate corporate social responsibility (CSR) report, the relevant information should still be included in the OFR to the extent necessary to enable members to assess the entity's development, performance and position. Any cross-referencing should be to additional information in the CSR or other report that is not essential for the purpose of the OFR.

2.87 The example in Table 2.9 shows that only certain aspects of its CSR reporting are included in the OFR and refers readers elsewhere for more in-depth information.

Table 2.9 – Cross reference to supplementary information

Centrica plc – Annual Report and Accounts – 31 December 2006

Corporate Responsibility (extract)

Information on our corporate responsibility (CR) activities over the last year is included in the reports on each of our business units. This section provides a summary of key themes, as well as performance information on group-wide activities. More detail will be provided in our 2006 CR Report, which will be available at www.centrica.com/responsibility in May 2007.

2.88 The reporting statement recommends that the OFR should be written in a clear and readily understandable style. [RS (OFR) para 21].

2.89 Management should consider what it needs to communicate, and what investors want to know, to prevent key messages from getting lost. For example, some form of narrative sequence and clear linkage from the company's markets to their strategy to their key performance indicators and future goals. An integrated structure, where important issues are linked throughout the report, can aid the reader's retention of the information provided.

2.90 Making the messages within the OFR understandable is imperative. Directors can help readers to navigate their reporting by explaining the critical issues for the company, highlighting them in quotes, titles, bullet points, etc. Graphical summaries can be used to present complex information visually. Use of plain English with clear explanations of technical terms and avoidance of jargon will help companies meet the aim of the principle of clarity and understandability.

2.90.1 This may be of particular application to industries where the product is of a highly technical or scientific nature. For example, while the use of technical terms and scientific names may be unavoidable in an explanation of a drug development pipeline, application of this principle might mean additional information being given to describe 'in layman's terms' what the drug does in relation to diseases or other conditions and how development will benefit both the company and the sufferers. Many pharmaceutical companies also include a brief description of the various stages (phases) of the approval process for new drugs.

2.91 Helpful navigation ensures that readers can find the information they need. A clear table of contents and an index, use of colour-coded sections or tabs and clarity in titles and sub-headings will all help achieve this. Companies can also repeat information or provide cross-referencing to other areas of the report to provide context and use box-outs to highlight key issues or figures.

Principle 6 — Balanced and neutral

2.92 Principle 6 states that *"The OFR should be balanced and neutral, dealing even-handedly with both good and bad aspects"*. [RS (OFR) para 22]. It means that directors should maintain a balance between good and bad news, give details of unfavourable events and include information about setbacks or misjudgements. [RS (OFR) para 23]. An example of disclosure that balances positive and negative aspects of the business is shown in Table 2.10.

Table 2.10 – Balanced reporting

ITV plc – Report and Accounts – 31 December 2006

Message from the Executive Chairman Michael Grade

On Monday, 8 January, 2007 I returned to work for ITV. From the moment I was approached by the Board last year, I had no doubt that I would accept this most stimulating and challenging position in British broadcasting.

ITV has not had an easy time in recent history, operating in the highly competitive and technology driven media sector. It faced a challenging advertising market and speculation over both its leadership and its ownership.

My brief is to restore the fortunes of the Group and thus return the business to growth.

Having been in post for two months it is too soon to conclude definitive plans for the business, but generally I have developed more positive impressions than negative ones, and the latter are mostly within our control to remedy.

On the positive side:

–   There are talented and dedicated people across all areas of the Company;

–   ITV Productions is a superb business of real scale with the ability to deliver outstanding content, from the Oscar winning film "The Queen" starring Dame Helen Mirren, to Coronation Street and Emmerdale, to Dancing on Ice;

–   ITV remains a much-loved brand and ITV1 is still the UK's most popular television channel in peak-time with the England v Sweden game during the football World Cup achieving the highest audience (18.5 million) on any channel in 2006;

–   Our strong regional presence is a greater asset than is recognised and the growth in regional advertising has been particularly buoyant against a depressed national TV advertising market. We need to find ways to sustain and even enhance this valuable public service. It is part of what binds ITV to its audiences throughout the UK and distinguishes us from our competitors.

–   Our digital channels are the most successful free to air commercial family of digital channels in the UK, each with distinctive branding and programming. We must ensure that they have the investment they need to grow their leading market position as we approach digital switchover;

–   The Consumer businesses represent an area of proven growth which we will seek to accelerate; and

–   The Board's strategy which I inherit is essentially sound. The businesses that have been recently acquired and developed are all natural extensions of the core operations.

On the negative side:

–   Whilst the strategy is sound, we are playing catch up in many areas, no doubt due to the efforts required to 'bed in' the successful Carlton/Granada merger. We have a valuable multichannel offering and exciting web opportunities – but still a long way to grow;

–   There is a lack of innovation in our programming, partly resulting from a fear of ratings failure and the punitive consequences that follow under the Contract Rights Renewal (CRR) remedy (described below);

–   The Company has developed a tendency towards bureaucracy. The cure for this lies with the example set by the leadership team within the businesses. I will improve delegation, and place emphasis on the need to make the ITV values (described on page 25) a reality in our actions;

– We need to continue strengthening the relationship between our commissioning teams and both internal and external producers. This is critical to ensure that the commissioning pipeline is filled with the high-quality programmes that deliver the audiences which in turn our commissioning team need to fulfil our advertisers' and viewers' aspirations; and

– Our regulatory environment needs to reflect the reality of our 21st century structure and the developing market in which we operate these days. ITV may have consolidated, but it is a long way from the advertising monopoly of yesteryear. The regulatory burden has yet fully to reflect this.

Principle 7 — Comparable

2.93 Principle 7 states that *"The OFR should be comparable over time"*. [RS (OFR) para 24]. This ensures that directors do not change from one performance measure to another from year to year depending on which gives the more favourable impression of the business. Similarly, if information is given in one year about a particular aspect of the business, similar information should be given in subsequent years if that aspect of the business remains significant. The aim is for information to be sufficient for members to compare it with similar information about the entity for previous financial years. Information on particular aspects of the business given over several years enables members to identify and analyse trends and other factors over successive years. [RS (OFR) para 25].

2.94 The example illustrated in Table 2.11 shows how performance indicators are measured over several years and highlights that a new measure will be developed and introduced in the following period.

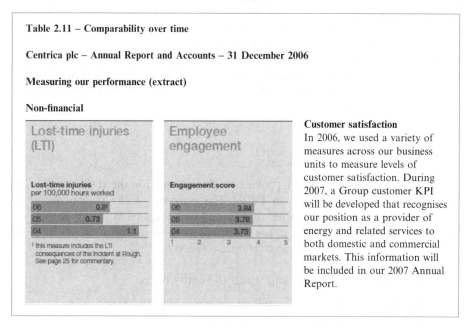

Table 2.11 – Comparability over time

Centrica plc – Annual Report and Accounts – 31 December 2006

Measuring our performance (extract)

Non-financial

Lost-time injuries (LTI)

Lost-time injuries per 100,000 hours worked

06	0.8[†]
05	0.73
04	1.1

[†] this measure includes the LTI consequences of the incident at Rough. See page 25 for commentary.

Employee engagement

Engagement score

06	3.84
05	3.78
04	3.73

1 2 3 4 5

Customer satisfaction
In 2006, we used a variety of measures across our business units to measure levels of customer satisfaction. During 2007, a Group customer KPI will be developed that recognises our position as a provider of energy and related services to both domestic and commercial markets. This information will be included in our 2007 Annual Report.

2.95 The reporting statement notes that directors may wish to consider the extent to which the OFR is consistent with reviews prepared by other entities in the same industry or geographical sector. [RS (OFR) para 25].

Table 2.12 – Comparability across industry sector

Prudential plc – Annual Report and Accounts – 31 December 2006

Directors report: Operating and financial review (extract)

Other corporate information (extract)

In May 2004, the CFO Forum, representing the Chief Financial Officers of 19 European insurers, published the European Embedded Value Principles (Principles) which are designed to improve the transparency and consistency of embedded value reporting.

Member companies, of which Prudential is one, agreed to adopt the Principles for supplementary reporting no later than the financial year end commencing 1 January 2005. Prudential fully adopted the Principles for the first time in respect of full-year 2005 results.

For Prudential, EEV reporting represents an evolution from achieved profits reporting and it welcomes the improved clarity and consistency of information that it provides to investors although there is still some way to go before achieving full consistency.

Compared to achieved profits, the principal differences are in respect of three areas:

- inclusion of an explicit allowance for the impact of options and guarantees. This typically requires stochastic calculations, under which a large number of simulations are performed that provide a representation of the future behaviour of financial markets;

- more active allowance for the combined impact of risk profile and encumbered capital in the selection of discount rates. This ensures that the risks to the emergence of shareholder cash flows are properly accounted for; and

- enhanced disclosure that enables informed investors to understand better the key risks within the business and the basis of preparation of the results.

The EEV basis not only provides a good indicator of the value being added by management in a given accounting period but it also demonstrates whether shareholder capital is being deployed to best effect. Indeed, insurance companies in many countries use comparable bases of accounting for management purposes.

Disclosure framework

2.96 The reporting statement provides a framework for the disclosures to be provided by the directors in an OFR. The purpose of the framework is to prescribe the key content elements that should be addressed in the OFR. It is for directors to consider how best to use the framework to structure the OFR, given the entity's circumstances. These circumstances may include:

- The industry or industries in which the entity operates.

- The range of products, services or processes that the entity offers.

- The number of markets served by the entity.

[RS (OFR) para 26].

2.96.1 Companies may also consider other criteria. For example, the company values adopted by Body Shop International PLC affect how the company presents its operating and financial review. The company's reputation and success is strongly linked to its social, environmental and ethical values on animal testing, community trade, self-esteem, human rights and protecting the planet. It aligns its business policies closely with its own and its customers' shared beliefs in these values and links the sale of its products, such as those relating to 'self esteem' with high profile campaigns, for example against domestic violence. As a result, the content and presentation of the OFR is more than usually devoted to social, environmental and ethical issues, because these are the issues that are of interest to its customers and members and which also contribute to the company's performance. This approach, 'profits with principles' is set out in Table 2.12A.

Table 2.12A – Profits with principles

Body Shop International PLC – Report and Accounts – 26 February 2005

Delivering Value to Stakeholders

The Body Shop has an established reputation as a socially and environmentally responsible company. We believe that our values are consistent with strong and sustained financial performance, and that profits with principles must be achieved in order to sustain the long-term future of the Group.

The Body Shop is committed to maintaining high standards of social and environmental performance. We believe in doing business with integrity and transparency. This means using our ethical principles to inform the way we do business, setting ourselves and our business partners clear standards of practice. It also involves engaging stakeholders with our business aims and publicly reporting on our performance within the overall context of our business strategy.

The overall strategic direction of the Group's values is reviewed periodically by the Board in consultation with the Director of Values. The Director of Values reports into the Chief Executive Officer and has overall responsibility for directing the Group's social and environmental programme. Strategic values objectives are aligned with the business objectives as well as stakeholder perceptions and expectations. These objectives are fully embraced by the senior management team, who have responsibility for balancing the interests of all key stakeholder groups. Sub-committees help direct the social and environmental approach of the business. These include an Issues Management Group, which reports into the Risk Committee; a Corporate Health and Safety Strategy Group; an Environmental Steering Group; and an Animal Protection Steering Group.

2.97 The OFR should provide information to assist members to assess the strategies adopted by the entity and the potential for those strategies to succeed. The key elements of the disclosure framework necessary to achieve this are:

- The nature of the business, including a description of the market, competitive and regulatory environment in which the entity operates and the entity's objectives and strategies.

- The business' development and performance, both in the financial year under review and in the future.

- The resources, principal risks and uncertainties and relationships that may affect the entity's long-term value.

■ Position of the business including a description of the entity's capital structure, treasury policies and objectives, and liquidity, both in the financial year under review and the future.

[RS (OFR) para 27].

2.98 To assist companies in structuring their OFR information more effectively, the reporting statement sets out the above disclosure framework, which can be represented in a logical flow as shown in Table 2.13.

Table 2.13 – Disclosure framework

The nature, objectives and strategies of the business	Resources, risks and uncertainties, and relationships	Current and future development of performance	Financial position
– Description of business and external environment. – Objectives to generate or preserve value over the longer term. – Strategies for achieving the objectives.	– Description of resources, tangible and intangible, available and how they are managed. – Description of principal risks and uncertainties and the directors' approach to them. – Information about significant relationships and stakeholders other than investors who may directly impact performance.	– Significant features of the development and performance of the business. – Main trends and factors likely to impact future performance.	– Analysis of the financial position and critical accounting policies. – Discussion of the capital structure. – Discussion of the cash inflows and outflows, ability to generate cash to meet commitments and fund growth. – Discussion of current and prospective liquidity.
Underpinned by the financial and non-financial KPIs used to assess progress against stated objectives, as well as other measures and evidence			

2.99 The OFR should also include the following information to the extent necessary to meet the recommendations set out in paragraph 27 of the reporting statement:

■ Environmental matters (including the impact of the entity's business on the environment).

■ The entity's employees.

■ Social and community issues.

■ Persons with whom the entity has contractual or other arrangements that are essential to the entity's business.

■ Receipts from, and returns to, the entity's members in respect of members' shareholdings.

■ All other matters the directors consider to be relevant.

[RS (OFR) para 28].

2.100 The OFR should also include the following items relating to environmental matters, the entity's employees and social and community issues:

■ The entity's policies in each area mentioned.

■ The extent to which those policies have been successfully implemented.

[RS (OFR) para 29].

Detailed guidance within the disclosure framework

The business' nature, objectives and strategies

2.101 The OFR should include a description of the business and the external environment in which it operates. This is to provide a context for the discussion and analysis of the entity's development, performance and financial position. [RS (OFR) para 30].

2.102 Depending on the nature of the business, the OFR should include discussion of matters such as:

■ The industries in which the business operates.

■ The entity's major markets and competitive position within those markets.

■ Significant features of the legal, regulatory, macro-economic and social environment that influence the business.

■ The main products and services, business processes and distribution methods.

■ The business' structure and its economic model, including an overview of the main operating facilities and their location.

[RS (OFR) paras 31, 32].

2.103 To understand and evaluate a company's strategy and performance, investors need a clear grasp of its business environment and the impact this has on the company now and in the future. Often, performance has been reported in isolation with only high level commentary on the business environment such as *"...against intensifying competition..."* or *"...prospects are good..."*.

2.104 Investors who are familiar with the company are interested in management's interpretation of market developments and trends; some may be less familiar and need the information to judge performance and the logic of strategies adopted by the company.

2.105 The example in Table 2.14 shows how the description of a business can be clearly presented, identifying the sectors it operates in, cross-referencing to further information for ease of navigation and highlighting the key messages for each sector. It also includes information on the entity's economic model – how it owns each type of property.

Table 2.14 – Description of business

Land Securities PLC – Annual Report – 31 March 2007

Report of the Directors (extract)

All you need to know (extract)

Land Securities is one of the world's five largest Real Estate Investment Trusts. Our national portfolio of commercial property includes some of UK's best-known shopping centres and landmarks.

We are leading urban renaissance through our multi-billion pound development programme, transforming regional city centres and key sites in Central London. We are also one of the leading names in Property Partnerships, and are involved in long-term, large-scale regeneration projects in the south east.

Land Securities Group

Retail Portfolio *See pages 34–44*
This business unit includes shopping centres, retail warehouses, shops outside London, shops held through the Metro Shopping Fund LP, regional offices and other regional properties.

Key points:

- 29 shopping centres and 31 retail parks
- 1.8 million m^2 of retail accommodation
- approximately 1,700 retailer occupiers
- nearly 300 million shopper visits per year
- development pipeline for some 255,000m^2 of retail led space

London Portfolio *See pages 44–53*
This business unit includes all London offices and London retail, but excludes those assets held in the Metro Shopping Fund LP.

Key points:

- over one million m^2 of office and retail accommodation
- more than 50,000 people work in offices owned by us
- provides accommodation for over 400 organisations
- potential to develop 600,000m^2 of commercial and residential space over next 10 years

Property Partnerships* *See pages 54–63*
This business unit is engaged in long-term property outsourcing partnerships with public sector organisations including DWP, DVLA and Royal Mail and with corporates including Norwich Union, Barclays and Accor Hotels. We have interests in 105 Public Private Partnership (PPP) projects in areas such as schools, hospitals, secure accommodation and offices.

Key points:

- 3.4 million m^2 across 2,024 properties in property outsourcing partnerships
- 1.4 million m^2 of PPP project floorspace average length of property outsourcing partnership contracts is 24 years with gross income of £794m
- Property Partnerships employs 919 people across the UK

*Land Securities Trillium, which we previously described as our property outsourcing business, is now known as Land Securities Trillium Property Partnerships as a result of our expansion into the PPP/Private Finance Initiative (PFI) markets.

2.105.1 From the business description, a user of the financial statements can expect to get an overall picture of the business. For example:

■ Whether it operates internationally.

■ Whether it operates in unstable economic and political regions.

■ The entity's relative strength in the markets/industry compared to its competitors, including its strongest and weakest business and geographic areas.

■ Whether the entity is highly regulated, or subject to significant legal actions against it.

■ The economic performance and outlook for the economies, markets and sectors in which the business operates.

■ The environmental and social factors that influence the business.

■ The products or services the entity provides, whether they involve significant R&D or advertising support and the product risk involved; whether there is significant dependency on a small number of customers or suppliers or scarcity of sources of supply for raw materials that affect the business.

■ Whether there are significant factors involved in manufacturing or distributing the entity's products.

■ How the business is organised and monitored by the board, for example by business or geographic sectors or a combination of both. Whether the business is run centrally or if the individual units have a high degree of autonomy.

■ Where the main operating facilities are located, their numbers, giving an idea of the business' size and the number of its employees.

2.106 The OFR should discuss the objectives of the business to generate or preserve value over the longer-term. [RS (OFR) para 33]. The reporting statement notes that objectives will often be defined in terms of financial performance, but that objectives in non-financial areas should also be discussed, where appropriate. [RS (OFR) para 34].

2.106.1 To some extent this understates the increasing importance to businesses of non-financial objectives. In the past such non-financial objectives have been of lesser importance. To take an extreme case, in the past a timber company might have obtained its product through flattening an area of rainforest, with little or no regard for the social, ecological or other consequences. The directors' concern would have been to make as much money as possible for the members. However, today such a policy would be extremely damaging to such an entity's reputation. In addition, it is likely that a significant number of customers would boycott the product, there would be legal action by deprived ethnic groups and environmental and regulatory authorities would impose fines or other sanctions. And that is before any action by environmental pressure groups. This is because there is a growing awareness of, and emphasis placed by both customers and members on, such non-financial elements of business operations. It is no longer just a question of making money, but also of how money is made.

2.106.2   For this reason the attitude of both directors and members is changing as they discover that in order to make the best return, their financial objectives and general interests are best served by having increased regard to social, environmental and other non-financial factors. As a result, an entity's objectives, whilst generally continuing to focus on achieving returns for members, include or refer to non-financial objectives or factors, particularly in those industries that have the potential to significantly affect the environment in which they operate. The theme of increasing responsibility is now a trend or factor that influences the development of businesses. It emerges even more clearly in the development of strategies.

2.106.3   A growing number of large companies now produce separate corporate social responsibility reports. Thus, whilst in some cases the OFR may contain details of a company's policy and performance in this area, in other cases a separate report is often prepared. Sometimes such a report is separate from the annual report and accounts, with only a summary appearing in the latter document. On other occasions a full corporate social responsibility report is included with the annual report, either separate from the OFR or incorporated within it.

2.106.4   Whilst discussion of corporate social responsibility is outside the scope of this chapter, it is worth noting that there are a number of organisations dedicated to improving corporate reporting in this area. Among them is Business in the Community and The Business Impact Review Group, who work together to develop a common approach to social and environmental reporting. As part of this work they developed guidance for disclosures under five major headings: marketplace, environment, workplace, community and human rights.

2.106.5   In relation to the importance of non-financial objectives, the example in Table 2.14A is an example of the disclosure of a company's non-financial policies and performance.

Table 2.14A – Social, environmental and other non-financial factors

Smiths Group plc – Annual Report and Accounts – 31 July 2007

Business Review (extract)

Corporate responsibility

Smiths has six fundamental strengths. Corporate responsibility for Smiths is enshrined in the sixth strength: 'doing business the right way'. Smiths defines 'the right way' in the Code of Corporate Responsibility and Business Ethics ('the Code'), which is based on 12 principles:

1   compliance with national laws and regulations;

2   fair and vigorous competition in the marketplace;

3   integrity and ethical conduct as the standard of individual and corporate business behaviour;

4   fair and honest treatment of suppliers and customers;

5   proper and respectful treatment of employees;

6   high standards for health and safety in the workplace;

7   respect for the environment;

8   contributions to the communities in which we live and work;

9   straightforward public information and activities;

10 respect for human rights;

11 prudent and transparent public accounting and reporting; and

12 a culture of compliance throughout the entire Smiths organisation – from the Chief Executive to the newest employee.

Translated into 13 languages, the Code applies to all Smiths businesses and employees worldwide and provides the framework for policies, programmes and procedures for a range of corporate responsibility issues. It is endorsed and fully supported by the Board.

Code compliance support to Smiths businesses worldwide is provided through a number of channels (including via the legal, human resources and internal audit functions) which provide advice, export control policies, education, training, guidance materials and risk assessment tools.

Managing corporate responsibility

The Code is set by the Board and monitored by the Code Compliance Council, chaired by the General Counsel, which reports at least twice a year to the Audit Committee of the Board. Responsibility for managing specific issues, however, lies at different levels within the Group, depending on the nature of the issue and how it can most effectively be managed:

● health, safety and environment issues are managed through a Group-wide steering committee and organisation;

● employee issues are managed through the human resources function and by line management;

● supplier and customer programmes are managed by each business; and

● community programmes are principally managed locally, although there is also some Group-level activity.

Environment

Smiths is committed to ensuring that, as far as is reasonably practicable, any detrimental effects of its activities, products and services upon the environment are minimised. In practice, this means using performance-based environmental management systems to drive improvement throughout the business.

Performance against targets

Target (set July 04)	2007 result	2006 result	Comment
ISO14001 certification for sites except small offices, with new acquisitions achieving certification within two years	**74 out of 75 currently eligible sites certified**	83 out of 104 eligible sites	All originally targeted sites all have been certified. Ongoing certified programme in place for certification of new sites
Energy consumption target set at 180MWh/£m sales (5% reduction over three years)	**145 MWh/£m sales**	176MWh/£m sales	Target achieved
Waste to landfill target set at 3.5 Tonnes/£m sales (6% reduction over three years)	**3.39 Tonnes/£m sales**	2.93 Tonnes/£m sales	Target achieved
Air emissions target set at 112kg/£m sales (6% reduction over three years)	**106kg/£m sales**	100kg/£m sales	Target achieved
Water consumption target set at 411m^3/£m sales (12% reduction over three years)	**258m^3/£m sales**	398m^3/£m sales	Target achieved

*Note that the 2004 baseline data includes Smiths Aerospace whereas 2007 does not. Whilst normalisation against sales makes the figures directly comparable, the changed mix of manufacturing processes can exaggerate to some extent an already positive level of achievement.

Health and safety

Smiths is committed to conducting all its activities in a manner which achieves the highest practicable standards of health and safety. This year, attention has been focused on the underperforming sites and improving cross-divisional sharing of good practice.

Performance against targets

Target (set July 04)	2007 results	2006 result	Comment
Recordable incident rate no target set	**1.96/200,000 man-hour**	2.58/200,000 man-hours	Ongoing year-on-year improvement achieved
Lost days rate no target set	**25.61/200,000 man-hours**	27.91/200,000 man-hours	Ongoing year-on-year improvement achieved
Lost time incident rate 1 incident/ 200,000 man-hours	**0.92/200,000 man-hours**	1.15/200,000 man-hours	Target achieved

New targets

We are pleased that the three-year targets set in 2004 have been achieved and new targets have been developed to drive improvement still further.

Environment

The major current public environmental issue worldwide is greenhouse gas emissions and their impact on climate change. Smiths most significant emissions source is from the generation of electrical energy purchased by and consumed in our facilities. We have in recent publications converted our energy consumption to carbon dioxide equivalent values and for the next three-year period it is appropriate to target our overall greenhouse gas emissions. This will include emissions from energy usage and VOC emissions and thus replace these former targets.

Formal international greenhouse regulatory systems do not consider normalisation. Instead, they target based on a fixed cap. It is appropriate that Smiths follows this trend and establishes a target of the same level of emissions or better in FY 2009 to 2010 as FY 2006 to 2007 for each individual facility. Additionally, total waste (net of recycled waste) and water consumption will continue to be targeted with an overall 9% improvement normalised against sales.

Health and safety

Building on the successful drive to reduce lost time incidents it has been decided to target 'recordable incidents'. This measure includes incidents that do not necessarily lead to lost time and thus is more challenging. Good practice is acknowledged as a recordable incident rate of better than 1.5 per 100 employees per year and this target has been set as the goal for the Group. Many parts of Smiths are already performing at this level but we will focus on those that do not whilst striving to maintain progress at all sites.

The implementation of the ISO14001 Environmental Management System plays a significant part in ensuring that our businesses have robust systems in place for managing environmental performance. Thus it has been decided to target implementation of the comparable OHSAS18001 Health and Safety Management System. At this stage the target has been set for external certification at two-thirds of our manufacturing sites with 50 or more employees within the next three years.

Employees

The Group's policy is to provide equal opportunities for employment. Smiths recruits, selects and promotes employees on the basis of their qualifications, skills, aptitude and attitude. In employment-related decisions, Smiths complies with anti-discrimination requirements in the relevant jurisdictions concerning matters of race, colour, national origin, gender, marital status, sexual orientation, religious belief, age, or physical or mental disability. Disabled people are given full consideration for employment and subsequent training, career development and promotion on the basis of their aptitudes and abilities.

All Smiths employees are treated with respect and dignity. Accordingly, any harassment or bullying is unacceptable. Smiths respects the right of each employee to join or not to join a trade union or other bona fide employee representative organisation. Smiths believes in good communications with employees and in promoting consultation, co-operation and teamwork on matters of mutual concern. Smiths offers all employees in the US and UK share schemes that enable employees to acquire an interest in the Company's shares and to align their interests more closely with those of shareholders.

Reaching Full Potential

Smiths invests in employees' skills and capabilities to help them reach their own Full Potential, which in turn helps the Company and its businesses to do likewise. Current priorities for Smiths to achieve full potential across the Group are talent development, succession planning and employee engagement.

Talent development

Smiths Group and the individual businesses continue to invest in identifying and developing the talents of our people. Smiths provides employees with challenging work that stretches their capabilities, backing that up with training and development activities tailored to individual needs. In 2006, Smiths introduced a new process for the most senior people, integrating the performance review with the overall 'Full Potential' goals of the business.

Smiths continues to be actively involved in all aspects of training and developing young people, including initiatives designed to ease the transition from school to work. Horizons is a two-year programme for new and recently appointed graduates. It provides an understanding of the Group and the business world in general, and develops personal and teamworking skills.

Succession planning

Smiths has a systematic succession management process for senior leadership roles. The Group identifies leadership talent and development needs, and follows this up with individual development plans that are monitored by senior management.

Employee engagement

Smiths provides information to and communicates with employees as an important part of doing business. Employees are regularly provided with a wide range of information concerning the performance and prospects of the business in which they are involved by means of employee councils, information and consultation forums, and other consultative bodies that allow their views to be taken into account.

Communities

Smiths is committed to contributing to the communities in which we operate. In addition to providing employment opportunities, we focus on community involvement through charitable giving, regeneration and education initiatives.

Smiths supports national and international charitable organisations from a central budget administered by the Charity and Donations Committee. This year's beneficiaries include the Royal Academy of Engineering, which helped to set up a new collaborative education initiative with Smiths in the UK – the Smiths Technology Education Programme (STEP) – which aims to provide able young people with the information and financial support they need to explore a career in technology. Individual businesses also support charity projects in a number of areas. For example, Smiths Medical supports medical research via the Smiths Medical Chair of Anaesthesia and Critical Care at University College London. In addition to corporate donations, Smiths businesses devote a time to local community projects around the world. For example, Smiths Medical recently participated in St Mungo's Putting Down Roots scheme, a gardening project for London's homeless.

For further information, please see the Corporate Responsibility Report 2007 at www.smiths.com/responsibility.

2.106.6   Examples of where financial objectives are qualified by non-financial considerations in the extractive industry, one of the industries where such factors are most significant, are given in Tables 2.14B and 2.14C. A further example, where the objectives are extended from the most common 'increasing value for members' to inclusion of all stakeholders in that objective, together with a strong emphasis on non-financial factors is quoted in Table 2.14D.

Table 2.14B – Social, environmental and other non-financial factors

Rio Tinto plc – Report and Accounts – 31 December 2006

Rio Tinto

Rio Tinto is a leading international mining group headquartered in the UK, combining Rio Tinto plc, a London listed public company, and Rio Tinto Limited, which is listed on the Australian Securities Exchange.

Rio Tinto's business is finding, mining and processing mineral resources. Major products are aluminium, copper, diamonds, energy (coal and uranium), gold, industrial minerals (borax, titanium dioxide, salt, talc) and iron ore. Activities span the world but are strongly represented in Australia and North America with significant businesses in South America, Asia, Europe and southern Africa.

The Group's objective is to maximise the overall long term return to shareholders through a strategy of investing in large, cost competitive mines, driven by the quality of each opportunity, not the choice of commodity.

Wherever Rio Tinto operates, the health and safety of its employees is the first priority. The Group seeks to contribute to sustainable development. It works as closely as possible with host countries and communities, respecting their laws and customs and ensuring a fair share of benefits and opportunities.

Rio Tinto (extract)

Objective, strategy and management structure

Our fundamental objective is to maximise the overall long term value and return to our shareholders. We do this by operating responsibly and sustainably in areas of proven expertise such as exploration, project evaluation and mining, where the Group has a competitive advantage.

Our strategy is to maximise net present value by investing in large, long life, cost competitive mines. Investments are driven by the quality of each opportunity, not by the choice of commodity.

Rio Tinto's management structure is designed to facilitate a clear focus on the Group's objective. This structure, reflected in this report, is based on the following principal product and global support groups:

- Iron Ore
- Energy
- Industrial Minerals
- Aluminium
- Copper
- Diamonds
- Exploration
- Operational and Technical Excellence (OTX).

The chief executive of each product group reports to the chief executive of Rio Tinto.

2043

Table 2.14C – Social, environmental and other non-financial factors

BHP Billiton plc – Report and Accounts – 30 June 2006

We are BHP Billiton, a leading global resources company

Our purpose is to create long-term value through the discovery, development and conversion of natural resources, and the provision of innovative customer and market-focused solutions.

Our seven strategic drivers assist us in achieving our objectives. These drivers are our people; our licence to operate; our world-class assets; the way we do business; our financial strength and discipline; our project pipeline; and growth options.

Underpinning our strategic drivers are the values that guide us. They are:

- An overriding commitment to health, safety, environmental responsibility and sustainable development.

- Integrity and doing what we say we will do.

- A commitment to achieving superior business results and stretching our capabilities.

- Having the courage to lead change in the face of adversity.

- The embracing of diversity and showing respect for and trust in each other.

3. Operating and financial review and prospects (extract)

Strategic drivers of our business

Our core purpose is to create long-term value through the discovery, development and conversion of natural resources and the provision of innovative customer and market-focused solutions.

Fundamentally, this means that our business will have:

- a focus on the upstream extraction of natural resources

- high-quality, long-life and low-cost assets with embedded growth options

- a diversified portfolio of commodities and assets and geographic regions that reduce the volatility of cash flows

- a focus on seaborne traded commodities

- a global portfolio of employees, assets and customers.

Our strategy is based around discovering or acquiring and developing large, low-cost, high reserve assets to produce stable cash flows that support an ongoing program of exploration and development of new assets, as well as providing consistent and growing returns to shareholders. In executing this strategy, we focus on seven strategic drivers:

- People – the foundation of our business is our people. We require people to find resources, develop those resources, operate the businesses that produce our products, and then deliver that product to our customers.

- Licence to operate – we ensure that those who are impacted by our operations also benefit by the operation. Licence to operate means win-win relationships and partnerships. This includes a central focus on health, safety, environment and the community, and being valued as a good corporate citizen.

- World-class assets – our world-class assets provide the cash flows that are required to build new projects, to pay our employees, suppliers, taxes and partners, and ultimately to pay dividends to our shareholders. We maintain high-quality assets by managing them in the most effective and efficient way. Taking care of our world-class assets is absolutely critical.

- The BHP Billiton way – this concept captures a series of Business Excellence processes, knowledge sharing networks and our customer-focused marketing organisation, which is applied to all of our assets and businesses. The development of these processes and sharing of the principles behind those concepts lead to increased economies of scale and shared best practices.

- Financial strength and discipline – we have a solid single 'A' credit rating, which balances financial flexibility with the cost of finance. Strong financial management is necessary in order to support the growth initiatives we are undertaking globally across all our businesses.

- Project pipeline – we are continuously identifying, prioritising and executing the next set of growth projects. It is a critical part of our strategy to successfully deliver our growth projects on time and on budget.

- Growth options – we use exploration, technology and our global footprint to identify the next generation of opportunities where we can invest and use our skills and strengths.

BHP Billiton Charter

Our purpose is to create long-term value through the discovery, development and conversion of natural resources, and the provision of innovative customer and market-focused solutions.

To prosper and achieve real growth, we must:

- actively manage and build our portfolio of high-quality assets and services,

- continue the drive towards a high-performance organisation in which every individual accepts responsibility and is rewarded for results,

- earn the trust of employees, customers, suppliers, communities and shareholders by being forthright in our communications and consistently delivering on commitments.

We value:

- **Safety and the Environment** – An overriding commitment to health, safety, environmental responsibility and sustainable development.

- **Integrity** – Doing what we say we will do.

- **High Performance** – The excitement and fulfilment of achieving superior business results and stretching our capabilities.

- **Win-Win Relationships** – Having relationships which focus on the creation of value for all parties.

- **The Courage to Lead Change** – Accepting the responsibility to inspire and deliver positive change in the face of adversity.

- **Respect for Each Other** – The embracing of diversity, enriched by openness, sharing, trust, teamwork and involvement.

We are successful in creating value when:

- our shareholders are realising a superior return on their investment

- our customers and suppliers are benefiting from our business relationships

- the communities in which we operate value our citizenship

- every employee starts each day with a sense of purpose and ends each day with a sense of accomplishment.

Table 2.14D – Non-financial factors

Barloworld Limited – Report and Accounts – 30 September 2006

"Our goal at Barloworld is sustainable value creation by focusing on a core group of businesses that demonstrate market leading characteristics."

Tony Phillips, CEO

VALUE BASED MANAGEMENT 4.8

"Value Based Management (VBM) was adopted in 1999 as our philosophy in doing business."

Tony Phillips, CEO

At Barloworld, sustainability is not just a section in the annual report. It lies at the heart of how we do business. We view sustainability in a holistic manner that treats both financial and non-financial performance as part of maintaining a stable profit stream from our businesses in a manner that benefits all stakeholders. This results in a long-term view of managing businesses. We are not portfolio traders, but rather try to build a core of businesses that are able to consistently achieve top-quintile performance through market leading characteristics.

"We structure our businesses to be able to profitably endure business cycles while growing at a pace that creates sustainable shareholder value."

Tony Phillips, CEO

Value Based Management was adopted in 1999 as our philosophy in doing business. While the principles contained in the VBM doctrine were already well entrenched in the way that Barloworld operates, the VBM framework allowed us to formalise what has essentially always been the Barloworld way of doing business.

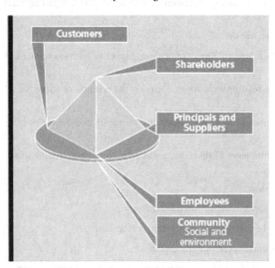

Barloworld's direct stakeholder groups are represented by the four points of a pyramid (see above). At its apex are our shareholders. At its base are our customers, our employees and our principals and suppliers. The pyramid is founded on the social and physical environment in which we operate. VBM is fundamentally different because it requires that we move beyond the traditional approach of tradeoffs between stakeholders, and search for solutions which add value for all.

2.106.7 The OFR should set out the directors' strategies for achieving the business' objectives. Although the reporting statement refers to 'objectives' and 'strategies', neither term is defined. In practice some entities refer only in very general terms to a single broad objective, such as 'to be the best' or 'to produce sustainable and responsible growth in value', and concentrate more on the business' detailed strategies. Others simply do not mention an objective at all, but discuss only strategies.

2.107 To assess the quality and sustainability of a company's performance, investors need to be clear about its objectives and the strategies for achieving those objectives. They need to know how management intends to address market trends and the threats and opportunities that they represent. They also need to understand the relationship between strategic objectives, management actions and executive remuneration. This enables them to judge the appropriateness and success of management actions in delivering the strategy and what to expect in the future.

2.108 Statements of objectives and strategies should provide the detail that enables investors to understand the priorities for action or the resources that must be managed to deliver results, as well as explaining how success will be measured and over what period of time it should be assessed.

2.109 The reporting statement notes that objectives will often be defined in terms of financial performance, but that objectives in non-financial areas should also be discussed, where appropriate. [RS (OFR) para 34].

2.110 Many strategic objectives focus on achieving value for shareholders and financial success. However, a company's strategy should also be based on an understanding of the key areas in which a company has competitive advantage, for example, a market-leading customer base or a highly skilled workforce. The company's success in creating value will depend on management's ability to invest resources in these areas and manage them so that they deliver the financial performance investors expect.

2.111 The example in Table 2.15 illustrates the company's key objectives, how they will measure success, the potential challenges to achieving that success and cross-references to where additional information can be found.

Table 2.15 – Objectives

Trifast plc – Report and Accounts – 31 March 2007

Business Review and Objectives (extract)

KEY OBJECTIVE	KEY PERFORMANCE INDICATORS	POTENTIAL CHALLENGES	WHAT ARE WE DOING?
To win key, large, profitable customers in Asia and Europe	New customer conversion rate	Raw material price increases Pressure from large customers to reduce prices	p.13, p.15, p.23
To introduce priced catalogues for transactional customers	Improve % revenue from transactional customers	Transactional sales in the fastener industry are highly competitive and tend to be served by local companies	p.8
To increase market penetration of TR branded products	Sales of TR branded products	Proprietary brands becoming commodity priced	p.9, p.17
To provide customers with engineering and design data	Number of engineers registered for our web-based solution	Maintaining and informative and relevant database.	p.16
To retain existing customers and strengthen customer relationships to maximise the available opportunities	Growth from existing customers and customer satisfaction results	Centrally controlled Group contracts Manufacturing migration to low-cost countries	p.8
To have the best trained, most committed, inspired workforce in the industry	Staff retention Staff satisfaction results	Talent management Career development	p.22, p.23
To improve the quality of our supply chain	Own manufactured spend as a % of total spend Number of quality rejects	Raw material availability Geographical spread of suppliers Meeting customer quality expectations	p.19
To continue to operate as a socially conscious company	% of profits committed to CSR activities Environmental audits	Cost implications Legislation	p.28, p.29
To generate cash	Reduction in debt funding organic growth Cash funding of acquisitions	Exchange rate risk Bad debts Working capital requirements for new accounts	p.26

2.112 Strategies and objectives may also embed environmental, social and ethical values of particular importance to the company, as shown in Table 2.16.

Table 2.16 – Embedding CRS in strategy and objectives

Marks and Spencer Group PLC – Annual Report and Financial Statements – 31 March 2007

Business Review (extract)

Plan A

In any company, the temptation can be to focus too narrowly on short-term business performance. Responsible companies have to look to the long term.

We set ourselves very high quality and ethical standards. Last year, we used our 'Look behind the label' campaign to describe the lengths we go to to ensure everything we sell is produced responsibly. But customers and staff wanted to understand our overall approach and our plan for the future. The result was Plan A, our five-year, £200m 'eco plan' launched in January 2007.

We've made 100 commitments across the five areas, including becoming carbon neutral, sending no waste to landfill, cutting our packaging by a quarter and only using fish and wood from sustainable sources. As well as addressing the wider issues, we continue to work closely with local communities through our 'Marks & Start' work experience programme, for example.

All of these commitments are described in our 'How we do business' report, published alongside this document at www.marksandspencer.com/howwedobusinessreport2007. Each year we will report on how far we have got in achieving them. To make sure Plan A is a success it is being completely integrated into our day-to-day operations. It will change how we operate forever.

PLAN A

Plan A is our five-year, 100-point plan to tackle some of the biggest challenges facing our business and our world.

Climate Change We aim to make our UK and Republic of Ireland operations carbon neutral in five years. We will minimise energy use, maximise the use of renewables and offset only as a last resort.

Waste We'll reduce packaging by 25%, find new ways to recycle and stop sending waste to landfill from our stores, offices and warehouses.

Sustainable Raw Materials From fish to forests, our goal is to make sure our key raw materials come from the most sustainable sources available.

Fair Partner By being a fair partner, we'll help improve the lives of hundreds of thousands of people in our worldwide supply chain and local communities.

Health We'll help customers and employees choose healthier lifestyles through healthy food ranges and clear labelling.

To find out more visit
www.marksandspencer.com/PlanA

2.113 The OFR should discuss the business' objectives to generate or preserve value over the longer-term. [RS (OFR) para 33].

2.114 The nature of the industry will affect the directors' determination of an appropriate time frame for the OFR. [RS (OFR) para 35]. The reporting statement gives, as an example, a business that focuses on long-term projects and that has to plan over the full project life cycle, which may be 20 years or more. It also states that if a project has a long-term impact on the environment, this is likely to affect long-term value and, therefore, determines the time perspective for reporting in the OFR. Industries with such long-term perspectives include, for example, the extractive industry, where the development and exploitation of a mine may extend for 20 years or more.

2.115   This contrasts with a service industry having few physical assets and depending on the supply of particular employee skills for its competitive advantage. Such an industry, it says, will plan over a period consistent with its ability to recruit, train and develop its staff, which may be a much shorter period than the industries cited above.

2.115.1   An example of the use of different time frames for different elements is BAA plc (see Table 2.17). BAA provides ten year forecasts, details of airport charges over five years and operating costs to be incurred over the following three years.

Table 2.17 – Different time scales

BAA plc – Report and Accounts – 31 March 2005

Passengers
Forecast growth in passenger numbers provides a critical input into capacity planning and other infrastructure decisions. The Group is forecasting average traffic growth of 3.0% per annum for its three London airports over the next ten years.

Total Passengers	Heathrow	Gatwick	Stansted	Total London
2004/05 (actual)	67.7	32.0	21.2	120.9
2005/06	69.5	33.4	22.2	125.1
2006/07	70.9	34.6	23.4	128.9
2007/08	72.3	36.0	24.7	133.0
2008/09	75.0	37.0	26.3	138.3
2009/10	78.0	38.0	28.0	144.0
2010/11	80.0	38.5	29.6	148.1
2011/12	81.5	39.5	30.9	151.9
2012/13	83.0	40.0	32.3	155.3
2013/14	84.5	40.5	33.7	158.7
2014/15	86.0	41.0	35.0	162.0

The key drivers and assumptions underlying the forecast growth at our London airports are:

- Traffic demand growth will average about 3.9% per annum

- Capacity constraints will restrict annual throughput growth to an average of 3.0% per annum. An element of traffic demand will, therefore, be lost from the London system as a result of these constraints

- UK GDP will grow in line with the historical trend, ie 2.0–2.5% per annum over the course of the forecasting period

- Real air fares will decline, on average, by 0.5–1.0% per annum. However, the rate of decline will vary between markets, eg. faster rate of fares decline has been assumed for those markets facing low-cost competition

- Major capacity developments are:

    – First full-year of Terminal 5 operation in 2008/09

- Further development of Heathrow non-Terminal 5 infrastructure

- Gatwick develops to handle at least 40 million passengers per annum on the existing runway

- Stansted develops to 35 million passengers per annum on the existing runway.

Regulated Airport Charges

Under the Airports Act, Heathrow, Gatwick and Stansted are subject to economic regulation whereby the Civil Aviation Authority (CAA) sets a price cap on airport charges for each airport every five years. The charges included within the price cap applied are the runway landing charge, the aircraft parking charge and the departing passenger charge. In February 2003, the CAA published its decision on the price caps that apply for the period 1 April 2003 until 31 March 2008:

Maximum Allowable Yield

	2003/04 out-turn	2004/05 out-turn	2005/06 RPI plus	2006/07 RPI plus	2007/08 RPI plus
Heathrow	£6.48	£7.08	+6.5%	+6.5%	+6.5%
Gatwick	£4.32	£4.44	+0.0%	+0.0%	+0.0%
Stansted	£4.89	£5.03	+0.0%	+0.0%	+0.0%

The pricing regime at Heathrow is linked to five triggers based on the completion of Terminal 5 and at Gatwick, linked to the completion of Pier 6. The trigger is an element of the price cap formula, and each trigger is equivalent to a 2% decrease in airport charges at Heathrow and 1% at Gatwick. The first two of the five triggers related to Terminal 5 were met by the 31 March 2005 deadline and Pier 6 at Gatwick was completed ten months ahead of schedule.

Impact of Business Developments on Operating Costs

Over the next three years the operating cost base of the Group will be impacted by some significant developments to our business.

Firstly, the opening of Heathrow Terminal 5 will impact the Group's operating costs. Over the next three years, BAA and its partners, will be increasingly focused on ensuring the operations are ready for Terminal 5's opening on 30 March 2008. This activity is focusing on three areas: planning for the new operations with our partners (including adapting organisational structures, work practices and processes); the recruitment and training of staff; and assisting our airline partners to integrate and reorganise operations across the five terminals. Accounting rules on pre-opening costs, under both UK GAAP and IFRS, mean that certain of these non-recurring costs will be included within the profit and loss account as opposed to being capitalised. Our initial estimate indicates a potential cost related to this activity of approximately £60 million over the next three years, the majority being incurred in the final year.

Once open, these non-recurring costs will fall away, however, the fifth terminal will significantly increase Heathrow's fixed cost base. The key contributors to this will be facility related expenditure, such as additional depreciation on the new assets, maintenance, rates and utilities. In addition, the nature of the activity in 2007/08 at Terminal 5 may require depreciation and interest to be charged against profit for approximately three months.

Secondly, the significant changes being planned in the way BAA organises its operations will lead to a more efficient application of resources and people. In making these changes, the Group will incur costs of reorganisation over a three-year period. £16 million of these have been recognised in 2004/05 (see explanation above).

2.115.2 The OFR should set out the directors' strategies for achieving the business' objectives. [RS (OFR) para 36].

2.115.3 As noted above, objectives and strategy are not clearly defined in the reporting statement and are often described as if they were the same thing. Consequently, much of the discussion above about objectives applies to strategies as well. The reporting statement says that disclosure of the directors' strategies is recommended in order for members to assess the current and past actions undertaken by directors in respect of the stated objectives. [RS (OFR) para 37].

2.115.4 When describing an entity's strategies, directors should include descriptions of any changes in strategies. This is particularly important where past strategies have not been successful, resulting in poor performance. In such circumstances, it is important for directors, in seeking to restore lost confidence in the entity, to spell out in detail the revised strategies for the future. In doing so, they may have particular regard, when discussing past strategy, to the principle that the OFR should be balanced and neutral, dealing even-handedly with both good and bad aspects.

2.116 When describing an entity's strategies, directors should include descriptions of any changes in strategies, for example as a result of a strategic review as shown in the example in Table 2.18.

Table 2.18 – Changes in strategy

Imperial Chemical Industries PLC – Annual Report and Accounts – 31 December 2006

Statement by the Chairman and the Chief Executive (extract)

Major business portfolio developments
As a result of the Quest and Uniqema disposals, ICI will have a focused portfolio of market-leading coatings, adhesives, starch and synthetic polymer businesses combined with a significantly stronger balance sheet.

The Uniqema disposal to Croda International Plc was completed in September for a gross consideration of £410m. We would like to thank all Uniqema employees for their great service to ICI, and their endeavours to improve the performance of the business during a challenging period.

In November, we announced the agreed sale of Quest to Givaudan SA for £1.2bn. The consideration obtained by ICI reflects the strategic value of Quest to Givaudan as it enables them to increase their leadership in the global flavours and fragrance industry. It also reflects the positive trend of Quest's performance in recent quarters.

We would like to thank the Quest team for their outstanding efforts in rebuilding the performance and value of the business over the past three years.

From Turnaround to Transformation
As a result of these recent developments combined with the performance improvements delivered through restructuring, ICI has moved from a **turnaround** strategy, which we embarked on in 2003, to one **of transformation**, which we signalled in part with our restructuring plans announced in May 2006. Delivery of our transformation strategy will focus on three important levers – **accelerating profitable growth**, sustaining our improvements in **operational effectiveness** and developing a **culture of sustainable improvement**.

2.117 To the extent necessary, the OFR should include the key performance indicators, both financial and non-financial, used by the directors to assess progress against their stated objectives. [RS (OFR) para 38]. The KPIs disclosed should be those that the directors judge are effective in measuring the delivery of their strategies and managing their business. Regular measurement using KPIs will enable an entity to set and communicate its performance targets and to measure whether it is achieving them. [RS (OFR) para 39]. Comparability will be enhanced if KPIs are widely used, either within the industry sector or more generally. [RS (OFR) para 40]. However, it is important that the KPIs used are appropriate for measuring the entity's performance from year to year.

2.118   KPIs are discussed from paragraph 2.192 and examples are given in Tables 2.44 and 2.45.

2.119   Directors should also consider the extent to which other performance indicators and evidence should be included. [RS (OFR) para 41]. Other performance indicators may be narrative evidence describing how the directors manage the business or indicators that are used to monitor the entity's external environment and/or its progress towards achieving its objectives. [RS (OFR) para 42]. Other performance indicators are discussed from paragraph 2.207 below.

Current and future development and performance

Development and performance in the year

2.120   The OFR should describe the significant features of the business' development and performance in the financial year, focusing on business (including geographical) segments that are relevant to an understanding of the development and performance as a whole. [RS (OFR) para 43].

2.121   Trends and factors in development and performance suggested by an analysis of current and previous financial years should be highlighted. Development and performance should be described in the context of the business' strategic objectives. [RS (OFR) para 44].

2.122   Comparison over a number of years may be appropriate where, for example, the entity has a particular strategic objective with a duration of several years. Table 2.19 illustrates the performance achieved on a reorganisation project, tracked over several years.

Table 2.19 – Performance on reorganisation project

Reuters Group PLC – Report and Accounts – 31 December 2004

Company information (extract)

Reuters strategy (extract)

On 18 February 2003 Reuters announced it was accelerating its transformation strategy to become a more competitive, focused and profitable information company. The three-year action plan, *Fast Forward,* is intended to strengthen Reuters core information business. It addresses the impact of structural changes in the financial services industry including consolidation, reduced headcount, growth in market data volumes and increasing regulation.

The five principal components of the *Fast Forward* plan are:

1. Supply information that customers value, by building on core strengths in providing content, analytics and trading and messaging capabilities in an open technology format. Reuters expects to; provide new company fundamental data and investment research through its pending acquisition of Multex.com, Inc. (Multex) (described below); increase its investment in analytics; continue to provide advanced tools to help customers communicate and share information; and build enhanced trading capabilities for the equities and fixed income markets into its premium information products.

2. Move to a single product delivery system, radically simplifying the way products and data are delivered by the use of a single, global technology platform.

3. Simplify and segment the product line, supplying the right product at the right price to profitable target markets, worldwide. During 2003 Reuters expects to launch a series of next generation products, offering specific data and tools required by different financial professionals. At the same time Reuters will speed up the withdrawal of numerous legacy products and platforms.

4. Focus Reuters solutions business, withdrawing from some elements of the established solutions business and actively managing Reuters portfolio of non-core investments. Going forward, Reuters solutions business will focus on three core areas of expertise – risk management, content management and treasury products – and Reuters will not seek further business from pure technology consulting or technology solutions that are not based on Reuters offerings.

See 'Operating and financial review' for information concerning the expected financial impact of the *Fast Forward* plan.

Operating and financial review (extract)

3. *Fast Forward*

As a result of the *Fast Forward* plan, the number of Reuters employees is expected to fall from 15,900 to around 13,000 by the end of 2006. Reuters expects to incur restructuring charges of £340 million between 2003 and 2005, with £160 million incurred in 2003. Reuters is targeting annualised savings from *Fast Forward* of approximately £440 million by 2006. The investment associated with *Fast Forward* measures such as building out the existing Bridge distribution system and building up Reuters content and analytics offerings is expected to come from the redirection of internal resources, rather than any incremental spend. Reuters estimates the amount of this internal investment at £120 million in each of 2003 and 2004.

CHIEF EXECUTIVE'S REVIEW (extract)

Q You say Reuters is being transformed – from what to what?

In short, from a company at the edge to a great company again. The Reuters of three years ago was at a crisis point. Our revenues were falling rapidly, we were losing market share, our costs were too high, and our organisation was too complex. Today, two-thirds of the way through Fast Forward, I'm pleased with our progress. We have strengthened our product line, we are meeting our cost savings targets and we have done much to simplify the company and reduce our portfolio. It's a tough process, and one that will continue this year, but it's worth it because I truly believe we are on the way to making Reuters a great company again.

COMPANY INFORMATION (extract)

02 STRATEGY (extract)

Reuters goal is to be the information company our customers value most, by offering indispensable content, innovative trading services and great customer service.

- First, complete and realise the benefits of Fast Forward, our business transformation programme – **'Fix it'**
- Second, complete the migration of our customers to our latest products, expand into areas of our market closely related to our current business, and make our business more resilient – **'Strengthen it'**
- Third, reposition our business over the longer term to take advantage of the structural changes and new opportunities in the global markets – **'Grow it'**.

'Fix it' through Fast Forward

The Fast Forward programme aims to transform Reuters into a more competitive, simpler, more customer service-driven and more efficient organisation. We have now completed two-thirds of the Fast Forward programme and have made real progress in each of these areas.

Our drive to become more competitive delivered a successful defence of our foreign exchange information and trading franchise, where the number of user positions grew in 2004 for the first time in seven years, despite increased competition.

To simplify the way we do business, we have made major changes to our product line and cut the number of products being actively sold by two-thirds, on the way to our target of 50 desktop financial information products.

We also continued to clear out our portfolio, and have now divested over 80 holdings. The most significant of these in 2004 was the sale of the majority of our stake in TIBCO Software Inc. (TSI).

To make Reuters more efficient, we exceeded our cost savings targets. At the end of 2004, we had cumulative savings of £234 million towards our goal of £440 million by the end of 2006.

We conduct an annual survey of 12,000 customers to measure their satisfaction with our products and service. Customer satisfaction continued to increase in 2004, following the trend from 2003, with users of the latest versions of our products ranking us more highly than users of our older products. However, a power disruption at our UK Docklands data centre in October caused a setback in the fourth quarter, and we immediately took corrective action to improve data centre resilience.

OPERATING AND FINANCIAL REVIEW (extract)

Restructuring

The Fast Forward programme resulted in a restructuring charge of £120 million in 2004 within operating profit. This compared with Fast Forward restructuring charges of £134 million, net of a £10 million release of legacy programme provisions, in 2003, and to previous business transformation plan charges of £112 million in 2002.

In 2004, Fast Forward delivered a further £159 million in cost savings leading to cumulative savings from the programme of £234 million. 900 employees were made redundant during the course of 2004, most of whom have already left the company, with the rest expected to leave in 2005.

2.123   The OFR should cover significant aspects of the statements of financial performance and, where appropriate, should be linked to other aspects of performance. [RS (OFR) para 45]. The example in Table 2.20 shows a graphical explanation of the revenue and profit from operations included in the financial statements. There is a clear indication of reasons for changes in these figures from one period to the next. Further information on each element of the movement is given in detailed narrative explanations of financial performance.

Table 2.20 – Explaining financial performance

Tomkins plc – Annual Report – 2 January 2010

OPERATING AND FINANCIAL REVIEW (extract)

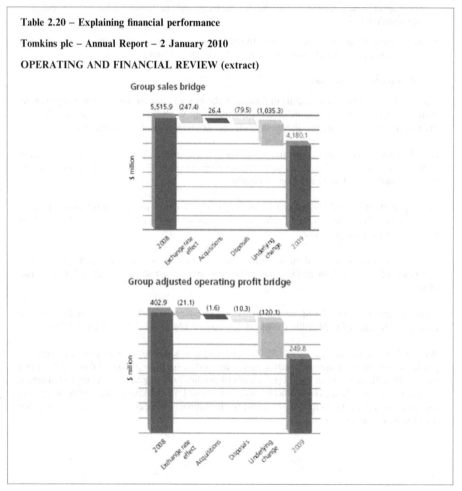

2.124 Unusual, non-recurring or exceptional items should be discussed and fully explained. Such items may include gains and losses on sales of businesses, reorganisation costs, fines and penalties, impairments, litigation costs and other material items that have been separately disclosed in the financial statements.

2.125 The OFR should include the directors' analysis of the effect on current development and performance of changes in the industry or external environment in which the business operates and developments within the business. Such changes include market conditions impacting the business and new products or services introduced by the company. [RS (OFR) para 46].

2.126 Competition, regulation and macro-economics can all affect a company's current development and performance. The introduction of a new competitor may result in changes to pricing decisions, as may regulatory pressure. Macro-economics and other broad market factors such as geopolitical events can also impact how the company has performed.

2.127 Table 2.21 provides an illustration of how market conditions have impacted a company's performance, considering market size and growth, market composition, competition and market share. Graphics are provided to illustrate elements of the disclosure.

Table 2.21 – Impact of market conditions on performance

Avis Europe plc – Annual Report and Accounts – 31 December 2006

Operating environment

Market size and growth

The latest independent market share data (Euromonitor IMIS Travel Database 2005) estimated the total car rental revenue generated in the 11 key corporate countries that the Group operated in during 2005 to be €8.8 billion. The largest of these countries by revenue were Germany (22.1%), the United Kingdom (19.6%), France (16.1%), Spain (15.2%) and Italy (9.9%). During this period, Euromonitor estimated that 40 million rentals were made and that a combined fleet of approximately 1.2 million vehicles was used.

Historically, the growth of the car rental market has been closely tied to general economic activity levels and, in the case of airport rentals, to airline passenger volume growth. Economic growth prospects for the Group's key markets are favourable, with the Economist Intelligence Unit forecasting Euro-area GDP to grow at an annual rate of between 2.1% and 2.2% from 2007 to 2010, and between 2.0% and 2.5% in the United Kingdom over the same period. The airline sector is particularly buoyant, driven in part by the rapid growth of low cost airlines. The International Air Transport Association forecasted growth in passenger arrivals for flights within Europe of just over 5% per annum from 2005 to 2009.

Euromonitor estimated that the total industry revenue in the key corporate countries grew at a compound rate of 1.4% per annum from 1999 to 2005 and forecasted growth of 3.0% per annum from 2005 to 2010.

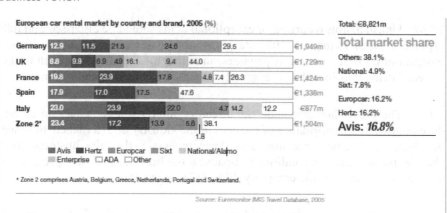

European car rental market by country and brand, 2005 (%)

Total: €8,821m

Country	Avis	Hertz	Europcar	Sixt	National/Alamo	Enterprise	ADA	Other	
Germany	12.9	11.5	21.5	24.6			29.5		€1,949m
UK	8.8	9.9	6.9	4.9	16.1	9.4	44.0		€1,729m
France	19.8	23.9	17.8	4.8	7.4	26.3			€1,424m
Spain	17.9	17.0	17.5	47.6					€1,338m
Italy	23.0	23.9	22.0	4.7	14.2	12.2			€877m
Zone 2*	23.4	17.2	13.9	5.8	1.8	38.1			€1,504m

■ Avis ■ Hertz ■ Europcar ■ Sixt □ National/Alamo
■ Enterprise □ ADA □ Other

Total market share

Others: 38.1%
National: 4.9%
Sixt: 7.8%
Europcar: 16.2%
Hertz: 16.2%
Avis: *16.8%*

* Zone 2 comprises Austria, Belgium, Greece, Netherlands, Portugal and Switzerland.

Source: Euromonitor IMIS Travel Database, 2005

Competition

Euromonitor research shows that the Group had the highest aggregate market revenue share in its 11 largest corporate countries in 2005 at 16.8%, followed by Hertz and Europcar with 16.2% each (please see the table on page 13). The recent merger between Europcar and Vanguard has given Europcar a leading position in this European market place.

In specific markets, the Group faces competition from Sixt in Germany and Enterprise in the United Kingdom, together with a large number of smaller-scale operators, with strength in particular markets (frequently the Mediterranean), examples being Maggiore in Italy and ADA in France.

On a global scale, the Group operates two of the three truly global brands, Avis, Budget and Hertz. The merger between Europcar and Vanguard referred to above creates a fourth global brand.

2.128   The introduction of new products or services is often a factor that has affected a company's development and performance. The example in Table 2.22 gives a pharmaceutical company's explanation of its product pipeline and its investment in research and development.

Table 2.22 – Effect of new products on performance

AstraZeneca PLC – Annual Report and Form 20-F Information – 31 December 2006

Business Review (extract)

REASEARCH AND DEVELOPMENT (extract)

WE HAVE A GLOBAL RESEARCH AND DEVELOPMENT ORGANISATION, WITH AROUND 12,000 PEOPLE AT 16 MAJOR CENTRES IN EIGHT COUNTRIES DEDICATED TO TRANSLATING LEADING-EDGE SCIENCE INTO INNOVATIVE, NEW MEDICINES THAT MAKE A DIFFERENCE IN THE LIVES OF PATIENTS.

In 2006, we spent $3.9 billion on research and development (2005 $3.38 billion, 2004 $3.47 billion) and approved $300 million of R&D capital investments including announcements of major new facilities in Sweden (safety pharmacology), the US (cancer and infection) and China (cancer).

We want to be among the best in the industry in terms of the quality of our work and the speed with which we get new medicines to market. During 2006 we continued our drive to improve the efficiency of our processes and the effectiveness of our decision-making, so that we can quickly eliminate weaker candidate drugs (CDs) and concentrate on the robust, rapid progress of the ones most likely to succeed as significant advances in healthcare.

In line with our strategy, we also continued to focus on accessing external innovation that complements our in-house capabilities, and on page 39 you can read more about our externalisation activities during the year.

PIPELINE STRATEGY
Our R&D strategy is geared to maintaining a flow of new products that will deliver sustained business growth in the short, medium and long term.

In the short term, our business needs will be met through successful delivery of the Phase III programmes and optimised life-cycle management for our key products.

In 2006, we experienced some setbacks with our Phase III portfolio with the termination of the programmes for Galida and NXY-059, as described in more detail on pages 18 and 25 respectively. Despite these setbacks, as at 1 February 2007 we still have 28 Phase III programmes compared with 29 at the end of January 2006.

Notable successes in the life-cycle management of our key marketed brands during the year included nine submissions and nine approvals in the US or EU and are described in the Therapy Area Review (pages 16 to 32).

In the mid term we will drive our pre-clinical and clinical Phase I and II projects towards proof of concept as rapidly as possible whilst recognising that we will need to continue our emphasis on externalisation to complement our internal R&D efforts. Our drug discovery effort is now a process that is much wider than our own laboratories, as we actively seek to make alliances and acquisitions with external partners to gain access to leading drug projects or technology platforms.

The progress we are making in our drive to increase productivity is reflected in the growth of our early development portfolio: during 2006 21 CDs were selected (compared with 25 in 2005 and 18 in 2004), and we have 92 development projects in the proof of principle phase (before Phase III, latestage development).

During 2006 we progressed 12 compounds into man.

In the long term, in addition to our current capabilities, we are also seeking to transform the AstraZeneca pipeline through a strategic move into biopharmaceuticals and by using biomarkers to help identify winning projects much earlier.

2.128.1   Where a company operates in a number of different territories and has a number of different product lines that are affected by different trends and factors (either economic or non-economic), analysis of performance showing this level of detail may be useful. Table 2.22A discloses changes in sales and sales volumes of global and local brands.

Table 2.22A – Market analysis for brand and geographic segment

Diageo plc – Report and Accounts – 30 June 2006

Operating and financial review (extract)

Europe (extract)

Summary:

- Net sales, after deducting excise duties, were unchanged year on year as growth in core spirits offset tough market conditions in beer and ready to drink

- Spirits demonstrated healthy volume growth at 3%

- Innovation is increasing brand visibility with new and existing customers

- Marketing spend was reduced by 4% and prioritised against specific opportunities such as Johnnie Walker throughout Europe and J&B in France

Key measures	2006 £ million	2005 £ million	Reported movement %	Organic movement %
Volume			2	1
Net sales after deducting excise duties	2,455	2,499	(2)	–
Marketing	389	403	(4)	(4)
Operating profit before exceptional items	737	702	5	6

Reported performance Net sales, after deducting excise duties, were £2,455 million in the year ended 30 June 2006, down by £44 million from the prior year. Operating profit before exceptional items increased by £35 million from £702 million to £737 million.

Organic performance Disposals net of the impact of acquisitions decreased net sales, after deducting excise duties, by £16 million and there was an organic decrease in net sales, after deducting excise duties, of £4 million and an adverse impact of exchange of £1 million. Transfers between business segments decreased prior year net sales, after deducting excise duties, by £23 million. Operating profit before exceptional items decreased by £5 million as a result of foreign exchange impacts. Acquisitions increased operating profit before exceptional items by £4 million and organic growth of £39 million was achieved. Transfers between business segments decreased prior year operating profit before exceptional items by £3 million.

	Reported volume movement %	Organic volume movement %	Reported net sales movement %	Organic net sales* movement %
Organic brand performance				
Global priority brands	1	1	(1)	(1)
Local priority brands	(2)	(2)	(1)	(1)
Category brands	6	2	(3)	2
Total	**2**	**1**	**(2)**	**–**
Key brands				
Smirnoff vodka		8	8	7
Smirnoff ready to drink		(22)	(21)	(21)
Johnny Walker		3	6	6
Baileys		1	–	–
J&B		(3)	(5)	(5)
Guinness		(3)	–	–
* after deducting excise duties				

Spirits demonstrated resilient growth with volume and net sales, after deducting excise duties, up 3%, while beer, volume down 3%, and ready to drink, volume down 22%, held back total performance. The shift from the on to the off trade in Ireland again negatively impacted overall beer performance. Wine volume grew 7% driven by Blossom Hill's robust growth in Great Britain and Ireland.

Smirnoff vodka, excluding ready to drink, continued to grow strongly, delivering volume growth of 8% and growth of net sales, after deducting excise duties, of 7%. A pan-European advertising campaign, focusing on the quality credentials of Smirnoff, continued to build the distinctiveness of the brand, although marketing spend was reduced by 9%.

Johnnie Walker Red Label volume grew 1% while net sales, after deducting excise duties, were flat. However, very strong volume growth of Johnnie Walker Black Label, up 14%, and Johnnie Walker Super Deluxe, up 21%, delivered overall growth in Johnnie Walker, with volume up 3%, and had a positive mix impact as net sales, after deducting excise duties, increased 6%. Growth was driven mainly by increased demand in Southern Europe, Russia and Eastern Europe and the favourable impact of advertising, especially the sponsorship of Team McLaren Mercedes Formula One. Marketing spend was up 19% as a result of increased activities in sports sponsorship.

Europe accounts for over half of Baileys volume worldwide and brand volume was up a further 1% year on year, driven by growth in France, Italy, Russia and Central and Eastern Europe. Net sales, after deducting excise duties, were flat. Excluding ready to drink, both volume and net sales, after deducting excise duties, grew by 1%.

The majority of J&B's volume in Europe is sold in Spain, where the decline of the scotch category led to a 3% decrease in overall volume of J&B. However, elsewhere in Europe, especially in France and Eastern Europe, J&B performed well.

Guinness volume declined 3% although pricing offset weak volumes and net sales, after deducting excise duties, were flat year on year. Guinness sales progressed well in Russia during the year following Diageo's agreement in July 2005 with Heineken NV for the production and distribution of Guinness in Russia.

Despite a year on year decline in ready to drink, Diageo has managed costs and increased the margin on ready to drink, even though contribution in absolute terms was down.

Total local priority brand performance was negatively impacted by the decline of Diageo's beer volume in Ireland.

Marketing spend was reduced by 4%, driven by a 23% reduction in spending on ready to drink.

Great Britain
Volume was flat and net sales, after deducting excise duties, were down 1% as the decline in ready to drink continued to cause a negative mix impact.

The total spirits market in Great Britain was broadly flat as growth in the off trade offset declines in the on trade. Diageo maintained leadership across all key categories and, excluding ready to drink, grew spirits volume by 2%.

Growth in spirits was attributable to Smirnoff vodka in particular, which continued to gain share as volume grew 6% and net sales, after deducting excise duties, grew 8%. Smirnoff performance was driven by marketing programmes focused on quality and on trade activity around signature cocktails. Smirnoff ready to drink volume declined 19%, a rate similar to the prior year.

Total Baileys volume declined 2% and net sales, after deducting excise duties, declined by 4%. Excluding Baileys Glide, Baileys volume declined 1% whilst net sales, after deducting excise duties, grew 1%. The majority of Baileys is sold in the off trade where there has been increased competition from value brands, however while volume declined, the brand maintained its value share. Baileys grew in the on trade driven by distribution gains and price increases.

Total Guinness volume declined 1% whilst net sales, after deducting excise duties, grew 1% driven by a price increase on Guinness Draught. While volume in the on trade beer market in Great Britain declined 3% as consumers shifted to consumption at home, Guinness Draught gained share in the on trade, growing volume 1% and net sales, after deducting excise duties, by 4%. Media activities were focused on quality attributes and Dublin brewed Guinness, as well as the first year of a four-year sponsorship of the rugby premiership. This helped to generate growth in the second half and increase share.

Local priority brand volume declined 2% and net sales, after deducting excise duties, fell 6%, mainly due to the decline in Archers ready to drink. Gordon's volume grew 1% and net sales, after deducting excise duties, were up 4%. Bell's Extra Special volume grew 2% although net sales, after deducting excise duties, were down.

Category brand volume grew 4% and net sales, after deducting excise duties, increased 2% driven by Blossom Hill, which continued to grow strongly with volume up 13%, and the launch in May 2006 of a new product, Quinn's, an alcoholic fruit ferment blended drink, into the on and off trade.

Ireland
The performance in Ireland reflects the continuing change in market dynamics from on to off trade, high levels of competitor investment, and consumer migration to value brands. While the total beverage alcohol market grew 2%, the on trade was down 3% and the off trade was up 7%. The on trade now represents 51% of the total market.

Volume declined 3% and net sales, after deducting excise duties, were down 1%. This was due to weak performance in beer, where volumes were down 6%, partly offset by growth in wine and spirits, where volume grew 18% and 7% respectively. The impact on net sales, after deducting excise duties, of declining beer volume was partly offset by price increases.

Guinness volume declined 8% whilst net sales, after deducting excise duties, declined 3% as a result of price increases introduced in June 2005 and May 2006. Guinness was impacted by increased levels of competitor investment and the movement to the off trade where Guinness' share is lower. In the year there was innovation on the Guinness brand with positive consumer response to the launch of the limited edition Brewhouse Series. In the second half, Guinness Mid-Strength, a lower alcohol by volume format, began consumer trials in 80 outlets.

The introduction of new packaging on Harp, new marketing executions on Carlsberg and Harp and increased distribution have helped reinvigorate both brands. As a result both Carlsberg and Harp have maintained volume year on year and net sales, after deducting excise duties, have increased 7% and 2% respectively.

Smirnoff continued to be the number one vodka in Ireland and outperformed the vodka category in both the on and off trade.

Baileys volume declined 2% and net sales, after deducting excise duties, fell 8% due to increased competition from lower value brands.

Iberia

In Iberia, volume and net sales, after deducting excise duties, both declined 3%. In Spain, spirits penetration is declining in all age groups versus other leisure categories and this has negatively impacted the Spanish business, whilst in Portugal trading conditions continued to be tough as a result of tightening consumer expenditure.

J&B faced increased pressure as the standard whisky segment in Spain continued to decline as consumers continued to switch to dark rums. Therefore, while J&B gained share in the Spanish on trade, overall Iberian volume declined 7% and net sales, after deducting excise duties, fell 10%. Marketing spend increased 3% behind J&B driven by investment in Spain.

Johnnie Walker volume declined 2%, however net sales, after deducting excise duties, were up 2% driven by the growth of Johnnie Walker Black Label, Super Deluxe and price increases throughout Iberia. Johnnie Walker Black Label and Super Deluxe combined grew volume by 4% and net sales, after deducting excise duties, by 11%. Johnnie Walker Red Label volume declined 3% despite a good performance in Spain, where it is the only standard whisky brand growing volume and share in the on trade. Total Diageo share in the standard scotch segment in Spain increased by 0.3 percentage points.

Across Iberia, Baileys volume was down 6% and net sales, after deducting excise duties, declined 5% driven by contraction in the on trade. José Cuervo volume grew 13% and net sales, after deducting excise duties, were up 15% due to continued consumer interest in the tequila category.

Local priority brand volume grew 5% and net sales, after deducting excise duties, were up 7%. Dark rums grew robustly in the on and off trade with Cacique volume up 6% and net sales, after deducting excise duties, up 9% as a result of repositioning the brand.

Category brand volume declined 8% and net sales, after deducting excise duties, fell 9%. Pampero volume declined 14% with net sales, after deducting excise duties, down 12% as marketing spend was focused on Cacique. In total, Diageo's rum brands grew volume 2% and net sales, after deducting excise duties, grew 5%.

Rest of Europe

In the rest of Europe, solid performances in Italy and Central and Eastern Europe and the growth of super premium brands in Russia drove volume growth of 6% and growth in net sales, after deducting excise duties, of 4%.

Johnnie Walker Red Label volume in the rest of Europe was up 2% and net sales, after deducting excise duties, were up 1%. Johnnie Walker Black Label and Super Deluxe experienced strong growth with volume up 25% and net sales, after deducting excise duties, up 28% from key markets such as Greece, Russia and Northern Europe.

Captain Morgan delivered volume growth of 29% driven by Northern Europe and Russia with net sales, after deducting excise duties, up 23%.

J&B performed well in France, its second largest market, with volume up 9% benefiting from effective on trade advertising and promotion. Baileys enjoyed strong sales in France and Italy.

Ready to drink volume in the rest of Europe declined by 27%, as a result of the continued decline in the segment in France.

Russia continued its momentum with robust volume growth of 25% and net sales, after deducting excise duties, up 26% driven by Johnnie Walker, as the trend towards premium products in Russia continued. Johnnie Walker is the number one scotch in Russia and Baileys holds the same position in the imported liqueur category.

Diageo has announced the acquisition of the Smirnov brand in Russia through a company in which Diageo holds a 75% stake. This company will unite the Smirnoff/Smirnov brands under common ownership and will be the exclusive distributor of Diageo spirits brands and the Smirnov vodka brand in Russia.

2.129 Another factor that can have significant impact on a company's current development and performance is changes in the business from acquisitions or disposals. The example in Table 2.23 clearly illustrates the impact of two significant acquisitions for a mining company, including the savings from synergies that have been achieved.

Table 2.23 – Trends in performance

Xstrata plc – Annual Report – 31 December 2006

Operational Review (extract)

Copper (extract)

Operations
The highlight of the 2006 financial year has been the acquisition and integration of the Tintaya and Falconbridge copper assets within the Xstrata Copper business unit, contributing 74% or $2.7 billion to the business unit's EBIT growth of $3.6 billion for the year.

During the Falconbridge integration planning process, Xstrata Copper identified approximately $60 million of annual synergy benefits from the integration of the former Falconbridge copper assets. The progressive implementation of integration plans will see these benefits fully realised during 2007. In addition, a once-off finance re-structuring benefit of $58 million was achieved as a result of the copper asset integration.

The synergies identified through the integration of the Tintaya operation into Xstrata Copper Peru, of $110 million of additional value, have been confirmed and are being progressively realised. A further $50 million of value uplift has already been realised through ongoing operational management initiatives, with a range of other significant initiatives being actively pursued in 2007.

2.129.1 Similarly, the disposal of operations will affect a company's development and performance. Table 2.23A discusses discontinued activities.

Table 2.23A – Disposal of significant operation

GKN plc – Report and Accounts – 31 December 2004

Discontinued operations

AgustaWestland
The Group completed the sale of its 50% shareholding in AgustaWestland on 30 November 2004. Figures for 2004 therefore reflect our share for the 11 months ended on that date and are based on accounts which reflect the contract margin and provision reviews which normally take place as part of the year-end procedures.

GKN's share of sales revenue in 2004 of £740 million was £136 million below the 2003 figure, reflecting the loss of one month's revenue, together with lower underlying sales largely as a consequence of the completion of the EH101 contract for the UK Ministry of Defence during the early part of 2003 and delivery of the final six Apaches for the British Army in 2004.

As a consequence, GKN's share of operating profit of £86 million was £16 million below last year.

As noted earlier, the Group also booked an exceptional profit of £652 million on disposal of the business.

2.129.2   Table 2.23B illustrates the effect of changes in exchange rates and inflation.

Table 2.23B – Exchange rate movements and inflation

Cadbury Schweppes plc – Report and Accounts – 31 December 2004

10 Effect of exchange rates and inflation on 2004 reported results
Over 80% of the Group's sales and profits in 2004 were generated outside the United Kingdom. The Group's reported results have been affected by changes in the exchange rates used to translate the results of non-UK operations. In 2004 compared with 2003, the biggest exchange rate impact on the Group's results was the 12% weakening of the US dollar followed by the weakening Mexican Peso, which fell by 16%. The weakness in the US dollar was partially offset by the Canadian dollar (up 4%) and the Australian dollar (up 2%).

The overall impact of exchange rate movements on the Group's Profit and Loss statement and free cash flow generation was adverse and is shown separately. In 2004, movements in exchange rates, primarily the US dollar reduced the Group's sales by 4%, underlying pre-tax profit by 7% and underlying earnings per share by 7%. There was a greater impact on underlying operating profit than turnover as the Group generated higher profits in the currencies that have weakened during the year compared to those that have strengthened.

The adverse impact of currency movements on free cash flow was 16%. The reason for the greater impact on free cash flow relative to profits was due to the higher margin generation of US Dollar sales in the Americas beverages region.

General price inflation in countries where the Group has its most significant operations remained at a low level throughout the year and in general terms was within the 1% to 3% range. In certain developing markets, notably Venezuela, Turkey, Brazil, Russia and Argentina, the rate of inflation was significantly higher than this range, but the impact was not material to the Group results.

2.129.3 Many companies express figures in the OFR in terms of constant currency, so as to show the trends in performance, excluding the effect of exchange rates. Where this is done, the reporting statement recommends that a reconciliation to reported figures is given.

2.130 The discussion and analysis should also include any other factors that have affected performance in the period under review. This includes those for which the effect cannot be specifically quantified, as well as any specific exceptional items that are quantified and disclosed in the financial statements. Events range from natural disasters that may affect entities operating in the geographical regions affected, to wars and terrorist attacks, fraud and other irregularities, major strategy changes involving acquisitions and disposals or major reorganisations, regulatory fines and sanctions and so on.

2.131 The OFR should analyse the main trends and factors that the directors consider are likely to affect future prospects. [RS (OFR) para 47]. The directors will, therefore, need to consider the potential future significance of issues in deciding whether or not to include an analysis of them in the OFR. [RS (OFR) para 49].

2.132 An example of disclosure relating to trends and factors likely to affect future prospects is given in Table 2.24. Market conditions are described for each segment, with an indication of the key parameters that the directors consider of potential significance for the company's future development and performance.

Table 2.24 – Future trends and factors

AMEC plc – Annual Report and Accounts – 31 December 2006

Business Review (extract)

Oil and gas services (extract)

Markets
Oil and gas are expected to remain the dominant sources of global energy supply for the foreseeable future, as shown in the chart below.

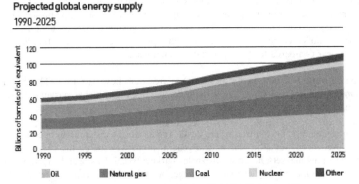

Projected global energy supply
1990-2025

Source: International Energy Outlook 1997, 1999, 2002, 2004, 2005 – Washingrton, DC,
US Department of Energy, Energy Information Administration

Major oil and gas company plans point to an investment increase of over 57 per cent in 2006-2010 compared to 2001-2005. If those plans are fully implemented and their spending forecasts prove accurate, oil and gas investment would rise from US$340 billion in 2005 to US$470 billion in 2010. The upstream sector will absorb almost two-thirds of total capital spending of which two-thirds will go towards maintaining or enhancing production from current fields. Beyond the current decade, higher investment in real terms will be needed to maintain growth in production capacity, with future projects likely to be more complex and remote, involving a higher unit cost. Slowing production declines at mature giant fields will require increased investment and enhanced recovery. (Source: IEA World Energy Outlook).

Building and Civil Engineering (extract)
AMEC offers integrated design, project management and construction services for hospitals, schools, rail, airports and commercial and government buildings. Clients include BAA, Transport for London, Defence Estates, South Lanarkshire Schools, Greater Manchester County Council, Marks & Spencer, Scottish Water and Welsh Water. This area of activities has synergies with the Building and Facilities Services and Investment businesses, both in relation to project tenders and in the construction phase of asset delivery. This business reported substantial losses in 2006, and significant actions have been taken to strengthen management and internal processes, together with increasing focus on higher quality work. The management team is committed to making a small profit in 2007 and the business is capable of achieving average margins of 1-3 per cent through the cycle.

Markets
This business is focused on UK markets which offer sound growth prospects (source: AMEC assessments) together with the right balance of risk and reward:

- Defence: The market available to AMEC is assessed at some £3 billion per annum and is expected to remain relatively stable.

- Healthcare: The UK Government is aiming to deliver 100 new hospitals by 2010; annual spending 2007/8 £4-5 billion.

- Education: The UK is committed to its largest schools capital investment programme for 30 years, with spending rising to £8 billion in 2008.

- Manufacturing: The UK market is stable, but growth opportunities exist with key clients as they invest overseas. Annual spending c. £3-4 billion.

- Transport: Growth in AMEC's available market in this sector is expected to be tempered as a result of the completion of the large terminal 5 project at London Heathrow Airport in 2007. AMEC has exited lump-sum roads contracts as this procurement route is unattractive.

2.133   Paragraph 48 of the reporting statement states:

"The main trends and factors likely to affect the future development and performance will vary according to the nature of the business, but could include the development of known new products and services or the benefits expected from capital investment. The OFR should discuss the current level of investment expenditure together with planned future expenditure and shall explain how that investment is directed to assist the achievement of business objectives. Any assumptions underlying the main trends and factors should be disclosed." [RS (OFR) para 48].

2.133.1   Investment expenditure is not defined in the reporting statement. The definition used by a company should be disclosed in the OFR to avoid ambiguity and should be wide enough that it enables users of financial statements to obtain an understanding of its impact on the company's future. The definition used may be wider than the definition of 'investing cash flows' used in the preparation of the cash flow statement (see further chapter 30 of the Manual of Accounting — IFRS for the UK and the Manual of Accounting — UK GAAP) and may include:

- Personnel policies and practices, including employee training.

- Pure and applied research that may lead to potential new products, services or processes.

- Development of new products and services.

- Investment in brand equity, for example through advertising and marketing activities.

- Refurbishment and maintenance programmes.

- Technical support to customers.

2.133.2   Discussion should also include explanations of variations in expenditure from year to year.

2.133.3   Table 2.24A shows discussion of movements in marketing and capital expenditure.

Table 2.24A – Investment expenditure

Cadbury Schweppes plc – Report and Accounts – 31 December 2004

Operating and Financial Review (extracts)

Marketing
Total marketing expenditure in 2003 was £702 million, an increase of 28% over 2002 (£547 million) and an increase of 30% at constant exchange rates. This represents a marketing to turnover ratio of 10.9% compared to 10.3% in 2002, with the increase being due to the acquisition of Adams, which had a higher marketing to turnover ratio.

Prior to acquisitions, the marketing to turnover ratio was 9.9%, with the year-on-year reduction reflecting the combination of exchange rate movements and lower spend during periods of unfavourable weather conditions in Americas Beverages and EMEA.

Capital Structure and Resources (extract)

(c) Capital Expenditure
Capital expenditure in 2004 was £285 million, a decrease of 6% from the level of expenditure in 2003 with key areas of expenditure being related to Fuel for Growth cost reduction programmes and IT spend related to the continued roll out of project Probe and the costs associated with transferring Adams businesses from Pfizer to Cadbury systems. All these projects were funded from internal resources.

For 2005, the Group expects capital spend to be in the region of £300 million, driven by investments behind the Fuel for Growth initiatives. The Group expects to continue to fund this from internal resources.

Capital expenditure in 2003 was £302 million, an increase of 8% over the level of expenditure in 2002 with key areas of expenditure being acquisition related capital expenditure in Adams in the

---

Americas, capital expenditure related to Fuel for Growth cost reduction programmes in the UK, Irish and French confectionery businesses and IT spend related to the continued roll out of Probe, and the costs associated with transferring Adams businesses from Pfizer to Cadbury systems. All these projects were funded from internal resources.

Capital expenditure in 2002 was £279 million, an increase of 16% over the level of expenditure in 2001. The Group continued to implement project Probe. This project was a significant contributor to the increased level of capital expenditure in 2002. The Group also carried out specific projects to increase production capacity in Mott's, Schweppes Spain and Cadbury Trebor Bassett. All these projects were funded from internal sources.

At 2 January 2005, the Group had capital commitments of £15 million. It is anticipated that these commitments will be financed out of the Group's operational free cash flow.

2.134 Table 2.25 illustrates how investing in training and development for employees helps this company to achieve its objectives around its key resource, its people.

Table 2.25 – Investing to meet objectives

Amlin plc – Annual Report – 31 December 2006

Operating and Financial Review (extract)

People – retaining, motivating and building skills (extract)

With regard to Amlin's employees our key objectives remain:

> A working environment where employees are well motivated and have a strong belief in the Company, its strategy and core values.

> The development of loyalty between the Company and employees.

> Continual improvement in the effective management of people and the skills and competency of staff at all levels and across all disciplines.

> The retention and growth of key skills which are critical to the business.

> Well constructed and fair reward systems which help drive superior performance and align employee and shareholder interests.

> The development and use of first class employment practices throughout the Group.

Training and development (extract)

Amlin Academy, now in its sixth year, provides training and development programmes for Group employees and selected open courses for others. The Academy's objective is to provide a core curriculum of training, while encouraging professional and personal development at every level throughout the organisation.

The Academy supports regulatory and compliance requirements and also provides a broad range of initiatives including technical training and management and personal development, to help staff realise their full potential. The number of employee days devoted to training increased by 21% to 1,252 days in 2006 as a result of increased personal development, much of which was associated with the roll out of our core values programme as referred to overleaf.

During 2006 a bespoke workshop was designed to educate all underwriting staff on the requirements of "Contract Certainty" with the primary objective of maintaining Amlin's position as a market leader in best practice and customer service.

Amlin Academy
Training days provided in 2005/6

- 2005
- 2006

- Professional qualifications
- Personal development
- Management development
- Information technology
- Business technical

0 100 200 300 400 500 600
Training days

Source: Amlin

A key initiative during 2006 was the development of a claims competency framework which incorporates a set of key behaviours specifically identified for claims staff, together with a technical know-how and skills matrix which categorises the skills required to perform the day job at various levels. This took longer to complete than originally envisaged, and is a high quality piece of work which will be used as a template for developing other competency frameworks across the business.

While fewer days in 2006 were devoted to management development than in 2005, Amlin continued to work closely with The Roffey Park Institute and The Coverdale Organisation in providing management development training. Both training providers have a good insight into the culture of Amlin, which adds a huge benefit when delivering their programmes.

Work commenced in 2006 on the design of a leadership development programme to provide directors and senior managers with tailored personal development and to raise the level of leadership capability across the Group. Completion of this in 2007 is a key priority.

Resources

2.135 The OFR should include a description of the resources available to the entity and how they are managed. [RS (OFR) para 50]. It should set out the key strengths and resources, tangible and intangible, available to the business that will assist it in pursuing its objectives. This should include, in particular, resources that are not reflected in the balance sheet. Depending on the business' nature, these may include:

- Corporate reputation.

- Brand strength.

- Natural resources.

- Employees.

- Research and development.

- Intellectual capital.

- Licences, patents, copyright and trademarks.

- Market position.

[RS (OFR) para 51].

Other examples not specifically referred to in the standard, include:

- Customer/supplier relationships.

- Strength of proprietary business processes, such as distribution systems.

- Web sites and databases.

- Non-financial aspects of reputation, such as environmental reputation or strength of involvement in and identification with the community.

- Strength of geographical spread or product range.

2.136   As noted in the reporting statement, resources to be disclosed will depend on the nature of the business and the industry the company operates in. The example in Table 2.26 shows how the company sees its brands as key assets and explains how it has developed them during the year.

Table 2.26 – Resources – brands

Diageo plc – Annual Report – 30 June 2008

Business review (extract)

Premium drinks (extract)

The collection of premium drinks comprises brands owned by the company as a principal and brands held by the company under agency or distribution agreements. They include:

Global priority brands

Smirnoff vodka and Smirnoff ready to drink products
Johnnie Walker scotch whiskies
Captain Morgan rum
Baileys Original Irish Cream liqueur
J&B scotch whisky
José Cuervo tequila (agency brand in North America and many other markets)
Tanqueray gin
Guinness stout

Other spirits brands include:

Crown Royal Canadian whisky
Buchanan's De Luxe whisky
Gordon's gin and vodka
Windsor Premier whisky
Bell's Extra Special whisky
Seagram's whiskey
Old Parr whisky
Bushmills Irish whiskey
Bundaberg rum

Cacique rum
Ketel One vodka (exclusive worldwide distribution rights)

Wine brands include:

Beaulieu Vineyard
Sterling Vineyards
Rosenblum Cellars
Chalone Vineyard
Blossom Hill
Piat d'Or

Other beer brands include:

Harp lager
Smithwick's ale
Malta Guinness non-alcoholic malt
Red Stripe lager
Tusker lager

Diageo's agency agreements vary depending on the particular brand, but tend to be for a fixed number of years. Diageo's principal agency brand is José Cuervo in North America and many other markets (with distribution rights extending to 2013). In the year ended 30 June 2008, Diageo signed a three-year agency agreement with Inversiones de Guatemala to distribute Zacapa ultra premium rums globally, other than in Central America (Guatemala, Guatemalan duty free, El Salvador, Honduras, Nicaragua, Costa Rica, and Panama), where Industrias Licoreras de Guatemala will retain the right to distribute the Zacapa brands. There can be no assurances that Diageo will be able to prevent termination of distribution rights or rights to manufacture under licence, or renegotiate distribution rights or rights to manufacture under licence on favourable terms when they expire.

Diageo also brews and sells other companies' beer brands under licence, including Budweiser and Carlsberg lagers in Ireland, Heineken lager in Jamaica and Tiger beer in Malaysia.

Global priority brands Diageo has eight global priority brands that it markets worldwide. Diageo considers these brands to have the greatest current and future earnings potential. Each global priority brand is marketed consistently around the world, and therefore can achieve scale benefits. The group manages and invests in these brands on a global basis. Figures for global priority brands include related ready to drink products, unless otherwise indicated. Net sales are sales after deducting excise duties.

In the year ended 30 June 2008, global priority brands accounted for 59% of total volume (86.3 million equivalent units) and contributed net sales of £4,614 million.

Smirnoff achieved sales of 29.6 million equivalent units in the year ended 30 June 2008. Smirnoff vodka volume was 25.1 million equivalent units. It was ranked, by volume, as the number one premium vodka and the number one premium spirit brand in the world. Smirnoff ready to drink volume totalled 4.5 million equivalent units.

Johnnie Walker scotch whiskies comprise Johnnie Walker Red Label, Johnnie Walker Black Label and several other brand variants. During the year ended 30 June 2008, Johnnie Walker Red Label sold 10.0 million equivalent units, Johnnie Walker Black Label sold 5.5 million equivalent units and the remaining variants sold 0.8 million equivalent units. The Johnnie Walker franchise was ranked, by volume, as the number one premium scotch whisky and the number three premium spirit brand in the world.

Captain Morgan was ranked, by volume, as the number two premium rum brand in the world with sales of 8.3 million equivalent units in the year ended 30 June 2008.

Baileys was ranked, by volume, as the number one liqueur in the world, having sold 7.5 million equivalent units in the year ended 30 June 2008.

Guinness is the group's only global priority beer brand, and for the year ended 30 June 2008 achieved volume of 11.4 million equivalent units.

Other global priority brands were also ranked, by volume, among the leading premium distilled spirits brands by Impact Databank. These include: J&B scotch whisky (comprising J&B Rare, J&B Reserve, J&B Exception and J&B Jet), ranked the number three premium scotch whisky in the world; José Cuervo, ranked the number one premium tequila in the world; and Tanqueray, ranked the number four premium gin brand in the world. During the year ended 30 June 2008, J&B, José Cuervo and Tanqueray sold 6.1 million, 5.0 million and 2.1 million equivalent units, respectively.

Other brands Diageo manages its other brands by category, analysing them between local priority brands and category brands. Local priority brands represent the brands, apart from the global priority brands, that make the greatest contribution to operating profit in a business area (North America, Europe, International or Asia Pacific), rather than worldwide. Diageo has identified 25 local priority brands. Diageo manages and invests in these brands within its business areas and, unlike the global priority brands, may not have a consistent marketing strategy around the world for such brands. For the year ended 30 June 2008, local priority brands contributed volume of 26.0 million equivalent units, representing 18% of total volume, and net sales of £1,734 million. Examples of local priority brands include Crown Royal Canadian whisky in North America, Buchanan's De Luxe whisky in International, Windsor Premier whisky in Asia Pacific, Gordon's gin in Europe, Bundaberg rum in Asia Pacific, Cacique rum in Europe, Malta Guinness non-alcoholic malt in International, Tusker lager in International, Seagram's 7 Crown whiskey and Seagram's VO whisky in North America, Bell's Extra Special whisky in Europe and Sterling Vineyards wines in North America.

The remaining brands are grouped under category brands. Category brands include spirits, beer and wine brands and for the year ended 30 June 2008, these category brands contributed volume of 32.8 million equivalent units, representing 23% of total volume, and net sales of £1,742 million. Of this, spirits achieved volume of 23.9 million equivalent units and contributed £1,120 million to Diageo's net sales in the year ended 30 June 2008. Examples of category spirits brands are Gordon's gin (all markets except Europe in which it is a local priority brand), Gordon's vodka, The Classic Malt whiskies and White Horse whisky.

In the year ended 30 June 2008, Diageo sold 13.2 million equivalent units of beers other than Guinness, achieving net sales of £765 million. Other beer volume was mainly attributable to owned brands, such as Red Stripe, Pilsner, Tusker and Harp lager, with a minority being attributable to beers brewed and/or sold under licence, such as Tiger beer in Malaysia and Heineken lager in Jamaica.

In addition, Diageo produces and markets a wide selection of wines. These include well known labels such as Beaulieu Vineyard, Sterling Vineyards, Rosenblum Cellars and Chalone Vineyard in the United States, Blossom Hill in the United Kingdom, and Barton & Guestier and Piat d'Or in Europe. For the year ended 30 June 2008, other wine volume was 2.3 million equivalent units, contributing net sales of £275 million.

2.137   A further example is given in Table 2.27 where a company reports on four key resources it must manage in order to achieve profitable growth.

Table 2.27 – Resources – brands

The Capita Group Plc – Annual Report and Accounts – 31 December 2006

Business review (extract)

Our business strategy How do we manage and measure our growth? (extract)

c) Resource and operational controls

Our continued growth and financial performance depends on having the right resources in place. To sustain our high contract win and retention rates, we have to satisfy clients that we have the operational scale and capability to deliver our promises – whether on relatively simple contracts or large scale, multi-service packages. Through the MOB process we continuously assess the needs of each business unit to ensure that we have the necessary people, infrastructure and resources for current and future development.

Each month, we monitor and review comprehensive operational management information enabling us to manage the business in a way that delivers our key financial aims.

4 key areas of attention:

Core operational indicators	Aim	Progress Year end 2006	Year end 2005
Retaining the right people	Senior management retention (top 250 earning over £90k) – attract and retain the appropriate level of senior management to drive the strategic direction of the Group	**91%**	92%
	Overall employee retention – attract and retain the right people to deliver Group strategy, maintaining employee retention at or above industry average (81.7%)	**82%**	81%
Creating extensive infrastructure	Continue to grow our infrastructure of business centres to meet the needs of our growing business	**52 business centres: Onshore 46 Nearshore 4 Offshore 2**	47 business centres: Onshore 42 Nearshore 3 Offshore 2
	Extend our offshore capability – have at least 10% of our people based in India by 2009	**3%**	1.6%
Using ICT and innovation to add value	Generate economies of scale by maximising use and growing number of shared technology platforms	**11 shared platforms**	9 shared platforms

Ensuring effective procurement	Monitor and build relationships with key strategic suppliers through our Supplier Development Programme	**Introduced comprehensive Supplier Development Programme**	–
	Continue to audit all existing suppliers against Capita's standards of business – 50% of all suppliers to be audited by December 2007	**Supplier audit commenced – targets set**	Supplier profiling project undertaken

Principal risks and uncertainties

2.138 The OFR should include a description of the principal risks and uncertainties facing the entity, together with a commentary on the directors' approach to them. [RS (OFR) para 52].

2.139 It is important that companies distinguish their principal risks and uncertainties rather than listing all possible risks without highlighting to the reader which are the most important in assessing the potential success of the company's strategy.

2.140 The example in Table 2.28 clearly illustrates four principal risks and uncertainties, referring to further commentary on them elsewhere.

Table 2.28 – Principal risks and uncertainties

Rentokil Initial plc – Annual Report – 31 December 2006

A Letter from the Chairman & CEO (extract)

The principal risks and uncertainties relating to our strategy are summarised below and discussed at greater length in the relevant parts of this review.

- Disruption in the businesses undergoing extensive organisational change.
- Ensuring acquisitions are integrated properly and meet the investment case.
- Resolving the challenges in the Textiles and Washroom Services division in some of its continental European markets.
- Retaining the management team.

2.140.1 Significant risks and uncertainties include both financial risks and non-financial risks. Indeed the two types are often indistinguishable because non-financial risk, such as the risk that a product may be faulty, may have serious financial consequences, such as the cost of withdrawing the product, penalties on long-term contracts, damage to the entity's reputation and so on. Other non-financial risks, which are increasingly referred to, reflect trends in consumer and social behaviour and potential regulatory actions. Examples include the health hazards of cigarettes, obesity risk and possible health risks from the use of mobile phones. Product risk is, therefore, often significant.

2.141 Entities should disclose the strategic, commercial, operational and financial risks where these may significantly affect the entity's strategies and development of the entity's value. [RS (OFR) para 53]. Specific risks facing entities will vary according to the nature of the business, but some risks, such as reputational risks, will be common to all. [RS (OFR) para 54]. Description of the principal risks should cover both exposures to negative consequences as well as potential opportunities. The directors' policy for managing principal risks should also be disclosed. [RS (OFR) para 55]. The OFR should cover the principal risks and uncertainties necessary to understand the business' objectives and strategy both where they constitute a significant external risk to the entity and where the entity's impact on other parties through its activities, products or services, affects its performance. Directors will need to consider the full range of business risks. [RS (OFR) para 56].

2.142 Table 2.29 illustrates a company reporting its key external and internal risks, encompassing strategic and commercial areas such as its business environment, operational issues such as customer service and financial risks such as diversifying revenue sources. Management also explains the actions the company is taking to manage the six principal risks, four of which are shown in Table 2.29.

Table 2.29 – Principal risks and uncerainties

Reuters Group PLC – Annual Report and Form 20-F – 31 December 2006

Business review (extract)

Our 'risk radar', reviewed by the Board, captures key external and internal risks that could affect Reuters ability to reach its full potential and the actions and plans in place to mitigate them.

Risk	Inpact	Action
Financial markets are cyclical.	Downturn in the financial markets could make it more difficult for us to achieve our financial goals.	• Diversify revenues through emphasis on Core Plus. • Prioritise initiatives that help customers achieve greater efficiency through business automation. See 'Strategy' on pages 44–45; 'Enterprise division' on page 61.
The financial services industry is undergoing rapid structural and regulatory evolution.	We need to keep pace with structural changes if we are to maintain a strong market position.	• Continue to develop Core Plus electronic trading initiatives. • Implement services which address MiFID and Reg NMS requirements. • Monitor industry shifts closely. • Engage with customers' strategies and ensure our own strategy remains aligned with theirs. • Launch FXMarketSpace with CME. • Experiment with new business models within our Innovation portfolio. See 'Markets' on pages 45–47; 'Divisional performance' on pages 58–62; 'Strategy' on pages 44–45.
The integrity of our reputation is key to our ability to remain a trusted source of news and information.	We need to protect our brand in order to sustain our credibility as a neutral supplier of content.	• Set appropriate 'tone at the top' from senior management. • Provide training on ethics and Reuters Trust Principles. • Enforce clear accountability. • Ensure regular Board review. See 'Corporate governance' on pages 22–23; 'Our commitment to ethics and compliance' on pages 48–49; 'People' on pages 47–48.
Our customers demand high levels of service to help them perform effectively.	We need to anticipate and respond to our customers' needs if we are to improve our competitiveness.	• Measure and monitor service levels. • Execute service improvement and content quality plans. • Continue to promote a service-driven culture. • Complete investments in data centre and capacity improvements. See 'Strategy' on pages 44–45; 'People' on pages 47–48.

2.143 Table 2.30 is an example of a company quantifying its risks in a graphical format, to indicate the relationship between likelihood and impact. It also specifically assigns accountability to individual directors for managing each risk, sets targets for risk mitigation and monitors progress against these. Disclosure is also made of risks additional to the small group identified as key risks.

Table 2.30 – Risk mitigation and quantification

Speedy Hire plc – Annual Report and Accounts – 30 June 2007

Corporate governance (extract)

Risk map

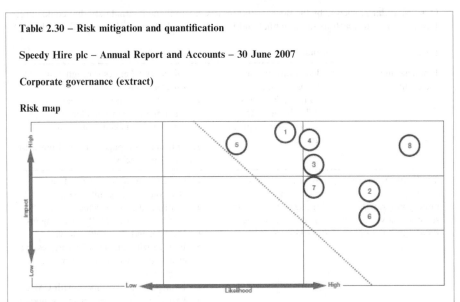

The table below summarises the small group of risks that were identified as key, together with a short description of monitoring/mitigation activities and sponsorship at Board level.

Risk no.	Risk area	Board Sponsor	Risk monitoring/ mitigation	Progress 06/07 & target 07/08
1	IT/business	Neil O'Brien	Detailed testing and phased, budgeted roll-out. Ongoing internal audit implementation review. Weekly call on project performance.	Third company going live. Roll-out phase to be implemented during 2007/8. Project risk analysis to be monitored on a regular basis.
2	Effective communication	Steve Corcoran	One Speedy initiative. Full review of internal/external marketing structures and strategies.	Feedback from staff on internal communication programme to be sought. Major risks to the One Speedy initiative to be identified and managed.

3	Business co-ordination	Steve Corcoran	Implementation by Executive Management Team. Sales training and in-house marketing.	Improved cross-selling through training.
4	Major acquisition: risk of poor performance	Mike McGrath	Consideration of project impact as part of all major acquisition programmes. Monitoring of performance against integration plan with reporting to the Board.	Ongoing review of impact on Senior Management resources/time.
5	Major acquisition integration	Mike McGrath	Documented procedures, with alignment of deal and integration teams. Formal review and reporting to the Board following the acquisition.	Continue to monitor and manage existing controls.
6	Employee training and development	Mike McGrath	Training and development plans in place, supported by internal communication programme.	Joint venture entered into with the leading training provider Carter & Carter. Mandatory training line to support current standard operating procedures.
7	Market competition	Neil O'Brien	Market developments continuously monitored and reported monthly to the Board.	Continue to monitor and manage existing controls.
8	Co-ordination/implementation of key strategic projects	All	Phased strategic projects, monitored by Strategy Steering Committee and overseen by CEO.	Implement key findings of integration project. Undertake talent review against strategic growth plans.

Other risks which do not feature on the above table nevertheless are regularly reviewed. For example:

1   The Board's belief is that the outlook for the construction industry remains strong (see Stratton report and OFR).

2 The Group is aware of the risk of product obsolescence and mitigates this by continually monitoring developments in technology relevant to the industry and discussing customers' needs with its suppliers.

3 The Board is also conscious of the potential for the expansion of off-site construction reducing the demand for hired tools to site. However, this is perceived to be a medium to long-term risk.

2.144   Management should disclose uncertainties as well as risks. These may include contingent liabilities relating to specific operational uncertainties, such as outstanding litigation; or market uncertainty, for example whether a new product will be successful. There are also inherent uncertainties that surround the preparation of the financial statements, which may require significant estimates and judgements. These may be referred to in the description of risk factors, but are more often dealt with in the description of critical accounting policies. Disclosure of critical accounting policies is addressed below under 'Accounting policies'. In addition, under IFRS, IAS 1 requires disclosure in the financial statements of significant judgements made by directors and of key sources of estimation uncertainty. [IAS 1 paras 113 and 116].

2.145   As well as the recommendation in the reporting statement to disclose risks and uncertainties, including financial risks, IAS 32, 'Financial instruments: Presentation', and IFRS 7, 'Financial instruments: Disclosures', and FRS 25 and FRS 29 (the UK equivalents) all require such disclosure for financial policies and risks. IAS 32, for example, requires an entity to *"describe its financial risk management objectives and policies, including its policy for hedging each main type of forecast transaction for which hedge accounting is used"*. [IAS 32 para 56]. The Manual of Accounting – Financial instruments deals with these requirements.

Relationships

2.146   Information should be included in the OFR about significant relationships with stakeholders other than members, where they are likely to influence, directly or indirectly, the business performance and its value. This information should be given to the extent necessary to enable members to assess the entity's strategies and their potential to succeed. [RS (OFR) para 57].

2.147   Stakeholders other than members may include customers, suppliers, employees, contractors, lenders, creditors, regulators and tax authorities. They may also include the community in which the entity operates and society generally, as well as those entities with which the entity has strategic alliances. [RS (OFR) para 58].

2.148   The types of significant relationships that may be appropriate to disclose include:

■ Customers – this may include management of customer service, details of losses or gains of customers, in particular those on which the company has a degree of reliance, and of new business developments with customers.

- Suppliers – including management of procurement activities, ability to source appropriate suppliers, consideration of raw material availability and prices, vetting of supplier behaviour and policy regarding child labour, fair wages etc.

- Employees – including satisfaction surveys, recruitment and retention, training and development, diversity, health and safety, employee communications, productivity, human rights, ethical trading.

- Impact on society and communities – including environmental impact (for example, noise, pollution, waste), product safety, product responsibility, charitable donations and community projects.

- Lenders and creditors – for example, negotiations of credit facilities and other arrangements with lenders, impact of macro-economic factors on availability of credit.

- Regulators – for example licences to operate, pricing restrictions, tax negotiations, government discussions on legislation impacting the company.

- Strategic alliances – such as joint ventures, sub-contractors, franchises.

2.149   The reporting statement notes that in deciding what should be included in the OFR, directors will need to take a broad view in determining the extent to which the actions of stakeholders other than members may affect the entity's performance and value. [RS (OFR) para 58]. Each of the examples of relationships set out in the previous paragraph may impact the company more or less depending on its circumstances. The following paragraphs highlight just a few of these. Management should decide which are important to them and explain how managing those relationships contributes to the potential future success of their strategies.

2.150   The example in Table 2.31 illustrates how customer relationships pose a key risk to the strategy of Cadbury Schweppes plc.

Table 2.31 – Relationships – customers

Cadbury Schweppes plc – Annual Report and Accounts – 31 December 2007

Consumer demand

Consumer demand for the Group's products may be affected by factors including changes to consumer preferences, unseasonable or unusual weather, or longer-term climatic changes. The Group has made substantial investments in understanding consumer preferences and in its ability to respond to consumer needs through innovation, and also has products appealing to a wide range of consumers. However, it may be unable to respond successfully or at reasonable cost to rapid changes in demand or consumer preferences, which may adversely affect its performance.

2.151   A major change in the customer base may have a significant effect on the business, because the extent and direction of operations may have to be materially curtailed or expanded and the entity's strategy may have to be modified to meet changed circumstances.

2.152   Table 2.33 illustrates management's efforts to manage relations with its employees, including the values underpinning the relationship and the ways in which it engages its workforce.

Table 2.33 – Relationships – employees

Alfred McAlpine plc – Annual Report and Accounts – 31 December 2006

Business review (extract)

People
Our employee strategy remains focused on supporting delivery and customer service, through a motivated and engaged workforce. The key differentiator in the service we provide to our customers is the quality and motivation of our employees. This is visibly demonstrated through their performance: through productivity, quality, safety and customer service.

To achieve a motivated and engaged workforce, we support our employees through excellent leadership, skilled management, investment in development and training, involvement through inclusive consultation and innovative internal communications as well as a reward package that motivates and supports them.

In addition, we utilise our HR, time management, routing and knowledge management systems to ensure that we provide our customers with the right person, with the right skills and motivation, at the right location, at the right time, with all the knowledge of the Company at their disposal.

Culture and values
 We believe that a positive culture is essential to high-quality customer service. Our values of winning, passion, honesty, collaboration and enjoyment have to be reflected in all our practices and procedures. Our reputation has been built on our people and we believe that employees whose behaviours reflect our values deliver excellent customer service.

The five values are:

Winning Alfred McAlpine values winners – people who want to create success for themselves, their company, and their customers; people with real commitment.

Passion Superior performance is born out of passion. Alfred McAlpine values people who are passionate about their work and about doing the very best job for their customers.

Honesty Alfred McAlpine demands honesty – honesty in dealing with each other and honesty in dealing with all external stakeholders.

Collaboration The Company values people who work openly and productively with each other, clients and partners – people who listen, people who explore new ideas and create new value.

Enjoyment The Company values job satisfaction. People who enjoy what they do put more in – and get more out.

Achieving an engaged workforce

Leadership
Motivated employees require great leaders and we have continued to focus on facilitating and nurturing leadership. We have established talent management programmes covering the majority of our management team and these provide both awareness of those who will benefit from accelerated development and, more importantly, focus the development needs of participants. Our 360 degree feedback process, our performance management and our employee survey all give us insight into the behaviour of our leaders. Our employee survey demonstrates that the improvements are visible to our employees.

Training and development
We run a series of training and development programmes operating across the core businesses which ensure that we obtain maximum value from our employees by helping them reach their full potential.

When asked through the MORI survey whether employees felt they had a clear career path, MORI recorded the highest score that they have recorded for any company.

Employee forums and consultation
We consult employees and listen to their feedback through the annual employee survey and a regular employee forum in each Business Stream. We also publish a range of internal magazines and newsletters across the Group and use web-based knowledge management systems. We also hold regular team briefings and toolbox talks.

2.153 There are many ways in which an entity's operations may affect the community in which it operates. How the entity interacts with society generally and those who are affected by its operations, has a significant effect on its reputation and, consequently, on its business performance. The non-financial matters range widely, from the 'big issues', such as ethical trading, human rights and environment, to the smaller but valuable involvement in the community through, for example, donations and secondments of employees to charities and help given to aid organisations dealing with natural disasters. The example shown in Table 2.34 illustrates one company's approach to managing its environmental and social impacts.

Table 2.34 – Relationships – society

Royal Dutch Shell plc – Annual Report and Form 20-F – 31 December 2006

OPERATING AND FINANCIAL REVIEW (extract)

Environment and society

INTRODUCTION
We recognise that our continuing business success depends on finding environmentally and socially responsible ways to help meet the world's growing energy needs. Managing today's business risks, delivering our strategy and achieving our goals all critically require maintaining the trust of a wide range of stakeholders. To keep the trust of stakeholders, we must do many things, including: behaving with integrity at all times, in line with the Shell General Business Principles (Business Principles); operating our facilities safely; being a good neighbour; contributing to development in the societies where we operate; and helping to find effective solutions to the problem of growing CO_2 emissions. In this section we discuss our overall

approach to managing environmental and social impacts, how we are addressing our main risks and opportunities and our performance in this area in 2006.

OUR APPROACH TO MANAGING ENVIRONMENTAL AND SOCIAL IMPACTS

We take a systematic approach to managing environmental and social impacts as part of the Shell Control Framework, through a combination of Group wide standards and processes, controls, incentives and our governance. In 2006, we took additional steps to clarify what we expect from staff, and how to increase their skills, and share our knowledge better around the Group.

STANDARDS AND PROCESSES

Our Business Principles include our commitment to contribute to sustainable development. This requires balancing short- and long-term interests and integrating economic, environmental and social considerations into business decision-making.

All companies and joint ventures where we have control over operations – for example as majority shareholder or operator – must apply the Business Principles, our new Code of Conduct (Code) launched in 2006, and the rest of the Shell Control Framework. The Business Principles and Code require compliance with all applicable laws and support for human rights. They forbid, among other things, bribery, fraud and anti-competitive behaviour. The commitment to contribute to sustainable development includes engaging with external stakeholders and being a good neighbour. These companies and joint ventures must also apply Shell-wide environmental and social standards. These include the Group Health, Safety and Environment (HSE) policy and commitment, requiring the systematic management of HSE, as well as our standards for animal testing, biodiversity, climate change, environmental management, health management, incident reporting, security, ship quality and our relationship with our people. We require contractors to manage HSE in line with our standards and expect them to follow our Business Principles or equivalent ones by including these expectations in our contract terms and conditions. We also encourage suppliers and ventures where we do not have a controlling interest to adopt and follow equivalent principles and HSE standards. If these contractors, suppliers and ventures cannot meet our expectations within a reasonable timeframe, we are required to review the relationship.

Our Business Principles and standards are reflected in our business processes. For example, they are included in the criteria used to assess investment proposals and in the planning and design of major new projects. All major new investments must include the expected future costs of emitting carbon in their financial calculations. We require an Impact Assessment to be carried out before we begin significant work on a project or at an existing facility. The actions identified must be part of the project's design and operation. All our major refining and chemicals facilities, and upstream operations with potential for high social impact, must also have social performance plans in line with Group guidance. These plans spell out how the operation will manage its social impacts and generate benefits for the local community.

In 2006, our Exploration & Production business clarified and tightened its requirements for identifying and managing environmental and social impacts when developing new projects – particularly at the earliest stages of project design. Experts from the business and central functions now review the top 70 new Exploration & Production prospects for environmental and social risks and opportunities. These include projects still in early concept or design phases.

CONTROLS AND INCENTIVES

Following our environmental and social standards is part of the duties of line managers, with support provided by HSE, social performance, security, human resources and finance specialists. Each Shell business is responsible for complying with our requirements and achieving its specific targets in this area.

We monitor compliance through an annual assurance letter process, internal audits and performance appraisals. The assurance letter process requires the relevant senior manager to report to the Chief Executive on the performance of their business or function in following our Business Principles and Group Standards. Results are reported to the Audit Committee of the Board. Sustainable development performance is an important component of appraisals and compensation, as it comprises 20% of the Group Scorecard.

GOVERNANCE
The Chief Executive counts sustainable development among his responsibilities. On his behalf, the Corporate Affairs Director chairs the Group Sustainable Development and HSE Executive Committee, which reviews performance and sets priorities, key performance indicators (KPIs) and targets. The Group HSE Function, central Social Performance Management Unit and issues management staff provide the needed challenge and support to our businesses to develop the necessary skills, share lessons learned and deal with issues in a consistent way. The Social Responsibility Committee is one of four committees of the Royal Dutch Shell plc Board. It reviews our policies and performance with respect to our Business Principles, Code of Conduct, HSE policy, and other relevant environmental and social standards, and major issues of public concern. It is composed of three Non-executive Directors, including its chair, Wim Kok, former Prime Minister of the Netherlands.

2.154 Details should be given of receipts from and returns to shareholders in relation to their shareholdings. This should include a description of distributions, capital raising and repurchases of shares. The information should be given to the extent necessary to give an understanding of the business. [RS (OFR) para 59].

2.155 An entity's dividend policy can impact which investors are interested in the company, depending on whether they are looking for income growth or capital growth. An example disclosure of dividend policy is given in Table 2.35.

Table 2.35 – Relationships – shareholders

Prudential plc – Annual Report – 31 December 2006

Directors' report: Operating and financial review (extract)

Group overview (extract)

Dividend per share
The Board has reviewed its longer-term dividend policy in light of its expectation that the overall operating cash flow of the Group will be positive from 2008.

The directors recommend a final dividend for 2006 of 11.72 pence per share payable on 22 May 2007 to shareholders on the register at the close of business on 13 April 2007. The interim dividend for 2006 was 5.42 pence per share. The total dividend for the year, including the interim dividend and the recommended final dividend, amounts to 17.14 pence per share compared with 16.32 pence per share for 2005, an increase of five per cent. The total cost of dividends in respect of 2006 was £418 million.

The full-year dividend is covered 1.5 times by post-tax IFRS operating profit from continuing operations.

Dividend cover is calculated as operating profit after tax on an IFRS basis, divided by the current year interim dividend plus the proposed final dividend.

The Board will focus on delivering a growing dividend, which will continue to be determined after taking into account the Group's financial flexibility and opportunities to invest in areas of the business offering attractive returns. The Board believes that in the medium term a dividend cover of around two times is appropriate.

2.156 Significant share issues and repurchases affect members' interests as they may dilute those interests or require members to make further investment, for example in a rights issue. The reasons for such changes in capital may include:

■ The need for additional finance for acquisitions or for organic expansion of the business.

■ Changing the capital structure to one that the directors consider to be more appropriate to the business' needs by increasing capital and using the proceeds to reduce debt or by repurchasing shares and increasing debt.

■ Returning capital as part of cash flow management.

2.157 An example of how share buybacks and dividends are used to help achieve strategic objectives, in this case effective cash management, is shown in Table 2.36.

Table 2.36 — Relationships — shareholders

Imperial Tobacco Group PLC – Annual Report and Accounts – 30 September 2006

Operating and Financial Review (extract)

Our Strategy
Our strategy is to create sustainable shareholder value by growing both organically and through acquisitions.

Our Strategic Objectives
We actively pursue three primary objectives which underpin our strategy:

● Sales development.

● Cost optimisation and efficiency improvements.

● Effective cash management.

Total Shareholder Return (extract)
In the past ten years we have returned more than £2.8 billion to shareholders by way of dividends and share buybacks.

Financial position

2.158   The OFR should include an analysis of the entity's financial position. [RS (OFR) para 60].

General

2.159   An entity's financial position – for example, plans for future capital expenditure and acquisitions and the robustness of its funding position to achieve those plans – is often contained in a separate section of the OFR, usually called the financial review or the finance director's review. In larger entities with diversified operations, additional financial information may be given elsewhere, for example by dividing the OFR into sections covering each of the main business segments, which describe the operations and financial position of each segment. Even where that form of presentation is adopted, however, there is usually a separate financial review dealing with the group's overall financial position.

2.160   The analysis of financial position in the OFR, while based upon the financial statements, should supplement the disclosures required by accounting standards and comment on events that impacted the entity's financial position during the year. This is particularly relevant when a large part of the company operates in an area of economic instability. The analysis should also comment on future factors that are likely to affect the financial position going forward. The reporting statement refers specifically to supplementing disclosures required by FRS 25 (IAS 32) or FRS 29 (IFRS 7). [RS (OFR) para 61]. The use of derivatives and the requirement of the standards to fair value certain types of instrument means that there can be significant volatility in the reported results. Requirements to classify certain instruments and arrangements involving shares as debt, may also have significant effects on the balance sheet presentation. This is why particular emphasis is placed on the need to further explain the entity's policies and practices in the OFR. The guidance contained in the Manual of Accounting – Financial instruments may be useful when preparing disclosure in this area.

2.161   A number of the measures used to monitor the company's financial position may be directly taken from the financial statements, but directors often supplement these with other measures common to their industry to monitor their progress towards stated objectives. Such disclosure may reflect non-GAAP measures (see paras 2.73 to 2.78) and may include sensitivity analysis, for example in respect of financial instrument values where volatility can have a significant impact on the company's financial position.

2.162   Table 2.37 shows how this company supplements the disclosures required by accounting standards with those financial position measures that it uses to manage the business. In particular, it records the significant judgements that are taken in accounting for the company's financial position.

Table 2.37 – Financial position

Capital & Regional plc – Annual Report – 30 December 2006

Operating and financial review – Results (extract)

Balance sheet, debt and hedging

Balance sheet: we look at our balance sheet in three ways:

- The enterprise balance sheet shows the £6,497 million portfolio we manage, financed by £913 million of shareholder equity and a further £2,288 million of institutional equity invested directly into our funds.

- The see through balance sheet gives our economic exposure to different market segments, and is the one we use for managing the business. It is notable that we have an increasing proportion of our exposure in the German and FIX UK portfolios.

- Our statutory balance sheet follows the accounting rules. Under these rules the three funds and various joint ventures are consolidated on an equity basis. The debt on this balance sheet excludes our share of fund and JV debt.

Three balance sheets	Enterprise £m	See through £m	Statutory £m
Shopping centres	3,185	772	398
Retail parks	1,568	430	245
Leisure property	1,252	359	210
German big box retail	382	359	382
FIX UK	110	110	110
Total property	6,497	2,030	1,345
Working capital	(57)	21	25
Debt	(3,239)	(1,138)	(457)
Net assets	3,201	913	913
C&R shareholders	913	913	913
Fund investors	2,288	–	–
Total equity	3,201	913	913
Loan to value	50%	56%	34%
Gearing (debt/equity)	101%	125%	50%

Balance sheet judgements: the key judgements in the balance sheet relate to:

1. Property valuations; all of which are carried out by independent valuers. For 69% of our property exposure held through the three funds, there is a further layer of scrutiny by the Fund Managers, Morley and Hermes.

2. Development provisioning; it often takes some years after a development is completed before all commercial issues are resolved and judgement is therefore needed on the level of provision required for completion costs.

3. Tax provisioning; it normally takes two or more years after each year end for all tax liabilities to be settled with the Inland Revenue. Judgement is needed on the correct level of provision required.

2.163   The reporting statement also suggests that discussion should focus on future factors that are likely to affect the position going forward. [RS (OFR) para 61]. Forward-looking statements are discussed above from paragraph 2.53.

Accounting policies

2.164   The OFR should highlight the entity's critical accounting policies. The critical accounting policies are key to understanding the entity's performance and financial position. The focus should be on those that require the particular exercise of judgement in their application to which the results are most sensitive. Discussion of accounting policies should include changes in accounting policies during the year. [RS (OFR) para 62].

2.165   Often this disclosure is a lengthy list of detailed accounting policies – similar to those found in risk disclosures. However, the example above in Table 2.37 shows another approach by highlighting the key areas in which judgements that are made in applying accounting policies relate to the balance sheet. As with risks, emphasising those accounting policies that are truly key to the company's performance and position can make it easier for investors to understand the context in which those results are presented.

2.166   The accounting policies disclosed and discussed will vary from entity to entity and from industry to industry. Critical accounting policies may include the following:

■   Revenue recognition – particularly in assessing revenue and profit to be recognised on long-term contracts and multiple component sales.

■   Impairment – where choice of discount rates and other assumptions can have significant effects on calculations.

■   Taxation – particularly where the entity has international operations and engages in significant tax planning activities.

■   Provisions – certain types of provisions, particularly for long-term environmental obligations require significant judgements and estimates.

■   Pensions – similar to provisions above, but pensions is an area where there is also additional volatility owing to the effects of stock market fluctuations.

■   Intangible assets including goodwill and development expenditure – goodwill and intangibles may comprise a large element of an entity's net assets, particularly in certain industries, such as advertising and publishing. Significant estimates and judgements are often required in assessing recoverability of such intangibles.

2.166.1   Although the critical accounting policies should be outlined in the OFR, it may be appropriate to cross-refer to the detailed descriptions contained in the notes to the financial statements.

Capital structure and treasury policies

2.167　The OFR should discuss the entity's capital structure and should set out its treasury policies and objectives. [RS (OFR) paras 63, 65].

2.168　This could include:

- Type of capital instruments used.

- Balance between equity and debt.

- Regulatory capital.

- Maturity profile of debt.

- Currency.

- Interest rate structure.

2.169　The discussion should include comments on short- and long-term funding plans to support the directors' strategies to achieve the entity's objectives. In addition, the discussion should comment on why the entity has adopted its particular capital structure.

2.170　For many listed companies, this section of the OFR could be relatively complex. Discussion may include reference to inter-linking issues. For example, a discussion could:

- Start with a description of the gearing and capital structure at the beginning of the year.

- Observe that the gearing level was lower or higher than normal.

- Discuss capital expenditure plans.

- Explain that ten-year debt was raised to finance that expenditure.

- Explain that long-term debt was raised because the investment was in long-term assets, but also acknowledge that:

  - The group was overly reliant on short-term debt.

  - The group wanted to take advantage of the historically low rate of interest on long-term debt.

Finally, this could lead to a discussion of the group's policy regarding fixed or floating rate finance. If interest rate swaps had been taken out as part of this policy, this fact could be explained.

2.171　In another example, a group might have overseas subsidiaries and may have changed the way in which these subsidiaries are financed. For example, the discussion could deal with the opening position, which might be that all funding was in sterling, and explain that the directors had decided during the year that, particularly in the light of their ambitions for overseas expansion, this gave rise to unduly high exchange rate exposure. The discussion could add that the directors had, therefore, decided to finance the overseas operations by a mixture of US dollar and euro borrowings. Alternatively, it might be explained that the group had retained its sterling borrowings, but taken out derivative contracts to hedge the overseas investments.

2.171.1 An example of disclosure relating to capital structure and treasury policy is provided in Table 2.38. This example also shows the group's market capitalisation and the highs and lows of the share price during the year. This information is commonly given by entities as part of the financial review as it enables members to assess the market's view of the entity's value at the end of, and during, the year.

Table 2.38 – Capital structure and treasury policy

Hilton Group plc – Report and Accounts – 31 December 2004

Capital structure and treasury policy

Financial risk management
The Group's treasury function provides a centralised service for the provision of finance and the management and control of liquidity, foreign exchange and interest rates. The function operates as a cost centre and manages the Group's treasury exposures to reduce risk in accordance with policies approved by the Board.

Derivative financial instruments, such as spot and forward foreign exchange contracts, currency swaps and interest rate swaps, are used to assist in the management of the Group's financial risk. These instruments are also used, where appropriate, to generate the desired effective currency and interest rate profile. It is not the policy of the Group to trade in or enter into speculative transactions.

Group operations are primarily financed from retained earnings, bank borrowings and long-term loans. Debt is principally raised centrally by the group finance company and then lent on to operating subsidiaries on commercial terms.

In addition to the primary financial instruments mentioned above, the Group also has other financial instruments, such as trade debtors, trade creditors, accruals and prepayments, that arise directly from the Group's operations.

The Group has a £2 billion Euro Medium Term Note (EMTN) programme, which is used to increase the flexibility of funding with regards to source, cost, size and maturity. As at 31 December 2004, three public Eurobond issues had been made under this programme – a £175 million 7.25% bond, maturing July 2008; a E500 million 6.5% bond, maturing July 2009; and a £250 million 7.125% bond, maturing July 2012. Several private placements have been issued under the programme in a variety of currencies. As at 31 December 2004, these private placements had an equivalent value of £36.8 million. Funds raised via the EMTN programme have been used to repay bank debt.

In October 2003, the Group issued £300 million 3.375% convertible bonds, maturing 2010. The bonds were issued by a subsidiary company and are convertible into exchangeable redeemable preference shares of the issuer, which are guaranteed by, and exchangeable for ordinary shares of, Hilton Group plc.

The main risks managed by the Group's treasury function are interest rate risk, liquidity risk, currency risk and credit risk. The Board reviews and agrees policies for each of these risks as summarised below. Note 20 to the accounts provides further disclosures with regard to these risks.

Interest rate risk The Group's exposure to interest rate fluctuations on its borrowings and deposits is managed by using various interest related derivatives, primarily interest rate swaps. The Group borrows in several currencies and operates a policy of fixing the interest rate of at least 25% of core debt for more than 12 months. Non-core debt and cash are kept at short-term interest rates. At 31 December 2004, after taking account of interest rate swaps, the proportion of the Group's gross borrowings at fixed rates was 40% (2003: 44%) fixed for a weighted average period of 2.7 years (2003: 3.2 years). The annual average interest rate on fixed rate debt was 5.2% (2003: 5.4%).

Liquidity risk The Group aims to maintain a balance between continuity and flexibility of funding through the use of borrowings with a range of maturities. The Group's policy on liquidity is to ensure that there is sufficient medium and long-term committed borrowing facilities to meet the medium-term funding requirements. At 31 December 2004, there were undrawn committed borrowing facilities of £341.4 million (2003: £588.9 million). Total committed facilities had an average maturity of 4.5 years (2003: 4.5 years).

Currency risk Due to the international nature of its core activities, the Group's reported profits, net assets and gearing are all affected by foreign exchange rate movements. The Group seeks to mitigate the effect of any structural currency exposure that may arise from the translation of the foreign currency assets by borrowing in foreign currencies to match at least 75% of the foreign currency assets. At 31 December 2004, foreign currency borrowings represented 93% (2003: 96%) of the net carrying value of foreign currency assets.

Although the Group carries out operations through a number of foreign enterprises, Group exposure to currency risk at a transactional level is minimal. The day to day transactions of overseas subsidiaries are carried out in local currency.

Credit risk Counterparty risk arises from the investment of surplus funds and from the use of derivative instruments. This risk is managed by restricting those transactions to banks that have a defined minimum credit rating and to limit the exposure to a maximum per bank. All derivative transactions are executed under agreements conforming to the International Swaps and Derivatives Association (ISDA) standards.

Share price and market capitalisation
The closing share price of the Group on 31 December 2004 was 284.50 pence (2003: 224.75 pence) and market capitalisation of the Group was £4.51 billion (2003: £3.56 billion). The high and low prices during the year were 285.25 pence and 214.50 pence respectively.

Going concern
The directors consider the Group has adequate resources to continue in operational existence for the foreseeable future and that it is therefore appropriate to adopt the going concern basis in preparing the financial statements.

Cash flows

2.172 The OFR should discuss the cash inflows and outflows during the financial year, together with the entity's ability to generate cash, to meet known or probable cash requirements and to fund growth. [RS (OFR) para 68].

2.173 The discussion should supplement the information in the financial statements around operating, investing and financing cash flows. [RS (OFR) para 69]. Specific commentary should be given on cash flows by segment where this is different from profit by segment. [RS (OFR) para 70]. This would be relevant, for example, in a long-term contracting business where the agreed timing of billings and cash receipts is out of line with profit recognition.

2.174 The OFR should comment on any special factors that have influenced cash flows in the period and that may have a significant effect on future cash flows. This could include the existence and timing of commitments for capital expenditure and other known or probable cash requirements. [RS (OFR) para 69]. An example of the latter might be the need to repay a large tranche of debt at a particular date in the future. Unusual or non-recurring cash flows should be highlighted where material, such as proceeds of a sale and leaseback or the termination of an interest rate swap.

2.175 Where an entity has cash that is surplus to its future operating requirements and its current levels of distributions to members, the OFR should discuss the entity's plans for making use of the cash. [RS (OFR) para 69]. Table 2.35 above indicates an example of a company reporting on its use of surplus cash.

2.176 For many users of financial statements cash flow is a key measure of performance and entities often develop KPIs that relate to cash flow. Some measures focus on cash flow from operations after meeting the entity's obligations for interest, tax and dividends and after capital expenditure, which is sometimes termed 'free cash flow'. However, definitions of 'free cash flow' (a non-GAAP measure) often vary from entity to entity and should, therefore, be fully explained. An example of disclosure of free cash flow is provided in Table 2.40, together with a reconciliation from the GAAP cash flow measures.

Table 2.40 – Free cash flow

Lonmin Plc – Annual Report – 30 September 2006

Free cash flow
We believe that a key metric of how successful we are as a business is ultimately the amount of cash we produce. We measure this by looking at our free cash flow. We define our free cash flow as cash flow from operations less interest and tax paid, less net capital expenditure and less dividends paid to our minority. We believe this measure indicates what cash we have which is free to fund equity dividends or make returns to shareholders, to pay down debt or to make discretionary investments.

Financials for the year 2002 to 2004 are as prepared under UK GAAP. For 2005 and 2006 the financials are prepared under IFRS. Details of the nature of the changes under IFRS can be found in Note 35 to the Accounts in the Annual Report.

Cash flow
The following table summarises the main components of the cash flow during the year:

	2006 Total $m	2005 Total $m
Cash flow from operations	722	377
Interest and finance costs	(31)	(27)
Tax	(185)	(79)
Trading cash flow	506	271
Capital expenditure	(182)	(190)
Proceeds from disposal of assets held for sale	28	–
Dividends received from associate	–	2
Dividends paid to minority	(62)	(27)
Free cash flow	290	56
Acquisitions*	(14)	(212)
Financial investments	(36)	1
Shares issued	15	6
Equity dividends paid	(124)	(102)
Cash inflow/outflow	131	(251)
Opening net debt	(585)	(272)
Exchange	(4)	(2)
Net debt in subsidiaries acquired	–	(60)
Closing net debt	(458)	(585)
Trading cash flow (cents per share)	354.9c	191.2c
Free cash flow (cents per share)	203.4c	39.5c

* 2005 comparative includes $15 million on intangible non-current assets acquired in 2005.

Liquidity

2.177 The OFR should discuss the entity's current and prospective liquidity. This should include, where relevant, a commentary on the level of borrowings, the seasonality of borrowing requirements (indicated by the peak level of borrowings during the period) and the maturity profile of borrowings and undrawn committed borrowing facilities. [RS (OFR) para 73].

2.178 The discussion should cover the entity's ability to fund its current and future operations and stated strategies. [RS (OFR) para 72]. This is consistent with the increased emphasis on the need for a forward-looking orientation.

2.179 An example of disclosure of current and future liquidity is shown in Table 2.41, including explanations of the impact of the seasonality of its business.

Table 2.41 – Liquidity

Signet Group plc – Annual Report and Accounts – 53 weeks ended 3 February 2007

Financial review (extract)

Liquidity and capital resources
It is the objective of the Group to maintain a strong balance sheet, after implementing its 8% – 10% new store space growth strategy in the US, the continuing programme of store refurbishments and relocations on both sides of the Atlantic, payment of dividends, and any repurchase of shares. Factors which could affect this objective would be the acquisition of a business or a change in the Group's distribution policy to shareholders or if there was a variation in the operating performance of the Group.

The cash flow performance of the Group depends on a number of factors, such as the:

• operating performance of the business;

• rate of space expansion, which influences both fixed and working capital investment;

• level of store refurbishment and relocations;

• level of inventory investment; and

• proportion of US sales made on the in-house credit card and the average monthly collection rate of the credit balances.

Investment in new space requires significant investment in working capital, as well as fixed capital investment, due to the slow inventory turn, and the additional investment required to fund sales in the US utilising the in-house credit card.

In years when the rate of new store space expansion in the US is towards the lower end of the planned 8% – 10% range, or the level of store refurbishment and relocation is below normal, the Group will have reduced levels of investment in fixed and working capital. In 2006/07 a faster rate of new store space growth in the US, and increased dividend payments, more than offset a lower level of refurbishment in the UK and meant that there was a cash outflow of £16.3 million (2005/06: £6.7 million) before the repurchase of shares amounting to £33.7 million (2005/06: £2.0 million) and proceeds from the issue of shares of £4.1 million (2005/06: £3.9 million).

The Group's working capital requirements fluctuate during the year as a result of the seasonal nature of its business. As inventory is purchased for the Christmas season there is a working capital outflow which reaches its highest levels in late autumn. This position then reverses over the key selling period of November and December. The working capital needs of the business are then relatively stable from January to August. The rough diamond sourcing initiative will require

---

> the Group to hold an element of its inventory for approximately an additional 60 days. The timing of the payment of the final dividend, normally in July, is also material to working capital requirements during the year.

2.180 Beyond information on liquidity, our research has shown that investors also want a clear picture of a company's debt position in order to understand management's plans for servicing it and any risks associated with it. Companies have to give information about how they are funded, but this can be scattered throughout the annual report – both in the OFR and in the financial statements. In addition, some of the information relating to debt is not provided in the annual report at all – investors get the information outside the regulatory model.

2.181 The problem of determining a company's credit risk profile is even greater if it has a number of subsidiaries. In this case, investors need a clear debt profile of the group and its individual business units, as well as an understanding of any restrictions on the transfer of funds between business units. Such internal sources of liquidity should be discussed. If there are restrictions on the group's ability to transfer funds from one part of the group to meet the obligations of another part of the group – for example as a result of exchange controls or tax consequences of transfers – this should be discussed. This applies where the restrictions *"...represent, or might foreseeably come to represent..."* a significant restraint on the group. [RS (OFR) para 73]. The restrictions could be in the form of legal barriers, such as exchange controls, that preclude or limit repatriation of profits, or they could be commercial obstacles, such as where funds could be repatriated, but unduly high rates of withholding or other taxes would have to be paid.

2.182 Investors' view of debt does not stop at financial instruments or borrowings. They want to know about other debt-like liabilities. These could include revenues paid in advance by customers, operating leases, pensions, or other liabilities such as decommissioning costs that could trigger major cash outflows in the future.

2.183 We suggest that companies should include an analysis of net debt that incorporates financial debt, operating debt in off balance sheet leases and other debt-like liabilities. Although not a requirement, investors have indicated that they value such disclosure. Investors believe all instruments that the company views as debt should be incorporated in this statement, including instruments that accounting standards classify as equity. By the same token, instruments classified by accounting standards as debt, but which the company sees as equity, should be excluded. A comprehensive maturity table of all components, analysis by currency and by subsidiary and details of any collateral or other restrictions are also highly desirable to investors.

2.184 Examples of such financing net debt analyses are becoming more common amongst UK companies – most often within the notes to the financial statements. Table 2.42 shows a company that has included a separate 'analysis of net debt' after its 'consolidated cash flow statement' and cross-references to other financial statement notes for further details of maturities etc.

Table 2.42 – Analysis of net debt

Home Retail Group plc – Annual Report & Financial Statements – 3 March 2007

Consolidated Cash Flow Statement (extract)

Analysis of Net Debt
For the short period 1 April 2006 to 3 March 2007

Non-GAAP Measures	Notes	2007 £m
Financing net debt:		
Cash at bank and in hand	21	283.8
Loans and borrowings	23	(223.6)
Total financing net debt		60.2
Operating net debt:		
Property leases		(2,920.1)
Total operating net debt		(2,920.1)
Total net debt		(2,859.9)
Deduct:		
Operating leases that are off balance sheet		2,920.1
Total net debt reflected in balance sheet		60.2

The Group uses the term net debt which provides the Group's aggregate net indebtedness to banks and other financial institutions together with debt-like liabilities, notably property leases.

The capitalised value of these property leases is £2,920.1m (2006: £2,795.0m) based upon discounting the current rentals at the estimated current long term cost of borrowing of 5.4%.

The analysis of net debt has not been provided for the prior year, as it is non comparable given the demerger of the Group from GUS plc in 2006.

2.185   Table 2.43 illustrates a company that views its pension deficit as being 'debt-like' in nature and reports on it as such in the OFR.

Table 2.43 – Identification of 'debt-like' liabilities

Tomkins Group plc – Annual Report – 30 December 2006

Operating and Financial Review (extract)

Funding policy
The Group remains committed to funding pensions responsibly. In the UK, this means satisfying the funding agreements made with the trustees of the schemes in order to eliminate deficits over a reasonable period of time. In the US, funding objectives generally seek to avoid Pension Benefit Guaranty Corporation variable rate premiums and accelerated funding charges mandated by the Employee Retirement Income Security Act of 1974 ("ERISA"), and remain above the ERISA required minimum funding levels. Accordingly, most of the US plans are funded on the basis of reaching or exceeding a 90% funded level on a current liability basis.

The Pension Protection Act of 2006 will impact the rate at which the deficit of the US plans is eliminated, with deficits generally required to be eliminated over a period of seven years from the

2008 plan year. Tomkins is assessing the impact of the funding provisions of The Pension Protection Act and will adapt its funding policy accordingly.

Tomkins recognises its responsibility to fund defined benefit pension plan deficits and views these deficits as being debt-like in nature. Accordingly, where beneficial, Tomkins plc issues guarantees in respect of certain UK defined benefit pension plan deficits in order to improve the credit standing of these plans. This also has the effect of minimising the cost of the Pension Protection Fund's risk-based levy.

2.185.1 Another example of disclosure of current and future liquidity is shown in Table 2.43A. This example also gives details of cash flows and of funding, such as operating leases that are not treated as debt.

Table 2.43A – Current and future liquidity

Tate & Lyle PLC – Report and Accounts – 31 March 2004

Cash Flow and Balance Sheet

Cash flow and debt
Operating cash flow totalled £289 million compared with £323 million in the previous year. There was an operating working capital outflow of £31 million (2003 – £6 million outflow). Contributions to the Group's pension funds, both regular and supplementary, reduced from £61 million in the previous year to £34 million. A net £115 million (2003 – £97 million) was paid to providers of finance as dividends and interest. Net taxation paid increased from £7 million, which included a number of refunds, to £74 million, reflecting higher payments in the UK and North America.

Plant replacement, improvement and expansion expenditure of £118 million was above depreciation of £106 million. Investment expenditure was £26 million, being primarily an investment of £15 million in the astaxanthin joint venture and an injection of funds into the Tate & Lyle Employee Benefit Trust which purchases shares to satisfy options granted under the Executive Share Option Scheme. Disposals of fixed assets and businesses generated cash of £63 million. Exchange translation, and other non-cash movements, reduced net debt by £64 million.

The Group's net borrowings fell from £471 million to £388 million.

The ratio of net borrowings to earnings before exceptional items and before interest, tax, depreciation and goodwill amortisation (EBITDA) improved from 1.4 times to 1.2 times and the gearing ratio reduced to 38% at 31 March 2004 (2003 – 45%). During the year net debt peaked at £498 million in April 2003 (April 2002 during the year ended 31 March 2003 – £605 million).

Funding and liquidity management
The Group funds its operations through a mixture of retained earnings and borrowing facilities, including capital markets and bank borrowings.

In order to ensure maximum flexibility in meeting changing business needs the Group seeks to maintain access to a wide range of funding sources. Capital markets borrowings include the €300 million 5.75% bond maturing in 2006, the €150 million Floating Rate Note maturing in 2007 and the £200 million 6.5% bond maturing in 2012. At 31 March 2004 the Group's long-term credit ratings from Moody's and Standard and Poor's were Baa2 and BBB respectively.

The Group ensures that it has sufficient undrawn committed bank facilities to provide liquidity back-up for its US commercial paper and other short-term money market borrowing for the foreseeable future. The Group has committed bank facilities of US$510 million which mature in 2008 with a core of highly rated banks. These facilities are unsecured and contain common

---

financial covenants for Tate & Lyle PLC and its subsidiary companies that the interest cover ratio should not be less than 2.5 times and the ratio of net debt to EBITDA should not be greater than four times. The Group monitors compliance against all its financial obligations and it is Group policy to manage the consolidated balance sheet so as to operate well within covenanted restrictions at all times.

The majority of the Group's borrowings are raised through the Group treasury company and are then on-lent to the business units on an arm's-length basis.

The Group manages its exposure to liquidity risk by ensuring a diversity of funding sources and debt maturities. Group policy is to ensure that, after subtracting the total of undrawn committed facilities, no more than 30% of gross debt matures within 12 months and at least 50% has a maturity of more than two and a half years. At the end of the year, after subtracting total undrawn committed facilities, there was no debt maturing within 12 months and all debt had a maturity of two and a half years or more (2003 – 0% and 100%). The average maturity of the Group's gross debt was 4.9 years (2003 – 5.4 years).

At the year-end the Group held cash and current asset investments of £154 million (2003 – £172 million) and had undrawn committed facilities of £277 million (2003 – £348 million). These resources are maintained to provide liquidity back-up and to meet the projected maximum cash outflow from debt repayment and seasonal working capital needs foreseen for at least a year into the future at any one time.

Funding not treated as debt
In respect of all financing transactions, the Group seeks to optimise its financing costs. The following items are not included in net debt under UK accounting conventions.

At Amylum, the Group receives cash from selling amounts receivable from customers. The facility allows the sale of up to US$85 million (£46 million) of receivables, and was fully utilised at both 31 March 2004 and 31 March 2003. Where financially beneficial, operating leases are undertaken in preference to purchasing assets. Commitments under operating leases to pay rentals in future years totalled £180 million (2003 – £209 million) and related primarily to railcar leases in the USA.

Net debt of joint ventures and associates totalling £66 million at 31 March 2004 (2003 – £60 million) is not consolidated in the Group balance sheet. After counter indemnities, £22 million of this debt was subject to recourse to the Group. Tate & Lyle's share of net debt of joint ventures and associates totalled £32 million.

2.186   Management should disclose when borrowing covenants are in place that restrict the use of financing arrangements or credit facilities and *"...negotiations with the lenders on the operation of these covenants are taking place or are expected to take place"*. The reporting statement also states that *"where a breach of a covenant has occurred or is expected to occur, the OFR should give details of the measures taken or proposed to remedy the situation"*. [RS (OFR) para 74].

2.186.1   The meaning of the second quote is clear, although there is some judgement involved in addressing whether a breach of covenant is expected to occur. But the meaning of the first quote is clear. It recommends disclosure when negotiations are being held, perhaps to change the covenants, in a situation where there is neither a breach nor any expectation of a breach. An example might be where a covenant is being renegotiated, not because of financial difficulty, but following the introduction of a new accounting standard that alters the ratios without any change in the underlying economic position.

2.186.2   Take an example where an entity's year end borrowings were £450,000, peak borrowings were £550,000 and its facilities were £500,000, that is, it had temporarily exceeded its borrowing facilities and breached its covenants. The reporting statement's recommendation in such circumstances is for the entity to give details about "...measures taken or proposed to remedy the situation". This could lead to awkward disclosures if the company and its bankers have not agreed what the remedial measures might be. Disclosure in these circumstances is of course exactly what the reporting statement is aiming for and exactly what investors would welcome. An example of disclosure of a breach of covenant is given in Table 2.43B.

Table 2.43B – Breach of covenant

Regent Inns plc – Report and Accounts – 3 July 2004

Chairman's Statement (extract)

Discussions with Banks
Just prior to the scheduled preliminary results announcement on 14 September 2004, it came to the attention of the Board that the calculation of one of the covenant tests under the banking facility had not been performed in strict accordance with the terms of the facility agreement. As a result we decided to delay the announcement until today to enable us to clarify this issue with our bankers.

On 15 September 2004, we appointed Paul Felton-Smith as Interim Finance Director, and he has led discussions with our lending banks. The Company has now notified its banks that on the basis of the strict application of the agreement, it will, on delivery to them of these financial statements, be in breach of its interest cover covenant and that therefore an event of default will occur. The banks have confirmed that they are supportive of the Company in its current situation and have indicated (whilst reserving their rights) that it is their current intention to enter into negotiations in respect of the facilities with the objective of having in place facilities sufficient for the Group's currently estimated needs. The banks have agreed to waive temporarily the default while they consider the Company's financial position generally. The Board is confident that the negotiations will result in a successful outcome.

Financial Review (extract)

Post Balance Sheet Event
As referred to in the Chairman's statement, on 14 September 2004 the Company delayed the preliminary announcement of its results pending clarification of the strict terms of the facility agreement in calculating the interest cover covenant. Subsequently it has been clarified that on the basis of the strict application of the agreement, the Company will, on delivery to the banks of these financial statements, be in breach of its interest cover covenant and that therefore an event of default will occur. However, notwithstanding the above, the banks have indicated (whilst reserving their rights) that it is their current intention to enter the negotiations with the Company with the objective of having in place facilities sufficient for the Group's currently estimated needs. Furthermore, the banks have agreed to waive temporarily the default while they consider the Company's financial position generally.

2.186.3 FRS 18, 'Accounting policies', and IAS 1, 'Presentation of financial statements', require disclosure (by all companies) of any material uncertainties, of which directors are aware, that may cast significant doubt on the entity's ability to continue as a going concern. [FRS 18 para 61; IAS 1 para 23]. In addition, both IAS 32 and IFRS 7 require disclosures of any defaults and breaches of principal, interest, sinking fund or redemption provisions on loans payable and of any other breaches of loan agreements where the breaches can permit the lender to demand repayment (except where the breaches have remedied before the balance sheet date). [IAS 32 para 94(j); IFRS 7 paras 18, 19].

2.187 Management should discuss any seasonality in its liquidity position. If the level of borrowings at the year end is not representative of the normal level during the year, this should be disclosed. If the level of cash is unrepresentative of the year as a whole this should also be disclosed. An examples of disclosure of seasonality of borrowings and of cash levels is provided in Table 2.43C.

Table 2.43C – Seasonality of cash and borrowings

Imperial Chemical Industries plc – Report and Accounts – 31 December 2006

Liquidity and investments (extract)

The Group's net debt position has historically changed over the course of a year, and, in particular, short-term debt has generally increased in the early part of the year to fund working capital requirements. These working capital needs arise principally from the seasonality of the Paints business, which experiences higher sales of products used on the exterior of buildings, and thus working capital, during the North American and European summer (the second and third quarters of the year). The Group's commercial paper programmes and other short-term borrowings are normally used to fund these working capital fluctuations. At 31 December 2006, the Group had £16m of short-term borrowings outstanding (as shown in note 23 relating to the Group accounts).

23 Financial liabilities (extract)

(a) Short-term borrowings

	2006 £m	2005 £m	Average interest rate * 2006 £m	2005 £m
Bank borrowings				
Secured – by floating charge	3	–		
Unsecured	13	14		
	16	14	2.6	2.5
Other borrowings				
Unsecured	–	–		
	–	–	–	–
	16	14		
Maximum short-term borrowings outstanding during year	277	455		

* Based on borrowings outstanding at 31 December.

Various short-term lines of credit, both committed and uncommitted, are available to the Group and are reviewed regularly. There are no facility fees payable on uncommitted lines nor is there a requirement for an equivalent deposit to be maintained with any of the banks.

Going concern

2.188   The FSA's Listing Rules require a listed company to make a statement that it is a going concern, as part of its corporate governance disclosures. [LR 9.8.6R (3)]. Often the required statement is made in the OFR, usually in the financial review section.

2.189   Guidance on the form of going concern statement that companies might use was published in November 1994 in a document entitled 'Going concern and financial reporting — guidance for directors of listed companies registered in the UK'. An example of disclosure given in the document was:

> *"After making enquiries, the directors have a reasonable expectation that the company has adequate resources to continue in operational existence for the foreseeable future. For this reason, they continue to adopt the going concern basis in preparing the accounts."*

2.190   Most going concern statements do no more than reproduce with minor variations the suggested wording of the guidance. Table 2.43D shows an example that points out that in the business' particular circumstances, there are a number of fundamental uncertainties in relation to going concern. Details of the uncertainties are further described in the chairman's statement, the notes to the financial statements and are also referred to in the auditors' report.

Table 2.43D – Fundamental uncertainties

Jarvis plc – Report and Accounts – 31 March 2004

8. Going concern
After making appropriate enquiries, the Directors have a reasonable expectation that the Company and the Group have adequate resources to continue in operational existence for the foreseeable future. For this reason they continue to adopt the going concern basis in preparing the financial statements. However, Note 1(a) to the financial statements includes a number of fundamental uncertainties which might affect the basis on which the financial statements have been prepared.

[The next paragraph is 2.192.2]

Key performance indicators

2.192   To the extent necessary to meet the requirements set out in paragraph 2.114 above, the OFR should disclose the key performance indicators (KPIs), both financial and non-financial, used by the directors to assess progress against their stated objectives. [RS (OFR) para 38].

2.193   Key performance indicators are those the directors judge are effective in measuring the entity's development, performance or position. They are quantified measurements that reflect the entity's critical success factors and disclose progress towards achieving a particular objective or objectives. [RS (OFR) para 3].

What is key?

2.194 The reporting statement does not prescribe specific KPIs that entities should disclose. However, comparability will be enhanced if the KPIs are accepted and widely used, either within an industry sector or more generally. [RS (OFR) para 40]. The performance indicators that are key to a particular company are those that the directors use to manage the business.

2.195 A challenge is whether the KPIs currently presented to the board are those that allow them to assess progress against stated strategies, and when reported externally, allow readers to make a similar assessment. If not, is this because the information is simply not available or because it is not yet escalated to the board but may instead be assessed by management of individual business units?

2.196 In addition, the KPIs will, to a degree, be conditioned by the industry in which a company operates. Comparability will be enhanced if the KPIs are accepted and widely used, either within an industry sector or more generally. [RS (OFR) para 40]. However, management should not feel compelled to create KPIs to match those reported by their peers. The overriding need is for the KPIs to be relevant to that particular company. Management should explain its choice in the context of the chosen strategies and objectives and provide sufficient detail on measurement methods to allow readers to make comparisons to other companies' choices where they want to.

How many KPIs?

2.197 Where multiple performance measures are disclosed, management should explain which are key to managing the business. The choice of which ones are key is unique to each company and its strategy; it is impossible to specify how many KPIs a company should have. However, between four and ten measures are likely to be key for most types of company.

Segmental or group KPIs?

2.198 Management should consider how KPIs are collated and reported internally; whether they make sense when aggregated and reported at a group level, or would be more usefully reported at business segment level. In some instances it may be more appropriate to report KPIs for each business segment separately if the process of aggregation renders the output meaningless. For example, it is more informative to report a retail business segment separately rather than combining it with a personal financial services segment.

How flexible is the choice of KPIs?

2.199 Management should reflect on whether the KPIs chosen continue to be relevant over time. Strategies and objectives develop over time, making it inappropriate to continue reporting on the same KPIs as in previous periods. Equally, more information may become available to management, facilitating reporting of new KPIs that provide a deeper understanding of the business, or changing how an existing KPI is calculated.

Does reliability matter?

2.200 Management may sometimes be concerned about the reliability of some of the information reported on KPIs, particularly as they are encouraged to move beyond the more traditional financial KPIs that are usually the output of established systems and controls processes and routine audit. There is no specific narrative reporting requirement for KPIs to be reliable, but the nature of the information should be clear to the users of narrative reports.

2.201 In order to address this issue and provide readers with useful information, it is more important that the limitations of the data and any assumptions made in providing it are clearly explained. Readers can then judge the reliability for themselves and make any necessary adjustments in their own analysis. Where data has been specifically assured by independent third parties, identifying this may also assist the reader.

2.202 Readers are often as interested in the trend of a KPI as the absolute performance being reported.

Reporting KPIs – a model for effective communication

2.203 The reporting statement does not prescribe either the types or the methods of calculating KPIs. However, to ensure that the KPIs can be understood by readers and properly used by them to assess the strategies adopted by the entity and the potential for those strategies to succeed, it sets out a model for effective communication of KPIs, recommending certain disclosures to be given for each KPI reported in the OFR, as follows:

- The KPI definition and its calculation method. Given the rapidly increasing use of industry-specific terminology, clear definitions of performance indicators add greatly to the reader's understanding of exactly what is being measured and allows comparisons between companies within an industry. An explanation of a metric's components and how it is calculated should be included, given the absence of standards for the measurement of many industry-specific indicators and with many companies also applying their own indicators.

- The KPI's purpose. Management should explain why it believes a performance indicator is relevant. This may be because it measures progress towards achieving a specific strategic objective.

- The source of underlying data and, where relevant, assumptions. To enable readers to make their own assessment of the reliability of the information, management should identify the sources of the data used in calculating performance indicators and any limitations on that data. Any assumptions made in measuring performance should be explained so that readers can reach an informed view of judgements made by management. An indication of the level, if any, of independent assurance of the data would also be valuable.

■ Quantification or commentary on future targets. Some performance indicators are best suited to a quantification of future targets. Expectations and aims for other indicators may be better explained in commentary. Either way, a forward-looking orientation is essential for readers to assess the potential for strategies to succeed and to give them a basis against which to assess future performance.

■ Where information from the financial statements has been adjusted for inclusion in the OFR, that fact and a reconciliation should be provided. Performance indicators may be financial or non-financial. Where the amounts measured are financial, but are not 'traditional' measures required by accounting standards (that is, GAAP measures), it is good practice to explain any differences. A reconciliation should, therefore, be provided between accounting measures and non-GAAP measures.

■ Corresponding amounts, where available, should be given for the previous year. Measurement of performance in isolation over a single period does not provide the reader with useful information. An indication of how performance has improved or worsened over time is much more valuable in assessing the success of management's strategies. It is also beneficial to explain to the reader what a particular trend in the data means (for example, an increasing measure is not always a sign of strength) and to explain management's actions to address or maintain such trends.

■ Any changes to KPIs and the calculation method used compared to previous years should be identified and explained, including significant changes in the underlying accounting policies adopted in the financial statements. Comparability over time is a key principle of good corporate reporting. It is recognised that KPIs may evolve over time as strategies change or more information becomes available. When such changes are made to the KPIs being monitored, either in terms of the KPIs used or how they are calculated, these changes should be explained.

[RS (OFR) paras 75, 76, 77].

2.204 The following information is also useful to investors and management when considering reporting around KPIs:

■ Link to strategy: the primary reason for including performance indicators in corporate reporting is to enable readers to assess the strategies adopted by the company and their potential to succeed. KPIs presented in isolation from strategies and objectives, or *vice versa*, cannot fulfil this requirement and will fail to provide the reader with the level of understanding they need.

■ Segmental: often KPIs make little sense when consolidated at group level. Corporate reporting users may want more detailed segmental information to assess progress towards specific segmental strategic aims. Performance indicators that are relevant to a specific segment's industry or strategy should, therefore, be provided in addition to those with a more group-wide focus.

■ Benchmarking: performance benchmarked against a relevant peer group, with an explanation of why these peers were chosen, is valuable to users. It provides a clear indication of who management believes the company's competitors to be, as well as setting the company's own performance in the context of a well defined peer group.

2.205 The implementation guidance contains 23 examples of types of KPI. Each of the examples in the guidance follows the disclosure recommendations described above. But the layout shown in the examples is not prescriptive and directors should decide how best to present the information, perhaps by presenting some of the details in footnotes or in a separate section of the OFR.

2.206 Many companies in the UK are now reporting their KPIs. The following examples, in Tables 2.44 and 2.45, were chosen on the basis of their ability to align their KPIs with specific group strategies and objectives and to illustrate a variety of content aspects from the model for effective communication set out above and a variety of presentation styles.

Table 2.44 – Key performance indicators

Taylor Wimpey plc – Annual report – 31 December 2009

Business Review (extract 1)

Our Group Strategy

A combination of the actions taken within the business over the last 18 months and our improved financing position now allows us to shift our focus to creating value by returning to profitability on existing and future sites.

Long term objectives

- Provide growth in earnings per share, in light of market conditions.
- Deliver a return on capital employed above the level of our cost of funding.
- Return the Group to an investment grade credit rating.
- Attract and retain the highest calibre of employees and strive to be a company that people want to work for.

Short term priorities

- Return the Group to profitability following the recent downturns in both of our main markets through:
  - Focusing on sales price increases rather than volume growth.
  - Continued focus on build cost reduction.
  - Maintaining tight control on overhead costs.
- Deliver value from our existing landbank.
- Continue to generate cash from operations through reduced level of investment in land and work in progress spend.
- Maximise the potential of our employees through training and development programmes.
- Deliver operating cash flows in excess of the levels set out within our financial covenants.

Our Group Key Performance Indicators at a glance

The following key financial and non-financial KPIs are the most appropriate basis on which to measure the Group's current performance:

Adjusted loss per share	Return on average capital employed	Operating cash flow covenant	Employee turnover
(4.3)p	1.5%	£457m inflow	6%
for 2009	for 2009	for 2009	for 2009
(7.2p loss for 2008)	(2.6% for 2008)	(Target: £51m outflow)	(16% for 2008)

For more information see page 9

Business Review (extract 2)

Our Group Key Performance Indicators

Given the significant changes in our operating environment during the economic downturn and the changes to our financial covenants, we have reviewed our suite of KPIs during 2009.

We believe that the KPIs below are the most appropriate basis on which to measure our current performance

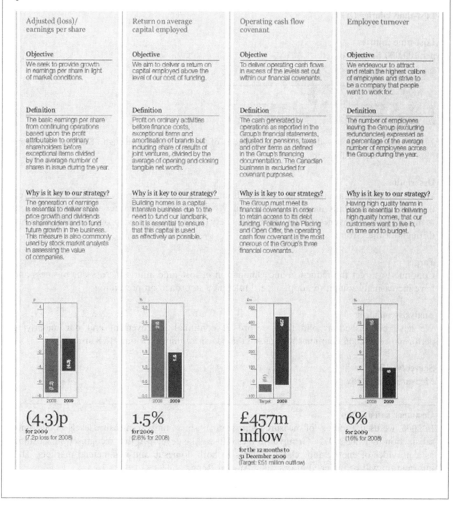

Adjusted (loss)/ earnings per share	Return on average capital employed	Operating cash flow covenant	Employee turnover
Objective	**Objective**	**Objective**	**Objective**
We seek to provide growth in earnings per share in light of market conditions.	We aim to deliver a return on capital employed above the level of our cost of funding.	To deliver operating cash flows in excess of the levels set out within our financial covenants.	We endeavour to attract and retain the highest calibre of employees and strive to be a company that people want to work for.
Definition	**Definition**	**Definition**	**Definition**
The basic earnings per share from continuing operations based upon the profit attributable to ordinary shareholders before exceptional items divided by the average number of shares in issue during the year.	Profit on ordinary activities before finance costs, exceptional items and amortisation of brands but including share of results of joint ventures, divided by the average of opening and closing tangible net worth.	The cash generated by operations as reported in the Group's financial statements, adjusted for pensions, taxes and other items as defined in the Group's financing documentation. The Canadian business is excluded for covenant purposes.	The number of employees leaving the Group (excluding redundancies) expressed as a percentage of the average number of employees across the Group during the year.
Why is it key to our strategy?	**Why is it key to our strategy?**	**Why is it key to our strategy?**	**Why is it key to our strategy?**
The generation of earnings is essential to deliver share price growth and dividends to shareholders and to fund future growth in the business. This measure is also commonly used by stock market analysts in assessing the value of companies.	Building homes is a capital intensive business due to the need to fund our landbank, so it is essential to ensure that this capital is used as effectively as possible.	The Group must meet its financial covenants in order to retain access to its debt funding. Following the Placing and Open Offer, the operating cash flow covenant is the most onerous of the Group's three financial covenants.	Having high quality teams in place is essential to delivering high quality homes, that our customers want to live in, on time and to budget.
(4.3)p	1.5%	£457m inflow	6%
for 2009	for 2009	for the 12 months to 31 December 2009	for 2009
(7.2p loss for 2008)	(2.6% for 2008)	(Target: £51 million outflow)	(16% for 2008)

2.206.1 Table 2.45 illustrates the type of information that can be provided for each KPI, as well as providing an example of how to communicate a new KPI that will be introduced during the year.

Table 2.45 – Key performance indicators

Centrica Plc – Annual Report and Accounts – 31 December 2006

Group Key Performance Indicators
In this section, as part of our commitment to enhanced narrative reporting, the Board and the Executive Committee have set out the key performance indicators (KPIs) that we use to monitor progress against our strategy.

Measuring our performance

Non-financial (extract)

Lost-time injuries (LTI)

Lost-time injuries
per 100,000 hours worked

† this measure includes the LTI consequences of the incident at Rough. See the Corporate responsibility section for commentary.

Description
We measure lost time injuries per 100,000 hours worked. The majority of these are incurred through slips, trips, falls and manual handling. We use both incidence rates and active indicators to monitor the effectiveness of the health and safety (H&S) preventative programmes that we run throughout the Group.

Target
Continue to target the reduction and elimination of lost time injuries across our business and have increasingly sought to adopt a 'zero tolerance' approach on prevention.

Analysis/comment
We have established a solid track record of continual improvement and our underlying performance in 2006 continues to indicate the beneficial impact of our H&S strategy.

Source/verification
Measured internally.

Customer satisfaction
In 2006, we used a variety of measures across our business units to measure levels of customer satisfaction. During 2007, a Group customer KPI will be developed that recognises our position as a provider of energy and related services to both domestic and commercial markets. This information will be included in our 2007 Annual Report.

Other performance indicators

2.207 Disclosure may also be given of other quantified measures that management use to monitor trends and factors and that can provide further context to their narrative reporting. However, if they are not considered by management to be KPIs and/or are outside the entity's control, the level of information about each one should be less than for a KPI.

2.208 The reporting statement includes less stringent disclosure recommendations for other performance indicators that are not KPIs. It states that where quantified measures other than KPIs are included, the OFR should disclose:

■ The definition and calculation method.

■ Where available, corresponding amounts for the previous financial year.

[RS (OFR) para 78].

'Seriously prejudicial'

2.209 The reporting statement recommends that disclosure should not be made in the OFR of information about impending developments or about matters in the course of negotiation if the disclosure would, in the directors' opinion, be seriously prejudicial to the entity's interests. [RS (OFR) para 79].

2.210 The reporting statement notes that this is consistent with existing practice in informing the markets on such matters. This is a reference to the UK Listing and Prospectus Rules, which contain exemptions from disclosure of information that would be seriously detrimental to a company. [PR 2.5.2].

2.211 Instances where non-disclosure is justified tend to include those where the omission is unlikely to mislead investors with regard to facts and circumstances that are essential for an informed assessment. This means that for information to be excluded on 'seriously prejudicial' grounds, the omission itself should not give rise to a misleading impression.

2.212 Situations where non-disclosure on seriously prejudicial grounds might apply are likely to be rare. They include those where a company's position might be seriously prejudiced in relation to disputes with other parties on the subject matter of a provision, contingent liability or contingent asset. FRS 12 and IAS 37, 'Provisions, contingent liabilities and contingent assets', contain an exemption from disclosure of some of the information otherwise required by those standards but require disclosure of the general nature of the dispute, together with the fact that the information has not been disclosed and the reason why. [FRS 12 para 97; IAS 37 para 92].

2.213 Although not mentioned in the reporting statement, disclosure of the fact that information on a particular matter has not been disclosed and the reasons for non-disclosure may be useful to shareholders, where such disclosure would not itself be prejudicial. For example, an entity may have let it be known that it would welcome offers for a particular segment of its business that it wishes to dispose of. It may be in negotiation with several parties who may be unaware of each other's interest. The company might disclose in the OFR that the segment is for sale, but it may consider that it would be seriously prejudicial to disclose that it is negotiating with more than one party. Non-disclosure of that information would be unlikely to mislead investors. It might instead (voluntarily) state that details of the negotiations have not been disclosed, but the outcome will be announced when the negotiations have been concluded.

Statement of compliance

2.214   Although not required, the OFR should, as good practice, include a statement as to whether it has been prepared in accordance with the reporting statement. [RS (OFR) para 80]. An example of such a statement is Table 2.46.

Table 2.46 – Statement of compliance with OFR reporting statement

Xstrata plc – Annual Report and Accounts – 31 December 2009

Cautionary note regarding forward-looking statements (extract)

The Business Review section of this report, comprising the Business, Strategy, Financial and Operating Reviews, has been prepared in accordance with the Accounting Standards Board Reporting Statement on Operating and Financial Review (January 2006), as applicable best practice guidance for UK companies required to prepare a business review.

International developments

2.215   In June 2009, the IASB published an exposure draft on management commentary (MC). The exposure draft sets out a non-binding framework for preparing and presenting management commentary. MC provides an opportunity for management to outline how an entity's financial position, financial performance and cash flows relate to management's objectives and its strategies for achieving those objectives.

2.216   The exposure draft follows the IASB's consideration of its discussion paper, 'Management commentary', issued in October 2005, responses to that discussion paper, developments in narrative reporting in a variety of jurisdictions and other recent work by the IASB on the objective and qualitative characteristics of financial reporting (the exposure draft issued in May 2008, 'An improved conceptual framework for financial reporting: Chapter 1: The objective of financial reporting, and Chapter 2: Qualitative characteristics and constraints of decision-useful financial reporting information').

2.217   Many of the principles and proposed disclosures in the draft standard are consistent with those of the ASB's reporting statement on the OFR. For example, the principles for preparing an MC are to:

- Provide management's view of the entity's performance, position and development.

- Supplement and complement information presented in the financial statements.

- Have an orientation to the future.

2.218 The proposed standard states that a decision-useful MC includes information that is essential to an understanding of:

- The nature of the business.

- Management's objectives and strategies for meeting those objectives.

- The entity's most significant resources, risks and relationships.

- Results of operations and prospects.

- Critical performance measures and indicators that management uses to evaluate the entity's performance against stated objectives.

2.219 The exposure draft acknowledges that management commentary is already an important part of communication with the market. The proposals present a broad framework for MC reporting and management will need to decide how best to apply this reporting framework to the business' particular circumstances.

2.220 The IASB received over 100 responses to its MC exposure draft. The comment period closed on 1 March 2010 and, at the time of writing, the IASB expects to publish completed MC guidance during the second half of 2010.

Directors' report

Directors' report

Introduction

3.1 The directors' report is one of the mandatory components of a company's annual financial statements and reports for members. It must also be delivered to the Registrar of Companies by all companies except those entitled to the small companies exemption (see from para 3.143). [CA06 Secs 444(1), 444A(1), 445(1), 446(1), 447(1)].

3.2 The duty to prepare a directors' report is contained in section 415 of the Companies Act 2006. However, the 2006 Act does not contain all the disclosure requirements: many of the detailed requirements are contained in Schedule 5 to SI 2008/409, 'The Small Companies and Groups (Accounts and Directors' Report) Regulations 2008', for companies or groups falling within the definition of 'small' (see chapter 31 of the Manual of Accounting — UK GAAP) and Schedule 7 to SI 2008/410, 'The Large and Medium-sized Companies and Groups (Accounts and Reports) Regulations 2008' for all other companies.

3.3 Directors have a responsibility to prepare the report even if none of the directors at the time the report is produced were directors during the period covered by the report. They cannot avoid this responsibility simply because they were not responsible for all or some of the activities that are being reported on.

3.4 The principal objectives of the directors' report are to supplement the financial information in the income statement (UK – profit and loss account) and the balance sheet with discussions and explanations about the company's activities and its future and also to provide details of other non-financial matters. The purpose of the narrative information is to give the user of the financial statements a more complete picture of the company than would otherwise be obtained.

3.5 Listed companies regard the annual report and financial statements as an important mode of communication with shareholders. They, therefore, take the opportunity to provide shareholders with information about all aspects of the company's activities and the environment in which it operates, the company's objectives and its values. Such voluntary information may be presented outside the statutory directors' report, for example, in the chairman's statement or in a separate operating and financial review (see further chapter 2). However, the 2006 Act introduced provisions that give directors a 'safe harbour' in respect of civil liability arising out of the content of the directors' report and the directors' remuneration report (see further from para 3.142). Thus, companies may wish to include voluntary disclosures within the directors' report in order to benefit from the 'safe harbour' provisions.

[The next paragraph is 3.11.]

Companies reporting under IFRS

3.11   The requirements relating to the directors' report are contained within the body of the Companies Act and, thus, apply to all companies, regardless of whether the financial statements are prepared under IFRS or UK GAAP.

Consolidated financial statements

3.12   The 2006 Act requires that, where an entity is a parent company and the directors prepare consolidated financial statements, the directors' report must be a consolidated report covering the company and its subsidiary undertakings included in the consolidation. [CA06 Sec 415(2)].

3.13   Where appropriate, the consolidated report should give greater emphasis to matters that are significant to the company and its subsidiary undertakings included in the consolidation, taken as a whole. [CA06 Sec 415(3)].

[The next paragraph is 3.16.]

Matters to be dealt with in the directors' report

Principal activities

3.16   The principal activities of both the company and of its subsidiaries during the year should be stated. [CA06 Sec 416(1)]. It is appropriate to include details of any significant change in the group's activities.

3.17   The term 'principal activities' is not defined in the 2006 Act, but is generally taken to mean the diverse industry segments or classes of business in which the entity operates. Guidance is provided in SSAP 25, 'Segmental reporting', which defines a separate class of business as the distinguishable component of the entity that provides a separate product or service or a separate group of related products or services. [SSAP 25 para 11]. Distinguishable components of an entity may include, for example, mining, textiles, electrical etc. Broad categories such as manufacturing, wholesaling and retailing are not indicative of the industries in which the entity operates. Those terms should not generally be used to describe an entity's industry segments without identification of the products or services. IFRS 8, 'Operating segments', considers segments entirely differently and uses a 'through the eyes of management' approach.

[The next paragraph is 3.19.]

3.19   The categories of principal activities described in the directors' report should, as far as possible, be consistent with the information that is provided for segmental reporting purposes. There are various factors that should be taken into account when deciding whether or not an entity operates in different industry segments and these are discussed further in chapter 10 on segmental reporting in both the Manual of Accounting – UK GAAP and the Manual of Accounting – IFRS for the UK.

3.20   A change in activity should be reported whenever there has been a commencement of a new activity or a complete withdrawal from a previous activity rather than a change in the degree of the activity undertaken. Such a change may be brought about by the acquisition or disposal of a subsidiary undertaking. In order to provide meaningful disclosure of the changes in activities, the extent to which the acquisition or disposal has impacted on any resultant change in the group's activities should be considered. Indeed, FRS 3, 'Reporting financial performance', requires that if an acquisition, a sale or a termination has a material impact on a major business segment, this impact should be disclosed and explained. [FRS 3 para 53]. IFRS 8's predecessor, IAS 14, 'Segment reporting', encouraged entities to disclose the nature and amount of any items of segment revenue and segment expense that were of such size, nature or incidence that their disclosure was relevant to explain the performance of each reportable segment for the period. [IAS 14 para 59]. Although there are no equivalent requirements in IFRS 8 or in UK GAAP, we consider such disclosure to be strongly recommended.

3.21   The degree of detail that should be given under principal activities will obviously depend upon the nature of the company's business. For companies operating in one or two business segments, the relevant information is normally given in the directors' report. Multinational corporations engaged in a wide range of business activities tend to include the relevant details elsewhere in the annual report and accounts, for example, in a separate statement that sets out a detailed review of their operations. Where this is done, a reference should be given in the directors' report to where the necessary information can be found. Table 3.1 provides an illustration of the disclosure of principal activities.

Table 3.1 — Principal activities

Smiths Group plc — Annual report and accounts — 31 July 2009

Group directors' report (extract)

Principal activities

The principal activities of the Company and its subsidiaries (the Group) are and, during the year ended 31 July 2009, were the development, manufacture, sale and support of:

- advanced security equipment, including trace detection, millimetre-wave, infrared, biological detection and diagnostics, that detect and identify explosives, narcotics, weapons, chemical agents, biohazards and contraband;

- mechanical seals, seal support systems, engineered bearings, power transmission couplings, specialist filtration systems and other hardware for the oil and gas, chemical, pharmaceutical, pulp and paper and mining sectors;
- medical devices aligned to specific therapies, principally airway, pain and temperature management, infusion, needle protection, critical care monitoring and vascular access;
- specialised electronic and radio frequency products that connect, protect and control critical systems for the global wireless telecommunications, aerospace, defence, space and medical markets; and
- engineered components including ducting, hose assemblies and heating elements that move and heat fluids for the aerospace, medical, industrial, construction and domestic markets.

The main manufacturing operations are in the UK, the Americas, Continental Europe and China.

Business review

3.22 Unless the company is entitled to the small companies exemption (see from para 3.143), the directors should include in their report a review of the business of the company and its subsidiaries. [CA06 Sec 417(1)].

3.23 Business review reporting requirements include a fair review of the entity's business, a description of principal risks and uncertainties and analysis using financial and, where appropriate, non-financial key performance indicators (KPIs). Quoted companies also need to give an indication of the main trends and factors likely to affect the future development, performance and position of the business, information about contractual and other essential relationships and information about environmental matters, employees and social and community issues.

3.23.1 In addition, for financial years beginning on or after 29 June 2010, the UK Corporate Governance Code (2010) introduces a recommendation for listed companies that the annual report should include an explanation of the basis on which the company generates or preserves value over the longer term (the business model) and the strategy for delivering the company's objectives. It states that it would be desirable if the explanation were located in the same part of the annual report as the business review. [UK CGC C.1.2].

3.24 It is acceptable to cross-refer from the directors' report to a business review elsewhere in the annual report, for example, in the operating and financial review (OFR), provided that the cross-reference clearly refers (by page numbers, paragraph numbers or headings) to the specific location. Guidance on business review disclosure requirements and the UK Corporate Governance Code (2010)'s recommendations for the business review are provided in chapter 2 of this publication.

Likely future developments

3.25   Paragraph 7(b) of Schedule 7 to SI 2008/410 requires the directors' report to contain an indication of likely future developments in the business of the company.

3.26   In addition, for quoted companies, section 417(5)(a) of the 2006 Act requires the directors' report to contain an indication of the main trends and factors likely to affect the future development, performance and position of the company's business. The 2006 Act contains no amplification as to the extent and the scope of this commentary. In practice, directors tend to interpret this requirement by providing information that will have a significant impact on future earnings and profitability of the company or the group. For example, information on such matters as development of new products or services, business expansion or rationalisation plans, capital expenditure plans and proposed disposals and acquisitions, is fairly common. A limited exemption from disclosure is available – see further paragraph 3.35 below.

3.27   The ASB's reporting statement on the operating and financial review provides some guidance in this area. (See further chapter 2).

Contracts, environmental and social matters

3.28   The 2006 Act requires the directors of quoted companies to disclose the following in their directors' report:

■   Information about persons with whom the company has contractual or other arrangements that are essential to the company's business (but see from para 3.35).

■   Information about:

   ■   environmental matters (including the impact of the company's business on the environment),

   ■   the company's employees; and

   ■   social and community issues,

including information about any policies of the company in relation to those matters and the effectiveness of those policies. [CA06 Sec 417(5)].

3.29   The disclosures are required *"to the extent necessary for an understanding of the development, performance or position of the company's business"*. If the review does not contain information about environmental and employee matters and social and community issues, it must state so.

3.30   The government expressed the view that the additional disclosures would add value to the quality of reporting without imposing unnecessary costs. These provisions have effectively reinstated a number of the requirements of the (now withdrawn) OFR regulations, albeit for disclosure within the directors' report as opposed to the OFR. Further guidance on making disclosures in these areas is included below and also in chapter 2.

3.31 In recent years there has been a growing tendency on the part of listed companies to comment on environmental issues in their annual report and accounts. Although environmental reporting, like health and safety, was not specifically required by the previous Act, the Companies Act 1985, or the Listing Rules, public pressures matched by legislation, in particular the Environmental Protection Act 1990 and various EC Regulations, have been instrumental in many companies submitting their environmental practice to external scrutiny.

3.32 As mentioned above, section 417(5)(b)(i) of the Companies Act 2006 requires quoted companies to disclose information about environmental matters (including the impact of the company's business on the environment) in their directors' report. As noted in paragraph 3.24, companies producing an OFR are not required to repeat the information that is given in the OFR, for example on environmental matters, in their directors' report provided that a reference is given in the directors' report to the specific paragraph or section in the OFR.

3.33 Because disclosure of environmental issues was previously voluntary, it was not surprising that the level of disclosure in annual reports varied from company to company. However, not all companies in the industrial sector discuss the impact their businesses have on the environment. Some companies are good at identifying environmental impacts and risks that are most relevant to their circumstances and the way in which they are addressing, or intend to address, those concerns. Many leading companies go further and publish separate environmental or corporate social responsibility (CSR) reports. Other companies are merely keen to emphasise the good works they do for the community and the environment. Guidance on what is regarded as good practice can be found on the PwC web site (www.corporatereporting.com). In January 2006, the government's Department of the Environment, Food and Rural Affairs (Defra) issued 'Environmental reporting guidelines – key performance indicators' (available via www.defra.gov.uk). The guidelines aim to help companies measure, manage and report on their environmental impacts.

3.34 An example of disclosure of essential (and other) contractual relationships is set out in Table 3.2.

Table 3.2 – Essential contractual relationships

Stagecoach Group plc – Annual report – 30 April 2009

3.4.2 Relationships

Stagecoach Group works closely with a range of bodies in each of the markets where we provide public transport services. Our stakeholders include:

- Our People – we have established strong working relationships with trade unions and work in partnership with them on a range of issues, including training and development, occupational

---

health matters, pensions and other employee benefits. We also communicate with our people face to face and through a number of internal publications.

- Investors and the Financial Community – our shareholders and lenders are critical to our business success. We have a regular programme of meetings with investors and provide frequent updates to the markets and financial community on our performance. We are a constituent of the FTSE4Good index, which sets standards and tracks the performance of the leading socially responsible companies around the globe.

- Customers – millions of people use our services every day. We conduct extensive customer research to monitor our performance and to determine how we can improve the delivery and accessibility of our services.

- Customer Interest Groups – our businesses have a regular and ongoing dialogue with bus and rail user groups. This includes presentations from managers on detailed aspects of our service as well as consultation and information sharing on particular issues.

- Government – our managers have an ongoing dialogue with national and local government in all our countries of operation to ensure the effective delivery of government transport policy and to assist in meeting wider objectives. In the UK, we work closely with the DfT, the Scottish Executive, Transport Scotland, the Welsh Assembly, and Transport for London ("TfL").

- Transport Authorities – we work closely with local authorities, including passenger transport executives, regional transport committees and transit authorities, in the delivery and planning of bus and rail services. Many of our businesses have partnership agreements in place to improve the delivery of public transport in their areas.

- Government Advisory Bodies and Lobbying Groups – we also have constructive dialogue with organisations such as the Commission for Integrated Transport, which provides advice to the UK Government, and lobbying groups such as the Campaign for Better Transport.

- Transport and Industry Representation Groups – we are active members of industry groups, such as the Confederation of Passenger Transport UK (which covers buses and light rail), the Association of Train Operating Companies and the American Bus Association.

- Suppliers – we rely on a range of suppliers to provide goods and services linked to our bus and rail operations. These include vehicle and rolling stock manufacturers, fuel suppliers, IT companies and clothing manufacturers.

We have contractual relationships with a number of parties which are essential to the business of the Group, including:

- The operation of our rail franchises depends upon a number of contractual relationships, the most critical of which include: contracts with the DfT governing the terms of the franchises; contracts with Network Rail governing station and track access arrangements; leases with rolling stock companies for the lease of trains and; maintenance contracts for the maintenance of trains.

- All of our businesses have various contractual relationships including purchase contracts with fuel suppliers, vehicle suppliers, IT companies and spare part suppliers.

- We have contracts with local authorities, government bodies and other parties for the supply of bus services on a contracted or tendered basis.

- We have contractual arrangements with banks and other finance providers for the provision of funds and financial products to the Group.

We are committed to conducting business in a socially responsible way and we believe this to be consistent with our business objectives and strategy. Indeed, by taking a responsible approach towards the environment and the wider community, we believe we will enhance our objective to deliver organic growth.

Seriously prejudicial

3.35 A limited exemption has been provided under the Companies Act 2006 such that disclosure of information is not required regarding *"information about impending developments or matters in the course of negotiation if the disclosure would, in the opinion of the directors, be seriously prejudicial to the interests of the company"*. [CA06 Sec 417(10)].

3.36 In addition, quoted companies need not disclose information about essential contractual or other arrangements if such disclosure would, in the directors' opinion, be seriously prejudicial to the counterparty of those arrangements or contrary to the public interest. [CA06 Sec 417(11)].

[The next paragraph is 3.43.]

Dividends

3.43 The amount (if any) that the directors recommend should be paid as dividend must be stated except in the case of a company that is entitled to the small companies exemption under the 2006 Act (see from para 3.143). [CA06 Sec 416(3)]. Where the directors do not propose a dividend, then it is customary to state this fact. An example of the relevant disclosure is given in Table 3.3 below.

Table 3.3 – Dividend payment

Imperial Tobacco Group PLC – Annual Report – 30 September 2009

Directors' Report: Other Information (extract)

Financial Results and Dividends
We include a review of our operational and financial performance, current position and future developments in our Business Review on pages 6 to 32.

The profit attributable to equity holders of the Company for the financial year was £663 million as shown in our consolidated income statement on page 74. Note 1 to the financial statements gives an analysis of revenue and profit from operations and net assets.

The Directors have declared dividends as follows:

In £s million	2009	2008
Ordinary Shares		
Interim paid, 21.0p per share (2008: 18.2p[1])	**213**	161
Proposed final, 52.0p per share (2008: 42.2p)	**527**	427
Total ordinary dividends, 73.0p (2008: 63.1p[1])	**740**	588

[1] The 2008 interim dividend has been adjusted to reflect the bonus element of the Rights Issue in June 2008.

The final dividend, if approved, will be paid on 19 February 2010 to our shareholders on the Register of Members at the close of business on 22 January 2010. The associated ex dividend date will be 20 January 2010. We paid an interim dividend on 19 August 2009 to shareholders on the register at the close of business on 19 June 2009.

3.43.1 Listed entities are required by the Listing Rules to give details of arrangements under which any shareholder has waived or agreed to waive any dividends. See paragraph 3.138 for further details.

Post balance sheet events

3.44 Particulars of any important events affecting the reporting entity that have occurred since the end of the financial year must be disclosed by all companies other than those subject to the small companies regime under the 2006 Act. [SI 2008/410 7 Sch 7(1)(a)]. This requirement gives rise to two potential inconsistencies between the law and FRS 21, 'Events after the balance sheet date' and IAS 10, 'Events after the reporting period'.

■ FRS 21 and IAS 10 distinguish between events that require adjustments to the amounts reported in the financial statements ('adjusting events') and events that are only required to be noted ('non-adjusting events' and the reversal of window dressing transactions). However, the law does not make such a distinction and requires disclosure of important post balance sheet events whether adjusting or non-adjusting. In practice, disclosure in the directors' report of the financial effects of material non-adjusting post balance sheet as *pro forma* information is not uncommon as indicated in Table 3.4 below.

■ The law requires material events after the balance sheet date to be disclosed in the directors' report, whereas FRS 21 and IAS 10 require disclosure of non-adjusting events in the notes to the financial statements. Where a post balance sheet event requires disclosure under both the 2006 Act and the standard, then theoretically disclosure ought to be made both in the directors' report as well as in the notes to the financial statements. In practice, however, companies normally disclose the information only in one place – usually the notes – so as to avoid duplication. A cross-reference should be given in the directors' report to the precise location of the information. The example in Table 3.4 below illustrates disclosure given in both the directors' report and the notes.

These standards are considered further in the Manual of Accounting – UK GAAP and the Manual of Accounting – IFRS for the UK.

Table 3.4 – Post balance sheet event

J Sainsbury plc – Report and Accounts – 27 March 2004

Report of the Directors (extract)

Post balance sheet events
On 30 April 2004, the Company announced that it had completed the sale of Shaw's, its US supermarkets business, to Albertson's Inc. for $2,475 million. Subject to obtaining shareholder approval, the Company intends to return 35 pence per share to shareholders, representing approximately £680 million. This return of capital will be made by way of a B share scheme,

---

providing shareholders with maximum flexibility in terms of tax treatment by allowing them to choose whether to receive the return as either income or capital.

The B share scheme will be accompanied by a share capital consolidation. A resolution to effect the B share scheme and the share consolidation will be proposed at an EGM to be held immediately following the AGM on 12 July 2004. A circular explaining the details of the B share scheme and the consolidation has been sent to shareholders with this Report, together with the notice of the EGM.

Notes to the accounts (extract)

36 Post balance sheet event
Sale of Shaw's Supermarkets Inc.
On 26 March 2004 the Group signed a conditional contract to sell its US supermarkets business (Shaw's) to Albertson's Inc. for a consideration of $2,475 million, including $368 million in assumed lease liabilities.

The sale, which was subject to a price adjustment mechanism and competition clearance, completed on 30 April 2004, when proceeds of £1,177 million (net of expenses) were received by the Group.

The profit on disposal is estimated to be in excess of £250 million and will be recognised in the 2004/05 accounts.

Of the total proceeds, the Company proposes to return 35 pence per share to shareholders, representing approximately £680 million.

The trading results of Shaw's have been included within discontinued operations (note 3 on page 29), as under FRS 3, the sale of Shaw's represents a material reduction in the Group's operating facilities in the US market.

Research and development activities

3.45   An indication of the activities (if any) of the reporting entity in the field of research and development should be provided in the directors' report by all companies except those subject to the small companies regime. [SI 2008/410 7 Sch 7(1)(c)].

3.46   As the law does not indicate how much detail needs to be given, the extent of disclosure varies considerably in practice. Some companies, particularly those in the pharmaceutical sector, give significant details about their research and development activities whilst others give a fairly minimal amount of disclosure on the subject. As research and development activities are particularly sensitive matters, companies are understandably reluctant to disclose too much information on the subject. However, in order to meet the requirements, the statement need not be technically elaborate or esoteric. A broadly-based note that considers the commercial aspects of the research and development activities and their impact on the activities of the company or group would be sufficient in most situations. An illustration of this disclosure is shown in Table 3.5.

Table 3.5 – Research and development

Molins plc – Annual report and accounts – 31 December 2009

DIRECTORS' REPORT (extract)

RESEARCH AND DEVELOPMENT
Group policy is to retain and enhance its market position through the design and development of specialist machinery and support services. To achieve this objective, engineering and product development facilities are maintained in the UK and overseas. Research and development expenditure incurred in 2009, net of third party income, amounted to £1.5m (2008: £1.9m), of which £0.4m (2008: £0.4m) was charged to the consolidated income statement and £1.1m (2008: £1.5m) was capitalised and included in development costs.

3.47 The requirement to give an indication of the research and development activities of the company and its subsidiaries does not mean that the accounting policy for research and development should be disclosed in the directors' report. It should, instead, supplement the accounting policy and the other disclosure requirements of SSAP 13, 'Accounting for research and development' (see also the Manual of Accounting – UK GAAP), and IAS 38, 'Intangible assets' (see also the Manual of Accounting – IFRS for the UK).

Differences between market and balance sheet value of land

3.48 Substantial differences between the market value and the balance sheet value of any interest in land held by the reporting entity should be disclosed in the report of any company other than one subject to the small companies regime if, in the opinion of the directors, the difference is of such significance that it should be brought to the shareholders' or debenture holders' attention. 'Land' includes the buildings and other structures. [Sch 1 Interpretation Act 1978]. The difference has to be shown with such degree of precision as is practicable. [SI 2008/410 7 Sch 2]. Although there is no requirement to make a negative statement that the difference is not significant, many companies do make this statement where there might otherwise be doubt. An example of disclosure is provided in Table 3.6.

Table 3.6 – Differences between market and book value of land

Marks and Spencer Group plc – Report and accounts – 3 April 2010

Directors' report (extract)
Other disclosures (extract)

Market value of properties
The last formal valuation of the Group's properties was carried out in September 2006. Taking into account movements in the Group's property portfolio since that date, the directors are of the opinion that the market value of the Group's properties, at 3 April 2010 exceeded their net book value (including prepayments in respect of leasehold land) of the fixed asset and leasehold properties by approximately £0.8bn.

3.49   It is recommended that, where there are several interests in land, the aggregate market value and the aggregate book value should be compared to see if the difference is substantial. When it is considered that a substantial difference exists, it is preferable to state both the aggregate market value and the basis on which the market value has been arrived at. In this regard, for financial statements prepared in accordance with UK GAAP, FRS 19 also requires disclosure of the tax effects, if any, that would arise if the asset were realised at a price equal to the estimated market value. [FRS 19 para 64(b)]. There is no equivalent requirement in IAS 12, 'Income taxes', for financial statements prepared in accordance with IFRS. An independent professional valuation is not required if the directors are competent to arrive at the market value themselves, but the wording should make the position clear in this respect. Where property is situated overseas, especially in territories subject to political unrest or where the remittance of currencies is restricted, it may not always be practicable, and may be misleading, to give the information required. In such circumstances, the wording should make this clear.

Details of directors

3.50   Disclosure is required of the names of the persons who were directors of the company at any time during the financial year. [CA06 Sec 416(1)(a)]. This can be achieved either by listing the names of the directors in the report or by referring to the page where this information may be found (for example, see Table 3.7 below). When cross-referring to a list elsewhere in the annual report, the list of directors is often at the balance sheet date or at the date the report and accounts were approved and so where there have been changes in directors during the year (or since the year end if the list is at the date the report and accounts were approved), it is necessary to provide details. In group financial statements, disclosure is required of the names of the parent company's directors only. Identification of directors and their roles is also required by the DTR – see paragraph 3.127.7.

3.51   Although not required by law, it has become customary to include the following information:

■   The dates of appointments or resignations of directors occurring during the financial year.

■   Changes in the directors since the end of the financial year.

■   Retirement of directors at the AGM and whether they offer themselves for election.

[The next paragraph is 3.57.]

Directors' service contracts for listed companies

3.57   Information on service contracts is usually given in the directors' remuneration report with a cross-reference from the directors' report as in the example in Table 3.7. The directors' remuneration report for listed companies must state the unexpired term of the directors' service contracts of any director who is proposed for election or re-election at the forthcoming AGM (see Table 3.7 below). If the directors proposed for election or re-election do not have service contracts, the directors' remuneration report must state that fact. [LR 9.8.8R (9)]. Directors' service contracts for this purpose are defined by reference to section 227 of the 2006 Act. For further guidance on the directors' remuneration report, see chapter 5.

Table 3.7 – Directors' service contracts

Cookson Group plc – Annual Report – 31 December 2009

DIRECTORS' REPORT (extract)
DIRECTORS
Messrs Beeston, Butterworth, Hewitt, Oosterveld, Perry, Salmon and Sussens all served as Directors of the Company during the year. Messrs Hill and Wanecq were appointed as Directors on 1 February 2010. Biographical information for all the Directors of the Company is given on page 30. In accordance with the Company's Articles of Association ("the Articles") Messrs Hill and Wanecq will retire at the Annual General Meeting and will offer themselves for election. Further information on the contractual arrangements of the executive Directors, including Mr Wanecq, is given on page 52. The Non-executive Directors, including Mr Hill, do not have service agreements.

DIRECTORS' REMUNERATION REPORT (extract)
DIRECTORS' CONTRACTS
Executive Directors
The following paragraphs summarise the main conditions of the contracts of the Directors:

In line with the policy of the Committee, Messrs Butterworth and Salmon have UK service contracts which have 12 month unexpired terms and provide for 12 months' notice being given. Mr Salmon's contract was dated 14 June 2004 and Mr Butterworth's 25 May 2005. Each contract provides for compensation to be paid on early termination by the Company based on one times salary, pension allowance and benefits payable half in a lump sum and the balance in six separate monthly instalments commencing six months after leaving, mitigated by any salary earned from any new paid occupation. Mr Wanecq is contracted to Vesuvius Group NV/SA, under a Belgian services agreement dated 1 March 2006 for which his remuneration is in the form of fees. His appointment to the Cookson Group plc Board is subject to a separate appointment agreement for which no fee is payable. His termination arrangements are structured to effectively mirror Messrs Butterworth's and Salmon's arrangements including the effective notice period and mitigation obligations.

None of the executive Directors' contracts contain any change of control provisions and they all contain a duty to mitigate should the Director find an alternative paid occupation in any period during which the Company must otherwise pay compensation on early termination. Other than as described for Mr Wanecq, no Directors had any material interest in a contract of significance (other than service agreements) with the Company or any subsidiary company during the year.

Non-executive Directors
In accordance with the Code, each Non-executive Director is appointed for an initial fixed term of three years subject to their election at the Company's first Annual General Meeting following their appointment. Thereafter, subject to approval of the Board and their re-election at the appropriate Annual General Meeting, they are appointed for a further three-year term.

	Date of appointment	Date of retirement	Annual General Meeting at which term expires	Unexpired notice period
Non-executive Directors				
Jeff Hewitt	01/06/05	–	2012	Not required
Peter Hill	01/02/10	–	2013	Not required
Jan Oosterveld	15/06/04	–	2013	Not required
Barry Perry	01/01/02	–	2011	Not required
John Sussens	01/05/04	–	2013	Not required

The Group Chairman, Mr Beeston, was appointed on 1 April 2003 for a fixed period which was due to expire at the conclusion of the Annual General Meeting in 2008. This was extended in 2007 and was due to expire at the conclusion of the Annual General Meeting in 2011. However, Mr Beeston has waived his entitlement to any notice from the Company. Non-executive Directors are not entitled to receive compensation for loss of office at any time.

All Directors are subject to retirement, and election or re-election, in accordance with the Company's Articles of Association.

The Board sets the remuneration of the Non-executive Directors after considering the role and responsibilities of each Director and the practice of other companies. The Non-executive Directors do not participate in Board discussions on their own remuneration. The Chairman's remuneration is set by the Remuneration Committee with reference to the fees of non-executive chairmen within two FTSE 250 comparator groups, the first focusing on sector comparators and the second on companies of similar size.

3.58   The UK Corporate Governance Codes (2008) and (2010) state that notice or contract periods should be set at one year or less. If it is necessary to offer longer notice or contract periods to new directors recruited from outside, such periods should reduce to one year or less after the initial period. [CC B.1.6; UK CGC D.1.5].

3.59   If a service contract does not specify a term, the term can be ascertained in one of the following ways:

■   If the contract is terminable on giving of notice, the expiration of the notice period will indicate the earliest date at which the contract could end.

■   If no notice period is stated in the contract, there may be a custom or practice as to the length of the notice.

■   In the absence of an express provision as to duration or expiry of a customary arrangement, there is a presumption in common law that (subject to the statutory minimum entitlements to notice) every contract of employment is terminable on reasonable notice by either party.

Where the length of the unexpired period of a director's service contract has been determined in one of the ways above, the details should be fully disclosed in the directors' report.

Directors' interests in contracts

3.60   Under the 2006 Act, disclosure of directors' interests in contracts is not required in the directors' report. Disclosure is required in the accounts of transactions and arrangements in which the director of a company has, directly or indirectly, a material interest (for example, contracts between a director and a company for the sale of non-cash assets). [SI 2008/410 1 Sch 72]. The disclosure requirements of contracts or substantial property transactions in which a director has a material interest are considered in detail in chapter 6.

3.61   In addition, the Listing Rules require listed entities to disclose in the annual report and accounts particulars of any contract of significance subsisting during the period under review. The disclosure does not have to be provided in the directors' report, but in practice is often given there. See paragraph 3.137.11 for further details.

Corporate governance for listed companies

3.62   In May 2010, the FRC published the UK Corporate Governance Code (2010), applicable for financial years beginning on or after 29 June 2010. For financial years beginning prior to 29 June 2010, the UK Corporate Governance Code (2008), formerly known as the Combined Code (2008), applies. The Listing Rules require companies to give a two part narrative statement, to explain how they have applied the applicable code's main principles and confirm that they have complied throughout the year with its provisions – or provide an explanation where they have not complied.

3.63   The Disclosure and Transparency Rules require the corporate governance statement to be included in the directors' report. [DTR 7.2.1R]. In practice, many companies prepare a separate corporate governance statement. Where this is the case, a cross-reference should be provided in the directors' report to the specific location of the corporate governance statement elsewhere in the annual report. [DTR 7.2.9R].

3.64   DTR 7.2.10R states that the directors' report must include a description of the main features of the group's internal control and risk management systems in relation to the process for preparing consolidated accounts.

3.65   See chapter 4 for further discussion of corporate governance matters, including the principles and provisions of the UK Corporate Governance Codes (2008) and (2010) and the disclosures required by the DTR in the corporate governance statement.

[The next paragraph is 3.75.]

Purchase of own shares and sales of treasury shares

3.75 Where the company has an interest in its own shares, the directors' report is required to include certain information. The directors' report must contain the details set out in paragraph 3.76 below where any of the following circumstances occur:

Acquisition of shares by the company

- A company purchases its own shares (including treasury shares) or otherwise acquires them by forfeiture, or by surrender in lieu of forfeiture, or by way of a gift, or in a reduction of capital duly made, or by order of the Court. [SI 2008/409 5 Sch 6(1)(a); SI 2008/410 7 Sch 8(a); CA06 659(1)(2)].

Acquisition of shares in a public company by another person

- A nominee of a public company acquires shares in the company from a third party without the company providing any financial assistance directly or indirectly and the company has a beneficial interest in those shares. [SI 2008/409 5 Sch 6(1)(b); SI 2008/410 7 Sch 8(b); CA06 Sec 662(1)(d)].

- Any person acquires shares in a public company with the financial assistance of the company and the company has a beneficial interest in those shares. [SI 2008/409 5 Sch 6(1)(b); SI 2008/410 7 Sch 8(b); CA06 Sec 662(1)(e), 671].

Lien or charges on own shares held by the company

- A company takes a lien or a charge (either express or implied) on its own shares for any amount that is payable in respect of those shares. [SI 2008/409 5 Sch 6(1)(c), SI 2008/410 7 Sch 8(c); CA06 Sec 670(2)].

- A company that has re-registered under section 1040 of the 2006 Act, holds a lien or a charge (either express or implied) on its own shares, and that lien or charge existed immediately before the company applied to be re-registered as a public company. [SI 2008/409 5 Sch 6(1)(c); SI 2008/410 7 Sch 8(c); CA06 Sec 670(4)].

3.76 Where any of the above circumstances has occurred, the directors' report must state the following details:

In respect of shares purchased

- The number and the nominal value of the shares that have been purchased in the financial year and the percentage of the called-up share capital which shares of that description represent.

- The aggregate amount of consideration paid and the reasons for their purchase.

An example is given in Table 3.8 below.

In respect of shares acquired other than by purchase or charged

- The number and the nominal value of any shares that have been otherwise acquired (whether by the company or by its nominee or any other person) or charged at any time during the financial year.

- The maximum number and the nominal value of shares which, having been so acquired or charged (whether or not during the year) are held at any time during the financial year.

- The number and the nominal value of such shares that were disposed of by the company (or any other person holding them on behalf of the company) during the year, or that were cancelled by the company during the year.

- For each of the above, the percentage of the called-up share capital which shares of that description represent.

- The amount of any charge.

In addition to the above, there should be disclosed the amount or the value of any consideration for any shares that either the company or the other person disposed of during the financial year that the company or the other person acquired for money or money's worth.

[SI 2008/409 5 Sch 6(2); SI 2008/410 7 Sch 9].

Table 3.8 – Repurchase of own shares

Compass Group PLC – Annual Report and Accounts – 30 September 2009

Directors' report (extract)

Share capital (extract)

Repurchase of shares

In 2008, the Company announced that it intended to buy back £400 million of ordinary shares in order to maintain an efficient capital structure whilst at the same time retaining the flexibility to fund further infill acquisitions. This followed buy-back programmes in 2007 and 2008 which had taken place following the disposals of Select Service Partner and the Selecta vending business in 2006 and 2007 respectively. During the year ended 30 September 2009 3,975,000 ordinary shares of 10 pence each of the Company (representing 0.216% of the ordinary shares in issue on 1 October 2008) were purchased and cancelled for a consideration of £12.58 million (including expenses), representing all of the ordinary shares purchased to date.

Resolution 12 set out in the Notice of Meeting will be proposed as a Special Resolution to renew the directors' limited authority last granted in 2009 to repurchase ordinary shares in the market. The authority sets the minimum and maximum prices which may be paid and it will be limited to a maximum of 10% of the Company's issued ordinary share capital at the date of this Report. This authority will enable your directors to reactivate, if appropriate, the £400 million share buy-back programme announced in 2008. Furthermore, this authority will enable your directors to continue to respond promptly should circumstances arise in which they consider such a purchase would result in an increase in earnings per share and would be in the best interests of the Company.

Any purchases of ordinary shares will be by means of market purchases through the London Stock Exchange and any shares so purchased may be cancelled or may be placed into treasury in

---

accordance with the Companies (Acquisition of Own Shares) (Treasury Shares) Regulations 2003. The Company currently holds no shares in treasury but the Regulations allow shares repurchased by the Company to be held as treasury shares that may be subsequently cancelled, sold for cash or used for the purpose of employee share schemes. The directors consider it desirable for these general authorisations to be available to provide flexibility in the management of the Company's capital resources.

Additional disclosure under the Listing Rules for companies purchasing own shares or selling treasury shares

3.77 A listed company must give the following additional information concerning purchases or proposed purchases of the company's own shares and sales of treasury shares:

- Particulars of any authority given by the shareholders in general meeting for the company to purchase its own shares that is still effective at the year end (that is, authority that has not yet been exercised and has not expired).

- In relation to purchases other than through the market or by tender to all shareholders, the names of the sellers of the shares that have been purchased, or are to be purchased, by the company.

- If the company has purchased any of its own shares since the year end, or has either been granted an option or entered into a contract to purchase its own shares since the year end, then the directors' report should disclose the equivalent information to that required under the Act as detailed in paragraph 3.76 above.

- In relation to sales of treasury shares made other than through the market, or in connection with an employees' share scheme, or other than pursuant to an opportunity available to all shareholders on the same terms, the names of the purchasers of such shares sold, or proposed to be sold, during the year.

[LR 9.8.6R (4)].

3.78 Examples of the relevant disclosures are given in chapter 7 of this publication dealing with the acquisition by a company of its own shares and chapters 23 of the PwC Manual of Accounting – UK GAAP and the Manual of Accounting – IFRS for the UK dealing with treasury shares.

Employee information

3.79 All companies are required to include in the directors' report information regarding the company's policy in respect of the employment of disabled persons. In addition, companies other than those subject to the small companies regime must include information regarding the health, safety and welfare at work of employees, and the involvement of employees in the management of the company.

Employment of disabled persons

3.80 If the company employed, on average, more than 250 employees in the UK in each week of the financial year, the directors' report must contain a statement that describes the company's policy during the year in respect of the following:

■ Giving full and fair consideration (having regard to the persons' particular aptitudes and abilities) to applications for employment that disabled persons (as defined in the Disability Discrimination Act 1995) make to the company. The definition of 'disabled person' in the 1995 Act is a person who has a physical or mental impairment that has a substantial and long term adverse effect on their ability to carry out normal day-to-day activities. [Disability Discrimination Act 1995 Sec 1.]

■ Continuing the employment of, and arranging appropriate training for, any of the company's employees who have become disabled during the period in which the company employed them.

■ Otherwise providing for the training, the career development and the promotion of those disabled persons the company employs.

[SI 2008/409 5 Sch 5; SI 2008/410 7 Sch 10].

An illustration of this disclosure is given in Table 3.9 below.

Table 3.9 – Employment of disabled persons

Yell Group plc – Annual report – 31 March 2009

Directors' Report (extract)

People with disabilities

Yell is an Equal Opportunities Employer. We are committed to the employment of people with disabilities and guarantee an interview for those who meet minimum selection criteria. We provide training and development for people with disabilities, tailored where appropriate, to ensure they have the opportunity to achieve their potential. If a Yell person becomes disabled while in our employment, we will do our best to retain them, including consulting them about their requirements, making appropriate adjustments, and providing alternative suitable provisions.

Employee involvement

3.81 The directors' report of any company other than one subject to the small companies regime should describe the action the company has taken during the financial year to introduce, maintain, or develop arrangements aimed at:

■ Providing employees systematically with information on matters of concern to them as employees.

■ Consulting employees or their representatives on a regular basis, so that the company can take the views of employees into account in making decisions that are likely to affect their interests.

- Encouraging the involvement of employees in the company's performance through (for example) an employees' share scheme.

- Achieving a common awareness on the part of all employees of the financial and the economic factors that affect the company's performance.

[SI 2008/410 7 Sch 11].

3.82 The above requirements apply only to the directors' report of a reporting entity that employs, on average, more than 250 employees in the UK each week during the financial year. [SI 2008/410 7 Sch 11(1)]. Table 3.10 gives an example of the information to be shown.

Table 3.10 – Employee involvement

Marks and Spencer Group plc – Annual Report and financial statements – 3 April 2010

Directors' report (extract)

Employee involvement

We have maintained our commitment to employee involvement throughout the business.

Employees are kept well informed of the performance and objectives of the Group through personal briefings, regular meetings, personal letters to their home, email and Chairman broadcasts at key points in the year to all head office employees and store management. In addition many of our store colleagues can join the briefings by telephone to hear directly from the Board. These types of communication are supplemented by our employee publications including, 'Your M&S' magazine, Plan A updates and DVD presentations. More than 3,500 employees elected onto Business Involvement Groups ('BIGs') across every store and head office location represent their colleagues in two-way communication and consultation with the Company. They have continued to play a key role in a wide variety of business changes, in what has been a very challenging year.

The fifteenth meeting of the European Works Council ('EWC') (established in 1995) will take place in September 2010. This Council provides an additional forum for informing, consulting and involving employee representatives from the countries in the European Community. The EWC includes members from our joint venture companies established in the Czech Republic and Greece, as well as representatives from the Republic of Ireland and the UK. By holding the meeting in September this year, the new Chief Executive will have the opportunity to address EWC and update on his observations following his first four months in office.

Directors and senior management regularly attend National BIG meetings and visit stores and discuss with employees matters of current interest and concern to them and the business through meetings with local Business Involvement Groups, specific listening groups and informal discussion.

Share schemes are a long-established part of our total reward package, encouraging and supporting employee share ownership. In particular, around 25,000 employees currently participate in Sharesave, the Company's all employee Save As you Earn Scheme. Full details of all schemes are given on pages 95 to 97.

We maintain contact with retired staff through communications from the Company and the Pension Trust. Member-nominated trustees have been elected to the Pension Trust Board, including employees and pensioners. We continue to produce a regular Pensions Update newsletter for members of our final salary pension scheme and the M&S Retirement Plan.

Equal opportunities

The Group is committed to an active Equal Opportunities Policy from recruitment and selection, through training and development, performance reviews and promotion to retirement.

It is our policy to promote an environment free from discrimination, harassment and victimisation, where everyone will receive equal treatment regardless of gender, colour, ethnic or national origin, disability, age, marital status, sexual orientation or religion. All decisions relating to employment practices will be objective, free from bias and based solely upon work criteria and individual merit. The Company is responsive to the needs of its employees, customers and the community at large and we are an organisation which uses everyone's talents and abilities and where diversity is valued. For example, we are one of the few major retailers or companies to operate without a Normal Retirement Age and are experiencing a number of employees continuing to work with us past the state retirement age.

Creditor payment policy

3.83 Company law requires a reporting entity to disclose its payment policy for its suppliers. The provision applies to public companies and large private companies (that is, neither small nor medium-sized companies) that are members of a group whose parent is a public company. [SI 2008/410 7 Sch 12(1)(a)(b)]. The provisions apply at a company level and not to the group as a whole. The requirement is for the directors to state with respect to the financial year *following* that covered by the annual report whether it is the company's policy to follow any code or standard on payment practice. Only where a company follows a particular code does it have to give the name of the code or standard together with an indication of where information about, and copies of, the code or standard can be obtained. [SI 2008/410 7 Sch 12(2)(a)]]. The directors also have to state whether it is the company's policy in respect of some or all of its suppliers:

- To settle the terms of payment with those suppliers when agreeing the terms of each transaction.

- To ensure that those suppliers are made aware of the terms of payment.

- To abide by the terms of payment.

[SI 2008/410 7 Sch 12(2)(b)].

3.84 Where the company's policy is different in respect of some or all of its suppliers from that outlined above, the directors must also state the company's policy in respect of those suppliers. In addition, where the company's policy is different for different suppliers or classes of suppliers, the directors must identify in their report the suppliers or classes of suppliers to which the different policy applies. [SI 2008/410 7 Sch 12(2)]. Examples of payment policies are given in Tables 3.11 and 3.12.

3.85 The directors' report is also required to state the number of days represented by trade creditors falling due for payment within one year at the year end (for example, UK GAAP balance sheet Format 1 item E4) compared to the total amounts invoiced to suppliers during the year. The requirement is to disclose the number of days that bears to the number of days in the financial year in the same proportion as X bears to Y where:

- X = the aggregate of the amounts that were owed to trade creditors at the end of the year.

- Y = the aggregate of the amounts invoiced by suppliers during the year.

[SI 2008/410 7 Sch 12(3)].

3.86   The calculation of the number of creditor days is illustrated in the example below.

> **Example**
>
> Trade creditors (all due within one year) at the end of the year are £30 million. Amounts invoiced during the year by suppliers are £300 million. Number of days in the financial year is 365.
>
> $$\frac{30 \times 365}{300} = 36.5 \text{ days}$$

3.87   For the purposes of the above provisions, a person will be a supplier of the company at any time if:

- At the time, the person is owed an amount in respect of the goods and services supplied.

- The amount owed would be included within trade creditors (item E4 in Format 1) if the financial statements were prepared at that time, were prepared in accordance with Schedule 1 to SI 2008/410 and that format was adopted.

[SI 2008/410 7 Sch 12(4)].

3.88   If a company does not draw up its accounts under balance sheet Format 1 in Schedule 1 to SI 2008/410, it still has to comply with the disclosures outlined above. If, for example, the company prepares its financial statements in accordance with IFRS or is a banking or insurance company, the disclosure has to be given in respect of creditors for goods and services that would have been included under trade creditors, had the company drawn up its financial statements in accordance with Schedule 1. Therefore, for an insurance company, although insurance and reinsurance creditors would not be classified as trade creditors, creditors for stationery and rent would be and the required disclosure has to be given in respect of these creditors.

3.88.1   There is no requirement to disclose comparative information in the directors' report but it is common and best practice to do so.

Table 3.11 — Creditor payment policy

Barclays Bank PLC — Annual report and accounts — 31 December 2009

Directors' report (extract)

Creditors' Payment Policy

Barclays values its suppliers and acknowledges the importance of paying invoices, especially those of small businesses, in a timely manner. Barclays policy follows the Department for Business, Innovation & Skills' Prompt Payment Code, copies of which can be obtained from the Prompt Payment Code website at www.promptpaymentcode.org.uk. Part 5 of Schedule 7 of the Large and Medium-sized Companies and Groups (Accounts and Reports) Regulations 2008 requires disclosure of trade creditor payment days. The Company's accounts are prepared in accordance with IFRS. The components for the trade creditor calculation are not easily identified. However, by identifying as closely as possible the components that would be required if item E.4 (trade creditors) in format I of Schedule 1 of these Regulations applied, the trade creditor payment days for Barclays Bank PLC for 2009 were 27 days (2008: 24 days). This is an arithmetical calculation and does not necessarily reflect our practice, which is described above, nor the experience of any individual creditor.

Table 3.12 — Creditor payment policy

Marks and Spencer Group plc — Annual report and financial statements — 3 April 2010

Directors' report (extract)

Creditor payment policy

For all trade creditors, it is the Group's policy to:

- agree the terms of payment at the start of business with that supplier;

- ensure that suppliers are aware of the terms of payment; and

- pay in accordance with its contractual and other legal obligations.

The main trading company, Marks and Spencer plc, has a policy concerning the payment of trade creditors as follows:

- general merchandise payments are received between 19 and 26 days after the stock was delivered;

- food payments are received between 18 and 25 days after the stock was delivered; and

- distribution suppliers are paid monthly, for costs incurred in that month, based on estimates, and payments are adjusted quarterly to reflect any variations to estimate.

Trade creditor days for Marks and Spencer plc for the year ended 3 April 2010 were 18 days, or 12 working days (last year 20.5 days, or 13.7 working days), based on the ratio of Company trade creditors at the end of the year to the amounts invoiced during the year by trade creditors.

3.89   To assist companies to honour their contract payment terms BIS (formerly known as BERR) issued the Better Payment Practice Code, which is available on http://www.payontime.co.uk/.

[The next paragraph is 3.100.]

Political and charitable donations

Summary of the provisions for disclosure and control

3.100   Company law requires a company to make disclosure in the directors' report of political donations and expenditure in the UK/EU and outside the EU. [SI 2008/409 5 Sch 2, 3; SI 2008/410 7 Sch 3, 4]. It also requires a company to control its political donations and expenditure in the UK and in other EU Member States by requiring directors to seek prior shareholder authorisation.

Definitions

3.101   Sections 362 to 379 of the Companies Act 2006 concern political donations and expenditure in the UK and Northern Ireland.

3.101.1   The legislation relates to political expenditure and to political donations made by companies to:

■   Political parties (both those registered in the UK and those acting in connection with any election to public office in any other EU member State).

■   Political organisations other than political parties, which are any organisation:

   ■   Carrying on, or proposing to carry on, activities capable of being reasonably regarded as intended to affect public support for any political party (as defined in the first bullet point in this paragraph) or for independent candidates at elections to public office held in an EU Member State other than the UK.

   ■   Carrying on, or proposing to carry on, activities capable of being reasonably regarded as intended to influence voters in national or regional referendums held under the law of any EU Member State.

■   Independent election candidates at any election to public office in the UK or another EU Member State.

[CA06 Sec 363].

3.101.2   The definition of a political donation is wide. It includes:

■   Any gift of money or other property.

■   Any sponsorship provided to cover expenses relating to any party conference, meeting or event, the preparation, publication or dissemination of any party publication or any party political study or research (or to ensure that such expenses are not incurred).

■   Any fee or subscription paid for membership of or affiliation to a political party or organisation.

- Any money spent in paying expenses incurred directly or indirectly by a political party, organisation or election candidate.

- Any money lent to a political party, organisation or election candidate otherwise than on a commercial basis.

- The provision (other than on a commercial basis) of property, services or facilities (including the services of any person).

The definition includes donations to any officer, member, trustee or agent of a political party, in his/her capacity as such. Further, it includes any donation made through a third party. [CA06 Sec 364].

3.101.3   Section 364 of the 2006 Act defines a 'political donation' by reference to sections 50 to 52 of the Political Parties, Elections and Referendums Act 2000 (disregarding amendments made by the Electoral Administration Act 2006, which remove from the definition of 'donation' loans made otherwise than on commercial terms).

3.101.4   Political expenditure means any expenditure incurred by a company in respect of:

- the preparation, publication or dissemination of advertising, promotional or publicity material of any kind that is capable of being reasonably regarded as intended to affect public support for a political party or other political organisation, or an independent election candidate; or

- any of the company's activities of the kind referred to in the definition of 'political organisation' (second bullet point of para 3.101.1).

[CA06 Sec 365].

Prohibition on political donations and expenditure

3.102   A company is prohibited from making any political donation to a political party, political organisation or independent election candidate, or incurring any political expenditure unless the donation or EU political expenditure has been authorised by the company using an 'approval resolution' (see para 3.105). [CA06 Sec 366(1)].

3.103   This resolution must be passed before the donation or political expenditure is made or incurred or, if earlier, any relevant contract entered into. See also the special rules for subsidiaries in paragraph 3.107. Shareholder approval is not required of donations or expenditure for purposes that are not connected with party politics in any EU Member State, but these still require disclosure.

[The next paragraph is 3.105.]

3.105 An approval resolution is a resolution passed by the company that:

■ Authorises the company to make donations not exceeding a specified total or incur political expenditure (including EU political expenditure) not exceeding a specified total for a period of not more than four years beginning with the date on which the resolution is passed.

■ Is expressed in general terms (accordingly, it must not purport to authorise particular donations or expenditure).

[CA06 Sec 367, 368].

Exemptions for donations

3.106 Sections 374 to 378 of the Companies Act 2006 set out five exemptions from the requirement for prior shareholder authorisation:

■ Donations to trade unions (including those in countries other than the UK). The exemption covers donations such as the provision of company rooms for trade union meetings, the use of company vehicles by trade union officials and paid time off for trade union officials to act in that capacity. However, a donation to a trade union's political fund is not covered by the exemption. [CA06 Sec 374].

■ Subscriptions paid to EU trade associations for membership (including trade associations that carry out their activities outside the EU). [CA06 Sec 375].

■ Donations to all-party parliamentary groups. [CA06 Sec 376].

■ Political expenditure that is exempt by virtue of an order by the Secretary of State. [CA06 Sec 377].

■ Small political donations: authorisation is not required unless the political donation and the aggregate amount of the political donations by the company in the 12 months ending on the date of the donation exceeds £5,000. Donations by other group companies (including subsidiaries) must be taken into account in calculating whether the £5,000 threshold has been exceeded. [CA06 Sec 378].

Subsidiaries incorporated in Great Britain and Northern Ireland

3.107 If the company is a subsidiary of another company (its holding company), an approval resolution may need to be passed by the holding company's shareholders as well as or instead of those of the company. This is relevant where the company is not a wholly-owned subsidiary of a UK-registered company. In addition to the resolution of the company, a resolution must be passed by its 'relevant holding company'. The relevant holding company is the ultimate holding company or, where such a company is not a UK-registered company, the holding company highest up the chain that is a UK-registered company. [CA06 Sec 366].

3.108   A wholly-owned subsidiary of a UK-registered company is not required to pass a resolution approving political donations or expenditure, although its relevant holding company is required to do so. [CA06 Sec 366(3)].

Example 1

X limited wishes to make a political donation. It is an 80% subsidiary of Y limited, which is a subsidiary of Z plc. Approval resolutions must be passed by X limited (the company) and Z plc (the ultimate holding company).

Example 2

The facts are the same as in example 1 except that entity Z is incorporated outside the UK. Approval resolutions must be passed by X limited and Y limited (the highest UK-registered holding company of X limited).

Example 3

The facts are the same as in example 2 except that X limited is a 100% subsidiary of Y limited. An approval resolution must be passed by Y limited, but need not be passed by X limited.

Directors' liability

3.109   There are no criminal sanctions in relation to making unauthorised political donations or incurring unauthorised political expenditure. Civil remedies are available to a company in the event of a breach of the prohibitions and may be pursued in the normal manner by the company.

3.110   If the company makes an unauthorised payment, the directors and (unless they took all available steps to prevent the political donation being made or the political expenditure being incurred), the directors of the relevant holding company are liable to reimburse the company for the amount of the political donation or political expenditure and damages for any loss it suffers together with interest until the amount is repaid to the company. [CA06 Sec 369].

3.111   Action may be taken against the directors for reimbursement by not less than 50 members or members holding not less than five per cent of the issued share capital. In addition, in any such action, the members are entitled to require the company to provide all relevant information. If the company refuses to do so, the court may make an order directing the company or its officers or employees to provide the information. [CA06 Secs 370(3), 373(1)].

Disclosure of political donations and expenditure

3.112   There are separate disclosure regimes for:

- Political donations and expenditure within the UK/EU area.

- Contributions to political parties in the rest of the world.

Company with no subsidiaries — not wholly-owned by a UK parent

3.113   If a company has made any donation to a political party, other political organisation or independent election candidate or has incurred any political expenditure, and the aggregate of those exceeds £2,000 in a financial year, it must disclose the following particulars in the directors' report for the year:

- For political donations, the name of each political party, political organisation or independent election candidate and the amount given to each in the financial year.

- The total amount of political expenditure incurred in the financial year.

[SI 2008/409 5 Sch 2(2); SI 2008/410 7 Sch 3(2)].

3.114   All contributions made by the company to non-EU political parties also require disclosure (although there is no requirement to name the parties). There is no threshold for these disclosures. Therefore, if the company has in the financial year made any contribution to a non-EU political party the directors' report for the year must contain:

- A statement of the amount contributed.

- If it has made more than one contribution in the year, a statement of the total contributions.

[SI 2008/409 5 Sch 3(1); SI 2008/410 7 Sch 4(1)].

Company with subsidiary — not wholly-owned by a UK parent

3.115   The following applies where the company has subsidiaries. If the amount of the combined political donations and the political expenditure of the company and its subsidiaries exceeds £2,000, the directors' report for the year must disclose the particulars mentioned in paragraph 3.114 above in relation to the company and each subsidiary by whom any such political donation or political expenditure has been made or incurred. [SI 2008/409 5 Sch 2(3); SI 2008/410 7 Sch 3(3)].

3.116   Where the company has subsidiaries that have made any contributions to a non-EU political party in the financial year the following applies. The directors' report of the company is not required to disclose the amount of the company's own contributions, but should instead contain a statement of the total amount of the contributions made by the company and its subsidiaries in the year. There is no threshold for these disclosures. [SI 2008/409 5 Sch 3(2); SI 2008/410 7 Sch 4(2)].

Company that is a wholly-owned subsidiary of a UK parent

3.117   A wholly-owned subsidiary of a company incorporated in the UK does not have to disclose its donations, expenditure or contributions in its own directors' report, but these must be disclosed by its holding company as mentioned above.

3.117.1   An example of disclosure is given in Table 3.13.

> **Table 3.13 – Political and charitable donations**
>
> **Rolls-Royce Group plc – Report and Accounts – 31 December 2009**
>
> **Donations and sponsorship**
>
> The Group's charitable donations policy is to 'directly support causes primarily relating to educational, engineering and scientific objectives, as well as social objectives connected with the Group's business and place in the wider community'.
>
> The Group's charitable donations amounted to £2.3 million, of which £1.5 million were made in the UK. These included support for Community Foundations, Emmaus for homeless people, and the main armed service benevolent funds. Rolls-Royce made charitable donations of US$800,000 in North America, €135,000 in Germany and £200,000 in other regions. These donations included support for the work of United Way in North America and for the victims of natural disasters in Vietnam, India, Indonesia and Brazil.
>
> **Political donations**
>
> In line with its established policy, the Group made no political donations pursuant to the authority granted at the 2009 AGM. Although the Company does not make, and does not intend to make, donations to political parties, within the normal meaning of that expression, the definition of political donations under the Companies Act 2006 is very broad and includes expenses legitimately incurred as part of the process of talking to members of parliament and opinion formers to ensure that the issues and concerns of the Group are considered and addressed. These activities are not intended to support any political party and the Group's policy is not to make any donations for political purposes in the normally accepted sense.
>
> A resolution will therefore be proposed at the 2010 AGM seeking shareholder approval for the directors to be given authority to make donations and incur expenditure which might otherwise be caught by the terms of the Companies Act 2006. The authority sought will be limited to a maximum amount of £25,000 per Group company but so as not to exceed £50,000 for the entire Group in aggregate.
>
> During the year, one of our US subsidiaries made a contribution towards the running expenses of a political action committee (PAC) organised by its employees in an amount of US$24,636 (2008: US$23,700). PACs are a common feature of the US political system and are governed by the Federal Election Campaign Act. The Rolls-Royce PAC is independent of the Company and independent of any political party. Its funds are contributed voluntarily by employees and the Company cannot affect how they are applied. Such contributions do not require authorisation by shareholders under the Companies Act 2006 and therefore do not count towards the £25,000 and £50,000 limits for political donations and expenditure for which shareholder approval will be sought at the AGM.

Disclosure of charitable gifts

3.118   The disclosures required in relation to charitable gifts are as follows:

■   *By a company that is not a wholly-owned subsidiary of a company incorporated in the UK.*

  If such a company has given money exceeding £2,000 for charitable purposes in a financial year, its directors' report for the year must contain, for each of the purposes for which money has been given, a statement of the amount of money given for that purpose. [SI 2008/409 5 Sch 4(1); SI 2008/410 7 Sch 5(1)].

- *By a company, that is not a wholly-owned subsidiary of a company incorporated in the UK, with subsidiaries that have given money for charitable purposes.*

  In this case, the requirements in the bullet point above do not apply to the company. But if the amount given in the year for charitable purposes by the company and its subsidiaries exceeds £2,000, the directors' report for the year must contain, for each of the purposes for which money has been given by the company and its subsidiaries between them, a statement of the amount given for that purpose. [SI 2008/409 5 Sch 4(2); SI 2008/410 7 Sch 5(2)].

3.119 For these disclosures 'charitable purposes' means purposes that are exclusively charitable and in Scotland, 'charitable' is defined in section 7(2) of the Charities and Trustee Investment (Scotland) Act 2005. Money given for charitable purposes to a person, who at the time of the gift, was ordinarily resident outside the UK is to be left out of account for these purposes. [SI 2008/409 5 Sch 4(3)(4); SI 2008/410 7 Sch 5(3)(4)].

3.120 Money given for purposes that include either a political or a commercial element would not come within the disclosure of charitable donations. However, a donation with a political element may be disclosable as a political donation and require shareholder approval. Some companies may consider it good practice to seek shareholders' approval for charitable gifts, although, unlike political donations, this is not a statutory requirement.

3.121 An example of disclosure is provided in Table 3.13 above (see para 3.117.1).

Financial instruments

3.122 Companies (other than those subject to the small companies regime) are required to provide the following disclosures in the directors' report in relation to the entity as a whole:

- The entity's financial risk management objectives and policies, including the policy for hedging each major type of forecasted transaction for which hedge accounting is used.

- The entity's exposure to price risk, credit risk, liquidity risk and cash flow risk.

The disclosure is not required where such information is not material for the assessment of the entity's assets, liabilities, financial position and profit or loss. [SI 2008/410 7 Sch 6(1)].

3.123   These requirements are consistent with IFRS 7 and FRS 29, both called 'Financial instruments: Disclosures'. Although not all companies preparing Companies Act financial statements are required to comply with FRS 29, the standard provides additional guidance as to appropriate disclosure.

3.124   FRS 29 and IFRS 7 require an entity to provide disclosures *"that enable users to evaluate: (a) the significance of financial instruments for the entity's financial position and performance; and (b) the nature and extent of risks arising from financial instruments to which the entity is exposed during the period and at the reporting date, and how the entity manages those risks"*. [FRS 29 para 1; IFRS 7 para 1]. Extensive quantitative and qualitative disclosures of each type of risk arising from financial instruments (credit risk, market risk and liquidity risk) are required. [FRS 29 paras 31-42; IFRS 7 paras 31-42]. (See the Manual of Accounting – Financial instruments.)

3.125   Both IFRS 7 and FRS 29 require the disclosures to be given in the notes to the financial statements. For companies that comply with either IFRS 7 or FRS 29, to avoid the need for duplication, a specific cross-reference may be included in the directors' report to the relevant note.

Disclosure of overseas branches

3.126   Companies (other than unlimited companies and those subject to the small companies regime) must give an indication of the existence of branches that they operate outside the UK. [SI 2008/410 7 Sch 7(1)(d)]. For this purpose, a branch is defined in section 1046(3) of the 2006 Act to mean only branches within the EU (see further the Manual of Accounting – UK GAAP). Therefore, branches operated in the US, for example, would not require disclosure. It should be noted that disclosure is required only of the company's branches, not those of its subsidiaries. This means that the directors' report of a parent company need only refer to the existence of branches that it operates outside the UK and not to those that are operated outside the UK by its subsidiaries. Branches operated by its subsidiaries would fall to be disclosed in the subsidiaries' directors' reports.

Directors' responsibility statements

3.127   There is no Companies Act requirement for a company's directors to include a statement of their responsibilities anywhere in the annual report. For listed companies, however, there has been a recommendation since 1992, now incorporated into the UK Corporate Governance Code (2008) and, for financial years beginning on or after 29 June 2010, the UK Corporate Governance Code (2010), for directors to make a statement of their responsibilities. [CC C.1.1; UK CGC C.1.1]. In addition, for accounting periods beginning on or after 20 January 2007, the Disclosure and Transparency Rules of the FSA require listed companies to make certain disclosures about directors' responsibilities (see further from para 3.127.5).

3.127.1 ISA (UK&I) 700 (revised), 'The auditor's report on the financial statements (2009)', refers to the responsibilities of those charged with governance (which, in a UK context, is the company's directors) and states that:

"The auditor's report should include a statement that those charged with governance are responsible for the preparation of the financial statements and a statement that the responsibility of the auditor is to audit and express an opinion on the financial statements in accordance with applicable legal requirements and International Standards on Auditing (UK and Ireland)." [ISA (UK&I) 700 (revised) para 15].

3.127.2 To complement ISA (UK&I) 700 (revised), the APB has included specimen wording describing the directors' responsibilities for inclusion in the annual report of a non-publicly traded company applying UK GAAP. This wording is found in Appendix 11 of Bulletin 2009/02, 'Auditor's reports on financial statements in the United Kingdom'. In addition, the example financial statements for GAAP UK Plc, IFRS GAAP Plc and UK GAAP Ltd (see 'Illustrative financial statements: IFRS and UK GAAP 2009') each contain example wording for directors' responsibility statements.

3.127.3 In more complicated situations, for example, where the company is listed in a market outside the UK where different requirements may apply, the directors may need to take legal advice on what to include in the statement of directors' responsibilities.

3.127.4 It is now usual for a company to post its financial reports on its web site — indeed, it is a requirement for quoted companies — see further chapter 8. [CA06 Sec 430]. The example in the APB's previous Bulletin (2006/06) on the same subject included a statement that the directors take responsibility for the maintenance and integrity of financial information contained on the company's web site, which should be included where that web site includes financial reports and it continues to be appropriate to include such a statement. Table 3.13A shows an example from published financial statements that reflects such responsibility. The inclusion of this responsibility in the directors' responsibilities statement negates the requirement to include it in the audit report.

Table 3.13A – Directors' responsibilities

DSG International plc – Annual Report and Accounts – 2 May 2009

Directors' Report: Corporate Governance

Directors' Responsibilities
The directors are responsible for preparing the Annual Report and the financial statements in accordance with applicable law and regulations. They are required to prepare accounts for the Group in accordance with International Financial Reporting Standards (IFRSs) as adopted by the European Union and have chosen to prepare unconsolidated company financial statements in accordance with United Kingdom Generally Accepted Accounting Practice (UK GAAP).

In the case of the consolidated IFRSs financial statements, International Accounting Standard 1 requires that financial statements present fairly for each financial year the Group's financial position, financial performance and cash flows. This requires the faithful representation of the effects of transactions, other events and conditions in accordance with the definitions and recognition criteria for assets, liabilities, income and expenses set out in the International Accounting Standards Board's 'Framework for the preparation and Presentation of Financial Statements'. In almost all circumstances, a fair presentation will be achieved by compliance with all applicable IFRSs. The directors are also required to:

- properly select and apply accounting policies;

- present information, including accounting policies, in a manner that provides relevant, reliable, comparable and understandable information; and

- provide additional disclosures when compliance with the specific requirements of IFRSs is insufficient to enable users to understand the impact of particular transactions, other events and conditions on the financial position and financial performance.

In the case of the unconsolidated Company financial statements prepared under UK GAAP, the directors are required by UK company law to prepare financial statements which give a true and fair view of the state of affairs of the Company for each financial period as at the end of that financial period and of the profit or loss of the Company for that period.

In preparing both the consolidated Group financial statements and the unconsolidated Company financial statements, suitable accounting policies have been used and applied consistently, and reasonable and prudent judgements and estimates have been made. Applicable accounting standards have been followed. The financial statements have been prepared on the going concern basis as disclosed in the Directors' Report.

The directors are responsible for maintaining adequate accounting records and sufficient internal controls to safeguard the assets of the Company and to take reasonable steps for the prevention and detection of fraud or any other irregularities and for the preparation of a Directors' Report and directors' Remuneration Report which comply with the requirements of the Companies Act 2006. The directors are responsible for the maintenance and integrity of the corporate and financial information included on the Company's website. Legislation in the United Kingdom governing the preparation and dissemination of financial statements may differ from legislation in other jurisdictions.

Responsibility statement
We confirm to the best of our knowledge:

- the Group and unconsolidated Company financial statements give a true and fair view of the assets, liabilities, financial position and loss of the Group and Company, respectively; and

- the Performance Review includes a fair review of the development and performance of the business and the position of the Group together with a description of the principal risks and uncertainties they face.

By Order of the Board

John Browett
Chief Executive
25 June 2009

Nicholas Cadbury
Group Finance Director
25 June 2009

3.127.5   For entities that are included in the official list maintained by the FSA, the Disclosure and Transparency Rules of the FSA require the annual financial report to include a responsibility statement. [DTR 4.1.5R]. The DTR require that the persons responsible within the listed company (that is, the directors) state that, to the best of their knowledge:

- The financial statements, prepared in accordance with the applicable set of accounting standards, give a true and fair view of the assets, liabilities, financial position and profit or loss of the listed company and the undertakings included in the consolidation taken as a whole.

- The management report includes a fair review of the development and performance of the business and the position of the company and the undertakings included in the consolidation taken as a whole, together with a description of the principal risks and uncertainties that they face (the same wording as is used in the directors' report business review requirements in Section 417 of the 2006 Act – see further chapter 2).

[DTR 4.1.12R].

This requirement does not extend to companies traded on AIM or the Plus Market's PLUS-quoted market.

3.127.6   The directors already have a responsibility under section 393 of the 2006 Act to provide financial statements, prepared in accordance with applicable accounting standards that give a true and fair view. They are also responsible for preparing a business review (see further from para 3.22). The DTR simply require the directors to make positive statements regarding their responsibilities.

3.127.7   The name and function of each person making a responsibility statement under the DTR must be clearly indicated in the responsibility statement. [DTR 4.1.12R]. If the responsibility statement is provided collectively by the board (and, for example, signed by the company secretary or a director on its behalf), all directors are, in substance, making the responsibility statement. It is usual for the directors' names and job titles to be listed elsewhere in the annual report and hence, to avoid duplication, a specific cross-reference from the directors' report would fulfil the DTR requirements.

Statement on disclosure of information to the auditors

3.127.8   Unless the entity is exempt from the requirement to audit the accounts and has taken advantage of that exemption, the directors' report must contain a statement to confirm, for all directors in office at the time the report is approved, the following:

- So far as each director is aware, there is no relevant audit information of which the company's auditors are unaware. Relevant information is defined as *"information needed by the company's auditor in connection with preparing his report"*.

- Each director has taken all the steps that he ought to have taken in his duty as a director in order to make himself aware of any relevant audit information and to establish that the company's auditor is aware of that information.

Steps that a director ought to have taken would include making enquiries of other directors and the auditor and any other steps required by the director's duty to exercise due care, skill and diligence.

[CA06 Secs 418(1) to (4)].

3.127.9   Table 3.13B gives an example of disclosure.

Table 3.13B – Statement on disclosure to auditors

Diageo plc – Report and accounts – 30 June 2009

DIRECTORS' REPORT (extract)
DISCLOSURE OF INFORMATION TO THE AUDITOR
The directors who held office at the date of approval of this directors' report confirm that, so far as they are each aware, there is no relevant audit information of which the company's auditor is unaware; and each director has taken all the steps that they ought to have taken as a director to make themselves aware of any relevant audit information and to establish that the company's auditor is aware of that information.

3.127.10   In determining the extent of each director's duty, the 2006 Act states that the following considerations are relevant:

- The knowledge, skill and experience that may reasonably be expected of a person carrying out the functions of the company director.

- The knowledge, skill and experience that the director actually has.

[CA06 Sec 174].

3.127.11   The penalty for *'knowingly or recklessly'* making a false statement in this regard, and failing to take reasonable steps to prevent the directors' report being approved, may be imprisonment or a fine, or both, for each director indicted. [CA06 Sec 418(5)(6)].

Re-appointment of auditors

3.128   It is customary, but not a statutory requirement, to state at the end of the directors' report that a resolution will be put to the general meeting, regarding the appointment or re-appointment of the auditors. Where a private company is deemed to have reappointed its auditors in accordance with section 487(2) of the 2006 Act, such a statement will of course not be relevant. In that situation, companies may wish to include a statement indicating that in the absence of a notice proposing that the appointment be terminated, the auditors will be deemed to be re-appointed for the next financial year.

Disclosure of qualifying third party and pension scheme indemnity provisions

3.128.1   Where a qualifying third party indemnity provision and/or a qualifying pension scheme indemnity provision (made by the company or otherwise) was in force for the benefit of one or more directors at any time during the financial year, or at the time when the report is approved, a statement should be made in the directors' report to confirm this fact. [CA06 Sec 236(2)(3)]. An example of disclosure is provided in Table 3.13C.

Table 3.13C – Disclosure of directors' indemnities

Mitchells & Butlers plc – Report and accounts – 26 September 2009

Directors' report (extract)
Directors' indemnity
As permitted by the Articles of Association, the Directors have the benefit of an indemnity which is a qualifying third party indemnity provision as defined by Section 234 of the Companies Act 2006. The indemnity was in force throughout the last financial year and is currently in force. The Company also purchased and maintained throughout the financial year Directors' and Officers' liability insurance in respect of itself and its Directors. No indemnity is provided for the Company's auditors.

3.128.2   A statement is also required in the directors' report where a qualifying indemnity provision has been made during the year, or at the time when the report is approved, by the company for the benefit of one or more directors of an associated company. [CA06 Sec 236(4)(5)]. An associated company is defined in section 256 of the 2006 Act. A holding company is associated with all its subsidiaries and a subsidiary is associated with its holding company and all the other subsidiaries of its holding company.

3.128.3   Section 234 of the 2006 Act defines a qualifying third party indemnity provision as one where the provision does not provide indemnity for any liability incurred by the director in respect of each of the following:

■   An amount due to the company or any associated company.

■   A fine imposed by criminal proceedings.

■   A penalty payable to a regulatory authority in respect of non-compliance with any requirement of a regulatory nature.

■   An amount payable.

    ■   in defending criminal proceedings in which the director is convicted;

    ■   in defending civil proceedings brought by the company (or an associated company) in which judgement is given against the director; or

    ■   in connection with any application in which the court refused to grant the director relief.

[CA06 Sec 234(2)(3)].

3.128.4   The 2006 Act defines a qualifying pension scheme indemnity provision as a provision indemnifying a director of a company that is a trustee of an occupational pension scheme against liability incurred in connection with the company's activities as a trustee of the scheme, provided the provision does not provide indemnity against any liability of the director:

- To pay a fine imposed by criminal proceedings.

- To pay a sum to a regulatory authority due to a penalty in respect of non-compliance with any regulatory requirement.

- Incurred by the director in defending criminal proceedings in which he is convicted.

[CA06 Sec 235(2)(3)].

Additional matters for publicly traded companies

3.129   The directors' report of companies with publicly traded securities should give information on further matters in addition to those already discussed above. These additional matters are considered in the paragraphs that follow.

Control and share structures

3.129.1   These are general requirements designed to bring greater transparency to the market and apply to companies whether or not they are involved in a takeover. The disclosure requirements apply to companies with voting shares that were admitted to trading on a regulated market at the end of the year. [SI 2008/410 7 Sch 13(1)].

3.129.2   The specific disclosure requirements must be provided either in the directors' report or, by virtue of DTR 7.2.9R, in a document accompanying the annual report provided that there is a specific cross-reference to the disclosures from the directors' report. The disclosure requirements are set out in Part 6 of Schedule 7 to SI 2008/410 and include the following, which are to be given by reference to the end of the financial year:

- The structure of the company's capital, including the rights and obligations attached to the shares.

- Any restrictions on the transfer of securities.

- Any restriction on voting rights.

- Where a person has a significant direct or indirect holding, the identity of the person, the size of the holding and the nature of the holding (see further from para 3.130).

- Where any person holds shares with specific rights regarding control of the company:

- the identity of the person; and

- the nature of those rights.

- Where the company has an employee share scheme but shares relating to that scheme have rights regarding the control of the company that are not directly exercisable by the employees, how those rights are exercisable.

- Agreements between holders of securities known to the company that may result in restrictions on the transfer of securities or voting rights.

- Any rules that the company has about the appointment of directors, powers of directors or amendments to the company's articles of association.

- Significant agreements that the company is a party to that will be affected by a change in control of the company, together with the effects of such agreements (see further from para 3.129.4).

- Any agreements with employees (including directors) of the company providing for compensation for loss of office or employment on the takeover of the company.

3.129.3   Failure to include either the information concerning control and share structures or explanatory material in the annual report will attract criminal sanctions under sections 415(4), (5), and 419(3), (4) of the 2006 Act (directors responsible for the failure to comply with provisions related to the directors' report are liable to a fine).

Agreements affected by a change of control

3.129.4   The extent to which agreements that a company has entered into will be affected by a change of control will vary, as will the nature of those contracts. Examples of agreements that may be affected (other than those specifically mentioned by the Act) are:

- Bank loan/facility agreements.

- Convertible and listed debt.

- Sale/supply agreements.

- Leases.

- Joint venture agreements.

An example showing both disclosure of agreements that would be affected by a change of control and a restriction of voting rights (that is also affected by a change of control) is given in Table 3.14.

Table 3.14 – Disclosure of agreements affected by change of control

British Sky Broadcasting Group plc – Annual Report – 30 June 2009

Directors' report – review of the business (extract)
The business, its objectives and its strategy (extract)

Significant agreements
The Companies Act 2006 requires us to disclose the following significant agreements that take effect, alter or terminate on a change of control of the Company:

PL
In August 2006, British Sky Broadcasting Limited (a group subsidiary) entered into an agreement (the "2006 PL Licence") with The Football Association Premier League Limited (the "PL"), pursuant to which the Group was awarded four of six available packages of live audio-visual rights for Premier League football (the six packages are together the "Live Packages").

The PL will not award all of the Live Packages to a single licensee (either on its own or as part of a consortium or through one or more of its related parties) (the "Single Buyer Rule"). Pursuant to the 2006 PL Licence, the PL can suspend and/or terminate all of the rights which are included in, or exercisable as part of, one of the six available Live Packages in the event that a change of control of the Company occurs at any time prior to the expiry of the 2006 PL Licence which, if it had occurred prior to the award of the Live Packages to the Group, would have resulted in a breach of the Single Buyer Rule.

In February 2009 we successfully bid for five of the six available packages of live audio-visual rights for Premier League football in the UK from the beginning of the 2010/11 season to the end of the 2012/13 season. We expect the licence in respect of those packages to include a change of control provision as set out above in relation to the 2006 PL Licence.

Revolving Credit Facility
On 3 November 2004, the Company, British Sky Broadcasting Limited and Sky Subscribers Services Limited entered into a revolving credit facility agreement with Barclays Capital, Citigroup Global Markets Limited, Deutsche Bank AG London, JP Morgan plc and the Royal Bank of Scotland plc (as mandated lead arrangers) and certain other financial institutions (as "Lenders") pursuant to which the Lenders agreed to make available to the Company £1 billion to refinance existing facilities and for general corporate purposes (the "RCF").

On 19 June 2009, the Company entered into a £750 million forward starting syndicated credit facility available for drawing from 30 July 2010 and expiring on 31 July 2012 (the "Forward Start RCF").

Pursuant to both the RCF and the Forward Start RCF, the Lenders can require all amounts outstanding under the RCF and the Forward Start RCF (respectively) to be repaid in the event of a change of control of the Company (other than in the event that News Corporation or any subsidiary or holding company thereof acquires such control).

News Corporation voting agreement
On 21 September 2005, the Company, BSkyB Holdco Inc., News UK Nominees Limited and News Corporation entered into a voting agreement, pursuant to which News UK Nominees Limited's voting rights at any general meeting are capped at 37.19% (the "Voting Agreement"). The provisions of the Voting Agreement cease to apply inter alia, on a change of control of the Company.

EMTN bond issue
On 3 April 2007, the Group established a Euro medium term note programme (the "EMTN Programme") which provides the Group with a standardised documentation platform to allow for senior debt issuance in the Eurobond markets. The maximum potential issuance under the EMTN Programme is £1 billion.

On 14 May 2007, the Company issued Eurobonds consisting of £300 million guaranteed notes paying 6.000% interest and maturing on 14 May 2027 (the "Notes"). The Notes were issued under the Group's EMTN Programme.

Pursuant to the final terms attaching to the Notes, a holder of the Notes has the option to require the Company to redeem or (at the Company's option) purchase its Notes at its principal amount plus interest for the relevant period if there is a change of control of the Company (i) which, if the Notes carry an investment grade credit rating, results in a downgrade to a non-investment grade rating or a withdrawal of that rating; or (ii) where, if the Notes carry a non-investment grade rating, results in a downgrade by one or more notches or a withdrawal of that non-investment grade rating; or (iii) where, if the Notes do not carry a credit rating, the Company does not seek such a rating or is unable to achieve such a rating.

February 2008 and November 2008 bond issues

In February 2008, the Group entered into an indenture in respect of US$750 million 6.10% senior unsecured notes due 2018.

In November 2008, the Group entered into an indenture in respect of US$600 million 9.5% senior unsecured notes due 2018.

Pursuant to the final terms attaching to the securities, a holder of the securities has the option to require the Company to redeem or purchase its securities at a price equal to 101% of their principal amount plus accrued and unpaid interest up to the date of repurchase, if there is a change of control of the Company (i) which, if the securities carry an investment grade credit rating, results in a downgrade to a non-investment grade rating or a withdrawal of that rating; or (ii) which, if the securities carry a non-investment grade rating, results in a downgrade by one or more notches or a withdrawal of that non-investment grade rating; or (iii) where if the securities do not carry a credit rating, the Company does not seek such a rating or is unable to achieve such a rating.

UK broadcasting licences

The Group is party to a number of Ofcom broadcasting licences for the broadcast of the Sky Channels.

The Broadcasting Act 1990 (as amended by the Broadcasting Act 1996 and the Communications Act) lays down a number of restrictions on those parties permitted to hold Ofcom broadcasting licences. Among those restricted from holding Ofcom broadcasting licences or from controlling a licensed company are (a) local authorities, (b) political bodies, (c) religious bodies, (d) any company controlled by any of the previous categories or by their officers or associates, (e) advertising agencies or any company controlled by such an agency or in which it holds more than a 5% interest.

Licensees are obliged to comply with these ownership restrictions. Failure by a licensee to do so (either by the licensee becoming a "disqualified person" or any change affecting the nature, characteristics or control of the licensee which would have precluded the original grant of the licence) may constitute a breach of the licence and, if not rectified, could result in revocation of the licence.

Matters for listed companies

3.129.5 The following requirements apply to those companies that are subject to the UKLA's Listing Rules (for example, companies traded on the main market of the LSE or the Plus Market's PLUS-listed market).

Major interest in company's shares

3.130   A statement should be given of particulars of the nature and extent of the interests of any person, in any holding of three per cent or more of the nominal value of any class of capital carrying rights to vote in all circumstances at general meetings of the company. The statement must be made at a date not more than one month prior to the date of notice of the annual general meeting. [LR 9.8.6R (2)]. The three per cent threshold is higher for certain entities, for example market makers only disclose interests of ten per cent or more. [DTR 5.1.3R].

3.131   The particulars to be disclosed include the names of the persons and the amount of their interests. This information should be that which has been disclosed to the company in accordance with DTR 5. If there is no such interest, that fact should also be stated. [LR 9.8.6R (2)]. It is customary to give this information in the directors' report. An example is given in Table 3.15 below. It should be noted that the Companies Act requirement to disclose significant shareholdings (described in para 3.129.2 above) requires such holdings to be disclosed as at the end of the financial year, whereas the Listing Rules require disclosures as at not more than one month prior to the date of the notice of AGM. The Companies Act requirement also requires the nature of the interest (direct or indirect) to be disclosed.

Table 3.15 — Major interest in company's shares

3i Group plc – Report and accounts – 31 March 2009

Directors' report – statutory and corporate governance information (extract)

Major interests in ordinary shares
Notifications of the following voting interests in the Company's ordinary share capital had been received by the Company (in accordance with Chapter 5 of the FSA's Disclosure and Transparency Rules) as at 31 March 2009 and 1 May 2009:

	As at 31 March 2009	% of issued share capital	As at 1 May 2009	% of issued share capital	Nature of holding
AXA S.A. and its group of companies	15,580,556	4.06	15,580,556	4.06	Direct and indirect
The Goldman Sachs Group, Inc	22,865,000	5.97	22,865,000	5.97	Indirect
BlackRock, Inc.	19,653,461	5.11	19,653,461	5.11	Indirect
Deutsche Bank AG	22,407,866	5.84	22,407,866	5.84	Direct and indirect
Lehman Brothers International (Europe)	11,550,096	3.01	11,550,096	3.01	Direct
Lloyds Banking Group Plc	26,677,335	6.95	19,736,041	4.68	Direct and indirect
Legal & General Group plc	23,209,163	6.04	25,253,140	5.98	Direct
Prudential plc group of companies	11,865,771	3.09	Below 3%	Below 3%	Direct
Schroder Plc	19,370,309	5.05	19,370,309	5.05	Indirect

3.132 Although there is no requirement in the Companies Act 2006 for a company to maintain a shareholders' register, it will be necessary to do so in order to meet this Listing Rule disclosure requirement. In order to ensure that the register is up to date, the Companies Act 2006 gives listed companies the right to write to any person who it believes is (or has been during the previous three years) interested in the company's shares and ask them to confirm that fact, or to state the person to whom the interest was transferred. [CA06 Sec 793]. Further, the DTR require holders of more than three per cent (or a higher threshold in certain circumstances – see para 3.130) of a company's qualifying financial instruments to notify the company if that holding increases above or falls below any integer percentage holding equal to or higher than three percent (see further chapter 8).

[The next paragraph is 3.135.]

Transactions with a controlling shareholder

3.135 The annual report should include particulars of any contract of significance between the company (or one of its subsidiary undertakings) and a controlling shareholder subsisting during the year. [LR 9.8.4R (10)(b)]. For this purpose, a 'contract of significance' is one which is determined in accordance with the rules set out in paragraph 3.137.11 below. An example is given in Table 3.16 below.

3.135.1 A 'controlling shareholder' is defined within the definition of an associate in the Listing Rules and is taken to mean any person who is:

■ entitled to exercise, or control the exercise of, at least 30 per cent of the voting power at the company's general meetings; or

■ is in a position to control the composition of a majority of the company's board of directors.

[LR App 1.1].

3.135.2 In addition, the directors' report should disclose details of any contract with a controlling shareholder (as defined above) to provide services to the company or to one of its subsidiaries (see Table 3.16 below). This information is not required if the shareholder is providing services that it normally provides as part of its principal business and it is not a contract of significance that is required to be disclosed. [LR 9.8.4R (11)].

Table 3.16 — Contract with a controlling shareholder

Premier Foods plc — Annual Report and Accounts — 31 December 2004

Directors' Report (extract)

Contracts of significance with controlling shareholder
Details of related transactions with related parties are set out in notes 24 and 29 to the financial statements on pages 71 to 73.

29. Related party transactions (extract)
Prior to the IPO HMTFPL had a controlling interest in the Group. As a consequence of which a number of related party arrangements existed between the Group and HMTFPL and its affiliates, which included Hicks, Muse & Co Partners L.P. ("Hicks, Muse & Co."). Save as disclosed elsewhere in these financial statements, details of these arrangements with HMTFPL and its affiliates are shown below:

Monitoring and Oversight agreement
In 1999, Premier Foods Holdings Limited and Premier Financing Limited entered into a 10-year agreement (the "Monitoring and Oversight agreement") with Hicks, Muse & Co. pursuant to which the Group pays Hicks, Muse & Co. an annual fee of £1.2m for providing financial oversight and monitoring services to the Group. The annual fee is adjustable at the end of each financial year to an amount equal to one tenth of one per cent of the Group's budgeted consolidated annual net sales, but in no event may the fee be less than £1.2m. In addition, the Group has agreed to indemnify Hicks, Muse & Co. and its shareholders and their respective directors, officers, agents, employees and affiliates from and against all claims, actions, proceedings, demands, liabilities, judgements, assessments, losses and costs, including fees and expenses, arising out of or in connection with the services rendered by Hicks, Muse & Co. under the Monitoring and Oversight agreement. The Monitoring and Oversight agreement makes available to the Group the resources of Hicks, Muse & Co. concerning a variety of financial and operational matters. The services that had been provided until IPO, when the agreement was terminated, could not otherwise be obtained by the Group without the addition of personnel or the engagement of outside professional advisers. In management's opinion, the fees provided for under the agreement reasonably reflect the benefits received by the Group. The Group paid £0.6m and £1.2m in the years ended 31 December 2004 and 2003 respectively under the Monitoring and Oversight agreement.

The Monitoring and Oversight agreement was terminated on 23 July 2004.

Financial Advisory agreement
In 1999, Premier Brands Foods Limited, Premier Financing Limited and Hicks, Muse & Co. entered into an agreement ("the Financial Advisory agreement") pursuant to which Hicks, Muse & Co. will be entitled to receive a fee equal to 1.5% of the transaction value for each acquisition, sale, merger, recapitalisation, restructuring or other similar transaction involving the Group. The Financial Advisory agreement makes available to the Group the resources of Hicks, Muse & Co. concerning a variety of financial and operational matters. The services that had been provided until IPO, when the agreement was terminated, could not otherwise be obtained by the Group without the addition of personnel or the engagement of outside professional advisers. In management's opinion, the fees provided for under the Financial Advisory agreement reasonably reflect the benefits received by the Group. The Group paid £nil and £1.6m in the years ended 31 December 2004 and 2003 respectively under the Financial Advisory agreement.

The Financial Advisory agreement was terminated on 23 July 2004.

Golden Share
A Golden Share was issued by Premier Financing Limited with voting rights, which entitled the holder of the Golden Share to block the passing of resolutions for the winding-up or administration of Premier Financing Limited or resolutions approving other matters that would constitute a breach of the Senior Credit Facility. Upon repayment of the Senior Credit Facility

during the year (see note 19(b)), the Golden Share was automatically converted at IPO into a deferred ordinary share of Premier Financing Limited with limited rights.

At the date of the IPO HMTFPL reduced its stake in the ordinary share capital of the Company to approximately 20%. In addition, they appointed Mr. Lyndon Lea as a non-executive director of the Company.

On 15 October 2004 HMTFPL sold all its interests in the ordinary share capital of the Company.

[The next paragraph is 3.137.]

Disclosure of directors' interests

3.137 The UKLA's Listing Rules require a listed company's annual financial report to include a statement setting out all the interests, as at the year end, of each person who is a director of the company as at the end of the period under review including:

- all changes in the interests of each director that have occurred between the end of the period under review and a date not more than one month prior to the date of the notice of the annual general meeting; or

- if there have been no changes in the interests of each director in the period described above, a statement that there have been no changes.

Interests of each director include the interests of 'connected persons' of which the listed company is, or ought upon reasonable enquiry to become, aware (see para 3.137.7 below).

[LR 9.8.6R (1)].

3.137.1 An example of disclosure is set out in Table 3.17.

Table 3.17 – Directors' share interests

3i Group plc – Report and accounts – 31 March 2009

Directors' report – statutory and corporate governance information (extract)

Directors' interests
In accordance with FSA Listing Rule 9.8.6(R)(1), Directors' interests in the shares of the Company (in respect of which transactions are notifiable to the Company under FSA Disclosure and Transparency Rule 3.1.2(R)) as at 31 March 2009 are shown below:

	Ordinary shares	B shares
Baroness Hogg	32,956	0
O H J Stocken	30,714	0
M J Queen	420,453	121,851
R H Meddings	5,583	0
W Mesdag	50,000	0
C J M Morin-Postel	7,985	0
Lord Smith of Kelvin	14,186	0
R W A Swannell	15,350	0
J S Wilson	1,986	1,037

The share interests shown for Mr M J Queen include a Super-performance Share award (over 70,175 ordinary shares) which is subject to forfeiture and is included in the table on page 87 and the share interests shown for Mr M J Queen and Mrs J S Wilson include ordinary shares held by them in the 3i Share Incentive Plan, as shown in the table on page 87. These interests do not include other share options or awards under the Company's share plans, details of which are shown in the Remuneration Report.

In the period from 1 April 2009 to 1 May 2009, Mrs J S Wilson and Mr M J Queen became interested in an additional 120 ordinary shares each.

Save as detailed above, there have been no changes in the above interests between 1 April 2009 and 1 May 2009.

3.137.2   The interests required to be disclosed are those in respect of transactions that are notifiable to the company under DTR 3.1.2R. Under that rule, persons discharging managerial responsibilities (which includes, but is not restricted to, directors) and their connected persons, must notify the issuer in writing of the occurrence of all transactions conducted on their own account in the shares of the issuer, or derivatives or any other financial instruments relating to those shares within four business days of the day on which the transaction occurred. Connected persons are considered further from paragraph 3.137.7.

3.137.3   Persons who are directors during, but not at the end of, the period under review need not be included. [LR 9.8.6AG (1)].

3.137.4   The UKLA's Listing Rules note that a listed company unable to compile the statement in LR 9.8.6R (1) from information already available to it may need to seek the relevant information, or confirmation, from the director, including that in relation to connected persons, but would not be expected to obtain information directly from connected persons. [LR 9.8.6AG (2)].

[The next paragraph is 3.137.6.]

3.137.6   Listed companies are required by Schedule 8 to SI 2008/410, 'The Large and Medium-sized Companies and Groups (Accounts and Reports) Regulations 2008', to make detailed disclosure in the directors' remuneration report about directors' share options. These are considered in detail in chapter 5. In practice, the disclosure of directors' interests in shares and options are sometimes combined and presented in a tabular manner, usually in the directors' remuneration report. A cross-reference may be given in the directors' report to the precise location of the information. Examples of how a company discloses its directors' interests in accordance with the Listing Rules are included in chapter 5.

Connected persons

3.137.7   The definition of 'connected persons' contained in the Listing Rules is wider than that contained in section 252 of the Companies Act 2006 (see para 3.137.10).

3.137.8 The definition of 'connected persons' in the Companies Act 2006 includes:

■ Members of the director's family, including:

   ■ The director's spouse, civil partner or any other person with whom the director lives as a partner in an enduring family relationship.

   ■ The director's children or step-children.

   ■ Any children or step-children (under the age of 18) of the director's enduring life partner who live with the director.

   ■ The director's parents.

■ A body corporate with which the director is connected (see para 3.137.9).

■ A trustee of a trust of which the beneficiary is (or can be, at the discretion of the trustee) the director (or a family member or connected body corporate as defined above) other than a trust for the purposes of an employee share scheme or pension scheme.

■ A person acting in capacity as partner of the director (or any person connected with him).

■ A partnership that is a legal person in which the director (or any person connected with him) is a partner.

■ A partnership that is a legal person with a partner that is, itself, a partnership, where the director (or a connected person of his) is a partner.

[CA06 Secs 252, 253].

3.137.9 A body corporate is a connected person of a director if the director and his connected persons are interested in at least 20 per cent of the nominal value of the body corporate's equity share capital (excluding treasury shares), or are entitled to control at least 20 percent of the voting power at any general meeting (excluding votes attached to treasury shares). [CA06 Sec 254]. For this purpose, an 'interest' in shares is defined in Schedule 1 to the 2006 Act and is taken to mean any interest whatsoever and includes any right to acquire shares or control of the voting rights attached to the shares. The definition of 'equity share capital' is contained in section 548 of the 2006 Act and is considered further in chapter 23 of the Manual of Accounting – IFRS for the UK and chapter 23 of the Manual of Accounting – UK GAAP.

3.137.10 In addition to those that fall within the 2006 Act's definition of connected persons, the Listing Rules definition includes:

■ Any relative of the director who, on the date of the transaction in question has shared the same household as the director for at least 12 months.

■ A body corporate in which the director (or a person connected to him under the 2006 Act or the bullet point above) is a director or a senior executive who has the power to make management decisions affecting the future development and business prospects of that body corporate.

[LR Glossary].

Directors' interests in contracts of significance

3.137.11   The Listing Rules require disclosure of particulars of any contract of significance (including substantial property transactions) subsisting during the period under review, to which the company, or one of its subsidiary undertakings, is a party and in which a director of the company is, or was, materially interested. [LR 9.8.4R (10)]. In this context, 'a contract of significance' is one which represents in value a sum equal to one per cent or more, calculated on a group basis where relevant, of:

■   The aggregate of the group's share capital and reserves for a capital transaction or for a transaction of which the principal purpose is the granting of credit.

■   The group's total purchases, sales, payments or receipts, as appropriate for other transactions.

[LR App 1.1].

Waiver of dividends

3.138   Particulars of any arrangements under which any shareholder has waived or agreed to waive any dividends should be disclosed. This requirement applies to waivers of future dividends as well as to waivers of dividends payable during the past financial year. Waivers of dividend of less than one per cent of the total value of any dividend may be disregarded provided that some payment has been made on each share of the relevant class during the year. [LR 9.8.5G].

[The next paragraph is 3.140.]

Special business

3.140   Holders of listed securities who are sent a notice of a meeting that is to occur on the same day as an AGM, which includes business that is considered not to be routine business of an AGM must be provided with an explanation in the directors' report of such business, unless an explanatory circular accompanies the notice. [LR 13.8.8R (1)]. An example of matters that are regarded as special business in an AGM is given in Table 3.18 below.

Table 3.18 — Special business in an AGM

WH Smith PLC — Annual report and accounts — 31 August 2009

DIRECTORS' REPORT AND BUSINESS REVIEW (extract)

Annual General Meeting

The AGM of the Company will be held at JPMorgan Cazenove, 20 Moorgate, London EC2R 6DA on 27 January 2010 at 11.30am. The Notice of Annual General Meeting is given, together with explanatory notes, in the booklet which accompanies this report.

NOTICE OF WH SMITH PLC

Annual General Meeting (extract)

SPECIAL BUSINESS

The following 2 resolutions will be proposed as ordinary resolutions.

Authority to make political donations

Resolution 7: to resolve that, in accordance with Section 366 of the Companies Act 2006, the Company and all companies that are subsidiaries of the Company at any time during the period for which this resolution has effect be and are hereby authorised to:

(a) make political donations to political parties or independent election candidates not exceeding £100,000 in total;

(b) make political donations to political organisations other than political parties not exceeding £100,000 in total; and

(c) incur political expenditure not exceeding £100,000 in total,

during the period from the date of passing this resolution up to and including the conclusion of the next Annual General Meeting or 28 February 2011, whichever is the earlier.

For the purpose of this resolution the terms "political donations", "political parties", "independent election candidates", "political organisations" and "political expenditure" have the meanings set out in Sections 363 to 365 of the Companies Act 2006.

Authority to allot shares

Resolution 8: to resolve that:

(a) the directors be generally and unconditionally authorised, in accordance with Section 551 of the Companies Act 2006, to exercise all powers of the Company to allot shares in the Company or grant rights to subscribe for, or convert any security into, shares in the Company:

　(i) up to a maximum nominal amount of £11,506,657; and

　(ii) comprising equity securities (as defined in Section 560 of the Companies Act 2006) up to a maximum nominal amount of £23,016,767 (including within such limit any shares allotted or rights granted under paragraph (i) above) in connection with an offer by way of a rights issue:

　　(A) to holders of ordinary shares in proportion (as nearly as may be practicable) to their existing holdings; and

　　(B) to holders of other equity securities if this is required by the rights of those securities or, if the directors consider it necessary, as permitted by the rights of those securities; and so that the directors may make such exclusions or other arrangements as they consider expedient in relation to any treasury shares, fractional entitlements, record dates, legal or practical problems under the laws in any territory or the requirements of any relevant regulatory body or stock exchange or any other matter;

(b)   this authority shall expire at the conclusion of the next Annual General Meeting of the Company after the passing of this resolution or, if earlier, on 28 February 2011;

(c)   the Company may, before this authority expires, make an offer or agreement which would or might require shares to be allotted or rights to be granted after it expires and the directors may allot shares or grant rights in pursuance of such offer or agreement as if this authority had not expired; and

(d)   all previous unutilised authorities under Section 80 of the Companies Act 1985 shall cease to have effect (save to the extent that the same are exercisable by reason of any offer or agreement made prior to the date of this resolution which would or might require shares to be allotted or rights to be granted on or after that date).

The following 4 resolutions will be proposed as special resolutions.

Disapplication of pre-emption rights

Resolution 9: to resolve that:

(a)   the directors be and are hereby empowered pursuant to Sections 570 and 573 of the Companies Act 2006:

    (i)   subject to the passing of resolution 8 set out in the Notice convening the Annual General Meeting of which this resolution forms part to allot equity securities (as defined in Section 560 of the Companies Act 2006) for cash pursuant to the authority conferred by resolution 8; and

    (ii)   to allot equity securities (as defined in Section 560(3) of the Companies Act 2006) for cash,

in either case as if Section 561 of the Companies Act 2006 did not apply to the allotment but this power shall be limited to:

    (A)   the allotment of equity securities in connection with an offer or issue of equity securities to or in favour of:

        (i)   holders of ordinary shares in proportion (as nearly as may be practicable) to their existing holdings; and

        (ii)   holders of other equity securities if this is required by the rights of those securities or, if the directors consider it necessary, as permitted by the rights of those securities, and so that the directors may make such exclusions or other arrangements as they consider expedient in relation to any treasury shares, fractional entitlements, record dates, legal or practical problems under the laws in any territory or the requirements of any relevant regulatory body or any stock exchange or any other matter; and

    (B)   the allotment of equity securities pursuant to the authority granted under resolution 8 (a)(i) and/or by virtue of Section 560(3) of the Companies Act 2006 (in each case otherwise than under paragraph (A) above) up to a maximum nominal amount of £1,726,171; and

(b)   this power shall expire at the conclusion of the next Annual General Meeting of the Company or on 28 February 2011, whichever is the earlier, save that the Company may before such expiry make an offer or agreement which would or might require equity securities to be allotted after such expiry and the directors may allot such equity securities in pursuance of such offer or agreement as if the power hereby conferred had not expired; and

(c)   all previous authorities under Section 95 of the Companies Act 1985 shall cease to have effect.

Market purchases of ordinary shares

Resolution 10: to resolve that, pursuant to Section 701 of the Companies Act 2006, the Company be and is hereby generally and unconditionally authorised to make market purchases (as defined in Section 693(4) of the Companies Act 2006) of any of its own ordinary shares in such manner and on such terms as the directors may from time to time determine provided that:

(a) the maximum aggregate number of ordinary shares authorised to be purchased is 23,365,125;

(b) the minimum price which may be paid for each ordinary share is 226/67p (exclusive of all expenses);

(c) the maximum price which may be paid for each ordinary share is an amount (exclusive of all expenses) equal to the higher of:

   (i)   105 per cent of the average of the middle market quotations for an ordinary share as derived from the London Stock Exchange Daily Official List for the five business days immediately preceding the day on which the ordinary share is purchased; and

   (ii) the price stipulated by Article 5(1) of the Buy-back and Stabilisation Regulation 2003;

(d) the authority shall, unless previously varied, revoked or renewed, expire at the conclusion of the next Annual General Meeting of the Company or on 28 February 2011, whichever is the earlier, save that the Company shall be entitled under such authority to make at any time before such expiry any contract to purchase its own shares which will or might be executed wholly or partly after such expiry and make a purchase of shares in pursuance of any such contract or contracts; and

(e) all existing authorities for the Company to make market purchases of ordinary shares are revoked, except in relation to the purchase of shares under a contract or contracts concluded before the date of this resolution and which has not been executed.

Notice of General Meetings

Resolution 11: to resolve that a general meeting (other than an annual general meeting) may be called on not less than 14 clear days' notice.

Articles of Association

Resolution 12: to resolve that with effect from the conclusion of the meeting:

(A) the Articles of Association of the Company be amended by deleting all the provisions of the Company's Memorandum of Association which, by virtue of Section 28 of the Companies Act 2006, are to be treated as provisions of the Company's Articles of Association; and

(B) the Articles of Association produced to the meeting and initialled by the Chairman of the meeting for the purposes of identification be adopted as the new Articles of Association of the Company in substitution for, and to the exclusion of, the current Articles of Association.

EXPLANATORY NOTES

[Not reproduced in this example.]

Additional disclosures for listed companies purchasing own share or selling treasury shares

3.141   The annual report of a listed company must give additional information concerning purchases or proposed purchases of the company's own shares and sales of treasury shares. The disclosure requirements are set out in paragraph 3.77 above.

Directors' liability: safe harbour

3.142　A further amendment provided by the Companies Act 2006 arising from the consultation on narrative reporting is for directors to be given safe harbour from civil liability for statements or omissions in the directors' report and the directors' remuneration report (including any summary financial statements derived from those reports). These provisions are considered further in chapter 8.

Small companies exemption

3.143　A company that is entitled to prepare its financial statements in accordance with the small companies regime (see further chapter 31 of the Manual of Accounting – UK GAAP), or would be if it were not a member of an ineligible group, is permitted, but not required, to exclude the directors' report from the financial statements filed with the Registrar of Companies. [CA06 Secs 444(1), 444A(1)]. These companies (that is, both categories of company) are described in the 2006 Act as being *"entitled to a small companies exemption in relation to the directors' report"*. [CA06 Sec 415A]. The 2006 Act also refers to these companies simply as companies entitled to the 'small companies exemption'.

3.144　An ineligible group is a group in which any of its members is (or was, at any time within the financial year) any one of the following:

■　A public company.

■　An authorised insurance company, a banking company, an e-money issuer, a MiFiD investment firm or a UCITS management company.

■　Carrying on insurance market activity.

■　A body corporate (other than a company, but including a foreign company) whose shares are admitted to trading on a regulated market in an EEA member State.

[CA06 Sec 384(2)].

3.145　This does not affect the requirement for companies to *prepare* a directors' report: all companies are required to do so, although those entitled to the small companies exemption are permitted to exclude certain disclosures contained in the main body of the 2006 Act while those subject to the small companies regime (see further chapter 31 of the Manual of Accounting – UK GAAP) do not have to give some of the disclosures contained in Schedule 7 to SI 2008/410 and so required by larger companies. The application of each of the requirements is considered throughout the chapter.

3.145.1　If, in preparing the directors' report, advantage has been taken of the small companies exemption, a statement to that effect must be included in the directors' report in a prominent position above the signature. [CA06 Sec 419(2)].

Approval and signing of directors' report

3.146   The board of directors must formally approve the directors' report and it must be signed on behalf of the board by a director or the secretary of the company. [CA06 Sec 419(1)].

3.147   Every copy of the directors' report that is laid before the company in general meeting, or that is otherwise circulated, published or issued, must state the name of the person who signed it on behalf of the board. [CA06 Sec 433(1) to (3)]. A copy of the directors' report that is to be delivered to the Registrar of Companies must also be signed on behalf of the board by a director or secretary of the company. [CA06 Sec 444 to 447].

3.147.1   As noted in paragraph 3.145.1 above, a directors' report prepared in accordance with the small companies regime must contain a statement to that effect in a prominent position above the signature. [CA06 Sec 419(2)].

Liability for contravention

3.148   Every person who was a director of the company at the end of the period within which the company's financial statements must be laid before the company in general meeting and be delivered to the Registrar of Companies may be guilty of an offence if the directors' report fails to comply with the Act's requirements (see further chapter 8). This offence is punishable by a fine. [CA06 Secs 415(4)(5), 419(3)(4)].

3.149   It is a defence in such a situation for a director to prove that he took all reasonable steps to ensure that the directors' report complied with all the Act's requirements. [CA06 Secs 415(4), 419(3)].

3.150   Furthermore, where the company does not comply with the requirements for the approval and signing of the directors' report as set out in paragraphs 3.146 and 3.147 above, the company and every officer of it who is in default will be guilty of an offence and liable to a fine. [CA06 Secs 419(4), 433(5)].

Position of the auditor

3.151   The auditors are required to state in their report whether, in their opinion, *"the information given in the directors' report for the financial year for which the accounts are prepared is consistent with those accounts"*. [CA06 Sec 496]. There is no exemption from this requirement for auditors of small and medium-sized companies (other than those exempt from the audit requirement – see further chapter 8).

3.152   Auditors have a statutory responsibility to review the directors' report for consistency with the financial statements. This approach is supported by the Auditing Practices Board's ISA (UK&I) 720B (revised), 'The auditor's statutory reporting responsibility in relation to directors' reports (2009)', and by APB

Bulletin 2009/02, 'Auditor's reports on financial statements in the United Kingdom'.

3.153 ISA (UK&I) 720B (revised) deals specifically with the auditor's statutory reporting responsibility in relation to directors' reports and requires the auditor to read the information in the directors' report and assess whether it is consistent with the financial statements.

3.154 The auditor should seek to resolve any inconsistencies identified between the information in the directors' report and the financial statements. If a material inconsistency between the directors' report and the financial statements is not resolved, details should be provided in the audit report. In addition, a qualified or adverse opinion would be necessary where an amendment that is necessary to the financial statements has not been made.

3.155 ISA (UK&I) 720B (revised) confirms that the information given in the directors' report includes information that is included by way of a cross reference to other information presented separately from the directors' report. For example the auditor has a statutory responsibility to review a business review presented within a separate voluntary OFR for consistency with the financial statements. [ISA (UK & I) 720B (revised) para 3].

Enforcement

3.156 The Financial Reporting Review Panel (FRRP), part of the Financial Reporting Council, is responsible for ensuring that both public and large private companies comply with relevant reporting requirements including the directors' report (and, thus, the business review). The Secretary of State (through Companies House) is responsible for enforcement in respect of other companies. [Companies (Audit, Investigation and Community Enterprise) Act 2004 Sec 14].

3.157 Under the existing enforcement regime in respect of defective accounts, a company may be required to revise its directors' report where it is not compliant with the Act's requirements. In cases of non-compliance the FRRP will have the power, if necessary, to go to the court to compel a company to revise its report. Revision of defective accounts is considered in chapter 8 of this publication.

Chapter 4

Corporate governance

Chapter 4

Corporate governance

History and development of corporate governance in the UK

Introduction

4.1 In 1992 the Cadbury Committee defined corporate governance in its report 'The financial aspects of corporate governance' as *"the system by which companies are directed and controlled. Boards of directors are responsible for the governance of their companies. The shareholders' role in governance is to appoint the directors and the auditors and to satisfy themselves that an appropriate governance structure is in place. The responsibilities of the board include setting the company's strategic aims, providing the leadership to put them into effect, supervising the management of the business and reporting to shareholders on their stewardship. The board's actions are subject to laws, regulations and the shareholders in general meeting"*. [CR]. In 2010, the latest version of the UK Corporate Governance Code still quotes this as the classic definition of the context of the Code.

4.2 Most UK companies have a single 'unitary' board of directors. Corporate governance in the UK corporate sector is, therefore, primarily concerned with:

- The procedures adopted by the board and its committees to discharge its duties (for example, membership of the board; frequency of, and procedures at, board meetings; the role of non-executive directors; constitution and terms of reference of audit and remuneration committees; and the role of the company secretary).

- The board's accountability to shareholders and other stakeholders (for example, annual reporting; use of AGMs; and shareholder voting rights).

- The manner in which the board controls the company or group (for example, management structures; group legal structure; and internal control philosophy and practice).

4.3 Corporate governance potentially covers a very wide range of issues and disciplines from company secretarial and legal, through to business strategy and risk management, executive and non-executive management, investor relations, and accounting and information systems.

4.4 Governance went higher up the corporate agenda in the early 1990s partly in response to a series of scandals, fuelled by the recession. Business failures heightened concerns about effective governance and led amongst other things to the development of corporate governance disclosures. More recently, corporate governance has again been in the spotlight following the perceived failures of companies in the banking sector during the economic downturn which began in 2008. Corporate governance and the reporting of that governance has become more of a pressing issue for listed companies, in particular in relation to going concern, risk management, internal controls, board balance and activities and directors' remuneration.

4.5   The importance of corporate governance disclosures is that, provided the information can be relied upon, they should help determine a company's value and be useful to stakeholders wishing to assess their risk exposure before deciding whether to commit resources to, or withdraw resources from, a company. Company failures have highlighted the need for stakeholders to obtain assurance on governance. They have also heightened the need for directors to be able to give such assurance if they are to continue to attract funds.

4.6   Some governance issues have attracted significant political and public interest, because they strike at the root of the objectives of companies – none more so than the accountability of boards to shareholders in relation to executive pay.

4.7   Improvements in governance disclosures over the last few years have meant that UK public companies are among the most accountable of organisations. In addition to publishing their results and having their financial statements audited, public companies are required to disclose detailed information about their operations, relationships, remuneration and governance.

The development of corporate governance disclosures

4.8   The response to the scandals and failures of the late 1980s was a series of committees, reports and recommendations. The first of these was the Committee on the Financial Aspects of Corporate Governance, generally referred to as the Cadbury Committee, after its chairman Sir Adrian Cadbury. Its report was issued in December 1992 and, as a result, major changes occurred in the way in which governance was viewed by companies as well as in the disclosures that they give.

4.9   Whilst board remuneration was one of a number of issues addressed by Cadbury, it was not the main focus. Nonetheless, the level of board remuneration continued to attract a high profile, particularly in relation to levels of pay in privatised utilities. In response to this a separate group was set up to study the matter and the result was 'Directors' remuneration: report of a study group chaired by Sir Richard Greenbury'. This is known as the Greenbury report and was published in July 1995. The Greenbury Report led to additional disclosure requirements being included in the Listing Rules. Remuneration disclosures are discussed in chapter 5.

4.10   One of Cadbury's recommendations was that a successor body should be set up to review progress and it identified a number of issues which that body might consider. The successor body, 'The Committee on Corporate Governance' (the 'Hampel committee') was set up in November 1995 under the chairmanship of Sir Ronald Hampel.

4.11   The final version of the Hampel report was published in January 1998. The recommendations aimed to ensure a balance between business prosperity and accountability.

4.12   Following the completion of its report, the Hampel Committee co-operated with the London Stock Exchange in producing 'The Combined Code – Principles of Good Corporate Governance and Code of Best Practice' in June 1998. The Combined Code (1998) embraced the Cadbury and Greenbury Reports, and took into account the Hampel Committee's Report and changes made by the London Stock Exchange, with the committee's agreement, following consultation.

4.13   The original Combined Code, published in June 1998, contained both principles and detailed Combined Code provisions and was in two parts, part 1, 'Principles of good governance' and part 2, 'Code of best practice'. Each part of the Combined Code (1998) was split into two sections. Section 1 contained the corporate governance principles and Combined Code provisions applicable to companies incorporated in the UK. Section 2 contained the principles and Combined Code provisions applicable to institutional shareholders with regard to their voting, dialogue with the company and evaluation of governance arrangements.

4.14   The Combined Code (1998) was appended to the Listing Rules (although it did not form part of those rules) and a new listing rule required companies to include a two part disclosure statement in their annual report describing how they had applied the principles of the Combined Code (1998) and whether or not they had complied with its detailed provisions throughout the accounting period, with details of any non-compliance. Although the changes to the Listing Rules in June 1998 only addressed the principles and Combined Code (1998) provisions in section 1 (that is for companies), the Hampel Committee regarded section 2 as an integral part of the recommendations and it encouraged institutional investors to make voluntary disclosure to their clients and the public based on these recommendations.

4.15   Also during 1998 the government announced a new initiative to modernise company law, known as the Company Law Review, which was completed in July 2001. In 2002 the government issued a White Paper outlining potential new legislation covering various matters including a statutory statement outlining directors' duties. The government did not advocate legislating for corporate governance requirements and disclosures, but has supported the best practice approach of having a code for companies and investors to follow. Following the White Paper, the Companies Act 2006 received Royal Assent in November 2006. The Companies Act 2006 represents a major overhaul of company law, with all provisions coming into force by 1 October 2009.

4.16   In February 2002 the government announced that Sir Derek Higgs was to carry out a review of the role and effectiveness of non-executive directors. This review was in part building on the work of the company law review that noted a growing body of evidence from the USA suggesting that companies with a strong contingent of non-executives produced superior performance. Therefore, this review was focused on improving UK performance by progressive strengthening of the quality and role of non-executive directors. The terms of reference of the review noted that in the decade following the introduction of the Cadbury Code the role of non-executives had been seen to strengthen. The government sought recommendations from Higgs as to how to further strengthen the quality, independence and effectiveness of non-executive directors in the UK.

4.17 Another strong influence on the review was the timing of its launch, since it took place when company accounting scandals and collapses, predominantly taking place in the USA, were shocking investors and the public. Shortly after Higgs' review was announced, the government also formed a co-ordinating group to consider the implications for the arrangements for financial reporting and auditing in the UK in the light of the US scandals. This group requested the Financial Reporting Council ('FRC') to set up a working group to consider whether the remit of audit committees under the existing Combined Code (1998) needed to change. The working group was chaired by Sir Robert Smith and worked closely with Higgs. The group's output was known as the Smith Guidance. The group suggested new provisions for the Combined Code (1998) around the role and responsibilities of audit committees. These were incorporated into the revised draft Combined Code published as part of the Higgs Report in January 2003. The Smith Guidance was later revised in 2008 and further discussion of this can be found in paragraph 4.145.

4.18 The FRC approved the new Combined Code on Corporate Governance on 23 July 2003, hereafter referred to as the Combined Code (2003). The format of the Combined Code (2003) was slightly different to the original, containing both main and supporting principles with the provisions. The division into two sections, companies and institutional shareholders, remained the same.

4.19 The Combined Code (2003) applied for reporting years beginning on or after 1 November 2003. Initially the Financial Services Authority ('FSA') replaced the Combined Code (1998) that was annexed to the Listing Rules with the Combined Code (2003). Since 1 July 2005, the Combined Code (2003) has not been appended to the Listing Rules (although it remains linked to them), because it was recognised as being the responsibility of the FRC, rather than the UK Listing Authority.

4.20 The FRC performed an informal review of the implementation of the Combined Code (2003) during 2004 and a formal review in 2005. In its review, the FRC found no appetite for major change to the Combined Code (2003). The Code was reported to have bedded down well and to have had a positive impact on the quality of corporate governance amongst listed companies. This outcome resulted in the FRC proposing only a few minor modifications to the Code in early 2006, concluding that major change was unnecessary. Following a period of consultation on these minor modifications, the FRC issued a revised Combined

Code on Corporate Governance, hereafter referred to as the Combined Code (2006), in June 2006.

4.21   In 2007, the FRC performed a further review of the Combined Code. The review's main objective was to assess whether the Code was *"appropriately enabling UK listed companies to be led in a way which facilitates entrepreneurial success and the management of risk"*. The results of the consultation were published in November 2007 and concluded that the Combined Code continued to be broadly beneficial to the governance of UK listed companies, without undermining boards' entrepreneurial leadership.

4.21.1   Following the 2007 review of the Combined Code and a further consultation, the FRC issued a revised Combined Code on Corporate Governance, hereafter referred to as the Combined Code (2008). There were two changes from the 2006 Code: (i) removal of the restriction on an individual chairing more than one FTSE 100 company and (ii) a relaxation for smaller companies outside the FTSE 350 allowing the company chairman to be a member, but not chair, of the audit committee provided that he/she was considered independent on appointment. The Combined Code (2008) is applicable for accounting periods beginning on or after 29 June 2008 and is discussed further from paragraph 4.95.

4.22   In June 2008 the FSA revised the Listing Rules by introducing its Corporate Governance Rules to implement the recent EU Company Law 4th and 8th Directives requiring companies to have an audit committee (or similar body) and to publish a corporate governance statement. The FSA Corporate Governance Rules (which are equivalent to chapter 7 of the Disclosure Rules and Transparency Rules (DTR)) are also applicable for accounting periods beginning on or after 29 June 2008. Furthermore, the corporate governance compliance statement requirement of the Listing Rules was restricted to compliance with the main principles of the Code only and not the supporting principles as previously required (the requirement to explain departures from the Code's provisions remains).

4.23   In 2010, the FSA's Listing Regime was restructured into two new segments (premium and standard listed companies) with the objective of providing more clarity about the regime for market participants. The new listings regime changed the applicability of the FSA Corporate Governance Rules with effect from 6 April 2010. The FSA rules are discussed further from paragraph 4.43.

4.24   As noted earlier, the 2008 financial crisis triggered widespread reappraisal of the governance systems, which might have helped to alleviate it. In the UK, Sir David Walker was appointed by the UK government in 2009 to review the governance of banks and other financial industry entities (BOFIs), and the FRC brought forward its regular review of the Combined Code so that corporate governance for other sectors could be assessed at the same time. The final report by Sir David Walker, published in November 2009, includes 39 recommendations. The FSA is implementing those recommendations that are specific to BOFIs. The recommendations that apply to all listed companies have been implemented by the FRC as part of its review of the Combined Code. The Walker report is further discussed in paragraph 4.39.

4.25 The 2009-10 FRC review of the Combined Code resulted in publication of the revised UK Corporate Governance Code on 28 May 2010, hereafter referred to as the UK Corporate Governance Code (2010) (or UKCGC). This new edition of the Code applies to all premium listed companies for financial years beginning on or after 29 June 2010, including overseas companies. The purpose of renaming the Code is to avoid confusion among overseas companies and investors. As a result of changes to the FSA's Listing Regime, overseas companies with a premium Listing need to report against the Code for financial years beginning after 31 December 2009. Therefore, the change of name makes the Code's status as the UK's recognised corporate governance standard clearer to overseas investors and companies. As the UK Corporate Governance Code (2010) only starts to apply for financial years beginning on or after 29 June 2010, the Combined Code (2008) will still be applicable for December 2010 year-end reporters. See paragraph 4.77 for further information on the changes for overseas companies.

4.26 The overriding view emerging from the 2009-10 FRC review as a whole was that the governance code is effective and that the 'comply or explain' approach is sufficiently flexible to embrace different companies' circumstances. However, the FRC also concluded that much more attention needs to be paid to following the spirit of the Code as well as its letter and that the quality of corporate governance ultimately depends on board behaviour not process.

4.27 The FRC, therefore, made structural and wording changes, aimed at changing the 'tone' of the Code by giving more prominence to factors that underpin an effective board, such as the pivotal role of the chairman in leading the board, the responsibility of the non-executive directors to provide constructive challenge, the directors' expected time commitment, the board's composition and the board's responsibility for risk. Additionally, there are strengthened provisions on director development and two new provisions for FTSE 350 companies: externally facilitated performance reviews of boards at least every three years and annual re-election of all directors. The main changes in the UKCGC are further discussed from paragraph 4.221 onwards.

4.28 The FRC hopes that these changes will promote greater clarity and understanding with regard to the tasks of an effective board and that communication with shareholders will be more effective as a result. The FRC has also taken responsibility for a Stewardship Code for institutional investors to enhance shareholder engagement following Sir David Walker's recommendations. This resulted in the FRC publishing the first UK Stewardship Code in July 2010 with immediate effect. The previous Section 2 'Institutional Investors' of the Combined Code (2008), therefore, ceases to apply. The purpose of the Stewardship Code is to improve the quality of corporate governance through promoting better dialogue between shareholders and company boards, and more transparency about the way in which investors oversee the companies they own. The FRC is encouraging all institutional investors to report publicly on the extent to which they follow the UK Stewardship Code. Paragraph 4.343 onwards deals further with the UK Stewardship Code.

Corporate governance concepts

4.29   The concepts of the Hampel Report that led to the original Combined Code (1998) are still applicable to the Combined Code (2008) and the UK Corporate Governance Code. The key concepts are discussed below.

Avoidance of 'box ticking'

4.30   Hampel argued for flexibility when considering corporate governance standards and a proper regard for the individual circumstances of the companies concerned. Too often companies' experience of Cadbury and Greenbury was that the Codes had been treated as sets of prescriptive rules with shareholders and their advisors following a 'box ticking' approach focusing only on whether a rule had been complied with rather than considering the particular circumstances involved.

4.31   In Hampel's view this 'box ticking' approach did not take account of the diversity of circumstances and experience among different companies and within the same company. Although Hampel agreed with Cadbury that there are guidelines that are appropriate in most cases, Hampel considered that there will often be valid reasons for exceptions and companies should not be penalised for this. A focus by those considering corporate governance arrangements on 'box ticking' draws attention away from the diligent pursuit of corporate governance objectives and becomes an objective in itself. Compliance with every Code recommendation does not guarantee that a business will not fail. It is possible for a company to arrange matters so that the letter of every governance rule is complied with, but not the substance.

'Comply or explain'

4.32   As noted above, it was recognised that not all listed companies would be able to comply with all the provisions of the Combined Code, given their different circumstances, and that there would be valid reasons for such non-compliance. Therefore the 'comply or explain' principle was adopted so that if the company had not complied with the Combined Code's provisions during the year it could provide an explanation in respect of those provisions with which it did not comply. This principle allows companies to demonstrate proper consideration of the Combined Code without forcing them to adopt a 'box ticking' approach to compliance and is a key characteristic of a code-based (as opposed to legislation-based) governance framework.

4.33   Listing Rule 9.8.6 requires a premium listed company to give a two-part compliance statement in its annual financial report; first to explain how it has *applied* the Code's main principles and, secondly, how it has *complied* with its provisions. It is supported by companies, investors and regulators in the UK and has increasingly been adopted as a model in other financial markets. This is discussed further from paragraph 4.60 onwards.

Shareholder/stakeholder engagement

4.34 Hampel recognised that the board's relationship with the company's shareholders is different to that with other stakeholders. The board of directors is responsible for relations with stakeholders, but because the shareholders elect the directors the board is accountable to the shareholders. Although the directors' primary responsibility is to the shareholders, both present and future, different types of companies will have different relationships with stakeholders and the objective of enhancement of long-term shareholder value can only be met by directors developing and sustaining their relationship with stakeholders.

4.35 The Hampel Committee considered that if companies do not let their investors know what they are doing and how, the investors will look elsewhere for information on whether or not the board is managing the company's affairs well. As there is a risk that investors will draw erroneous conclusions, and as it is the investors who influence the company's market value, it is in the directors' interests to be open and transparent. The theme of the directors having a dialogue with investors based on mutual understanding of objectives appeared in the Higgs Report and was carried through into the Combined Code (2003).

4.36 This underlying philosophy is responsible for the inclusion of a section in all four Combined Codes (1998, 2003, 2006 and 2008) on institutional shareholders. Transparency and openness are less effective if the communication is a one-way process. Investors have duties and responsibilities too. Included in section 2 of each Combined Code are three main principles relating to institutional shareholders. These cover dialogue with companies, evaluation of governance disclosures and shareholder voting. In 2010 this section was replaced by the first UK Stewardship Code for institutional investors published by the FRC, which is discussed from paragraph 4.343.

Recent corporate governance reviews

4.37 As discussed in paragraph 4.24, the UK saw two corporate governance reviews in 2009-10: the Walker review of governance of banks and other financial industry entities; and the FRC review of the Combined Code (so that corporate governance for other sectors could be assessed at the same time). The output of the FRC review of the Combined Code is discussed from paragraph 4.221 and the Walker review is discussed from paragraph 4.39.

Themes of recent corporate governance reviews

4.38 Similar themes emerged from both Walker and the FRC reviews around:

- Board behaviour – Were non-executive directors (NEDs) sufficiently robust in their challenge to management? Commentators questioned whether they spent sufficient time in the business to enable them to fully understand the business and ask the necessary probing questions.

- Board balance in terms of skills and experience rather than independence – It was thought that there was too much emphasis on the independence of directors without taking into account the directors' expertise. Bank boards in particular were getting larger, in part, arguably, driven by the independence rules. Large boards create challenges, as decision-making and arriving at consensus is more difficult.

- Engagement between boards and shareholders – Was there effective engagement? What were the investors doing to hold boards to account for their actions? It was recognised that for the 'comply or explain' mechanism to work effectively, there needed to be good two-way communication between boards and investors. Both companies and shareholders reported frustration over the quality of engagement. Companies criticised investors for taking a box-ticking approach, while investors criticised boards for approaching communication as a presentation, rather than a dialogue.

- Board's oversight of risk management – Did some boards lose sight of the level of risk being taken? Was risk oversight undertaken by the board, or delegated to the audit committee or the risk committee? It became apparent that there were serious deficiencies in prudent oversight of risk management in banks and financial institutions.

- Performance-related pay – In some cases, reward was not linked to the company's long term interests and reward was not compatible with the company's risk policies.

These themes drove the Walker recommendations and the changes to the Combined Code that are reflected in the UK Corporate Governance Code.

The Walker Review

4.39   Sir David Walker was appointed in 2009 by the UK Government to lead a review of corporate governance in banks and other financial industry entities (BOFIs). The terms of reference of the Walker Review included considering:

- The effectiveness of risk management at board level, including the incentives in remuneration policy to manage risk effectively.

- Board balance in banks, in terms of skills, experience and independence.

- Effectiveness of board practices and performance of committees.

- Institutional investor engagement.

- Degree of consistency of UK with international practice and how to promulgate best practice.

4.40 The final Walker Report, published in November 2009, highlighted five key themes and included 39 recommendations. The five key themes are summarised below:

- Both the UK unitary board structure and the FRC Combined Code remain fit for purpose. Combined with tougher capital and liquidity requirements and a tougher regulatory stance on the part of the FSA, the 'comply or explain' approach to guidance and provisions under the Combined Code provides the surest route to better corporate governance practice, with some additional BOFI-specific elements to be taken forward through the FSA.

- The principal deficiencies in BOFI boards related much more to patterns of behaviour than to organisation. The most critical need is for an environment in which effective challenge of the executive is expected and achieved in the boardroom before decisions are taken on major risk and strategic issues.

- Given that the overriding strategic objective of a BOFI is the successful management of financial risk, board-level engagement in the high-level risk oversight should be materially increased with particular attention to the monitoring of risk and discussion leading to decisions on the entity's risk appetite and tolerance.

- There is a need for fund managers and other major shareholders to engage more productively with their investee companies.

- Substantial enhancement is needed in board level oversight of remuneration policies, in particular in respect of variable pay and in associated disclosures. The remit and responsibility of board remuneration committees should be extended beyond board members to cover the remuneration structure and levels for all senior employees whose role puts them in a position of significant influence on the entity's risk profile.

4.41 Walker made 39 recommendations. The key recommendations for BOFIs included:

- To enhance risk management, have a separate risk committee and strengthen the chief risk officer's role .

- The chairman to face annual re-election and the chairman of the remuneration committee to face re-election if the remuneration report gets less than 75 per cent approval of the shareholders.

- Non-executives to spend substantially more time on the job. An induction process to be introduced for all non-executive directors and regular training. Non-executive directors to face tougher scrutiny under the FSA authorisation process.

- On remuneration, to defer incentive payments to align reward with sustainable performance and consider clawback provision to reclaim amounts in cases of misstatement or misconduct.

- New remuneration disclosure of 'high end' remuneration on a banded basis for those earning over £1 million.

- A Stewardship Code for institutional investors under FRC.

4.42 The FSA is currently in the process of implementing those recommendations that are specific to banks and other financial industry entities. The recommendations that apply to all listed companies have been implemented by the FRC as part of its review of the Combined Code (2008). The FRC has published the first UK Stewardship Code; see paragraph 4.343.

FSA corporate governance rules

Revised FSA Corporate Governance Rules — impact of Disclosure Rules and Transparency Rules

4.43 On 27 June 2008, the FSA released revisions to the Listing Rules and the DTR to implement amendments to the EU 4th and 8th Company Law Directives and chapter 7 of the DTR became the FSA Corporate Governance Rules. The revised requirements are effective for accounting periods beginning on or after 29 June 2008 and are discussed further below.

4.44 The advent of the Disclosure Rules and Transparency Rules (DTR)/ FSA Corporate Governance Rules adds another set of rules governing parts of the front end of the annual report to the principles and provisions of the Combined Code (CC) or UK Corporate Governance Code (UKCGC), the Listing Rules (LR), and the legislative requirements of the Companies Act 2006 (CA 2006) and its accompanying regulations and instruments. Key elements of the DTR/ FSA Corporate Governance Rules are set out from paragraph 4.46.

4.45 The table below summarises the corporate governance requirements under the Codes, Listing Rules and DTR for each type of listed company. The UKCGC applies to financial years starting on or after 29 June 2010 and the CC applies to periods prior to this date.

	UK premium	UK standard	Overseas premium	Overseas standard
Listing Rule 9.8.6 (5) and (6) (Compliance statement)	■	x	■	x
The CC or UKCGC ('comply or explain')	■	x	■ (for financial years beginning after 31/12/09)	x
Listing Rule 9.8.6 (3) (Going concern statement)	■	x	x (though CC provision C.1.2 and UKGCG provision C.1.3 requires similar going concern disclosures)	x
FSA Corporate Governance Rules				
■ DTR 7.1 Audit Committee	■	■	x	x
■ DTR 7.2 Corporate Governance Statement	■	■	■	■
Auditors' Report (LR 9.8.10) (9 Code provisions)	■	x	■ (though APB guidance relates only to UK companies)	x

Requirement to have an audit committee (DTR 7.1)

4.46 The DTR requires certain companies (see para 4.47) to have an audit committee (or a body performing equivalent functions). At least one member must be independent and at least one member (who may, but need not be, the same person) must have competence in accounting and/or auditing. [DTR 7.1.1R].

As a minimum the relevant body must:

■ Monitor the financial reporting process.

■ Monitor the effectiveness of the internal control, internal audit where applicable and risk management systems.

■ Monitor the statutory audit of the annual and consolidated financial statements.

■ Review and monitor the independence of the statutory auditor and, in particular, the provision of additional services provided by the auditors.

The FSA has indicated that there are a number of overlaps between the Combined Code/ UKCGC and the DTR. These have been summarised in paragraph 4.59.

4.47 DTR 7.1 applies to UK incorporated companies with transferable securities admitted to trading on either the London Stock Exchange or the PLUS-listed markets and that are required to appoint a statutory auditor. There are exemptions to this requirement for:

■ A listed company whose parent is subject to this rule (or an equivalent rule of any EEA State).

■ An issuer whose sole business is to act as the issuer of asset-backed securities, provided that the issuer makes a public statement explaining why it is not appropriate to have an audit committee.

■ A credit institution whose shares are not admitted to trading if the total nominal value of its listed debt securities is less than €100 million and the company has not prepared a prospectus in accordance with section 85 of the Financial Services and Markets Act 2000.

4.48 The FSA has applied DTR 7.1 only to UK incorporated issuers, not to overseas issuers.

Requirement to present a corporate governance statement (DTR 7.2)

4.49 For accounting periods beginning on or after 29 June 2008, companies (see para 4.51) are required to present a corporate governance statement in one of the following ways. It may be included: as part of the directors' report (or incorporated by reference into the directors' report); separately issued to accompany the annual report and financial statements; or made available on the company's web site, but with cross-references from the directors' report. Where a company chooses to present its corporate governance statement separately there are new Companies Act requirements in respect of the approval, signing and filing of the separate governance statement. These requirements are discussed further in paragraph 4.334.

4.50 It should be noted that the Listing Rules (LR 9.8.9) require the corporate governance statement to be included in the company's annual report; in effect this currently prevents the statement being presented separately from the annual report in the UK. The FRC consulted on this issue to consider whether to change the Code and allow companies a choice of whether to place the corporate governance statement on the company website or in the annual report, but did not resolve the point when it published the final UKCGC.

4.51 DTR 7.2 applies to all companies with shares admitted to trading on the London Stock Exchange or PLUS-listed markets or traded on a multi-lateral trading facility. [DTR 1B.1.5, 1B.1.6]. In this respect, it is different from DTR 7.1, which applies only to UK incorporated issuers under the FSA Corporate Governance Rules.

4.52 The DTR contains a number of disclosures that must be given in the corporate governance statement. Many of those requirements are also dealt with elsewhere in UK legislation or guidance. The requirements are listed below, together with any overlap with other legislation or guidance.

4.53   The corporate governance statement must contain a reference to:

■   Any corporate governance code to which the company is subject.

■   Any corporate governance code which the company may have voluntarily decided to apply.

■   All relevant information about the corporate governance practices applied beyond the requirements under national law.

■   Where any corporate governance code that is applied (either mandatorily or voluntarily) is publicly available.

■   An explanation of any departure from any corporate governance code applied. (This overlaps with the 'comply or explain' rule in LR 9.8.6 R(5) – see further para 4.70).

[DTR 7.2.2R, 7.2.3R].

4.54   In addition, the corporate governance statement must contain:

■   A description of the main features of the company's internal control and risk management systems in relation to the financial reporting process. [DTR 7.2.5R]. (See para 4.56.)

■   The information required to be included in the directors' report by paragraphs 13(2)(c), (d), (f), (h) and (i) of Schedule 7 to the Large and Medium-sized Companies and Groups (Accounts and Reports) Regulations 2008, resulting from the EU Takeover Directive. [DTR 7.2.6R]. (These requirements are discussed further in chapter 3.) Whilst these disclosures now need to be made in both the corporate governance statement *and* the directors' report, the disclosure may continue to be given once and appropriate cross-reference made.

■   A description of the composition and operation of the company's administrative, management and supervisory bodies and their committees. [DTR 7.2.7R].

4.55   The FSA has indicated that compliance with provisions A.1.1, A.1.2, A.4.6, B.2.1 and C.3.3 of the Combined Code (or A.1.1, A.1.2, B.2.4, D.2.1 and C.3.3 of UKCGC) will ensure compliance with DTR 7.2.7R. See the summary table of overlapping provisions in paragraph 4.59 for more details.

4.56   Over and above the recommendations of the Combined Code/UKCGC, there is a requirement in DTR 7.2.5R for a *description* of the main features of the company's internal control and risk management systems *in relation to the financial reporting process*. The FRC has indicated that while this requirement in DTR 7.2.5R differs from the recommendation in the Combined Code/UKCGC provision C.2.1 (see below), the FRC envisages that both the Code and the DTR can be satisfied by a single internal control statement.

> "*The board should, at least annually conduct a review of the effectiveness of the group's system of internal controls and should report to shareholders that they have done so. The review should cover all material controls, including financial, operational and compliance controls and risk management systems*".

[CC C.2.1].

The wording of C.2.1 has been updated slightly in the UKCGC to place more emphasis on the risk management systems:

> "*The board should, at least annually, conduct a review of the effectiveness of the company's risk management and internal control systems and should report to shareholders that that have done so. The review should cover all material controls, including financial, operational and compliance controls.*"

[UKCGC, C.2.1].

4.57   For a group, there is also a requirement to include a *description* of the main features of the group's internal control and risk management systems *in relation to the process for preparing consolidated financial statements*. [DTR 7.2.10R].

Table 4.1

Centrica plc – Annual Report – 31 December 2009

Corporate Governance Report (extract)

The Centrica Controls Board, whose members are the Group Finance Director, Director of Financial Control, Head of Audit and Risk and Business Unit Finance Directors, is responsible for ensuring appropriate internal controls are in place over financial reporting processes and the related IT systems. Its responsibilities are discharged through the Centrica Controls Steering Group (CCSG) which met five times during 2009.

The CCSG monitors the risks and associated controls over financial reporting processes, including the consolidation process. The financial reporting controls are monitored and maintained through the use of internal control frameworks which address key financial reporting risks, including risks arising from changes in the business or accounting standards. Effectiveness is assessed through quarterly self-certification and independent testing of the controls.

The integrity of the Company's public financial reporting is further supported by a number of processes and steps to provide assurance over the completeness and accuracy of the content, including:

- review by members of the Executive Team;
- verification exercises;
- review and recommendation by the Audit Committee; and
- review and approval by the Board.

Interaction between the FSA Rules and the Corporate Governance Code

4.58 Although many of the DTR requirements overlap with provisions of the Combined Code/UKCGC, the FRC has indicated that, where a company chooses to 'explain' rather than 'comply' with any of the overlapping provisions, it will need to ensure that it, nonetheless, meets the requirements in the FSA Rules. It is possible to comply with Combined Code/UKCGC provision C.2.1 but still be in breach of DTR 7.2.5R and, therefore, the Listing Rules. Conversely, if a smaller listed company has only one independent non-executive director on the audit committee, the company will need to explain a departure from Combined Code/UKCGC provision C.3.1, but it will have complied with DTR 7.1.1R. In this case, non-compliance with the Combined Code/UKCGC does not necessarily mean a breach of the DTR.

4.59 The table below shows the overlapping provisions between the DTR and the Combined Code / UKCGC:

DTR	Combined Code / UKCGC
DTR 7.1.1R: Minimum requirements on composition of the audit committee or equivalent body.	Provision C.3.1: Recommended composition of the Audit Committee.
DTR 7.1.3R: Minimum functions of the Audit Committee or equivalent body.	Provision C.3.2: Recommended minimum terms of reference for the Audit. Committee.
DTR 7.1.5R: Disclosure of composition and function of Audit Committee (or equivalent) in the annual report. DTR 7.1.7G states that compliance with Code provisions A.1.2, C.3.1, C.3.2 and C.3.3 will result in compliance with DTR 7.1.1R to DTR 7.1.5R.	Provision A.1.2: The annual report should identify members of the board and board committees. Provision C.3.1 and C.3.2: See above. Provision C.3.3: The annual report should describe the work of the audit committee (also see further recommendations in the FRC Guidance on Audit Committees).
DTR 7.2.5R: The corporate governance statement must include a description of the main features of the company's internal control and risk management systems in relation to the financial reporting process. While this requirement differs from the Combined Code/UKCGC requirement, it is envisaged that both could be met by a single internal control statement. See paragraph 4.56.	Provision C.2.1: The Board must report that a review of the effectiveness of the risk management and internal control systems has been carried out. Further recommendations on the content of the internal control statement are set out in the Turnbull Guidance. NB 'risk management' is a new requirement brought in with the UKCGC Provision C.2.1.

DTR 7.2.7R: The corporate governance statement must include a description of the composition and operation of the administrative, management and supervisory bodies and their committees. DTR 7.2.8G states that compliance with Combined Code provisions A.1.1, A.1.2, A.4.6, B.2.1 and C.3.3 (UKCGC provisions A.1.1, A.1.2, B.2.4, D.2.1 and C.3.3) will result in compliance with DTR 7.2.7R.	This requirement overlaps with a number of different provisions of the Code: A.1.1: the annual report should include a statement of how the board operates. A.1.2: the annual report should identify members of the board and board committees. A.4.6 (2008)/ B.2.4 (UKCGC): the annual report should describe the work of the nomination committee. B.2.1 (2008)/ D.2.1 (UKCGC): a description of the work of the remuneration committee should be made available. [Note: in order to comply with DTR 7.2.7R this information will need to be included in the corporate governance statement.] C.3.3: the annual report should describe the work of the audit committee.

Governance reporting

UK premium listed companies — Listing Rules — two-part statement

4.60 A premium listed company is required to include in its annual report and accounts a two-part statement on corporate governance. Whether reporting under the Combined Code (2008) or the UKCGC, the first part of the statement requires the company to make a statement explaining how it has applied the main principles. This statement is to provide sufficient information to enable the company's shareholders to evaluate how the principles have been applied. [LR 9.8.6R(5)].

4.61 In practice, few companies list out every main principle and discuss specifically how each has been applied. However, it should be possible to deduce this from the content of the corporate governance statement as a whole. The Combined Code (2008) includes guidance in its preamble to assist boards in applying this Listing Rule requirement. See also paragraph 4.66.

Statement 1 — Applying the main principles (Combined Code (2008))

4.62 The main principles in Section 1 of the Combined Code are included in the following table. These must all be applied by the listed company to comply with the Code. The supporting principles and specific Code provisions are designed to assist the preparer in addressing each of the main principles. The table below also shows the paragraph number where they are discussed in more detail.

Section	Area	Main principle
A Directors	A.1 The board	Every company should be headed by an effective board, which is collectively responsible for the success of the company. (See paragraph 4.100 for supporting principles and disclosure requirements.)
	A.2 Chairman and chief executive	There should be a clear division of responsibilities at the head of the company between the running of the board and the executive responsibility for the running of the company's business. No one individual should have unfettered powers of decision. (See para 4.100.)
	A.3 Board balance and independence	The board should include a balance of executive and non-executive directors (and in particular independent non-executive directors) such that no individual or small group of individuals can dominate the board's decision taking. (See para 4.119.)
	A.4 Appointments to the board	There should be a formal, rigorous and transparent procedure for the appointment of new directors to the board. (See para 4.127.)
	A.5 Information and professional development	The board should be supplied in a timely manner with information in a form and of a quality appropriate to enable it to discharge its duties. All directors should receive induction on joining the board and should regularly update and refresh their skills and knowledge. (See para 4.127.)
	A.6 Performance evaluation	The board should undertake a formal and rigorous annual evaluation of its own performance and that of its committees and individual directors. (See para 4.113.)
	A.7 Re-election	All directors should be submitted for re-election at regular intervals, subject to continued satisfactory performance. The board should ensure planned and progressive refreshing of the board. (See para 4.109.)

B Remuneration	B.1 The level and make up of remuneration	Levels of remuneration should be sufficient to attract, retain and motivate directors of the quality required to run the company successfully, but a company should avoid paying more than is necessary for this purpose. A significant proportion of executive directors' remuneration should be structured so as to link rewards to corporate and individual performance. (See para 4.153.)
	B.2 Procedure	There should be a formal and transparent procedure for developing policy on executive remuneration and for fixing the remuneration packages of individual directors. No director should be involved in deciding his or her own remuneration. (See para 4.153.)
C Accountability and audit	C.1 Financial reporting	The board should present a balanced and understandable assessment of the company's position and prospects. (See para 4.192.)
	C.2 Internal control	The board should maintain a sound system of internal control to safeguard shareholders' investment and the company's assets. (See para 4.161.)
	C.3 Audit committee and auditors	The board should establish formal and transparent arrangements for considering how they should apply the financial reporting and internal control principles and for maintaining an appropriate relationship with the company's auditors. (See para 4.138.)
D Relations with shareholders	D.1 Dialogue with institutional shareholders	There should be a dialogue with shareholders based on the mutual understanding of objectives. The board as a whole has responsibility for ensuring that a satisfactory dialogue with shareholders takes place. (See para 4.210.)
	D.2 Constructive use of the AGM	The board should use the AGM to communicate with investors and to encourage their participation. (See para 4.217.)

Statement 1 — Applying the main principles (UKCGC)

4.63 The main principles in the UKCGC are included in the following table. These must all be applied by the listed company to comply with the Code. The supporting principles and specific Code provisions are discussed later in this chapter, and are designed to assist the preparer in addressing each of the main principles. The table below also shows the paragraph number where they are discussed in more detail.

Section	Area	Main principle
A Leadership	A.1 The role of the board	Every company should be headed by an effective board which is collectively responsible for the long-term success of the company. (See para 4.237.)
	A.2 Division of responsibilities	There should be a clear division of responsibilities at the head of the company between the running of the board and the executive responsibility for the running of the company's business. No one individual should have unfettered powers of decision. (See para 4.237.)
	A.3 The chairman	The chairman is responsible for leadership of the board and ensuring its effectiveness on all aspects of its role. (See para 4.237.)
	A.4 Non-executive directors	As part of their role as members of a unitary board, non-executive directors should constructively challenge and help develop proposals on strategy. (See para 4.237.)
B Effectiveness	B.1 The composition of the board	The board and its committees should have the appropriate balance of skills, experience, independence and knowledge of the company to enable them to discharge their respective duties and responsibilities effectively. (See para 4.262.)
	B.2 Appointments to the board	There should be a formal, rigorous and transparent procedure for the appointment of new directors to the board. (See para 4.274.)
	B.3 Commitment	All directors should be able to allocate sufficient time to the company to discharge their responsibilities effectively. (See para 4.274.)

	B.4 Development	All directors should receive induction on joining the board and should regularly update and refresh their skills and knowledge. (See para 4.274.)
	B.5 Information and support	The board should be supplied in a timely manner with information in a form and of a quality appropriate to enable it to discharge its duties. (See para 4.274.)
	B.6 Evaluation	The board should undertake a formal and rigorous annual evaluation of its own performance and that of its committees and individual directors. (See para 4.251.)
	B.7 Re-election	All directors should be submitted for re-election at regular intervals, subject to continued satisfactory performance. (See para 4.246.)
C Accountability	C.1 Financial and business reporting	The board should present a balanced and understandable assessment of the company's position and prospects. (See para 4.306.)
	C.2 Risk management and internal control	The board is responsible for determining the nature and extent of the significant risks it is willing to take in achieving its strategic objectives. The board should maintain sound risk management and internal control systems. (See para 4.300.)
	C.3 Audit committee and auditors	The board should establish formal and transparent arrangements for considering how they should apply the corporate reporting and risk management and internal control principles and for maintaining an appropriate relationship with the company's auditor. (See para 4.287.)
D Remuneration	D.1 The level and components of remuneration	Levels of remuneration should be sufficient to attract, retain and motivate directors of the quality required to run the company successfully, but a company should avoid paying more than is necessary for this purpose. A significant proportion of executive directors' remuneration should be structured so as to link rewards to corporate and individual performance. (See para 4.294.)

	D.2 Procedure	There should be a formal and transparent procedure for developing policy on executive remuneration and for fixing the remuneration packages of individual directors. No director should be involved in deciding his or her own remuneration. (See para 4.294.)
E Relations with shareholders	E.1 Dialogue with shareholders	There should be a dialogue with shareholders based on the mutual understanding of objectives. The board as a whole has responsibility for ensuring that a satisfactory dialogue with shareholders takes place. (See para 4.316.)
	E.2 Constructive use of the AGM	The board should use the AGM to communicate with investors and to encourage their participation. (See para 4.321.)

Statement 2 — compliance throughout the period

4.64　In the second part of the corporate governance statement required by the Listing Rules, premium listed companies have to report whether or not the company has complied throughout the accounting period with the provisions set out in section 1 of the Code. Where a company has not complied with the Combined Code (2008) or UKCGC provisions, or has only complied with some of these provisions or (in the case of provisions whose requirements are of a continuing nature) has complied for only part of an accounting period, the compliance statement must identify the Code provisions with which the company has not complied, for what part of the period such non-compliance continued (where relevant) and give reasons for any non-compliance. [LR 9.8.6 R(6)].

4.65　There is no requirement in either Code specifying where the statement of compliance should be located within the annual report. Such statements are commonly included within a separate section dealing with corporate governance just after the directors' report, or within the directors' report itself. Occasionally, the issue is dealt with or referred to within the chairman's statement. It is not appropriate to include the statement within the audited financial statements. See paragraph 4.49 for discussion of the impact of the Companies Act 2006 on these requirements.

4.66　For a company that complies with the provisions of the Combined Code (2008) or the UKCGC in their entirety, it is reasonable to assume that, in doing so, they have applied the main principles.

4.67　Where an explanation of non-compliance with one or more of the Code's provisions is given in respect of one particular main principle, it will be necessary to include an explanation of how the company has, nonetheless, applied that particular main principle.

4.68   At the extreme, where an explanation of non-compliance with a number of the Code's provisions is given and those provisions support the application of a number of main principles, it may be appropriate for the company to explain how it has nevertheless applied the Code's main principles.

4.69   In support of the compliance statement, boards or audit committees may expect to see a paper that sets out how the company complies with each aspect of the Combined Code/UKCGC, supported by relevant documentation. It is helpful for the board or audit committee to minute its approval of such a paper.

Statements of non-compliance with Code provisions

4.70   Any element of non-compliance with Code provisions for any part of the period must be identified, giving reasons. The specific aspect of the Code must be identified. This does not mean that the paragraph number in the relevant Code must be used, although some companies might do so. It would not be adequate simply to list the paragraph numbers of the Code, because the reader would have to refer elsewhere to discover the significance of the statement.

4.71   Statements of non-compliance might become quite lengthy where there are a significant number of departures from the relevant Code's recommendations. However, it would be very rare indeed for a company to fail to comply with all aspects. For example, under the Combined Code (2008) few boards would wish to suggest that they do not *'meet sufficiently regularly'*, do not include directors who are *'independent in character and judgement'*, or that the aim of the remuneration committee is *'rewarding poor performance'*. [CC A.1.1, A.3.1, B.1.5].

4.72   The shortest way to make a statement of non-compliance is to provide a list of areas of non-compliance with individual provisions or overall reasons for non-compliance. However, such a minimalist approach will be very negative, because it focuses on the areas of non-compliance. It is preferable to give a more balanced statement which gives information on compliance and/or on areas where the company is moving towards compliance or has decided that compliance will not best suit the circumstances of the company and, therefore, a departure from the Combined Code or UKCGC provisions is appropriate.

4.73   There could be valid reasons why some of the provisions have not been followed or some alternative procedures may have been adopted. As long as the company explains and has reasonable justification for any non-compliance with specific aspects and governance is effective in practice, then in the spirit of transparency, it is hoped that the market will react in a positive way.

4.74   However, as discussed in paragraph 4.58, it is necessary to bear in mind that, for accounting years beginning on or after 29 June 2008, where a company is explaining a departure from any of the Code's provisions that overlap with that disclosure requirement of the DTR, then this departure from the Code may result in a breach of the DTR.

4.75 It is recommended that shareholders and others monitoring compliance with the Combined Code (2008) or UKCGC should do so with flexibility, common sense and with regard to the individual company's circumstances, for example, in a newly listed company in its first year of reporting compliance with the relevant Code. Effective shareholder engagement is one of the areas that recent corporate governance reviews have focussed on and viewed as being of critical importance. In general it is argued that, on the one hand, there need to be sufficient institutional investors willing and able to engage actively with the companies in which they invest and, on the other hand, that companies must be willing to welcome communication with investors as an opportunity to obtain external views on their performance. Further discussion of the corporate governance reviews and recent developments in respect of the UK Stewardship Code can be found in paragraph 4.290.

UK standard listed companies

4.76 UK standard listed companies are required to comply with both DTR 7.1, 'Audit Committees', and DTR 7.2, 'Corporate governance'. UK standard listed companies are not, however, required to report under the Combined Code (or UKCGC). See paragraphs 4.45 to 4.57 for details of the DTR requirements.

Overseas companies — standard and premium listed companies

4.77 As discussed above, from 6 April 2010, the Listing Rules were amended to reclassify listed entities from having either 'primary' or 'secondary' listings to 'premium' or 'standard'. One effect of the changes in the Listing regulations is that overseas companies, which did not previously have to comply with the Combined Code, are now required under the Listing Rules to report against the Code if they have a premium listing.

4.78 Whilst only premium listed companies (both UK and overseas) are required to comply with the Combined Code (2008) or UKCGC, all listed companies, whether standard or premium, are required to comply with the DTR requirements in respect of corporate governance (DTR 7.2).

4.79 Where a standard listed overseas company applies any corporate governance code, DTR 7.2.2R and 7.2.3R require it effectively to 'comply or explain' against that code. This could significantly increase the scope of its governance disclosures in some cases.

4.80 The FSA has not applied Listing Rule 9.8.6 (3), which requires "*a statement made by the directors that the business is a going concern*" to overseas incorporated premium listed companies (and Listing Rule 9.8.6 (3) does not apply to any standard listed company). However, provision C.1.2 of the Combined Code (2008), or provision C.1.3 of the UKCGC, states that "*the directors should report. . . . . that the business is a going concern. . .*" so any failure to do this would need to be explained under Listing Rule 9.8.6 (6) by an overseas premium listed company.

Other aspects of reporting and compliance

Good practice reporting

4.81   A number of UK listed companies have gone above and beyond the disclosure recommendations of the Combined Code (2008) in their corporate governance statement. PricewaterhouseCoopers' compendium, 'Corporate governance: Best practice reporting' last issued in January 2010, features a wide range of good practice disclosures from the corporate governance statements published in annual reports. It provides examples of good practice disclosure in terms of both format and content and may be used as a practical guide to preparing corporate governance statements. Companies should, however, ensure that their statements reflect their own particular circumstances and are specific to the company and its activities during the year or period under review.

Structure of front end, quality of reporting and compliance

4.82   To improve the quality of their reporting, companies often want to bring together all the required disclosures relating to a topic in one place. This approach is also specifically advocated by the regulators: for instance, the October 2009 FRC publication, 'Going concern and liquidity risk: guidance for directors of UK companies', advocates bringing together in one place in the annual report the various disclosures around going concern.

4.83   The challenge for this approach is that the various pieces of legislation and guidance often specify where certain information must be given – usually in the directors' report or in the governance statement. For instance, the disclosure requirements of DTR 7.2.5R around internal control over the financial reporting process must be dealt with in the governance statement and the disclosures on risk management and internal control required by the 2005 Turnbull guidance are also normally included in the governance statement, but the principal risk disclosures required by section 417(3)(b) of the Companies Act 2006, (to which the Turnbull disclosures should relate) must be in the directors' report.

4.84   To address this, many companies follow the principle of DTR 7.2.1R and include the corporate governance statement within the directors' report: in practice, they frequently include in the annual report a section entitled, 'Report of the directors' (or similar) which has, as subsections within it, the governance statement, remuneration report, and the technical requirements of the directors' report. It should be noted that this approach may also allow the directors to take advantage of the 'safe harbour' provisions of section 463 of 2006 Act in relation to the other statements included within the report of the directors.

Use of cross-references and 'incorporation by reference'

4.85　Where the governance statement is included within the directors' report (or the 'report of the directors'), it will often be necessary to provide cross-references to other parts of the directors' report to ensure regulatory requirements are met.

4.86　Where it is not a subsection of the directors' report, companies may 'incorporate by reference' the governance statement within the directors' report. In this situation, the mechanism used to link the two should be more formally worded than a simple cross-reference and should include a phrase such as *"the governance statement is incorporated by reference into"* or *"the governance statement forms part of"* the directors' report. Whether this mechanism would bring with it the safe harbour protections is a legal matter on which companies may wish to take advice.

4.87　Companies may also incorporate by reference into the governance statement parts of other components of the front end of the annual report. For instance, the risk management and internal control disclosures may be given in the business review, but certain parts may relate to the Turnbull guidance and allow the company to comply with the related Code provision on internal control. These specific parts may be incorporated by reference into the governance statement.

Differences for smaller and FTSE 350 listed companies

4.88　The Combined Code (2008) provides a small number of concessions specific to smaller listed companies (those below the FTSE 350 for all of the preceding year):

- The board, the audit committee and the remuneration committee should have at least two independent non-executive directors. [CC A.3.2, CC B.2.1, CC C3.1].

- The company chairman may be a member of, but not chair, the audit committee so long as he or she was considered independent on appointment as chairman. This appointment would be in addition to the existing independent non-executive members of the committee.

4.89　These concessions are carried forward into the UKCGC. The UKCGC also introduced two new Code provisions that apply only to FTSE 350 companies:

- Evaluation of the board of FTSE 350 companies should be externally facilitated at least every three years. A statement should be made available of whether an external facilitator has any other connection with the company. [UKCGC B.6.2].

- All directors of FTSE 350 companies should be subject to annual election by shareholders. All other directors should be subject to election by shareholders at the first annual general meeting after their appointment, and to re-election thereafter at intervals of no more than three years. Non-executive directors who have served longer than nine years should be subject to annual re-election. The names of directors submitted for election or re-election should be accompanied by sufficient biographical details and any other relevant information to enable shareholders to take an informed decision on their election. [UKCGC B.7.1].

Non-listed organisations and AIM

4.90   Where non-listed organisations choose voluntarily to report on compliance with the Combined Code (2008) or UKCGC, we recommend that they report fully as though they were listed. We, therefore, advise against phrases such as: "*We comply with all aspects of the Combined Code relevant to the organisation*".

4.91   This form of disclosure on its own provides the reader with no indication of what aspects of the Code the organisation has considered relevant and, therefore, is of no real value. Some organisations, such as the National Health Service Management Executive, have issued their own code of governance. In these situations, reference will of course be made to such codes instead.

4.92   Although non-listed organisations are encouraged to aim at meeting the Combined Code or UKCGC's recommendations, this has been rare to date outside of public interest entities and financial services institutions.

4.93   Companies that are considering the possibility of a listing will need to consider establishing appropriate governance procedures well in advance of coming to the market. In particular, they should review and, if necessary, improve their systems of internal control. In seeking a listing, companies are expected to make a statement of 'support' for the principles of the relevant Code. It is also usual to describe the steps the company has taken to comply in the areas of non-executive directors, audit, remuneration and nomination committees (describing their composition and principal functions), even if they have only recently been appointed or established. The sponsors will also normally expect to see significant moves toward compliance in other areas. In their first period following listing, the UK Listing Authority has generally permitted new registrants to make a statement of compliance for the period from the date of listing only, rather than for the full accounting period. Nevertheless, it will be important to be well prepared, because certain procedures can take some time to implement.

4.94   Companies that are considering listing on AIM should also consider establishing appropriate governance procedures. Although AIM companies are not required to follow the recommendations in the Code it is considered best practice, with the focus being on applying the 'comply or explain' principle to key areas such as board composition, audit and remuneration committees, board effectiveness and internal control.

The Combined Code (2008)

Overview of the contents of the Combined Code (2008)

4.95 The Combined Code (2008) comprises main principles, supporting principles and provisions. The structure is as follows:

- Section 1 – Companies:
  - A – Directors.
  - B – Remuneration.
  - C – Accountability and audit.
  - D – Relations with shareholders.
- Section 2 – Institutional shareholders:
  - E – Institutional shareholders.

4.96 Section 1 of the Combined Code (2008) contains the corporate governance main and supporting principles and the provisions applicable to all premium listed companies. It is this section that is covered by the company's two-part statement required by the Listing Rules (discussed further in para 4.60). Section 2 of the Combined Code (2008) contains main and supporting principles applicable to institutional shareholders with regard to dialogue with companies, evaluation of a company's corporate governance arrangements and shareholder voting. This section ceased to apply on 2 July 2010 when the UK Stewardship Code for institutional investors came into effect. The UK Stewardship Code is discussed from paragraph 4.343.

Schedules forming part of the Combined Code

4.97 In the Combined Code (2008) three schedules provide further information:

- Schedule A – Provisions on the design of performance related remuneration.
- Schedule B – Guidance on liability of non-executive directors: care, skill and diligence.
- Schedule C – Disclosure of corporate governance arrangements.

Schedule A was part of the Combined Code (1998). Schedules B and C were introduced as part of the Combined Code (2003). Schedule B provides a useful summary of the liability issues that impact non-executive directors. Schedule C focuses on disclosure and has been modified by the Combined Code (2008) and the FSA Rules on Corporate Governance. It summarises the information that should be included in a company's annual report and that which should be 'made available' (that is, *via* the company's web site). In addition, it contains details of the information that the board should set out to shareholders in relation to election or re-election of directors and when recommending appointment or reappointment of an external auditor.

4.98   The Listing Rules requirements in relation to the Combined Code have been included within Schedule C of the Combined Code (2008) for clarity and convenience.

4.99   Key areas of governance covered by Section 1 of the Combined Code (2008) are set out below. For each area, the following information is provided, where applicable:

■   The main and supporting principles.

■   Specific disclosure requirements.

■   Other related provisions or guidance which the company should apply.

■   Details of any other guidance that should be considered when dealing with the relevant area.

■   Trends in best practice disclosures, in some cases addressing themes of the 2009 governance reviews (see para 4.38). Such disclosures, while not mandatory, may help to avoid a 'box-ticking' approach to governance reporting.

Disclosures required under DTR 7 are not included below other than for comparative purposes against Code disclosures. See paragraphs 4.46 to 4.57 for details of these.

The board

Principles

4.100   The main principles that should be applied in relation to the board are as follows:

■   Every company should be headed by an effective board, which is collectively responsible for the success of the company. [CC Main principle A.1].

■   There should be a clear division of responsibilities at the head of the company between the running of the board and the executive responsibility for the running of the company's business. No one individual should have unfettered powers of decision. [CC Main principle A.2].

4.101   The supporting principles relevant to the board set out that:

■   The board's role is to provide entrepreneurial leadership of the company within a framework of prudent and effective controls which enables risk to be assessed and managed. The board should set the company's strategic aims, ensure that the necessary financial and human resources are in place for the company to meet its objectives and review management performance. The board should set the company's values and standards and ensure that its obligations to its shareholders and others are understood and met. [CC Supporting principle A.1].

■ All directors must take decisions objectively in the interests of the company. [CC Supporting principle A.1].

■ As members of a unitary board, non-executive directors should constructively challenge and help develop proposals on strategy. They should scrutinise management's performance in meeting agreed goals and objectives and monitor the reporting of performance. They should satisfy themselves on the integrity of financial information and that financial controls and systems of risk management are robust and defensible. They are responsible for determining appropriate levels of remuneration of executive directors and have a prime role in appointing, and where necessary removing, executive directors, and in succession planning. [CC Supporting principle A.1].

■ The chairman is responsible for the board's leadership, ensuring effectiveness on all aspects of its role and setting its agenda. The chairman is also responsible for ensuring that the directors receive accurate, timely and clear information. He/she should ensure effective communication with shareholders, facilitate the effective contribution of non-executive directors in particular and ensure constructive relations between executive and non-executive directors. [CC Supporting principle A.2].

Disclosures

4.102 The following disclosures in relation to the board are required within the annual report:

■ A statement should be made about how the board operates, including a high level statement of which types of decisions are taken by the board and which are delegated to management. [CC provision A.1.1].

■ Combined Code provision A.1.2 requires that the annual report should identify:

   ■ The chairman.

   ■ The deputy chairman (where applicable).

   ■ The chief executive.

   ■ The senior independent director.

   ■ The chairmen and members of each of the nomination, audit and remuneration committees.

This provision also requires that the annual report includes the number of meetings of the board and each committee and individual attendance by directors.

4.103 There are a number of Code provisions which overlap with the requirements of the DTR, as noted in paragraph 4.59. The DTR confirms that if a company provides the information specified by CC A.1.1, A.1.2, A.4.6, B.2.1 and C.3.3 it will satisfy the relevant requirements of DTR 7.1.5R and 7.2.7R.

Other related provisions

4.104 The following provisions are not disclosure provisions, however it is envisaged that compliance with these detailed provisions will mean that the main principle has been applied.

- The board should meet sufficiently regularly to discharge its duties effectively. There should be a formal schedule of matters reserve for the board. [CC A.1.1].

- The roles of chairman and chief executive should not be exercised by the same individual. The division of responsibilities between the chairman and chief executive should be clearly established, set out in writing and agreed by the board. [CC A.2.1].

- Where directors have concerns which cannot be resolved about the running of the company or a proposed action, they should ensure that their concerns are recorded in the board minutes. On resignation, a non-executive director should provide a written statement to the chairman, for circulation to the board, if they have any such concerns. [CC A.1.4].

- The company should arrange appropriate insurance cover in respect of legal action against its directors. [CC A.1.5].

- The terms of reference of the nomination, audit and remuneration committees, including each committee's role and authority delegated to it by the board, should be made available. The recommendation can be met by making the information available on the company's website. [CC A.4.1, B.2.1, C.3.3].

- A chief executive should not go on to be chairman of the same company. If exceptionally a board decides that a chief executive should become chairman, the board should consult major shareholders in advance and should set out its reasons to shareholders at the time of the appointment and in the next annual report. [CC A.2.2].

- The chairman should on appointment meet the independence criteria set out in A.3.1. [CC A.2.2].

4.105 FRC guidance on the role of the chairman is included in the 'Good practice suggestions from the Higgs Report' (the 'Higgs Guidance') issued in June 2006. While boards are not required to follow this guidance, it is intended to assist them in when implementing the relevant provisions of the Code. This guidance is currently undergoing a review with the intention of issuing revised guidance by the end of 2010.

4.106 The Higgs Guidance (2006) provides guidance on the role of the chairman, explaining that the he/she is pivotal in creating the conditions for overall board and individual director effectiveness in and outside of the boardroom. The responsibilities of the director are:

- To run the board and set its agenda. Agendas should take into account issues and concerns of all board members. In addition, the agendas should be forward looking and concentrate on strategic matters rather than approving proposals which can be delegated to management.

- To ensure that information received by board members, particularly about the company's performance, is accurate, timely and clear. This should enable the board to take sound decisions, monitor effectively and provide advice to promote the company's success.

- To ensure effective communication with shareholders and ensure that the board members develop an understanding of the views of the major investors.

- To manage the board to ensure that sufficient time is allowed for discussion of complex or contentious issues. Where it is appropriate to do so, the chairman should arrange for informal meetings beforehand to enable thorough preparation for the board discussion. Non-executive directors must have sufficient time to consider critical issues and should not have to face unrealistic deadlines when making difficult decisions.

- To lead the process to provide a properly constructed induction programme for new directors that is comprehensive, formal and tailored and facilitated by the company secretary.

- To take the lead in identifying and meeting the development needs of individual directors. The company secretary has a key role in facilitating the provision of training. It is the responsibility of the chairman to address the development needs of the board as a whole with a view to enhancing its overall effectiveness as a team.

- To ensure evaluations of the performance of individuals and of the board as a whole and its committees are performed at least once a year.

- To encourage active engagement by all the members of the board.

[Good practice suggestions from the Higgs Report, June 2006].

4.106.1 The Higgs guidance also suggests specific actions for a chairman to be effective. The chairman should:

- Uphold the highest standards of integrity and probity.

- Set the agenda, style and tone of board discussions to promote both constructive debate and effective decision-making.

- Promote effective relationships and open communication between non-executive directors and executive team. This should be both inside and outside the boardroom.

- Build a board that is effective and that initiates change and planning succession in board appointments, subject to approval by the board and shareholders.

- Promote the highest standards of corporate governance and seeks to comply with the Code provisions wherever possible.

- Ensure clear structure for and the effective running of board committees.

- Ensure that board decisions are effectively implemented.

- Establish a close relationship with the chief executive. The chairman should be able to provide support and advice while at the same time respecting executive responsibility.

- Provide a coherent leadership of the company, including representing the company and understanding the views of shareholders.

[Good practice suggestions from the Higgs Report, June 2006].

4.107   Best practice trends in this area include:

- Explaining how appropriate board behaviours and dynamics are encouraged, acknowledging behavioural aspects of a successful board.

- Describing how the actual activities undertaken by the board as well as matters reserved for it.

- Describing all board activities, not just scheduled meetings.

- Explaining the differing responsibilities between chairman and chief executive in a manner tailored to the circumstances of the business.

4.108   The following table is an extract from the Great Portland Estates plc annual report which sets out very clearly the principal activities undertaken by the Board Committees during the year.

Table 4.1 – Principle activities of the board

Great Portland Estates plc – Annual report – 31 March 2009

Month	Committees	Principal activity
January	Audit	Review of the Interim Management Statement
		• Meeting with the Valuers
January/March	Remuneration	Review of Remuneration Policy
		• Remuneration structure for Executive Directors, including bonus and share-based long-term incentive plans
March	Audit	Year end planning meeting
		• Meeting with the Auditors
		Review of:
		• Audit Plan
		• independence of Auditors
		• audit/ non-audit fees
		• Review developments in accounting and reporting requirements
		• Review of internal controls and risk management processes
		• Consideration of need for internal audit
March/April	Nomination[1]	Review of Board evaluation and succession planning
April/ May	Remuneration	Review of performance and remuneration
		• Review of:
		• Year end appraisals of Executive Directors and Senior Managers below board level and their objectives and targets set for forthcoming year
		• Senior Manager bonuses
		• Senior Manager salary, bonus and long-term incentive levels for forthcoming year
		• Review of:
		• Executive Director bonuses
		• Executive Director salary, bonus and long-term incentive levels for forthcoming year
		• Executive Director and employee corporate bonus plan targets
May	Remuneration	Approval of Remuneration Report
May	Audit	Review of year end results
		• Review of annual report/ Preliminary Announcement
		• Meeting with the Valuers
		• Meeting with the Auditors

		• Review of internal controls and risk management process
May/June	Remuneration	Review of LTIP and SMP performance and vesting of awards
		Approval of LTIP and SMP awards
July	Audit	Review of Interim Management Statement
		• Meeting with the Valuers
September	Audit	Half year planning meeting
		• Meeting with the Auditors
		Review of:
		• Audit plan
		• Independence of Auditors
		• Audit/ non-audit fees
		• Review developments in accounting and reporting requirements
October/ November	Audit	Review of half year results
		• Review of half year results announcement
		• Meeting with the Valuers
		• Meeting with the Auditors
		• Review of internal controls and risk management process
		• Review of pension plan annual accounts

1 Additional Nomination Committee meetings held as appropriate where Board appointments required.

Re-election of directors

Principles

4.109   The main principle that should be applied in relation to the re-election of directors is as follows:

■   All directors should be submitted for re-election at regular intervals, subject to continued satisfactory performance. The board should ensure planned and progressive refreshing of the board. [CC Main principle A.7].

Disclosures

4.110   Disclosures in relation to the re-election of directors which are required within the annual report are as follows:

■   The names of directors submitted for election or re-election should be accompanied by sufficient biographical details and any other relevant information to enable shareholders to take an informed decision on their election. [CC A.7.1].

Other related provisions

4.111 The following detailed provisions should be implemented:

- There should be a nomination committee, which should lead the process for board appointments and make recommendations to the board. [CC A.4.1].

- The nomination committee should have a majority of independent non-executive directors. The chairman or an independent non-executive director should be chair of the committee. The chairman should not chair the nomination committee when it is dealing with the appointment of a successor to the chairmanship. [CC A.4.1].

- Non-executive directors should be appointed for specified terms subject to re-election and to Companies Act provisions relating to the removal of a director. Any term beyond six years for a non-executive director should be subject to particularly rigorous review, and should take into account the need for progressive refreshing of the board. For terms in excess of nine years (for example, three three-year terms), non-executive directors should be subject to annual re-election with consideration given to on-going independence (refer to provision A.3.1). The board should set out to shareholders in the papers why they believe an individual should be elected as a non-executive director. When proposing re-election, the chairman should confirm that, following formal performance evaluation, the individual's performance continues to be effective and to demonstrate commitment to the role. [CC A.7.2].

- All directors should be subject to election by shareholders at the first AGM following their appointment, and to re-election thereafter at intervals of no more than three years. [CC A.7.1].

- The board should establish both an audit committee and a remuneration committee of at least three, or in the case of smaller companies (that is, those below the FTSE 350 throughout the year immediately prior to the reporting year) two independent non-executive directors. [CC C.3.1 and B.2.1].

- The company chairman may also be a member of, but not chair, the remuneration committee if he or she was considered independent on appointment. [CC B.2.1].

- For smaller companies, the company chairman may also be a member of, but not chair, the audit committee if he or she was considered independent on appointment. This is in addition to the two independent non-executive directors. [CC C.3.1].

4.112 The UK Corporate Governance Code (2010) introduced annual re-election for all directors of FTSE 350 companies. Companies may wish to explain how they plan to address this change.

Performance evaluation

Principles

4.113   The main principle that should be applied in relation to evaluation of the board is as follows:

■   The board should undertake a formal and rigorous evaluation of its own performance and that of its committees and individual directors. [CC Main principle A.6].

4.114   The supporting principle relevant to performance evaluation explains that individual evaluation should aim to show whether each director continues to contribute effectively and to demonstrate commitment to the role (including commitment of time for board and committee meetings and any other duties). The chairman should act on the results of the performance evaluation by recognising the strengths and addressing the weaknesses of the board and, where appropriate, proposing new members be appointed to the board or seeking the resignation of directors. [CC Supporting principle A.6].

Disclosures

4.115   Disclosures relevant to performance evaluation are that the annual report should state how performance evaluations of the board, its committees and its individual directors have been conducted. [CC A.6.1].

Other related provisions

4.116   The following related detailed provision should be addressed:

■   The chairman should hold meetings with the non-executive directors without the executive directors present. The non-executive directors, led by the senior independent director, should be responsible for the performance evaluation of the chairman, taking into account the views of the executive directors. [CC A.1.3, A.6.1].

4.117   The Higgs Guidance issued in June 2006 includes guidance on performance evaluation including questions to consider in a performance evaluation of the board, the chairman and the non-executive directors. Under the UKCGC (but not under the Combined Code (2008)), FTSE 350 companies are required to have external facilitation of their performance reviews at least every three years.

4.118   Best practice disclosures may include:

■   Details of the outcome of the evaluation and any follow up action proposed; this indicates commitment to improvement and transparency.

- What use the company makes, or plans to make in future, of externally facilitated performance reviews.

Board balance and independence

Principles

4.119   The main principle that should be applied in relation to board balance and independence is as follows:

- The board should include a balance of executive and non-executive directors (and in particular independent non-executive directors) such that no individual or small group of individuals can dominate the board's decision taking. [CC Main principle A.3].

4.120   The supporting principles relevant to the board set out that:

- The board should not be unwieldy, but of sufficient size that the balance of skills and experience is appropriate for the requirements of the business and that changes to the board's composition can be managed without undue disruption. [CC Supporting principle A.3].

- There should be a strong presence on the board of both executive and non-executive directors to ensure that power and information are not concentrated in one or two individuals. [CC Supporting principle A.3].

- When deciding chairmanship and membership of committees there is value in ensuring that committee membership is refreshed and that undue reliance is not placed on particular individuals. [CC Supporting principle A.3].

- No one other than committee chairman and members is entitled to be present at a meeting of the nomination, audit or remuneration committee, but others may attend at the invitation of the committee. [CC Supporting principle A.3].

Disclosures

4.121   Disclosures in relation to board balance and independence that are required within the annual report are as follows:

- The board should identify in the annual report each non-executive director it considers to be independent. If the board considers a director to be independent, despite circumstances or relationships existing that may appear relevant to that decision, disclosure should be made of the reasons for determining that director to be independent. [CC A.3.1].

Other related provisions

4.122   The following are the detailed provisions related to the principles above:

- Circumstances that could appear to affect a director's independence will include:

- employment with the company or group within the last five years;

- a material business relationship within the last three years between the company and the director, or a body of which he/she is a partner, shareholder, director or senior employee;

- any entitlement to remuneration from the company other than a director's fee or participation in the company's share option or a performance-related pay scheme or membership of the company's pension scheme;

- close family ties between the director and any of the company's advisers, directors or senior employees;

- a cross-directorship or significant links with other directors through involvement in other companies or bodies;

- representing a significant shareholder; or

- more than nine years' service on the board.

[CC A.3.1].

- At least half the board, excluding the chairman, should comprise independent non-executive directors. A smaller company (that is, a company below the FTSE 350 throughout the year immediately prior to the reporting year) should have at least two independent non-executive directors. [CC A.3.2].

- An independent non-executive director should be appointed by the board as the senior independent director. This director should be available to shareholders if they have concerns, which contact through the normal channels of chairman, chief executive or finance director has failed to resolve or for which such contact is inappropriate. [CC A.3.3].

4.123 Provision A.3.2 requires that at least half the board (excluding the chairman) should comprise independent non-executive directors. Thus a board that comprises a chairman, three executive directors and four independent non-executive directors would comply with this provision; at least half the board excluding the chairman (that is, four independent directors out of seven directors) are independent. This provision does not apply to smaller companies (defined as those companies categorised as falling outside of the FTSE 350 throughout the year immediately prior to the reporting year), which instead should have at least two independent non-executive directors. These recommendations can be difficult for smaller companies to comply with, given the practical difficulty of attracting and retaining high quality independent non-executives. The relaxations introduced by the Combined Code (2008) outlined in paragraph 4.88 should help to ease this difficulty.

4.124 The recommendation that a senior independent non-executive director should be identified in the annual report, provides an additional route for concerns to be conveyed to the board and/or an early warning system that may highlight poor management.

4.125 FRC guidance on the role of the non-executive director is included in the Higgs Guidance issued in June 2006. This guidance distinguishes explains that all directors are required to fulfil a number of requirements. These include providing entrepreneurial leadership of the company within a controlled framework which enables risk to be identified and managed, set the company's strategic aims, and set the company's values and standards.

- To assist in developing strategy and be able to constructively challenge to promote debate.

- To scrutinise the performance management in attaining their goals and monitor the reporting of this performance.

- To satisfy themselves that the financial information has integrity and that financial control and risk management systems are sufficiently robust.

- To appoint and remove directors where necessary and to be responsible for determining appropriate levels of remuneration.

[Good practice suggestions from the Higgs Report, June 2006].

4125.1 To be effective, the non-executive director should:

- Be well informed about the company and the environment in which it operates. This may be attained by a comprehensive, formal and tailored induction, which the director should insist upon. This induction may include site visits rather than be restricted to formal briefings. The director should ensure that this knowledge is continually updated in order to ensure their contribution to the board remains relevant.

- Be independent in judgement and have an enquiring mind. The non-executive director should support executives in their leadership of the business while monitoring their conduct. He or she should also be able to listen to the views of others both inside and outside the board.

- Insist that information is received sufficiently in advance of meetings to enable thorough consideration of the issues facing the board.

- Understand the views of major investors both through the chairman and the senior independent director.

- Promote the highest standards of corporate governance and seek to comply with Code provisions wherever possible.

- Question intelligently, debate constructively, challenge rigorously and decide dispassionately.

[Good practice suggestions from the Higgs Report, June 2006].

4.126   Companies may wish to consider including the following examples of best practice disclosures:

■   Personal statements or examples from non-executive directors to demonstrate commitment to appropriate behaviours and constructive challenge of the executives.

■   Clear explanation of why the senior independent director is suitable for the role, including any explanations around independence.

■   Description of succession planning to ensure ongoing balance is appropriate.

■   Indication of future plans for succession for non-executives serving more than 9 years.

■   Description of criteria used for independence judgements.

Appointments to the board

Principles

4.127   The main principles that should be applied in relation to appointments to the board are as follows:

■   There should be a formal, rigorous and transparent procedure for the appointment of new directors to the board. [CC Main principle A.4].

■   The board should be supplied in a timely manner with information in a form and of a quality appropriate to enable it to discharge its duties. All directors should receive induction on joining the board and should regularly update and refresh their skills and knowledge. [CC Main principle A.5].

4.128   The supporting principles relevant to appointments to the board state that:

■   Appointments to the board should be made on merit and against objective criteria. Care should be taken to ensure that appointees have enough time available to devote to the job (particularly important for chairmen). [CC Supporting principle A.4].

■   The board should be satisfied that plans are in place for orderly succession for appointments to the board and senior management to maintain an appropriate balance of skills and experience within the company and on the board. [CC Supporting principle A.4].

■   The chairman is responsible for ensuring that the directors receive accurate, timely and clear information and management has an obligation to provide such information (but directors should seek clarification or amplification where necessary). [CC Supporting principle A.5].

- The chairman should ensure that the directors continually update their skills, knowledge and familiarity with the company required to fulfil their role both on the board and on board committees. The company should provide the necessary resources for developing and updating its directors' knowledge and capabilities. [CC Supporting principle A.5].

- Under the direction of the chairman, the company secretary's responsibilities include ensuring good information flows within the board and its committees and between senior management and non-executive directors, as well as facilitating induction and assisting with professional development as required. [CC Supporting principle A.5].

- The company secretary should be responsible for advising the board through the chairman on all governance matters. [CC Supporting principle A.5].

Disclosures

4.129 Disclosures should be made of the chairman's other significant commitments before his/her appointment. Any changes to these should be reported to the board as they arise and their impact explained in the annual report. [CC A.4.3].

Other related provisions

4.130 The following detailed provisions should be addressed:

- The nomination committee should prepare a job specification for the appointment of a chairman, including an assessment of the time commitment expected, recognising the need for availability in the event of crises. [CC A.4.3].

- The terms and conditions of appointment of non-executive directors should be made available for inspection (at the company's registered office during business hours and at the AGM for 15 minutes before the meeting and during the meeting). [CC A.4.4].

- Letters of appointment should set out the expected time commitment. Non-executive directors should undertake that they will have sufficient time to meet what is expected of them. Their other significant commitments should be disclosed to the board before appointment, and upon subsequent changes. [CC A.4.4].

- The board should not agree to a full time executive director taking on more than one non-executive directorship in a FTSE 100 company nor the chairmanship of such a company. [CC A.4.5].

- Where a company releases an executive director to serve as a non-executive director elsewhere, the remuneration report should include a statement as to whether or not the director will retain such earnings and, if so, what the remuneration is. [CC B.1.4].

■ All directors, especially non-executive directors, should have access to independent professional advice at the expense of the company where they judge it necessary to discharge their responsibilities as directors. Committees should be provided with sufficient resources to undertake their duties. [CC A.5.2].

■ All directors should have access to the advice and services of the company secretary, who is responsible to the board for ensuring that board procedures are complied with. The appointment and removal of the company secretary should be a matter for the board as a whole. [CC A.5.3].

■ The chairman should ensure that new directors receive a full, formal and tailored induction on joining the board, part of which should be an opportunity for major shareholders to meet new non-executive directors. [CC A.5.1].

4.130.1   Another point of focus of recent governance reviews has been the extent of the induction, training and on-going professional development of non-executive directors. If the non-executive directors are expected to challenge constructively and question sensibly, they need to have sufficient knowledge and understanding of the business and its issues.

4.130.2   Best practice disclosure trends include:

■ The specific arrangements for tailored induction and ongoing professional development for directors.

■ Opportunities provided for non-executives to understand the business more fully.

■ How executive directors take on non-executive roles to enhance their experience and development.

■ Descriptions of the specific information packs that board members receive.

4.131   Time commitment also remains a real focus for companies in this area. Current best practice reporting in this area may cover:

■ The expected time commitment for new non-executive directors (with or without numbers of days).

■ Whether the company has a policy restricting the number of other directorships held by non-executive directors.

■ A table of directors' attendance at board and committee meetings. This also gives clarity to director changes and board and committee appointments.

4043

Report of the nomination committee

Disclosures

4.132   Disclosures in relation to the nomination committee which are required within the annual report are as follows:

■   A separate section of the annual report should describe the work of the nomination committee, including the process it has used in relation to board appointments. An explanation should be given if neither an external search consultancy nor open advertising has been used in the appointment of a chairman or a non-executive director. [CC A.4.6].

The above disclosure provision overlaps with the DTR and the DTR confirms that, if a company provides the information specified by CC A.4.6 above, it will satisfy the requirements of DTR 7.2.7R in respect of this committee.

Other related provisions

4.133   The following are the relevant detailed provisions:

■   The nomination committee should lead the process for board appointments and make recommendations to the board. The majority of the committee should be independent non-executive directors. The chair of the nomination committee should be either the chairman or an independent non-executive director. The chairman should not chair the committee when dealing with the appointment of a successor to the chairmanship. [CC A.4.1].

■   The nomination committee should make its terms of reference available, these terms of reference should explain the committee's role and the authority delegated to it by the board. [CC A.4.1].

■   The nomination committee should evaluate the balance of skills, knowledge and experience on the board. In the light of this evaluation, the committee should prepare a description of the role and capabilities required for a particular appointment. [CC A.4.2].

4.134   The nomination committee is responsible for board composition, new appointments and succession planning; it therefore fulfils a vital role in effectively creating an effective board. The Higgs Guidance issued in June 2006 includes a summary of the principal duties of the nomination committee, a pre-appointment due diligence checklist for new board members and a sample letter of non-executive director appointment.

4.135   Best practice disclosures and practice on nomination committees may include:

■   A description of the skills and experience criteria for new board appointments; in future reporting with due regard for diversity.

■ The setting up of a specialised nomination committee which brings benefits for making key appointments, such as chairman appointments.

[The next paragraph is 4.138.]

Audit committee and auditors

Principles

4.138 The main principle that should be applied in relation to the audit committee is as follows:

■ The board should establish formal and transparent arrangements for considering how they should apply the financial reporting and internal control principles and for maintaining an appropriate relationship with the company's auditors. [CC Main principle C.3].

Disclosures

4.139 Disclosures in relation to audit committees arising from both the Combined Code and the FRC guidance on audit committees, formerly known as the Smith guidance, have been summarised below. The Smith guidance is discussed further from paragraph 4.145 onwards.

■ The terms of reference of the audit committee, including its role and the authority delegated to it by the board, should be made available. A separate section in the annual report should describe the work of the committee in discharging its responsibilities. [Smith para 5.1, CC C.3.3].

■ The audit committee section should include:

■ A summary of the role of the audit committee.

■ The names and qualifications of all members of the audit committee during the period.

■ The number of audit committee meetings.

■ A report on the way the audit committee has discharged its responsibilities.

[Smith para 5.2]

■ Where there is no internal audit function, the reasons for its absence should be explained. [Smith para 4.9, CC C.3.5].

■ The audit committee should have primary responsibility for making a recommendation to the board on the appointment, reappointment and removal of the external auditors. If the board does not accept the audit committee's recommendation, the annual report should include a statement from the audit committee explaining its recommendation and the reasons why the board has taken a different position. [Smith para 4.17, CC C.3.6].

- The audit committee section of the annual report should explain to shareholders how it reached its recommendation to the board on the appointment, reappointment or removal of the external auditors. This explanation should normally include supporting information on tendering frequency, the tenure of the incumbent auditor, and any contractual obligations that acted to restrict the audit committee's choice of external auditors. [Smith para 4.22].

- If the auditor provides non-audit services, it should be explained how the auditor's objectivity and independence is safeguarded. [Smith para 4.34, CC C.3.7].

The above disclosure provisions overlap with the DTR and the DTR confirms that, if a company provides the information specified by CC A.1.2, C.3.1, C.3.2 and C.3.3 above, it will satisfy the requirements of DTR 7.1.1R to 7.1.5R in respect of this committee.

Other related provisions

4.140   The following detailed provisions and guidance relate to this area:

- The audit committee should consist of at least three, or in the case of smaller companies, (that is, those below the FTSE 350 throughout the year immediately prior to the reporting year), two independent non-executive directors. In smaller companies the company chairman may be a member of, but not chair, the committee in addition to the independent non-executive directors, provided he or she was considered independent on appointment as chairman. The board should satisfy itself that at least one member of the audit committee has recent and relevant financial experience. [CC C.3.1, Smith paras 2.1 and 2.3]. See paragraph 4.144 for further discussion of 'recent and relevant' financial experience.

  The audit committee should have written terms of reference setting out its responsibilities that should include:

  - Monitoring the integrity of the financial statements of the company, and announcements relating to the company's financial performance and reviewing significant financial reporting judgements contained in them.

  - Reviewing the company's financial and non-financial internal controls and risk management systems (to the extent that these are not delegated to another committee made up of independent non-executive directors).

  - Monitoring and reviewing the effectiveness of the company's internal audit function.

  - Making recommendations to the board relating to the appointment, re-appointment and removal of the external auditor and approving the remuneration and terms of engagement of the external auditor.

- Reviewing and monitoring the external auditor's and effectiveness of the audit process.

- Developing and implementing a policy on the engagement of the external auditor to supply non-audit services and reporting to the board, identifying matters in where action or improvement is needed.

[CC C.3.2 and Smith para 2.2].

- The audit committee should monitor and review the effectiveness of the internal audit activities. Where there is no internal audit function, the audit committee should consider annually whether there is a need for one and make a recommendation to the board. [CC C.3.5 and Smith para 4.9].

- The audit committee should review arrangements by which staff of the company may, in confidence, raise concerns about possible improprieties in matters of financial reporting or other matters. It should ensure the proportionate and independent investigation of such matters and follow-up action. [CC C.3.4].

[The next paragraph is 4.142.]

4.142   Other relevant guidance is included in 'FRC guidance on challenges for audit committees arising from current economic conditions' which is discussed from paragraph 4.151. In addition there are DTR requirements on audit committees which are discussed in paragraph 4.46.

Recommendations for best practice disclosure

4.143   Current best practice reporting on audit committees may include:

- Details of the qualifications and experience of audit committee members to confirm their suitability and recent and relevant financial experience.

- Specific examples of audit committee activities in the year and how these addressed developments in the business.

Provision C.3.1 – 'Recent and relevant' financial experience

4.144   Some companies feel that identifying one individual as having recent and relevant financial experience may increase that individual's exposure to liability and as a result choose not to identify one individual, but rather explain that audit committee members collectively have recent and relevant financial experience. If this is the case, it is a departure from the Code and requires an explanation. The revised FSA Rules, which are discussed further in paragraph 4.46, provide that at least one member of the audit committee (or the equivalent body) must have competence in accounting and/or auditing.

FRC guidance on audit committees (the 'Smith Guidance')

4.145   The Smith Guidance was designed to assist company boards in making suitable arrangements for their audit committees and to assist directors serving on audit committees in carrying out their role. While boards are not required to follow this guidance, it is intended to assist them when implementing the relevant provisions of the Combined Code.

4.146   In March 2008, the FRC announced the launch of a consultation on the Smith Guidance on Audit Committees following the release of recommendations by the FRC Market Participants Group (MPG) report on promoting choice in the audit market. The new guidance was published in October 2008 and companies were encouraged to adopt best practice from that date, with the recommendations on disclosures applying to periods ending on or after 30 June 2009. The main changes to the guidance are:

■   Recommended disclosure in the annual report of how the audit committee reached its recommendation to the board on the appointment, re-appointment or removal of the external auditor, including supporting information on tendering frequency, the tenure of the incumbent auditor and any contractual obligations that acted to restrict the audit committee's choice of external auditor.

■   Encouragement to audit committees to consider the need to include the risk of the withdrawal of their auditor from the market in their risk assessment process.

■   Amendments to the information that audit committees should seek from the external audit firm about the independence of its staff, its policies for maintaining staff independence and monitoring compliance with relevant requirements (including the rotation requirements for partners and staff) and its safeguards in relation to provision of non-audit services. These changes simply ensure consistency with the existing APB Ethical Standards for auditors.

■   Introduction of the suggestion that it may be appropriate for the audit committee of a group to consider using audit firms from more than one network of firms, with additional guidance on considerations relevant to such a decision, including the option of joint audits.

■   A suggestion that the audit committee, as well as obtaining a report on the audit firm's own internal quality control procedures, gives consideration to the audit firm's annual transparency report, where available.

4.147   In July 2010, a new consultation paper on the Smith Guidance was issued. The paper acknowledges a perception amongst investors that confidence in the audit can be reduced where non-audit services are provided by the auditor and emphasises the need to address this perception issue through improved transparency and disclosure of non-audit services provided, and governance around the decision as to whether a company's auditors should be engaged to provide such services. The most significant proposed updates relate to the following parts of the guidance:

- governance around the policy on appointing the external auditor to carry out non-audit services;

- guidance on types of non-audit services that it may be appropriate to pre-approve; and

- enhanced disclosure of how auditor objectivity and independence is safeguarded where the auditor provides non-audit services.

4.148 There is specific additional guidance on audit engagement partner rotation and using the external auditor to undertake aspects of the internal audit function.

4.149 Following the consultation period, revised guidance is expected to be issued in December 2010. This guidance may change again in 2011 following the completion of the FRC's ongoing review of the Turnbull guidance. This is due to the overlap between these two sets of guidance on the Audit Committee's role in relation to risk management and internal controls.

4.150 Audit committees should also consider the FRC Audit Quality Framework published in February 2008, which is designed to support effective communication between auditors, audit committees, investors and other stakeholders on audit quality. The Framework is intended to be complementary to existing regulations and guidelines and to assist audit committees in undertaking annual assessments of the effectiveness of external audits.

Challenges for audit committees arising from the current economic crisis

4.151 In November 2008, the FRC issued guidance entitled 'Challenges for audit committees arising from current economic conditions', to assist audit committees in meeting their responsibilities relating to financial statements in difficult economic conditions. This guidance was updated in November 2009 because the FRC believed that, although the current economic outlook appeared to be less depressed than in 2008, significant economic risks remained and would present challenges for many audit committees during the 2009/10 reporting season. The FRC specifically highlighted that past experience showed insolvencies increased after the technical end of recessions as companies ran out of working capital. Such conditions could increase the risk that annual reports and accounts misreport facts and circumstances and contain unidentified errors and omissions. The updated guidance does not establish any new requirements, nor does it alter the role of an audit committee, which is outlined in the Combined Code (2008); but it offers a number of questions that committee members may wish to consider when fulfilling their responsibility to "*monitor the integrity of the financial statements of the company and any formal announcements relating to the company's financial performance, reviewing significant financial reporting judgements contained in them*". [CC.3.2].

4.152 The key areas in both the 2008 and 2009 guidance suggests that audit committees may wish to consider are:

■ Year end planning – prompt action by audit committees will better enable them to ensure that they, and the company, have sufficient resources and expertise in place to ensure the financial statements' integrity, particularly with regard to areas of difficult year end judgements.

■ Liquidity and going concern – when market conditions mean that many companies face difficulties servicing debt or securing financing, audit committees may wish to examine in more detail the rigour of the analysis supporting the use of the going concern assumption, as well as the integrity of the disclosures about going concern in the financial statements and other market communications. In some cases, detailed consideration will need to be given as to whether there are, or are not, material uncertainties leading to significant doubt about whether the business is a going concern (see from para 4.197).

■ Reliance on assumptions – in times of market volatility, audit committees are likely to want to better understand the assumptions that support cash flow and other forecasts on which asset valuations and impairment assessments rely. They will need to ensure that a wide range of reasonably possible outcomes are considered when performing sensitivity analysis on estimates.

■ Significant judgements – in times of uncertainty, audit committees are likely to want to be assured that key judgments are supported by a greater degree of rigour and analysis than in more normal circumstances.

Remuneration Committee

Principles

4.153 The main principles that should be applied in relation to remuneration are as follows:

■ Levels of remuneration should be sufficient to attract, retain and motivate directors of the quality required to run the company successfully, but a company should avoid paying more than is necessary for this purpose. A significant proportion of executive directors' remuneration should be structured so as to link rewards to corporate and individual performance. [CC Main principle B.1].

■ There should be a formal and transparent procedure for developing policy on executive remuneration and for fixing the remuneration packages of individual directors. No director should be involved in deciding his or her own remuneration. [CC Main principle B.2].

4.154 The supporting principles relevant to remuneration are as follows:

- The remuneration committee should judge where to position their company relative to other companies. But they should use such comparisons with caution, in view of the risk of an upward ratchet of remuneration levels with no corresponding improvement in performance. They should also be sensitive to pay and employment conditions elsewhere in the group, especially when determining annual salary increases. [CC Supporting principle B.1].

- The remuneration committee should consult the chairman and/or chief executive about their proposals relating to the remuneration of other executive directors. The remuneration committee should also be responsible for appointing any consultants in respect of executive director remuneration. Where executive directors or senior management are involved in advising or supporting the remuneration committee, care should be taken to recognise and avoid conflicts of interest. [CC Supporting principle B.2].

- The chairman of the board should ensure that the company maintains contact as required with its principal shareholders about remuneration in the same way as for other matters. [CC Supporting principle B.2].

Disclosures

4.155 Disclosures in relation to the remuneration committee that are required within the annual report are as follows:

- The remuneration report should include a description of the work of the remuneration committee, including, where an executive director serves as a non-executive director elsewhere, whether or not the director will retain such earnings and, if so, what the remuneration is. [CC provision B.1.4].

- Where remuneration consultants are appointed, a statement should be made available of whether they have any other connection with the company. [CC B.2.1].

The above disclosure provision overlaps with the DTR and the DTR confirms that, if a company provides the information specified by CC B.2.1, as well as A.1.1, A.1.2, A.4.6 and C.3.3, it will satisfy the requirements of DTR 7.2.7R in respect of this committee.

Other related provisions

Policy

4.156 The following detailed provisions in relation to the make up of remuneration should be complied with, or explanations given:

- Performance-related elements of remuneration should form a significant proportion of an executive director's total remuneration package. This package should be designed to align directors' interests with those of shareholders and to give these directors keen incentives to perform at the highest levels. In designing schemes of performance-related remuneration, the remuneration committee should follow the provisions in Schedule A of the Code. [CC B.1.1].

■ Executive share options should not be offered at a discount unless permitted by the relevant provisions of the Listing Rules. [CC B.1.2].

■ Remuneration for non-executive directors should reflect the time commitment and responsibilities of the role and should not include share options. If, exceptionally, options are granted, shareholder approval should be sought in advance and any shares acquired by exercise of the options should be held until at least one year after the non-executive director leaves the board. Holding of share options could be relevant to determining a non-executive director's independence (as set out in provision A.3.1). [CC B.1.3].

Service contracts and compensation

4.157 Service contracts and compensation have also been considered within the Code in the following detailed provisions:

■ The remuneration committee should carefully consider what compensation commitments (including pension contributions and all other elements) their directors' terms of appointment would entail in the event of early termination. The aim should be to avoid rewarding poor performance. They should take a robust line on reducing compensation to reflect departing directors' obligations to mitigate loss. [CC B.1.5].

■ Notice or contract periods should be set at one year or less. If it is necessary to offer longer notice or contract periods to new directors recruited from outside, such periods should reduce to one year or less after the initial period. [CC B.1.6].

Procedure

4.158 The Code also includes specific provisions regarding the procedures relating to remuneration:

■ The board should establish a remuneration committee of at least three, or in the case of smaller companies, two independent non-executive directors. The company chairman may be a member of, but not chair, the committee if he or she was considered independent on appointment as chairman. [CC B.2.1].

■ The responsibility for setting remuneration for all executive directors and the chairman, including pension rights and any compensation payments, should be delegated to the remuneration committee. The committee should also recommend and monitor the level and structure of remuneration for senior management. The definition of 'senior management' for this purpose should be determined by the board but should normally include the first layer of management below board level. [CC B.2.2].

- The board itself or, where required by the Articles of Association, the shareholders should determine the remuneration of the non-executive directors within the limits set in the Articles of Association. The board may however delegate this responsibility to a committee, which might include the chief executive, where permitted by the Articles. [CC B.2.3].

- Shareholders should be invited specifically to approve all new long-term incentive schemes (as defined in the Listing Rules) and significant changes to existing schemes, save in the circumstances permitted by the Listing Rules. [CC B.2.4].

[The next paragraph is 4.160.]

4.160   Disclosure of the remuneration committee's activities throughout the year is considered to be good practice. The Combined Code (2008) principles and best practice provisions concerning directors' remuneration are considered in more detail in chapter 5.

Internal control

Principles

4.161   The main principle that should be applied in relation to internal controls is as follows:

- The board should maintain a sound system of internal control to safeguard shareholders' investment and the company's assets. [CC Main principle C.2].

Summary of guidance

4.162   The Combined Code (2008) recommends that the directors should at least annually review the effectiveness of all material controls, including operational, financial and compliance controls and risk management systems. Guidance was issued to directors in 1999 in order to assist them in complying with the internal control provision in the Combined Code (1998), known as the Turnbull guidance. In 2005, following a consultation process, the Turnbull guidance was updated. The Turnbull guidance (2005) supersedes and replaces the Turnbull guidance (1999).

4.163   The purpose of the review of controls effectiveness is to ensure that there is a strong control framework through which the organisation can both protect and increase shareholder value. For many companies this may be the most onerous aspect of the Combined Code (2008) and will require the active involvement of senior management. This, and the disclosure required by the Turnbull guidance, is discussed further from paragraph 4.182.

4.164   The importance of internal control to good governance is well recognised and the Combined Code recommends that all companies, regardless of their size, consider the need for an internal audit function annually. [CC C.3.5]. Modern internal audit should be focussed on all aspects of internal control including business risk assessment and response, financial management, safeguarding assets and compliance with laws and regulations. In addition, internal audit can also add value to the organisation as well as providing assurance on the control environment.

4.165   The requirement for boards to review the effectiveness of all material controls also affects the company's auditors, who are currently required by the Listing Rules to review the directors' statement of compliance with that provision of the Combined Code. [LR 9.8.10R(2)(b)].

Reporting on internal control

4.166   The Combined Code states that:

> *"The board should, at least annually, conduct a review of the effectiveness of the group's system of internal controls and should report to shareholders that they have done so. The review should cover all material controls, including financial, operational and compliance controls and risk management systems."* [CC C.2.1].

4.167   The recommendation for directors to review the effectiveness of all material controls goes further than the original Cadbury Code recommendation to review financial control and requires the active involvement of senior management.

4.168   For many companies that had already accepted that in practice it is difficult to distinguish financial from other controls, this wider risk and control review may already have been well established. For others, when this provision was introduced, compliance with the Combined Code may have required a significant extension of the work previously done to review and report on internal financial control. Past experience shows that the review of internal financial control was one of the more onerous requirements of Cadbury. It was also one of the more fruitful where undertaken effectively.

4.169   The remit for the review to cover risk management and operational, financial and compliance controls provides an ideal opportunity to review the effectiveness of the existing processes, taking into account developments in risk management thinking that have occurred in recent years. High level integrated risk management approaches that take account of strategy, organisation and people as well as business processes have, for some time, been seen by leading corporations as offering clear potential for enhancing shareholder value.

4.170   Companies with a listing in the US are required to provide an internal control report containing an assessment by management of the effectiveness of controls and financial reporting procedures under section 404 of the Sarbanes-Oxley Act.

Turnbull guidance (2005) for directors

4.171   The Turnbull guidance specifically outlines broad principles rather than boxes to be ticked, requiring directors to use their judgement to decide whether or not they have complied. Listed companies are expected to embrace the spirit of the guidance, rather than just follow the letter of it. The aim is to help companies to achieve their own business objectives. This challenges boards to develop an approach that fits the operating style of their organisation and builds upon any practices already in place. The Turnbull guidance deliberately does not attempt to set out prescriptive procedures that will fit all companies, as the 'right' procedures will be those that support the individual businesses.

4.172   The framework of the Turnbull guidance is that companies adopt a risk-based approach to setting and managing their internal control processes. Throughout the guidance the importance of an embedded ongoing process of identifying and responding to risk is emphasised. This integrated approach will need to include procedures to:

■   Establish business objectives.

■   Identify the key risks associated with these.

■   Agree on the risk profiles to be adopted and the control processes to address the accepted risks.

■   Set up a system to implement the decisions, which will include regular feedback.

■   Ensure that the company's implementation of the Turnbull guidance and the related disclosures are aligned with their risk register and other disclosures around risk in the annual report.

4.173   The internal control system to be implemented should encompass all the policies and procedures that, taken together, facilitate the effectiveness and efficiency of a company's operations and enable it to respond to significant business, operational, financial, compliance and other risks. The internal control system is a crucial element in managing risks which if not operating effectively may adversely affect the fulfilment of business objectives.

4.174   The main issues to address are that:

■   The identification and management of risks needs to be linked to the achievement of business objectives and enhancing shareholder value.

■   There should be a risk based approach to internal control including evaluation of the likelihood and impact of risks becoming a reality.

■   Business, operational and compliance risks must be addressed as well as financial risks.

■   Risk assessment must be embedded within ongoing operations.

- The board should receive regular reports during the year on internal control and risk (not just annually).

- The principal results of risk identification, evaluation and management review should be reported up to, and reviewed at, board level.

4.175   The appendix to the Turnbull guidance includes questions to consider and related examples that will assist companies when implementing the guidance.

The board's role

4.176   The role of the board is crucial under the Turnbull guidance. The onus is on the board to sponsor and take ownership of internal control. Specifically, it is important that the board defines the process to be adopted for its ongoing review of the effectiveness of internal control. There needs to be regular reporting to the board during the year and the board must set out both the scope and frequency of the reports it wishes to receive during the year.

4.177   The Turnbull guidance includes a preface highlighting to boards the importance of having a continuous process to review and update the system of internal controls. In addition, it encourages boards to take the opportunity to explain the specific risk and control issues facing the company, how the company maintains a framework of internal controls to address these issues and how the board has reviewed the effectiveness of that framework. The board should exercise the standard of care generally applicable to directors in the exercise of their duties when forming a view on the effectiveness of the internal control.

4.178   The board reports may cover particular business or risk areas rather than the whole system. They will, however, need to provide a balanced assessment of the significant risks relevant to the particular area and the effectiveness of the procedures put in place to manage those risks. Any significant control failings or weaknesses identified should be discussed in the reports, as the board will need to be aware of these and their implications, including the need for actions to rectify them. The board should confirm that necessary action has been (or is being) taken to remedy any significant failings or weaknesses identified from their review of the effectiveness of the internal control system. The board will also be interested in the financial or business impact that these failings have had or could have had, and the actions being taken.

4.179   By setting out a requirement for full and open reporting, and defining the scope of such reports, the board should be able to build up a picture of the internal control system and its operation during the year. The board should be comfortable that it is aware of the significant risks and how these have been identified, evaluated and managed; it has been able to assess the effectiveness of the management of these risks, notably by considering how significant failings or weaknesses have occurred, been reported and rectified; and it has put in place any additional monitoring which may be required.

4.180   Such regular reporting may be made to a board committee rather than the full board, but the board is still required to take responsibility and ownership of the overall issue. In addition to the regular reviews, the board also needs to undertake a separate assessment each year to enable it to make the public statements required by the Turnbull guidance. This annual assessment will cover the issues raised during the regular reporting process and any other issues necessary to ensure all significant aspects of the internal control process have been covered. In particular, the annual assessment should consider any changes in the risk profiles of the company; the company's ability and effectiveness in responding to such changes; the scope and results of the ongoing monitoring of the internal controls including the significance and response to any failings or weaknesses identified; and the extent and frequency of reports to the board and how comprehensive a picture has been obtained through this process.

Disclosures

4.181   Disclosures in relation to internal controls which are required within the annual report are as follows:

■   The board should, at least annually, conduct a review of the effectiveness of the group's system of internal controls and should report to shareholders that they have done so. The review should cover all material controls, including financial, operational and compliance controls and risk management systems. [CC- C.2.1].

As a reminder, the DTR also requires the following additional disclosures (see paragraph 4.56):

■   The corporate governance statement must include a description of the main features of the company's internal control and risk management systems in relation to the financial reporting process. [DTR 7.2.5R].

■   Where the issuer is required to prepare a group directors' report, they should include a description of the main features of the group's internal control and risk management systems in relation to the process for preparing consolidated financial statements. [DTR 7.2.10R].

The DTR requirements differ from the Combined Code; however, the FRC envisages that both could be met by a single internal control statement.

Disclosures required under Turnbull

4.182   The Turnbull guidance proposes the inclusion in the annual report and financial statements of a statement by the board on internal control. The recommended content is simple disclosure with the intention of avoiding boilerplate descriptions of high level controls, which had become somewhat common previously.

4.183 The Turnbull guidance states that *"the annual report and accounts should include such meaningful, high-level information as the board considers necessary to assist shareholders' understanding of the main features of the company's risk management processes and system of internal control, and should not give a misleading impression"*.

4.184 Regarding the application of principle C.2 of the Combined Code, the board should disclose that there is an ongoing process for identifying, evaluating and managing the significant risks faced by the company, that this process has been in place for the year under review, and up to the date of approval of the annual report, that it is regularly reviewed by the board and accords with the Turnbull guidance (2005). This is the minimum disclosure acceptable, but additional information can be given, particularly if it would assist understanding of the company's risk management processes and system of internal control. Some companies, therefore, may take this as an opportunity to describe their significant risks (including opportunities) and how these are managed.

4.185 There should be a specific acknowledgement that the board is responsible for the company's system of internal control and for reviewing its effectiveness. The board should confirm that it has reviewed the effectiveness of controls during the year. It should also explain that such a system is designed to manage rather than eliminate the risk of failure to achieve business objectives and can only provide reasonable, and not absolute, assurance against material misstatement or loss.

4.186 In relation to provision C.2.1 of the Combined Code, the board needs to summarise the process undertaken to review the effectiveness of the internal control system. In addition, if any significant problems have been noted in the annual report and accounts (for example, in the chairman's statement) the process applied to deal with any material internal control aspects of these need to be identified. This is an area of disclosure that needs to be specifically addressed by boards prior to approving the annual report.

4.187 The board should confirm that necessary actions have been or are being taken to remedy any significant failings or weaknesses identified from that review. The Turnbull Review Group's published deliberations indicated that it considered requiring companies to provide details of material or significant changes made to the internal control system as a result of the board's annual review of effectiveness. However, the Review Group recognised that if this was imposed on companies, then in effect it would be asking them to disclose any material weaknesses, with consequences for market perceptions. It was precisely in order to avoid any such concerns, that the Review Group acknowledged that this may result in boilerplate disclosures, but at least it would provide investors with some additional assurance that the outcome of the annual review process was action-oriented.

4.188 Where a board cannot make one or more of the disclosures listed in the Turnbull guidance, it should state this fact and provide an explanation. The

Listing Rules require the board to disclose if it has failed to conduct a review of the effectiveness of the company's system of internal control.

Application of Turnbull guidance to groups

4.189 The Turnbull guidance refers throughout to the 'company'. It states, however, that this should be taken to mean the group of which the reporting company is the parent company. The disclosures made and the reviews of internal control should be in relation to the group as a whole. This may not be possible for some joint ventures or associates. If those have not been dealt with as part of the group when undertaking internal control reviews, this fact should be disclosed by the board in the annual report.

Recommendations for best practice disclosure

4.190 Current best practice reporting in this area includes:

■ A tailored description of the company's internal control and risk management framework. The use of diagrams adds clarity and allows complex concepts to be presented effectively.

■ Clear linkage between business and industry risks and the system of internal control.

■ An explanation of how the judgements and inherent uncertainties underlying risk management systems are handled.

■ An explanation of the roles and remit of any other committees within the internal control framework.

4.191 The FRC is carrying out a limited review of the Turnbull guidance in the second half of 2010.

Financial reporting

Principles

4.192 The main principle that should be applied in relation to financial reporting is as follows:

■ The board should present a balanced and understandable assessment of the company's position and prospects. [CC Main principle C.1].

4.193 The supporting principle relevant to financial reporting states that the board's responsibility to present a balanced and understandable assessment extends to interim and other price-sensitive public reports and reports to regulators as well as to information required to be presented by statutory requirements. [CC Supporting principle C.1].

4.194   Disclosures in relation to financial reporting which are required within the annual report are as follows:

■   There should be a statement from the directors explaining their responsibility for preparing the financial statements. [CC C.1.1].

■   There must be a statement by the directors that the business is a going concern, with supporting assumptions or qualifications as necessary. This statement should cover both the parent company and the group as a whole. [LR 9.8.6(3); CC C.1.2].

Reporting on going concern

4.195   The Combined Code (2008) states that *"the directors should report that the business is a going concern, with supporting assumptions or qualifications as necessary"*. [CC C.1.2].

4.196   A going concern statement became a separate requirement of the Listing Rules effective for accounting periods beginning on or after 31 December 1995 and this requirement remains in the Listing Rules. [LR 9.8.6R(3)]. See paragraph 4.80 for the position regarding overseas companies in this respect.

FRC guidance — Going concern and liquidity risk: guidance for directors of UK companies 2009

4.197   In November 2008 the FRC published guidance for directors entitled 'An update for directors of listed companies: going concern and liquidity risk' ('FRC guidance'), to assist directors of listed companies preparing and approving annual reports in a difficult economic environment.

4.198   Subsequently, in October 2009, the FRC published updated guidance on going concern for directors of UK companies, which brings together in one place the requirements of company law, accounting standards and the Listing Rules on going concern and liquidity risk for small, medium and large UK companies.

4.199   The guidance provides a framework to assist directors, audit committees and finance teams, of all sizes of company, in determining whether it is appropriate to adopt the going concern basis for preparing financial statements (both annual and half-yearly) and in making balanced, proportionate and clear disclosures. The FRC guidance for directors is effective for accounting periods ending on or after 31 December 2009

[The next paragraph is 4.201.]

4.201   The FRC guidance is principles-based, with supporting detailed information bringing together the requirements of company law, accounting standards and the Listing Rules on going concern, and providing further information on their application. The three principles are:

1 Assessing going concern

Directors should make and document a rigorous assessment of whether the company is a going concern when preparing annual and half-yearly financial statements. The process carried out by the directors should be proportionate in nature and depth depending upon the size, level of financial risk and complexity of the company and its operations.

2 The review period

Directors should consider all available information about the future when concluding whether the company is a going concern at the date they approve the financial statements. Their review should usually cover a period of at least twelve months from the date of approval of annual and half-yearly financial statements.

3 Disclosures

Directors should make balanced, proportionate and clear disclosures about going concern for the financial statements to give a true and fair view. Directors should disclose if the period that they have reviewed is less than twelve months from the date of approval of annual and half-yearly financial statements and explain their justification for limiting their review period.

[FRC Going concern and liquidity risk: guidance for directors of UK companies 2009].

4.202 The principles should be applied by directors of all companies when preparing annual and half-yearly financial statements but do not apply when preparing interim management statements in accordance with the Disclosure and Transparency Rule (DTR) 4.3.

4.203 The appendices to the guidance provide examples of going concern disclosures for small companies; for companies other than small companies (including subsidiary companies of large private or listed groups) and key questions for boards to consider.

4.204 The form of disclosure depends on the directors' conclusions having undertaken procedures in relation to going concern. There are three basic conclusions:

- no material uncertainties exist that lead to significant doubt concerning the entity's ability to continue in operational existence for the foreseeable future;

- material uncertainties exist that may cast significant doubt over the company's ability to continue in operation but, nonetheless, the directors consider it appropriate to use the going concern basis in preparing the financial statements; or

- the going concern basis of accounting is not appropriate.

4.205 Where no uncertainties (material or otherwise) exist over the company's ability to continue as a going concern, the Going Concern and Financial Reporting (GCFR) guidance published in November 1994 suggests the appropriate form of words to be:

> *"After making enquiries, the directors have a reasonable expectation that the company has adequate resources to continue in operational existence for the foreseeable future. For this reason, they continue to adopt the going concern basis in preparing the accounts."* [GCFR para 49].

4.206 This form of disclosure has historically been adopted by most companies, although a significant number of blue chip companies, especially in the financial services sector, have chosen to give rather more detail in the current uncertain economic conditions. Principle 3 of the FRC guidance set out in paragraph 4.201 above should lead to this basic statement being expanded to explain more about the enquiries made by the directors and the basis for their 'reasonable expectation'.

4.207 The GCFR guidance recommends that the disclosure should be located in an operating and financial review (OFR) recognising that the OFR provides a context for a going concern statement. Despite this, it is quite common for the going concern statement to be included within the corporate governance statement or the business review with a separate sub-heading.

4.208 If the directors conclude that the company is unlikely to continue in operational existence for the foreseeable future, a non-going concern basis will be required in preparing the financial statements and this will require disclosure. Directors will generally wish to take legal advice before making such a disclosure, in particular in relation to whether the directors may be liable for wrongful trading.

4.209 Further discussion of going concern matters is included in chapter 2 'Business review'.

Dialogue with institutional shareholders

4.210 The main principle that should be applied in relation to a dialogue with institutional shareholders is as follows:

- There should be a dialogue with shareholders based on the mutual understanding of objectives. The board as a whole has responsibility for ensuring that a satisfactory dialogue with shareholders takes place. [CC Main principle D.1].

4.211 The supporting principles relevant to this dialogue are:

- Whilst recognising that most shareholder contact is with the chief executive and finance director, the chairman (and the senior independent director and other directors as appropriate) should maintain sufficient contact with major shareholders to understand their issues and concerns. [CC Supporting principle D.1].

■ The board should keep in touch with shareholder opinion in whatever ways are most practical and efficient. [CC Supporting principle D.1].

Disclosures

4.212   In relation to this dialogue disclosure should be made of the steps that the board has taken to ensure that the board members, and in particular the non-executive directors, develop an understanding of the views of the major shareholders (for example through direct face-to-face contact, analysts' or brokers' briefings and surveys of shareholder opinion) about their company. [CC D.1.2].

4.213   The following detailed provisions should be observed:

■ The chairman should ensure that the views of shareholders are communicated to the board as a whole. [CC D.1.1].

■ The chairman should discuss governance and strategy with major shareholders. Non-executive directors should be offered the opportunity to attend meetings with major shareholders and should expect to attend them if requested by major shareholders. The senior independent director should also attend sufficient meetings with a range of major shareholders to listen to their views. [CC D.1.1].

4.214   One of the themes of recent governance reviews has been that there needs to be appropriate two-way communication between the board and its investors if the 'comply or explain' mechanism of the Code is to work effectively.

4.215   As recommended in the Walker Report, the FRC has issued a Stewardship Code for institutional investors, which came into effect in July 2010. As a result the previous section E of the Combined Code (2008) ceased to be applicable. See from paragraph 4.343 for a discussion of the UK Stewardship Code. Section D on the company side continues to be applicable.

4.216   Current best practice and transparent reporting in this area may include:

■ The use of an independent third party to assist the board in obtaining investor views; this demonstrates commitment and encourages openness.

■ Company-specific disclosure about two-way communication and the investor relations process.

■ Recognition in practice and in the annual report of the importance of the whole investor base, including non-institutional investors, where applicable.

■ Effective use of technology to enhance shareholder communications, such as reference to websites where investor relations information is held.

Constructive use of the AGM

Principles

4.217   The main principle that should be applied in relation to constructive use of the AGM is as follows:

■   The board should use the AGM to communicate with investors and to encourage their participation. [CC Main principle D.2].

Other related provisions

4.218   There are no disclosure provisions associated with constructive use of the AGM, however the following detailed provisions should be implemented by the company:

■   The chairman should arrange for the chairmen of the audit, remuneration and nomination committees to be available to answer questions at the AGM and for all directors to attend. [CC D.2.3].

■   The company should propose a separate resolution on each substantially separate issue and should in particular propose a resolution at the AGM relating to the report and accounts. For each resolution, proxy appointment forms should provide shareholders with the option to direct their proxy to vote either for or against the resolution or to withhold their vote. The proxy form and any announcement of the results of a vote should make clear that a 'vote withheld' is not a vote in law and will not be counted in the calculation of the proportion of the votes for and against the resolution. [CC D.2.1].

■   The company should ensure that all valid proxy appointments received for general meetings are properly recorded and counted. For each resolution, after a vote has been taken, except where taken on a poll, the company should ensure that the following information is given at the meeting and made available as soon as reasonably practicable on the company's website:

■   the number of shares in respect of which proxy appointments have been validly made; and

■   the number of votes (i) for, and (ii) against the resolution, and (iii) the number of shares in respect of which the vote was directed to be withheld.

[CC D.2.2].

■   The company should arrange for the Notice of the AGM and related papers to be sent to shareholders at least 20 working days before the meeting. [CC D.2.4].

4.219   Current best practice reporting in this area may explain that the company:

- Ensures shareholders are aware of meeting protocol, such as by referring to a separate Notice of Meeting booklet.

- Appoints an independent assessor to scrutinise the AGM to strengthen reporting and enhance transparency.

The UK Corporate Governance Code (2010)

Introduction

4.220   In June 2010 the Financial Reporting Council (FRC) published the revised UK Corporate Governance Code ('UKCGC') to replace the 2008 Combined Code. The new edition of the Code applies to all premium listed companies for financial years beginning on or after 29 June 2010, including overseas companies.

Main changes from the Combined Code (2008)

4.221   The overriding view emerging from the FRC consultation during 2009-2010 as a whole was that the governance code is effective and that the 'comply or explain' approach is sufficiently flexible to embrace different companies' circumstances. However the FRC also concluded that much more attention needs to be paid to following the spirit of the Code as well as its letter and that the quality of corporate governance ultimately depends on board behaviour not process. The new Code therefore puts greater emphasis on the leadership and effectiveness of boards, and on the board's responsibility for the management of risk. It also recognises that there needs to be better communication and engagement with shareholders.

4.222   In general, the new Code includes points of re-emphasis and re-focus rather than fundamental change. The main changes are summarised below:

For FTSE 350 companies only

- Annual re-election of all directors to increase accountability to shareholders.

- Externally facilitated performance reviews of boards at least every three years to help enhance the board's performance and awareness of its strengths and weaknesses.

For all listed companies

- To encourage boards to be well balanced and avoid 'group think', there are new principles on the composition and selection of the board, including the need to appoint members on merit, against objective criteria, and with due regard for the benefits of diversity, including gender diversity.

- To promote proper debate in the boardroom, there are new principles on the leadership of the chairman, the responsibility of the non-executive directors to provide constructive challenge, and the time commitment expected of all directors.

■ To help enhance the board's performance and awareness of its strengths and weaknesses, the chairman should hold regular development reviews with each director.

■ To increase accountability to shareholders, chairmen are encouraged to report personally on how the principles relating to the leadership and effectiveness of the board have been applied.

■ To improve risk management, the board should be responsible for determining the nature and extent of the significant risks it is willing to take (and there must be specific reporting on the company's business model in the annual report).

■ Performance-related pay should be aligned to the company's long-term interests and its risk policies and systems.

■ There are significant structural changes: the section on directors is divided into two sections 'Leadership' and 'Effectiveness' and the preamble is updated to form a new introductory section reinforcing important messages about the way the Code should be viewed and applied.

4.223   The FRC has confirmed separately how a 'FTSE 350 company' will be defined for the purposes of the Code provisions on re-election of directors and board performance evaluations. The definition is the converse of that for a 'smaller company' elsewhere in the Code: that is, it is a company that is within the FTSE 350 throughout the year immediately prior to the reporting year.

4.224   The FRC hopes that the changes will promote greater clarity and understanding with regard to the tasks of an effective board and that communication with shareholders will be more effective as a result. In addition, the FRC has also taken responsibility for a code for institutional investors to enhance shareholder engagement. This resulted in the FRC publishing the first UK Stewardship Code in July 2010, with immediate effect. See paragraph 4.343 onwards for a discussion of the UK Stewardship Code.

4.225   The FRC has amended the Code to adopt those recommendations from the Walker review that it believes apply to all listed companies. In particular, there are revised principles on the roles of the chairman and non-executive directors, the composition of the board, the commitment expected of directors and the board's responsibility for risk. The new provisions on annual re-election and performance evaluation are also consistent with Walker. Examples of Walker recommendations that have not been applied outside the banking sector include having a board risk committee and risk officer and stipulating a minimum time commitment for non-executive directors.

4.226   More commentary on the changes in the UK Corporate Governance Code is included under each area of governance in the sections that follow.

Reporting under the Code and 'comply or explain'

4.227 The Listing Rules continue to require a two-part compliance statement:

- one statement explaining how the main principles have been applied; and

- a second on whether the company has complied with the related provisions, or explaining why this is not the case. For requirements under the DTR, compliance is mandatory.

The descriptions together should give shareholders a clear and comprehensive picture of a company's governance arrangements in relation to the Code. See from paragraph 4.60 for a discussion on compliance statements.

4.228   Current best practice corporate governance reporting in terms of 'comply or explain' statements show:

- Companies getting behind the principles-based environment provided by the Code.

- A commitment to transparent reporting, tailored to the circumstances of the business. This aids effective engagement between investors and boards.

4.229   One of the main themes of the FRC review was that there needs to be better communication and engagement with shareholders. The FRC believes there is a need for boards to make communications with shareholders more confident and persuasive, and it encourages board chairmen, and the chairmen of the main board committees, to see the corporate governance statement as an opportunity to demonstrate to current and potential investors why they can have confidence in the board. The FRC hopes particularly that chairmen will choose to report personally in their annual statements how the principles of the Code relating to the role and effectiveness of the board have been applied.

Overview of the contents of the UK Corporate Governance Code (2010)

4.230   The UK Corporate Governance Code (2010) structure is as follows:

- Preamble covering: Governance and the Code; Preface; Comply or Explain

- The main principles of the Code

- Section A – Leadership

- Section B – Effectiveness

- Section C – Accountability

- Section D – Remuneration

- Section E – Relations with shareholders

4.231   Sections A to E contain the main principles and provisions to be reported against in the two-part compliance statement as required by the Listing Rules (discussed further in para 4.60).

Schedules forming part of the UK Corporate Governance Code

4.232   In the UKCGC three schedules provide further information:

- Schedule A – The design of performance-related remuneration for executive directors

- Schedule B – Disclosure of corporate governance arrangements

- Schedule C – Engagement principles for institutional shareholders

4.233   Schedule B summarises the disclosure requirements of corporate governance arrangements including the FSA Listing Rules and Disclosure Rules and Transparency Rules. Disclosure requirements are discussed from paragraph 4.49. Schedule B also summarises the information that should be 'made available' (which may be met *via* placing it on the company's web site) and the information that should be set out to shareholders in relation to election/re-election of directors and appointment /re-appointment of an external auditor.

4.233.1   Schedule C ceased to apply on 2 July 2010 when the UK Stewardship Code for institutional investors came into effect. The UK Stewardship Code is discussed from paragraph 4.343.

Structure of sections that follow

4.234   Key areas of governance covered by the UKCGC are set out below. For each area, the following information is provided, where applicable:

- The main and supporting principles.

- Specific disclosure requirements.

- Other related provisions or guidance which the company should apply.

- Details of any other guidance that should be considered when dealing with the relevant area.

- Trends in best practice disclosures, in some cases addressing themes of the 2009 governance reviews (see para 4.38). Such disclosures, while not mandatory, may help to avoid a 'box-ticking' approach to governance reporting.

Disclosures required under DTR 7 are not included below other than for comparative purposes against Code disclosures. See paragraphs 4.46 to 4.57 for details of these.

The board

4.235 The UKCGC's principles on leadership cover the role of the board, division of responsibilities and responsibilities of the chairman and non-executive directors.

4.236 One of the main topics of discussion in the corporate governance reviews during 2009 concerned the role and activity of the board and whether there was sufficient oversight from the non-executive directors. Questions were raised such as:

- Was the board effective in its decision making?

- Was sufficient attention paid to risk management or was this an area that was delegated to the audit committee?

- What did the board spend their time discussing at their board meetings?

- What role were the non-executive directors expected to fill and did they spend enough time getting to know the business?

Personal behaviours by directors underpin this area. The FRC, therefore, made structural changes to the Combined Code (2008) by splitting the previous section 'Directors' into two separate sections ('Leadership' and 'Effectiveness') and revising the principles and provisions within them. This was to give more prominence to the factors that underpin an effective board.

Principles

4.237 The main principles that should be applied in relation to the board are as follows:

- Every company should be headed by an effective board which is collectively responsible for the long-term success of the company. [UKCGC Main principle A.1].

- There should be a clear division of responsibilities at the head of the company between the running of the board and the executive responsibility for the running of the company's business. No one individual should have unfettered powers of decision. [UKCGC Main principle A.2].

- The chairman is responsible for leadership of the board and ensuring its effectiveness on all aspects of its role. [UKCGC Main principle A.3].

- As part of their role as members of a unitary board, non-executive directors should constructively challenge and help develop proposals on strategy. [UKCGC Main principle A.4].

4.238 The supporting principles relevant to the board go on to explain that:

- The board's role is to provide entrepreneurial leadership of the company within a framework of prudent and effective controls that enables risk to be assessed and managed. The board should set the company's strategic aims, ensure that the necessary financial and human resources are in place for the company to meet its objectives and review management performance. The board should set the company's values and standards and ensure that its obligations to its shareholders and others are understood and met. [UKCGC Supporting principle A.1].

- All directors must act in what they consider to be the company's best interests, consistent with their statutory duties. [UKCGC Supporting principle A.1].

- The chairman is responsible for setting the board's agenda and ensuring that adequate time is available for discussion of all agenda items, in particular strategic issues. The chairman should also promote a culture of openness and debate by facilitating the effective contribution of non-executive directors in particular and ensuring constructive relations between executive and non-executive directors. [UKCGC Supporting principle A.3].

- The chairman is responsible for ensuring that the directors receive accurate, timely and clear information. The chairman should ensure effective communication with shareholders. [UKCGC Supporting principle A.3].

- Non-executive directors should scrutinise the management's performance in meeting agreed goals and objectives and monitor the reporting of performance. They should satisfy themselves on the integrity of financial information and that financial controls and systems of risk management are robust and defensible. They are responsible for determining appropriate levels of remuneration of executive directors and have a prime role in appointing and, where necessary, removing executive directors, and in succession planning. [UKCGC Supporting principle A.4].

Disclosures

4.239 Disclosures in relation to the board that are required within the annual report are as follows:

- A statement should be made about how the board operates, including a high level statement of which types of decisions are to be taken by the board and which are to be delegated to management. [UKCGC A.1.1].

- UKCGC provision A.1.2 requires that the annual report should identify:

  - The chairman.

  - The deputy chairman (where applicable).

  - The chief executive.

  - The chairmen and members of each of the nomination, audit and remuneration committees.

This provision also requires that the annual report includes the number of meetings of the board and each committee and individual attendance by directors.

4.240   There are a number of Code provisions that overlap with the requirements of the DTR, as noted in paragraph 4.59. The DTR confirms that if a company provides the information specified by CC A.1.1, A.1.2, B.2.4, C.3.3 and D.2.1 it will satisfy the relevant requirements of DTR 7.1.5 R and 7.2.7 R.

Other related provisions

4.241   The following provisions are not disclosure provisions. However, it is envisaged that compliance with these detailed provisions will mean that the main principle has been applied.

- The board should meet sufficiently regularly to discharge its duties effectively. There should be a formal schedule of matters specifically reserved for its decision. [UKCGC A.1.1].

- The roles of chairman and chief executive should not be exercised by the same individual. The division of responsibilities between the chairman and chief executive should be clearly established, set out in writing and agreed by the board. [UKCGC A.2.1].

- The company should arrange appropriate insurance cover in respect of legal action against its directors. [UKCGC A.1.3].

- Where directors have concerns which cannot be resolved about the running of the company or a proposed action, they should ensure that their concerns are recorded in the board minutes. On resignation, a non-executive director should provide a written statement to the chairman, for circulation to the board, if they have any such concerns. [UKCGC A.4.3].

- The terms of reference of the nomination, audit and remuneration committees, including each committee's role and authority delegated to it by the board, should be made available. The recommendation can be met by making the information available on the company's website. [UKCGC B.2.1, C.3.3, D.2.1].

4.242   Best practice trends in this area include:

- Explaining how appropriate board behaviours and dynamics are encouraged, acknowledging behavioural aspects of a successful board.

- Describing the actual activities undertaken by the board as well as matters reserved for it.

- Describing all board activities, not just scheduled meetings.

4.243   Both Walker and the FRC review recognise the crucial role of the chairman in setting the 'tone at the top' for the rest of the board, including determining the board agenda and ensuring sufficient time for issues to be debated between executives and non-executives. The FRC therefore:

- brought the existing material on the role of the chairman from main principle A.2 of the Combined Code (2008) under a new main principle A.3;

- amended the supporting principle to include that the chairman is responsible for ensuring that adequate time is available for discussion of all agenda items, in particular strategic issues; and

- stated that the chairman should promote a culture of openness and debate.

4.244 FRC guidance on the role of the chairman is included in the 'Good Practice Suggestions from the Higgs Report' (the 'Higgs Guidance') issued in June 2006; see paragraph 4.106. While boards are not required to follow this guidance, it is intended to assist them in implementing the relevant provisions of the Code. This guidance is currently undergoing a review with the intention of revised guidance being issued by the end of 2010.

4.245 Current disclosures in this area tend to focus on the division of responsibilities between chairman and chief executive, with best practice examples showing clear explanations of the responsibilities of the respective roles, in a manner tailored to the circumstances of the business. As the role of the chairman has been brought under a new main principle, we expect future disclosures to further highlight the pivotal role of the chairman in defining the 'culture' of the board and ensuring its effectiveness. As noted above, the FRC hopes particularly that chairmen will choose to report personally in their annual reports how the Code's principles relating to the board's role and effectiveness have been applied. Best practice reporting often features at least an introduction to the corporate governance statement from the chairman and it is likely that this type of personal reporting will increase.

Re-election of directors

Principles

4.246 The main principle that should be applied in relation to the re-election of directors is as follows:

- All directors should be submitted for re-election at regular intervals, subject to continued satisfactory performance. [UKCGC Main principle B.7].

Disclosures

4.247 Disclosures in relation to the re-election of directors that are required within the annual report are as follows:

- The names of directors submitted for election or re-election should be accompanied by sufficient biographical details and any other relevant information to enable shareholders to take an informed decision on their election. [UKCGC B.7.1].

Other related provisions

4.248 The following detailed provisions should be implemented:

- There should be a nomination committee that should lead the process for board appointments and make recommendations to the board. [UKCGC B.2.1].

- The nomination committee should have a majority of independent non-executive directors. The chairman or an independent non-executive director should chair the committee. The chairman should not chair the nomination committee when it is dealing with the appointment of a successor to the chairmanship. [UKCGC B.2.1].

- The board should set out to shareholders in the papers why they believe an individual should be elected as a non-executive director. When proposing re-election, the chairman should confirm to shareholders that, following formal performance evaluation, the individual's performance continues to be effective and to demonstrate commitment to the role. [UKCGC B.7.2].

- Non-executive directors should be appointed for specified terms subject to re-election and to statutory provisions relating to the removal of a director. Any term beyond six years for a non-executive director should be subject to particularly rigorous review, and should take into account the need for progressive refreshing of the board. [UKCGC B.2.3].

- All directors of FTSE 350 companies should be subject to annual election by shareholders. All other directors should be subject to election by shareholders at the first annual general meeting after their appointment, and to re-election thereafter at intervals of no more than three years. Non-executive directors who have served longer than nine years should be subject to annual re-election. [UKCGC B.7.1].

- The board should establish both an audit committee and a remuneration committee of at least three, or in the case of smaller companies (that is, those below the FTSE 350 throughout the year immediately prior to the reporting year) two independent non-executive directors. [UKCGC C.3.1, D.2.1].

- The company chairman may also be a member of, but not chair, the committee if he or she was considered independent on appointment as chairman. [UKCGC D.2.1].

- For smaller companies, the company chairman may be a member of, but not chair, the audit committee if he or she was considered independent on appointment as chairman. This is in addition to the independent non-executive directors. [UKCGC C.3.1].

4.249 To enhance accountability to, and the influence of, shareholders the Walker review recommended the annual re-election of the board chairman and

the re-election of the remuneration committee chair if the remuneration report fails to secure 75% support. The FRC extended these Walker recommendations by introducing a new provision requiring re-election for all directors of FTSE 350 companies on the basis that it is appropriate for shareholders to have an annual opportunity to express their views on the performance of all the directors. The FRC recognises the concern that smaller companies with a more concentrated shareholder base might be exposed to disagreements between their major shareholders and, therefore, has limited the new provision to FTSE 350 companies. The FRC also note in the preface to the 2010 Code that: "...
companies are free to explain rather than comply if they believe that their existing arrangements ensure proper accountability and underpin board effectiveness, or that a transitional period is needed before they introduce annual re-election. The boards of smaller companies are also encouraged to consider their policy on director re-election."

4.250   Although the FRC has stated that there was widespread support from the investor community for annual re-election of all directors during the process of consulting on the new Code, initial indications are that some institutional investors will not be insisting upon the change on the grounds that it may create instability.

Performance evaluation

Principles

4.251   The main principle that should be applied in relation to evaluation of the board is as follows:

■   The board should undertake a formal and rigorous annual evaluation of its own performance and that of its committees and individual directors. [UKCGC Main principle B.6].

4.252   The supporting principles relevant to the board set out that:

■   The chairman should act on the results of the performance evaluation by recognising the strengths and addressing the weaknesses of the board and, where appropriate, proposing new members be appointed to the board or seeking the resignation of directors. [UKCGC Supporting principle B.6].

■   Individual evaluation should aim to show whether each director continues to contribute effectively and to demonstrate commitment to the role (including commitment of time for board and committee meetings and any other duties). [UKCGC Supporting principle B.6].

Disclosures

4.253   Disclosures relevant to performance evaluation are as follows:

- The board should state in the annual report how performance evaluation of the board, its committees and its individual directors has been conducted. [UKCGC B.6.1].

- Where an external facilitator is used to evaluate the board, a statement should be made as to whether the facilitator has any other connection with the company. [UKCGC B.6.2].

Other related provisions

4.254   The following related detailed provisions should be addressed:

- All FTSE 350 companies should engage an externally party to evaluate the board's performance at least every three years. [UKCGC B.6.2].

- The chairman should hold meetings with the non-executive directors without the executive directors present. The non-executive directors, led by the senior independent director, should be responsible for the chairman's performance evaluation, taking into account the views of executive directors. [UKCGC A.4.2, B.6.3].

4.255   Performance evaluation can be an effective way of assessing the board's performance and bringing issues to light where remedial action should be taken. The FRC followed Walker by including a new provision requiring FTSE 350 companies to perform an externally facilitated evaluation every three years, although it acknowledges that in the short to medium term there will continue to be concerns about the availability of board evaluation services, and for that reason has limited the new provision to FTSE 350 companies only. The FRC will also consider whether there are any steps it should take to raise standards among service providers.

4.256   The Higgs Guidance issued in June 2006 includes guidance on performance evaluation including questions to consider in a performance evaluation of the board, the chairman and the non-executive directors.

Forms of performance evaluation

4.257   The most common forms of board evaluation are paper questionnaires and interviews. An externally facilitated evaluation will generally involve one-to-one interviews with each member of the Board and, possibly, senior management or other third parties who interact with the Board. Interviews may be complemented by the completion of questionnaires or may be based around high level questions. An internal board evaluation will most commonly involve the completion of a questionnaire or checklist, which will be facilitated by the Chairman. However, in some cases, board evaluation is simply an informal discussion of the board's strengths and weaknesses and its achievements and shortcomings. Companies may also consider a similar approach for Committee reviews.

4.258 A formal externally facilitated board evaluation will usually include one-to-one interviews, completion of questionnaires (with examples to support responses), desk-top review of board papers and constitution and observation of board and/or committee meetings. For individual director (and Chairman) performance evaluation, peer evaluation questionnaires are often used that require individual directors to assess the performance of themselves and their peers on a number of different criteria.

4.259 The UKCGC requires companies to report how their performance evaluation has been conducted. Currently, most companies include a short piece in their corporate governance statement, confirming that a board evaluation has taken place and, in some cases, explain the methodology and highlight some of the findings. We expect the extent of these disclosures to increase going forward.

4.260 Existing good practice disclosures may include:

■ Details of the outcome of the evaluation and any follow up action proposed, this indicates commitment to improvement and transparency.

■ What use the company makes, or plans to make in future, of externally facilitated performance reviews.

Board balance and independence

4.261 One focus of recent governance reviews was the importance of having an appropriate balance of skills, experience, independence and knowledge amongst the directors. The FRC has made this the main principle to replace the former one on the balance of executive and non-executive directors to emphasise that the over-riding consideration for assessing board composition is that the board is fit for purpose rather than independence criteria.

Principles

4.262 The main principle that should be applied in relation to board balance and independence is as follows:

■ The board and its committees should have the appropriate balance of skills, experience, independence and knowledge of the company to enable them to discharge their respective duties and responsibilities effectively. [UKCGC Main principle B.1].

4.263 The supporting principles relevant to board composition are:

■ The board should be of sufficient size that the requirements of the business can be met and that changes to the board's composition and that of its committees can be managed without undue disruption, and should not be so large as to be unwieldy. [UKCGC Supporting principle B.1].

- The board should include an appropriate combination of executive and non-executive directors (and, in particular, independent non-executive directors) such that no individual or small group of individuals can dominate the board's decision taking. [UKCGC Supporting principle B.1].

- The value of ensuring that committee membership is refreshed and that undue reliance is not placed on particular individuals should be taken into account in deciding chairmanship and membership of committees. [UKCGC Supporting principle B.1].

- No one other than the committee chairman and members is entitled to be present at a meeting of the nomination, audit or remuneration committee, but others may attend at the invitation of the committee. [UKCGC Supporting principle B.1].

Disclosures

4.264 Disclosures in relation to board balance and independence that are required within the annual report are:

- The annual report should identify each non-executive director that the board considers to be independent. If the board considers a director to be independent, but circumstances or relationships exist that may appear relevant to that decision, disclosure should be made of the reasons for determining that director to be independent. [UKCGC B.1.1].

4.265 The following are the detailed provisions related to the principles above:

- Circumstances that could appear to affect a director's independence will include:
- employment with the company or group within the last five years;
- a material business relationship within the last three years between the company and the director, or a body of which he/she is a partner shareholder, director or senior employee;
- any entitlement to remuneration from the company other than a director's fee or participation in the company's share option or a performance-related pay scheme or membership of the company's pension scheme;
- close family ties between the director and any of the company's advisers, directors or senior employees;
- a cross-directorship or significant links with other directors through involvement in other companies or bodies;
- representing a significant shareholder; or
- more than nine years' service on the board.

[UKCGC B.1.1].

- At least half the board, excluding the chairman, should comprise independent non-executive directors. A smaller company (that is, a company below the FTSE 350 throughout the year immediately prior to the reporting year) should have at least two independent non-executive directors. [UKCGC B.1.2].

- An independent non-executive director should be appointed by the board as the senior independent director. This director should provide a sounding board for the chairman and serve as an intermediary for the other directors. This directors should also be available to shareholders if they have concerns that contact through the normal channels of chairman, chief executive or finance director has failed to resolve or for which such contact is inappropriate. [UKCGC A.4.1].

- A chief executive should not go on to be chairman of the same company. If exceptionally a board decides that a chief executive should become chairman, the board should consult major shareholders in advance and should set out its reasons to shareholders at the time of the appointment and in the next annual report. [UKCGC A.3.1].

- The chairman should on appointment meet the independence criteria set out in B.1.1. [UKCGC A.3.1].

4.266 Although the main principle is now wider than independence, provision B.1.2 still requires that at least half the board (excluding the chairman) should comprise independent non-executive directors. Thus a board that comprises a chairman, three executive directors and four independent non-executive directors would comply with this provision; at least half the board excluding the chairman (that is, four independent directors out of seven directors) are independent.

4.267 This provision does not apply to smaller companies (defined as those companies categorised as falling outside of the FTSE 350 throughout the year immediately prior to the reporting year), which instead should have at least two independent non-executive directors. These recommendations can be difficult for smaller companies to comply with, given the practical difficulty of attracting and retaining high quality independent non-executives.

4.268 Best practice disclosures in this area tend to include:

- A description of succession planning to ensure ongoing balance is appropriate.

- An indication of future plans for succession for non-executives serving more than nine years (which remains relevant despite the new provision for FTSE 350 directors to be subject to annual re-election).

- A description of the criteria used for independence judgements.

4.269 The corporate governance reviews during 2009-10 questioned the role and activity of the board and whether there was sufficient oversight from the non-executive directors. The FRC, therefore, aimed in the new Code to emphasise the responsibility of non-executives and encourage appropriate behaviours by bringing the existing material on the role of the non-executives from supporting principle A.1 of the Combined Code (2008) under a new main principle A.4 stating that non-executives should constructively challenge and help develop proposals on strategy. In addition, the FRC adopted the Walker recommendation to expand the role of the Senior Independent Director (SID) to provide a sounding board for the chairman and serve as intermediary for other directors.

4.270   FRC guidance on the role of the non-executive director is included in the Higgs Guidance issued in June 2006; see paragraph 4.125.

4.271   Best practice disclosures in this area may include:

- Personal statements or examples from non-executive directors to demonstrate commitment to good board behaviours and constructive challenge of the executives.

- Clear explanation of why the senior independent director is suitable for the role including any explanations around independence.

Appointments to the board

4.272   Under the UKCGC, the FRC is encouraging boards to avoid 'group think' by considering diversity when making board appointments. The FRC, therefore, amended supporting principle B.2 by explicitly providing that due regard must be had to the benefits of diversity on the board, including gender, when searching for board candidates and making appointments.

4.273   One of the areas of focus in recent governance reviews was whether non-executive directors spend enough time to fulfil their role. The Walker recommendations discuss minimum time commitments: 30 to 36 days for a non-executive director in a major bank and, for a chairman of a major bank, around two-thirds of their time. The FRC has steered away from stipulating a minimum time commitment for non-executive directors, but a theme from previous supporting principle A.4 of the Combined Code (2008) has been elevated to new main principle B.3, emphasising the importance of this area.

Principles

4.274   The main principles that should be applied in relation to appointments to the board are as follows:

- There should be a formal, rigorous and transparent procedure for the appointment of new directors to the board. [UKCGC Main principle B.2].

- All directors should be able to allocate sufficient time to the company to discharge their responsibilities effectively. [UKCGC Main principle B.3].

- All directors should receive induction on joining the board and should regularly update and refresh their skills and knowledge. [UKCGC Main principle B.4].

- The board should be supplied in a timely manner with information in a form and of a quality appropriate to enable it to discharge its duties. [UKCGC Main principle B.5].

4.275 The supporting principles relevant to appointments to the board state that:

- The search for board candidates should be conducted, and appointments made, on merit, against objective criteria and with due regard for the benefits of diversity on the board, including gender. [UKCGC Supporting principle B.2].

- The board should satisfy itself that plans are in place for orderly succession for appointments to the board and to senior management, so as to maintain an appropriate balance of skills and experience within the company and on the board and to ensure progressive refreshing of the board. [UKCGC Supporting principle B.2].

- The chairman should ensure that the directors continually update their skills and the knowledge and familiarity with the company required to fulfil their role both on the board and on board committees. The company should provide the necessary resources for developing and updating its directors' knowledge and capabilities. [UKCGC Supporting principle B.4].

- To function effectively, all directors need appropriate knowledge of the company and access to its operations and staff. [UKCGC Supporting principle B.4].

- The chairman is responsible for ensuring that the directors receive accurate, timely and clear information. Management has an obligation to provide such information, but directors should seek clarification or amplification where necessary. [UKCGC Supporting principle B.5].

- Under the direction of the chairman, the company secretary's responsibilities include ensuring good information flows within the board and its committees and between senior management and non-executive directors, as well as facilitating induction and assisting with professional development as required. [UKCGC Supporting principle B.5].

- The company secretary should be responsible for advising the board through the chairman on all governance matters. [UKCGC Supporting principle B.5].

Disclosures

4.276 Disclosures should be made of the chairman's other significant commitments before his/her appointment. Any changes to these should be reported to the board as they arise and their impact explained in the annual report. [UKCGC B.3.1].

Other related provisions

4.277   The following detailed provisions should be addressed:

■   The nomination committee should prepare a job specification for the appointment of a chairman, including an assessment of the time commitment expected, recognising the need for availability in the event of crises. [UKCGC B.3.1].

■   The terms and conditions of appointment of non-executive directors should be made available for inspection (at the company's registered office during business hours and at the AGM for 15 minutes before the meeting and during the meeting). [UKCGC B.3.2].

■   Letters of appointment should set out the expected time commitment. Non-executive directors should undertake that they will have sufficient time to meet what is expected of them. Their other significant commitments should be disclosed to the board before appointment, and upon subsequent changes. [UKCGC B .3.2].

■   The board should not agree to a full time executive director taking on more than one non-executive directorship in a FTSE 100 company nor the chairmanship of such a company. [UKCGC B.3.3].

■   Where a company releases an executive director to serve as a non-executive director elsewhere, the remuneration report should include a statement as to whether or not the director will retain such earnings and, if so, what the remuneration is. [UKCGC D.1.2].

■   All directors, especially non-executive directors, should have access to independent professional advice at the expense of the company, where they judge it necessary to discharge their responsibilities as directors. Committees should be provided with sufficient resources to undertake their duties. [UKCGC B.5.1].

■   All directors should have access to the advice and services of the company secretary, who is responsible to the board for ensuring that board procedures are complied with. Both the appointment and removal of the company secretary should be a matter for the board as a whole. [UKCGC B.5.2].

■   The chairman should ensure that new directors receive a full, formal and tailored induction on joining the board. As part of this, directors should avail themselves of opportunities to meet major shareholders. [UKCGC B.4.1].

■   The chairman should regularly review and agree with each director their training and development needs. [UKCGC B.4.2].

4.278   Current best practice reporting in this area may address:

■   The expected time commitment for new non-executive directors (with or without numbers of days).

■   Whether the company has a policy restricting the number of other directorships held by non-executive directors.

■   A table of directors' attendance at board and committee meetings. This also gives clarity to director changes and board and committee appointments.

Induction, training and ongoing professional development

4.279   Another point of focus of recent governance reviews was the extent of the induction, training and ongoing professional development of non-executive directors. If the non-executive directors are expected to challenge constructively and question sensibly, they need to have sufficient knowledge and understanding of the business and its issues. The FRC has, therefore, split a previous main principle into two main principles 'Development' and 'Information and support' to recognise that they are two separate activities of an effective board. Within the development section the FRC also included:

■   A new provision that the chairman should regularly review and agree with each director their training and development needs.

■   A new supporting principle recognising the importance of directors acquiring appropriate knowledge of the company. This recognises that non-executive directors would be better able to provide constructive challenge if they spent more time in the operational parts to gain a better understanding of its activities and challenges.

■   Descriptions of the specific information packs that board members receive.

4.280   The Higgs Guidance issued in June 2006 includes an induction checklist for non-executive directors.

4.281   Companies may wish to explain as part of best practice disclosures:

■   The specific arrangements for tailored induction and ongoing professional development for directors.

■   Opportunities provided for non-executives to understand the business more fully.

■   How executive directors take on non-executive roles to enhance their experience and development.

4.282   The Walker Review recommended a dedicated support for non-executives of banks and financial institutions on any matter relevant to the business. The FRC did not change the existing provisions, so that the arrangement above continues to apply.

Disclosures

4.283   Disclosures in relation to the nomination committee that are required within the annual report are as follows:

■   A separate section of the annual report should describe the work of the nomination committee, including the process it has used in relation to board appointments. An explanation should be given if neither an external search consultancy nor open advertising has been used in the appointment of a chairman or a non-executive director. [CC B.2.4].

The above disclosure provision overlaps with the DTR and the DTR confirms that, if a company provides the information specified by CC B.2.4 above, it will satisfy the requirements of DTR 7.2.7 R in respect of this committee.

Other related provisions

4.284   The following are the relevant detailed provisions:

■   The nomination committee should lead the process for board appointments and make recommendations to the board. The majority of the committee should be independent non-executive directors. The chair of the nomination committee should be either the chairman or an independent non-executive director. The chairman should not chair the committee when dealing with the appointment of a successor to the chairmanship. [UKCGC B.2.1].

■   The nomination committee should make its terms of reference available — these terms of reference should explain the committee's role and the authority delegated to it by the board. [UKCGC A.4.1].

■   The nomination committee should evaluate the balance of skills, knowledge and experience on the board. In the light of this evaluation, the committee should prepare a description of the role and capabilities required for a particular appointment. [UKCGC B.2.2].

4.285   The nomination committee is responsible for board composition, new appointments and succession planning; it therefore fulfils a vital role in effectively creating an effective board. The Higgs Guidance issued in June 2006 includes a summary of the principal duties of the nomination committee, a pre-appointment due diligence checklist for new board members and a sample letter of non-executive director appointment.

4.286   Current best practice disclosures and practices on nomination committees include:

■   A description of the skills and experience criteria for new board appointments; in future these will need to show due regard for diversity.

■ The setting up of a specialised nomination committee for key appointments, such as chairman.

Audit committee and auditors

Principles

4.287 The main principle that should be applied in relation to the audit committee is as follows:

■ The board should establish formal and transparent arrangements for considering how they should apply the corporate reporting and risk management and internal control principles and for maintaining an appropriate relationship with the company's auditors. [UKCGC Main principle C.3].

4.288 Disclosures in relation to audit committees arising from both the UKCGC and the FRC guidance on audit committees, formerly known as the Smith guidance, have been summarised below. The Smith guidance is discussed further from paragraph 4.145 onwards.

■ The terms of reference of the audit committee, including its role and the authority delegated to it by the board, should be made available. A separate section in the annual report should describe the work of the committee in discharging its responsibilities. [Smith para 5.1; UKCGC C.3.3].

  ■ The audit committee section should include:

  ■ A summary of the role of the audit committee.

  ■ The names and qualifications of all members of the audit committee during the period.

  ■ The number of audit committee meetings.

  ■ A report on the way the audit committee has discharged its responsibilities.

  [Smith para 5.2].

■ Where there is no internal audit function, the reasons for its absence should be explained. [Smith para 4.9; UKCGC C.3.5].

■ The audit committee should have primary responsibility for making a recommendation to the board on the appointment, reappointment and removal of the external auditors. If the board does not accept the audit committee's recommendation, the annual report should include a statement from the audit committee explaining its recommendation and the reasons why the board has taken a different position. [Smith para 4.17; UKCGC C.3.6].

- The audit committee section of the annual report should explain to shareholders how it reached its recommendation to the board on the appointment, reappointment or removal of the external auditors. This explanation should normally include supporting information on tendering frequency, the tenure of the incumbent auditor, and any contractual obligations that acted to restrict the audit committee's choice of external auditors. [Smith para 4.22].

- If the auditor provides non-audit services, it should be explained how the auditor's objectivity and independence is safeguarded. [Smith para 4.34; UKCGC C.3.7].

Other related provisions

4.289   The following detailed provisions and guidance relevant to this area:

- The audit committee should consist of at least three, or in the case of smaller companies, (that is, those below the FTSE 350 throughout the year immediately prior to the reporting year), two independent non-executive directors. In smaller companies the company chairman may be a member of, but not chair, the committee in addition to the independent non-executive directors, provided he or she was considered independent on appointment as chairman. The board should satisfy itself that at least one member of the audit committee has recent and relevant financial experience. [UKCGC C.3.1; Smith paras 2.1 and 2.3]. See paragraph 4.291 for further discussion of 'recent and relevant' financial experience.

- The audit committee should have written terms of reference setting out its responsibilities that should include:

  - monitoring the integrity of the company's financial statements, and announcements relating to the company's financial performance and reviewing significant financial reporting judgements contained in them;

  - reviewing the company's financial and non-financial internal controls and risk management systems (to the extent that these are not delegated to another committee made up of independent non-executive directors);

  - monitoring and reviewing the effectiveness of the company's internal audit function;

  - making recommendations to the board relating to the appointment, re-appointment and removal of the external auditor and approving the remuneration and terms of engagement of the external auditor;

  - reviewing and monitoring the external auditor's and effectiveness of the audit process;

  - developing and implementing a policy on the engagement of the external auditor to supply non-audit services and reporting to the board, identifying matters in where action or improvement is needed.

[UKCGC C.3.2; Smith para 2.2].

- The audit committee should monitor and review the effectiveness of the internal audit activities. Where there is no internal audit function, the audit committee should consider annually whether there is a need for one and make a recommendation to the board. [UKCGC C.3.5; Smith para 4.9].

- The audit committee should review arrangements by which staff of the company may, in confidence, raise concerns about possible improprieties in matters of financial reporting or other matters. It should ensure the proportionate and independent investigation of such matters and follow-up action. [UKCGC C.3.4].

4.290 In banks and other financial industry entities the role of a separate risk committee and the need for a chief risk officer have been key areas of discussion and Walker has specific recommendations around these. The FRC has not extended these recommendations to all listed entities. The audit committee retains responsibility for elements of risk and control and the main principle on audit committees has been reworded to reflect the committee's role in risk management. Otherwise there have been no changes to this part of the UK Corporate Governance Code. Further guidance is included in the FRC guidance on challenges for Audit Committees arising from current economic conditions, discussed from paragraph 4.151. In addition there are DTR requirements on audit committees, which are discussed in paragraph 4.46.

Provision C.3.1 'Recent and relevant' financial experience

4.291 Some companies feel that identifying one individual as having recent and relevant financial experience may increase that individual's exposure to liability and as a result choose not to identify one individual, but rather explain that audit committee members collectively have recent and relevant financial experience. If this is the case, it is a departure from the Code and requires an explanation. The FSA Rules, which are discussed further in paragraph 4.46, also provide that at least one member of the audit committee (or the equivalent body) must have competence in accounting and/or auditing.

4.292 Current best practice reporting on audit committees may include:

- Details of the qualifications and experience of audit committee members to confirm their suitability and recent and relevant financial experience.

- Specific examples of audit committee activities in the year and how these addressed developments in the business.

DTR overlap summary

4.293 Refer to paragraph 4.59 for an explanation of the overlapping provisions between the UKCGC and the DTR requirements on audit committees.

Principles

4.294   The main principles that should be applied in relation to remuneration are as follows:

- Levels of remuneration should be sufficient to attract, retain and motivate directors of the quality required to run the company successfully, but a company should avoid paying more than is necessary for this purpose. A significant proportion of executive directors' remuneration should be structured so as to link rewards to corporate and individual performance. [UKCGC Main principle D.1].

- There should be a formal and transparent procedure for developing policy on executive remuneration and for fixing the remuneration packages of individual directors. No director should be involved in deciding his or her own remuneration. [UKCGC Main principle D.2].

4.295   The supporting principles relevant to remuneration are as follows:

- The performance-related elements of executive directors' remuneration should be stretching and designed to promote the long-term success of the company. [UKCGC Supporting principle D.1].

- The remuneration committee should judge where to position their company relative to other companies. But they should use such comparisons with caution in view of the risk of an upward ratchet of remuneration levels with no corresponding improvement in performance. [UKCGC Supporting principle D.1].

- They should also be sensitive to pay and employment conditions elsewhere in the group, especially when determining annual salary increases. [UKCGC Supporting principle D.1].

- The remuneration committee should consult the chairman and/or chief executive about their proposals relating to the remuneration of other executive directors. The remuneration committee should also be responsible for appointing any consultants in respect of executive director remuneration. Where executive directors or senior management are involved in advising or supporting the remuneration committee, care should be taken to recognise and avoid conflicts of interest. [UKCGC Supporting principle D.2].

- The chairman of the board should ensure that the company maintains contact as required with its principal shareholders about remuneration. [UKCGC Supporting principle D.2].

Disclosures

4.296   Disclosures in relation to the remuneration committee that are required within the annual report are as follows:

■   The remuneration report should include a description of the work of the remuneration committee, including, where an executive director serves as a non-executive director elsewhere, whether or not the director will retain such earnings and, if so, what the remuneration is. [UKCGC D.1.2].

■   Where remuneration consultants are appointed, a statement should be made available of whether they have any other connection with the company. [UKCGC D.2.1].

The above disclosure provision overlaps with the DTR and the DTR confirms that, if a company provides the information specified by UKCGC D.2.1 above, it will satisfy the relevant requirements of DTR 7.2.7R in respect of this committee as long as this information is given within the corporate governance statement itself.

Other related provisions

The level and components of remuneration

4.297   The following detailed provisions in relation to the level and components of remuneration should be complied with, or explanations given:

■   In designing schemes of performance-related remuneration for executive directors, the remuneration committee should follow the provisions in Schedule A to the Code. [UKCGC D.1.1].

■   Levels of remuneration for non-executive directors should reflect the time commitment and responsibilities of the role. Remuneration for non-executive directors should not include share options or other performance-related elements. If, exceptionally, options are granted, shareholder approval should be sought in advance and any shares acquired by exercise of the options should be held until at least one year after the non-executive director leaves the board. Holding of share options could be relevant to determining a non-executive director's independence (as set out in provision B.1.1). [UKCGC D.1.3].

■   The remuneration committee should carefully consider what compensation commitments (including pension contributions and all other elements) their directors' terms of appointment would entail in the event of early termination. The aim should be to avoid rewarding poor performance. They should take a robust line on reducing compensation to reflect departing directors' obligations to mitigate loss. [UKCGC D.1.4].

■   Notice or contract periods should be set at one year or less. If it is necessary to offer longer notice or contract periods to new directors recruited from outside, such periods should reduce to one year or less after the initial period. [UKCGC D.1.5].

Procedure

4.298   The Code includes specific provisions regarding the procedures relating to remuneration. These provisions should be applied:

- The remuneration committee should have delegated responsibility for setting remuneration for all executive directors and the chairman, including pension rights and any compensation payments. The committee should also recommend and monitor the level and structure of remuneration for senior management. The definition of 'senior management' for this purpose should be determined by the board, but should normally include the first layer of management below board level. [UKCGC D.2.2].

- The board itself or, where required by the Articles of Association, the shareholders should determine the remuneration of the non-executive directors within the limits set in the Articles of Association. Where permitted by the Articles, the board may however delegate this responsibility to a committee, which might include the chief executive. [UKCGC D.2.3].

- Shareholders should be invited specifically to approve all new long-term incentive schemes (as defined in the Listing Rules) and significant changes to existing schemes, save in the circumstances permitted by the Listing Rules. [UKCGC D.2.4].

4.299   Performance-related pay was much discussed during the recent governance reviews. Walker made several recommendations in this area and the FRC implemented the following in the new Code:

- performance-related remuneration to be stretching and designed to promote the company's long term success (supporting principle and provision);

- incentives to be compatible with risk policies and systems (provision); and

- consideration to be given for the company to claw-back variable components of remuneration in exceptional circumstances (provision).

Provision D.1.3 has also been strengthened to clarify that all forms of performance-related remuneration are discouraged for non-executives, not just share options. No changes were made to the remuneration 'procedure' part of the Code.

Principles

4.300   The main principle that should be applied in relation to internal controls is as follows:

- The board is responsible for determining the nature and extent of the significant risks it is willing to take in achieving its strategic objectives. The board should maintain sound risk management and internal control systems. [UKCGC Main principle C.2].

Disclosures

4.301   Disclosures in relation to internal controls that are required within the annual report are as follows:

- The board should, at least annually, conduct a review of the effectiveness of the company's risk management and internal control systems and should report to shareholders that they have done so. The review should cover all material controls, including financial, operational and compliance controls. [UKCGC C.2.1].

4.302   As a reminder, the DTR also requires the following additional disclosures (see para 4.56):

- The corporate governance statement must include a description of the main features of the company's internal control and risk management systems in relation to the financial reporting process. [DTR 7.2.5 R].

- Where the issuer is required to prepare a group directors' report, they should include a description of the main features of the group's internal control and risk management systems in relation to the process for preparing consolidated financial statements. [DTR 7.2.10 R].

The DTR requirements differ from the UKCGC; however, the FRC envisages that both could be met by a single internal control statement.

4.303   Another of the themes of recent corporate governance reviews was in relation to boards taking greater responsibility for assessing the company's risk profile, tolerance of risk and oversight of risk management systems. The FRC, therefore, enhanced the relevant main principle by adding that the "... *board is responsible for determining the nature and extent of the significant risks it is willing to take in achieving its strategic objectives*". In the financial sector, this is usually referred to as a company's 'risk appetite'. In the accompanying provision it has also been made explicit that the annual effectiveness review over internal control should include the risk management system.

4.304 The main guidance to assist directors in complying with the annual effectiveness review provision is the Turnbull guidance. Turnbull, and the disclosures required by it, are discussed further from paragraph 4.171.

4.305 Current best practice reporting in this area includes:

■ A tailored description of the company's internal control and risk management framework. The use of diagrams adds clarity and allows complex concepts to be presented effectively.

■ Clear linkage between business and industry risks and the system of internal control.

■ An explanation of how the judgements and inherent uncertainties underlying risk management systems are handled.

■ An explanation of the roles and remit of any other committees within the internal control framework.

Financial reporting

Principles

4.306 The main principle that should be applied in relation to financial reporting is as follows:

■ The board should present a balanced and understandable assessment of the company's position and prospects. [UKCGC Main principle C.1].

4.307 The supporting principle relevant to financial reporting states that the board's responsibility to present a balanced and understandable assessment extends to interim and other price-sensitive public reports and reports to regulators as well as to information required to be presented by statutory requirements. [UKCGC Supporting principle C.1].

4.308 Disclosures in relation to financial reporting that are required within the annual report are as follows:

■ There should be a statement from the directors explaining their responsibility for preparing the financial statements. [UKCGC C.1.1].

■ The directors should include in the annual report an explanation of the basis on which the company generates or preserves value over the longer term (the business model) and the strategy for delivering the objectives of the company. [UKCGC C.1.2].

■ The directors should report in annual and half-yearly financial statements that the business is a going concern, with supporting assumptions or qualifications as necessary. [UKCGC C.1.3].

4.309 The recent corporate governance reviews emphasised the need for boards to take greater responsibility for risk management. Concerns were also expressed about the quality of risk reporting. The FRC has, therefore, included a new provision in the new Code that the Business Review section of the annual report should include an explanation of the business model and strategy for delivering the company's objectives. The FRC has also amended the provision on going concern disclosures to clarify that these disclosures should be made both in half-yearly and annual financial statements. Paragraph 4.197 onwards discusses the FRC guidance on going concern and liquidity risk that suggests means of applying this provision. The Listing Rules also require a statement on going concern (see para 4.312.)

Directors' responsibility statements

4.310 Refer to chapter 3 for a discussion on directors' responsibility statements.

Business model

4.311 The FRC refers to paragraphs 30 to 32 of the ASB's Reporting Statement on the Operating and Financial Review for guidance as to the matters that should be considered in an explanation of a business model. These paragraphs are discussed in 'The business' nature, objectives and strategies' section of chapter two. The FRC has made it clear that companies reporting in line with the ASB's Reporting Statement will have met the requirements of UKCGC C.1.2 (see para 2.37.20.1.)

Going concern reporting

4.312 The sources of regulation and guidance that should be applied by companies include:

- Listing Rule 9.8.6 R (3), which requires a statement that the business is a going concern (see para 4.196).

- FRC guidance on going concern and liquidity risk (see para 4.197).

- FRC guidance relating to the challenges for audit committees arising from current economic conditions (see para 4.151).

4.313 The FRC guidance on going concern and liquidity risk emphasises the importance of balanced, proportionate and clear disclosures about going concern issues and the key assumptions being made in one place in the annual report (which may not be in the governance statement itself). Along with the withdrawal of the 'boilerplate' language for the going concern confirmation statement, this should result in a more meaningful confirmation statement by companies.

Communication

4.314   One of the themes of recent governance reviews has been that there needs
to be appropriate two-way communication between the board and its investors if
the 'comply or explain' mechanism of the Code is to work effectively. Too often,
both companies and shareholders have reported frustration over the quality of
'engagement'. Companies criticise investors for taking a box-ticking approach to
monitoring their investees, while shareholders criticise companies for preferring
presentations to dialogue.

4.315   As recommended in the Walker Report the FRC has issued a Stewardship
Code for institutional investors, which came into effect in July 2010. As a result
section E of the Combined Code ceased to be applicable. See from
paragraph 4.343 for discussion of UK Stewardship Code. Section D on the
company side continues to be applicable and is carried forward in section E of the
UKCGC.

Dialogue with institutional shareholders

Principles

4.316   The main principle that should be applied in relation to dialogue with
institutional shareholders is as follows:

- There should be a dialogue with shareholders based on the mutual
  understanding of objectives. The board as a whole has responsibility for
  ensuring that a satisfactory dialogue with shareholders takes place.
  [UKCGC E.1].

4.317   The supporting principles relevant to this dialogue include the following:

- Whilst recognising that most shareholder contact is with the chief executive
  and finance director, the chairman (and the senior independent director and
  other directors as appropriate) should maintain sufficient contact with
  major shareholders to understand their issues and concerns. [UKCGC
  Supporting principle E.1].

- The board should keep in touch with shareholder opinion in whatever ways
  are most practical and efficient. [UKCGC Supporting principle E.1].

Disclosures

4.318   Disclosures in relation to this dialogue that are required within the annual
report are as follows:

- Disclosure should be made of the steps that the board has taken to ensure
  that the members of the board, and in particular the non-executive directors,
  develop an understanding of the views of the major shareholders (for

example through direct face-to-face contact, analysts' or brokers' briefings and surveys of shareholder opinion) about their company. [UKCGC E.1.2].

Other related provisions

4.319   The following provisions are not disclosure provisions. However it is envisaged that compliance with these detailed provisions will mean that the main principle has been applied.

■   The chairman should ensure that the views of shareholders are communicated to the board as a whole. [UKCGC E.1.1].

■   The chairman should discuss governance and strategy with major shareholders. Non-executive directors should be offered the opportunity to attend meetings with major shareholders and should expect to attend them if requested by major shareholders. The senior independent director should also attend sufficient meetings with a range of major shareholders to listen to their views. [UKCGC E.1.1].

4.320   Current best practice and transparent reporting in this area may include the following:

■   The use of an independent third party to assist the board in obtaining investor views; this demonstrates commitment and encourages openness.

■   Company-specific disclosure about two-way communication and investor relations process.

■   Recognition in practice and in the annual report of the importance of the whole investor base, including non-institutional investors, where applicable.

■   Effective use of technology to enhance shareholder communications, such as reference to websites where investor relations information is held.

Constructive use of the AGM

Principles

4.321   The main principle that should be applied in relation to constructive use of the AGM is as follows:

■   The board should use the AGM to communicate with investors and to encourage their participation. [UKCGC Main principle E.2].

Other related provisions

4.322   There are no disclosure provisions associated with constructive use of the AGM. However, the following detailed provisions should be implemented by the company:

- The chairman should arrange for the chairmen of the audit, remuneration and nomination committees to be available to answer questions at the AGM and for all directors to attend. [UKCGC E.2.3].

- The company should propose a separate resolution on each substantially separate issue and should in particular propose a resolution at the AGM relating to the report and accounts. For each resolution, proxy appointment forms should provide shareholders with the option to direct their proxy to vote either for or against the resolution or to withhold their vote. The proxy form and any announcement of the results of a vote should make clear that a 'vote withheld' is not a vote in law and will not be counted in the calculation of the proportion of the votes for and against the resolution. [UKCGC E.2.1].

- The company should ensure that all valid proxy appointments received for general meetings are properly recorded and counted. For each resolution, after a vote has been taken, except where taken on a poll, the company should ensure that the following information is given at the meeting and made available as soon as reasonably practicable on the company's website:

    - the number of shares in respect of which proxy appointments have been validly made; and

    - the number of votes (i) for, and (ii) against the resolution, and (iii) the number of shares in respect of which the vote was directed to be withheld.

  [UKCGC E.2.2].

- The company should arrange for the Notice of the AGM and related papers to be sent to shareholders at least 20 working days before the meeting. [UKCGC E.2.4].

4.323 The AGM is the main formal opportunity for dialogue and communication between the company and its shareholders. From the company's point of view, the AGM provides a forum for the board to inform its shareholders about what the company does and how well it has performed during the year. For investors, it provides a forum to learn more about the business and ask questions of the directors, (particularly the chairmen of the audit, remuneration and nomination committees) and to use their votes responsibly.

4.324 Current best practice reporting in this area may explain that the company:

- Ensures shareholders are aware of meeting protocol, such as by referring to a separate Notice of Meeting booklet.

- Appoints an independent assessor to scrutinise the AGM to strengthen reporting and enhance transparency.

Practical implications around implementing the new Code

4.325   The practical implications of the changes to the Code include the following. These may require companies to take specific action in advance of the first period of reporting under the UKCGC, once they have determined whether they plan to comply.

■   Annual re-election for directors of FTSE 350 companies: A change in the company's Articles of Association may be needed to implement this provision. If a change of Articles takes place during the first year to which the new Code applies then the annual report would still need to explain non-compliance for the period up to the change of the Articles.

■   External facilitation of board evaluation: When will this start and what will be done in the intervening years?

■   Diversity: How will this be addressed, including gender diversity?

■   Risk appetite: Ensure the board determines nature and extent of significant risks it is willing to take and that risk management is a regular feature of board agenda.

■   Induction programme: Ensure non-executive directors have the opportunity for site visits and to meet staff and major shareholders.

■   Training: The Chairman should start to regularly review and agree training and development needs for all directors.

■   Description of business model: Consider how this requirement will be addressed for the next annual report.

■   Communicating shareholders' concerns: Ensure all directors are made aware of major shareholders' concerns.

■   Going concern statement: Include a statement on going concern in the next half-year report.

Auditor review of compliance with the Combined Code and UKCGC

Listing Rules requirement

4.326   The Listing Rules include reference to the Code and explain auditor responsibilities in relation to it. The Listing Rules were amended with effect of from August 2010 to include reference to the new name of the Code. The Listing Rules' transitional provisions (FSA 2010/39) state that: "*References to provisions in the UK Corporate Governance Code are to be read as references to the equivalent provisions in the Combined Code for accounting periods beginning before 29 June 2010*".

4.327   There is no other change in the auditor responsibilities as a result of the introduction of the UKCGC.

4.328   The Listing Rules state that auditors should review companies' disclosures in relation to nine provisions of the UK Corporate Governance Code. This excludes provision C.1.2, relating to going concern, because this provision is covered by Listing Rule 9.8.6R(3). The provisions covered by the auditors' review requirement are stated in Listing Rule 9.8.10R(2) and are as follows:

■   The directors should explain in the annual report their responsibility for preparing the financial statements and there should be a statement by the auditors about their reporting responsibilities. [CC and UKCGC C.1.1].

■   The board should, at least annually, conduct a review of the effectiveness of the group's system of internal controls and should report to shareholders that they have done so. The review should cover all material controls, including financial, operational and compliance controls and risk management systems. [CC C.2.1].

Or, under UKCGC:

The board should, at least annually, conduct a review of the effectiveness of the company's risk management and internal control systems and should report to shareholders that they have done so. The review should cover all material controls, including financial, operational and compliance controls. [UKCGC C.2.1].

■   The board should establish an audit committee of at least three, or in the case of smaller companies two, independent non-executive directors. In smaller companies the company chairman may be a member of, but not chair, the committee in addition to the independent non-executive directors, provided he or she was considered independent on appointment as chairman. The board should satisfy itself that at least one member of the audit committee has recent and relevant financial experience. [CC and UKCGC C.3.1].

■   The main role and responsibilities of the audit committee should be set out in written terms of reference and should include:

■   To monitor the integrity of the company's financial statements and any formal announcements relating to the company's financial performance, reviewing significant financial reporting judgements contained in them.

■   To review the company's internal financial controls and, unless expressly addressed by a separate board risk committee composed of independent directors, or by the board itself, to review the company's internal control and risk management systems.

■   To monitor and review the effectiveness of the company's internal audit function.

■   To make recommendations to the board, for it to put to the shareholders for their approval in general meeting, in relation to the appointment, re-appointment and removal of the external auditor and to approve the remuneration and terms of engagement of the external auditor.

- To review and monitor the external auditor's independence and objectivity and the effectiveness of the audit process, taking into consideration relevant UK professional and regulatory requirements.

- To develop and implement policy on the engagement of the external auditor to supply non-audit services, taking into account relevant ethical guidance regarding the provision of non-audit services by the external audit firm.

- To report to the board, identifying any matters in respect of which it considers that action or improvement is needed and making recommendations as to the steps to be taken.

[CC and UKCGC C.3.2].

- The terms of reference of the audit committee, including its role and the authority delegated to it by the board, should be made available. A separate section of the annual report should describe the work of the committee in discharging those responsibilities. [CC and UKCGC C.3.3].

- The audit committee should review arrangements by which the company's staff may, in confidence, raise concerns about possible improprieties in matters of financial reporting or other matters. The audit committee's objective should be to ensure that arrangements are in place for the proportionate and independent investigation of such matters and for appropriate follow-up action. [CC and UKCGC C.3.4].

- The audit committee should monitor and review the effectiveness of the internal audit activities. Where there is no internal audit function, the audit committee should consider annually whether there is a need for an internal audit function and make a recommendation to the board, and the reasons for the absence of such a function should be explained in the relevant section of the annual report. [CC and UKCGC C.3.5].

- The audit committee should have primary responsibility for making a recommendation on the appointment, re-appointment and removal of the external auditors. If the board does not accept the audit committee's recommendation, it should include in the annual report, and in any papers recommending appointment or re-appointment, a statement from the audit committee explaining the recommendation and should set out reasons why the board has taken a different position. [CC and UKCGC C.3.6].

- The annual report should explain to shareholders how, if the auditor provides non-audit services, auditor objectivity and independence is safeguarded. [CC and UKCGC C.3.7].

4.329   In addition to the review requirement under the Listing Rules, the scope of the auditor's report on the financial statements must cover certain disclosure requirements concerning directors' remuneration. These include the disclosures required by Listing Rules 9.8.11R(1), (2), (3) and (4) (see further chapter 5). The auditor must state in the audit report if in his or her opinion the company has not complied with the disclosures specified above and, where this information has not been given, must include in the report, so far as he/she is reasonably able to do so, a statement giving the required information. [LR 9.8.12R].

4.330 Detailed guidance on how to perform the auditors' review in relation to companies' reporting under the Combined Code was issued by the APB in Bulletin 2006/05, 'The Combined Code on corporate governance: requirements of auditors under the Listing Rules of the Financial Services Authority and the Irish Stock Exchange'. This sets out specific procedures to be followed in relation to each relevant provision. The auditors' responsibilities in respect of the directors' statement on going concern are set out in APB Bulletin 2009/04, 'Developments in corporate governance affecting the responsibilities of auditors of UK companies'.

4.331 The guidance in APB Bulletin 2006/05 covers the auditors' review responsibilities in relation to the directors' statement on internal control.

4.332 There is no requirement, in either the UK Corporate Governance Code, Combined Code or the Listing Rules for publication of an auditors' report on corporate governance. In 1999 the APB concluded that such a report could be seriously misleading for readers. They were of the view that the narrow scope of the auditors' review and the introduction of a statement of auditors' responsibilities meant that it was no longer appropriate for auditors' reports on the directors' compliance statement to be published in the annual report. For listed companies this position resulted in the discontinuance of published auditors' reports on corporate governance matters in annual reports of listed companies.

4.333 Instead of a separate report on corporate governance matters, auditors of premium listed companies report in an 'Other matters' section of the report on the annual report and financial statements that they have reviewed the nine provisions specified and the going concern statement.

4.334 As discussed in paragraph 4.49, the DTR requires certain companies to present a corporate governance statement, which may be included as part of the directors' report. Alternatively, it can be separately issued to accompany the annual report or may be made available on the company's web site, but with cross-references in the directors' report. Where the company publishes a separate corporate governance statement, there are new requirements for the auditors under the Companies Act 2006, which have been introduced by SI 2009/1581, 'The Companies Act 2006 (Accounts, Reports and Audit) Regulations 2009'. This SI amends Parts 15 and 16 of the Companies Act 2006 to deal with the approval, signing and filing of the corporate governance statement where companies choose to present such a statement separately, rather than including it in the directors' report and includes additional duties for the auditors. The auditor is required to give an opinion on whether certain information in the corporate governance statement is consistent with the financial statements. Where the company chooses to present a separate corporate governance statement, the auditor has to give a separate opinion in the audit report.

Approval, signing and filing of separate corporate governance statement

4.335   When the corporate governance statement is included as part of the directors' report it will be approved on behalf of the board and filed with the Registrar of Companies as part of the directors' report. For companies presenting a separate corporate governance statement, the SI is effectively putting into law the same provisions regarding approval, signing and filing that would apply had the corporate governance statement been included within the directors' report.

4.336   A new section 419A has been inserted after section 419 of the Companies Act 2006 (approval and signing of directors' report), which requires that any separate corporate governance statement must be approved by the board of directors and signed on behalf of the board by a director or the company secretary.

4.337   Sections 446 and 447 of the Companies Act 2006 have been amended to provide that the directors of a quoted or an unquoted company must deliver to the Registrar of Companies a copy of any separate corporate governance statement, in addition to the company's annual financial statements, the directors' remuneration report (for quoted companies only) and the directors' report. The separate corporate governance statement must state the name of the person who signed it on behalf of the board under section 419A and must be signed on behalf of the board by a director or the company secretary. They must also deliver a copy of the auditors' report on any separate corporate governance statement.

Auditors' report and auditors' duties on separate corporate governance statement

4.338   There are different requirements of auditors depending on which option a company exercises for the publication of its corporate governance statement.

4.339   (Under DTR 7.2.1 R) – If the corporate governance statement is included as part of the directors' report, the audit requirement is that of existing section 496 of the Companies Act 2006. That is, the auditors are required to state in their report on the company's annual financial statements whether, in their opinion, the information given in the directors' report for the financial year for which the financial statements are prepared is consistent with those accounts.

4.340   (Under DTR 7.2.9 R) – A new section 497A has been inserted after section 497 of the Companies Act 2006, which provides that if the corporate governance statement is not included within the directors' report, the auditor must state in their report whether, in their opinion, the information given in the corporate governance statement in compliance with rules 7.2.5 and 7.2.6 of the FSA's Disclosure Rules and Transparency Rules (Corporate Governance Rules) regarding internal control and risk management systems and certain disclosures on share capital structures is consistent with the annual financial statements for the year. For the other information in the corporate governance statement, the auditor must check that the information has been included.

4.341   A new section 498A has been inserted after section 498 of the Companies Act 2006 (duties of auditor), which provides that, where a company is required to prepare a corporate governance statement, and has neither included such a statement as part of its directors' report nor prepared a separate corporate governance statement, the auditors must state that fact in their report.

4.342   The APB recommends that prior to the release of the annual report, the auditor communicates, and discusses, with the directors the scope and factual findings of their review.

The UK Stewardship Code

4.343   The FRC agreed to take on responsibility for oversight of a code to enhance shareholder engagement following Sir David Walker's recommendations. The FRC subsequently published the first Stewardship Code for institutional investors in 2 July 2010, following a consultation process. The purpose of the Code is to improve the quality of corporate governance through promoting better dialogue between shareholders and company boards, and more transparency about the way in which investors oversee the companies they own.

Who should apply the Code

4.344   The Code is addressed in the first instance to firms who manage assets on behalf of institutional shareholders such as pension funds, insurance companies, investment trusts and other collective investment vehicles. The FSA is consulting on whether to introduce a 'comply or explain' disclosure requirement that would apply to those firms authorised by the FSA to manage assets on behalf of institutional investors.

4.345   The responsibility for monitoring company performance does not rest with fund managers alone. The FRC, therefore, strongly encourages all institutional investors to publicly report if and how they have complied with the Code. Pension funds and other owners may not wish to become directly involved in engagement, but they can make a significant contribution by, for example, mandating their fund managers to do so on their behalf.

4.346   Principle 1 of the Code (see Content of the UK Stewardship Code below) states that institutional investors that make use of proxy voting and other advisory services should disclose how they are used. The FRC encourages those service providers in turn to disclose how they carry out the wishes of their clients by applying the principles of the Code that are relevant to their activities.

4.347   The FRC also hopes that investors based outside the UK will commit to the Code. It is recognised that, in practice, local institutions usually take the lead in engagement.

Comply or explain

4.348   Like the UK Corporate Governance Code, the UK Stewardship Code is to be applied on a 'comply or explain' basis. In reporting terms this currently entails providing a statement on the institutional investor's website containing:

■   a description of how the principles of the Code have been applied; and

■   disclosure of the specific information listed under Principles 1, 5, 6 and 7; or

■   an explanation if these elements of the Code have not been complied with.

Content of the UK Stewardship Code

4.349   The UK Stewardship Code is based on the Institutional Shareholders' Committee (ISC) Code and consists of the following seven principles and further guidance on each of them.

The principles are as follows. Institutional investors should:

1.   Publicly disclose their policy on how they will discharge their stewardship responsibilities.

2.   Have a robust policy on managing conflicts of interest in relation to stewardship and this policy should be publicly disclosed.

3.   Monitor their investee companies.

4.   Establish clear guidelines on when and how they will escalate their activities as a method of protecting and enhancing shareholder value.

5.   Be willing to act collectively with other investors where appropriate.

6.   Have a clear policy on voting and disclosure of voting activity.

7.   Report periodically on their stewardship and voting activities.

4.350   The amendments made to the ISC Code to arrive at the UK Stewardship Code are intended to incorporate guidance to institutional investors previously contained in Section E of the 2008 Combined Code, and to align this Code with the guidance on engagement provided to companies in the new UK Corporate Governance Code. Specifically, the guidance on Principle 3 (on the monitoring of companies) has been amended to encourage investors to:

■   meet the chairman of investee companies, and other board members where appropriate, as part of their ongoing monitoring and not only when they have concerns;

- attend the General Meetings of companies in which they have a major holding, where appropriate and practicable; and

- consider carefully explanations given by investee companies for departure from the UK Corporate Governance Code, and advise the company where they do not accept its position.

Reporting to clients

4.351 Under the Stewardship Code, investment firms and other agents should report regularly to their clients on how they have discharged their responsibilities. The Code also recommends that investors who sign up to it should consider obtaining an independent audit opinion on their engagement and voting processes and that the existence of such assurance reports should be publicly disclosed. The most relevant existing reporting standard is the Audit and Assurance Faculty (AAF) 01/06 guidance, produced by the ICAEW.

4.352 Guidance on reporting is currently being developed by the ICAEW in conjunction with a stakeholder panel. The FRC have stated that asset managers may wish to wait until this guidance has been finalised before considering whether to comply with this part of the Code.

Monitoring

4.353 From the end of September 2010 the FRC plans to retain on its website a list of those institutions that have published a statement on their compliance or otherwise with the Stewardship Code.

4.354 The FRC will undertake further work to develop a proposed approach to monitoring. It is envisaged that the first full monitoring exercise, looking at the take-up and application of the Code, will be carried out in the second half of 2011.

4.355 As an interim measure, the Investment Management Association (IMA) is continuing with its regular engagement survey, which is being tailored to cover adherence to the Code by those institutions that sign up, and is introducing some independent oversight to the survey process. Its intention is to review adherence in 2010 and provide initial benchmarking data. The FRC is liaising with the IMA on this and is to chair the steering group set up to oversee this survey, without prejudice to the approach that may be followed in future years.

Future corporate governance developments

4.356 Ongoing activities associated with the FRC's 2009-10 review of the Combined Code include:

- A review by the Institute of Chartered Secretaries and Administrators (ICSA) to update the good practice guidance from the Higgs Report (which addresses, for example, the roles of the chairman and non-executive directors); the second stage of the consultation ends on 14 October 2010. The intention is for the FRC to publish the revised guidance by the end of 2010.

■ A limited review of the Turnbull Guidance on internal control during the second half of 2010.

4.357 In addition, the APB is currently considering issues relating to the provision by audit firms of non-audit services to their audit clients. As a result, changes are proposed to the FRC Guidance on Audit Committees and this is currently subject to separate consultation. The intention is to publish revised guidance in December 2010. See paragraph 4.147 for the changes currently proposed.

The role of Europe

4.358 The uncertain economic climate discussed earlier in this chapter is of course not restricted only to the UK; rather it is a global crisis presenting challenges for companies on a worldwide basis. Many countries across the EU have established their own corporate governance practices and many have their own equivalents of the UK Corporate Governance Code. Some of these Codes were inspired by the UK's ground-breaking Cadbury and Hampel reforms and contain similar principles, including 'comply or explain'. Compliance with these national Codes is often voluntary except where, as in the UK, the requirements have been incorporated in local listing rules.

4.358.1 The implementation of European Directives in the UK has a direct impact on UK governance requirements, as the Disclosure Rules and Transparency Rules demonstrate (see para 4.43 onwards). The current activities of the EC relating to governance, which are associated with the G20 agenda for reform in the financial services sector, may well have a very significant impact on UK governance requirements in the future. The impact would be unlikely to be restricted to the financial sector.

European Commission Green Papers

4.359 On 2 June 2010 the EC launched a public consultation on its *Green Paper on Corporate Governance in Financial Institutions and Remuneration Policies* (the Green Paper). The Green Paper is part of the G20 agenda for reform in the financial services sector, but the section on remuneration is not limited to that sector and covers all listed companies.

4.360 A further green paper on corporate governance of listed companies more widely will follow in autumn 2010. This is expected to deal with the place and role of shareholders, the distribution of duties between shareholders and boards with regard to supervising senior management teams, the composition of boards and corporate social responsibility.

4.361 The Consultation on the content of the first Green Paper was open until 1 September 2010. Following the consultation the Commission will decide in the first quarter of 2011 on the need for any legislative or non-legislative proposals. As the Green Paper proposes several compulsory measures, this could lead to further changes to UK corporate governance arrangements and rules.

4.362 The first Green Paper addresses the following issues:

- How to improve the functioning and the composition of boards of financial institutions in order to enhance their supervision of senior management.

- How to establish a risk culture at all levels of a financial institution in order to ensure that long-term interests of the business are taken into account.

- How to enhance the involvement of shareholders, financial supervisors and external auditors in corporate governance matters.

- How to change remuneration policies in listed companies in order to discourage excessive risk taking.

4.363 The Green Paper's main suggestions to improve corporate governance in financial institutions include:

- Limit the number of directors' memberships of boards (possibly to three).

- Require more expertise on boards.

- Widen the 'fit and proper test' to include evaluation of expertise and individual qualities of candidates.

- Enhance the role of supervisors in the review of corporate governance structures.

- Mandate risk committees at board level tasked with setting policy on risk appetite to be disclosed publicly through a risk statement.

- Strengthen the legal liability of directors *via* an expanded 'duty of care'.

- Strengthen the authority of the risk management function potentially giving the Chief Risk Officer equal standing to the Chief Financial Officer.

- Separate the functions of the Chairman and of the Chief Executive Officer.

- Reduce or suspend the variable component of remuneration in financial institutions that have received public funding.

- Put in place a stricter duty for auditors to flag certain serious matters to boards and supervisors and to look at whether they should have an enhanced role to check risk-related financial information. This enhanced role would be in addition to the planned review by the Commission of auditors' existing role on which a green paper is expected in autumn 2010.

- Mandate that institutional investors publish their voting and engagement policies and records and adhere to stewardship codes.

■   Regulate conflicts of interests.

4.364   In the UK several of these suggestions are addressed by recommendations resulting from Sir David Walker's review of corporate governance in banks and other financial industries and by the revised UK Corporate Governance Code in general. However, the Green Paper's suggestions include several compulsory measures rather than being 'comply or explain' based.

4.365   In terms of remuneration of directors of listed companies, the Green Paper notes that previous recommendations have not been applied by Member States in a uniform or satisfactory manner. As a result, the Green Paper raises questions on the following: possible additional measures at EU level on remuneration; regulating or prohibiting directors' stock options and severance packages; whether favourable tax treatment of stock options in certain Member States encourages excessive risk-taking; and strengthening the role of shareholders and employees in establishing remuneration policy.

Chapter 5

Disclosure of directors' remuneration

Disclosure of directors' remuneration

Introduction

5.1   Directors' remuneration is one of the most sensitive and closely regulated aspects of financial reporting. Generally, directors are well rewarded and it is inevitable, given their stewardship role, that comparisons will be made by investors and others between the company's performance and the level of the directors' remuneration. One facet of this subject is the extent of the disclosure of remuneration in financial statements.

5.2   The legal rules relating to disclosure of directors' remuneration are contained in the Companies Act 2006 in the 'Small Companies and Groups (Accounts and Directors' Report) Regulations 2008' (SI 2008/409) and the 'Large and Medium-sized Companies and Groups (Accounts and Reports) Regulations 2008' (SI 2008/410) for accounting periods beginning on or after 6 April 2008. The rules fall broadly into three main sections; those that apply to all companies; those that apply only to unquoted companies and those that apply to quoted companies. AIM companies, whilst largely treated as unquoted companies, have to give more information than other unquoted companies in relation to share option gains and long-term incentives received in shares. In addition, for periods ending on or after 31 March 2010, AIM companies are required to provide additional details of remuneration by individual director. The scope of the requirements is dealt with from paragraph 5.6 onwards.

5.3   Under UK company law, remuneration should be disclosed when it is paid to or receivable by a director in respect of qualifying services to the company and its subsidiaries. Generally, disclosure is required in respect of:

■   The aggregate amount of remuneration (including salary, fees, bonuses and benefits in kind).

■   Share options.

■   Long-term incentive schemes.

■   Pension schemes.

■   Compensation for loss of office.

■   Sums paid to or receivable by third parties for making available directors' services.

These disclosure requirements are covered in detail in this chapter.

5.4 Directors' remuneration disclosures made by quoted companies are extensive. They include information on policy and details of remuneration given by individual director. The legal requirements for quoted companies substantially reproduce the requirements in the Listing Rules relating to disclosure of directors' remuneration, but they also contain additional disclosures over and above those in the Listing Rules. In addition, there are some differences between the legal requirements and those of the Listing Rules, which are discussed later in the chapter.

5.4.1 For financial years beginning on or after 29 June 2010, the UK Corporate Governance Code (2010), issued by the FRC, contains principles and provisions relating to directors' remuneration. For periods beginning prior to 29 June 2010, the UK Corporate Governance Code (2008), formerly the Combined Code on Corporate Governance (2008), applies. UK listed entities are required by the Listing Rules to disclose how they have applied the principles of the applicable code and confirm that they have complied with its provisions – or provide an explanation where they have not done so. The UK Corporate Governance Codes (2008) and (2010) are discussed further in chapter 4.

5.5 In addition, for companies preparing their financial statements under IFRS, IAS 24, 'Related party disclosures', requires disclosure of 'key management compensation' in the notes to the financial statements.

Scope of the requirements

5.6 Disclosure of directors remuneration is governed by:

■ The Companies Act 2006.

■ The Listing Rules of the FSA.

■ The UK Corporate Governance Code (2008), for financial years beginning prior to 29 June 2010, and the UK Corporate Governance Code (2010), for financial years beginning on or after 29 June 2010, both published by the FRC.

5.6.1 In addition, as noted in paragraph 5.5 above, for companies that are preparing their financial statements in accordance with IFRS, IAS 24 requires disclosure of 'key management compensation' in the notes to the financial statements. The requirements of IAS 24 differ from those contained in both the 2006 Act and the Listing Rules. The requirements are considered in chapter 29 of the Manual of Accounting – IFRS for the UK.

5.6.1.1 In addition to the requirements set out above in paragraphs 5.6 and 5.6.1, various organisations such as the National Association of Pension Funds (NAPF), the Association of British Insurers (ABI) and RiskMetrics Group have published good practice guidance on remuneration. Further details are provided from paragraph 5.223.1 below.

5.6.2   As noted in paragraph 5.2 above, the legal rules relating to disclosure of directors' remuneration are contained in the Companies Act 2006, in Schedule 5 and Schedule 8 to the 'Large and Medium-sized Companies and Groups (Accounts and Reports) Regulations 2008' (SI 2008/410). The rules in the 2006 Act fall broadly into three main sections; those that apply to all companies; those that apply only to unquoted companies and those that apply to quoted (as defined in section 385(2) of the 2006 Act) companies. AIM companies, whilst largely treated as unquoted companies, have to give more information than other unquoted companies in relation to share option gains and long-term incentives received in shares. In addition, for periods ending on or after 31 March 2010, AIM companies are required to provide additional details of remuneration by individual director (see from para 5.120.1).

5.6.3   The definition of quoted company for the purposes of disclosure is:

'...a company whose equity share capital –

(a)   has been included in the official list in accordance with the provisions of Part VI of the Financial Services and Markets Act 2000; or

(b)   is officially listed in an EEA State; or

(c)   is admitted to dealing on either the New York Stock Exchange or the exchange known as Nasdaq;

and in paragraph (a) 'the official list' shall have the meaning given it by section 103(1) of the Financial Services and Markets Act 2000.'

[CA06 Sec 385(2)].

5.6.3.1   The 2006 Act clarifies that "a company is a quoted company in relation to a financial year if it is a quoted company immediately before the end of the accounting reference period by reference to which that financial year was determined". [CA06 Sec 385(1)]. Our view is that if a company is quoted at the year end then any disclosures required by the 2006 Act (or accounting standards) that are applicable to quoted companies must be complied with. In this respect a delisting is regarded as a non-adjusting post balance sheet event.

5.6.4   'Company' means a company formed and registered under any Companies Act since 1929. The definition of quoted company applies only to UK companies. [CA06 Sec 1(1)]. Quoted, as defined above, effectively means listed on the London Stock Exchange or officially listed in the European Economic Area (which includes EU Member States plus Iceland, Norway and Liechtenstein) or admitted to dealing on the New York Stock Exchange or on Nasdaq. For the purpose of this definition, therefore, companies listed on AIM are not included.

5.6.5   The requirements of Schedule 8 to SI 2008/410 substantially reproduce the requirements of Listing Rule 9.8.8R relating to disclosure of directors' remuneration, although there are some differences. The requirements of LR 9.8.8R are set out in Section IV below, but as its requirements are generally similar to Schedule 8 to SI 2008/410, these are not discussed in detail in this chapter. However, because there are some differences between the requirements of the Listing Rules and those of the 2006 Act, the disclosures can be complicated. An illustrative example is given in the directors' remuneration report for IFRS GAAP plc (see separate publication containing illustrative financial statements). Other Listing Rules relating to directors' remuneration that are not covered by Schedule 8 to SI 2008/410 are also dealt with in section IV below. Annex 1 sets out the principles and provisions of the UK Corporate Governance Code (2008) and, for periods beginning on or after 29 June 2010, the UK Corporate Governance Code (2010), that relate to directors' remuneration.

5.6.6   Where a company is not quoted, but has debt or fixed income shares listed in the UK, it does not have to comply with the requirements of Schedule 8 to SI 2008/410. Such an entity has to comply with the disclosures relating to directors' remuneration contained in Schedule 5 to SI 2008/410. Although such a company has to comply with the Listing Rules, it is not required to comply with the requirements concerning directors' remuneration in LR 9.8.8R (see annex 2).

5.6.7   Where a company is quoted on an overseas exchange, but has debt or fixed income shares listed in the UK, it has to comply with the directors' remuneration requirements contained in part 1 of Schedule 5 and in Schedule 8 to SI 2008/410. In addition, such an entity is exempt from the Listing Rule requirement concerning the disclosure of directors' remuneration in LR 9.8.8R (see annex 2). [LR 9.8.6R].

5.6.8   As noted in paragraph 5.6.2 above, AIM companies are not treated as quoted companies for the purpose of disclosure of directors' remuneration.

Example – AIM companies and directors' remuneration

Are AIM companies required to present a directors' remuneration report in accordance with Schedule 8 to SI 2008/410?

No. The requirement in Section 420(1) of the Companies Act 2006 is that quoted companies should prepare a directors' remuneration report compliant with Schedule 8 to SI 2008/410. The definition of a quoted company is given in paragraph 5.6.3 above.

A company with equity shares listed on AIM does not fall within the definition of a quoted company, so is not required to prepare a directors' remuneration report compliant with Schedule 8 to SI 2008/410.

However, AIM companies, whilst largely treated as unquoted companies, have to give more information than other unquoted companies in relation to share option gains and long-term incentives received in shares. In addition, for periods ending on or after 31 March 2010, AIM companies are required to provide additional details of remuneration by individual director. The requirements for AIM-listed companies are dealt with from paragraph 5.118.

5.7   The Companies Act 2006 replaces all the provisions of the Companies Act 1985. Implementation of the 2006 Act was staggered and different parts had different commencement dates. The requirements under the 2006 Act (including those in SI 2008/410) relating to disclosure of directors' remuneration are generally applicable for accounting periods commencing on or after 6 April 2008.

5.8 The disclosure of directors' remuneration can be considered under a number of headings and sub-headings:

- Section I – All companies.
- General Rules.
  - Directors' and auditors' duties.
  - Payment for directors' services.
  - Disclosure in which year.
  - Other matters.
- Aggregate remuneration and other benefits.
  - Aggregate remuneration.
  - Benefits in kind.
  - Gains made on exercise of share options and amounts received or receivable under long-term incentive schemes.
  - Pension contributions.
- Section II – Unquoted companies (including AIM companies).
  - Highest paid director's emoluments and other benefits.
  - Excess retirement benefits of directors and past directors.
  - Compensation for loss of office.
  - Sums paid to third parties in respect of directors' services.
  - Companies Act 2006 disclosure requirements.
  - AIM Rules disclosure requirements.
- Section III – AIM companies.
  - Companies Act 2006 disclosure requirements.
  - AIM Rules disclosure requirements.
- Section IV – Quoted companies (excluding companies listed on AIM).
  - Remuneration report.
  - Information not subject to audit.
    - Composition of remuneration committee and advisors.
    - Statement of policy on directors' remuneration.
    - Performance graph.

- Service contracts.

- Compensation for past directors.

- Appendix – UK Corporate Governance Codes (2008) and (2010).

■ Information subject to audit.

- Individual directors' emoluments and compensation.

- Share options.

- Long-term incentive schemes.

- Pensions.

- Excess retirement benefits of directors and past directors.

- Compensation for past directors.

- Sums paid to third parties in respect of directors' services.

- Approval of remuneration report.

■ Section V – Audit requirements.

■ Section VI – Group situations.

Each of these is considered in turn below and annex 2 to the chapter includes a directors' remuneration decision tree, which shows for different companies the parts of the 2006 Act that apply and whether the Listing Rules need to be followed.

Section I — All companies

General rules — all companies

Directors' and auditors' duties

5.9 A company's directors have a duty to give information about their remuneration (including pensions, compensation for loss of office and sums paid to third parties) to the company so that the information discussed below can be disclosed in the financial statements. This requirement also applies to a person who has been a director of the company within the preceding five years. Any director failing to give notice of the required information to the company is liable to a fine. [CA06 Sec 412(5),(6)].

5.10 If the required information is not disclosed in the financial statements or if information subject to audit that is required to be included in the directors' remuneration report of a quoted company is not disclosed in that report, the auditors have a duty to include the information (so far as they are reasonably able to do so) in their audit report. [CA06 Sec 498(4)].

Payment for directors' services

5.11   The remuneration to be disclosed should include all amounts paid to a director for his services as a director of the company and any subsidiary, or for managing the company and its subsidiaries while a director. [SI 2008/409 3 Sch 12(1); SI 2008/410 5 Sch 15(1); SI 2008/410 8 Sch 17(1)]. All payments should be included, whether those payments are made by the company, or by a subsidiary undertaking of the company or by any other person, unless the director has to account in turn to another group company, or to members under section 219 of the 2006 Act (directors' duty to make disclosure on company takeover and consequences of non-compliance), for the receipt of the remuneration. [SI 2008/409 3 Sch 5(2); SI 2008/410 5 Sch 8(1); SI 2008/410 8 Sch 19(2)]. This also applies to payments by way of compensation for loss of office.

> **Example – Director paid by non-group company**
>
> Mr Smith spends part of his time as an executive director of company A and part of his time as an employee of company B, which is controlled by him. Company B pays Mr Smith's salary and it invoices company A for an amount to cover that part of the time that Mr Smith spends working for company A. Although Mr Smith is paid by company B (and not by company A of which he is a director), the amount that he receives from company B is partially in respect of his services as a director of company A.
>
> Consequently, Mr Smith should disclose to company A, and company A should disclose in its financial statements as remuneration, the proportion of his salary that relates to his services as a director of company A. This figure may or may not be the same as the amount that company B has invoiced company A. This will depend on whether the invoiced amount is intended to cover an amount that is either more or less than the actual cost of the director's services to company A.

5.12   Overlooking this point can have serious consequences as illustrated by the findings of the Financial Reporting Review Panel (FRRP) on the financial statements of Foreign & Colonial Investment Trust plc (FCIT) for the year ended 31 December 1991. The FRRP found that the financial statements of FCIT reflected the remuneration receivable by the directors from the company and its subsidiaries. However, remuneration receivable by five directors from the company's investment manager, an associate of one of its subsidiaries, relating to services provided to FCIT and its subsidiaries had not been disclosed in FCIT's financial statements. Following discussions with the Panel, the directors agreed to provide, in the 1992 financial statements, additional information concerning that proportion of remuneration receivable by the directors from the company's investment manager, which related to services to FCIT and its subsidiary undertakings. Appropriate comparative figures for 1991 were also presented in the 1992 financial statements.

5.13   The disclosure in the 1992 financial statements is shown in Table 5.1.

Table 5.1 — Payment for directors' services

Foreign & Colonial Investment Trust PLC — Report and Accounts — 31 December 1992

Directors' emoluments (extract)

Mr A.C. Barker, Mr O.N. Dawson, Mr E.C. Elstob, Mr M.J. Hart and The Hon. James Ogilvy receive emoluments from Foreign & Colonial Management Limited for their services to that company. The proportion of their emoluments which relates to the management of the affairs of the Company or any of its subsidiary undertakings amounts to approximately £227,000 (1991—£195,000). This amount has been taken into account, together with the £106,000 (1991—£100,000) paid directly by the Company to the non-executive directors, in providing the following disclosure:

Directors' emoluments (including payments by all subsidiary undertakings but excluding pensions contributions).

Comparatives for 1991 have been restated.

	1992	1991
Chairman	**£29,000**	£25,000
Highest paid director	**£138,000**	£114,000
£1-£5,000	**1**	–
£10,001-£15,000	**6**	7
£15,001-£20,000	**1**	1
£25,001-£30,000	**2**	2

5.14   There is also nothing in the Companies Act 2006 to suggest that the director must receive payments personally in order that they should be subject to disclosure as remuneration. Amounts paid to or receivable by a director, including amounts paid in respect of compensation for loss of office, will include amounts paid to or receivable by a person connected with, or a body corporate controlled by that director (but such amounts should not be counted twice). [SI 2008/409 3 Sch 5(3); SI 2008/410 5 Sch 7(3); SI 2008/410 8 Sch 19(3)]. The definitions of connected persons and body corporate controlled by a director are set out in sections 252 to 255 of the 2006 Act. [SI 2008/410 5 Sch 15(2); SI 2008/410 8 Sch 17(4)]. Consequently, even where a director sets up another company specifically to receive remuneration, that remuneration will be deemed to be remuneration received by him if that company is controlled by him.

5.15   Furthermore, if the company has nominated (either directly or indirectly) the director to be a director of another company, that other company is treated as if it were a subsidiary undertaking for the purposes of determining the amounts to be disclosed for directors' remuneration, compensation for loss of office and payments to third parties for directors' services. Accordingly, the director's remuneration and compensation for loss of office should include any amount he receives as a director of that other company (whether or not that other company is a subsidiary of the company). [SI 2008/409 3 Sch 11; SI 2008/410 5 Sch 14; SI 2008/410 8 Sch 16(1), 17(1)]. Any sums that the other company pays to third parties in respect of his services should be disclosed as sums paid to third parties.

Example – Nominated director of an associate

Company A has nominated one of its directors to the board of its associate, company B. Company B pays £20,000 per year to the director in respect of his services to that company. Does this £20,000 have to be disclosed as directors' remuneration in company A's financial statements?

The Companies Act 2006 requires disclosure of remuneration received by a director of a company for qualifying services, which includes services as a director of the company or its subsidiaries. This might appear to exclude services to associates, but paragraph 14 of Schedule 5 to SI 2008/410 (and paragraph 11 of Schedule 3 to SI 2008/409 for small companies), or for quoted companies paragraph 17(1) of Schedule 5 to SI 2008/410, states that reference to a subsidiary undertaking, in relation to a person who whilst a director of the company is also a director of any other undertaking by virtue of the company's nomination, includes that other undertaking whether or not it is in fact a subsidiary undertaking.

This means that because the director has been nominated by company A as a director of the associate, the associate is deemed for the purposes of directors' remuneration disclosure to be a subsidiary. The director is performing qualifying services for company A by being its representative on company B's board. Therefore, in this situation, the director must disclose to company A, as remuneration, the amount of £20,000 that he receives from company B. Company A will need to disclose, as directors' remuneration, the aggregate of the amount paid to the director in respect of his services as director of company A and the amount of £20,000 he receives from company B.

If, on the other hand, the amount of £20,000 is paid to company A (that is, as a sum to be accounted for to the company, see para 5.11) and not to the director personally, then this amount need not be included as directors' remuneration in company A's financial statements. However, company B will need to disclose the payment of £20,000 in its own financial statements as a sum paid to a third party in respect of the director's services.

Note that the answer would be the same if company B was not related to company A, but company A had nominated one of its directors to company B's board (for example, if it was able to do this because of a significant trading relationship).

5.15.1   Further practical guidance in relation to group situations is provided in section VI, from paragraph 5.233 below.

Disclosure in which year

5.16   A director's remuneration that should be disclosed in the financial statements for a particular year is the remuneration receivable by the director in respect of that year, regardless of when it is paid to the director. [SI 2008/409 3 Sch 5(4); SI 2008/410 5 Sch 7(4); SI 2008/410 8 Sch 20(1)]. For example, if a bonus is receivable by a director in respect of services performed in year one, but is not paid to the director until year two, it is disclosable as that director's remuneration in year one.

5.17   In the case of remuneration that is receivable by a director in respect of a period that extends beyond the financial year, for example, a long-term incentive scheme covering a period of three years, where the only condition is for the director to remain in service, disclosure should be made in the year it is paid. [SI 2008/409 3 Sch 5(4); SI 2008/410 5 Sch 7(4); SI 2008/410 8 Sch 20(1)]. Whilst not explicitly stated, the implication of this is that where remuneration is receivable in respect of a period, be that a period of one year or more than one year, it should be disclosed when due, that is, in the year in which it becomes receivable.

[The next paragraph is 5.19.]

5.19   Where remuneration is not receivable in respect of a period, whether of a single financial year or a period of over one financial year, it should be disclosed in the financial statements of the period in which it is paid. This might apply, for instance, when a single *ex gratia* payment is made to a director that is unrelated to a financial year or other period. An example might be a payment made as compensation for a reduction in the length of a director's service contract.

5.20   One problem that sometimes arises in respect of long-term incentive schemes is where the performance period lasts three years, but a director must then remain with the company for a further period, say six months, before he becomes entitled to receive any amounts under the scheme. The question that arises in such a case is whether the amounts due under the scheme are receivable in respect of the three-year performance period and are, therefore, disclosable in the third year of the scheme, or whether they are receivable only after a further six months, when the additional service period has been completed, in which case they would be disclosable in the fourth year.

5.21   The answer to the question may depend on the particular terms of the scheme and on when the remuneration becomes a firm entitlement. If, for instance, the additional service period has no real effect in practice, and the director would receive the remuneration whether or not he stayed for the extra six months, this would imply that the substance was that the remuneration was effectively a firm entitlement in respect of the three-year performance period and should be disclosed in the third year. If, however, the additional service period was of real significance, for instance if the director would get nothing if he were to leave the company within that additional period, then it is probable that the remuneration should be disclosed in the fourth year.

5.22   In practice, there is some variation on the way that companies apply the rules to the situation described in paragraphs 5.20 and 5.21 above, with some companies preferring to disclose when all performance conditions have been satisfied, even when there is a further service period. For quoted companies, where the problem mainly arises, Schedule 8 to SI 2008/410 requires disclosure of full details of long-term incentive schemes, which means that, whichever approach is taken, there is still full disclosure of the benefits arising, or the benefits that have arisen, under such schemes during the period for which they operate. This is discussed further in paragraph 5.185.

5.23 The above rules apply to remuneration generally and also extend to compensation for loss of office.

Other matters

5.24 Under the 2006 Act, a company is permitted to end its financial year on the same day in the week rather than on the same date, if it wishes to (see further chapter 8). Therefore, a financial year (and, consequently, the financial statements) may cover a period slightly longer than one year. In this situation, the amounts disclosed for directors' remuneration are those in respect of the longer period, as explained in the following example.

> **Example – Remuneration for a 53 week period**
>
> A company has a 53 week financial year this year. Can the disclosure of directors' remuneration be given for a 52 week (365 day) period, rather than for 53 weeks?
>
> For unquoted companies, paragraph 7(4) of Schedule 5 to SI 2008/410 (or paragraph 5(4) of Schedule 3 to SI 2008/409 for small companies) and for quoted companies paragraph 20(1) of Schedule 8 to SI 2008/410 require that the amounts of remuneration to be shown for any financial year are the sums receivable in respect of that year (whenever paid).
>
> Section 390(3) of the Companies Act 2006 states that *"subsequent financial years begin with the day immediately following the end of the company's previous financial year and end with the last day of its next accounting reference period or such other date, not more than seven days before or after the end of that period, as the directors may determine".* Therefore, the company's financial year is 53 weeks and so the amounts to be disclosed must be for the 53 weeks of the financial year.
>
> As an analogy, if the company prepares statutory accounts for a short period (for example, nine months), the amounts to be disclosed under the Act is the remuneration for that period (that is, nine months).

5.24.1 Where a director is appointed during the year, only the remuneration while he is a director of the company is disclosable as director's remuneration, as explained in the example in paragraph 5.167.

5.24.2 If it is necessary to apportion remuneration and compensation for loss of office paid to a director between the matters in respect of which it has been paid or is receivable, the directors may apportion it in any way that they consider appropriate. [SI 2008/409 3 Sch 5(6); SI 2008/410 5 Sch 7(6); SI 2008/410 8 Sch 21].

5.25 In certain situations, directors' remuneration might not be included in the notes to the financial statements (or in the directors' remuneration report, in the case of a quoted company) for a period because either the director is liable to account for it to the company or to another group company, or because it is considered to be an expense allowance not chargeable to UK income tax. Where this is so, and these reasons are subsequently found not to be justified, the remuneration must be disclosed in a note to the first financial statements (or in the first directors' remuneration report, in the case of a quoted company) in which it is practicable for this to be done, and the remuneration must be identified separately. This also applies to compensation for loss of office. [SI 2008/409 3 Sch 5(5); SI 2008/410 5 Sch 7(5); SI 2008/410 8 Sch 20(2)].

5.26   An example of disclosure is given in Table 5.2.

Table 5.2 – Corrections to emoluments disclosed in previous years

The Plessey Company plc – Report and Accounts – 1 April 1988

Directors and senior employees (extract)

The emoluments of the Chairman, who in 1988 was the highest paid director, amounted to £391,956. The emoluments of the highest paid director in 1987 amounted to £237,347.

The above amount of £391,956 includes an adjustment of £93,750 resulting from the reclassification of expenses in respect of the financial years 1979/80 to 1986/87 following a settlement agreed with the Inland Revenue.

Aggregate remuneration and other benefits — all companies

Aggregate remuneration and other benefits

5.27   The Act requires the following information to be disclosed in the notes to the annual financial statements:

■   The aggregate amount of emoluments paid to or receivable by directors in respect of qualifying services. [SI 2008/409 3 Sch 1(1)(a); SI 2008/410 5 Sch 1(1)(a)].

■   The aggregate of the amount of gains made by directors on the exercise of share options (but see para 5.28 below). [SI 2008/410 5 Sch 1(1)(b)].

■   The aggregate of the following:

■   the amount of money paid to or receivable by directors under long-term incentive schemes in respect of qualifying services; and

■   the net value of assets (other than money and share options) received or receivable by directors under such schemes in respect of such services (but see para 5.28 below).

[SI 2008/409 3 Sch 1(1)(b); SI 2008/410 5 Sch 1(1)(c)].

■   The aggregate value of any company contributions paid, or treated as paid, to a pension scheme in respect of directors' qualifying services, being contributions by reference to which the rate or amount of any money purchase benefits that may become payable will be calculated. [SI 2008/410 5 Sch 1(1)(d)].

■ In the case of each of the following:

■ money purchase schemes; and

■ defined benefit schemes.

The number of directors (if any) to whom retirement benefits are accruing under such schemes in respect of qualifying services. [SI 2008/409 3 Sch 2; SI 2008/410 5 Sch 1(2)].

5.28 The above requirements relate to *all* companies other than small companies reporting under SI 2008/409 (see further the Manual of Accounting – UK GAAP) with the following additional exception. Companies which are not quoted (see para 5.6.3) and are not listed on AIM do not have to disclose either the aggregate of the amount of gains made by the directors on the exercise of share options or the net value of shares received or receivable under long-term incentive schemes in respect of qualifying services. Instead, such companies must disclose:

■ the number of directors who exercised share options; and

■ the number of directors in respect of whose qualifying services shares were received or receivable under long-term incentive schemes.

[SI 2008/410 5 Sch 1(3)].

[The next paragraph is 5.31.]

5.31 Each of the elements of the disclosure described above is discussed in turn in the following paragraphs.

Aggregate remuneration

All companies

5.32 All companies (that is, quoted, and unquoted, including AIM) have to disclose aggregate remuneration paid to or receivable by directors in respect of qualifying services.

5.33 Qualifying services means:

■ Services as a director of the company.

■ Services as a director of any subsidiary undertaking of the company, during the time in which a person is a director of the company.

■ Services in connection with the management of the affairs of either the company or any subsidiary undertaking of the company, during the time in which a person is a director of the company.

[SI 2008/409 3 Sch 12(1); SI 2008/410 5 Sch 15(1)].

5.34 In addition, qualifying services includes services, while a director of the company, as a director of any other undertaking of which he is a director by virtue of the company's nomination (direct or indirect). [SI 2008/409 3 Sch 11(1); SI 2008/410 5 Sch 14(1)]. See further paragraph 5.15 above.

5.35 If an undertaking is a subsidiary undertaking at the time the service is rendered by the directors, it should be included even where the undertaking is no longer a subsidiary at the reporting date. [SI 2008/409 3 Sch 11(2); SI 2008/410 5 Sch 14(2)].

5.36 For this purpose, 'remuneration' paid to or receivable by a director includes not only his salary, but also the following:

■ Fees and bonuses.

■ Any expense allowances (to the extent that they are chargeable to UK income tax).

■ The estimated money value of any other benefits received otherwise than in cash (but see para 5.37 below).

■ Remuneration in respect of a person accepting office as director.

[SI 2008/409 3 Sch 7; SI 2008/410 5 Sch 9(1), 15(3)].

5.37 In this context, the term remuneration does not include the value of share options granted to or exercised by directors. It does not include any company pension contributions paid on behalf of directors (although it does include contributions that directors themselves pay by way of a compulsory deduction from salary) nor any benefits to which directors are entitled under any pension scheme. Also excluded from the definition are money or other assets paid to or receivable by directors under long-term incentive schemes. [SI 2008/409 3 Sch 12(2); SI 2008/410 5 Sch 9(2)].

5.38 The reason for excluding those elements from the disclosure of aggregate remuneration is, quite simply, that they are picked up by separate disclosure requirements that are discussed below.

5.39 The term 'paid to or receivable by' is discussed from paragraph 5.16 above.

5.40 Whether the director receives remuneration for services as a director of the company or in connection with the management of its affairs is a question of fact. It should be presumed that all payments made to a director, except for reimbursement of expenses, will generally fall within one of these categories, unless it can clearly be demonstrated otherwise. However, an exception could be where payments have been made to a director in a self-employed or professional capacity. Consider the following example:

Example – Director paid on a self-employed basis

A director of a company is paid for technical services supplied on a 'self-employed persons' basis. How should this be disclosed?

Provided that it can be clearly established that the fees are genuinely for technical services and that they are not connected with management services (which they might be if the director were a technical director), then the amounts paid need not be disclosed as remuneration. However, the transaction may need to be disclosed as a related party transaction (see the Manual of Accounting – UK GAAP or the Manual of Accounting – IFRS for the UK). In practice, however, it is often difficult to make such a precise distinction and the remuneration for other services is often included with directors' remuneration.

5.41   When considering directors' remuneration, there is no need to distinguish between a director's service contract and a contract for services that a director has with the company. Remuneration received in either capacity will fall to be disclosed in the company's financial statements as directors' remuneration. However, a director's service contract makes him essentially an employee of the company and, therefore, such remuneration will have to be included in staff costs. On the other hand, a contract for services puts the director in essentially the same position as a third party hired to do a particular job. Amounts invoiced to the company should be recognised as an expense, but should not be classified as 'staff costs'.

Benefits in kind

5.42   The estimated money value of a benefit in kind that must be included in directors' remuneration should be taken as the market value of the facility that is provided for the director's private benefit, less any contribution the director pays. The amount used to assess the taxable benefit should be used *only* where it is an approximation of the market value of the benefit. However, in practice the value of the taxable benefit is often a good starting point for considering the value that should be placed on the amounts for accounting disclosure purposes.

5.43   Where there is a tax concession such that part of a benefit is not taxable even though it is a benefit for the director (as opposed to a valid business expense), the value of the taxable benefit will not be an appropriate starting point. If there is a benefit to the director, the total amount receivable by a director is disclosable as a benefit in kind. The fact that the tax rules allow some of this benefit to be tax-free (for instance, certain relocation allowances) does not change the position.

5.44   Benefits in kind may include: provision of accommodation at below market rates; provision of a car or health benefits; and share options. Gains on exercise of share options are dealt with separately (see para 5.47 below).

Example – Premium paid for director's life assurance cover

A company pays a premium to an insurance company to purchase life assurance cover for a director. This life cover is in addition to the life cover provided by the pension scheme and is an entirely separate arrangement. The beneficiary would be the next of kin of the director. How should this be disclosed for the purpose of directors' remuneration?

The premium should be included as a benefit in kind in arriving at the aggregate directors' remuneration and will be included in the aggregate of remuneration to be disclosed (for all companies) under paragraphs 1(1) and 7 of Schedule 3 to SI 2008/409 and paragraphs 1(1) and 9(1) of Schedule 5 to SI 2008/410. If the company is quoted the benefit would also be disclosed in the total of benefits received by the director, which is required to be shown separately in the table of individual directors' remuneration in the directors' remuneration report, together with the nature of the benefit (see further para 5.164). [SI 2008/410 8 Sch 7(1), 7(3)].

5.44.1   Where a company pays a director's tax liability on benefits, the amount disclosed in respect of benefits should be grossed up for the tax paid, that is, the amount disclosed should reflect the gross amount payable in cash to leave the director in the same position had the company not paid the tax on his behalf. For example, if the benefit received is £100,000 and the director is taxed at 40% (that is, the director would expect to receive a net amount of £60,000, even though this would be disclosed as £100,000 in the remuneration disclosure). However, where the company pays the tax, such that the benefit received is actually a net amount of £100,000, then the gross amount the director would receive is $100,000/(1-0.4) =$ £167,000 and hence it is the £167,000 that should be disclosed as part of the director's remuneration.

5.45   Whilst separate disclosure of expenses or benefits in kind is not required by SI 2008/409 or SI 2008/410, some companies do so. An example is given in Table 5.4. As noted in the example in paragraph 5.44 above, for quoted companies separate disclosure of benefits by individual director is required (see para 5.164 onwards).

Table 5.4 – Benefits in kind

National Westminster Bank Plc – Annual Report and Accounts – 31 December 1993

Emoluments of directors (extract)

The total remuneration and benefits of the highest paid director in the UK, Mr R K Goeltz, were £554,238 (1992 £383,900), which comprised £230,564 basic salary and other emoluments (inclusive of director's fee), a performance related bonus of £72,739, expenses and disbursements amounting to £242,170 incurred by the Bank and Mr Goeltz in connection with his relocation from New York to London and £8,765 of benefits in kind. Mr Goeltz participates in the Bank's pension fund.

5.46   Remuneration in respect of a person accepting office as director (see the last point in para 5.36) requires disclosure of incentive payments (so-called 'golden hellos') that are made by companies to attract people to join the board of directors.

Gains on share options and amounts receivable under long-term incentive schemes

Quoted and AIM companies

5.47   For quoted (see para 5.6.3) and AIM companies, separate totals for the aggregate of gains made by directors on exercising share options and for the aggregate of amounts of money and the net value of other assets received or receivable under long-term incentive schemes must be disclosed. [SI 2008/410 5 Sch 1(1)(b), (c)]. This disclosure requirement would be met if the information can be readily ascertained from other information provided – see further paragraph 5.72. An example of disclosure of gains made on the exercise of share options is given in Table 5.5.

Table 5.5 – Gains made on the exercise of share options and amounts receivable under long-term incentive plans

ARM Holdings plc – Annual Report & Accounts – 31 December 2009

Notes to the financial statements (extract)

3 Key management compensation and directors' emoluments (extract)

Directors' emoluments
The aggregate emoluments of the directors of the Company are set out below:

	2009 £'000	2008 £'000
Aggregate emoluments in respect of qualifying services	3,842	3,602
Aggregate Group pension contributions to money purchase schemes	203	194
Aggregate gains on exercise of share options	976	12
Aggregate amounts receivable under the Long Term Incentive Plan	477	635
	5,498	4,443

Detailed disclosures of directors' emoluments are shown on page 53. Details of directors' interests in share options and awards are shown on pages 49 to 52 which form part of the financial statements.

5.48   The amount of the gain on exercising share options (quoted and AIM companies only) is the difference between market price of the shares on the day of exercise and the price actually paid for the shares. [SI 2008/410 8 Sch 17(1)].

Example – Market price of shares

A quoted company (see para 5.6.3 for definition) is disclosing gains on exercise of directors' share options in accordance with the Companies Act disclosure rules. In the rules the gain is defined as the difference between the market price of the shares on the day the option was exercised and the exercise price. A company wishes to know what price it should take as market price, as there was considerable price movement on the day in question, for instance can the definition in taxes legislation be used?

We consider that the mid-market price is the price that should be used. By way of support for this the FSA Listing Rules define market value as the middle-market quotation for a share as derived from the Daily Official List of the London Stock Exchange. [LR 9.5.10R (2)]. It seems to us this is a straight forward and sensible interpretation of the term 'market value' in the absence of a more precise definition in the Companies Act. The definition of market value in taxes legislation is not relevant to this disclosure issue.

5.49 Share options granted in respect of a person's accepting office as a director are to be treated as share options granted in respect of that person's services as a director. [SI 2008/410 5 Sch 15(3)]. Accordingly, the exercise of such options requires disclosure by quoted and AIM companies of the amount of the gain made in accordance with the requirement in paragraph 5.47 above.

Unquoted companies excluding companies listed on AIM

5.50 Unquoted companies, excluding companies listed on AIM, are not required to include the amount of gains made by directors on the exercise of share options. Nor do they have to include the value of any shares received or receivable under long-term incentive schemes. Instead they should give the aggregate amount of money and net value of other assets (excluding shares) received and receivable under long-term incentive schemes and disclose separately:

■   The number of directors who exercised share options.

■   The number of directors in respect of whose qualifying services shares were received or receivable under long-term incentive schemes.

[SI 2008/410 5 Sch 1(3)].

This does not apply to small companies reporting under SI 2008/409.

Example – Exercise of share options by director of unquoted company

A director of an unquoted subsidiary of a quoted company (see para 5.6.3 for definition) has share options convertible into shares of the parent company. The director has exercised some of these options in the year. Do the gains on the exercise (which can be measured because the parent is quoted) need to be disclosed in the subsidiary's financial statements in the directors' remuneration note under the disclosure rules set out in Schedule 5 to SI 2008/410?

No. The Act's disclosure rules for unquoted companies (unless they are AIM companies) specifically exclude gains on the exercise of share options, even if they can be measured. Instead, the subsidiary should disclose the number of directors who exercised share options. [SI 2008/410 5 Sch 1(3)].

Similarly, for an unquoted company (unless it is an AIM company), disclosure of the highest-paid director's remuneration does not include an amount for gains on exercise of share options, but the fact that the highest-paid director exercised options must be disclosed. [SI 2008/410 5 Sch 2(3)(a)].

5.51   The accounting implications under IFRS 2 and FRS 20, 'Share-based payment', of share options in a group situation are dealt with in the Manual of Accounting – IFRS for the UK and the Manual of Accounting – UK GAAP.

5.52   In addition, for companies reporting under IFRS, IAS 24, requires disclosure of remuneration (in total and split into five categories) for key management personnel in respect of services provided to the entity. One of the categories is share-based payment and would include the share options, because the remuneration includes *"all forms of consideration paid, payable or provided by the entity, or on behalf of the entity in exchange for services rendered to the entity"*. The options are provided by the quoted parent to the director of the subsidiary in return for his services to the subsidiary. Therefore, in so far as it relates to directors and key managers, amounts charged in the subsidiary's financial statements under IFRS 2 would be disclosed as part of key management personnel compensation under the category 'share-based payment'.

Definitions

5.53   Share options are defined as the right to acquire shares. [SI 2008/409 3 Sch 9; SI 2008/410 5 Sch 12(b)]. We interpret this to include the right to acquire shares through subscription, by way of gift, by purchasing shares from an ESOP or indeed any other form of acquisition. It should be noted that there is a difference between the definition in Schedule 3 to SI 2008/409 and Schedule 5 to SI 2008/410 of share options for the purpose of disclosure of aggregate gains and the definition in Schedule 8 to SI 2008/410 for the purpose of disclosure of individual directors' share options in the directors' remuneration report. See further paragraph 5.178.

5.54   A long-term incentive scheme is defined as *'an agreement or arrangement (a) under which money or other assets may become receivable by a director, and (b) which includes one or more qualifying conditions with respect to service or performance which cannot be fulfilled within a single financial year'*. [SI 2008/409 3 Sch 8(1); SI 2008/410 5 Sch 11(1)]. The definition specifically excludes:

■   Bonuses the amount of which is determined by reference to service or performance within a single financial year.

■   Compensation for loss of office, payments for breach of contract and other termination payments.

■   Retirement benefits.

[SI 2008/409 3 Sch 8(2); SI 2008/410 5 Sch 11(2)].

5.55   Amounts received or receivable means amounts that become due to directors during the financial year. For example, if a long-term incentive scheme runs for three years and amounts or other assets become due to the directors at the end of the third year, they are disclosable in that year, even if they are not actually paid over to or received by the directors until the following year (see from para 5.16 above).

5.56 Other assets received or receivable under long-term incentive schemes may include all sorts of non-cash items, for example, diamonds, gold, wine or works of art. Most commonly, however, such assets will be in the form of shares. Shares are defined as shares (whether allotted or not) in the company, or any undertaking which is a group undertaking in relation to the company and it includes share warrants. [SI 2008/409 3 Sch 9(a); SI 2008/410 5 Sch 12(a)]. A share warrant is a warrant that states that the bearer of the warrant is entitled to the shares specified in it. The phrase *'any undertaking which is a group undertaking in relation to the company'* would, we believe, include the parent undertaking and fellow subsidiary undertakings as well as subsidiary undertakings of the company. The 'value' of the shares received or receivable is defined elsewhere in the Act as the market price of the shares on the day the shares are received or receivable. [SI 2008/410 8 Sch 17(1)].

5.57 The net value of other assets received or receivable by a director under a long-term incentive scheme means the value after deducting any money paid or other value given by the director. [SI 2008/409 3 Sch 12(1); SI 2008/410 5 Sch 15(1)].

Pension contributions

5.58 Company pension contributions do not form part of aggregate remuneration described from paragraph 5.32 above. Instead, the Act requires separate disclosure of the aggregate value of company contributions paid, or treated as paid, to a money purchase pension scheme in respect of directors' qualifying services by a person other than the director. Contributions mean those according to which the rate or amount of any money purchase benefits that may become payable will be calculated. [SI 2008/409 3 Sch 1(1)(c); SI 2008/410 5 Sch 1(1)(d)].

5.59 In addition, a company must separately disclose the number of directors to whom retirement benefits are accruing under money purchase schemes and under defined benefit schemes in respect of qualifying services. [SI 2008/409 3 Sch 1(2); SI 2008/410 5 Sch 1(2)].

5.60 Although disclosure of contributions to money purchase schemes gives a reasonable indication of the benefit to a director, disclosure of contributions to defined benefit schemes may often not do so, as the level of funding will depend upon whether the scheme is in surplus or deficit. Schedule 8 to SI 2008/410 requires quoted companies (see para 5.6.3) to make detailed disclosures about directors' pension entitlements under defined benefit schemes (see section IV below). Because of the cost of obtaining information to satisfy the requirements of Schedule 8 to SI 2008/410, which would be considered unduly onerous for unquoted companies, disclosure of the number of directors to whom benefits are accruing must be disclosed to, at least, put members on notice that such schemes exist.

5.61   Pension schemes are defined as meaning the same as a retirement benefits scheme under section 611 of the Income and Corporation Taxes Act 1988 (ICTA). [SI 2008/409 3 Sch 10(1); SI 2008/410 5 Sch 13(1)]. Section 611 of ICTA defines a retirement benefits scheme as a scheme for the provision of benefits consisting of or including relevant benefits, but not including any national scheme providing such benefits. References to a scheme include references to a deed, agreement, series of agreements or other arrangements providing for relevant benefits notwithstanding that it relates or they relate only to:

- A small number of employees, or to a single employee (including company payments to personal pension plans – see example below).

- The payments of a pension starting immediately on the making of the arrangements.

Example – Payments to director's personal pension plan

A company makes a payment to a personal pension plan for one if its directors. The pension plan was arranged by the director some time before joining the company. Should these payments be disclosed under the Companies Act 2006 requirement to disclose company contributions to money purchase schemes?

Yes, if the company makes the payments to the pension scheme, the payments should be disclosed in the aggregate of company contributions to money purchase schemes in respect of directors' qualifying services. [SI 2008/409 3 Sch 1(1)(c); SI 2008/410 5 Sch 1(1)(d)]. (If the company is quoted there should also be disclosure of the contributions in respect of each individual director – see further para 5.194.)

5.62   The definition of pension schemes above is generally interpreted as extending to unfunded pension arrangements. Accordingly, where a company makes provisions in respect of unfunded pensions of a money purchase type, it should disclose the amounts provided as contributions to money purchase schemes. Where it makes provisions in respect of unfunded pensions of a defined benefit type, it should take the related benefits provided to directors into account when determining the amounts to be disclosed in respect of directors' pension entitlements under defined benefit schemes.

5.63   Retirement benefits has the meaning given by section 612 of ICTA 1988. [SI 2008/409 3 Sch 10(1); SI 2008/410 5 Sch 13(1)]. That is, any pension, lump sum, gratuity or other like benefit given or to be given:

- on retirement; or
- on death; or
- in anticipation of retirement; or
- in connection with past service, after retirement or death; or
- to be given on or in anticipation of or in connection with any change in the nature of the service of the employee in question;

except that it does not include any benefit which is to be afforded solely by reason of the disablement by accident of a person occurring during his service or of his death by accident so occurring and for no other reason.

5.64 'Money purchase benefits' for the purpose of the requirement set out in paragraph 5.58 above means retirement benefits payable under a pension scheme the rate or amount of which is calculated by reference to payments made, or treated as made, by the director or by any other person in respect of the director and which are not average salary benefits. [SI 2008/409 3 Sch 10(3); SI 2008/410 5 Sch 13(4)].

5.65 'Company contributions' do not have to be paid by the company itself as the definition states that the term means any payments (including insurance premiums) made, or treated as made to the scheme in respect of the director by a person other than the director. [SI 2008/409 3 Sch 10(2); SI 2008/410 5 Sch 13(3)]. Thus, for instance, contributions paid by the company's parent undertaking would qualify for disclosure as company contributions.

5.66 A 'money purchase scheme' for the purpose of the requirement set out in paragraph 5.59 above means a pension scheme under which all of the benefits that may become payable to or in respect of the director are money purchase benefits. A 'defined benefit scheme' is a pension scheme that is not a money purchase scheme. [SI 2008/409 3 Sch 10(3); SI 2008/410 5 Sch 13(4)].

5.66.1 The disclosure for the purpose of directors' remuneration is based on the legal form of the pension scheme. This is particularly relevant where a company does not account for a pension scheme as defined benefit (where it is entitled to an exemption in the relevant accounting standard for pensions), as illustrated in the following example.

Example – Industry-wide pension scheme

Company F, a private company reporting under SI 2008/410, participates in an industry-wide defined benefit pension scheme. Company F is unable to identify its share of the scheme's underlying assets and liabilities and has taken the exemption available to it to account for the scheme as a defined contribution scheme, with the appropriate disclosure.

In the disclosure of directors' remuneration required by the Companies Act 2006, should the scheme be treated as a defined contribution scheme so that the disclosures are consistent?

The disclosure of the directors' remuneration required for a private company by Schedule 5 to SI 2008/410 is determined by the pension scheme's legal form and not by the accounting treatment. Company F should not make disclosure of the contributions paid to the industry-wide scheme as 'company contributions to money purchase schemes'.

Disclosure should be made of the number of directors to whom benefits are accruing under the defined benefit scheme and, if the aggregate remuneration of the directors exceeds £200,000, the accrued benefit and accrued lump sum at the end of the year for the highest paid director. [SI 2008/410 5 Sch 1(2)(b), 2(2)].

It may be useful to include some disclosure in the directors' remuneration note to the financial statements to explain the apparent inconsistency.

5.67   Where a pension scheme is a hybrid scheme and provides that any benefits that become payable will be the greater of money purchase benefits as determined under the scheme and defined benefits as determined, then the company may elect to treat the scheme as a money purchase scheme or as a defined benefit scheme, whichever seems more likely at the end of the financial year. [SI 2008/409 3Sch 10(4); SI 2008/410 5 Sch 13(6)].

5.68   The effect of the provision in the preceding paragraph is that where a pension scheme has both money purchase and defined benefit elements the company has an option as to how directors' remuneration disclosure is made. It can either take advantage of the provision and classify the scheme as money purchase or defined benefit in its entirety according to the type of benefits which appear to be higher in respect of the director at the end of the year. If the scheme is classified as a money purchase arrangement, the relevant disclosures as described in paragraph 5.58 above are made. If the scheme is classified as a defined benefit arrangement, the disclosure required by paragraph 5.59 is made.

5.69   Alternatively, the company can elect not to take advantage of the option and make separate disclosure of information relating to the money purchase element of the scheme following the requirement in paragraph 5.58 above. If this is done then the scheme is counted as a defined benefit scheme for the purpose of the requirement in paragraph 5.59.

5.70   The choice between the two alternatives may also be influenced by the requirement (discussed below from para 5.84) to disclose the pension entitlement of the highest paid director under any defined benefit scheme.

5.71   For the purpose of determining whether a pension scheme is a money purchase or defined benefit scheme any death in service benefits provided by the scheme are disregarded. [SI 2008/409 3 Sch 10(5); SI 2008/410 5 Sch 13(7)].

General — readily ascertainable from other information

5.72   Where the information discussed in the above sections is readily ascertainable from the other information that is shown, this satisfies the disclosure requirements. [SI 2008/409 3 Sch 4(2); SI 2008/410 5 Sch 6(2)]. For example, a quoted company that gives detailed information by individual director in its directors' remuneration report (as required by Schedule 8 to SI 2008/410) could satisfy the Schedule 5 to SI 2008/410 requirement for disclosure of the aggregate remuneration (described above) if the total is readily ascertainable, provided that there is a cross-reference from the notes to the financial statements (where the Schedule 5 to SI 2008/410 disclosure is required to be given) to the relevant part of the directors' remuneration report.

[The next paragraph is 5.74.]

Section II — Unquoted companies (including AIM companies)

5.74 In addition to the requirements described in section I, unquoted companies (other than small companies reporting under SI 2008/409 but including companies listed on AIM) must comply with the following requirements. Quoted companies (for definition see para 5.6.3) must comply instead with the requirements described in section IV.

Highest paid director's emoluments and other benefits

5.75 SI 2008/410 requires details of the highest paid director's emoluments and other benefits to be disclosed.

5.76 Quoted companies have to give details of individual directors' emoluments and other benefits (see section IV below) and so for them there is no requirement to give details of the highest paid director's emoluments separately, as such a requirement would be superfluous.

5.77 For unquoted (and AIM) companies the requirement to disclose additional information on the highest paid director enables the reader of the financial statements at least to determine the maximum amounts received or receivable by any director and thus to assess and evaluate this against company performance or whichever other criteria the reader chooses. Requirements recently introduced for AIM companies (see from para 5.120.1) include a breakdown of remuneration by individual director, but the three disclosure categories are slightly different to those required by the Act for highest paid director (see para 5.78), hence, a company meeting the AIM requirements is likely to need additional disclosure to meet the highest paid director disclosure requirements.

Ascertaining the highest paid director

5.78 There is a *de minimis* level below which the highest paid director's emoluments and other benefits need not be disclosed. If the total of the following items shown for all directors exceeds or is equal to £200,000, the information on the highest paid director must be given. These items are:

- Aggregate emoluments paid to or receivable by directors in respect of qualifying services.

- Aggregate amount of gains made by directors on exercise of share options (but see para 5.82).

- Aggregate amount of (a) money paid to or receivable by directors under long-term incentive schemes in respect of qualifying services and (b) net value of assets (other than money and share options) received or receivable by directors under such schemes in respect of such services (but see para 5.82).

[SI 2008/410 5 Sch 2(1)].

5.79 The highest paid director is the director with the greatest part of the total calculated in paragraph 5.78 above. [SI 2008/410 5 Sch 10]. Note that only the elements listed above are included in the calculation. Other items, for example compensation for loss of office and company pension contributions, are not included in determining the highest paid director.

5.80 The total of the amounts listed in paragraph 5.78 is the figure to be taken into account in determining whether the £200,000 level is reached or exceeded.

5.81 The threshold figure of £200,000 is not increased or decreased when the financial year for which financial statements are prepared exceeds or is less than 12 months. This is because it is determined by reference to the actual figures disclosed (see para 5.78 above) which are those for the financial period, whether that period is 12 months or not.

5.82 For unquoted companies other than companies listed on AIM, the items described do not include the amounts of gains made on exercise of share options or the value of shares received under long-term incentive schemes, because these amounts do not have to be calculated or disclosed by such unquoted companies (see para 5.28 above).

Disclosure

5.83 If the limit of £200,000 is reached or exceeded, the following two amounts must be disclosed in respect of the highest paid director:

- The total of the aggregate amounts described in paragraph 5.78 above that is attributable to the director.

- The amount of any company contributions paid, or treated as paid to a money purchase pension scheme in respect of the director's qualifying services.

[SI 2008/410 5 Sch 2(1)].

5.84 If the highest paid director has also participated in a defined benefit pension scheme, in respect of his qualifying services during the year, then the following information must also be disclosed:

- The amount at the end of the year of his accrued pension.

- Where applicable, the amount at the end of the year of his accrued lump sum.

[SI 2008/410 5 Sch 2(2)].

5.85 Where a company is unquoted and not listed on AIM and, therefore, does not include details of gains on options exercised or the value of shares awarded under long-term incentive schemes, it must disclose:

- Whether the highest paid director exercised any share options.

- Whether any shares were received or receivable by that director in respect of qualifying services under a long-term incentive scheme.

[SI 2008/410 5 Sch 2(3)].

5.86   However, if the director has not been involved in any such transactions there is no need to state that fact. [SI 2008/410 5 Sch 2(4)].

5.86.1   Comparative figures are required for the director's emoluments information in the normal way – see paragraph 5.92 onwards below.

'Accrued pension' and 'accrued lump sum'

5.87   The terms 'accrued pension' and 'accrued lump sum' mean the amount of the annual pension and the amount of the lump sum that would be payable to the director when he reaches normal pension age if:

- He had left the company's service at the end of the financial year.

- There were no increase in the general level of prices during the period from the end of the year to the director's pension age.

- There was no question of there being any commutation of the pension or inverse commutation of the lump sum.

- Any amounts attributable to voluntary contributions (AVCs) paid by the director to the scheme, and any money purchase benefits payable under the scheme were disregarded.

[SI 2008/410 5 Sch 13(2)].

5.88   'Normal pension age' is the earliest date at which the director is entitled to receive a full pension on retirement of an amount determined without reduction to take account of its payment before a later age (but disregarding any entitlement to pension upon retirement in the event of illness, incapacity or redundancy). [SI 2008/410 5 Sch 13(5)]. This means that a pension is not a 'full pension' if the benefits are reduced to take account of early payment and that any entitlement in the event of illness, incapacity or redundancy is disregarded for these purposes.

5.89   The third bullet point in paragraph 5.87, which refers to commutation of the pension or inverse commutation of the lump sum, should be interpreted as follows. Disclosure of the amount of accrued lump sum should only be made where, under the pension scheme rules, the director will automatically receive a lump sum on retirement. No disclosure should be made of a lump sum when a lump sum may be payable by way of commutation (that is, reduction) of rights to an annual pension. In the same way, disclosure of the amount of accrued pension should not include any reverse commutation of a lump sum entitlement. In practice, schemes that have both lump sums and pensions are extremely rare outside the public sector.

5.90   If, for example, a director was entitled at the end of the year to an accrued pension of £30,000, but could commute that into a pension of £20,000 per annum and a lump sum of £100,000, the only disclosure to be made would be the accrued pension of £30,000. If he was entitled to a pension of £30,000 and a lump sum of £50,000 (without any reduction in the pension), both figures would be disclosed. If he was entitled to a pension of £30,000 and a lump sum of £50,000, but could commute the lump sum such that he could instead take a pension of £35,000 and no lump sum, then the figures to be disclosed would be £30,000 and £50,000, that is ignoring the right to the reverse commutation of the lump sum.

Example 1 – Accrued pension (no entitlement to lump sum)

The highest paid director is 50 at the beginning of the year. He joined the company when he was 40 and is entitled to retire at 60. His salary in the previous year was £120,000 per annum. In the current year his salary is also £120,000. His maximum pension is 20/30 of his final salary after 20 years, but he has no entitlement to a lump sum (although he may commute part of his pension and take a lump sum in place of the amount commuted).

The pension accrual would be calculated as follows:

Accrued pension at the end of the previous year	$10/30 \times £120,000 = £40,000$
Accrued pension at the end of the current year	$11/30 \times £120,000 = £44,000$

The disclosure would, therefore, be:

Accrued pension of the highest paid director	£44,000 (previous year £40,000)

Example 2 – Accrued pension and lump sum

The highest paid director is 50 at the beginning of the year. He joined the company at 20 and is entitled to retire at 60. His salary in the previous year was £150,000 and is £160,000 in the current year. His maximum pension is 40/80 of his final salary after 40 years and he is also entitled to a maximum lump sum of 120/80 of his final salary after 40 years. (He may commute the lump sum by taking an increased pension instead of all or part of the lump sum.)

The pension accrued and accrual of the lump sum entitlement would be as follows:

Accrued pension at the end of the previous year	$30/80 \times £150,000 = £56,250$
Accrued pension at the end of the current year	$31/80 \times £160,000 = £62,000$
Accrued lump sum at the end of the previous year	90 (being $120 \times 30/40$ years)/ $80 \times £150,000 = £168,750$
Accrued lump sum at the end of the current year	93 (being $120 \times 31/40$ years)/ $80 \times £160,000 = £186,000$

The disclosure would, therefore, be:

Accrued pension of highest paid director	£62,000 (previous year £56,250)
Accrued lump sum of highest paid director	£186,000 (previous year £168,750)

5.90.1   The examples below consider the implications for disclosure in respect of the highest paid director's pension entitlements when the director is appointed or retires in the year.

Example 1 – director appointed in the year

A director was appointed during the year. He had previously been an employee of the (unquoted) company for many years. He is the highest paid director. In disclosing his accrued pension entitlement (in accordance with the requirements of Schedule 5 to SI 2008/410 for unquoted companies) should it be calculated on the basis of the period for which he has been a director or on the basis of the whole period for which he has been both an employee and a director?

The accrued pension entitlement disclosed under Schedule 5 to SI 2008/410 should be calculated and disclosed, based on the whole period of his service as an employee and a director. However, the company could add a note to explain how much of the entitlement was earned prior to his becoming a director.

This is further explained in the similar example for a quoted company – see further paragraph 5.203.

Example 2 – director retires in the year

The highest paid director of an unquoted company retired during the year and started drawing his pension. What should be disclosed as the pension entitlement of the highest paid director at the year end under Schedule 5 to SI 2008/410?

For the purposes of the Schedule 5 to SI 2008/410 disclosure, the amount of the annual pension payable to the director should be disclosed, because up until his retirement he performed qualifying services by reference to which the final pension was calculated. A note could be given to explain that the figure disclosed was the pension entitlement at the date of retirement.

Examples of disclosure

5.90.2   The examples below illustrate disclosures in respect of the highest paid director.

Example 1 – Disclosure for highest-paid director (AIM company)

An example of disclosure in respect of the highest paid director that incorporates all of the above elements would be as follows for an AIM company:

Highest paid director	20X2	20X1
	£	£
Aggregate emoluments, gains on share options exercised and benefits under long-term incentive schemes	200,000	180,000
Company pension contributions to money purchase scheme	2,000	2,000
Defined benefit scheme:		
Accrued pension at end of year	30,000	25,000
Accrued lump sum at end of year	60,000	50,000

Example 2 – Disclosure for highest-paid director (unquoted company)

For an unquoted company that is not listed on AIM disclosure that incorporates all the above elements would be:

Highest paid director	20X2	20X1
	£	£
Aggregate emoluments and benefits (excluding gains on exercise of share options and value of shares received) under long-term incentive schemes	250,000	240,000
Company pension contributions to money purchase scheme	2,000	2,000
Defined benefit scheme:		
Accrued pension at end of year	60,000	53,000
Accrued lump sum at end of year	100,000	90,000

The highest paid director exercised share options during the year and received shares under the executive long-term incentive scheme.

General – readily ascertainable from other information

5.91 Where information on the highest paid director's emoluments is readily ascertainable from the other information that is shown, this satisfies the disclosure requirements. [SI 2008/410 5 Sch 6(2)].

Comparative figures

5.92 Comparative figures are required for the highest paid director's emoluments information in the normal way.

5.92.1 Where the highest paid director in the current year was not the highest paid in the previous year, we consider that the comparative figure disclosed should be the emoluments of the actual highest paid director last year. Therefore, the comparative figures may relate to a different person from the highest paid director this year. Where this is the case, the company may wish to indicate this in the disclosure.

5.92.2   Where a company reaches the £200,000 threshold (see para 5.78) in the current year and so is required to disclose the highest paid director's emoluments, the requirement to disclose comparatives applies even where the company did not reach the £200,000 threshold in the previous year and the information has not previously been disclosed.

5.92.3   Where a company is below the £200,000 threshold in the current year, it is not required to disclose the highest paid director's emoluments in the current year. However, if the company reached the £200,000 threshold in the prior year, our view is that it will not be exempt from disclosure for that year and so the comparative should be disclosed, together with an explanation that the company is exempt from disclosure in the current year. Furthermore, if the company is likely to reach the £200,000 threshold in the next year, it will be required to disclose information for that year with comparatives (see para 5.92.1). Therefore, the company should consider giving the disclosure for the current year, so that this is then available for the comparatives in next year's financial statements.

5.92.4   The above requirements for disclosure of comparatives in respect of the highest paid director's emoluments are summarised in the table below.

Current year	Prior year	Disclosure
£200,000 or more	£200,000 or more	Disclose highest paid director's emoluments for both years.
£200,000 or more	Less than £200,000	Disclose highest paid director's emoluments for both years (para 5.92.2).
Less than £200,000	£200,000 or more	No disclosure of highest paid director's emoluments for current year, but comparative disclosure required for prior year (para 5.92.3).
Less than £200,000	Less than £200,000	No disclosure of highest paid director's emoluments for both years.

Excess retirement benefits of directors and past directors

5.93   Except for small companies reporting under SI 2008/409, if retirement benefits paid to or receivable by directors or past directors are in excess of the retirement benefits to which they were entitled at the time when the benefits first became payable or 31 March 1997 (whichever is the later) the notes must disclose the aggregate amount of:

■   The amount of the excess benefits paid to or receivable by directors under pension schemes.

■   The amount of the excess benefits paid to or receivable by past directors, again under pension schemes.

[SI 2008/410 5 Sch 3(1)].

5.94 The excess amounts referred to above do not include amounts paid or receivable if:

■ The scheme's funding was such that the amounts were or could have been paid without recourse to additional contributions; and

■ The amounts were paid to or receivable by all pensioner members of the scheme on the same basis ('pensioner members' being persons entitled to the present payment of retirement benefits under the scheme).

[SI 2008/410 5 Sch 3(2), 3(3)].

5.95 The exception described above means that the excess retirement benefits disclosed do not include retirement benefits paid to all pensioners on the same basis out of an adequately funded pension scheme.

5.96 'Retirement benefits' for the purpose of the above includes benefits otherwise than in cash, and where benefits other than in cash are given the amount should be calculated as their estimated money value. The nature of any such benefit should also be disclosed. [SI 2008/410 5 Sch 3(4)].

Compensation for loss of office

5.97 Disclosure must be made of the aggregate amount of any compensation received or receivable by directors or past directors in respect of loss of office. [SI 2008/409 3 Sch 2(1); SI 2008/410 5 Sch 4(1)]. This disclosure should include amounts received or receivable in respect of the loss of office by the director of the reporting company. It should also include amounts received or receivable in respect of loss, while a director of the reporting company or in connection with ceasing to be a director of that company, of office as a director of any subsidiary undertaking or of any office that involved management of the affairs of the company or of any subsidiary undertaking. [SI 2008/409 3 Sch 2(2); SI 2008/410 5 Sch 4(2)]. 'Subsidiary undertaking' includes an undertaking at the time the services were rendered and a subsidiary undertaking immediately before the loss of office as a director. It also includes an undertaking where the director was a director, whilst being a director of the company, by virtue of the company's nomination (direct or indirect), whether or not it was in fact a subsidiary undertaking. [SI 2008/409 3 Sch 11; SI 2008/410 5 Sch 14].

5.98 Compensation for loss of office includes compensation for or in connection with a person's retirement from office. Where such retirement is caused by a breach of the person's contract with the company or with a subsidiary undertaking compensation includes payments made by way of damages for the breach or payments made in settlement or compromise of any claim in respect of the breach. [SI 2008/409 3 Sch 2(2); SI 2008/410 5 Sch 4(3)].

General – readily ascertainable from other information

5.99 Where information on compensation for loss of office is readily ascertainable from the other information that is shown this satisfies the disclosure requirements. [SI 2008/409 3 Sch 4(2); SI 2008/410 5 Sch 6(2)]. For example, if compensation had been paid to two people and each person's compensation is shown separately, but the aggregate can be readily ascertained this would satisfy the requirement to disclose the aggregate.

Pension scheme top ups

5.100 We consider that a payment made to top up a pension scheme for the benefit of a director on his retirement is disclosable as it is effectively a benefit in kind (see para 5.102 below). This would be so even if the top up were funded out of an existing scheme surplus [SI 2008/409 3 Sch 5(2); SI 2008/410 5 Sch 7(2)], because the reduction in the surplus would involve the company paying increased contributions to the scheme and the top up is, therefore, even in that case, indirectly a cost to the company.

Example – Enhanced pension on retirement

A director retired in the year and as part of his leaving package the company enhanced his pension by giving him extra years of pensionable service. The enhancement was funded out of a surplus in the company's pension scheme and the capital value of the added pension entitlement was £250,000. How should this be disclosed in the financial statements? Would the answer be different if the company had paid £250,000 into the pension scheme?

Since the pension enhancement was given in connection with the director's retirement, it should be included as part of the director's compensation for loss of office for disclosure under SI 2008/410. The amount to be disclosed would be £250,000, the capital value of the increase, because this is the value of the benefit to the retiring director. The disclosure would be the same, irrespective of whether the director's enhanced pension was funded out of a surplus in the scheme or by a special company contribution to the scheme.

5.101 An example of disclosure of a top up payment made by the company is given in Table 5.6.

Table 5.6 – Top up payment

XYZ Group Limited – Annual Report – 31 March 20X1

Directors' emoluments (extract)

During the year, Mr X, the previous chief executive, left the company. Mr X had a service contract with the company terminable by the company on one years' notice. The company has agreed to pay Mr X as compensation for loss of office an amount approximately equivalent to one year's salary and other benefits. This amount was £398,400, which is subject to deduction of tax, and includes a sum of £60,000 in respect of Mr X's pension arrangements.

(Note: This example is made up, but includes features from a real example of disclosure.)

Benefits in kind

5.102 In addition to any monetary payment, the term compensation for loss of office includes benefits received or receivable otherwise than in cash. The value of the benefit should be determined according to its estimated money value. [SI 2008/ 410 5 Sch 4(4)]. Except for small companies reporting under S1 2008/409 where compensation is given in kind, the company's financial statements should disclose its nature. [SI 2008/410 5 Sch 4(4)]. For example, the compensation might be the gift to the director of a car that he had previously used, but that was owned by the company. In this situation, the money value of the car and the fact that the compensation is in the form of a car will have to be disclosed. Normally, the market value of the car at the time of transfer should be used for this purpose. If, however, compensation includes both cash and a car, only the nature and not the amount of the benefit relating to the car needs to be separately disclosed. The cash and the amount of the benefit may be shown as one figure.

Ex gratia payments

5.103 The statutory description of 'compensation to directors for loss of office' is widely drawn. In deciding whether compensation to a director or a former director is required to be disclosed, regard should be had to both the nature of the compensation and the circumstances in which it was made, rather than just to the description the company gives to it. For example, *'ex gratia'* payments made on either a director's retirement or his removal from office can be regarded not as gratuitous payments, but as payments in compensation for loss of office and they should be disclosed as such.

Payments made on retirement

5.104 In some cases, directors may have terms in their service contracts which entitle them to continue to receive remuneration for a period after they cease to be directors, perhaps in their capacity as employees. In other cases, they may have more than one service contract with different companies in a group. In such cases, the company may be obliged to make payments for periods after the directors cease to act as directors of the parent company. Where such arrangements exist or where they are terminated by payment of an additional lump sum on retirement as director we consider that the amounts should be disclosed as part of the compensation for loss of office disclosure.

5.105 Additionally, on retirement a director might enter into a consultancy agreement with a company whereby he is paid an annual retainer for one or more years. Again we consider that such arrangements should be disclosed. In some cases, where genuine services are to be provided, disclosure may be as a transaction in which a director is interested (caught by related party disclosures). In others where no genuine services will be provided or the services to be provided have a fair value that is less than the compensation payable by the company, we consider that the amounts payable under the arrangement are, in substance, compensation for loss of office. For quoted companies, see also paragraph 5.214.

5.106   A further benefit sometimes allowed to directors on retirement is that they may retain share options previously granted to them where such options would normally lapse on their leaving the company. Alternatively, they may be entitled to keep the options as a result of the terms in their service contract. Again, where there is a benefit to the retiring director to which he is not entitled under the scheme rules, the value of this benefit should be included in 'compensation' for loss of office and its nature disclosed in accordance with paragraph 5.102, disclosure should be made (see Table 5.7).

5.107   Further examples of disclosure of compensation which include the above features are set out in Tables 5.7 to 5.10 below.

Table 5.7 – Compensation for loss of office

XYZ plc (AIM company) – Annual Report and Accounts – 30 June 20X1

Remuneration of directors (extract)

Mr X resigned as a Director on 16th February 20X1 and his contracts of employment with the Company and a Group subsidiary undertaking in the USA were terminated with effect from 31st March 20X1. Under the terms of his contract with the Company, he has been paid £105,000 upon termination of that contract. Under the terms of his contract with the US subsidiary undertaking he is entitled, subject to certain conditions, to continue to receive his annual salary of US$635,000 and certain other incidental benefits for a period of up to three years from 31st March 20X1; these salary payments have been fully provided for in these accounts and are disclosed as payments for termination of executive office when paid. He will retain his participation in the cycle of the long-term performance-related incentive plan ending on 30th June 20X1, pro rata to the period during which he was an employee of the Group. Payments to him under this plan will be disclosed as payments to a former Director when paid. He retains his right to share options, numbering 93,217 at 31st March 20X1, which expire on dates up to 20th March 20X4.

(Note: This example is made up but includes features from a real example of disclosure.)

Table 5.8 – Compensation for loss of office

XYZ Limited – Report and Accounts – 31 December 20X1

7. EMOLUMENTS OF THE DIRECTORS OF THE HOLDING COMPANY (extract)

Mr. X, a former Director of the Company and of Subsidiary Y, resigned on 12 October 20X1. He will continue to receive cash and non-cash benefits under the terms of his contract of employment dated 19 March 199X for the two year period to 31 October 20X3. As compensation for his loss of office as Managing Director of Subsidiary Y, this contract was changed so that over the two year period he is free to undertake other employment, subject to certain non-compete conditions, and is to be available for consultation by the Company. The estimated money value of the benefit to Mr. X, being the estimated total cash and non-cash benefits, is £670,000.

(Note: This example is made up but contains features from a real example of disclosure.)

Table 5.9 – Compensation for loss of office

XYZ Limited – Annual Report and Accounts – 31 December 20X1

Directors and employees (extract)

Following Mr X's resignation as director on 6 July 20X1, Mr X and Associates, of which Mr X is a partner, entered into a consultancy agreement with the company. The agreement has a term of two years from 1 August 20X1. Under the provisions of the agreement, Mr X and Associates will provide consultancy services as required by the company and receive remuneration comprising a day rate and payments at specified intervals. The agreement also provides for the partnership to receive a start-up loan of £50,000 free of interest but repayable by three instalments at specified dates in 20X2 and 20X3. The amount paid to the partnership for the services rendered in 20X1 was £95,750. The amount payable in 20X2 and 20X3, provided the agreement is not terminated, will depend on the work undertaken but will include specified payments which may total a maximum of £145,000.

(Note: This example is made up but contains features from a real example of disclosure.)

Table 5.10 – Disclosure of compensation for loss of office

X plc (AIM company) – Annual Report and Accounts – 2 April 20X3

SUPPLEMENTARY PROFIT AND LOSS INFORMATION (extract)

The value of the compensation received by a former director for loss of office amounted to £100,000 (20X2 — £1,162,536 relating to five directors). He also retained and has exercised options over 113,732 shares (granted under the executive share option scheme in May 20X1), and 144,975 shares (granted in May 20X2).

(Note: This example is made up but contains features from a real example of disclosure.)

Requirement for member approval

5.108   The Companies Act 2006 requires companies to obtain member approval for payments made to a director (or former director) or to persons connected with them relating to loss of office. This includes payments by way of compensation for loss of office and those in connection with the directors' retirement and includes payments relating to the loss of office from a subsidiary undertaking or any other office in connection with the company's management. The provisions are set out in sections 215 to 222 of the Companies Act 2006, including some exceptions, for wholly-owned subsidiaries and non-UK incorporated entities, and are effective for retirements occurring on or after 1 October 2007.

5.109   In addition to the exemptions for wholly-owned subsidiaries and non-UK incorporated entities, certain further exceptions to the requirement for shareholder approval are set out in the Act. A company will not be required to seek shareholder approval where the payment is made in good faith:

■   in discharge of an existing legal obligation (namely an obligation that was not entered into in connection with, or in consequence of, the event giving rise to the payment for loss of office);

- by way of damages for breach of an existing legal obligation;

- by way of settlement or compromise of any claim arising in connection with the termination of a director's office or employment; or

- by way of pension in respect of past services.

[CA06 Sec 220].

5.109.1   There is also a *de minimis* exception, such that shareholder approval is not required if the total value of the payment does not exceed £200. [CA06 Sec 221].

Example – Compensation for loss of office to be approved at the next AGM

An ultimate parent company with a 31 December 20X8 year end is proposing to make a payment to a director for loss of office. The payment is to be approved by the members at the AGM on 15 March 20X9.

No expense should be charged in the 2008 financial statements for this proposal. Compensation for loss of office proposed to be paid by the directors is not a liability of the company until approved by the members. The payment for compensation for loss of office should be accrued for in the 31 December 20X9 financial statements. This is similar to the situation for the accounting for final dividends (see chapters 22 of the Manual of Accounting – IFRS for the UK and the Manual of Accounting – UK GAAP).

Consideration should also be given to providing disclosure in the directors' remuneration note to the accounts or the remuneration report under Schedules 5 and 8 to SI 2008/410 respectively.

Disclosure in the financial statements

5.110   Amounts to be disclosed include all relevant sums paid by or receivable from the company, the company's subsidiary undertakings and any other person, unless the director has to account for the sums to the company, its subsidiaries or to members. [SI 2008/409 3 Sch 5(2); SI 2008/410 5 Sch 7(2)].

5.111   For this purpose, a subsidiary undertaking includes a company that was a subsidiary undertaking immediately before the date on which the director lost office. It also includes an undertaking of which the director, while a director of the company, was a director by virtue of the company's nomination (direct or indirect), whether or not it is or was in fact a subsidiary undertaking of the company. [SI 2008/409 3 Sch 11(1); SI 2008/410 5 Sch 14(1)].

5.112   Compensation paid to a director for loss of office should not be included in the disclosure of that person's aggregate remuneration as described from paragraph 5.32.

Sums paid to third parties in respect of directors' services

5.113   Paragraph 3 of Schedule 3 to SI 2008/409 and paragraph 5 of Schedule 5 to SI 2008/410 require companies to disclose in their financial statements any consideration paid to or receivable by third parties for making available the services of any person:

- As a director of the company.

- While a director of the company, as director of any of its subsidiary undertakings, or otherwise in connection with the management of the affairs of the company or any of its subsidiary undertakings.

[SI 2008/409 3 Sch 3(1); SI 2008/410 5 Sch 5(1)].

5.114   In this context, third parties do not include:

- The director himself or a person connected with him or a body corporate controlled by him.

- The company or any of its subsidiary undertakings.

[SI 2008/409 3 Sch 3(3); SI 2008/410 5 Sch 5(3)].

5.115   For the purpose of this disclosure 'subsidiary undertaking' includes an undertaking which is a subsidiary undertaking at the time the services were rendered and an undertaking where the director, while a director of the company, was a director by virtue of the company's nomination (direct or indirect), whether or not it is or was in fact a subsidiary undertaking. [SI 2008/409 3 Sch 11; SI 2008/410 5 Sch 14(1)]. See further paragraph 5.15.

5.116   For the purposes of this disclosure, the definition of consideration includes non-cash benefits. Where a benefit is given, its amount should be determined by reference to its estimated money value. The nature of the non-cash benefit must also be disclosed. [SI 2008/409 3 Sch 3(2); SI 2008/410 5 Sch 5(2)].

5.117   The requirement to disclose amounts paid to third parties for making available the services of a director is illustrated in the following example.

Example – Amounts paid to third party

Company A borrows money from a venture capital company. As part of the financing arrangement, a director of the venture capital company has been appointed to the board of directors of company A. Company A pays £10,000 per year to the venture capital company in respect of the director's services. The director is remunerated by the venture capital company and does not receive the money paid in respect of his services by company A personally. In this situation, the amount of £10,000 would be disclosed in company A's financial statements as sums paid to third parties in respect of directors' services in accordance with paragraph 3 of Schedule 3 and paragraph 5 of Schedule 5 to SI 2008/410.

5.117.1   A further example is given in Table 5.11.

Table 5.11 – Sums paid to third parties in respect of directors' services

XYZ Limited – Report and Accounts – 2 May 20X2

EMOLUMENTS OF DIRECTORS (extract)

ABC Bank plc, of which Mr X was a director, were paid fees of £23,000 during the period for the release of Mr X's services during the illness of the then Chairman.

(Note: This example is made up but contains features from a real disclosure example.)

5.117.2   The disclosure applies where third parties make available the services of a director. It does not apply to other services, as illustrated in the following example.

> **Example – Payments to a head hunter**
>
> Company B is looking to recruit a new director and agrees to use the services of a head hunter. Once the director has been employed, should the payments made to the head hunter be included with the emoluments disclosures?
>
> Paragraph 3 of Schedule 3 to SI 2008/409 and paragraph 5 of Schedule 5 to SI 2008/410 (for small and medium and large unquoted companies respectively) require disclosure of the aggregate amount of any consideration paid to or receivable by third parties for making available the services of any person as a director of the company. (Note that paragraph 16 of Schedule 8 to SI 2008/410 (for quoted companies) requires the information to be disclosed by individual director.)
>
> Where the fees paid by company B to a head hunter relate solely to services to the company for finding and introducing the person, we consider that a head hunter is not making available the services of a person as director in the sense envisaged in SI 2008/410. The head hunter receives a fee for finding the person who the company appoints to perform the services, but is not being paid in respect of the services. Our interpretation is that SI 2008/410 only applies to third parties who make the services of the director available (for instance, where another company lends a director part-time).

Disclosure examples

5.117.3   An example of directors' remuneration disclosure under the 2006 Act by an unquoted company not listed on AIM is given below.

Example – Disclosure of directors' remuneration (unquoted company)

	20X2	20X1
	£	£
Aggregate emoluments	350,000	320,000
Amounts (excluding shares) receivable under long-term incentive schemes	50,000	40,000
Company pension contributions to money purchase schemes	5,000	5,000
Compensation for loss of office	100,000	—
Sums paid to third parties for directors' services	—	20,000
Excess retirement benefits		
– current directors	5,000	5,000
– past directors	10,000	10,000

Two directors exercised share options in the year (20X1: two) and one director became entitled to receive shares under the long-term incentive scheme (20X1: three). Retirement benefits are accruing to two directors under the company's money purchase pension scheme (20X1: two) and to one director under a defined benefit scheme (20X1: one).

(Note: details of the highest paid director's emoluments must also be disclosed. An example of disclosure is given in para 5.90.2.)

An example of disclosure under the Act by an AIM company is given in the next section in paragraph 5.120.

Section III — AIM companies

5.118   AIM companies are effectively treated as unquoted companies by the Companies Act 2006. Therefore, unlike quoted companies (see para 5.6.3) they are not required to produce a directors' remuneration report in the form set out in Schedule 8 to SI 2008/410.

5.119   However, AIM companies do have to give certain information that other unquoted companies not listed on AIM do not have to give. The additional requirements are set out in the Companies Act 2006 and, for financial years ending on or after 31 March 2010 onwards, the AIM Rules, as follows.

Companies Act 2006 disclosure requirements

5.119.1   Schedule 5 to SI 2008/410 requires AIM companies to provide disclosures of aggregate gains made by directors on the exercise of share options and the aggregate net value of shares received or receivable under long-term incentive schemes. [SI 2008/410 5 Sch 1(b), (c)].

5.119.2   In addition, in their disclosure of highest paid director's emoluments, AIM companies also have to include amounts in respect of gains on the exercise of share options and the net value of shares received or receivable under long-term incentive schemes. [SI 2008/410 5 Sch 2(1)(a)].

5.120 These points are dealt with in section I and section II above, which distinguish, where applicable, the provisions relating to AIM companies from those relating to unquoted companies not listed on AIM. In general, however, the requirements for AIM companies are, with the above exceptions, the same as those for other unquoted companies. An example of disclosure under the 2006 Act by an AIM company is given below.

Example – Disclosure of directors' remuneration (AIM company)

	20X2 £	20X1 £
Aggregate emoluments	650,000	580,000
Gains made on exercise of share options	50,000	—
Amounts receivable under long-term incentive schemes	400,000	350,000
Company pension contributions to money purchase schemes	50,000	50,000
Compensation for loss of office	—	100,000
Sums paid to third parties for directors' services	20,000	20,000
Excess retirement benefits		
– current directors	5,000	5,000
– past directors	10,000	10,000

Retirement benefits are accruing to two directors under the company's money purchase pension scheme and to one director under a defined benefit scheme.

(Note: details of highest paid director's emoluments must also be disclosed. An example of the disclosure is given in para 5.90.2. In addition, disclosure of three categories of remuneration by individual director must be disclosed under the AIM Rules, as explained from paragraph 5.120.1.)

AIM Rules disclosure requirements

5.120.1 In February 2010, the London Stock Exchange introduced a requirement into the AIM Rules for the financial statements of AIM-listed entities to include details of individual directors' remuneration. Previously, the AIM Rules were silent in this area and, as a result, entities merely had to present directors' remuneration in total, and for the highest paid director, as described from paragraph 5.119.2 above.

5.120.2 Revised AIM Rule 19 requires the following to be disclosed for each director:

■ Emoluments and compensation (this will include both cash and non-cash benefits).

- Details of share options and other long-term incentive schemes (this will include information on all outstanding options and awards).

- The value of any company contribution made to a pension scheme.

5.120.3   There is limited detailed guidance on the new requirements, for example, there is little clarity on the extent of the detail to be provided in relation to share options and long-term incentive schemes. AIM-listed entities may, therefore, wish to look to the current requirements in Schedule 5 (requirements for all entities) and Schedule 8 (requirements for quoted entities) to SI 2008/410 for further guidance. Detailed guidance on these schedules is set out from paragraphs 5.27 (Schedule 5) and 5.163 (Schedule 8).

5.120.4   Revised AIM Rule 19 refers to the requirement to disclose remuneration earned *"by each director of the AIM company acting in such capacity during the financial year"*. The definition in Schedule 5 to SI 2008/410 is more specific, requiring all companies to disclose aggregate remuneration paid to or receivable by directors in respect of qualifying services. Qualifying services are defined in paragraph 5.33. We believe that, consistent with SI 2008/410's definition, disclosures should be in respect of remuneration of directors for their work for the whole group, not just work for the parent company.

Position of the auditor

5.120.5   While the notice issued by the London Stock Exchange states that the AIM Rules do not require the new directors' remuneration disclosures to be audited, the location of the disclosure could mean that the additional information on individual directors' remuneration is subject to audit. In addition, given the nature of the disclosures, and the following analysis, it is likely in practice that such balances would be audited.

- The introductory sentence to amended AIM Rule 19 states: *"an AIM company must publish annual audited accounts..."*. Therefore, the later reference in Rule 19 stating that *"the accounts produced in accordance with this rule must provide disclosure of...directors' remuneration..."* could be read as implying that these disclosures are subject to audit, despite the contradiction to the explicit statement in the London Stock Exchange's notice that the disclosures are not required to be audited.

- If the directors' remuneration disclosures required by AIM Rule 19 are included within the notes to the financial statements, these would need to be audited, consistent with other notes (unless headed up as 'unaudited', which would be unusual).

- AIM-listed entities are not required to prepare a remuneration report in accordance with Schedule 8 to SI 2008/410 because they do not meet the definition of a quoted company under section 385(2) of the Companies Act 2006. However, if a voluntary remuneration report were produced or the disclosures were included within the directors' report, then section 496 of the

Act and ISA (UK&I) 720A (revised), 'The auditor's responsibilities relating to other information in the documents containing audited financial statements (2009)', would apply. Section 496 of the Act requires the auditor to opine on *"whether the information given for the financial year of which the accounts are prepared is consistent with those accounts"*, including seeking to resolve any identified inconsistencies and providing details in the audit report if any material inconsistency is not resolved.

■ As mentioned above, AIM Rule 19 states that the disclosures are required to be made in the 'accounts' and this could be interpreted as meaning the financial statements. In any event, given the nature of the disclosures it is likely in practice that such balances would be audited even if included in the front end of the financial statements.

Effective date

5.120.6   The revised AIM Rule 19 applies for 31 March 2010 year ends onwards.

Section IV — Quoted companies (excluding companies listed on AIM)

Remuneration report

5.121   SI 2008/410 contains requirements for quoted companies (for definition see para 5.6.3) which substantially duplicates the requirements contained in the FSA Listing Rules. The requirements of SI 2008/410 also contain additional disclosures over and above those contained in the Listing Rules. As explained in paragraph 5.6.5, there are some differences between the requirements of the Listing Rules and those of SI 2008/410 and so the disclosures could be complicated. An illustrative example is given in the directors' remuneration report for IFRS GAAP plc (see separate publication containing illustrative financial statements). The requirements of the Listing Rules are covered in this section in addition to those in SI 2008/410.

5.122   Quoted companies must comply with the disclosure requirements that are applicable to all companies, and these are described above in section I of this chapter. Sections 420 to 422 of the Companies Act 2006 require that the directors of a quoted company prepare a directors' remuneration report that contains the information specified in Schedule 8 and complies with any requirement of that Schedule as to how the information is to be set out in the report. Section 421 of the Companies Act 2006 gives the Secretary of State power to make provision by regulations as to the information that must be contained in a directors' remuneration report and how it should be set out. These matters are set out in Schedule 8 to SI 2008/410.

5.123   The directors' remuneration report must be approved by the board and signed on its behalf by a director or the secretary of the company. [CA06 Sec 422(1)].

5.124   Schedule 8 to SI 2008/410 contains four parts:

■   Introductory.

■   Information not subject to audit — information about remuneration committees, performance related remuneration and liabilities in respect of directors' contracts.

■   Information subject to audit — detailed information about directors' remuneration.

■   Interpretation and supplementary.

5.125   This section of the chapter considers the provisions of Schedule 8 to SI 2008/410 in two parts: first the information that is not subject to audit and second the information that is subject to audit, which was mainly derived from the requirements of the Listing Rules, but with some changes – notably on pensions disclosure.

5.126   The introductory part of Schedule 8 to SI 2008/410 merely states that the directors' remuneration report shall show the information specified in the Schedule and that information required to be shown in the report for, or in respect of, a particular person shall be shown in the report in a manner that links the information to that person identified by name. [SI 2008/410 8 Sch 1].

5.127   The information not subject to audit covers:

■   Consideration by the directors of matters relating to directors' remuneration.

■   A statement of policy on directors' remuneration.

■   Statement of consideration of conditions elsewhere in the company and group.

■   Performance graph.

■   Service contracts.

■   Compensation for past directors (explanation for awards).

There is also some discussion on the interaction between the UK Corporate Governance Codes (2008) and (2010) and the remuneration report at the end of this section.

5.128   The information that is subject to audit covers:

■   Individual directors' emoluments and compensation.

■   Share options.

■   Long-term incentive schemes.

■   Pensions.

- Excess retirement benefits of directors and past directors.

- Compensation for past directors (details of awards).

- Sums paid to third parties in respect of directors' services.

5.129 Each of these above requirements is considered below and finally the approval and audit requirements are described.

Information not subject to audit

Consideration by the directors of matters relating to directors' remuneration

5.130 SI 2008/410 requires that if a committee of a company's directors has considered matters relating to directors' remuneration for the year, the names of each of the directors on the committee must be given in the remuneration report. [SI 2008/410 8 Sch 2(1)(a)].

5.131 An example of such disclosure is provided in Table 5.12.

Table 5.12 – Remuneration committee composition

National Grid plc – Annual report – 31 March 2010

Remuneration Committee

The Remuneration Committee members are John Allan, Ken Harvey, Stephen Pettit and George Rose. Each of these Non-executive Directors is regarded by the Board as independent and served throughout the year.

5.132 The name must be given of anyone (which may include a director who was not a member of the committee) who provided advice or services that materially assisted the committee in considering any matter relating to directors' remuneration. For anyone so named, who is not a director of the company, further information must be given as follows:

- The nature of any other services that the person provided to the company during the year.

- Whether the person was appointed by the committee.

[SI 2008/410 8 Sch 2(1)(b)(c)].

5.132.1 This requirement is illustrated in the following examples.

Example 1 – Report benchmarking remuneration

The remuneration committee of a quoted company engaged an HR consultant to prepare a report benchmarking the remuneration of the company's directors against the remuneration of directors of comparable companies. Does this constitute material assistance for the purpose of disclosure under Schedule 8 of SI 2008/410?

This would be material assistance. The HR consultant prepared a report with the purpose of assisting the remuneration committee in their consideration of directors' remuneration by benchmarking against similar companies.

Example 2 – Independent benchmarking survey

A different HR consultant has prepared and published widely an independent benchmarking survey that the remuneration committee has used when considering whether the relative importance of performance-related and non-performance-related remuneration is appropriate. Would this constitute material assistance?

This would not be material assistance. The HR consultant prepared a report for the purposes of general publication, which the remuneration committee used to assist itself in its consideration of directors' remuneration. No assistance was given by the HR consultant to this remuneration committee.

Example 3 – Preparation of performance graph

A third HR consultant was engaged by the same remuneration committee to prepare the total shareholder return graph for inclusion in the directors' remuneration report. Would this constitute material assistance?

This would not be material assistance. The HR consultant is putting together a graph of factual information, all of which is publicly available, for the purposes of disclosure and not to assist the remuneration committee in its consideration of directors' remuneration.

Example 4 – Auditors' review of remuneration report

During the course of an audit, the auditors reviewed the directors' remuneration report and made some comments to the directors on the presentation and content of the remuneration report. Would this constitute material assistance?

This would not be material assistance. The review of the directors' remuneration report is undertaken by the auditor as part of the audit and does not assist the remuneration committee in its consideration of directors' remuneration.

5.133   An example of disclosure that complies with the requirement to provide details of anyone who provided advice or services to the remuneration committee is given in Table 5.13.

Table 5.13 – Advisors to the remuneration committee

Anglo American plc – Annual Report 2009 – 31 December 2009

1 Remuneration Committee (extract)

1.2 Membership of the Committee (extract)

In 2009, the Committee was advised by the Company's Human Resources and Finance functions and, specifically, Mervyn Walker and Chris Corrin. It also took external advice as shown in Figure 1.

Certain overseas operations within the Group are also provided with audit related services from PwC's and Deloitte's worldwide member firms and non-audit related services from Mercer's worldwide member firms.

A summary of the letter from Mercer containing the conclusions of their review of the Committee's executive remuneration processes for 2009 can be found on page 91, while the full letter can be found on the Company's website.

Figure 1: External advice provided to the Remuneration Committee

Advisers		Other services provided to the Company
PricewaterhouseCoopers LLP (PwC)	Appointed by the Company, with the agreement of the Committee, to provide specialist valuation services	Investment advisers, actuaries and auditors for various pension schemes; advisers on internal audit projects; taxation, payroll and executive compensation advice
Monks Partnership (a subsidiary of PwC)	Appointed by the Company, with the agreement of the Committee, to provide market remuneration data	
Linklaters LLP (Linklaters)	Appointed by the Company, with the agreement of the Committee, to provide legal advice on long-term incentives and directors' service contracts	Legal advice on certain corporate matters
Mercer Limited (Mercer)	Engaged by the Committee to review the Committee's processes on an annual basis, in order to provide shareholders with assurance that the remuneration processes the Committee has followed are in line with stated policy and that the Committee has operated within its Terms of Reference	Investment advisers and actuaries for various pension schemes
Deloitte LLP (Deloitte)		In their capacity as Group auditors, Deloitte undertakes an audit of sections 10 and 11 of the remuneration report annually. However, they provide no advice to the Committee

Statement of policy on directors' remuneration

5.134 The directors' remuneration report should contain a statement of the company's policy on directors' remuneration for the following year and for subsequent financial years. [SI 2008/410 8 Sch 3(1)]. For companies listed in the UK, the Listing Rules also require a statement of the company's policy on executive directors' remuneration. [LR 9.8.8R (1)]. The policy statement required under the Act should include:

- For each director, a detailed summary of any performance conditions to which the director's entitlement to share options or long-term incentive awards is subject, together with an explanation as to why those performance conditions were chosen.

- A summary of the methods to be used to assess whether the performance conditions are met and an explanation of why those methods have been chosen.

- If any of the performance conditions involves comparison with factors external to the company, a summary of the factors to be used in the comparison. If any of the factors relates to the performance of another company, or of two or more companies, or of an index on which a company or companies are listed, the identity of the company or companies or of the index must be given.

- A description of, and explanation for, any significant amendment that is proposed to the terms and conditions of any entitlement of a director to share options or under a long-term incentive scheme.

- If there are no performance conditions attached to the entitlement of a director to share options or under a long-term incentive scheme, an explanation as to why that is the case.

[SI 2008/410 8 Sch 3(2)].

5.135 The policy statement must, in respect of each director's terms and conditions relating to remuneration, explain the relative importance of the elements that are related to performance and those that are not. [SI 2008/410 8 Sch 3(3)].

5.136 The Listing Rules also require an explanation and justification of any element of remuneration, other than basic salary, which is pensionable. [LR 9.8.8R (7)].

5.136.1 In addition to the above disclosure required by the Act in respect of performance conditions and of any significant amendments to the terms of share options or long-term incentive schemes, the Listing Rules also require a statement of the company's policy on the granting of options or awards under its employees' share schemes and other long-term incentive schemes, explaining and justifying any departure from that policy in the period under review and any change in the policy from the preceding year. [LR 9.8.8R (10)].

5.137   As detailed in paragraph 5.134, SI 2008/410 requires certain disclosures in respect of performance conditions to which the director's entitlement to share options or long-term incentive awards is subject. SI 2008/410 does not distinguish between performance conditions and additional service conditions that have to be met before an award vests. This is considered in the example below.

> **Example – Service conditions outstanding**
>
> A quoted company is preparing a directors' remuneration report. A director has been awarded share options that vest if the company meets certain targets for the first three years of the scheme and he remains employed by the company for a further two years. Is the requirement for him to stay for the further two years a performance condition?
>
> SI 2008/410 does not distinguish between performance conditions and service conditions that must be met before an award under a share option scheme is exercisable or under an LTIP is receivable. Although it is possible to interpret the Act to have a narrow definition of 'performance conditions', we believe that the intention of the Act is that service conditions should be included within the umbrella of 'performance conditions'. This is consistent with both the company's perspective that during the period in which the director is fulfilling his service conditions, the company is receiving qualifying services. It is also consistent with IFRS 2 (FRS 20), 'Share-based payment', which recognises the charge to the income statement (UK – profit and loss account) for employee services received over the vesting period which includes the performance and service periods.
>
> Hence, given that the director is not entitled to exercise his share options unless he remains employed by the company for a period of five years, it would be appropriate to explain this fact in the remuneration report. We believe that it is good practice to disclose the service condition as a performance condition under paragraph 3 of Schedule 8 to SI 2008/410.

5.137.1   An example of disclosure of long-term incentive awards, explaining why no performance conditions are attached, is given in Table 5.15.

Table 5.15 – Explanation of reason for no performance conditions

EMI Group plc – Annual Report – 31 March 2003

Remuneration Report (extract)

Long-term incentive arrangements (extract)
Mr Bandier was also granted a restricted share award under the SEIP of 662,500 shares. These shares will vest no earlier than 31 March 2006. The award was in lieu of additional base salary and is not, therefore, subject to performance requirements. The aim of the award was to bring Mr Bandier's basic annual remuneration into line with competitive practice in the US, where he is based, whilst aligning his interests more closely with those of the shareholders and providing him with a strong incentive to remain with the Group. No further awards of this nature are envisaged.

5.137.2   The directors who are covered by the detailed requirements in paragraphs 5.134 to 5.135 above are those who are serving as directors at any time in the period from the end of the financial year to the date on which the directors' remuneration report is laid before the company in general meeting. [SI 2008/410 8 Sch 3(5)].

5.137.3 Further disclosure requirements in respect of share options are given from paragraph 5.170 onwards and in respect of long-term incentive schemes are given from paragraph 5.180.

5.138 The remuneration policy statement must also summarise and explain the company's policy on:

■ The duration of contracts with directors.

■ Notice periods and termination payments under such contracts.

[SI 2008/410 8 Sch 3(4)].

5.139 We believe that this requirement relates to the company's general policy on contracts and notice periods and, therefore, would apply to anyone who is a director during the year or in the period up to the date that the remuneration report is signed.

5.140 Examples of notes that deal with policy for service contracts and termination payments are given in Table 5.16 and Table 5.16A. Further disclosure requirements in respect of service contracts are given from paragraph 5.149.

Table 5.16 – Policy on service contracts and termination payments

Standard Life plc – Annual report and accounts 2009 – 31 December 2009

Directors' remuneration report

Policy on executive contracts
The current executive Directors' service contracts were issued in 2006 and the Remuneration Committee seeks to strike the right balance between the Company's interests and those of the executive Directors, while ensuring that they comply with best practice, legislation and the remuneration principles. Contracts are not for a fixed term, but provide for notice periods in line with the executive's role. The main terms are:

Provision	Policy
Notice periods	• Six months by the Director • 12 months by the Company or a payment in lieu of notice can be made
Termination payment	• Any payment in lieu of notice will be up to 12 months' salary, pension contributions and the value of other contractual benefits • A duty to mitigate applies • The payment may be made in phased instalments and the policy is to do this for notice periods in excess of six months • Rights to bonus and existing LTIP awards are governed by the rules of the respective plans

---

Remuneration	• Salary, pension and benefits are mentioned in the contracts and are treated as described above
	• There is no contractual entitlement to annual bonus and LTIP awards and instead individuals are told of these discretionary schemes at the beginning of each year
Non-compete	• Apply during the contract and for up to six months after leaving at the Company's choice

Contract dates	Sir Sandy Crombie[1]	31 March 2006 (expires 30 April 2010)
	David Nish[2]	31 October 2006[3]
	Keith Skeoch	3 April 2006

1 Sir Sandy Crombie stepped down as Group Chief Executive and resigned as a director of Standard Life plc and other Group companies on 31 December 2009. He will remain an employee of the Group until 30 April 2010 to assist in the handover to David Nish.

2 Appointed Chief Executive with effect from 1 January 2010. Jackie Hunt was appointed as interim Chief Financial Officer in November 2009 and is not a member of the Standard Life plc Board and as such is not covered by this report.

3 David Nish signed a new contract on 16 October 2009, reflecting his appointment as Chief Executive from 1 January 2010.

Table 5.16A – Statement of policy for service contracts and termination payments

EMI Group plc – Annual Report – 31 March 2007

Directors' service contracts

The Code recommends that notice or contract periods should be set at one year or less. It is the Group's policy to achieve that, where possible.

The Committee endorses the principle of mitigation of loss on early termination of a service contract and recognises the advantage of service contracts including an explicit calculation, subject to mitigation, of compensation payable upon early termination, other than for misconduct or in other circumstances justifying summary termination. The Committee's policy is that such compensation should generally be calculated by reference to base salary, annual bonus at target level and other benefits, including pension contributions, for the notice period or unexpired term of the service contract. The contract should also include an explicit obligation to mitigate and to offset earnings from alternative employment undertaken during the notice period or unexpired term of the contract against all or part of the compensation payment.

However, the Committee is conscious that fixed-term contracts of three or more years are common for senior executives in the global entertainment industry and such agreements often include no (or only a limited) obligation to mitigate. The Committee, therefore, considers that it is in the best interests of EMI and its shareholders to retain the flexibility to compete for top executive talent, where necessary, through the ability to offer contract terms in excess of one year. However, as an alternative, the Committee may agree compensation payments calculated without mitigation in order to limit contract terms or notice periods to one year.

Group CEO and Group CFO — Eric Nicoli and Martin Stewart

The service contracts of Mr Nicoli and Mr Stewart, dated 11 April 2003 and 5 January 2005, respectively, are terminable by the Company on one year's notice.

In the case of gross misconduct or other circumstances justifying summary dismissal, the Company may terminate their service contracts without payment of compensation. Termination by the Company in other circumstances, without the required notice being given, entitles the departing executive to compensation, calculated on:

- his then base annual salary (currently £788,000 pa for Mr Nicoli and £551,250 pa for Mr Stewart) for one year; plus,

- the value of retirement benefits and either the continued enjoyment of, or the value of, benefits in kind provided to him for one year (the accrued value of such retirement contributions and the benefits in kind would have been £471,695 for Mr Nicoli and £229,405 for Mr Stewart had either one of them been dismissed on 31 March 2007); plus,

- a sum in respect of lost annual bonus opportunity, being 50% of his maximum bonus for the period from the date of his departure to the end of the contractual notice period.

Their entitlement to such compensation is subject to both a duty to mitigate and, also, offset for any earnings which they derive from other employment during the unworked part of the notice period for which they have been compensated.

Chairman and CEO EMI Music Publishing — Roger Faxon

Mr Faxon was reappointed as a Director on 1 April 2006 and became Chairman and sole CEO of EMI Music Publishing on 6 March 2007. His employment agreement, which is effective as of 1 February 2005, allows EMI to terminate the contract at any time on 30 days' notice. If termination is for cause (as defined in the contract), no compensation is payable. If termination is without cause or Mr Faxon terminates the agreement for good reason (for example, breach by EMI), he is entitled to compensation based on one year's pay, as follows:

- continued payment of his base annual salary (currently US$1,7,00,000 pa) for one year; plus,

- continued provision of retirement benefits and the continued enjoyment of benefits in kind provided to him for one year (the annual value of such retirement contributions and the benefits in kind would have been US$914,884 had he been dismissed on 31 March 2007); plus,

- a lump sum equal to his target annual bonus opportunity for the next following financial year, being not less than 50% of his base salary in effect immediately prior to termination.

In the light of competitive music industry practice, and in recognition of Mr Faxon's agreement, when he was promoted to Group CFO on 2 February 2002, to reduce his basic contract term from two years to one year, there is no obligation on him to mitigate, or to offset against the compensation payment any earnings from alternative employment during the year following termination. However, the Company's obligation to continue to provide insurance benefits will cease to the extent that similar benefits are provided by another employer during the 12 months following termination.

5.141   To a large extent, the above requirements are drawn from the UK Corporate Governance Codes (2008) and (2010). The principles of the UK Corporate Governance Codes (2008) and (2010) that relate to directors' remuneration are described in Annex 1 to this chapter. Whilst the legal requirements above set out what must be disclosed, the UK Corporate Governance Codes (2008) and (2010) also contain best practice provisions for a range of issues including setting remuneration levels, awarding options and service contracts.

5.141.1   A number of other organisations, including industry commentators such as the NAPF, ABI and RiskMetrics Group have also published good practice guidance on remuneration. This guidance is discussed from paragraph 5.223.1 below.

Statement of consideration of conditions elsewhere in the company and group

5.142 Under the Companies Act 2006, there is a new requirement for quoted companies to report in their directors' remuneration report on how they have taken pay and employment conditions elsewhere in the group into account when determining directors' remuneration for the relevant financial year. [SI 2008/410 8 Sch 4]. This new requirement will only have to be included in reports for financial years beginning on or after 6 April 2009. An example of disclosure of consideration of conditions elsewhere in the group is given in Table 5.16B.

Table 5.16B Mitchells & Butlers – Annual report – 26 September 2009

Remuneration report (extracts)

Committee remit and membership (extract)

The Committee takes into account a range of factors, including remuneration policy, incentive arrangements and percentage increases awarded across the Group.

Executive Directors' remuneration

The proportion of the Group's basic salary bill attributable to the Executive Directors and other members of the Executive Committee in 2009 was 0.6% (2008 0.7%).

The Committee is regularly updated on pay and conditions applying to other Group employees; these are taken into consideration when setting Executive Director remuneration.

The average earnings (base salary and annual performance bonus) of the Executive Directors were £414,600 (2008 £422,551) and the average earnings, on a full time equivalent basis, per non-Board employee were £13,979 (2008 £13,810); the ratio is therefore 1:30 (2008 1:31). The Board and the Committee do not have a policy on this ratio, but aim to reward all employees fairly according to the nature of their role, their performance and market forces.

In the year under review the average base salary increase, excluding promotional increases, for members of the Executive Committee which includes the Executive Directors was 4.7%, whereas the average increase for other employees including retail staff and management was 3.4%.

The total emoluments, including benefits in kind, earned by those members of the Executive Committee who were employed in the Group at the year end and who were not main Board Directors, are shown in the table below:

Number of executives	£000
1	201-250
1	251-300
4	301-350
2	351-400

Performance graph

5.143 The directors' remuneration report is required to include a performance graph showing the total shareholder return for the company against an index.

5.144 The detailed requirement is for a line graph to be presented that shows the total shareholder return for each of:

- A holding of shares of the company's equity share capital whose listing or admission to dealing has led to the company being defined as a quoted company (for definition see para 5.6.3 above).

- A hypothetical holding of shares made up of shares of the same kind and number as those by reference to which a broad based equity market index is calculated.

[SI 2008/410 8 Sch 5(1)(a)].

5.145 The name of the index selected for the purpose of the graph and the reason for selecting that index should be disclosed. [SI 2008/410 8 Sch 5(1)(b)].

5.146 The line graph should cover five financial years of which the last is the current financial year (that is, the year for which financial statements are being presented). However, if the company has been in existence for less than five years, a shorter period may be given comprising only the number of financial years completed since the company came into existence. For example, if the current financial year is the company's third, the graph would cover three financial years. [SI 2008/410 8 Sch 5(2)(3)]. The situation where the company has been listed for less than five years, despite existing for longer is dealt with in paragraph 5.148.2 below. The situation where the index itself has existed for less than five years is considered in paragraph 5.148.4 below.

5.147 Total shareholder return is calculated using a fair method that:

- Starts with the percentage change in the market price of the holding over the period.

- Makes the following assumptions as to reinvestment of income:

  (a) That any benefit in the form of shares of the same kind as those in the holding is added to the holding when that benefit becomes receivable.

  (b) That any benefit in cash, and the value of any benefit not in cash and not falling into (a) above, is used when the benefit becomes receivable to purchase shares of the same kind as the existing holding at market price and that the notional shares so purchased are added to the existing holding at that time.

  (c) 'Benefit' in paragraphs (a) and (b) means any benefit (including dividends) receivable in respect of the holding from the company of whose share capital the holding forms part.

- Makes the following assumptions as to the funding of liabilities:

  (a) Where the holder has a liability to the company of whose share capital the holding forms part, shares are sold from the holding:

    (i) immediately before the time by which the liability is due to be settled; and

> (ii) they are sold in such numbers that, at the time of sale, the market price of the shares sold equals the amount of the liability in respect of the shares in the holding that are not sold.

(b) in paragraph (a) 'liability' means a liability in respect of any shares in the holding or from the exercise of a right attached to any of those shares.

[SI 2008/410 8 Sch 5(4)-(8)].

■ Makes provision for any replacement of shares in the holding by shares of a different description.

The same method must be used for each of the holdings mentioned in paragraph 5.144.

[SI 2008/410 8 Sch 5(4)-(8)].

5.148 In general there are a number of indices that are widely available and which show total returns. For example the UK Series of the FTSE Actuaries Share indices include Total Return indices. As noted in paragraph 5.145, SI 2008/410 requires disclosure of the name of the index, therefore, it is not acceptable to use an index created by the company alone, although it may be possible to give some disclosure as additional information. This is considered in the example below.

Example – Selection of index for total shareholder return graph

A quoted company is preparing its directors' remuneration report and is selecting the index to use in the total shareholder return graph. Can the company 'create' an index of companies of a similar size and nature? If not, which index should it use?

Given the Companies Act's requirement for disclosure of the name of the index (see para 5.145 above), using an index created by the company alone is not acceptable.

There are a number of published indices for total shareholder return that are publicly available. These include indices that are industry-based, such as the TechMark index, as well as indices that are size-based, such as the FTSE 100.

We consider that when selecting an index, the directors should generally use an index of which the company is a constituent and that they use internally to measure the company's performance against its peers. The remuneration committee should consider a range of appropriate indices and, based on the relative merits of each, select the index that is, in their opinion, most appropriate.

However, we also consider that, if a company has also devised a more specific index for a peer group of companies, that it actually uses for the purpose of setting performance targets, a total return graph, plotting the company's performance against the performance of the peer group, could be given as additional information. The composition of the peer group, the basis of preparation of the graph and reasons for producing it, should be given.

5.148.1   A straightforward example of disclosure is given in Table 5.17 below. See also the example in Table 5.18, which gives the information required by the legislation in the first graph and additional information in subsequent graphs. The example compares the company's performance with three indices, each of which is relevant because each gives a different perspective on the group's performance.

Table 5.17 – Performance graph

Rolls-Royce Group plc – Annual Report – 31 December 2009

Performance graph

The Company's TSR performance over the previous five years compared to a broad equity market index is shown in the graph opposite. The FTSE 100 index has been chosen as the comparator index because it contains a broad range of other leading UK listed companies.

This graph shows the growth in value of a hypothetical £100 holding in Rolls-Royce Group plc ordinary shares over five years, relative to the FTSE 100 index. The values of the hypothetical £100 holdings at the end of the five-year period were £227.60 and £135.40 respectively.

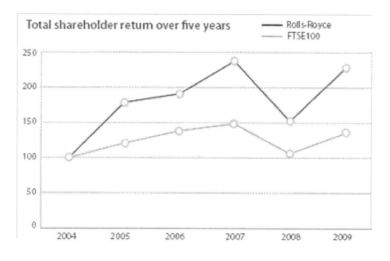

Table 5.18 – Performance graph

Pearson Plc – Annual Report – 31 December 2009

Total shareholder return performance

Below we set out Pearson's total shareholder return on three bases. Pearson is a constituent of all the indices shown.

First, we set out Pearson's total shareholder return performance relative to the FTSE All-Share index on an annual basis over the five-year period 2004 to 2009. We have chosen this index, and used it consistently in each report on directors' remuneration since 2002, on the basis that it is a recognisable reference point and an appropriate comparator for the majority of our investors.

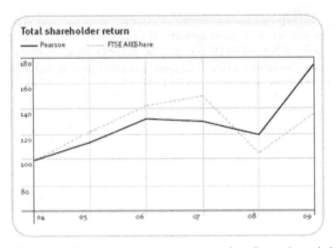

Secondly, to illustrate performance against our sector, we show Pearson's total shareholder return relative to the FTSE Media index over the same five-year period.

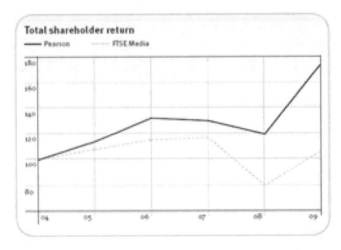

And thirdly, we show Pearson's total shareholder return relative to the FTSE All-Share and Media indices on a monthly basis over 2009, the period to which this report relates.

5.148.2 SI 2008/410 requires that the line graph should cover five financial years and it deals with the situation where the company has been in existence for less than five years (see para 5.146 above). The situation where the company has existed for more than five years, but been listed for less than five years in considered in the example below.

> **Example – Performance graph for company listed less than five years**
>
> A quoted company is preparing its directors' remuneration report for the year ended 31 December 20X2. Paragraph 5 of Schedule 8 to SI 2008/410 requires the company to present, in the remuneration report, a line graph showing, for the previous five years and for each of the securities that results in the company being a quoted company, the Total Shareholder Return (TSR) for a holding of those shares and the TSR for a hypothetical holding of shares on a broad equity market index. The company listed in April 20X0 and, consequently, the TSR for the company cannot be calculated prior to that date. Is it acceptable to present the TSR graph only from the date of listing?
>
> Within paragraph 5 of Schedule 8 to SI 2008/410 there is an exemption from presenting the full five year history when the company has been in existence for less than five years, but there is no similar exemption where the company has been listed for less than five years.
>
> However, paragraph 5(4) of Schedule 8 to SI 2008/410 states that TSR is calculated taking as the starting point the percentage change in the market price over the period. As the shares have only been listed since April 2000 and, therefore, only have a listed market price since that date, we consider that the Act would require the company's TSR to be calculated taking the change in the period from April 20X0 to 31 December 20X0 as the starting point.

5.148.3 Another situation where a company's total shareholder return may not be available for the five year period is where there has been a demerger. In Table 5.19 reference is made to how the company has chosen to overcome the complication caused by a demerger in the five year period. Another example of a company's total shareholder return compared to a related index, in this instance showing the period since demerger, is provided in Table 5.19A.

Table 5.19 – Performance graph

Peninsular and Oriental Steam Navigation Company – Annual Report and Accounts – 31 December 2002

PERFORMANCE GRAPH

In line with the Regulations, the following graph compares the performance of the Company's deferred stock on a TSR basis for the past five years against the FTSE 350 Index. This index has been selected as P&O is a constituent of the FTSE 350 and uses this index for their comparator group for the Matching Plan. However, the line representing the FTSE 350 on the graph is based on the market index weighted by market capitalisation whereas the Matching Plan is based on the performance of the companies comprising the FTSE 350 at the commencement of the relevant performance period. TSR is shown as the value of £100 invested in P&O and in the FTSE 350 index over the five year period.

The demerger of P&O Princess Cruises occurred on 23 October 2000. There are a number of different accepted methodologies that are used to take account of such a demerger in assessing how much £100 invested in P&O at the beginning of 1998 would be worth at the end of 2002. Therefore two methods are shown on the performance graph:

- P&O's TSR including the TSR performance of P&O Princess Cruises; and

- P&O's TSR using data which has been adjusted to exclude the value attributable to P&O Princess Cruises by reference to the proportionate value of the two businesses at the demerger date.

TSR is calculated for each year relative to the base date of 1 January 1998 and taking the percentage change of the market price over the relevant period, reinvesting any dividends at the ex-dividend date.

Table 5.19A – Performance graph

Home Retail Group plc – Annual report – 28 February 2009

Directors' remuneration report

Performance graph

The graph below compares the TSR for Home Retail Group against the FTSE 350 index of general retailers for the period from demerger to the end of the period under review. The directors feel that the FTSE 350 index of general retailers is the most appropriate choice of index as it is a relevant comparator group for a retail business. The graph has been prepared in accordance with the assumptions contained in the relevant legislation.

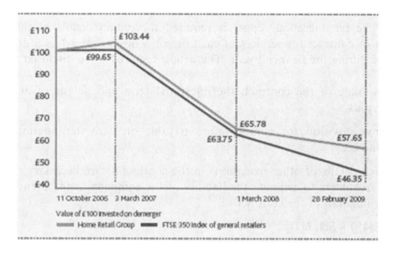

5.148.4 The situation can also arise where the index being used has existed for less than five years. This is considered in the following example.

Example – New index used for total shareholder return graph

A quoted company is preparing its directors' remuneration report for the year ended 31 December 20X2 and is selecting the index to use in the total shareholder return graph. The remuneration committee consider that the most appropriate index to use would be a new index, but this has only existed since 20X1. The remuneration committee consider that the second most appropriate index would be the FTSE All Share index. The remuneration committee do not want to have to use the FTSE All Share index until 20X6 and then change to the new index and explain the change. What should they do?

As the information for the new index is not available for the full five year period, then to select this index would not comply with the Act's requirements.

SI 2008/410 does not prohibit the presentation of two performance graphs: one showing a five year comparison against the FTSE All Share index and one showing a two year comparison with the new index. The remuneration committee can disclose both graphs and explain the reasoning, then in 20X6 when a five-year history for the new index is available, they can drop the disclosure of the FTSE All Share index.

5.148.5 In other examples, not reproduced here, several companies have given explanations of how their long-term incentive scheme criteria differ from the measure of performance provided by comparison with stock exchange indices and this provides useful additional information. Others, as in Table 5.19 above, have given explanations of how significant changes in the composition of the group, such as mergers or demergers, have been dealt with. Where companies have been listed for only part of the five year period required, and thus a market price has not been available, the shorter period since listing has generally been used as explained in paragraph 5.148.2 above.

Service contracts

5.149 The remuneration report is required to contain details of the service contract or contract for services of each person who has served as a director at any time during the financial year. The details required to be disclosed are:

■ The date of the contract, the unexpired term and details of any notice periods.

■ Any provision for compensation payable on early termination of the contract.

■ Such details of other provisions in the contract as are necessary to enable shareholders to estimate the liability of the company in the event of early termination of the contract.

[SI 2008/410 8 Sch 6(1)].

5.149.1 The requirement to disclose any provision for compensation payable on early termination of the contract refers to the contract's terms and includes 'golden parachute' provisions in service contracts, that is, where the directors receive a payment if they leave, for example, following a hostile take-over bid (see also para 5.149.2 below).

5.149.2 In addition, a UK company that has securities carrying voting rights admitted to trading on a regulated market at the end of its financial year is required to disclose, in its directors' report, details of any agreement with employees (including directors) of the company providing for compensation for loss of office on the takeover of the company. [SI 2008/410 7 Sch 13(2)(k)]. Disclosures in respect of contracts relating to takeovers are dealt with in chapter 3 of this publication.

5.149.3 The above disclosure requirements in the Act apply equally to executive and non-executive directors, because the Act does not differentiate between the two roles that directors take within a quoted company. This is illustrated in the following example.

Example – Details of contracts with non-executive directors

A quoted company is preparing its directors' remuneration report. Paragraph 6 of Schedule 8 to SI 2008/410 requires the company to present, in the remuneration report, details of directors' service contracts. Is this just for the executive directors or should details of contracts with non-executive directors be disclosed as well?

As noted above, the disclosure requirements contained in Schedule 8 to SI 2008/410 apply equally to executive and non-executive directors, because the Act does not differentiate between the two roles that directors take within a quoted company.

The requirement in paragraph 6 of Schedule 8 to SI 2008/410 surrounds the disclosure of certain, specified, details of each "... *contract of service or contract for services of each person who has served as a director of the company at any time during the relevant financial year ...*". [SI 2008/410 8 Sch 6(1)]. We consider that the term 'contract for services' encompasses all written agreements between a director and the company under which the director agrees to perform services for the company, regardless of the legal form that those agreements may take.

5.150   In addition, for companies listed in the UK, the Listing Rules require disclosure of:

■   Details of any directors' service contract with a notice period in excess of one year or with provisions for pre-determined compensation on termination which exceeds one year's salary and benefits in kind, giving the reasons for such notice period.

■   The unexpired term of any directors' service contract of a director proposed for election or re-election at the forthcoming annual general meeting and, if any director proposed for election or re-election does not have a directors' service contract, a statement to that effect.

[LR 9.8.8R (8), (9)].

5.151   An example of disclosure in respect of all the matters in the bullet points in paragraph 5.149 is given in Table 5.20 below.

Table 5.20 – Details of service contracts

BG Group plc – Annual Report – 31 December 2009

Remuneration report (extracts)

SERVICE CONTRACTS

The Executive Directors' service contracts, including arrangements for early termination, are carefully considered by the Committee and are designed to recruit, retain and motivate Directors of the quality required to manage the Company. The Committee considers that a rolling contract with a notice period of one year is appropriate.

In line with the Company's policy, the Executive Directors' service contracts contain change of control provisions. Should the Directors' employment be terminated within 12 months of a change of control, they are entitled to liquidated damages. The amount of liquidated damages is equal to one year's gross salary and a credit of one year's pensionable service (less any deductions

---

the employer is required to make), which the Committee considers to be a genuine pre-estimate of loss. The Committee considers that these provisions assist with recruitment and retention and that their inclusion is therefore in the best interests of shareholders.

Other than change of control, the Executive Directors' service contracts do not contain provisions for compensation in the event of early termination. When calculating termination payments, the Committee takes into account a variety of factors, including individual and Company performance, the obligation for the Director to mitigate his or her own loss (for example, by gaining new employment) and the Director's length of service. Further details of the Executive Directors' service contracts can be found on page 57.

NON-EXECUTIVE DIRECTORS (extract)
The Board aims to recruit non-executive directors of a high calibre, with broad commercial, international or other relevant experience. Non-Executive Directors are appointed by the Board on the recommendation of the Nominations Committee. Their appointment is for an initial term of three years, subject to election by shareholders at the first annual general meeting (AGM) following their appointment. Upon the recommendation of the Nominations Committee, they are generally re-appointed for a second term of three years, subject to re-election by shareholders. There is no notice period and no provision for termination payments.

The terms of engagement of the Non-Executive Directors are set out in a letter of appointment.

DIRECTORS' SERVICE CONTRACTS
EXECUTIVE DIRECTORS
Details of the service contracts of the Executive Directors who served during the year are set out below:

	Contract date	Unexpired term	Notice period	Compensation payable upon early termination (a)
Ashley Almanza	01 Aug 02	rolling 1yr	1yr	n/a
Frank Chapman	14 Sep 00	rolling 1yr	1yr	n/a
Martin Houston	03 Feb 09	rolling 1yr	1yr	n/a

(a) Other than the change of control provisions, the Executive Directors' service contracts do not contain provisions for compensation payable upon early termination.

Change of control

As described on page 54, the Executive Directors' service contracts contain change of control provisions.

For the purposes of these provisions, a change of control is deemed to occur if the Company becomes a subsidiary of another company; or if 50% or more of the voting rights of the Company or the right to appoint or remove the majority of the Board of the Company become vested in any individual or body or group of individuals or bodies acting in concert; or if all or substantially all of the business, assets and undertakings of the Company become owned by any person, firm or company (other than a subsidiary or associated company). A change of control is also deemed to occur if the whole of the issued capital of BG Energy Holdings Limited or a substantial part of the undertaking of that Company (including its subsidiaries) is transferred to another company, unless that transferee company is a subsidiary of the Company, or a company ultimately owned by substantially the same shareholders as are the ultimate owners of the Company.

However, a change of control does not occur if (and only if) through a process of reconstruction the Company becomes a subsidiary of another company owned by substantially the same shareholders as are the shareholders of the Company. The Executive Directors' service contracts provide that any payments made pursuant to these provisions will be made, less any deductions the employer is required to make. Any such payments shall be in full and final settlement of any claims the Executive Director may have against the employer or any associated company arising out of the termination of employment, except for any personal injury claim, any claim in respect of accrued pension rights, or statutory employment protection claims.

CHAIRMAN AND NON-EXECUTIVE DIRECTORS

	Date of appointment or re-appointment	Expiry date
Sir Robert Wilson	1 Jan 10	Dec 12
Peter Backhouse	14 May 07	May 10
Jürgen Dormann	18 May 09	May 12
Baroness Hogg	14 May 08	May 11
Dr John Hood	14 May 08	May 11
Sir David Manning	1 July 08	May 11
Mark Seligman	3 Dec 09	Dec 12
Lord Sharman	14 May 07	May 10
Philippe Varin	18 May 09	May 12

The Non-Executive Directors' letters of appointment do not contain any notice period or provision for compensation in the event of early termination of their appointment.

Compensation for past directors

5.152 The remuneration report must contain an explanation for any significant award made in the circumstances described in paragraph 15 of Schedule 8 to SI 2008/410 to a past director, including, in particular, compensation for loss of office and pensions but excluding any sums shown separately in the table of individual directors' emoluments and compensation in accordance with the requirement of paragraph 7(1)(d) of Schedule 8 to SI 2008/410. [SI 2008/410 8 Sch 6(2)].

5.153 Paragraph 15 of Schedule 8 to SI 2008/410 contains a 'sweep-up' requirement to disclose any significant award to a past director that has not already been disclosed in the table of individual directors' emoluments and compensation (see below from para 5.209). This is disclosed in the 'auditable part' of the remuneration report. The requirement of paragraph 6(2) of Schedule 8 to SI 2008/410, which is outside the auditable part, is to give an explanation for any such payment.

5.154 The example in Table 5.21 below gives details of such a payment and an explanation (outcome of dispute in relation to employment which ceased in a previous year).

Table 5.21 – Outcome of dispute in relation to employment which ceased in a previous year

United Utilities PLC – Report and Accounts – 31 March 1999

Remuneration report (extract)

Directors emoluments (extract)

During the year the company settled its dispute with Brian Staples, the previous Chief Executive, whose employment with the company terminated on 31 July 1997. The company paid £60,000 (plus VAT) towards Mr Staples' legal fees. Mr Staples was allowed to exercise options granted on 18 September 1995 to subscribe for 124,435 ordinary shares at an exercise price of 530.12p per

---

ordinary share. All other options to subscribe for ordinary shares granted to him subsequently under the executive share option scheme and options granted to him under the employee sharesave scheme, lapsed. The mid market price of a share on the day of exercise was 895 pence. Mr Staples was reimbursed for previously incurred relocation expenses of £34,142 (inclusive of VAT) in accordance with the company's relocation policy. Pursuant to that policy, that amount was grossed up to take account of higher rate income tax payable by Mr Staples on receipt of that payment.

Interaction between the UK Corporate Governance Codes (2008) and (2010) and the remuneration report

5.155   The Listing Rules require a listed company to comply with the provisions of the applicable UK Corporate Governance Code ((2008) or (2010)), or to explain any departures (see chapter 4). The UK Corporate Governance Codes (2008) and (2010) recommend that where a company releases an executive director to serve as a non-executive director elsewhere, the remuneration report should include a statement as to whether or not the director will retain such earnings and, if so, what the remuneration is. [CC B.1.4; UK CGC D.1.2]. An example disclosure is provided in Table 5.21A. Further details on the principles and provisions of the UK Corporate Governance Codes (2008) and (2010) that relate to directors' remuneration are set out in annex 1.

Table 5.21A – Executive directors retain fees for services provided as non-executive directors elsewhere

Pearson plc – Annual report and accounts – 31 December 2009

Report on directors' remuneration (extract)

Executive directors' non-executive directorships

The committee's policy is that executive directors may, by agreement with the board, serve as non-executives of other companies and retain any fees payable for their services.

The following executive directors served as non-executive directors elsewhere and received fees or other benefits for the period covered by this report as follows:

	Company	Fees/benefits
Marjorie Scardino	Nokia Corporation	€150,000
	MacArthur Foundation	$24,000
Rona Fairhead	HSBC Holdings plc	£135,000
	Spencer Stuart Advisory Board	£10,000

Other executive directors served as non-executive directors elsewhere but did not receive fees.

[The next paragraph is 5.163.]

Information subject to audit

Individual directors' emoluments and compensation

5.163   Schedule 8 to SI 2008/410 requirements for disclosure of individual directors' emoluments and compensation are similar to those contained in the

Listing Rules. This section of the chapter deals mainly with the legal requirements for quoted companies, but also refers to the requirements of the Listing Rules where appropriate.

5.164 For quoted companies, the remuneration report is required to show, in tabular form, for each director of the company who served as such at any time in the financial year, each of the following:

- The total amount of salary and fees paid to or receivable by the director in respect of qualifying services (see para 5.33).

- The total amount of bonuses paid or receivable, the amount of which is determined by reference to service or performance within a single year (see para 5.181).

- The total amounts paid by way of expenses allowance that are:

    (a) chargeable to UK income tax, or would be if the person was an individual; and

    (b) paid to or receivable by the director in respect of qualifying services.

- The total amount of:

    (a) any compensation for loss of office paid to or receivable by the director (see para 5.168 below); and

    (b) any other payments paid to or receivable by the director in connection with the termination of qualifying services.

- The total estimated value of any benefits received by the director otherwise than in cash (see para 5.166 below) that:

    (a) do not fall within any of the bullet points above or which are not included in the other information required to be disclosed in the auditable part of the remuneration report in respect of share options and long-term incentive schemes;

    (b) are emoluments of the director; and

    (c) are received by the director in respect of qualifying services.

- The total of the sums mentioned in the bullet points above.

[SI 2008/410 8 Sch 7(1), 7(4)].

5.164.1 In respect of comparative amounts, the Act states that *"the directors' remuneration report shall show, for each person who has served as a director of the company at any time during the relevant financial year, the amount that for the financial year preceding the relevant financial year is the total of the sums mentioned in paragraphs (a) to (e) of sub-paragraph (1)"*. Therefore, comparative amounts for the total referred to in the last bullet point above must be given for each director. [SI 2008/410 8 Sch 7(2)]. Comparatives for each component of the total are not required.

5.164.2 Comparatives are required in respect of each person who has served as a director of the company at any time during the *relevant financial year*. The relevant financial year means the financial year in respect of which the report is prepared. [SI 2008/410 8 Sch 1(1)]. Therefore, strictly, SI 2008/410 does not require disclosure of the comparatives in respect of individual directors who retired last year. However, it is common practice for such disclosure to be made. It provides useful additional information for readers and it means that the figures in the directors' remuneration report can be reconciled to the aggregate figures disclosed in the notes to the financial statements under Schedule 5 to SI 2008/410.

5.165 For companies listed in the UK, the Listing Rules require disclosure of:

■ The amount of each element in the remuneration package for the period under review of each director by name, including, but not restricted to, basic salary and fees, the estimated money value of benefits in kind, annual bonuses, deferred bonuses, compensation for loss of office and payments for breach of contract or other termination payments.

■ The total remuneration for each director for the period under review and for the corresponding prior period.

■ Any significant payments made to former directors during the period under review.

[LR 9.8.8R (2)(a)-(c)].

5.165.1 In addition, the Listing Rules require listed companies to disclose particulars of any arrangement under which a director has either waived or agreed to waive any future or current emoluments and details of such waivers. This applies in respect of emoluments from either the company or any of its subsidiaries. [LR 9.8.4R (5)]. An example of disclosure of waivers is given in Table 5.22 below.

Table 5.22 – Disclosure of waivers

Saatchi & Saatchi Company PLC – Report and Accounts – 31 December 1993

Directors' and senior executives' emoluments (extract)

In addition to the emoluments shown above, certain Directors were entitled to the following amounts which were waived. These waivers were without prejudice to any existing entitlements to pension contributions and to entitlements of those Directors to emoluments in the future.

WAIVERS BY EXECUTIVE DIRECTORS	Year ended 31 Dec 1993 £	Year ended 31 Dec 1992 £
M. Saatchi (Chairman)	312,500	312,500
C. Saatchi	290,064	312,500
C.T. Scott	–	83,355
J.T. Sinclair	70,000	70,000
R.L.M. Louis-Dreyfus	53,420	230,473
	725,984	1,008,828

In addition, M. Saatchi and J.T. Sinclair have agreed to waive a portion of their emoluments, £312,500 and £70,000 respectively, for the year to 31st December 1994.

5.166   For quoted companies, separate disclosure of benefits by individual director is required. The nature of any element of each director's remuneration package that is not cash must also be stated. [SI 2008/410 8 Sch 7(3)]. However, the amount attributed to each non-cash element of a director's remuneration does not need to be disclosed. Further guidance on benefits is kind (applicable to all companies) is given from paragraph 5.42 onwards and in the example below.

Example – Flexible benefits scheme

A quoted company has a flexible benefits scheme, whereby a director may apply part of his/her salary in purchasing additional benefits, such as increased holiday or health cover. Assuming the director takes advantage of this and purchases, say, two weeks additional holiday, should the value of this be disclosed in the individual directors' remuneration table required by Schedule 8 to SI 2008/410 as salary/fees or as benefits in kind?

We consider that in a case such as this the basic salary figures should not be adjusted (reduced). This is because the director is entitled to the basic salary and it is his/her option to apply it in purchasing whatever he/she wants. The fact that holiday/other benefits are purchased from the company rather than from some third party is not relevant. If, however, the additional benefits and reduction in base salary were imposed on the director (that is, it was not at his/her option) the amounts would be adjusted and the benefit included in the total of his/her benefits disclosed in the individual directors' remuneration table with the nature of the benefit also being disclosed. [SI 2008/410 8 Sch 7(1), (3)].

5.167   Where a director is appointed during the year, only the remuneration while he is a director of the company is disclosable as director's remuneration, as explained in the following example.

Example – Employee appointed as director during year

As noted above, quoted companies are required to disclose details of each element of the remuneration of each director by name and the total for each director. If a person has been an employee for part of the year and is then appointed a director during the year, should the figures disclosed for him include remuneration paid to him whilst he was an employee or should it just include remuneration paid to or receivable by him whilst a director?

Schedule 8 to SI 2008/410 requires only the amounts paid to or receivable by the person in respect of 'qualifying services' to be disclosed. Qualifying services means services as a director of the company or whilst a director of the company, as a director of a subsidiary undertaking or as director of any other company of which he is a director as a result of the company's nomination (direct or indirect) or otherwise in connection with the management of the affairs of the company or any such subsidiary or other undertaking. Therefore, only the remuneration while he is a director of the company is disclosable as director's remuneration.

Note that for companies reporting under IFRS, additional disclosure for the whole period may be necessary. IAS 24 requires disclosure of remuneration (in total and split into five categories) for key management personnel in respect of services provided to the entity. In this context we consider that the services provided to the entity means services while the person is a member of key management personnel. Where a director fell into the key management classification prior to appointment as a director, remuneration for the whole period under review should be given in the aggregate IAS 24 disclosure.

5.167.1 In some situations, directors are remunerated in a currency that differs from the company's presentation currency. This is considered in the following example.

Example – Director paid in foreign currency

A quoted company is preparing its remuneration report. Although most of the directors are UK resident and are paid by the company in pounds sterling (which is both the company's functional and presentation currency), one of its directors is resident in the United States and is paid by the UK company in US dollars. Should his emoluments be disclosed in US dollars or pounds?

Paragraph 7 of Schedule 8 to SI 2008/410 requires disclosure of a table disclosing the emoluments paid to or receivable by each director in respect of qualifying services. The legislation is silent as to the currency in which the directors' remuneration should be denominated.

We consider, however, that it would be misleading and confusing to users of the remuneration report to denominate different directors' emoluments in different currencies, as it hinders the comparability of the information. We consider, therefore, that the directors' remuneration should all be disclosed in the company's presentation currency and that, where this results in translation of directors' remuneration, the exchange rate used for that translation should be disclosed. Each director's emoluments could also be disclosed in the currency in which the director is paid.

This enables users of the remuneration report to make meaningful comparisons of the directors' remuneration packages whilst fully understanding their nature.

5.167.2 Multi-national groups sometimes encourage directors to second over-seas. When directors work outside their home country, companies may 'equalise' their remuneration package to ensure that the individuals are neither advantaged nor disadvantaged as a result of working overseas. In such cases, the amounts requiring disclosure in the remuneration report may not be immediately obvious. An acceptable approach in this situation is considered in the following example.

Example – Equalisation of benefits

Entity X is a UK company with multi-national operations. The group's policy is to encourage divisional directors to spend two-year secondments in the UK to broaden their knowledge of the group at corporate level.

The divisional directors are subject to varying taxation regimes and costs of living in their home countries. However, whilst working in Britain, the directors will be subject to British taxes and costs of living. In order to ensure that no directors are advantaged or disadvantaged from an overseas secondment, entity X operates a 'benefits equalisation' scheme. The scheme works as follows.

Directors are awarded a salary in their home country. This is based in the currency of their home country and is the remuneration specified in their employment contract as authorised by the remuneration committee. The amount is translated into sterling (the functional currency of entity X). The sterling amount is referred to as the 'base salary'.

Using the base salary as a benchmark, the payroll department calculates a 'host country salary'. The host country salary aims to give the director the net equivalent amount in the host country that they would need to live in their home country, taking into account cost of living differences.

The host country salary comprises two elements:

■ Local cost of living allowance. This is an allowance to ensure that the expat employee is not disadvantaged when buying an average basket of goods (that is, food, petrol, entertainment and so on) and utilities.

■ Discretionary spend. This is the amount that an employee would be expected to have left over from their home country salary after deducting the costs of living in their home country and home country taxes.

The net host country salary is grossed up for tax, in this example, in sterling for UK tax rates as these rates are applicable whilst the directors are working in Britain.

The tax amount as calculated is settled with HMRC and the net host country salary amount is paid to the directors each month as their payroll.

To illustrate for one director:

■ Home country salary (gross):	USD 1,500,000
■ Home country salary (net of tax at 40%):	USD 900,000
■ Translated from USD to GBP into net base salary @ 1:1.5	GBP 600,000
■ Adjustment factor for cost of living between UK and US	4:3
■ Host country salary (net)	GBP 800,000
■ Host country salary (gross of tax @ 50%)	GBP 1,600,000
■ Tax payable to UK tax authorities	GBP 800,000

In this situation, the actual cost to the company of employing the director while on secondment is the host country gross amount (£1.6m). This drives the payroll expense in the income statement and the numbers for inclusion in the key management personnel compensation note under IAS 24, 'Related party disclosures'. [IAS 24 para 16].

However, for the remuneration report, the Companies Act requires disclosure of the *"total amount of salary and fees paid to or receivable by ... [the director].... in respect of qualifying services"*. [SI 2008/410 8 Sch 7(1)]. The Act's wording focuses on the value to a director as opposed to the cost to the company principle under IAS 24.

The cash that a director receives is based upon the gross home country salary. This is the amount written into the director's contract and the amount that is authorised by the remuneration committee. When a director works outside his home country, adjustments are made to the home country salary to equalise their remuneration. The equalisation adjustments seek to ensure that the net salary benefit to the director after deducting cost of living expenses is the same regardless of where the director is living and being remunerated.

Following the principal that the remuneration report focuses on the value of benefits to the directors in question, a reasonable approach is to include the gross home country salary in the remuneration report. The fact that this salary is then subject to adjustment is part of an internal equalisation process that does not alter the value of the benefits to a director.

The payments made to seconded directors are based upon the adjusted host country salary. Therefore the home country salaries disclosed in the remuneration report will be different to the cost to the company for each director. As mentioned above, the cost to the company will form the basis of the IAS 24 key management compensation disclosures in the notes to the financial statements.

In such a situation, consideration must also be given to whether any additional 'secondee' allowances are being paid to a director working overseas. These may either be shown as separate allowances or could be factored into the host country salary conversion factors. For example, any additional housing allowances, additional increases for school fees or other benefits in addition to the standard remuneration from a director's home country will need to be included in the disclosure.

5.168 As noted in paragraph 5.164 above, quoted companies are required to disclose for each director the total amount of compensation for loss of office paid to or receivable by the director and any other amounts paid or receivable in connection with the termination of qualifying services. This disclosure is required to be given in the table of directors' emoluments. The amount that should be disclosed when the compensation is conditional on uncertain future events is considered in the example below. Further guidance on compensation for loss of office (applicable to all companies) is given in paragraph 5.97 onwards. There is a further 'sweep-up' requirement for quoted companies, which is discussed in paragraph 5.209 onwards.

Example – Compensation contingent on uncertain future events

A director of a quoted company resigned during the year. Contractually, he is entitled to receive compensation for loss of office of one year's annual salary in twelve equal monthly instalments during the year post-resignation. If at any point during the twelve months immediately following his resignation he secures alternative employment on the same (or higher) salary, payments to the director will cease, but there are no provisions for the company to claw-back any payments already made to him pursuant to this arrangement.

The company's year end is 31 December, the director resigned on 31 August and the directors' remuneration report is signed on 28 February. The monthly instalment is £10,000. The company has recognised the full £120,000 as an expense in the income statement (UK – profit and loss account) for the period, as it considers it probable that the full amount will become payable.

What should be included as the director's compensation for loss of office in the annual report in the year in which he resigns?

Paragraph 7 of Schedule 8 to SI 2008/410 requires disclosure of compensation for loss of office, which is defined in terms of amount paid to or receivable by a director in connection with loss of office.

Of the full £120,000 that the director may be entitled to, £40,000 has been paid at the year end. Consequently, £40,000 meets the definition of compensation for loss of office and must be disclosed as compensation for loss of office.

Although the remaining £80,000 is not technically receivable by the director at the year end, our view is that it is to be paid to him in the future as part of his compensation for leaving office and should also be included in the remuneration table as compensation for loss of office, taking the total to £120,000. This is consistent with the accounting treatment. Disclosure should be made in a footnote to the table (that the amount in the table should be cross-referred to) of full details of the contingency, to draw readers' attention to the fact that an element of the amount disclosed may not become payable. The 'full details' in the footnote should include the nature of the contingency, the amount that was paid during the year (£40,000) and the amount that was paid between the year end and the date of signing of the remuneration report (£20,000).

An alternative view, which is also acceptable and compliant with the SI 2008/410, is to include only the £40,000 that technically meets the definition of compensation for loss of office in the emoluments table prepared in accordance with paragraph 7 of Schedule 8 to SI 2008/410. Full disclosure must be made in a footnote to the table (that the amount in the table should be cross-referred to) of full details of the arrangements to draw readers' attention to the fact that the total compensation payable may be higher. The 'full details' in the footnote should note that the amount included in the table is only that which was paid during the year, disclose the maximum that could become payable (an additional £80,000) and the amount that was paid between the end of the year and the date of signing of the remuneration report (£20,000). In the following year, the director may be omitted from the tabular disclosures required by paragraph 7 (see para 5.164.2), but all amounts paid to or receivable by him will meet the definition of an 'award to a former director' and will be required to be disclosed in the remuneration report (albeit outside the table) by paragraph 15 of Schedule 8 to SI 2008/410.

Under either option, there will be a 'payment to a former director' in the subsequent year, which must be disclosed in accordance with the Listing Rules (see para 5.165). [LR 9.8.8 R (2)(c)].

5.169   An example is given below of the sort of presentation that may be given to comply with the legislation. In Table 5.23 details are given by individual director of salaries/fees, bonuses, compensation for loss of office (referred to as termination payments), expense allowances, benefits and totals.

Table 5.23 – Directors' emoluments

BT Group plc – Annual Report – 31 March 2010

Directors' emoluments

Directors' emoluments for the 2009/10 financial year were as follows:

	Basic salary and fees £000	Pension allowance net of pension contributions £000	Total salary and fees £000	Annual bonus £000	Expense allowance £000	Other benefits excluding pension £000	Total 2010 £000	Total 2009 £000	Deferred bonus plan 2010 £000	2009 £000
Sir Michael Rake[c]	600	–	600	–	–	70	670	630	–	–
I Livingston[c]	850	10	860	1,206	–	39	2,105	1,174	1,206	343
T Chanmugam[c,d,e]	475	143	618	463	19	9	1,109	275	346	77
G Patterson[c,d]	500	100	600	487	19	27	1,133	698	365	121
T Ball[f]	53	–	53	–	–	–	53	–	–	–
C Brendish	80	–	80	–	–	–	80	80	–	–
J E Daniels	75	–	75	–	–	–	75	74	–	–
P Hewitt[g]	128	–	128	–	–	–	128	75	–	–
P Hodkinson	100	–	100	–	–	–	100	100	–	–
C G Symon[h]	150	–	150	–	–	24	174	150	–	–
H Lalani[c,d,I]	458	176	634	503	4	25	1,166	805	–	–
M Alahuhta[j]	12	–	12	–	–	–	12	70	–	–
D Lathen[h,k]	63	–	63	–	–	18	81	75	–	–
M van den Bergh[l]	44	–	44	–	–	–	44	150	–	–
F Barrault[m]	–	–	–	–	–	–	–	1,257	–	–
B Verwaayen[n]	–	–	–	–	–	–	–	577	–	–
	3,588	**429**	**4,017**	**2,659**	**42**	**212**	**6,930**	**6,190**	**1,917**	**541**

Termination payments		
H Lalani[o]	131	–
F Barrault[p]	10	1,599
B Verwaayen	–	700
	7,071	**8,489**

a Pension allowance paid in cash for the 2009/10 financial year – see 'Pensions' below.

b Deferred annual bonuses payable in shares in three years' time, subject to continued employment.

c Other benefits include some or all of the following: company car, fuel or driver, personal telecommunications facilities and home security, medical and dental cover for the director and immediate family, special life cover, professional subscriptions, personal tax advice, and financial counselling.

d Expense allowance in the above table includes a monthly cash allowance in lieu of a company car or part of such allowance which has not been used for a company car.

e Tony Chanmugam was granted a retention cash award in early 2008 prior to his appointment as a director. He will receive a payment of £315,000 in May 2010.

f Tony Ball was appointed as a director on 16 July 2009.

g Patricia Hewitt was appointed as Senior Independent Director on 16 July 2009.

h Includes an additional fee for regular travel from overseas to Board and Board committee meetings.

i Hanif Lalani resigned as a director on 7 January 2010 and left the company on 31 March 2010.

j Matti Alahuhta retired as a director on 31 May 2009.

k Deborah Lathen retired as a director on 31 January 2010.

l Maarten van den Bergh retired as a director on 15 July 2009.

m François Barrault resigned as a director on 30 October 2008 and left the company on 30 November 2008.

n Ben Verwaayen retired as a director on 30 June 2008.

o Hanif Lalani's contract was terminated on 11 January 2010. In accordance with his contract, his salary of £585,000 per annum and the value of all the benefits to which he is entitled, amounting to £195,000 per annum, will continue to be provided until the earlier of nine months from 31 March 2010 or his obtaining full-time employment.

p François Barrault continued to receive medical insurance until 30 November 2009, in accordance with the terms of his contract.

Share options

5.170   The remuneration report must contain details, by individual director, of share options granted in respect of qualifying services. The information in (a) to (d) of paragraph 5.170.1 below should be in tabular form, but may be aggregated to avoid excessively lengthy reports (see para 5.174). [SI 2008/410 8 Sch 8(1)-(3)]. The Listing Rules require disclosure of information on share options, including SAYE options, for each director by name in accordance with the requirements of Schedule 8 to SI 2008/410. [LR 9.8.8R (2)(d)].

5.170.1   The information to be given (in tabular form for (a) to (d) below) for each director who served as such at any time in the financial year is:

(a)   Number of shares subject to a share option at the beginning of the financial year or, if later, at the date of appointment as a director (differentiating between options having different terms and conditions).

(b)   Number of shares at the end of the financial year or, if earlier, at the date of ceasing to be a director (differentiating between options having different terms and conditions).

(c)   Details of options awarded, options exercised, options expiring unexercised and options whose terms and conditions have been varied in the financial year.

(d)   For each share option that is unexpired at any time in the financial year:

(i)   The price paid, if any, for its award.

(ii)   The exercise price.

(iii)   The date from which the option may be exercised.

(iv)   The date on which the option expires.

(e)   A description of any variation made in the year to the terms and conditions of a share option.

(f)   A summary of any performance criteria on which the award or exercise of an option is conditional and a description of any variation in such performance criteria made in the year.

(g) For each option that has been exercised in the financial year, the market price of the shares in relation to which the option was exercised, at the date of exercise (see also para 5.48 above).

(h) For each option that is unexpired at the end of the financial year:

(i)   The market price of the related shares at the end of that year.

(ii) The highest and lowest market prices of the related shares in that year.

[SI 2008/410 8 Sch 8, 9].

5.171 The following examples illustrate some of the disclosure requirements above. The examples are extracts only and, therefore, may not meet all of the above requirements, as information on, for example, performance conditions may have been included elsewhere in the remuneration report. In Table 5.24, performance conditions are explained and options are disclosed at the beginning and end of the year together with options granted and exercised.

Table 5.24 – Share options

AVEVA Group plc – Annual Report & Accounts – 31 March 2010

Directors' remuneration report

Share awards (extract)

Long Term Incentive Plan (LTIP)
The Company established the AVEVA Group plc Long Term Incentive Plan (LTIP) which was approved at the Extraordinary General Meeting held in 2004. Under the LTIP, options are granted to selected individuals to acquire ordinary shares at an exercise price equal to the nominal value of the shares; these options will be exercisable only if stringent performance criteria are met. There are no rules under the LTIP scheme which govern the maximum awards that can be made to participants. However in 2009/10 the market value of awards under the LTIP awarded to Richard Longdon and Paul Taylor amounted to 50% of basic salary (2009 – 50%). It is not expected that material changes will be made to the level of awards under the LTIP without consultation with shareholders.

Details of the outstanding awards under the LTIP are as follows:

2006/07 awards
In 2006/07 a total of 42,588 share options were awarded to the Executive Directors under the LTIP. The performance conditions were based on average growth in earnings per share (EPS) achieved over the three years from 2006/07 to 2008/09. If average EPS growth was greater than 15% per annum then all of the shares would vest. If average EPS growth was less than 7.5% per annum none of the shares would vest. If average EPS growth was between 7.5% and 15% then the number of shares that would vest would be determined by linear interpolation. The Remuneration Committee considered that these were challenging performance conditions in the context of the Company's budget and market expectations at the time of the awards. The performance conditions were measured in accordance with the terms of the grant and all awards vested in full.

2007/08 awards
In 2007/08, a total of 18,234 share options were awarded to the Executive Directors under the LTIP. The performance conditions are based on average growth in EPS over the years from 2007/08 to 2009/10. If average EPS growth is greater than 11.5% per annum then all of the shares shall vest. If average EPS is less than 9% per annum then none of the shares shall vest. If average EPS growth is between 9% and 11.5% per annum then the number of shares that shall vest shall

---

be determined by linear interpolation. The Remuneration Committee considered that these were challenging performance conditions in the context of Company's budget and external expectations at the time of the awards. Although the vesting date has not yet been reached, it is anticipated that the performance conditions attached to this award will be met following finalisation of the 2009/10 financial results. However this is still subject to the approval of the Remuneration Committee at the time of announcement of the results.

2008/09 awards

In 2008/09, a total of 17,929 share options were awarded to the Executive Directors under the LTIP. The performance conditions are based on average growth in EPS over the years from 2008/09 to 2010/11. If average EPS growth is greater than 14% per annum then all of the shares shall vest. If average EPS is less than 10% per annum then none of the shares shall vest. If average EPS growth is between 10% and 14% per annum then the number of shares that shall vest shall be determined by linear interpolation. The Remuneration Committee considered that these were challenging performance conditions in the context of internal and external expectations at the time of the awards.

2009/10 awards

In 2009/10, a total of 36,628 share options were awarded to the Executive Directors under the LTIP. In view of the general economic background, the Remuneration Committee gave especially careful consideration to what performance conditions would be appropriate and finally agreed that they should be based on average diluted EPS over the three years from 2009/10 to 2011/12. All shares under this option shall vest if average diluted EPS for the three years ending 31 March 2012 is equal to or above 52.14 pence. Should average diluted EPS for the period be below 52.14 pence, then no shares will vest and the option will lapse. The Remuneration Committee considered that these were challenging performance conditions in the context of internal and external expectations at the time of the awards.

Deferred annual bonus share plan

As described above, part of the annual bonus earned by Executive Directors in the year is used to determine eligibility for an award of deferred shares under the Deferred Share Scheme. In order to deliver shares under the Deferred Share Scheme, an Employee Benefit Trust (EBT) was established following shareholder approval at the 2008 Annual General Meeting. Awards of deferred shares are made by the trustee of EBT using shares purchased in the market. The awards, which take the form of nil-cost options, will normally deliver the deferred shares to participants in three equal tranches, one in each of the three years following the year in which an award is made by the EBT. These awards are made solely in respect of performance in the financial year immediately prior to their grant. Delivery of the deferred shares is not subject to further financial performance conditions provided that the participant remains an employee or Director of the Group. If the participant ceases to be an employee or Director, entitlement to all outstanding tranches would fall away unless the cessation occurs by reason of his or her death. Following the death of a bonus participant, or on a takeover, reconstruction or amalgamation, or voluntary winding up of the Company, the period for which the participant must remain an employee or Director would be reduced below the normal three years and entitlement to delivery of the shares would be accelerated. There are no arrangements for the delivery of additional matching shares to a participant in any circumstances.

On 27 May 2009 the EBT awarded 22,487 and 14,508 deferred shares to Richard Longdon and Paul Taylor respectively in respect of the bonus arrangements for the year ended 31 March 2009.

Following the achievement of the objectives for 2009/10, it is anticipated that 12,471 and 8,046 deferred shares will be awarded to Richard Longdon and Paul Taylor respectively in respect of the bonus arrangements for the year ended 31 March 2010.

Disclosure of directors' remuneration

Share options

The interests of Directors in options to acquire ordinary shares were as follows:

	Scheme	As at 1 April 2009 Number	Granted Number	Exercised Number	As at 31 March 2010 Number	Gain on exercise £	Exercise price Pence	Earliest date of exercise	Date of expiry
Richard Longdon	LTIP	25,548	–	(25,548)	–	252,368	3.33	28.06.09	28.06.13
	LTIP	11,083	–	–	11,083	–	3.33	02.07.10	02.07.14
	LTIP	10,891	–	–	10,891	–	3.33	07.07.11	07.07.15
	LTIP	–	22,264	–	22,264	–	3.33	07.07.12	07.07.16
	Deferred Share Scheme (2008)	12,282	–	–	12,282	–	0	26.05.09	Note
	Deferred Share Scheme (2009)	–	22,487	–	22,487	–	0	26.05.10	Note
Paul Taylor	LTIP	17,040	–	(17,040)	–	168,325	3.33	28.06.09	28.06.13
	LTIP	7,151	–	–	7,151	–	3.33	02.07.10	02.07.14
	LTIP	7,038	–	–	7,038	–	3.33	07.07.11	07.07.15
	LTIP	–	14,364	–	14,364	–	3.33	07.07.12	07.07.16
	Deferred Share Scheme (2008)	7,923	–	–	7,923	–	0	26.05.09	Note
	Deferred Share Scheme (2009)	–	14,508	–	14,508	–	0	26.05.10	Note

Note: The last date of the exercise is the end of the 42-day period following the announcement of the financial results of the Group in the third calendar year following that in which the option was granted or (if applicable) such later date as the Remuneration Committee may specify.

The market price as at 31 March 2010 was £11.85 (31 March 2009 – £5.64) with a high–low spread for the year of £5.35 to £11.92.

During the year Richard Longdon and Paul Taylor exercised options over 25,548 and 17,040 ordinary shares respectively at an exercise price of £0.03. The market price on the date of exercise was £9.91 which resulted in an aggregate gain on exercise of £252,368 for Richard Longdon and £168,325 for Paul Taylor. Mr Longdon retained 14,970 and Mr Taylor 9,984 of the resultant shares arising.

At 31 March 2010, Mr Longdon owned 364,970 ordinary shares (2009 – 350,000 ordinary shares) and options over 79,007 ordinary shares (2009 – 59,804 options). Mr Taylor owned 59,984 ordinary shares (2009 – 50,000 ordinary shares) and options over 50,984 ordinary shares (2009 – 39,152 options).

Options under the LTIP are normally exercisable in full or in part between the third and tenth anniversaries of the date of grant. Details of the performance conditions of share option awards are set out on pages 42 and 43.

5.172 In Table 5.25 details of performance conditions on which the exercise of options is conditional are given.

Table 5.25 – Performance conditions

Manchester United PLC – Annual Report – 31 July 2001

Report on Directors' Remuneration (extract)

Under the Executive Share Option Plan options over the Company's shares may be granted each year to executive directors and senior managers, on a discretionary basis, at not less than the prevailing market price and subject to an overall maximum holding of four times remuneration. All options granted under the Plan are subject to performance conditions on exercise as determined annually by the Remuneration Committee. Options granted prior to 25 September 1998 may not be exercised unless the percentage growth in adjusted earnings per share over a period of not less than three consecutive years exceeds the percentage growth in the retail price index over such period by an average of at least 3 per cent per annum. In addition to the percentage growth in adjusted earnings per share condition, options granted after 25 September 1998 may not be exercised unless the Company's Total Shareholder Return (defined as share price growth and net dividends paid) over a period of three consecutive years exceeds the Total Shareholder Return of a company placed in the median position of those companies in the FTSE Mid-250 at the start and still remaining in the FTSE Mid-250 at the end of the measurement period. Options must be held for three years before they are exercisable and lapse if not exercised within ten years from grant.

Under the Savings Related Share Option Scheme all Group employees are given an opportunity to acquire shares in the Company.

The details of each executive director's interests in share options arising from the Executive Share Option Plan and the Savings Related Share Option Scheme are set out below:

		Number at 1 August 2000	Granted	Exercised	Number at 31 July 2001	Exercise Price £	Date from which exercisable	Expiry date
P F Kenyon	(a)	500,000	–	–	**500,000**	1.59	20.11.2000	20.11.2007
P F Kenyon	(a)	–	137,711	–	**137,711**	2.36	17.11.2003	17.11.2010
D A Gill	(a)	400,000	–	–	**400,000**	1.59	20.11.2000	20.11.2007
D A Gill	(a)	–	95,338	–	**95,338**	2.36	17.11.2003	17.11.2010
D A Gill	(b)	11,101	–	–	**11,101**	1.52	01.02.2005	01.08.2005

(a) Executive Share Option Plan
(b) Savings Related Share Option Scheme

The Remuneration Committee have confirmed that the performance condition in respect of the options exercisable from 20 November 2000 has been met.

No options lapsed during the Year. The market price of the shares at 31 July 2001 was £1.75 (2000 – £3.21) and the range during the year was £1.46 to £3.30.

5.173 In Table 5.26 details are given of rebasing of share options as to volume and price terms. 324,000 options were rebased, which can be identified in the table as those with an exercise price (rebased) of 849p. Details of performance conditions are given elsewhere in the remuneration report.

Table 5.26 – Rebasing of share options

SurfControl plc – Annual Report – 30 June 2001

Remuneration Report (extract)

Share options The Group operated two share option schemes over the year that are referred to in note 18 to the financial statements. The Remuneration Committee determines the allocation of share options to both directors and employees subject to predetermined individual, product group, or corporate performance criteria that are usually based upon revenue targets. Share options are regarded as vital both to retain and motivate staff, and to more closely align their interests with those of shareholders. During the year options were granted under the Unapproved Schedule to the Company's 1998 Inland Revenue Approved Executive Share Option Scheme.

The following table shows the movement in interests in share options held by directors.

	Exercise price	Exercise period	1 June 2000 (after rebasing)	**Granted in the period (after rebasing)**	**Lapsed in period**	**Exercised in the period**	**30 June 2001**
Rob Barrow	434p	30/11/00-29/11/09	150,000	–	–	–	**150,000**
Rob Barrow	849p	14/6/01-13/6/10	–	**80,000**	–	–	**80,000**
Rob Barrow – non-beneficial	321p	5/10/00-4/10/09	–	**3,000**	**(3,000)**	–	**–**
Steve Purdham	29.4p	5/7/97-5/7/03	153,237	–	–	(153,237)*	–
Steve Purdham	331p	15/7/00-15/7/09	150,000	–	–	–	**150,000**
Steve Purdham	434p	30/11/00-29/11/09	150,000	–	–	–	**150,000**
Steve Purdham	849p	14/6/01-13/6/10	160,000	–	–	–	**160,000**
Steve Purdham – non-beneficial	321p	5/10/00-4/10/09	3,000	–	–	–	**3,000**
Steve Purdham – non-beneficial	849p	14/6/01-13/6/10	3,200	–	–	–	**3,200**
Shelagh Rogan	238p	30/4/00-29/4/09	102,000	–	–	(85,000)*	**17,000**
Shelagh Rogan	331p	15/7/00-15/7/09	150,000	–	–	–	**150,000**
Shelagh Rogan	434p	30/11/00-29/11/09	150,000	–	–	–	**150,000**
Shelagh Rogan	849p	14/6/01-13/6/10	80,000	–	–	–	**80,000**
George Hayter	186p	11/9/99-7/10/08	10,200	–	–	(5,000)*	**5,200**
George Hayter	849p	9/2/01-8/2/01	800	–	–	–	**800**

*Exercised on 31 October 2000 when the market price was £17.75.

Gains made on exercise of options totalled £2,674,905 for Steve Purdham; £1,306,450 for Shelagh Rogan and £79,450 for George Hayter.

Included in the above table were 324,000 share options with exercise periods in the range of 9 February 2001 to 26 February 2011 that were rebased in volume and price terms on 4 May 2001. The number of options held by the then option holders was decreased by 20% and the original exercise price reset at £8.49 per ordinary share, being 20% above the closing middle market price on 4 May 2001. The market price of the Company's shares at the end of the financial period was £3.65 and the range was between £26.625 and £3.225.

5.174   If disclosure of the details set out in paragraph 5.170.1 above would result in disclosure of excessive length, the disclosure may be summarised as follows:

■   Information disclosed in relation to an individual director need not differentiate between options having different terms and conditions (para 5.170.1 (a) and (b) above).

■   In respect of the disclosure of the price paid for the award and the exercise price of options that are unexpired at any time in the year (para 5.170.1 (d)(i) and (ii) above) and in respect of disclosure of the market price at the end of the year and the highest and lowest prices in the year for shares related to options unexpired at the end of the year (para 5.170.1 (h) above), share options may be aggregated and, instead of disclosing prices for each option, disclosure may be made of weighted average prices of aggregated share options.

■   In respect of disclosure of dates from which options may be exercised or of dates of expiry of options that are unexpired at any time in the year (para 5.170.1 (d)(iii) and (iv) above) options may be aggregated and, instead of disclosing dates for each option, disclosure may be made of ranges of dates for aggregations of share options.

[SI 2008/410 8 Sch 10(1)].

5.175   The relaxations in the last two bullet points above are, however, subject to the condition that options in relation to shares whose market price at the end of the year is below the option exercise price (out of the money options) may not be aggregated with options relating to shares whose market price at the end of the year is equal to or above the option exercise price (in the money options). [SI 2008/410 8 Sch 10(2)].

5.176   The relaxations in the bullet points above do not apply in respect of options that have been awarded or exercised or had their terms and conditions varied in the year. [SI 2008/410 8 Sch 10(3)].

5.177   The following examples illustrate aggregated disclosures as permitted by these provisions. In Table 5.27 aggregated disclosures are given for options, but the table shows separately options that are out of the money from those that are in the money.

Table 5.27 – Separate disclosure for out of the money options

AstraZeneca PLC – Annual Report and Accounts – 31 December 2009

Directors' Remuneration Report (extract)

Share options

The interests of Directors, and of former Directors who served during 2009, in options to subscribe for Ordinary Shares, granted under the SOP, the AstraZeneca Savings-Related Share Option Plan and the Zeneca Plan, are included in the following table. No options were exercised during 2009. All grants in 2009 were made under the SOP, unless otherwise indicated.

		Number of Ordinary Shares under option[1]	Exercise price per Ordinary Share[2]	First day exercisable[3,4]	Last day exercisable[3,4]
Håkan Mogren	At 1 January 2009	244,896	2848p	13.12.02	24.03.13
	– market price above option price	139,530	2499p	13.12.02	24.03.13
	- market price at or below option price	105,366	3309p	23.08.03	27.03.12
	At 30 April 2009[5]	244,896	2848p	13.12.02	24.03.13
	- market price above option price	65,551	2231p	25.03.06	24.03.13
	– market price at or below option price	179,345	3073p	13.12.02	27.03.12
David Brennan	At 1 January 2009 – options over Ordinary Shares	432,959	2410p	24.03.09	27.03.18
	– market price above option price (Ordinary Shares)	322,318	2226p	30.03.10	27.03.18
	– market price at or below option price (Ordinary Shares)	110,641	2949p	24.03.09	18.05.16
	Granted 27 March 2009 (Ordinary Shares)	160,016	2280p	27.03.12	26.03.19
	At 31 December 2009 – options over Ordinary Shares	592,975	2375p	24.03.09	26.03.19
	– market price above option price (Ordinary Shares)	505,244	2271p	19.05.09	26.03.19
	– market price at or below option price (Ordinary Shares)	87,731	2975p	24.03.09	23.03.16
	At 1 January 2009 – options over ADSs	355,246	$45.22	16.03.03	23.03.15
	– market price above option price (ADSs)	110,987	$40.35	24.03.08	23.03.15
	– market price at or below option price (ADSs)	244,259	$47.44	16.03.03	25.03.14
	At 31 December 2009 – options over ADSs	355,246	$45.22	16.03.03	23.03.15
	– market price above option price (ADSs)	210,255	$42.91	26.03.07	23.03.15
	– market price at or below option price (ADSs)	144,991	$48.58	29.03.04	27.03.12
Simon Lowth	At 1 January 2009	88,803	1951p	16.11.10	27.03.18
	– market price above option price	88,803	1951p	16.11.10	27.03.18
	– market price at or below option price	–	n/a	n/a	n/a
	Granted 27 March 2009	65,131	2280p	27.03.12	26.03.19
	At 31 December 2009	153,934	2090p	16.11.10	26.03.19
	– market price above option price	153,934	2090p	16.11.10	26.03.19
	– market price at or below option price	–	n/a	n/a	n/a

John Patterson	At 1 January 2009	305,396	2544p	25.03.02	27.03.18
	– market price above option price	213,606	2279p	25.03.02	27.03.18
	– market price at or below option price	91,790	3163p	23.08.03	23.03.16
	Lapsed	(2,916)	2674p	25.03.02	24.03.09
	At 31 March 2009[6]	**302,480**	**2543p**	**16.03.03**	**27.03.18**
	– market price above option price	122,213	1991p	24.03.08	27.03.18
	– market price at or below option price	180,267	2917p	16.03.03	29.03.17

1 Vesting is subject to satisfying the relevant performance conditions set out in each of the relevant share option plans. Further information on the performance conditions applicable to SOP is set out in the AstraZeneca Share Option Plan – Performance conditions section on page 109. As a Save-As-You-Earn scheme, the AstraZeneca Savings-Related Share Option Plan is not subject to any performance conditions. Awards granted under the Zeneca Plan are no longer subject to any performance conditions.

2 Exercise prices are weighted averages.

3 First and last exercise dates of groups of options, within which period there are shorter exercise periods.

4 UK date convention applies.

5 Håkan Mogren ceased to be a Director on 30 April 2009.

6 John Patterson ceased to be a Director on 31 March 2009.

Gains by Directors on exercise of share options

The aggregate amount of gains made by Directors on the exercise of share options during the year and the two previous years is set out below. No options were exercised during 2009.

Year	Gains made by Directors on the exercise of share options $	Gains made by the highest paid Director $
2009	–	–
2008	1,764.96	–
2007	783,858.08	–

During 2009, the market price of Ordinary Shares or ADSs was as follows:

Stock Exchange	Ordinary Share/ADS market price as at 31 December 2009	Range of the Ordinary Share/ADS market price during 2009
London	2910.5p	2147p to 2947p
Stockholm	307.00 SEK	261.50 SEK to 356.00 SEK
New York	$46.94	$30.24 to $47.54

5.178 It should be noted that there is a difference between the definition of share options required to be disclosed by quoted companies in the directors' remuneration report under Schedule 8 to SI 2008/410 and the definition of share options for the purposes of the requirement in Schedule 5 to SI 2008/410 for the disclosure of aggregate gains made on the exercise of share options. In Schedule 8 to SI 2008/410, share options are defined as options granted in respect of qualifying services of the person. [SI 2008/410 8 Sch 8(4)]. However, share options in Schedule 5 to SI 2008/410 are defined merely as rights to acquire shares (that is, it includes share options that are not in respect of qualifying services). [SI 2008/410 5 Sch 12(b)]. This is illustrated in the following example:

Example – Definition of share options

Three years ago, company A acquired 100 per cent of the share capital of company B from Mr C, a director of both companies. As part of the consideration, Mr C was granted options to subscribe for shares in company A at 25p per share. These options have recently been exercised at a time when the market price of company A's shares was 75p. Will the gain on exercising these options be disclosable as part of directors' emoluments in company A's financial statements?

Under paragraph 1(1)(b) of Schedule 5 to SI 2008/410 disclosure is required of the aggregate amount of gains – being the difference between the market price of the shares on the day on which the options were exercised and the price actually paid – on the exercise of any right to acquire shares. However, in the case of a company that is not quoted (as defined in section 385(2) of the 2006 Act) or listed on AIM, only the number of directors who exercised options should be shown.

If company A is quoted, it seems that disclosure of the gains made by Mr C would be required. Under the provisions of Schedule 5 to SI 2008/410, only aggregate disclosure would be required, so Mr C's gains could be combined with those of the other directors and a single figure disclosed. It is arguable that such disclosure does not belong in a note concerning directors' emoluments, as Mr C was granted the options only as consideration for the acquisition of company B. Indeed, each of the other requirements of paragraph 1 of Schedule 5 to SI 2008/410 (that is, other than the gains on the exercise of share options) refers specifically to 'qualifying services' and these options were not a reward for qualifying services. However, the fact that reference to qualifying services is not included in the requirement must be relevant. Hence, we consider that disclosure of Mr C's gains in the aggregate figure required by Schedule 5 to SI 2008/410 would be appropriate.

There is a further disclosure requirement in Schedule 8 to SI 2008/410 for quoted companies to disclose, in tabular form, by individual director, details of share options. In this case, however, paragraph 8(4) of Schedule 8 to SI 2008/410 specifically states that 'share option' (for the purpose of the Schedule 8 to SI 2008/410 disclosures) means a share option granted in respect of qualifying services of a person. Therefore, as the options were not granted in respect of Mr C's services to company A, the options do not require to be disclosed in the table of individual directors' share options.

5.179 The examples below consider the disclosure requirements when share options are exercised by a director after retirement.

Example 1 – Options exercised immediately after retirement

A director of a quoted company (for definition see para 5.6.3) resigned during the year. He was allowed to retain and exercise his share options early and did so one day after resignation (but still during the year). He is the only director who has exercised options. At present the company has not included the director in the disclosure table of directors' individual interests in options required by Schedule 8 to SI 2008/410, but has included a footnote with some but not all the information. For example, it has not disclosed the gain on exercise of the options. Should this be disclosed?

If the director had exercised his option whilst still a director then disclosure of the gain would be required by SI 2008/410 requirements for disclosure of aggregate gains made by directors on exercise of options. However, as he exercised them a day after resigning it is not caught by this requirement.

If the options were retained not as an entitlement of employment, but as part of compensation for leaving, they form part of the director's compensation for loss of office. The question arises generally as to whether if a director retains options on leaving the company, but exercises them in the following year, the gain needs to be disclosed. In that situation our view is that no disclosure is required, but there should have been full disclosure at the time of leaving (see example 2 below).

In this case, however, the early exercise of options is connected with the resignation and took place immediately afterwards. Therefore, we consider there should be disclosure of the exercise of the options in the compensation for loss of office note. This can be done by including the director in the individual directors' share options table which should cover directors during the year and not just those at the year end. Schedule 8 to SI 2008/410 requires disclosure (in tabular form) in the directors' remuneration report of interests in options of each person who has served as a director at any time in the financial year. It requires, therefore, that the director is included in the table and the director's interest should be disclosed as at the date of his resignation. [SI 2008/410 8 Sch 8, 9]. A note should then be added to say that the director was permitted to retain the options on resigning and that they have subsequently been exercised. In addition, we consider that the gain on exercise should be disclosed by way of a note. Schedule 8 to SI 2008/410 requires disclosure of compensation for loss of office not otherwise disclosed in the table of individual directors' emoluments. [SI 2008/410 8 Sch 15].

Example 2 – Options exercised by former directors

Two directors of a quoted company (for definition see para 5.6.3) retired in the previous financial year and, at the end of that year, the financial statements disclosed that they had retired and had been permitted to retain their share options, giving details as part of the disclosure on compensation for loss of office. In the course of this year, those former directors exercised their options. Does any disclosure have to be given under the Companies Act relating to directors' remuneration?

There is no Companies Act requirement to disclose the gains as the directors left before the end of the previous year. Schedule 8 to SI 2008/410 requires significant awards of compensation to former directors to be disclosed, but the exercise of share options after retirement is not the same as a payment or award made to the former director by the company. [SI 2008/410 8 Sch 15]. Therefore, there does not appear to be any requirement in the Act to disclose anything this year (given full disclosure of the retained options in last year's financial statements), but the company could disclose, if it wished, in the spirit of 'full disclosure'.

Long-term incentive schemes

5.180 A long-term incentive scheme is defined under SI 2008/410 as *'…any agreement or arrangement under which money or other assets may become receivable by a person and which includes one or more qualifying conditions with respect to service or performance that cannot be fulfilled within a single financial year'*. [SI 2008/410 8 Sch 11(5)].

5.181 A long-term incentive scheme does not include bonuses the amount of which fall to be determined by reference to service or performance within a single financial year. [SI 2008/410 8 Sch 11(5)]. A feature of many bonus arrangements is that a bonus is payable after the end of the financial year and only if the director is in office at the payment date. In such circumstances we consider that under SI 2008/410 the bonus may fall within the definition of a long-term incentive scheme.

> **Example – Bonuses paid after the end of the period**
>
> A company calculates its directors' bonuses by reference to the company's results for the year ended 31 December 20X5. However, under the terms of the bonus scheme, the bonuses are paid on 28 February 20X6. If the director is not in office at 28 February 20X6, entitlement to the bonus is forfeited.
>
> We consider that the amount of the bonus is not calculated by reference to service or performance conditions that can be fulfilled within a single financial year. Instead it is calculated by reference to the company's performance for the financial year ended 31 December 20X5 and the directors' service for the fourteen month period to 28 February 20X6. Thus, we consider that the most appropriate disclosure of these bonuses is as long-term incentive schemes.
>
> However, the definitions under the Listing Rules differ from those in the Act, which can impact on disclosure – see further the example in paragraph 5.188.1.

5.182 A long-term incentive scheme does not include compensation for loss of office, payments for breach of contract and other termination payments. Nor does it include retirement benefits. [SI 2008/410 8 Sch 11(5)].

5.183 Bonuses and deferred bonuses and compensation for loss of office would instead be disclosed in the table of each director's emoluments and compensation (see para 5.164 above). Pensions and other retirement benefits would be separately disclosed (see para 5.193 onwards below).

5.184 The difference between a long-term incentive scheme and a deferred bonus may sometimes be difficult to determine. For example, if a three-year performance scheme is introduced whereby a director is entitled to an award if the performance of the company over the three years satisfies certain conditions, this is a long-term incentive scheme. This is because the award relates to a three-year period and the conditions cannot be fulfilled within a single financial year.

5.184.1 The example below considers the disclosure requirements for a long-term incentive scheme where the performance conditions have been met, but the final award of shares is still subject to approval.

> **Example – Share awards subject to approval**
>
> A quoted company (for definition see para 5.6.3) operates a long-term incentive plan (LTIP) for directors based on performance conditions over a three-year period. At the end of the current reporting period, the performance conditions have been met, but the final award of shares will not be approved until after the date of approval of the financial statements. What should be disclosed for directors' remuneration?
>
> Paragraph 1(1)(c) of Schedule 5 to SI 2008/410 requires separate disclosure of the aggregate of (i) the amount of money paid to or receivable by directors under long-term incentive schemes in respect of qualifying services and (ii) the net value of assets (other than money and share options) received or receivable by directors under such schemes in respect of such services.
>
> Therefore, the Schedule 5 to SI 2008/410 disclosure will depend upon when the amounts were receivable (and can be quantified). The relevant amount would be measured as at the date the shares were receivable by the directors, that is, no longer contingent. If the award is subject to approval after the date of approval of the financial statements, the amounts would be contingent at that date and would, therefore, not be disclosed as finally awarded until the following year.
>
> The LTIP awards are not included in the table showing directors' individual emoluments, as Schedule 8 to SI 2008/410 requires separate disclosure (in tabular form) of details of any long-term incentive schemes (see para 5.189 below for the information to be disclosed).
>
> This disclosure, required by Schedule 8 to SI 2008/410, is similar to that in Listing Rule 9.8.8R (3) (see para 5.189.2 below) and so compliance with SI 2008/410 will also cover the requirements of the Listing Rules. If the awards were not receivable at the year end (because they are still awaiting formal approval), then the shares will be included in the scheme interests at the end of the year. A note should, however, be included to indicate that the performance conditions have been met, but that the award is still subject to formal approval after the date of approval of the financial statements and, therefore, further details of the final determination of the award will be included in the following year.

5.185   If, however, there is a scheme that lasts three years, but a director receives an award in each of those three years dependent on the performance of that year, this is a bonus. If the three years of bonus is only payable after the end of the three years it is a deferred bonus, but not a long-term incentive, because the conditions were satisfied by reference to performance in each of the three years, considered separately. However, if the three years of bonus, although earned by reference to each of the individual years is only payable if the director stays for the three years, this may fall within the definition of a long-term incentive scheme as there is then an additional service condition that cannot be satisfied within one year (see also para 5.188.1 below).

5.186   Sometimes a scheme may provide for a bonus payable in respect of the year, but where part of the bonus may be taken in shares, which have to be held for a further three years and are then supplemented by a further award of shares, dependent on cumulative performance over the three years. In this case, the whole of the initial bonus, whether reinvested in shares or not, is emoluments in year one because it is receivable in respect of that year, but the additional potential award may be treated as a long-term incentive.

5.187   The remuneration report is required to disclose details of long-term incentives by individual director in tabular form (see para 5.189). [SI 2008/410 8 Sch 11(1), (3)].

5.188   Details of share options are not required to be included. This is because they are separately disclosed (see from para 5.170 above). [SI 2008/410 8 Sch 11(2)]. Awards of long-term incentives are sometimes received in the form of options with a nil exercise price. Thus, there may sometimes be a cross over between the disclosure of long-term incentives and the disclosure of share options as illustrated in the example below. In such cases, full details of the options, often referred to as 'nil cost options', and a clear cross-reference between information contained in each of the tables should be given.

> **Example – Gain on exercise of nil cost options awarded under LTIP**
>
> A quoted company (for definition see para 5.6.3) has had a long-term incentive scheme in operation for three years, whereby three years ago directors were awarded the right to receive a number of shares that would vary depending on the company's performance over three years. The scheme has always, to date, been disclosed and described as a long-term incentive scheme. This year the final awards were made and the shares vested with the directors. Normally the disclosures required would be the value of the shares awarded on the date they vested. However, it transpires that the form of the award is the grant of nil cost options exercisable from that date. As these are options, is the requirement of the Act to give the total gain on the exercise of options, calculated as at the date of exercise and not, as with long-term incentive schemes, as at the date of vesting?
>
> In this case we consider that the substance of the scheme is a long-term incentive scheme and that there is no difference in reality between vesting the shares in the directors at a particular date and awarding them nil cost options exercisable from that date. For this reason we consider that the disclosures should be made as if the scheme were a long-term incentive scheme and not an option scheme. Thus the disclosures should be made, by individual director, of the value of the shares received on the vesting date. This is because the options are exercisable immediately so that it is the same as if an outright award of shares had been made on the same day. Details of the awards should be given in the table of individuals' interests in long-term incentive schemes required by paragraphs 11 and 12 of Schedule 8 to SI 2008/410 and the resulting options should then also be disclosed in the table of share options required by paragraphs 8 and 9 of Schedule 8 to SI 2008/410. There will need to be a note and cross-reference to describe the situation so that it is clear to a reader of the remuneration report.

5.188.1   A further complication can arise as a result of different definitions in SI 2008/410 and in the Listing Rules. This is explained in the example below.

Example – Deferred bonuses

The directors of a quoted company (for definition see para 5.6.3) have met performance targets for this financial year and have been allocated shares as a bonus. The shares will vest with the directors unconditionally in three years' time if the directors are still with the company. How should such bonuses be disclosed in the annual report?

Under SI 2008/410 an arrangement conditional on fulfilment of one or more qualifying conditions with respect to service or performance that cannot be fulfilled in a single financial year is classed as a 'long-term incentive scheme'. Bonuses whose amount can be determined by reference to service or performance within a single financial year are disregarded for this purpose. [SI 2008/410 8 Sch 11(5)].

Although the amount is initially determined by reference to performance within a single year, this amount is only provisional. The final amount receivable (all or nothing in this case) depends on a further service condition. Therefore, the final amount of the bonus cannot be determined by performance or service within one year and so qualifies as a long-term incentive scheme under SI 2008/410. Therefore, the award should be treated as a long-term incentive and disclosed by individual director in tabular form in the directors' remuneration report required by SI 2008/410.

If, in practice, the service conditions were not observed such that a director would receive the shares whether or not he stayed with the company for three years, this would not be a long-term incentive scheme. If the service condition either does not exist or is not observed, the bonus would be treated as an amount to be disclosed in the table of individual directors' emoluments as a bonus under paragraph 7(1)(b) of Schedule 8 to SI 2008/410.

Under the Listing Rules deferred bonuses are defined as *"any arrangement pursuant to the terms of which an employee or director may receive a bonus (including cash or any security) in respect of service and/or performance in a period not exceeding the length of the relevant financial year notwithstanding that the bonus may, subject only to the person remaining a director or employee of the group, be receivable by the person after the end of the period to which the award relates"*. This definition effectively requires the service period to be ignored and thus the bonus would be disclosed in the year as remuneration for the purpose of the Listing Rules.

There is, therefore, a difference between the disclosure under the legal requirements (as a long-term incentive) and the disclosure under the Listing Rules (as directors' emoluments for the year). We suggest that this is dealt with by excluding the amount from the detailed directors' remuneration table given under the Listing Rules, but including a note to that table to say that the amount is included in the long-term incentive scheme table given in accordance with SI 2008/410. The note to the detailed directors' remuneration table should also give the amount of the bonus by individual director and the total emoluments that would be disclosed under the Listing Rules, if the bonus were to be included in the table of emoluments required by the Listing Rules. The bonus should then be included in accordance with SI 2008/410 in the disclosure of directors' long-term incentive scheme interests.

In addition, for companies reporting under IFRS, there could be a further difference. Under IAS 24, long-term benefits include long-service, profit-sharing, bonuses and deferred compensation not payable wholly within 12 months of the end of the period. SI 2008/410 does not rigidly divide bonuses between amounts *payable* within a year of the period end and amounts payable thereafter as the IAS 24 definitions do, but rather divides them by reference to the *period of service to which they relate*. That is, SI 2008/410 divides them between the amounts payable in respect of the year and amounts not payable specifically in respect of the year.

5.189 For quoted companies, the information to be disclosed by individual director in tabular form is as follows:

- Details of the scheme interests of each director at the beginning of the financial year or date of appointment as director, if later. For this purpose and for the purpose of the remaining disclosure requirements 'scheme interest' means an interest under a long-term incentive scheme whereby assets may become receivable in respect of the director's qualifying services. [SI 2008/410 8 Sch 11(4)(a), 12(1)(a)].

- Details of scheme interests awarded to each director during the financial year, including (if shares may become receivable) the number of shares, the market price of those shares at the date of award and details of performance conditions. [SI 2008/410 8 Sch 12(2), 12(1)(b)].

- Details of scheme interests of each director at the end of the financial year or on ceasing to be a director, if earlier. [SI 2008/410 8 Sch 12(1)(c)].

- For each scheme interest referred to above:

  (i)   The end of the period over which the qualifying conditions for that interest have to be met (or the end of the last such period where there are different periods for different conditions).

  (ii) A description of any variation in the terms and conditions of the scheme interests in the year.

  [SI 2008/410 8 Sch 12(1)(d)].

- For each scheme interest that has vested in the year:

  (i)   the relevant details of any shares, that is the number of shares, the date on which the scheme interest was awarded, the market price of each of those shares when the scheme interest was awarded, the market price when the scheme interest vested and details of performance conditions;

  (ii) the amount of any money; and

  (iii) the value of any other assets;

  that have become receivable in respect of the interest. [SI 2008/410 8 Sch 12(1)(e), 12(3)].

- For the purpose of the disclosure in the last bullet point above a scheme interest vests at the earliest date when:

  (i)   It has been ascertained that the qualifying conditions have been met.

(ii)   The nature and quantity of the assets receivable under the scheme in respect of the interest have been ascertained.

[SI 2008/410 8 Sch 11(4)(b)].

5.189.1   It should be noted that there is a distinction between the disclosures required to be made by quoted companies and those by unquoted companies. Quoted companies have to disclose the amounts that *may* become receivable (the 'scheme interests') and also give information regarding performance conditions, so that the reader of the remuneration report can understand what will have to occur for the director to earn that amount. If the director earns the right to the award in the period (that is, it vests), this must also be disclosed. Unquoted companies only have to disclose the amount that is received or receivable by the director in the period (see para 5.27) — that is, the amount that the director has earned the right to (in other words, the amount that has vested).

5.189.2   For companies listed in the UK, the Listing Rules require disclosure of details of any long-term incentive schemes, other than share options (details of which are disclosed separately), including:

■   The interests of each director by name in the long-term incentive schemes at the start of the period under review.

■   Entitlements or awards granted and commitments made to each director under such schemes during the period, showing which crystallise either in the same year or subsequent years.

■   The money value and number of shares, cash payments or other benefits received by each director under such schemes during the period.

■   The interests of each director in the long-term incentive schemes at the end of the period.

[LR 9.8.8R (3) to (6)].

5.190   The example below considers the disclosure implications for long-term incentives where the incentive was awarded before appointment as a director.

Example – LTIP awarded before appointment as a director

A director of a quoted company (for definition see para 5.6.3) is appointed during the year. Immediately prior to being appointed a director, he had been awarded benefits under a long-term incentive plan (LTIP) and at the date of appointment and the year end date, the performance conditions remain unfulfilled.

(a) Does the director's interest in the LTIP need to be disclosed in the directors' remuneration report?

(b) If the award had been made a number of years ago and he had completed his performance criteria, but is required to remain in the company's employment for a further period, does this make any difference?

Paragraphs 11 and 12 of Schedule 8 to SI 2008/410 require disclosure of each director's interests in LTIPs that are receivable *"in respect of qualifying services"*.

(a) Where a director is appointed during the period and has outstanding performance conditions in respect of an award made under an LTIP prior to his appointment, we consider that the award is receivable in respect of qualifying services, because he must perform those qualifying services in order to be entitled to receive that award. Consequently, disclosure of the interest in the LTIP is required in the directors' remuneration report.

(b) SI 2008/410 does not distinguish between performance conditions and service conditions (see para 5.137). Where a director is required to remain in the company's employment in order for an entitlement under an LTIP to vest, the company is receiving performance from that director over that extended period, so it would be included as a performance condition under SI 2008/410. Consequently, if the director is required to remain in employment after his date of appointment in order to become entitled to receive the award, then we would consider that the award is in respect of qualifying services and disclosure of the interest in the LTIP is required in the directors' remuneration report. However, an explanation could be given in a note of the circumstances, that is, that the performance conditions were satisfied before becoming a director and only the service condition remains to be satisfied.

5.190.1   The example below summarises the disclosures required under SI 2008/410 in respect of performance conditions relating to awards that have not vested at the year end.

Example – Performance conditions

A quoted company is preparing a directors' remuneration report. Several of the directors have awards that have been granted to them under the company's share option scheme and Long-Term Incentive Plan (LTIP), but which are yet to vest. Do the performance criteria upon which vesting depends need to be disclosed in the remuneration report?

Paragraph 3 of Schedule 8 to SI 2008/410 requires disclosure of a policy statement that explains the company's policy on directors' remuneration for the following financial year and for financial years subsequent to that. The policy statement should include a summary of performance criteria to which any entitlement under a share option scheme or LTIP is subject and an explanation as to why those performance criteria were chosen (see para 5.134).

Paragraph 9(e) of Schedule 8 to SI 2008/410 also requires a summary of performance criteria on which the award or exercise of a share option is conditional, including a description of any variation in the year, to be given (see para 5.170.1).

Paragraphs 12(2) and 12(3) of Schedule 8 to SI 2008/410 require disclosure of performance conditions in respect of scheme interests awarded in the year and scheme interests that been received or become receivable in the year respectively (see para 5.189).

An award under a share option scheme or an LTIP forms part of the director's remuneration in the year in which the share options are exercised or when the awards under the LTIP are received or receivable.

Consequently, if an award under either a share option scheme or an LTIP is outstanding at the year end, it will form part of the director's remuneration in the following or subsequent periods and the performance criteria on which vesting depends should be disclosed, together with an explanation as to why those performance criteria were chosen.

5.191 Table 5.29 is an example of disclosure of performance conditions attaching to a scheme. In this case the performance condition is related to total shareholder return and adjusted earnings per share.

Table 5.29 – Performance conditions

Scottish and Southern Energy PLC – Annual Report 2009 – 31 March 2009

Remuneration Report – Remuneration Explained (extract)

Executive Directors' Remuneration 2008/09 (extract)

Performance Measure	Purpose – Link to Strategy	Award Policy
Long-term – Performance Share Plan Performance is measured against the following two elements over a three year period:	The two elements reflect both internal and external measures of performance.	Maximum award up to 150% of base salary each year. Awards released to the extent performance conditions are met.
Total Shareholder Return (TSR) against the FTSE 100	The relative TSR performance measure is dependent on the company's relative long-term share price performance and dividend return, and therefore brings a market perspective to the PSP. Further vesting of this element requires the Committee to be satisfied with the company's underlying financial performance.	50% based on TSR • 100% vests at or above the 75th percentile • 25% vests at median • straight-line basis between median and 75th percentile • no vesting of award if median performance is not achieved
Adjusted Earnings per Share (EPS)	Adjusted EPS growth is a key internal measure which is critical to the company's long-term success and ties in with the Group's strategic goals. These target ranges are designed to strike the right balance between being stretching at the top end, and being achievable and motivational at the lower end.	50% based on EPS • 100%: vests where EPS is RPI +9% above RPI • 25% vests where EPS is RPI +3% • straight-line basis between 3% and 9% above RPI • no vesting if EPS minimum growth of RPI +3% is not achieved

---

Long-term incentive scheme for an individual

5.192   Where the only participant of a long-term incentive scheme is a director (or a prospective director) and the arrangement is established specifically to facilitate, in unusual circumstances, the recruitment or retention of the relevant individual, disclosure of the following details are required to be given in the first annual report and accounts published by the company following the date on which the individual becomes eligible to participate in the arrangement:

■   The full text of the scheme or a description of its principal terms.

■   Details of trusteeship in the scheme or interest in the trustees, if any, of directors of the company.

■   A statement that the principal provisions of the scheme (set out in detail in rule 13.8.11R (3) of the Listing Rules) cannot be altered to the advantage of the participant without shareholders' approval.

■   A statement as to whether benefits under the scheme will be pensionable and if so the reasons for this.

■   The name of the sole participant.

■   The date on which he or she first became eligible to participate in the arrangement.

■   An explanation as to why the circumstances in which the arrangement was established were unusual.

■   The conditions to be satisfied under the arrangement's terms.

■   The maximum award(s) under the arrangement's terms, or, if there is no maximum, the basis on which the awards will be determined.

[LR 9.4.3R, 13.8.11R].

An example of disclosure is given in Table 5.31 below.

Table 5.31 – Long-term incentive scheme for a single director

First Leisure Corporation PLC – Annual report and financial statements – 31 October 1997

Report of the Remuneration Committee (extract)

(iv)   Senior executive long term incentive scheme

The Remuneration Committee approved the introduction of the senior executive long term incentive scheme as from 1st November 1994. The total potential bonus for each executive was fixed at the beginning of the scheme which covers the four financial years up to and including 1997/98. The maximum bonus payable in respect of each of the four years covered by the scheme increases evenly from 22% to 28% of the total potential bonus payable.

The scheme provides executives with the opportunity of earning significant cash bonuses if sustained real earnings per share growth and share price appreciation are achieved. In order to qualify for the maximum bonus in any year, the real growth in the Group's earnings per share and share price must exceed 6% over a maximum three year rolling period. Where

---

real growth is below 6% the maximum potential bonus is reduced on a sliding scale. Where real growth is below 1.2% no bonus is payable.

Each annual bonus is deferred for a minimum of two years, except for the final award which is deferred for a minimum of one year. Payment of the annual bonus is subject to the following further conditions:

- 25% of the annual bonus is contingent solely on the executive being in the Group's employment at the end of the minimum deferral period. This element of the bonus is accrued for in the year in which it is conditionally earned;

- the remaining 75% of the annual bonus is dependent upon an additional condition that there is a further increase in earnings per share over the deferral period. The maximum deferral period is unlimited. This element of the bonus is accrued for evenly over the minimum deferral period.

Currently, Mr Coles is the only scheme member. However, Mr Payne's service contract with the Company entitles him to receive bonuses equivalent to Mr Coles under the scheme, as though he was a scheme member.

For the annual awards in respect of the 1994/95 and 1995/96 financial years, the growth in earnings per share and share price were such that the maximum bonus in respect of these years will become payable if the further conditions relating to employment and further earnings per share growth are met. No annual award has been made in respect of the 1996/97 financial year since the required level of real growth in earnings per share and share price was not achieved. Accordingly, the total conditional interests of Mr Payne and Mr Coles, which relate to the 1994/95 and 1995/96 annual awards, are the same at the beginning and end of the year and amounted to £230,000 each.

The maximum average annual award payable to Mr Payne and Mr Coles over the life of the scheme is £125,000 each.

To date no amounts have been paid under the scheme to either Mr Coles or Mr Payne although the conditions attaching to the payment of the first 25% of 1994/95 have been satisfied and this amount is now payable. However, as regards the remaining 75% of the 1994/95 award, the required further increase in earnings per share was not achieved in 1996/97 and therefore this payment remains deferred.

Senior executive long term incentive scheme (1997).

The Remuneration Committee approved the introduction of the senior executive long term incentive scheme (1997) from 1st November 1997. Mr Grade is the sole participant. The terms and conditions to apply will reflect the advice received by the Remuneration Committee from independent remuneration consultants, and will be broadly the same as those described above except that the scheme will cover the four financial years from 1997/98 up to 2000/01 and the minimum real growth that must be achieved before an award can be made has been increased from 1.2% to 2%. The average maximum annual award payable under the scheme is £625,000.

As permitted by paragraph 13.13A of the Listing Rules, the scheme was not approved by shareholders in advance, since in establishing the scheme the Remuneration Committee considered that exceptional circumstances existed in that these arrangements needed to be put in place at the earliest opportunity to attract, motivate and retain the services of a senior executive of Mr Grade's calibre. For similar reasons the Remuneration Committee approved the grant of options to Mr Grade under the 1994 executive share option scheme set out on page 28.

Pensions

5.193 The definitions of pension scheme, money purchase scheme, money purchase benefits and retirement benefits are the same under Schedule 8 to SI 2008/410 as they are for the purpose of the requirement to disclose total emoluments under Schedule 5 to SI 2008/410. The definitions are described from paragraph 5.61 above.

5.194 The disclosure requirements for money purchase schemes are to show, by individual director, the details of company contributions paid or payable in respect of the director for the year or paid by the company in the year in respect of another financial year. [SI 2008/410 8 Sch 13(3)]. This is similar to the requirement in the Listing Rules for disclosure of details of the contribution or allowance payable or made by the company in respect of each director during the period under review. [LR 9.8.8R (11)].

5.195 'Company contributions' means any payments (including insurance premiums) made, or treated as made, to the scheme in respect of the director by anyone other than the director, that is the term would include payments by parties other than the company in respect of the director. [SI 2008/410 8 Sch 17]. This definition is consistent with that given for the purpose of disclosure of aggregate contributions by all companies (see para 5.65 above). See further paragraph 5.202 for practical application of the rules.

5.195.1 An example of disclosure of company contributions to money purchase schemes is given in Table 5.32.

Table 5.32 – Money purchase pension schemes

Aggreko PLC – Annual Report – 31 December 2009

Pension entitlements

Executive Directors participate in defined contribution plans that are designed to be in line with the median practice in the relevant country but Executive Directors who reside in the United Kingdom and who joined the Board before 1 April 2002 participate in a defined benefits plan.

Rupert Soames, Kash Pandya and Bill Caplan are members of the Aggreko plc Group Personal Pension Plan. Rupert Soames is entitled to a pension contribution from the Company of 25% of his basic salary and Kash Pandya and Bill Caplan are entitled to a Company contribution of 20%. Kash Pandya has chosen not to take his entire Company contribution into the Group Personal Pension Plan and takes a proportion as a cash payment, shown as Other Pay in the Emoluments table on page 65.

George Walker is entitled to participate in the Employees' Savings Investment Retirement plan and the Supplemental Executive Retirement plan of Aggreko LLC, which are governed by the laws of the United States. These plans allow contributions by the employee and the Group to be deferred for tax.

Contributions paid by the Company under the defined contribution plans during the year are as follows:

	Company contributions during 2009 £	Company contributions during 2008 £
Rupert Soames	125,000	125,624
George Walker	111,271	80,179
Kash Pandya	15,840	15,840
Bill Caplan	40,500	–

5.196 The Schedule 8 to SI 2008/410 disclosure requirements in respect of directors' rights under defined benefit schemes are to show, for each director of the company who has served as such at any time during the financial year, the following information:

- Changes in the director's accrued benefits during the year.

- Details of the director's accrued benefits at the end of the year.

- Transfer value of the director's accrued benefits at the end of the year, calculated in accordance with 'Retirement Benefit Schemes – Transfer Values (GN11)' published by the Institute of Actuaries and the Faculty of Actuaries and dated 6 April 2001.

- Transfer value of the director's accrued benefits, either at the end of the previous year as shown in the previous period's remuneration report or, if none was produced, as at the beginning of the financial year.

- The amount of the difference between the two transfer values disclosed in the previous two bullet points, less the amount of any contributions made to the scheme by the director during the year.

[SI 2008/410 8 Sch 13(1), (2)].

5.196.1 An example of disclosures required under Schedule 8 to SI 2008/410 might be as follows:

Director	Increase in accrued benefits	Accrued benefits at 31 December 2002	Transfer value 31 December 2002	Transfer value 31 December 2001	Increase in transfer value less director's contributions
	£	£	£	£	£
A Smith	2,000	30,000	216,000	190,000	21,000
B Jones	10,000	150,000	1,500,000	1,360,000	137,000

See further paragraph 5.203 for practical application of the rules.

5.197 For companies listed in the UK, the Listing Rules disclosure requirements in respect of directors' rights under defined benefit schemes are to show the following information:

- details of the amount of the increase during the period under review (excluding inflation) and of the accumulated total amount at the end of the period in respect of the accrued benefit to which each director would be entitled on leaving service or is entitled having left service during the period under review;

- and either:

  - the transfer value (less director's contributions) of the relevant increase in accrued benefit (to be calculated in accordance with Actuarial Guidance Note GN11, but making no deduction for any underfunding) as at the end of the period; or

  - so much of the following information as is necessary to make a reasonable assessment of the transfer value in respect of each director:

    - current age;

    - normal retirement age;

    - the amount of any contributions paid or payable by the director under the scheme's terms during the period under review;

    - details of spouse's and dependants' benefits;

    - early retirement rights and options, expectations of pension increases after retirement (whether guaranteed or discretionary); and

    - discretionary benefits for which allowance is made in transfer values on leaving and any other relevant information which will significantly affect the value of the benefits.

Voluntary contributions and benefits should not be disclosed.

[LR 9.8.8R (12)].

5.198 There is some overlap between the disclosure requirements in respect of defined benefit pensions in the Listing Rules and the legal requirements in SI 2008/410, but there are differences. The legal disclosure requirements go much further than the requirements of the Listing Rules. This is principally because SI 2008/410 specifically requires the transfer value of a director's accrued pension at the beginning and end of the year to be given, which is not a requirement of the Listing Rules. The difference between these two values less the director's contributions also has to be disclosed. Under the Listing Rules either the transfer value of the increase in accrued pension or sufficient information to enable it to be ascertained only has to be given. The main disclosures, which are considered further below, are as follows:

- The SI 2008/410 requires disclosure of any changes during the year in a director's accrued benefits under a pension scheme, which includes inflation, whereas the Listing Rules requirement excludes inflation (see para 5.199 below).

■ The SI 2008/410 requires disclosure of the change in the transfer value of accrued benefits (based on the opening and closing values of the transfer value), whilst the Listing Rules require the transfer value of the increase in the accrued benefit to be disclosed (or sufficient information about the Director's pension entitlements from which that value can be derived) (see para 5.200 below).

5.199 The Listing Rules require disclosure of the increase excluding inflation of the director's accrued benefit during the period under review, whereas SI 2008/410 requires disclosure of any changes during the relevant financial year in the person's accrued benefits under the scheme, which would include inflation. [LR 9.8.8 R (12)(a); SI 2008/410 8 Sch 13(2)(a)(i)]. Although the only difference between the disclosures is the inflationary element, they are aimed at telling different stories: the SI 2008/410 disclosure is aimed at telling the reader the difference between the annual pension that each director would have received if they had retired at the end of the year and the annual pension that they would have received if they had retired at the end of the previous year. However, the Listing Rules disclosure is designed to disclose the element of the director's increase in their accrued benefit that is earned during the year. If the director's annual pension entitlement increased only because of inflation, they would have earned no additional pension benefit by reason of employment, as their pension would have been increased by an inflationary element even if they had left. An example of an adjustment for inflation is given below.

Example – Adjustment for inflation

This example shows how the entitlement should be calculated for a director given the relevant facts as follows:

A director has ten years' service at the beginning of the year and earns £120,000 per annum. He is entitled to a pension of one-sixtieth of final pensionable salary for each year of pensionable service. At the end of the year his salary was £130,000. The increase for the year and the accumulated total at the year end are calculated as follows:

Accumulated totals
At the beginning of the year: $10/60 \times £120,000 = £20,000$
At the end of the year: $11/60 \times £130,000 = £23,833$
Calculation of increase in the year (excluding inflation)
Increase: $£23,833$ less $£20,000 = £3,833$
Inflation is assumed to be 5%.
The increase due to inflation is: $£20,000 \times 5\% = £1,000$
The increase excluding inflation is, therefore, £2,833.

Note: The inflation rate used should be that published by the Secretary of State for Social Security each year (Schedule 3 of the Pension Schemes Act 1993).

5.200 A further difference between the Listing Rules and the legal requirements is that the Listing Rules require disclosure of the transfer value (less director's contributions) of the relevant increase in accrued benefit as at the end of the period or sufficient information about the director's pension entitlements from which that value can be derived. [LR 9.8.8R (12)(b)]. SI 2008/410, however, requires disclosure of the amount obtained by subtracting the transfer value of the person's accrued benefits at the end of the previous period from the transfer value of his accrued benefits at the end of the current period, then subtracting the director's personal contributions from that total. [SI 2008/410 8 Sch 13(2)(d)]. The transfer value of the increase in accrued benefits, required by the Listing Rules, discloses the current value of the increase in accrued benefits that the director has earned in the period, whereas the change in the transfer value, required by SI 2008/410 discloses the absolute increase or decrease in the director's transfer value and includes the change in value of the accrued benefits that results from applying a different actuarial factor to the accrued benefits at the beginning of the period, as well as the additional value earned in the year.

5.201   The above differences between SI 2008/410 requirements and those of the Listing Rules are illustrated in the following example.

Example – Transfer values under SI 2008/410 and the Listing Rules

A UK listed company is preparing its directors' remuneration report in compliance with the disclosure requirements in the Listing Rules and Schedule 8 to SI 2008/410. The company's executive directors are members of the company's defined benefit pension scheme. The Listing Rules require disclosure of the transfer value of the increase in each director's accrued benefits under the scheme, excluding inflation, while SI 2008/410 requires disclosure of the increase in the transfer value of their accrued benefits less the director's personal pension contributions.

What is the difference between these disclosures and does the company need to disclose both figures?

A transfer value is an actuarially calculated value that measures the fair value of a pension scheme's liability in respect of a director's accrued benefit. The Listing Rules require disclosure of the transfer value of the increase in the director's accrued benefit excluding inflation. So, using an example, if a director's accrued benefit at the end of 20X2 was £100,000 and his accrued benefit at the end of 20X3 was £110,000, inflation was steady at 3% and the actuarially calculated 'factor' for this director to be applied is 9.27, the transfer value of the increase in accrued benefit excluding inflation is £64,890, being 9.27 × (£110,000 – (103% × £100,000)).

SI 2008/410 requires disclosure of the difference between the transfer value at the year end and the transfer value at the beginning of the year, less any personal contributions paid by the director. Using the same facts as in the example above and assuming that the 'factor' at the end of 20X2 was 8.5 and the director contributed £500 per month (gross), the figure disclosed will be £163,700 (the difference between the transfer value at the end of 20X3 (£110,000 × 9.27 = £1,019,700) and the transfer value at the end of 20X2 (£100,000 × 8.5 = £850,000), less the director's personal contributions of £6,000).

So, although the requirements of the Listing Rules and SI 2008/410 may appear similar, the resulting disclosures can be significantly different. The company will need to comply with both requirements.

5.201.1 An example of disclosure that gives the information required by both SI 2008/410 and the Listing Rules is Table 5.33 (note that Schedule 8 to SI 2008/410 has replaced Schedule 7A to the Companies Act 1985 for periods beginning on or after 6 April 2008).

Table 5.33 – Disclosure of directors' pension benefits

BT Group plc – Annual Report and Form 20-F – 31 March 2010

Pensions (extract 1)
The table below shows the increase in the accrued benefits, including those referred to above, to which each director who is a member of the BTPS has become entitled during the year, and the transfer value of the increase in accrued benefits.

Pensions (extract 2)
Increases in pension benefits at 31 March 2010

	Accrued pension		Transfer value of accrued benefits		Change in transfer value c-d less directors' contributions	Additional accrued benefits earned in the year	Transfer value of increase in accrued benefits in e less directors' contributions
	2010 £000 a	2009 £000 b	2010 £000 c	2009 £000 d	2010 £000	2010 £000 e	2010 £000 f
T Chanmugam[g,h]	180	140	3,536	2,419	1,117	35	693
H Lalanii[g,i]	166	161	2,382	1,742	640	–	–

a-d As required by the Large and Medium-sized Companies and Groups (Accounts and Reports) Regulations 2008.
a-b The values represent the deferred pension to which they would have been entitled had they left the company on 31 March 2010 and 2009, respectively.
c Transfer value of the deferred pension in column (a) as at 31 March 2010 calculated on the basis of actuarial advice in accordance with relevant legislation. The transfer value represents a liability of the BTPS rather than any remuneration due to the individual, and cannot be meaningfully aggregated with annual remuneration, as it is not money the individual is entitled to receive.
d The equivalent transfer value but calculated as at 31 March 2009 on the assumption that the director left the company on that date.
e The increase in pension built up during the year, net of inflation. The gross amount can be calculated by deducting the amount under column (b) from the amount under column (a).
f The transfer value of the pension in column (e), less directors' contributions.
g Directors' contributions in the financial year 2009/10 were as follows: Hanif Lalani £nil (2009: £nil); Tony Chanmugam, £nil (2009: £9,500).
h Tony Chanmugam was appointed as a director on 1 December 2008.
i Hanif Lalani resigned as a director on 7 January 2010 and left the company on 31 March 2010.

Practical application of pensions disclosures

5.202 As noted in paragraph 5.194, quoted companies are required to show, by individual director, the details of company contributions paid or payable in respect of the director to money purchase pension schemes. This requirement applies both to company pension schemes and to company payments to personal pension schemes (see further para 5.61 above).

5.202.1   However, contributions that directors themselves pay by way of a compulsory deduction from salary are disclosed as part of directors' emoluments, rather than pension contributions (see para 5.37 above). Similarly, payments made directly to a director, which the director then elects to pay into a pension scheme should be disclosed as emoluments, rather than pension contributions, as illustrated in the examples below.

Example 1 – Cash in lieu of pension contributions

A quoted company is preparing its directors' remuneration report in accordance with Schedule 8 to SI 2008/410. All but one of the directors have contributions paid by the company into its defined contribution scheme. One director elected instead to receive a direct payment through payroll, in lieu of the contributions that would have been made by the company to the defined contribution scheme. Although it is expected that he will use the cash in a personal pension scheme, he is under no obligation to do so. How should the payments be presented in the remuneration report?

Because the cash in lieu of pension contributions is paid directly to the director through the payroll system it cannot be classified as a company contribution to a pension scheme.

The cash received in lieu of pension contributions is remuneration and should be included appropriately in the tabular disclosure given under Schedule 8 to SI 2008/410. Although it is not a company pension contribution, in our view it is equally not salary, bonus, expense allowance or benefit in kind (which are required to be disclosed separately – see para 5.164). In the interests of transparency we believe that the company should disclose the amounts in the emoluments table in a separate column, explaining the nature of the payment.

Example 2 – Waiver of bonus in favour of pension contributions

A director of a quoted company is entitled to an annual salary and other benefits, including an annual bonus. After the end of the year, the value of his bonus is determined and he is given three options:

(a)   He receives the bonus in cash.

(b)   He waives the bonus and the company pays the same amount into his defined contribution pension arrangement.

(c)   He waives the bonus and the company pays the same amount into his final salary-based pension to buy additional years' service in the scheme.

What would be disclosed in the remuneration report under each of these options?

Would the answer be any different if he waived part of his salary, rather than his bonus?

Paragraph 7 of Schedule 8 to SI 2008/410 requires disclosure, in a table, of the emoluments (including bonus) paid to or receivable by each director in respect of qualifying services for the financial year.

The bonus was receivable by the director in respect of qualifying services and it would be his choice to convert the bonus into a pension contribution, so if this happens the amount should continue to be disclosed as emoluments.

If emoluments are waived, then they are excluded from the emoluments table, but disclosed in the remuneration report, as required by the Listing Rules. [LR 9.8.4R (5)]. However, the bonus has not, in substance, been waived as the director has received consideration (additional pension contributions) for the waiver, therefore, the amount should continue to be disclosed as emoluments.

5.203   The examples below consider the implications for disclosure in respect of pension entitlements in various situations, including when the director is appointed or retires in the year. The examples cover the following situations:

■   A director (who was previously an employee) is appointed during the year (example 1). (For unquoted companies see para 5.90.1.)

■   Serving director receives pension (example 2).

■   Retired director becomes non-executive director (example 3).

■   Director retires during year, but remains an employee (example 4).

■   Director retires and commutes pension (example 5).

Example 1 – Director (previously an employee) appointed during the year

A quoted company is preparing its directors' remuneration report. One of the directors has been an employee of the company and a member of its defined benefits pension scheme, for a number of years, but was appointed as a director of the company during this year.

(a) Under Schedule 8 to SI 2008/410, should the disclosures in respect of the benefits accruing to that director under the defined benefits scheme include all benefits accruing or just those that have accrued to him in respect of qualifying services?

Paragraph 13 of Schedule 8 to SI 2008/410 requires disclosure of specified information (see para 5.196) in respect of a director, where *"...the person has rights under a ... defined benefit scheme ... and any of those rights are rights to which he has become entitled in respect of qualifying services..."*. This means that the disclosures apply where any of the rights are earned in respect of qualifying services. As the director was appointed in the year and some of the benefits accrued at the year-end are in respect of the qualifying services performed since the appointment date, this means that the disclosures apply. These disclosure requirements do not state that they should be made only in respect of the period since appointment and they should, therefore, be calculated based on the director's total accrued benefit under the scheme and not just on the portion that has been earned in respect of qualifying services.

(b) Should the change in the director's accrued benefit disclosed under Schedule 8 to SI 2008/410 be the difference between his accrued benefit at the end of the year and at the beginning of the year or the date of appointment?

Paragraph 13 of Schedule 8 to SI 2008/410 requires disclosure of the change in the director's accrued benefit during the year and does not contain a *proviso* that where the director was appointed during the year the change should be given only since the date of appointment. Therefore, the change in the director's accrued benefit disclosed should be the total difference between the director's accrued benefit at the end of the year and at the beginning of the year. However, whilst disclosing the full year's increase an explanation could be added to the effect that the increase for the year of £x arose after the director became a director.

Example 2 – Serving director receives pension

The chairman of a quoted company is past retirement age and has been receiving a pension from the company for the whole of the current year, in addition to his emoluments (which are not pensionable). Does the table of accrued pension benefits, required by paragraph 13 of Schedule 8 to SI 2008/410 have to include, in respect of the chairman, details of the change (if any) in his accrued benefit, the accrued benefits at the end of the year and the transfer values?

The disclosure requirements for the chairman's defined benefit pension entitlement are the same as the requirements in respect of each of the other directors and are as set out in paragraph 13(2) of Schedule 8 to SI 2008/410. The Act requires disclosure of the information specified in paragraph 13 of Schedule 8 to SI 2008/410 in respect of each person's defined benefit pension entitlements where that person has performed qualifying services at any point during the year (which the chairman has) and has benefits accruing to him/her under a defined benefits scheme (which the chairman has), any of which were accrued in respect of qualifying services. So even though the chairman received no pensionable emoluments during the year (so no further benefits accrued to him during the year), full disclosure is required.

The requirement in Schedule 8 to SI 2008/410 differs from the requirement in Schedule 5 to SI 2008/410 (for unquoted companies) and from the Listing Rules (for UK listed companies).

Schedule 5 to SI 2008/410 requires disclosure (by unquoted companies) of the highest paid director's accrued benefits (and accrued lump sum where applicable) only if the director has performed qualifying services in the year that earn pension entitlements, which a director who is drawing his pension will normally not do. This requirement applies only to the highest paid director.

The Listing Rules require disclosure (by UK listed companies) of the increase in the accrued benefit (excluding inflation) and the transfer value of that increase (which can be substituted by specified details as outlined in the Listing Rules) for each director (or person who resigned as a director during the year). As the chairman is receiving a pension, there will be no increase in the accrued benefit and, consequently, no disclosure is required by the Listing Rules.

However, Schedule 8 to SI 2008/410 requires disclosure (by quoted companies) of pension entitlements where a director has rights under a scheme and any of those rights are rights to which he has become entitled in respect of qualifying services. However, it does not make disclosure conditional on his having performed qualifying services in the year that accrue pension entitlements.

Therefore, the Schedule 8 to SI 2008/410 requirements differ from those of the Listing Rules and under Schedule 8 to SI 2008/410, even if a person has retired and is performing non-qualifying services as a director of the company, perhaps in a non-executive capacity, such that the accrued benefit does not increase, all the pensions entitlement disclosures of Schedule 8 to SI 2008/410 are still required to be given in the directors' remuneration report, as he has rights under the pension scheme that were earned in respect of qualifying services in the past (before he retired).

Example 3 – Retired director becomes non-executive director

A director of a quoted company is a member of the company's defined benefit pension scheme. During the prior year, he reached retirement age, stood down as an executive director and was appointed a non-executive director. He is receiving his pension from the pension scheme in addition to fees in respect of his services as a non-executive director.

(a) Does the director's annual pension received need to be included in his emoluments?

Paragraph 7 of Schedule 8 to SI 2008/410 requires disclosure, in a table, of the emoluments paid to or receivable by each director in respect of qualifying services for the financial year. The pension payment is receivable by the director, but it was accrued in respect of qualifying services in years prior to his retirement, so is not receivable in respect of qualifying services for the period and should be excluded from the disclosure of his emoluments.

(b) Should the director be included in the defined benefit pension disclosures?

Paragraph 13 of Schedule 8 to SI 2008/410 requires disclosure of specified information (see para 5.196) in respect of a director, where *"...the person has rights under a ... defined benefit scheme ... and any of those rights are rights to which he has become entitled in respect of qualifying services..."*. This means that the disclosures apply where the director (the Act does not differentiate between executive and non-executive directors) has any entitlement under a defined benefit scheme and any of those rights are earned in respect of qualifying services.

As the director served as a director during the year and has an entitlement under a defined benefit scheme, some of which was accrued in respect of qualifying services (albeit in years prior to his retirement), the above disclosures are required in respect of him, even though pension entitlements were not accruing in respect of services during the period.

Example 4 – Director retires during year, but remains an employee

A quoted company is preparing its directors' remuneration report. One of the directors, who is a member of its defined benefits pension scheme, resigned as a director of the company during this year, but will remain an employee of the company, accruing further pensionable service.

(a) Should the disclosures in respect of the benefits accruing to that director under the defined benefits scheme include all benefits accruing or just those that have accrued to him in respect of qualifying services?

Schedule 8 to SI 2008/410 requires disclosure of specified information (see para 5.196) in respect of any person who has served as a director at any time during the year and has defined benefit pension entitlements, any of which were accrued in respect of qualifying services. This means that the disclosures apply where any of the rights are earned in respect of qualifying services. As the director resigned in the year and some of the benefits accrued at the year end are in respect of qualifying services, this means that the disclosures are required in respect of all benefits accrued (that is, determined as at the year end, rather than at the date of retirement).

(b) Should the change in the director's accrued benefit disclosed be the difference between his accrued benefit at the beginning of the year and at the end of the year or at the date of resignation?

Paragraph 13 of Schedule 8 to SI 2008/410 requires disclosure of the change in the director's accrued benefit during the year and does not contain a *proviso* that where the director resigned during the year the change should be given only until the date of resignation. Therefore, the change in the director's accrued benefit disclosed should be the total difference between the director's accrued benefit at the end of the year and at the beginning of the year.

Example 5 – Director retires and commutes pension

A quoted company is preparing its directors' remuneration report for the year ended 31 December 20X4. One of its directors retired during the year and, as permitted by the rules of the defined benefit pension scheme, commuted part of her pension entitlement into a tax-free lump sum. In the 20X3 remuneration report, her disclosed accrued benefit was £100,000 and the transfer value of her accrued benefit at that date was £950,000. When she retired, she elected to forfeit £25,000 of her annual pension entitlement in consideration for a cash receipt of £235,000. At 31 December 20X4, her accrued pension is £76,000 (the £1,000 increase being inflationary) and the transfer value is £724,000. She made no personal contributions during the year.

What should be disclosed in this year's remuneration report under the Companies Act?

Schedule 8 to SI 2008/410 requires disclosure of specified information (see para 5.196) in respect of any person who has served as a director at any time during the year and has defined benefit pension entitlements, any of which were accrued in respect of qualifying services. So full disclosure in accordance with paragraph 13 of Schedule 8 to SI 2008/410 is required of information about the director's pension entitlement.

A literal reading of SI 2008/410 requirements would lead to disclosure of her accrued benefits of £76,000, the reduction in accrued benefit of £24,000, the transfer values at 1 January 20X4 and 31 December 20X4 of £950,000 and £724,000 respectively and the reduction in transfer value (excluding personal contributions) of £226,000. However, disclosure of this information without disclosure of the cash lump sum of £235,000 would be misleading to the user of the remuneration report so disclosure of this must be given.

An alternative view is that a more representative disclosure would be based on her entitlement had she not commuted her benefit into cash. That is, disclosure of her accrued benefit of £101,000 and a transfer value at the end of the year calculated by reference to that amount. However, as this is not the benefit that she will actually receive, in order that the readers of the remuneration report are not misled, a footnote must be given, explaining that she has commuted 25% of her benefit and received a cash lump sum.

In our view, either disclosure is acceptable, but either disclosure must be clear to the users of the remuneration report.

Excess retirement benefits of directors and past directors

5.204   The remuneration report must disclose, for each director who served during the year and for each past director, the amount of excess retirement benefits paid to or receivable by that director or past director under pension schemes. [SI 2008/410 8 Sch 14].

5.205   The requirement for disclosure by individual director or past director in the remuneration report prepared by quoted companies is subject to similar criteria and definitions as the aggregate disclosure requirement that applies only to unquoted companies (see para 5.93). Thus, for example, the excess amounts referred to above do not include amounts paid or receivable if:

■   the scheme's funding was such that the amounts were or could have been paid without recourse to additional contributions; and

■   the amounts were paid to or receivable by all pensioner members of the scheme on the same basis ('pensioner members' being persons entitled to the present payment of retirement benefits under the scheme).

[SI 2008/410 8 Sch 14(3)].

5.206   Retirement benefits, for the purpose of the above, includes benefits otherwise than in cash and where benefits otherwise than in cash are given, the amount is their estimated money value. The nature of any such benefit should also be disclosed. [SI 2008/410 8 Sch 14(4)].

5.207   Retirement benefits means retirement benefits to which the director or past director became entitled in respect of his qualifying services. [SI 2008/410 8 Sch 14(2)].

5.208   An example of disclosure of excess retirement benefits by individual director or past director is given in Table 5.35. The example also includes other payments to former directors.

Table 5.35 – Excess retirement benefits paid to past director

Marks and Spencer Group p.l.c. – Annual report & financial statement – 29 March 2003

Remuneration report (extract)

4 Payments to former directors
Details of payments made under the Early Retirement Plan and other payments made to former directors during the year are:

	Paid in 2003 £000	Paid in 2002 £000
Early retirement pensions 1 (payable until)		
James Benfield (22 April 2009)	71	70
Lord Stone of Blackheath (7 September 2002)	47	93
Derek Hayes (19 November 2008)	66	65
Chris Littmoden (28 September 2003)	89	88
Keith Oates (3 July 2002)	59	174
Unfunded pensions		
Clinton Silver 2	89	88
Other		
Robert Colvill 3	19	177
Chris Littmoden	–	87
Sir David Sieff	–	13

1 Under the Early Retirement Plan the Remuneration Committee could, at its discretion, offer an unfunded Early Retirement Pension, separate from the Company pension, which was payable from the date of retirement to age 60. With effect from 31 March 2000, the Early Retirement Plan was withdrawn but payments continue for awards made before this date.

2 The pension scheme entitlement for Clinton Silver is supplemented by an additional, unfunded pension paid by the Company.

3 Robert Colvill continued to receive a fee as non-executive chairman of Marks & Spencer Financial Services until 31 August 2002.

Compensation for past directors

5.209   The general rules for disclosure of compensation for loss of office, applicable for all companies, are dealt with in paragraph 5.97 onwards. In addition, for quoted companies, the remuneration report is required to disclose details of compensation for loss of office for individual directors (see para 5.163). However, there may be other payments or benefits given to past directors that may not legally qualify as compensation for loss of office and so SI 2008/410 contains a 'sweep-up' requirement for such awards to be disclosed.

5.210   The requirement is to disclose details of any significant award made in the financial year to any director who was not a director at the time when the award was made, but was previously a director. This requirement covers, in particular, compensation for loss of office and pensions, but excludes any sums already disclosed in the table of individual directors' emoluments and compensation for loss of office. [SI 2008/410 8 Sch 15].

Example – Awards to former directors

(i) Paragraph 15 of Schedule 8 to SI 2008/410 requires disclosure of the details of any significant award made in the financial year to any director who was not a director at the time when the award was made, but was previously a director. How should this be interpreted for awards in the current period to:

(a) A director who retires in the period?

Paragraph 7(1) of Schedule 8 to SI 2008/410 requires disclosure in respect of each person who has served as a director of the company at any time during the year. Therefore, if a director retires in the period then his emoluments (for qualifying services) should be included in the analysis by individual director as normal. This analysis would also include any compensation for loss of office. Any further awards made after the person ceased to be a director that are not included in compensation would fall to be disclosed separately under paragraph 15 of Schedule 8 to SI 2008/410.

(b) A director who retired in the previous period?

We interpret significant awards to former directors during the year to include awards (cash or non-cash) to former directors who had ceased to be directors by the beginning of the current accounting period. These awards would be picked up by the paragraph 15 of Schedule 8 to SI 2008/410 requirement detailed above.

(ii) Do significant awards to former directors have to be disclosed by individual director, naming them, or can they just be disclosed in aggregate, without names?

If the awards are not already disclosed in the table by individual director as compensation under paragraph 7 of Schedule 8 to SI 2008/410, they would be separately disclosed by director under paragraph 15 of Schedule 8 to SI 2008/410. Disclosure by individual director is clearly required by the wording of paragraph 15 of Schedule 8 to SI 2008/410.

5.211 Of particular note is that the requirement also relates to pensions and so will lead to disclosure of any pension top-ups (see para 5.100 onwards) or benefits in respect of early retirement not disclosed elsewhere.

5.211.1 In addition, for companies listed in the UK, the Listing Rules require disclosure of any significant payments made to former directors during the period under review. [LR 9.8.8R (2)(c)].

5.212 Examples of items that may fall to be disclosed under these requirements are contained in Table 5.35 (see para 5.208 above). This example has been used above to illustrate disclosure of excess retirement benefits required to be disclosed separately (see from para 5.204), but also includes disclosure that may fall under this section of other significant awards to former directors that are not compensation for loss of office or excess retirement benefits.

5.213 Another example might be one such as that shown in Table 5.21 in paragraph 5.154 of a payment made in respect of a dispute with a former director, which is resolved several years after the director ceased to act as such.

5.214   Another example might be a consultancy contract entered into with a former director. This is considered in the example below.

> **Example – Consultancy contract with former director**
>
> A quoted company is preparing its directors' remuneration report. During the year it entered into a contract for services with a person who was previously a director of the company, but who had resigned as a director three years previously. The rate being paid to the former director is in excess of the market rate for the services he is contracted to provide.
>
> (a) Is there any disclosure requirement in the directors' remuneration report?
>
> (b) Would it make any difference if the payment for services was an arm's length rate?
>
> As noted in paragraph 5.210 above, paragraph 15 of Schedule 8 to SI 2008/410 requires disclosure in the directors' remuneration report of "...*any significant award made in the relevant financial year to any person who was not a director of the company at the time the award was made but had previously been a director of the company*...".
>
> Paragraph 6(2) of Schedule 8 to SI 2008/410 requires disclosure of an explanation for any significant award made in the circumstances described in paragraph 15 of Schedule 8 to SI 2008/410.
>
> (a) Where the director receives reward for the services he provides to the company at a value in excess of arm's length, this would be an award under the terms of paragraph 15 of Schedule 8 to SI 2008/410 and disclosure would be required of amounts received by him, together with an explanation.
>
> (b) Where the director receives payment at a value that is arm's length, the award of the contract to the former director would require disclosure under paragraph 15 of Schedule 8 to SI 2008/410, together with an explanation, in the year in which it is awarded. In subsequent accounting periods, there will be no SI 2008/410 disclosure requirements in respect of the ongoing arm's length contract because there will be no award in those years.
>
> In either case, the Listing Rules require disclosure of significant payments to former directors and would require disclosure of this payment in the directors' remuneration report (see para 5.165). [LR 9.8.8R 2(c)].

[The next paragraph is 5.216.]

Sums paid to third parties in respect of directors' services

5.216   SI 2008/410 contains a requirement for quoted companies to disclose, by individual director, the aggregate amount of any consideration paid to or receivable by third parties for making available the services of the director.

■   As a director of the company.

■   While a director of the company:

(i)   as director of any of its subsidiary undertakings;

(ii)   as director of any other undertaking of which he was a director by virtue of the company's nomination (direct or indirect); or

(iii) otherwise in connection with the management of the affairs of the company or any such other undertaking.

[SI 2008/410 8 Sch 16(1)].

5.217 In this context, third parties do not include:

■ The director himself or a person connected with him or a body corporate controlled by him.

■ The company or any other undertaking of which he is a director (while director of the company) by virtue of the company's nomination (direct or indirect).

[SI 2008/410 8 sch 16(3)].

5.218 This part of SI 2008/410 does not specifically exclude from the definition of third party the company's subsidiary undertakings, whilst the rule relating to disclosure of aggregate amounts by unquoted companies in paragraph 5(3) of Schedule 5 to SI 2008/410 does do so (see para 5.114 above). This may be an oversight and common sense would suggest that subsidiary undertakings should also be excluded.

5.219 The reference to consideration includes benefits otherwise than in cash and where such benefits are given the amount to be disclosed is the estimated money value of the benefit. [SI 2008/410 8 Sch 16(2)]. An example of disclosure of sums paid to third parties is given in Table 5.11 in paragraph 5.117.1 above.

5.220 The disclosure applies where third parties make available the services of a director. It does not apply to other services, for example, payments to a head hunter that relate solely to services to the company for finding and introducing a director. This is illustrated in the example in paragraph 5.117.2 above.

[The next paragraph is 5.222.]

Approval of remuneration report

5.222 Section 447 of the 2006 Act requires that the remuneration report (quoted companies only – see para 5.6.3 for definition) has to be approved by the board of directors and signed on behalf of the board by a director or the secretary of the company. [CA06 Sec 447(3)].

5.223 Quoted companies are required by section 439 of the 2006 Act to give notice to members, prior to the general meeting at which accounts are laid, of an ordinary resolution to approve the directors' remuneration report for the year. However, no entitlement of a director to remuneration is made conditional on the resolution being passed by reason only of the requirements in section 439 of the 2006 Act. [CA06 Sec 439(2)]. In other words, the success or failure of the resolution does not affect the entitlement of the directors to the remuneration disclosed in the report. This is because remuneration will already be the subject of contracts that cannot be overturned. However, any 'no vote' or significant opposition is likely to spell trouble for the company in terms of investor relations.

Good practice guidance from industry commentators

5.223.1   A number of organisations have issued good practice guidance on remuneration policy for consideration by both companies and investors. The discussion that follows provides a brief overview of some of the published guidance. Consistent themes across the guidance include aligning executive remuneration with business objectives and strategy, considering shareholders' long-term interests, avoiding reward for failure and poor performance, and the importance of timely, constructive dialogue with investors.

NAPF remuneration guidelines

5.223.2   In November 2009, the National Association of Pension Funds (NAPF) wrote to the chairmen of FTSE 350 entities encouraging restraint over executive remuneration and stating that remuneration should be aligned with the long-term interests of shareholders. The NAPF stated that it is *"in the interests of pension funds as long-term investors that company management be well rewarded for delivering outstanding performance"* and made clear that:

■   Pay and performance should be clearly aligned, with a focus on risk. Bonuses should reflect profit levels. For example, if profits have decreased, bonuses should also be lower.

■   Companies should explain in their annual reports how the longer-term interests of shareholders are balanced with those of management and how profits are allocated between capital, remuneration and dividends to shareholders.

■   A significant part of any bonus payment should be deferred into shares.

■   If performance conditions are adjusted because they are no longer realistic, companies should take account of the potential for economic recovery.

5.223.3   In addition to the recommendations described above, the NAPF has stated its support for the UK Corporate Governance Code (2008) and issued voting guidelines in relation to them. At the time of writing, no statement has been made in relation to the recently-issued UK Corporate Governance Code (2010), however, in July 2009 the NAPF stated its support for a progress review by FRC that formed part of the process resulting in the publication of the UK Corporate Governance Code (2010).

5.223.4 The NAPF has also stated its support for the global remuneration principles, a set of guidelines on executive remuneration prepared by a group of UK institutional investors in 2007, applicable to both UK and overseas markets.

5.223.5 The global remuneration principles set out guidelines in three areas as follows:

■ Formulation and implementation of policy. A clear statement of the objectives of remuneration policy should be provided. Companies should avoid paying more than is necessary and avoid rewarding departing directors for poor performance.

■ Dialogue with investors. Such dialogue should ensure that remuneration policy for senior employees and executives is aligned to deliver company strategy that provides the best return to shareholders. Good behaviour should be encouraged and good performance recognised.

■ Other factors. Where senior employees have significant equity holdings, the interests of directors and shareholders are better aligned. Remuneration should be appropriately balanced between long- and short-term elements and should incentivise and encourage retention. Care should be taken in benchmarking and any benchmarking process should be explained.

Further details of the global remuneration principles can be found within NAPF's 'Corporate Governance Policy and Voting Guidelines – 2009', available at www.napf.co.uk.

5.223.6 The NAPF refers to the ABI's guidelines for executive remuneration, anticipating that most institutional investors and issuers will use these as a benchmark for remuneration policy. The ABI's guidelines are described in the following section.

ABI guidelines for executive remuneration

5.223.7 The Association of British Insurers (ABI) published 'Executive remuneration — ABI guidelines on policies and practices' in December 2009. The principles, provisions and guidance represent best practice for listed entities and other entities are encouraged to observe the guidelines. The ABI summarised its views on executive remuneration in its position paper of the same date, as follows:

"Shareholders seek a constructive dialogue that results in remuneration policies that promote the creation of long-term sustainable value...

Shareholders seek remuneration policies that encourage management to deliver long-term business performance in line with corporate strategy to deliver long-term value creation. Structures should be transparent and simple. Remuneration committees should be accountable to shareholders for their decisions and the use of discretion..."

5.223.8   The core remuneration principles set out in the ABI's guidelines are:

■   Remuneration policies and practices should promote longer-term value for shareholders. Remuneration policies should be clearly aligned with the company's objectives and strategy.

■   Consistent with the UK Corporate Governance Code's recommendations, remuneration committees should comprise independent directors who scrutinise remuneration. High quality dialogue between boards and shareholders is important.

■   Remuneration should be aligned with shareholder interests. Remuneration should be set at levels to retain and motivate executives and linked to individual as well as company performance. Benchmarks should be used with caution.

■   The level of reward should be justified by performance and service contracts should be prepared appropriately to support this.

5.223.9   The ABI's more detailed provisions and guidance that support the principles described above cover remuneration committees and their responsibilities, guidance for base pay, bonuses, pensions and contracts and severance and guidance for share-based payment incentive schemes.

5.223.10   Full details of the ABI's guidance can be found at www.ivis.co.uk.

5.223.11   It is worth noting that in light of challenging economic conditions, in September 2008, the ABI drew specific attention to the following points:

■   Remuneration policy should be fully explained and justified, particularly when changes are proposed. Shareholders will carefully scrutinise increases in remuneration, particularly in relation to salaries or annual bonuses.

■   Where a company has underperformed and its share price dropped significantly, this should be taken into account when determining the level of awards under share incentive schemes. It is not appropriate for executives to receive awards of such a size that they are perceived as rewards for failure.

■   Shareholders generally do not favour additional remuneration in relation to succession or retention, particularly where no performance conditions are attached.

■   In the context of the consultation process for share incentive schemes, remuneration committees should ensure that shareholders have adequate time to consider the proposal and that their views are carefully considered. Relevant information related to the consultation should be clearly and fully disclosed.

RiskMetrics Group remuneration guidance

5.223.12 RiskMetrics Group's '2010 RiskMetrics U.K. Remuneration Guidance' is consistent with the NAPF's policy. It comprises general policies and practices as well as more detailed guidance on the components (basic salary, bonuses, long-term incentive plans and termination arrangements in service contracts) of remuneration packages. The general policies include the following:

■ Remuneration and performance measures should be clearly linked with business strategy in order to motivate executives appropriately. Consideration should be given to the attitude to risk and behaviour that a remuneration package may drive.

■ Shareholders should be fully consulted on remuneration policy proposals.

■ Rewards for failure or poor performance should be avoided.

■ Directors' remuneration should be consistent with pay and conditions across the company.

■ Total remuneration is not, generally, expected to increase where profits have declined.

■ One-off retention payments are not justified.

The full guidance can be found at www.riskmetrics.com.

Section V — Audit requirements

5.224 As indicated in the previous sections, SI 2008/410 requires part of the remuneration report ('the auditable part') to be audited. This requirement and the general provisions of the Act in relation to auditors' duties in respect of directors' remuneration information given in financial statements or accompanying them, are discussed below.

5.225 Section 412 of the Companies Act 2006 requires that the information in Schedule 5 to SI 2008/410 must be given in the notes to a company's annual accounts. [CA06 Sec 412]. Section 420 of the Companies Act 2006 requires that, in the case of quoted companies, a remuneration report must be prepared, which must contain the information required by Schedule 8 to SI 2008/410 and comply with any requirement of that Schedule as to how the information is to be set out in the report. [CA06 Secs 420(1); 412(1), (2)].

5.226 Section 498(1) and section 498(2) of the Companies Act 2006 require the auditors to determine whether the accounts (including the notes) and the auditable part of the company's directors' remuneration report (in the case of quoted companies) are in accordance with the accounting records and returns and are required to include a statement in their report if they are not in agreement. [CA06 Sec 498(1), (2)].

5.227 Section 498(4) of the 2006 Act requires that if the requirements of Schedule 5 to SI 2008/410 and, where a remuneration report is required to be prepared (that is, for quoted companies), the requirements of Schedule 8 to SI 2008/410 in respect of the auditable part of that report, are not complied with, the auditors must, so far as they are reasonably able to do so, include in their report the required information. [CA06 Sec 498(4)].

5.228 Section 497 of the 2006 Act requires that if a directors' remuneration report is prepared (that is, for quoted companies only – see para 5.6.3 for definition) the auditors shall report on the auditable part and state in their report whether in their opinion that part (the auditable part) of the directors' remuneration report has been properly prepared in accordance with the Companies Act 2006. [CA06 Sec 497(1)].

5.229 The auditable part of the directors' remuneration report is the part containing the information required by Part 3 of Schedule 8 to SI 2008/410. This has been discussed above under the heading 'Information subject to audit' from paragraph 5.163.

5.230 In October 2002, the APB issued Bulletin 2002/2, 'The United Kingdom Directors' Remuneration Report Regulations 2002'. The Bulletin discusses the auditors' responsibilities with respect to the unaudited part of the directors' remuneration report.

Example – Identification of auditable and non-auditable information

A quoted company is preparing its directors' remuneration report. The company is proposing to mix the auditable information and the non-auditable information within the remuneration report, rather than keeping them as separate parts. Is this acceptable under Schedule 8 to SI 2008/410?

There is no requirement in SI 2008/410 to separate the auditable and the non-auditable information within the remuneration report, or even to state in that report which information has been audited and which has not. However, APB Bulletin 2002/2, 'The United Kingdom Directors' Remuneration Report Regulations 2002', considers the practical difficulties in describing, in the audit opinion, the scope of the audit when part but not all of a section in the annual report has been audited. It is insufficient for the directors and auditors of a company to assume that the user of the financial statements has existing knowledge to be able to determine which information has and which has not been audited.

The bulletin suggests that the auditors should discuss the format of the directors' remuneration report with management before the year end and should agree, possibly by including terms in the letter of engagement, that the auditable and the non-auditable parts of the remuneration report will be clearly distinguished. Where this is the case, a cross-reference in the audit opinion to the identifiable audited part will satisfy the need to make clear the scope of the opinion.

However, where the remuneration report does not clearly distinguish the auditable and non-auditable information, the audit report should identify specifically, by page and paragraph number or heading if necessary, each section of the directors' remuneration report that has been audited. This will need to be sufficient to enable the user to identify the information that has and has not been audited.

5.231 Also, under the Listing Rules, the scope of the auditors' report on the financial statements must cover the disclosures specified below. The auditors must state in their report if, in their opinion, the company has not complied with any of these requirements and, in such a case, must include in their report, so far as they are reasonably able to do so, a statement giving details of the non-compliance. [LR 9.8.12R]. The relevant disclosures are as follows:

- Detail of elements in the remuneration package (see para 5.165).

- Information on share options (see para 5.170).

- Details of other long-term incentive schemes (see para 5.189.2).

- Details of defined benefit schemes (see para 5.197).

- Details of contributions to money purchase schemes (see para 5.194).

[The next paragraph is 5.233].

Section VI — Group situations

5.233 Common problems arise with the disclosure of directors' emoluments in a group context. Consider the following examples where a director of a parent company has also been nominated to the board of one of its subsidiaries. In all the situations it is assumed that the director is remunerated by the parent company in connection with his services as director of the parent company, but also receives payment for services to the subsidiary (as set out in the examples below). It is also assumed that all the relevant information concerning emoluments is available to the reporting company and that both companies are private companies (that is, the relevant disclosures are governed by Schedule 5 to SI 2008/410).

Example 1 – Director paid by subsidiary

Where the subsidiary pays the director directly in respect of his services as a director of the subsidiary.

In this situation the parent company will need to disclose, as directors' emoluments, the aggregate of the amount paid to the director in respect of his services as a director of the parent company and the amount he receives in respect of his services as a director of the subsidiary. [SI 2008/410 5 Sch 7(2)]. This will be the case even if the parent is not preparing consolidated financial statements.

The subsidiary will also need to disclose the amount paid to the director by the subsidiary in respect of the director's services to that subsidiary, as directors' emoluments, in its own financial statements.

Example 2 – Payment passed back to parent

Where the subsidiary pays the director, but the director is liable to account to the parent company for the remuneration he receives in respect of his services as director of the subsidiary.

In this situation, the notes to the financial statements of the parent company need only disclose, as directors' emoluments, the amounts paid to the director in respect of his services as director of the parent company.

The amount paid by the subsidiary in respect of the director's services to that subsidiary, needs to be disclosed, as directors' emoluments, in the subsidiary's financial statements. Where, however, the director is subsequently released from the obligation to account for the remuneration, the remuneration must be disclosed in a note to the first financial statements of the parent company in which it is practicable to show it, and the remuneration must be distinguished from other remuneration. [SI 2008/410 5 Sch 8(2)].

Example 3 – Parent recharges subsidiary

Where the parent company pays the director directly and recharges the subsidiary for his services as a director of the subsidiary.

The aggregate amount that needs to be disclosed, as directors' emoluments, in the parent company's financial statements is the same as in example 1.

The notes to the subsidiary's financial statements must disclose, as directors' emoluments, the amount receivable by the director for services to the subsidiary, that is, in this situation, the amount recharged by the parent company in respect of the director's services.

Example 4 – Parent does not recharge subsidiary

Where the parent company pays the director directly, but no recharge is made to the subsidiary.

Again, the aggregate amount that needs to be disclosed, as directors' emoluments, in the parent company's financial statements is the same as in example 1.

The notes to the subsidiary's financial statements, however, must include details of the remuneration paid by the parent company in respect of the director's services to the subsidiary. An explanation to the effect that the charge for director's remuneration has been borne by the parent company may be useful, although there is no requirement in the Act to do so. If it is necessary for the parent company to apportion the director's remuneration, the directors may apportion it in any way they consider appropriate. [SI 2008/410 5 Sch 7(6)].

Practical difficulties in ascertaining remuneration

5.234 Practical difficulties may arise in connection with disclosure of remuneration in a subsidiary's financial statements where a director of the subsidiary is also:

- a director or employee of the parent and is paid by the parent; or

- a director of another subsidiary and is paid by that other subsidiary.

5.235   In such cases, it is often difficult to ascertain the emoluments of the director that are paid to or receivable by him in respect of his services to the subsidiary in question. This difficulty may be aggravated if there is no charge made to the subsidiary by the payer of the emoluments. It may also sometimes be aggravated by a desire on the part of either the parent or the subsidiary to limit the amount of disclosure in the subsidiary's financial statements, if, for instance, the parent-appointed director is more highly rewarded than other directors.

5.236   Paragraph 6 of Schedule 5 to SI 2008/410 states that the schedule requires information to be given regarding emoluments, pensions and compensation for loss of office only so far as it is contained in the company's books and papers or the company has the right to obtain it from the persons concerned.

5.237   As noted in paragraph 5.9 above, section 412(5) of the Companies Act 2006 states that *"...it is the duty of any director of a company, and any person who is or has at any time in the preceding five years been a director of the company, to give notice to the company of such matters relating to himself as may be necessary for the purposes of regulations under this section"*.

5.238   Where, despite the requirements of section 412 of the 2006 Act, there are difficulties in obtaining information one or more of the steps described below might be taken.

5.239   If the subsidiary is a party to the directors' service agreement, and that agreement stipulates what the director is paid in respect of his services to the subsidiary, then the information is contained in the subsidiary's books and papers and the subsidiary should disclose it.

5.240   If the subsidiary is not a party to the service agreement (possibly because the agreement is with the parent or a fellow subsidiary), the subsidiary or its directors should *'make reasonable efforts'* to obtain the information, for instance by asking the parent or fellow subsidiary for details of the terms of the service agreement, or by obtaining a detailed breakdown of any management charge.

5.241   If any fellow director of the subsidiary has obtained the necessary information in his capacity as a director of the subsidiary, he should disclose it to the board of the subsidiary. The information will then be under the subsidiary's control and it should disclose it.

5.242   If the information needed is not obtainable by any of the above means, companies often make an apportionment. This is relatively simple where a director is a director of both the subsidiary and the parent, but spends the vast majority of his time in an executive capacity on the subsidiary's affairs. It is less easy if the director is also a director of a large number of different subsidiaries. Schedule 5 to SI 2008/410 permits apportionment (see para 5.24.2 above). We suggest that where apportionment is relatively straightforward it may be the best way of determining the emoluments to be disclosed in the subsidiary.

5.243   The above steps may be summarised as follows:

- Inspect the subsidiary's relevant books and papers including service contracts to which it is party.

- Analyse any management charges for details of emoluments charged.

- Request information from other group companies that have service contracts with directors to which the company is not a party or from the director himself.

- Apportion where total emoluments are known and the apportionment can be made with a high degree of confidence and accuracy.

These steps should result in disclosure in the majority of cases.

5.244   If, in rare circumstances, the necessary information is not contained in the company's books and papers and the company does not have the right to obtain it from the director, the company is not required to disclose it (see para 5.236 above). In addition, the auditors would not be able to give the information required in their report (see para 5.10 above).

5.245   Where this situation occurs it might be that the financial statements would not give a true and fair view if no disclosure were made of the facts. Hence, in these circumstances, if the financial statements are to give a true and fair view, some narrative needs to be given. Table 5.38 in paragraph 5.247 below is an example of such a note.

5.246   We suggest that example 1 below and examples 2 and 3 in paragraph 5.247 would be appropriate notes for three situations that may arise where no information is available.

Example 1 – Recharge cannot be separately identified

A recharge is made to the subsidiary by a parent company or fellow subsidiary, but the management charge includes other costs and the emoluments cannot be separately identified.

'The above details of directors' emoluments do not include the emoluments of Mr X, which are paid by the parent company (fellow subsidiary) and recharged to the company as part of a management charge. This management charge, which in 20XX amounted to £95,000 also includes a recharge of administration costs borne by the parent company (fellow subsidiary) on behalf of the company and it is not possible to identify separately the amount of Mr X's emoluments.'

5.247   It is envisaged that this situation would be very rare as normally a full breakdown of management charges should be possible.

Table 5.38 – Directors' emoluments in a group situation

The Telegraph plc – Annual Report and Accounts – 31 December 1994

Directors (extract)

During the year a charge of £871,192 was made by Hollinger Inc. under the services agreement referred to in note 26(c). It is not possible to identify whether any portion of the charge relates to services provided by any director of the company.

26(c) Services agreement

Under the terms of a services agreement with Hollinger Inc., for so long as Mr Black remains chairman of the board, the Telegraph will bear 66.7% of the cost of the office of the chairman incurred by Hollinger or such other proportion as may be agreed from time to time by the Audit Committee. Other services will be provided at cost and may include the arrangement of insurance, assistance in the arrangement of finance and assistance and advice on acquisitions, disposal and joint venture arrangements. Charges to the company in respect of Mr Black's office and these other services amounted to £871,192 in 1994 *(1993: £1,044,000)*.

32. Ultimate parent company

Hollinger Inc., incorporated in Canada and listed on the Toronto, Montreal and Vancouver stock exchanges, is regarded by the directors of the company as the company's ultimate parent company.

The largest group in which the results of the company are consolidated is that of which Hollinger Inc. is the parent company. The consolidated accounts of Hollinger Inc. may be obtained from Montreal Trust Company of Canada, 151 Front Street West, 8th Floor, Toronto, Ontario, Canada M5J 2N1.

The smallest such group is that of which DT Holdings Limited is the parent company, whose consolidated accounts may be obtained from 21 Wilson Street, London EC2M 2TQ. DT Holdings Limited is registered in England and Wales.

Example 2 – Non-executive role in subsidiaries

The director is an executive of the parent and also a director of a large number of other subsidiaries for which he carries on work. He is paid by the parent company which makes no recharge to the subsidiaries. His role is chiefly that of non-executive director of the subsidiaries overseeing the subsidiaries' affairs on behalf of the parent.

'The emoluments of Mr X are paid by the parent company. Mr X's services to this company and to a number of fellow subsidiaries are of a non-executive nature and his emoluments are deemed to be wholly attributable to his services to the parent company. Accordingly, the above details include no emoluments in respect of Mr X.'

Example 3 – Executive role in subsidiaries

The director is also a director of a number of other subsidiaries for which he carries on work. He is paid by the parent company that makes no recharge to the subsidiaries. His role is that of an executive director of each of the subsidiaries.

'The emoluments of Mr X are paid by the parent company which makes no recharge to the company. Mr X is a director of the parent company and a number of fellow subsidiaries and it is not possible to make an accurate

> *apportionment of his emoluments in respect of each of the subsidiaries. Accordingly, the above details include no emoluments in respect of Mr X. His total emoluments are included in the aggregate of directors' emoluments disclosed in the financial statements of the parent company.'*

5.248   It is suggested that where a similar situation applies, but the emoluments are paid by a fellow subsidiary, there should normally be a recharge. This is because the situation of a subsidiary paying emoluments of group directors normally only arises with a group services company and such a company would usually recharge for the services it performs. In such a case, the note would not be needed, because the appropriate amount to be disclosed should be ascertainable.

Annex 1 — UK Corporate Governance Codes (2008) and (2010)

The UK Corporate Governance Code (2008) (formerly the Combined Code on Corporate Governance (2008)), applicable for financial years beginning prior to 29 June 2010, and the UK Corporate Governance Code (2010), applicable for financial years beginning on or after 29 June 2010, are dealt with in detail in chapter 4. The main principles, supporting principles and related good practice provisions concerning directors' remuneration are set out below for each code.

UK Corporate Governance Code (2008) – financial years beginning prior to 29 June 2010

Section 1 of the UK Corporate Governance Code (2008) contains two main principles relating to directors' remuneration. The Listing Rules require UK listed entities to provide a statement on how they have applied the principles of the UK Corporate Governance Code (2008) and to give a statement confirming whether they have complied with its provisions (providing an explanation where they have not complied). The main principles, supporting principles and related best practice provisions are described below.

The level and make-up of remuneration

The first main principle concerning directors' remuneration states that levels of remuneration should be sufficient to attract, retain and motivate directors of the quality required to run the company successfully, but companies should avoid paying more than is necessary for this purpose. A significant proportion of executive directors' remuneration should be structured to link rewards to corporate and individual performance. [CC B.1].

This is supplemented by the supporting principle, which states that the remuneration committee should judge where to position their company relative to other companies, but should use comparisons with caution in view of the risk of an upward ratchet of remuneration levels with no corresponding improvement in performance. They should also be sensitive to pay and employment conditions elsewhere in the group, especially when determining annual salary increases. [CC B.1].

The following additional recommendations in relation to remuneration policy were made as part of the best practice provisions:

- Performance-related elements of remuneration should form a significant proportion of the total remuneration package of executive directors and should be designed to align their interests with those of the shareholders and to give those directors keen incentives to perform at the highest levels. The remuneration committee should follow the provisions in Schedule A of the UK Corporate Governance Code (2008), which offers additional guidance in designing performance-related remuneration schemes.

- Executive share options should not be offered at a discount, unless permitted by the relevant provisions of the Listing Rules.

- Levels of remuneration for non-executive directors should reflect the time commitment and responsibilities of the role. Remuneration for non-executive directors should not include share options but if, exceptionally, options are granted, shareholder approval should be sought in advance and any shares acquired by exercise of the options should be held until at least one year after the non-executive director leaves the board. Holding share options could be relevant to determining a non-executive director's independence.

- Where a company releases an executive director to serve as a non-executive director elsewhere, the remuneration report should include a statement as to whether or not the director will retain such earnings and, if so, what the remuneration is.

[CC B.1.1-B.1.4].

The best practice provisions also include the following relating to service contracts and compensation:

- Remuneration committees should carefully consider what compensation commitments (including pension contributions and all other elements) their directors' terms of appointment would entail in the event of early termination. The aim should be to avoid rewarding poor performance. They should take a robust line on reducing compensation to reflect departing directors' obligations to mitigate loss.

- Notice or contract periods should be set at one year or less. If it is necessary to offer longer notice or contract periods to new directors recruited from outside, such periods should reduce to one year or less after the initial period.

[CC B.1.5-B.1.6].

Procedure

The main principle in this area is that there should be a formal and transparent procedure for developing policy on executive remuneration and for fixing the remuneration packages of individual directors. No director should be involved in deciding his or her own remuneration. [CC B.2].

In support of this main principle are the following supporting principles:

■ The remuneration committee should consult the chairman and/or chief executive about their proposals relating to the remuneration of other executive directors. It should also be responsible for appointing any consultants in respect of executive director remuneration. Where executive directors or senior management are involved in advising or supporting the remuneration committee, care should be taken to recognise and avoid conflicts of interest.

■ The chairman of the board should ensure that the company maintains contact as required with its principal shareholders about remuneration in the same way as for other matters.

[CC B.2].

These principles are further supplemented by the following best practice provisions:

■ The board should establish a remuneration committee of at least three, or in the case of smaller companies (that is, those falling outside the FTSE 350 throughout the year immediately prior to the reporting year), two independent non-executive directors. In addition the company chairman may also be a member of, but not chair, the committee if he or she was considered independent on appointment as chairman. The remuneration committee should make available its terms of reference on request and on the company website, explaining its role and the authority delegated to it by the board. Where remuneration consultants are appointed, a statement should be made available (in the same way as described for the terms of reference) of whether they have any other connection with the company.

■ The remuneration committee should have delegated responsibility for setting remuneration for all executive directors and the chairman, including pension rights and any compensation payments. The committee should also recommend and monitor the level and structure of senior managements' remuneration. The definition of 'senior management' for this purpose should be determined by the board, but should normally include the first layer of management below board level. [Note that disclosure of the remuneration committee's activities throughout the year is considered to be good practice.]

■ The board itself or, where required by the articles of association, the shareholders should determine the non-executive directors' remuneration within the limits set in the articles of association. Where permitted by the articles, the board may, however, delegate this responsibility to a committee, which might include the chief executive.

- Shareholders should be invited specifically to approve all new long-term incentive schemes (as defined in the Listing Rules) and significant changes to existing schemes, save in the circumstances permitted by the Listing Rules.

[CC B.2.1-B.2.4].

Schedule A – Provisions on the design of performance-related remuneration

Schedule A of the UK Corporate Governance Code (2008), which is referred to above, deals with the design of performance-related remuneration and includes the following:

- The remuneration committee needs to consider whether the directors should be eligible for annual bonuses. If so, performance conditions should be relevant, stretching and designed to enhance shareholder value. Upper limits should be set and disclosed. There may be a case for part of the bonuses to be paid in shares to be held for a significant period.

- The remuneration committee needs to consider whether the directors should be eligible for benefits under long-term incentive schemes. Traditional share option schemes should be compared to other kinds of long-term incentive scheme. Generally, shares granted or other forms of deferred remuneration should not vest, and options should not be exercisable, in less than three years. Directors should be encouraged to hold their shares for a further period after vesting or exercise, subject to the need to finance any costs of acquisition and associated tax liabilities.

- Any new long-term incentive schemes that are proposed should be approved by shareholders and should preferably replace any existing schemes or at least form part of a well considered overall plan, which should incorporate existing schemes. Furthermore, the total rewards potentially available should not be excessive.

- Payouts or grants under all incentive schemes, including new grants under existing share option schemes, need to be subject to challenging performance criteria reflecting the company's objectives. Consideration needs to be given to criteria that reflect the company's performance relative to a group of comparator companies in some key variables, for example total shareholder return.

- Normally, grants under executive share option and other long-term incentive schemes should be phased rather than awarded in one large block.

- Generally, only basic salary should be pensionable.

- The remuneration committee needs to consider the pension consequences and associated costs to the company of basic salary increases and any other changes in pensionable remuneration, especially for directors close to retirement.

[CC Sch A].

UK Corporate Governance Code (2010) – financial years beginning on or after 29 June 2010

Section D of the UK Corporate Governance Code (2010) contains two main principles relating to directors' remuneration. The Listing Rules require all companies with a Premium Listing of equity shares to provide a statement on how they have applied the principles of the UK Corporate Governance Code (2010) and to give a statement confirming whether they have complied with its provisions (providing an explanation where they have not complied). The main principles, supporting principles and related best practice provisions are described below.

The level and make-up of remuneration

The first main principle concerning directors' remuneration states that levels of remuneration should be sufficient to attract, retain and motivate directors of the quality required to run the company successfully, but companies should avoid paying more than is necessary for this purpose. A significant proportion of executive directors' remuneration should be structured to link rewards to corporate and individual performance. [UK CGC D.1].

This is supplemented by a supporting principle, which states that performance-related elements of executive directors' remuneration should be stretching and designed to promote the long-term success of the company. The remuneration committee should judge where to position their company relative to other companies, but should use comparisons with caution in view of the risk of an upward ratchet of remuneration levels with no corresponding improvement in performance. They should also be sensitive to pay and employment conditions elsewhere in the group, especially when determining annual salary increases. [UK CGC D.1].

The following additional recommendations in relation to remuneration policy are made as part of the best practice provisions:

- The remuneration committee should follow the provisions in Schedule A of the UK Corporate Governance Code (2010), which offers additional guidance in designing performance-related remuneration schemes.

- Where a company releases an executive director to serve as a non-executive director elsewhere, the remuneration report should include a statement as to whether or not the director will retain such earnings and, if so, what the remuneration is.

- Levels of remuneration for non-executive directors should reflect the time commitment and responsibilities of the role. Remuneration for non-executive directors should not include share options but if, exceptionally, options are granted, shareholder approval should be sought in advance and any shares acquired by exercise of the options should be held until at least one year after the non-executive director leaves the board. Holding share options could be relevant to determining a non-executive director's independence.

[UK CGC D.1.1-D.1.3].

The best practice provisions also include the following relating to service contracts and compensation:

- Remuneration committees should carefully consider what compensation commitments (including pension contributions and all other elements) their directors' terms of appointment would entail in the event of early termination. The aim should be to avoid rewarding poor performance. They should take a robust line on reducing compensation to reflect departing directors' obligations to mitigate loss.

- Notice or contract periods should be set at one year or less. If it is necessary to offer longer notice or contract periods to new directors recruited from outside, such periods should reduce to one year or less after the initial period.

[UK CGC D.1.4-D.1.5].

Procedure

The main principle in this area is that there should be a formal and transparent procedure for developing policy on executive remuneration and for fixing the remuneration packages of individual directors. No director should be involved in deciding his or her own remuneration. [UK CGC D.2].

In support of this main principle are the following supporting principles:

- The remuneration committee should consult the chairman and/or chief executive about their proposals relating to the remuneration of other executive directors. It should also be responsible for appointing any consultants in respect of executive director remuneration. Where executive directors or senior management are involved in advising or supporting the remuneration committee, care should be taken to recognise and avoid conflicts of interest.

- The chairman of the board should ensure that the company maintains contact as required with its principal shareholders about remuneration.

[UK CGC D.2].

These principles are further supplemented by the following best practice provisions:

- The board should establish a remuneration committee of at least three, or in the case of smaller companies (that is, those falling outside the FTSE 350 throughout the year immediately prior to the reporting year), two independent non-executive directors. In addition the company chairman may also be a member of, but not chair, the committee if he or she was considered independent on appointment as chairman. The remuneration committee should make available its terms of reference, on request and on the company's website, explaining its role and the authority delegated to it by the board. Where remuneration consultants are appointed, a statement should be made available (in the same way as described for the terms of reference) of whether they have any other connection with the company.

■ The remuneration committee should have delegated responsibility for setting remuneration for all executive directors and the chairman, including pension rights and any compensation payments. The committee should also recommend and monitor the level and structure of senior managements' remuneration. The definition of 'senior management' for this purpose should be determined by the board, but should normally include the first layer of management below board level. [Note that disclosure of the remuneration committee's activities throughout the year is considered to be good practice.]

■ The board itself or, where required by the articles of association, the shareholders should determine the non-executive directors' remuneration within the limits set in the articles of association. Where permitted by the articles, the board may, however, delegate this responsibility to a committee, which might include the chief executive.

■ Shareholders should be invited specifically to approve all new long-term incentive schemes (as defined in the Listing Rules) and significant changes to existing schemes, save in the circumstances permitted by the Listing Rules.

[UK CGC D.2.1-D.2.4].

Schedule A – The design of performance-related remuneration for executive directors

Schedule A of the UK Corporate Governance Code (2010), which is referred to above, deals with the design of performance-related remuneration and includes the following:

■ The remuneration committee needs to consider whether the directors should be eligible for annual bonuses. If so, performance conditions should be relevant, stretching and designed to promote the long-term success of the company. Upper limits should be set and disclosed. There may be a case for part of the bonuses to be paid in shares to be held for a significant period.

■ The remuneration committee needs to consider whether the directors should be eligible for benefits under long-term incentive schemes. Traditional share option schemes should be compared to other kinds of long-term incentive scheme. Executive share option schemes should not be offered at a discount, except as permitted by the Listing Rules.

■ Generally, shares granted or other forms of deferred remuneration should not vest, and options should not be exercisable, in less than three years.

Directors should be encouraged to hold their shares for a further period after vesting or exercise, subject to the need to finance any costs of acquisition and associated tax liabilities.

- Any new long-term incentive schemes that are proposed should be approved by shareholders and should preferably replace any existing schemes or at least form part of a well considered overall plan, which should incorporate existing schemes. Furthermore, the total rewards potentially available should not be excessive.

- Payouts or grants under all incentive schemes, including new grants under existing share option schemes, need to be subject to challenging performance criteria reflecting the company's objectives, including non-financial performance metrics where appropriate. Remuneration incentives should be compatible with risk policies and systems.

- Normally, grants under executive share option and other long-term incentive schemes should be phased rather than awarded in one large block.

- Consideration should be given to the use of provisions that permit the company to reclaim variable components in exceptional circumstances of misstatement or misconduct.

- Generally, only basic salary should be pensionable. Remuneration committees need to consider the pension consequences and associated costs to the company of basic salary increases and any other changes in pensionable remuneration, especially for directors close to retirement.

[UK CGC Sch A].

Annex 2 — Directors' remuneration disclosure — decision tree

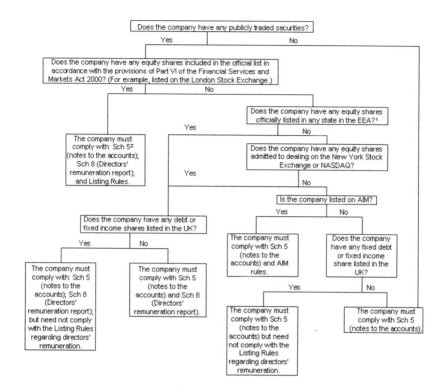

[1] At the time of writing the EEA comprises the member states of the European Union plus Norway, Iceland and Liechtenstein.

[2] Note that paragraphs 2 to 5 of Schedule 5 to the 'Large and Medium-sized Companies and Groups (Accounts and Reports) Regulations 2008' (SI 2008/410) do not apply to quoted entities.

All of the above entities have also to comply with the Companies Act 2006 requirements concerning the content of the Directors' report.

Loans and other transactions involving directors

Chapter 6

Loans and other transactions involving directors

Introduction

6.1   Transactions between a company and its directors are governed by company law to ensure that directors do not put themselves in a position where their personal interest and the interest of their company conflict.

6.2   The table below summarises the key items covered within this chapter and the relevant sections under the 2006 Act.

	2006 Companies Act requirements
Definition of a connected person (para 6.18)	Sections 252-255
Transactions with directors (loans, quasi-loans, credits and guarantees) (para 6.30)	Sections 197-214
Disclosure of transactions with directors (loans, quasi-loans, credits and guarantees) (para 6.82)	Section 413 and paragraph 72 of Schedule 1 to SI 2008/410 (related party transactions, see para 6.107)
Substantial property transactions (para 6.97)	Sections 190-196
Transactions with directors who are sole members (para 6.118)	Section 231
Money-lending and banking companies (para 6.121)	Section 413(8), paragraph 72 of Schedule 1 and paragraph 92 of Schedule 2 to SI 2008/410 (related party transactions, see para 6.107)
Penalties for failure to disclose transactions – Civil remedy – Criminal sanctions	Section 213, 214 Not applicable

6.3   Listed companies and those traded on AIM or the PLUS-quoted market are required to make additional disclosures of transactions between a company and its directors or their related parties to comply with the UKLA Listing and Disclosure and Transparency Rules, the AIM rules or the PLUS-quoted market rules (see from para 6.111). In addition, the transactions with directors and key management caught by the related party provisions of Schedule 1 to SI 2008/410 (refer to para 6.107) require disclosure. IFRS reporters complying with IAS 24, 'Related party disclosures', (see chapter 29 of Manual of Accounting – IFRS for the UK) will meet the related party disclosure requirements under the 2006 Act. This was clarified by the European Commission's Accounting Regulatory Committee (ARC) at its November 2007 meeting. For UK GAAP reporters, the 2006 Act may introduce additional disclosures over those contained within FRS 8, 'Related party disclosures' (see chapter 29 of Manual of Accounting – UK GAAP).

6.4 This chapter initially sets out key definitions, then deals with loans, quasi-loans and credit transactions as they apply to public and private companies. It explains their legality, the disclosure requirements for transactions with directors and officers and the sanctions imposed if the rules are breached. It deals with the procedural and disclosure requirements of other types of transactions or arrangements involving a company and a director. It also deals with the special provisions for such transactions that apply exclusively to money lending companies and banking companies. Lastly, it mentions declarations of interest to the board. In each case the requirements set out by the Companies Act 2006 are stated with any transitional provisions from the 1985 Act that still apply.

Definitions

6.5 The definitions that follow are essential to an understanding of the types of transaction that the Act regulates.

Director

6.6 The word 'director' as used in the Act includes any person who occupies the position of director by whatever name called. [CA06 Sec 250]. This means that it is the person's responsibilities and duties and not their title that determines whether or not somebody is a director. A director is a person who actively takes part in board meetings and votes at them. 'Directors' may be called governors, managers or trustees.

6.7 Directors can be of three kinds: *de jure* directors (that is, directors who have been validly appointed as such); *de facto* directors (that is, directors who assume to act as directors without having been appointed validly or at all); and shadow directors. Shadow directors and *de facto* directors are considered below.

Shadow director

6.8 A 'shadow director' is defined in the 2006 Companies Act as *"...a person in accordance with whose directions or instructions the directors of the company are accustomed to act"*. The section continues, *"a person is not to be regarded as a shadow director by reason only that the directors act on advice given by him in a professional capacity"*. [CA06 Sec 251(1), (2)]. There is a similar definition in section 22(5) of the Company Directors Disqualification Act 1986 (CDDA 1986). Important guidelines on the meaning of the definition in the CDDA 1986 were set out in *Secretary of State v Deverell [2000] 2BCLC 133*, which reviewed the earlier cases. The facts of this case were as follows. D and H had declared themselves consultants, but they were much more closely connected with the management of the company than that would suggest. The Court found that D bossed everyone around including the directors (who habitually followed what he said) and that H took the lead in important matters relating to the company's affairs, although not as directly as D. Both were held to be shadow directors. The guidelines are outlined briefly below.

6.9   'Directions and instructions' – For the purposes of the definition in section 22(5) of the CDDA 1986, the question whether a particular communication constituted a direction or instruction had to be answered in the light of the evidence. Non-professional advice could come within the definition. The proviso, excepting advice given '...*in a professional capacity*', appears to assume that advice given generally is, or may come, within that statutory description. Moreover, the concepts of direction and instruction do not exclude the concept of advice since all three share the common feature of 'guidance'. The directions or instructions do not have to extend over all or most of the company's corporate governance activities, but must cover at least those matters essential to the company's corporate governance, including its financial affairs. Frequent non-professional advice usually acted upon by the board would be sufficient.

6.10   'Accustomed to act' – It will not always be necessary (although it would be sufficient) to show that, in the face of the 'directions or instructions', the properly appointed directors (that is, the whole board of directors) cast themselves in a subservient role or surrendered their respective discretions. It is not necessary to demonstrate a degree of compulsion beyond the fact that the whole board was accustomed to act in accordance with the directions or instructions. Further, it is not necessary for the shadow director to lurk in the shadows although he/she might frequently do so. An example was given where a foreign resident owns all the shares in a company operating openly through a local board of directors. From time to time the owner gives directions to the local board what to do but takes no part in management himself/herself. The judge considered that the owner may be a shadow director although he or she takes no steps to hide the part played in the company's affairs.

6.11   The consequences of being found to be a shadow director have particular relevance if the company goes into insolvent liquidation. For instance, in an insolvent liquidation a shadow director may be liable with the directors and *de facto* directors (a) to be disqualified if their conduct makes them unfit to be concerned in the management of company; and (b) to contribute to the company's assets under the wrongful trading provisions.

De facto director

6.12 The distinction between a *de facto* director and a shadow director has been further clarified in the *Deverell* case mentioned above by subdividing *de facto* directors into two types: *de facto* directors type 1 (that is, directors who assume to act, claim to be and are held out by the company as being directors); and *de facto* directors type 2 (that is, directors who directly assume the functions of the directors and act on an equal footing with those who are but without having any sort of label). However, the judge expressed no view on whether the categories of shadow directors or *de facto* directors are mutually exclusive. The following cases indicate the factors that the courts will take into account in ascertaining whether a person is a *de facto* director.

6.13 It was held in *Secretary of State v Tjolle* [1998] IBCLC 333 that there is no one decisive test of whether a person is a *de facto* director. The Court had to take account of all the relevant factors, including whether or not the company considered the individual a director, whether the individual used the title, whether the individual had proper information (for example, access to management accounts) on which to base decisions, whether the individual had to make major decisions and so on. The question was then, whether the individual was part of the corporate governing structure. It followed that someone who had no, or only peripheral, knowledge of matters of vital company concern (for example, financial state) and had no right, legal or *de facto*, to access such matters would not be regarded by the law as in substance a director.

6.14 In the *Tjolle* case, K used the title director principally in the form 'sales and marketing director'. She did not have real access to, or responsibility for, the financial records. The Court held that the use of the title 'director' did not make her a *de facto* director, because she was not in fact directing the company. K was a manager, but she did not form part of the real corporate governance of the company. There was no function she performed that could only properly be discharged by a director. She was not, therefore, a *de facto* director.

6.15 In *Re Kaytech International plc* [1999] 2 BCLC 351 the Court had to decide whether P was a *de facto* or shadow director. P had been deeply and openly involved in the company's affairs. Although he had done his best to avoid being seen as a director, using his office as company secretary as a camouflage, on some very important occasions he acted as a director. For all practical purposes the company was run by K (who was a director) and P. Between them they were its owners. It was essentially a quasi-partnership although P, owning only 20 per cent, might be called the junior partner. K assumed the task of making the final decisions and had the casting vote. Even so, P was held to be a *de facto* director as he was openly acting as a director and was held out as such.

Alternate director

6.16 The position of an 'alternate director' is determined by the articles of association of a company. If the articles adopted are those of Table A under the

Companies (Tables A to F) Regulations of the 1985 or the 2006 Act, the alternate director has the following position:

- He/she is appointed and can be removed by the same director of the company.

- If the potential alternate director is not already a director, his/her appointment must be approved by a resolution of the board.

- If the director who appointed the alternate director ceases to be a director, the appointment of the alternate ceases immediately.

- The alternate director is, unless the articles provide otherwise, a director of the company, and can, at meetings of the board, fulfil all the functions of the director appointing him/her, in the absence of that director. Attendance and voting at board meetings is only permitted when the appointing director is absent.

6.17 Where the term 'director' is used in this chapter, it includes references to directors (both *de facto* and *de jure*), shadow directors, and alternate directors.

Connected persons

6.18 A 'connected person' is a person who is connected with a director of a company and is either an individual or a legal person (for example, a company). A connected person is defined by section 252 of the 2006 Act as any of the following:

(a) A member of the director's family (see further para 6.19). [CA06 Secs 252(2)(a), 253].

(b) A body corporate with which the director is connected (see further para 6.20). [CA06 Secs 252(2)(b), 254].

(c) A person acting in his capacity as a trustee of any trust in either of the following situations

  - The trust includes as a beneficiary the director, a member of the director's family or a body corporate with which the director is connected (see further from para 6.19).

  - The trust confers a power on the trustees that may be used to benefit the director, a member of the director's family or a body corporate with which the director is connected.[CA06 Sec 252(2)(c)].

  However, a person acting as trustee of either an employee share scheme or a pension scheme is not connected with a director merely by virtue of that trusteeship. [CA06 Sec 252(2)(c)].

(d) A partner of the director or of a person who is connected with him under (a), (b) or (c) above. [CA06 Sec 252(2)(d)].

(e) A firm that is a legal person in which one of the following applies:

- The director is a partner, or persons connected with him/her under (a), (b) or (c) above are partners.

- Another firm is a partner, and the director or persons connected with him/her under (a), (b) or (c) above are partners of that other firm. [CA06 Sec 252(2)(e)].

This is particularly relevant in Scotland, as in accordance with Scots law, a firm is a legal person distinct from the partners of whom it is composed, but each partner can still be compelled to pay the firm's debts.

However, none of the above persons are connected if they themselves are also directors of the company. [CA06 Sec 252(3)].

Members of a director's family

6.19   The members of a director's family are defined as:

- The director's spouse, civil partner or any other person with whom the director lives as a partner in an enduring family relationship.

- The director's children or step-children.

- The children or step-children of the directors' partner who the director lives with as a partner in an enduring family relationship and who live with the director and are under 18 (but are not themselves the director's children or step-children).

- The director's parents.

[CA06 Sec 253].

Body corporate with which a director is connected

6.20   A director is 'connected' with a body corporate if, the director, together with the persons connected with him, satisfy either of the following two conditions:

- They are *interested* (according to the rules set out in Schedule 1 to the 2006 Act) in at least 20 per cent of its equity share capital (excluding any shares held as treasury shares).

- They are entitled to *exercise or control the exercise* of more than 20 per cent of the voting power at any general meeting (excluding any voting rights attached to any shares held as treasury shares).

[CA06 Sec 254(2)-(5)].

For simplicity, a body corporate (that is, an entity incorporated in Great Britain or elsewhere, but excluding a Scottish firm) is referred to below as a company. A person connected with a director can be a foreign-registered company.

6.21 For the purposes of establishing whether a director is 'connected' with a company, a director's *interest* in at least 20 per cent of the equity share capital, or his ability to *exercise or control the exercise* of 20 per cent of the voting power, may be either *direct* (that is, he or his connected parties own the shares or control the votes) or *indirect* (that is, a company that he or his connected parties 'control' owns the shares or controls the votes). [CA06 Sec 254(4); CA06 1 Sch 5]. These rules are set out below.

Control of body corporate

6.22 In determining whether the director and those connected with him can *control the exercise* of more than 20 per cent of the voting power of a company in general meeting, any votes held *indirectly* by a director through another company are to be included in the calculation, but only if the director 'controls' that second company. [CA06 Sec 254(4), 255(4)]. A director of a company is deemed to 'control' that second company if, but only if, both the following two conditions in section 255(2) of the 2006 Act are satisfied:

■ The director, or any person connected with him/her is *interested* in any part of the equity share capital of that second company, or is entitled to *exercise or control the exercise* of any part of the voting power at any general meeting of that second company.

■ The director, the persons connected with him/her and the other directors of the first company, together, are *interested* in more than 50 per cent of the second company's share capital (excluding any shares in the company held as treasury shares) or are entitled to *exercise or control the exercise* of more 50 per cent of that voting power (excluding any voting rights attached to any shares in the company held as treasury shares).

[CA06 Sec 255(2), (5)].

Sections 254 and 255 of the 2006 Act are illustrated in example 4 in paragraph 6.25 below.

Interests in shares

6.23 Under the above provisions, a director's *interests* in shares must be aggregated with those of his connected persons. Schedule 1 to the 2006 Act lays down rules for determining whether a person is interested in shares. These state that a person is interested in shares if a company is interested in them and either of the following two conditions are met:

■ The person is entitled to exercise or control the exercise of more than 50 per cent of that company's voting power at general meetings.

■ That company or its directors are accustomed to act in accordance with his directions or instructions.

[CA06 1 Sch 5].

See also examples 2 and 3 in paragraph 6.25 below.

Limits on aggregation

6.24   For the purpose *only* of determining whether a company is connected with a director, another company with which the director is connected is not regarded as a connected person (see para 6.18 above), except where that company is:

- a partner of the director or of a person who is connected with the director under (a), (b) or (c) in paragraph 6.18 above [CA06 Secs 254(6), 255(6)]; or

- a trustee of a trust the beneficiaries of which include, or may include the persons mentioned in (c) of paragraph 6.18. [CA06 Secs 254(6), 255(6)].

Furthermore, a trustee of a trust the beneficiaries of which include (or may include) a company with which a director is connected is not to be treated as connected with a director by reason only of that fact [CA06 Secs 254(6), 255(6)].

6.25   The following examples illustrate the operation of the rules mentioned in the above paragraphs to establish whether a director is connected with a company – first, through an interest in shares and, secondly, through control of voting power:

Example 1 – Not connected through an interest in shares

Mr Jones owns 18% of company A's equity share capital, and he also owns 25% of company B's equity share capital. Company B owns 19% of company A's equity share capital.

Mr Jones is connected with company B, because he has an *interest* in more than 20% of the equity share capital of that company. [CA06 Sec 254(2)].

In the situation of company A, despite Mr Jones having an effective holding of 22.75% (that is, 18% + 25% × 19% = 22.75%), company A is *not connected* with him. This is because in deciding whether company A is connected with Mr Jones, company B's interest in company A's shares should be ignored. The reason for this is that, although company B is connected with Mr Jones, its interest in company A cannot be aggregated with Mr Jones' own interest for the purposes of section 254(2) of the 2006 Act. Company B is *not connected with* him for these purposes, because company B is not a partner or trustee of Mr Jones. [CA06 Secs 254(6), 255(6)].

Example 2 – Connected through an interest in shares

The facts are the same as in example 1 except that Mr Jones owns 5% of company A and he also owns 51% of company B.

In this situation, although Mr Jones has an effective holding of 14.69% (that is, 5% + 51% × 19% = 14.69%), company A is *connected* with him. This is because, although company B's interest in company A's shares should be ignored by virtue of section 254(6) of the 2006 Act, nevertheless, Mr Jones is taken to be *interested* in the shares of company A held by company B, because he is entitled to exercise, or control the exercise of, more than 50% of the voting power of company B. [CA06 Sec 255(2)]. Consequently, company A is *connected with* Mr Jones via the operation of section 254(2), because he has an interest in 24% (all of the 19% and not a proportion of it, together with a direct holding of 5%) that is greater than 20% of company A's equity share capital.

Example 3 – Not connected through control of voting power

Mr Williams owns 2% of company C's equity share capital. He also owns 100% of company D's £1 'A' equity shares, but none of the £1 'B' equity shares. The issued share capital of company D consists of 5,000 £1 'A' equity shares and 45,000 £1 'B' equity shares. Each 'A' share carries 3 votes and each 'B' share carries 1 vote. Company D owns 25% of company C's equity share capital (which represents 25% of company C's votes).

Although Mr Williams holds only 10% of the total equity share capital of company D, he is able to exercise 15,000 votes out of a maximum of 60,000 votes, which represent in total 25% of the voting power. Therefore, Mr Williams is connected with company D, because he is able to control more than 20% of the voting power of that company. [CA06 Sec 254(2)(b)].

In determining whether company C is connected with Mr Williams, the interest of company D in the shares of company C should be disregarded. [CA06 Sec 254(6)]. However, unlike in the second example above, Mr. Williams is also not taken to have an interest in the shares in company C held by company D for the purposes of the operation of section 255 of the 2006 Act, because he is only *entitled to exercise, or control the exercise of, 25% of the voting power* of company D. Because Mr Williams neither controls nor is presumed to control company D, company C is *not connected* with Mr Williams by the operation of section 255(2)(b) of the 2006 Act.

Example 4 – Connected through control of voting power

The facts are the same as in example 3, except that Mr Williams has acquired a further 18,000 £1 'B' equity shares in company D from some of the existing 'B' equity shareholders.

Mr Williams is now able to exercise 33,000 votes out of a maximum of 60,000 votes, which represent in total 55% of the voting power of company D. Therefore, Mr Williams is not only connected with company D, but because he is able to exercise more than 50% of its voting power the conditions in section 255(2) of the 2006 Act for determining whether he 'controls' are met. Because Mr Williams controls company D, he is regarded as controlling company D's exercise of its voting power in company C. [CA06 Secs 254(4)]. Because company D's *voting power exceeds 20%* of the potential voting power at company C's general meeting, company C is regarded as being connected with Mr Williams by the operation of section 254(2)(b) of the 2006 Act.

Associated company

6.26 Two companies or two bodies corporate are associated if one is a subsidiary of the other or both are subsidiaries of the same body corporate. [CA06 Sec 256].

Body corporate

6.27 This term includes a body incorporated outside the UK and limited liability partnerships, but does not include a corporation sole or a partnership that is not regarded as a company under local laws (for example, a Scottish partnership is considered a legal person under Scots law and, therefore, does not meet the definition of a body corporate) (see para 6.18(e)). [CA06 sec 1173(1)].

Company

6.28 A 'company' is a company formed and registered under the Companies Act 2006 or any of the former Companies Acts. [CA06 Sec 1(1)].

Holding company and subsidiary

6.29 These terms are defined in section 1159 of the 2006 Act. A company is a 'subsidiary' of another company, its 'holding company', if that other:

- holds a majority of the voting rights in it; or

- is a member of it and controls the board or a majority of voting rights in it.

It will also be a subsidiary if it is a subsidiary of a company which is itself a subsidiary of that other company. This is different from the definition of 'parent company' used for accounting purposes.

Loans, quasi-loans and credit transactions: Transactions with directors entered into prior to 1 October 2007

6.30 Section 330 of the 1985 Act prohibited a company from entering into certain types of transactions (listed below) for the benefit of its directors or persons connected with those directors, unless they fell within specific exemptions set out in sections 332 to 338 of the 1985 Act. The 2006 Act abolished this prohibition for transactions entered into on or after 1 October 2007. However, loans, quasi-loans, credit transactions and related arrangements between a company and its directors or persons connected with the director now require approval by the company's members. The transactions that were prohibited by the 1985 Act were:

- Loans.

- Quasi-loans.

- Credit transactions.

- Guarantees or securities in connection with any of the above transactions made by another person.

- Assignments or assumptions of rights, obligations or liabilities under the above types of transactions.

■ Indirect arrangements for the above.

The transactions requiring member approval under the 2006 Act and the exemptions to them for public and private companies, and money-lending and banking companies are considered in the next section.

Loans, quasi-loans and credit transactions: Transactions with directors entered into after 1 October 2007

Loans

Definition

6.31 Although the expression 'loan' is not defined in the 2006 Act, it was interpreted in a case brought under the Companies Act 1948. In that case it was held that the dictionary definition should be applied. The dictionary definition of a loan is *"a sum of money lent for a time to be returned in money or money's worth"*. [*Champagne Perrier-Jouet S.A. v H.H. Finch Ltd.* [1982] 1 WLR 1359]. Therefore, a loan arises when monies are advanced on the understanding that they will be repaid.

Value of loans

6.32 The value of a loan is the principal amount of the loan. [CA06 Sec 211(2)]. For these purposes, the interest due on the loans may be ignored. If the value cannot be ascertained as a specific sum, it is deemed to exceed £50,000. [CA06 Sec 211(7)]. The value is relevant for ascertaining the 'relevant amounts' to be aggregated for the purpose of establishing whether a proposed transaction is within the exceptions from requiring member approval. [CA06 Secs 204(2), 207(1), (2), 210(1)-(5)].

Member approval

6.33 Under the 2006 Act a company may not make a loan to a director or to a person connected with a director, of the company or its holding company, or provide a guarantee or security in connection with a loan, unless the transaction has been approved by a resolution of the company's members. [CA06 Secs 197(1), 200(2)]. If the director is also a director of the company's holding company, the transaction must also be approved by a resolution of the holding company's members. [CA06 Secs 197(2), 200(3)].

6.34 Prior to a resolution being passed to approve a loan to a director, a memorandum containing details of the nature of the transaction, the amount of the loan, its purpose and the extent of the company's liability must be made available to all members. In the case of a written resolution this memorandum must be sent to every eligible member (see para 6.35) at or before the time the proposed resolution is sent out. In the case of a resolution to be passed at a meeting, it must be made available at the company's registered office for at least 15 days prior to the meeting and at the meeting itself. [CA06 Secs 197(3), (4), 200(4), (5)].

Eligible member

6.35   The eligible members are the members who would have been entitled to vote on the resolution on the circulation date of the resolution. [CA06 Sec 289(1)]. This may also include persons who have been nominated by members to vote on their behalf as set out in section 145 of the 2006 Act.

6.36   Where a person has been nominated by a member of a company whose shares are admitted on a regulated market to enjoy information rights under section 146 of the 2006 Act, that person is not entitled to vote unless an agreement exists between the person and the member who nominated him. [CA06 Sec 149].

Exceptions

Small loans

6.37   There is a general exception from the need to obtain member approval for small loans. A company does not need to obtain member approval under sections 197, 198 or 200 of the 2006 Act for a company to make a loan or to give a guarantee or security in connection with a loan provided that the aggregate of the value of the transaction and any other relevant transactions does not exceed £10,000. [CA06 Sec 207(1)].

6.38   The relevant amounts to be aggregated are:

a   The value of the *proposed transaction(s)*.

b   The amount outstanding under *any existing transaction or arrangement* (described in para 6.61) by virtue of the relevant exception, by the company and any of its subsidiaries or where the director is a director of the holding company, by the holding company and any of its subsidiaries. Where the proposed transaction or arrangement is to be made for a director of the company or director of the holding company or a person connected with the director, the conditions are that the transaction or arrangement is entered into for that director (or a person connected with him). [CA06 Sec 210(2)-(4)].

The amount outstanding is the value less any amount by which the value has been reduced. [CA06 Sec 211(1)].

Example – Small loan exception

A subsidiary is asked to lend £8,000 to the director of its parent company. The director already has a loan of £2,500 from the parent company. The directors of the subsidiary are unsure whether this proposed loan requires member approval of either the parent or the subsidiary.

Section 210 of the 2006 Act requires that amounts lent by the parent company or any subsidiary should be added to any proposed additional loan to the director of the parent company in order to determine whether the new loan falls within any available exception. In this situation, the small loans exception from member approval is £10,000, which is less than the total of the two loans combined (£8,000 plus £2,500). Assuming that the amount outstanding on the parent company's loan is still £2,500, the subsidiary should restrict its proposed loan by £500 to £7,500 to fall within the small loans exception from member approval. If the loan was not restricted, member approval would be required from both the members of the parent and the subsidiary company. [CA06 Sec 197(2)].

6.39   There is a further limitation for the purposes of calculating the relevant amounts. Transactions entered into by a company that, at the time of entering into the transactions, was a subsidiary or fellow-subsidiary, but at the time when the calculation under section 210 of the 2006 Act has to be done, is no longer a subsidiary or fellow subsidiary, need not be taken into account in such calculation. [CA06 Sec 210(5)].

6.40   A foreign subsidiary (that is, one incorporated outside the UK) of a company formed and registered under the 2006 Act or its predecessor is not required under sections 197, 198, 200 and 201 of the 2006 Act to obtain member approval for a loan to a director of its UK parent, provided that the parent or any UK subsidiary does not compensate the foreign subsidiary for making the loan or guarantee it. This is because a foreign subsidiary does not fall within the definition of a 'company' (see para 6.28). Such a foreign subsidiary may, however, be subject to restrictions under the laws of its home state.

Groups

6.41   The second exception relates to loans to an associated body corporate (inter-company loans). An associated body corporate is defined in paragraphs 6.26 and 6.27. A company is not required to obtain member approval for a loan or quasi-loan to another company within the same group by reason only that a director of one of the group companies is connected with another group company. This also applies where the company enters into a guarantee, or provides any security in connection with a loan or quasi-loan made by any person to another group company. [CA06 Sec 208(1)].

6.42   A holding company is not required to obtain member approval to make loans to a director of its subsidiary. Similarly, a subsidiary is not required to obtain member approval to lend to a director of a fellow subsidiary. However, in these instances the subsidiary or the fellow subsidiary must not be a party to any indirect arrangement under which they provide any benefit or compensation to the lending company. Indirect arrangements are described in paragraph 6.66. The transaction might also be a related party transaction under the Listing Rules (see para 6.111 below).

6.43 In addition, although the 2006 Act requires member approval for loans to directors, a loan made before a person becomes a director does not automatically require approval. However, it would become disclosable as a loan to a director when he becomes a director.

6.44 More general exceptions which may also be available are set out from paragraph 6.70 below.

Quasi-loans

Definition

6.45 A quasi-loan is a transaction where one party (the creditor) either:

a   agrees to pay, or pays, a sum *for another* (the borrower); or

b   agrees to reimburse, or reimburses, expenditure another party incurs for another (the borrower);

and either of the following two conditions apply:

■   the transaction's terms are such that the borrower (or a person on his behalf) will reimburse the creditor; or

■   the circumstances surrounding the transaction give rise to a liability on the borrower to reimburse the creditor.

[CA06 Sec 199(1)].

The liabilities of a borrower under a quasi-loan include the liabilities of any person who has agreed to reimburse the creditor on the borrower's behalf. [CA06 Sec 199(3)].

The following are common examples of a quasi-loan:

Example 1 – Company credit card

A director uses a company credit card to buy goods for personal use and he does so on the understanding that the company will settle the liability and will be reimbursed by the director at a later date. The quasi-loan is the amount that the company has paid the credit card provider for the directors' personal expenditure.

Example 2 – Company buys goods directly

Companies in a group pay for goods and services for the personal use of a director of the parent company, on the basis that the director will reimburse those companies at a later date. The quasi-loan is the amount that is paid for the directors' personal expenditure.

Value of quasi-loans

6.46 The value of a quasi-loan is the amount, or maximum amount, that the person to whom it is made is liable to reimburse the creditor. [CA06 Sec 211(3)]. If the value is not ascertainable as a specific sum it is deemed to exceed £50,000. [CA06 Sec 211(7)]. The value is relevant in connection with the disclosure of quasi-loans to be made in the company's financial statements (see from para 6.82) as well as for ascertaining the 'relevant amounts' to be aggregated for the purpose of establishing whether a proposed transaction is within the exceptions from requiring member approval (see para 6.38).

Conditions for quasi-loans

6.47 A private company not associated with a public company is permitted to make a quasi-loan of any amount to a director of the company, or its holding company, or a person connected with such a director, without shareholder approval.

6.48 A public company, or a private company associated with a public company, may only make a quasi-loan, or provide a guarantee or security in connection with a quasi-loan made by any person to a director of the company, or its holding company, or a person connected with such a director, if the transaction is approved by a resolution of the members of the company. [CA06 Secs 198(1), (2), 200(1), (2)]. If the director is a director of the company's holding company or if the connected person is a person connected with a director of the company's holding company, the transaction must also be approved by a resolution of the holding company's members. [CA06 Secs 198(3), 200(3)].

6.49 Prior to a resolution being passed to approve a quasi-loan to a director, a memorandum containing details of the nature of the transaction, the amount of the quasi-loan, its purpose and the extent of the company's liability must be made available to all members. In the case of a written resolution this must be sent to every eligible member at or before the time the proposed resolution is sent out. In the case of a resolution to be passed at a meeting, it must be made available at the company's registered office for at least 15 days prior to the meeting and at the meeting itself. [CA06 Secs 198(4), (5), 200(4), (5)].

Exceptions

Small quasi-loans

6.50 Approval is not required under sections 198 or 200 of the 2006 Act for a company entering into a quasi-loan, or to give a guarantee or security in connection with a quasi-loan, if the aggregate of the value of the proposed transaction and the value of any other relevant transactions or arrangements does not exceed £10,000. [CA06 Sec 207(1)].

6.51 A quasi-loan is relevant for these purposes if it meets the criteria set out in paragraph 6.38 above.

6.52 More general exceptions that may also be available are set out from paragraph 6.70 below.

Credit transactions

Definition

6.53 A credit transaction is any transaction where one party (the creditor):

- supplies any goods or sells any land under a hire purchase agreement or a conditional sale agreement;

- leases or hires any land or goods in return for periodic payments; or

- otherwise disposes of land, or supplies goods or services, on the understanding that payment (whatever form it takes) is to be deferred.

[CA06 Sec 202(1)].

'Services' means anything other than goods or land. [CA06 Sec 202(3)].

Value of credit transactions

6.54 The value of a credit transaction is the price that it would be reasonable to expect could be obtained for the goods, land or services to which the transaction relates if they had been supplied in the ordinary course of the company's business and on the same terms (apart from price). [CA06 Sec 211(4)]. If the value of the transaction cannot be ascertained, it is deemed to exceed £50,000. [CA06 Sec 211(7)]. The value is relevant in connection with the exception for business transactions (see para 6.59), for ascertaining the 'relevant amounts' in connection with the exception for minor transactions (see para 6.58), and in connection with the information relating to credit agreements to be disclosed in the company's financial statements (see para 6.82).

Conditions for credit transactions

6.55 A private company not associated with a public company is permitted to enter into a credit transaction or give a guarantee or provide security in connection with a credit transaction entered into by another third party with a director or a person connected with the director of the company, or its holding company without shareholder approval.

6.56 A public company, or a private company associated with a public company, may only enter into a credit transaction or give a guarantee or provide security in connection with a credit transaction entered into by another third party with a director of the company, or its holding company or a person connected with such a director, if the transaction is approved by a resolution of the company's members. [CA06 Sec 201(1), (2)]. If the director or connected person is a director of the company's holding company or a person connected with such a director, the transaction must also be approved by a resolution of the holding company's members. [CA06 Sec 201(3)].

6.57 Prior to a resolution being passed to approve a credit transaction to a director or person connected with a director, a memorandum containing details of the nature of the transaction, the value of the credit transaction, the purpose for which the land, goods or services are required and the extent of the company's liability must be made available to all members. In the case of a written resolution this must be sent to every eligible member at or before the time the proposed resolution is sent out, or in the case of a resolution to be passed at a meeting, it must be made available at the company's registered office for at least 15 days prior to the meeting and at the meeting itself. [CA06 Sec 201(4), (5)].

Exceptions

Minor transactions

6.58 Approval is not required under section 201 of the 2006 Act for a public company or a private company associated with a public company entering into a credit transaction, or to give a guarantee or security in connection with a credit transaction for a person if the aggregate of the value of the proposed transaction and the relevant amounts under other credit transactions, guarantees and securities and arrangements relating to such transactions and made for any one director or his connected persons, does not exceed £15,000. [CA06 Sec 207(2)]. (Arrangements are discussed in para 6.61.) The 'relevant amounts' to be aggregated are set out in paragraph 6.38.

Business transactions

6.59 Approval is not required under section 201 of the 2006 Act for a public company or a private company associated with a public company entering into a credit transaction, or to give a guarantee or security in connection with a credit transaction for a person if:

■ the transaction in question was entered into in the ordinary course of its business; and

■ the value and the terms on which the company enters into the transaction are no more favourable, for the person for whom it is made, than those the company would have normally offered to a person who was of similar financial standing, but was unconnected with the company.

[CA06 Sec 207(3)].

The value of a credit transaction is considered in paragraph 6.54 above.

6.60 More general exceptions that may also be available are set out from paragraph 6.70 below.

Assignment or assumption of rights, obligations or liabilities

6.61 Both public companies and private companies associated with public companies are prohibited by section 203(1)(b) of the 2006 Act from arranging for the assignment to them, or the assumption by them, of any rights, obligations or liabilities under transactions which, had they, themselves, *entered into* them, would have required member approval under sections 197, 198, 200 or 201 of the 2006 Act, unless the arrangement is approved by resolution of the company's members (refer to para 6.33). The transactions mentioned in these sub-sections are loans, quasi-loans and credit transactions (and guarantees, indemnities and the provision of security in respect of such loans, quasi-loans or credit transactions).

6.62 In addition, private companies not associated with public companies are prohibited by section 203(1)(b) of the 2006 Act from arranging for the assignment to them, or the assumption by them, of any rights, obligations or liabilities under loans which, had they, themselves, *entered into* them, would have required member approval under section 197 of the 2006 Act, unless the loan is approved by resolution of the company's members (refer to para 6.33).

6.63 For the purposes of section 203 and the other provisions relating to loans, quasi-loans and credit transactions in sections 197, 198, 200 and 201 of the 2006 Act, the transaction will be treated as having been *entered into* on the date of the arrangement for the assignment or assumption of rights, obligations or liabilities mentioned above. [CA06 Sec 203(6)].

6.64 An illustration of an 'assignment' is given in example 1 below and an illustration of an 'assumption of liabilities' in example 2 below:

Example 1 – Loan assignment

A third party makes a loan to a director of a company and, subsequently, the director's company purchases the third party's rights to the loan. In this situation, the company has paid out resources to acquire an asset and the company purports to become a creditor of the director just as if it had advanced the loan itself.

Example 2 – Assumption of liabilities

A third party guarantees a loan that a fourth party makes to a director of a company and, subsequently, the director's company enters into an arrangement with the third and the fourth parties, whereby the third party is released from his guarantee, and the company purports to assume the liability under the guarantee. Again, in this situation, the company's resources are tied up by a contingent liability when the company purports to assume the guarantee on behalf of the director.

Value of assignment or assumption

6.65 The value of this type of arrangement is the value of the transaction to which the arrangement relates less any amount by which the liabilities of the person for whom the transaction or arrangement was made have been reduced. [CA06 Sec 211(6)]. If the value of the transaction cannot be ascertained as a specific sum, it is deemed to exceed £50,000. [CA06 Sec 211(7)]. The value is relevant in connection with the information regarding the arrangement to be disclosed in the company's financial statements and in the calculation of 'relevant amounts' (see para 6.38).

Indirect arrangements

6.66 Indirect arrangements are regulated by section 203 of the 2006 Act. Thus, a company cannot take part in an arrangement whereby another person:

- enters into a transaction that would have required member approval under sections 197, 198, 200 or 201 had the company itself entered into it; and

- that other person has obtained, or is to obtain, under the arrangement a benefit of any kind from the company, or a body corporate associated with it, unless the arrangement in question has been approved by a resolution of the company's members. [CA06 Sec 203(1)].

6.67 This provision expressly prevents a company's resources from being used to procure another person to provide one of the various forms of credit that require member approval without the company itself either entering into, or subsequently becoming a party to, the transaction.

6.68 As a consequence, the provision is very widely drafted and is intended to cover the wide variety of forms that these types of arrangement can take. For example, it covers the situation where a company agrees to make a loan to another company's director in return for that other company making a loan to one of the first company's directors. It also covers the situation where a director persuades a bank to make a loan on favourable terms to him/her in return for his company placing business with the bank. Furthermore, by the use of the term 'body' corporate it captures indirect arrangements using the company's foreign subsidiaries.

Value of indirect arrangements

6.69 The value of an indirect arrangement is ascertained in the same way as the value of an assignment or an assumption of rights considered in paragraph 6.65 above. The value is relevant for the same purposes.

General exceptions from the requirement for member approval for loans and similar transactions

6.70　In addition to the exceptions that apply only to particular types of transactions (for example, the *de minimis* exception for loans and quasi-loans totalling not more than £10,000, the Companies Act 2006 includes more general exceptions in respect of:

■　Intra-group transactions (see para 6.71).

■　Directors' business expenditure (see from para 6.72).

■　Director's expenditure on defending proceedings (see from para 6.75).

■　Director's expenditure in connection with regulatory action or investigation (see from para 6.79).

Intra-group transactions

6.71　The following transactions between associated companies are not covered by the requirement for member approval that sections 197, 198, 200 and 201 of the 2006 Act imposes on loans, quasi-loans and credit transactions:

■　A loan or a quasi-loan a company makes to an associated company, or a company's guarantee or provision of security to a third person who has made a loan or quasi-loan to an associated company.

■　A credit transaction a company enters into as creditor for an associated company, or a guarantee or security that a company provides in connection with a credit transaction a third party makes for an associated company.

[CA06 Sec 208].

This exception would apply, for instance, where the holding company is a director of the subsidiary.

Transactions that fall within the above provisions do not, therefore, require member approval.

Directors' business expenditure

6.72　Section 204 of the 2006 Act provides an exception from the requirement to obtain member approval for any action by a company to provide a director of the company, its holding company or a person connected with such a director, with funds to meet expenditure incurred or to be incurred by him/her for the purposes of the company, or to enable him/her to perform his duties properly as an officer of the company. [CA06 Sec 204(1)]. Furthermore, the company is not prohibited from doing anything to enable a director to avoid incurring expenditure of the kind described in section 204(1). [CA06 Sec 204(1)(b)]. The company may provide these funds by way of a loan, or a quasi-loan or a credit transaction, or by any other similar arrangement. This exception applies only if the aggregate of the transaction in question and the value of any other relevant transactions or arrangements does not exceed £50,000. [CA06 Sec 204(2)]. The relevant amounts to be aggregated are those referred to in paragraph 6.38.

6.73 The most common form of transaction of this nature relates to travelling expenses between different places of business. Another form of transaction of this nature is a bridging loan a company gives to a director, who changes location within the company and so is required to move house.

6.74 Section 204 of the 2006 Act does not restrict advances to an amount appropriate to the specific business expenditure it is anticipated the director will incur. However, where the amount is clearly excessive or remains unspent for an unduly long time, then the recipient is likely to have derived some personal benefit and the transaction takes on the nature of a loan. In such a case the amount may require member approval.

Funding of director's expenditure on defending proceedings

6.75 Member approval is not required for a company to provide a director of the company or its holding company with funds to meet expenses incurred or to be incurred in connection with:

■ Defending any civil or criminal proceedings in connection with any alleged negligence, default, breach of duty, or breach of trust in relation to the company or an associated company.

■ Any application to the courts for relief from a liability or claim under section 661(3) and (4) of the 2006 Act (acquisition of shares by innocent nominee) or section 1157 (general power to grant relief in case of honest and reasonable conduct).

[CA06 Sec 205(1), (5)].

6.76 Furthermore, approval is not needed for a company acting to enable a director to avoid incurring such expenditure. [CA06 Sec 205(1)(b)].

6.77 This exception is contingent as the terms of the arrangement requiring that the loan to the director or (if the transaction is a quasi-loan or credit transaction) the liability of the company is repaid or discharged no later than:

■ The date on which the director's conviction becomes final (if he is convicted).

■ The date on which judgement against the director becomes final (if judgement is found against him/her).

■ The date on which the court's refusal of relief becomes final (if an application for relief is refused).

[CA06 Sec 205(2)].

6.78 For the purpose of section 205(2) of the 2006 Act, a conviction, judgement or refusal becomes final when the period for bringing an appeal expires (if no appeal has been made) or when the appeal has been disposed of (that is, it is determined that the period for bringing any further appeal has ended or the appeal is abandoned or otherwise ceases to have effect). [CA06 Sec 205(3), (4)].

Funding of director's expenditure in connection with regulatory action or investigation

6.79 The Companies Act 2006 introduced a further exception to the requirement for member approval in relation to regulatory investigations. A company may, without member approval, provide a director of the company or its holding company with funds to meet expenditure incurred or to be incurred in defending himself in an investigation by a regulatory authority or against action proposed to be taken by a regulatory authority in connection with any alleged negligence, default, breach of duty or breach of trust by him in relation to the company or an associated company. [CA06 Sec 206(a)].

6.80 Furthermore, approval is not needed for a company acting to enable a director to avoid incurring such expenditure. [CA06 Sec 206(b)].

Civil consequences of contravention

6.81 The consequences of failing to comply with sections 197, 198, 200, 201 or 203 of the 2006 Act are set out in detail from paragraph 6.91.

[The next paragraph is 6.83.]

Disclosure requirements for loans, quasi-loans, credit arrangements and guarantees

Introduction

6.83 Section 413 of the 2006 Act (contained in Part 15: Accounts and reports) sets out the disclosure requirements for loans, quasi-loans, credit arrangements and guarantees granted to a company's directors. Somewhat confusingly, section 413 of the 2006 Act uses different terminology for the disclosure requirements from that used in sections 197, 198, 200, 201 and 203 of that Act dealing with the legality of such transactions. Section 413 refers to the transactions as advances, credits and guarantees. It requires disclosure of (a) advances and credits granted by the company to its directors and (b) guarantees of any kind entered into by the company on behalf of its directors.

6.84 The following section describes the disclosure requirements for advances, credits and guarantees under the 2006 Act.

Disclosure in financial statements

6.85   The 2006 Act removed the previous requirement included in the Companies Act 1985 to disclose transactions between the company and persons connected with the director. However, such transactions may fall to be disclosed under the related party disclosure requirements. IFRS reporters complying with IAS 24 (refer to the Manual of Accounting – IFRS for the UK) will meet these related party disclosure requirements. For UK GAAP reporters, additional related party disclosure requirements have been introduced by the 2006 Act over and above those within FRS 8 (refer to chapter 29 of the Manual of Accounting – UK GAAP).

6.86   The disclosure requirements in respect of advances (which include loans and quasi-loans), credit and guarantees entered into with directors are contained in section 413 of the 2006 Act. Where a company does not prepare consolidated financial statements, it is required to disclose details of advances and credits granted by the company to its directors and guarantees entered into by the company on behalf of its directors. Where a parent company prepares consolidated financial statements, it is required to disclose details of advances and credits granted to the directors of the parent company, by that company or by any of its subsidiaries and guarantees entered into on behalf of the directors of the parent company, by that company or by any of its subsidiaries. [CA06 Sec 413(1), (2)].

6.87   The details required to be disclosed in respect of an advance or credit are:

■   Its amount.

■   An indication of the interest rate.

■   Its main conditions.

■   Any amounts repaid.

[CA06 Sec 413(3)].

6.88   The 2006 Act also requires disclosure of the totals of the amounts of advances and credits and the total of the amounts repaid. [CA06 Sec 413(5)(a), (b)].

6.89   The disclosures required in respect of a guarantee are:

■   Its main terms.

■   The amount of the maximum liability that may be incurred by the company (or its subsidiary).

■   Any amount paid and any liability incurred by the company (or its subsidiary) for the purpose of fulfilling the guarantee (including any loss incurred by reason of enforcement of the guarantee).

[CA06 Sec 413(4)].

6.90 In respect of guarantees entered into on behalf of the directors, the 2006 Act also requires disclosure of the total amounts of the maximum liability that may be incurred and of the total amounts paid and any liability incurred for the purpose of fulfilling the guarantee. [CA06 Sec 413(5)(c), (d)].

Criminal sanctions under the 1985 Act

6.91 The 1985 Act imposed criminal sanctions for failure to comply with section 330 of the 1985 Act relating to directors' loans (see para 6.30). To be guilty of the offence, the director (or other person) must have known, or have had reasonable cause to believe, that the transaction contravened section 330 of the 1985 Act. [CA85 Sec 342]. A company could, as a civil remedy, seek to treat an unlawful transaction as voidable under section 341 of the 1985 Act.

6.92 These criminal penalties continue to apply under the 2006 Act for contraventions occurring before 1 October 2007. For transactions entered into after 1 October 2007, sections 330 to 342 of the 1985 Act have been repealed.

Civil consequences of contravention of the 2006 Act

6.93 If a company enters into a transaction or an arrangement that contravenes sections 197, 198, 200, 201 or 203 of the 2006 Act (members' approval for loans, quasi loans, credit transactions and related arrangements), the company may seek to treat the transaction as voidable.

6.94 A company may, as a civil remedy under section 213 of the 2006 Act, seek to treat an unlawful transaction as voidable. This means that a company does not need to regard itself as bound by any agreement that it has entered into with the director or any other person. However, because a transaction is not actually void, a company may wish to elect to affirm the agreement instead. [CA06 Sec 214]. Also, the company will not be entitled to treat the transaction as voidable if the subject matter of the transaction cannot be restored (for example, where the sum a company has lent to a borrower who is unable to repay has been used to buy goods which have been consumed), or if the person who benefited under the transaction has indemnified the company.

6.95 Similarly, a transaction will not be voidable if a third party has, *bona fide* for value and without actual notice of the contravention, acquired rights under the agreement and these rights would be affected if the company avoided the liability. [CA06 Sec 213(2)].

6.96 Moreover, whether or not an unlawful transaction has been avoided, the person who benefited from the unlawful transaction and any other director who authorised the transaction and, where the transaction was with a person connected with a director, the director so connected, have a statutory duty to reimburse the company. They are, consequently, liable to account to the company for any gain they have made (whether directly or indirectly) and also to indemnify the company for any loss or damage resulting from the transaction. [CA06 Sec 213(3)]. Their liability may, however, be limited if either of the following applies.

■ Where the transaction in question was made for a person connected with a director of the company or its holding company, that director is not liable to account to the company or to indemnify it if he shows that he/she took all reasonable steps to ensure that the transaction did not contravene sections 200, 201 or 203 of the 2006 Act, whichever is the relevant section. [CA06 Sec 213(6)].

■ A connected person who transacted with the company and a director who authorised the transaction will avoid civil liability if he can show that, at the time the company entered into the transaction, he did not know of the circumstances that amounted to a contravention. [CA06 Sec 213(7)].

Substantial property transactions

Introduction

6.97 In addition to the requirement for member approval for loans, quasi-loans and credit transactions between a company and its directors as set out above, a company's ability to contract with a director is similarly restricted where it wishes to enter into certain substantial property transactions.

Shareholders' approval of substantial property transactions

6.98 A company (whether a public or private company) is prohibited from entering into an arrangement whereby:

■ a director of the company or its holding company, or a person connected with the director, acquires one or more substantial non-cash assets from the company; or

■ the company acquires one or more substantial non-cash assets from such a director or connected person,

unless the prior approval by resolution of the company and (if the director is a director of the holding company) its holding company in general meeting is given, or is conditional on such approval being given. [CA06 Sec 190(1), (2)]. Consequently, unless such prior approval is given or the arrangement is affirmed by resolution of the company in general meeting within a reasonable period the transaction is voidable by the company. [CA06 Secs 195(2), 196].

6.99 Stricter rules apply to companies that are charities. In this case, the approval or affirmation by the company in general meeting of a substantial property transaction under section 190 of the 2006 Act is ineffective unless the prior written consent of the Charity Commission is obtained. [Charities Act 1993 Sec 66 as amended by Charities Act 2006 8 Sch 153].

Substantial property transaction value

6.100 A substantial non-cash asset is one whose value, at the time the arrangement is entered into, either exceeds 10 per cent of the company's asset value and is more than £5,000; or exceeds £100,000. [CA06 Sec 191(2)]. The 2006 Act does not define the criteria by which the non-cash asset's value is to be determined for the purpose of calculating the £5,000 or £100,000 threshold. However, it has been held that the aim of section 191 of the 2006 Act is the protection of shareholders in arrangements that would or might benefit directors to the detriment of the company. The company and its advisers valuing the asset should, therefore, have regard to its value to the director (or connected person) proposing to acquire it. For instance, any special value that the asset would have to such person would need to be taken into account. *Micro Leisure Ltd v County Properties & Developments Ltd & Anor* [2000] BCC 872. However, the 2006 Act defines the 'company's asset value' for the purposes of the 10 per cent threshold as meaning the value of the company's net assets as disclosed in its latest financial statements laid before shareholders. Where there are no such financial statements, the 'company's asset value' means the amount of the company's called-up share capital. [CA06 Sec 191(3)].

6.101 In the context of section 190 of the 2006 Act, 'non-cash asset' means any type or form of property, or any interest in property other than cash. (For this purpose, 'cash' includes foreign currency.) 'Property' means any type of asset of a company and is not only buildings or land. The acquisition or transfer of a non-cash asset also includes the creation or extinction of an interest in property (for example, a lease) and the discharge of any person's liability other than a liability for a liquidated sum. [CA06 Sec 1163]. For illustrations of 'non-cash assets' see Table 6.1 below and the example in paragraph 6.106.

6.102 Section 190 of the 2006 Act also affects certain intra-group transactions. Where, for example, a director of a company owns or controls a certain percentage of the shares in another group company, that other group company may fall within the definition of a connected person (see para 6.18). In these circumstances, all dealings between the company and any company that falls within the definition of a person connected with a director will require prior approval of the company in general meeting (see para 6.104 for the exemptions).

6.103 An example of a substantial property transaction is given in Table 6.1. It is worth noting that this disclosure was under the 1985 Act, however, the provisions under the 2006 Act are unchanged from those in the 1985 Act other than a change in the definition of connected person (see para 6.18), an increase in the financial thresholds, provisions relating to the aggregation of transactions and enabling a company to enter into a substantial property transaction that is conditional upon shareholder approval. Therefore, this example is still relevant.

Table 6.1 – Substantial property transaction

Fine Art Developments p.l.c. – Annual Report & Accounts – 31 March 1993

Directors' Report (extract)

Proposed transaction with an associated party

In accordance with their policy to dispose of businesses which are not considered core to the group, the directors have decided there should be a sale of Herbert Walker & Son (Printers) Limited. This company is engaged in commercial printing and, if it was retained, would require considerable investment in plant and equipment in the near future.

The profit before tax of Herbert Walker in the year to 31 March 1993 amounted to £66,450 and its net assets on completion of a sale are estimated to be £664,000. The independent directors have concluded that a fair value of the company would be £764,000. In reaching this conclusion it has been assumed that the group will continue to purchase printed products from Herbert Walker on normal commercial terms of no less than an annual total purchase price of £1.5m in each of the three years following completion of a sale. The independent directors have sought advice from BDO Binder Hamlyn who consider that the terms of the proposed disposal, taking into account all relevant factors, are fair and reasonable so far as concern the shareholders of Fine Art Development p.l.c.

Mr K Chapman, a director, has agreed to purchase and Britannia Products Limited, a subsidiary of Fine Art Developments p.l.c. and the holder of the whole of the issued share capital of Herbert Walker, has agreed to sell the whole of such capital for a cash consideration of £764,000 payable on completion, subject to approval of the transaction by shareholders in general meetings as required under Section 320 of the Companies Act 1985. The contract for sale will contain a provision that Fine Art Developments p.l.c. shall procure that the group place orders for printed products with Herbert Walker on the terms referred to above.

An ordinary resolution to approve the sale is set out in the notice of annual general meeting on page 11.

Exemptions from obtaining approval

6.104   Although a company must comply with the disclosure requirements set out in paragraph 6.107, the shareholders' approval is not required for a substantial property transaction of the type described in paragraph 6.100 where one of the exceptions set out below applies:

■   The body corporate in question is not a company formed and registered under the Companies Act 2006. [CA06 Sec 190(4)].

■   The company in question is a wholly-owned subsidiary of any company, wherever incorporated. [CA06 Sec 190(4)(b)]. In these circumstances, in practice, the holding company's directors have control over the subsidiary's directors.

■   The director is entitled to the property as part of his/her service contract or if the property relates to payment for compensation for loss of office as defined in section 215 of the 2006 Act (payments requiring members approval – see chapter 5). [CA06 Sec 190(6)].

■   The non-cash asset is to be acquired:

- By a holding company from any of its wholly-owned subsidiaries.

- By a wholly-owned subsidiary from its holding company.

- By a wholly-owned subsidiary from a fellow wholly-owned subsidiary.

[CA06 Sec 192].

In effect, this exemption relieves companies that would otherwise be required by section 190 of the 2006 Act to obtain approval at a general meeting for intra-group transactions that take place in a wholly-owned group.

- The arrangement is entered into by a company that is being wound up, and the winding-up is not a members' voluntary winding-up, or the company is in administration. [CA06 Sec 193].

- The following two conditions are satisfied:

  - A member of the company acquires an asset from the company.

  - The arrangement was made with that person (for example, a director of the company or the holding company or a person connected with such a director) in his capacity as a member of the company.

[CA06 Sec 192(a)].

- The transaction is effected on a recognised investment exchange by a director, or a person connected with him/her, through an independent broker. [CA06 Sec 194].

Liabilities for contravention of section 190

6.105 An arrangement for which the shareholder approval required by section 190 of the 2006 Act has not been obtained (and any transaction pursuant thereto) may be treated as voidable by the company unless one of the following three conditions is satisfied:

- it is no longer possible to obtain the return of the subject matter of the transaction;

- the company has been indemnified for any loss or damage it has suffered; or

- a third party has acquired rights, in good faith and for value, and without having notice of the contravention, which would be affected. [CA06 Sec 195(2)].

6.106 A director who contravenes section 190 of the 2006 Act may incur civil penalties. The director and any connected person who entered into the arrangement, and any director who authorised it may all be liable to account to the company for any gain they have received. They may also be liable to indemnify the company from any resultant loss or damage it has incurred. [CA06 Sec 195(3), (4)]. However, a director will not be liable if the arrangement was made with a person connected to them and if the director took all reasonable steps to secure the company's compliance. In addition, any person with whom the company entered into the arrangement in contravention of section 190 who is connected with the director or any director who authorised the arrangement is not liable if they can show that at the time the arrangement was entered into, they did not know the relevant circumstances constituting the contravention. [CA06 Sec 195(6), (7)].

> **Example – Transaction that would contravene section 190 of the 2006 Act**
>
> Although the transaction was determined to be in contravention of section 320 of the 1985 Act, it nevertheless remains as relevant case law for the purposes of section 190 of the 2006 Act.
>
> C and his wife owned company O. Company O agreed to buy a property for £495,000 and paid a deposit of £49,500. On completion the property was conveyed to another company, D, of which C was also a director on the basis that company O would take 50% of any profit but not bear any loss. D borrowed £350,000 to fund the purchase. Company D paid the balance of the purchase price and reimbursed company O the deposit. Company D then sought to avoid the transaction, as the value of the property had subsequently fallen, on the grounds that it had not been approved by the members of company D. It was held that company D was connected to C and that the transaction contravened section 320 (of the 1985 Act). There was an inquiry as to what damage D had suffered, as the property was subsequently sold for £177,970.
>
> It was held that the indemnity D was entitled to under section 322(3)(b) (of the 1985 Act) was the loss caused by the depreciation of the property. A further hearing established that this loss was limited to the difference between the cost of the property and the proceeds of sale plus interest on that sum. [*Re Duckwari plc (No.3) Duckwari v Offerventure (No.3)* [1999] 1BCLC 168].

Disclosure requirements for substantial property transactions

6.107   There are no specific disclosure requirements relating to substantial property transactions under the 2006 Act. However, paragraph 72 of Schedule 1 to the 'Large and Medium-sized Companies and Groups (Accounts and Reports) Regulations 2008' (SI 2008/410) sets out disclosure requirements for related party transactions that may include substantial property transactions. Details may be given of transactions that the company has entered into with related parties, and must be given if such transactions are material and have not been concluded under normal market conditions. The details that are required to be disclosed are:

■   The amount of the transaction.

■   The nature of the related party relationship.

■   Other information about the transactions necessary to understand the company's financial position.

6.108   The disclosure requirements do not apply to medium-sized companies. [SI 2008/410 reg 4(2)(b)]. In addition, there is an exemption for transactions entered into between two or more members of a group, provided that any subsidiary undertaking which is a party to the transaction is wholly-owned. [SI 2008/410 1 Sch 72(4)].

6.109   For the purpose of this disclosure, 'related party' has the same meaning as under IFRS. Therefore, compliance with IAS 24 ensures compliance with this Companies Act requirement, as confirmed by the ARC in its meeting in November 2007. The requirements of IAS 24 are dealt with in chapter 29 of the Manual of Accounting – IFRS for the UK.

6.110   The UK GAAP definition of a related party was amended to reflect certain changes to the Act resulting from the introduction of EU Directive 2006/ 46/EC into SI 2008/410. As a consequence, for periods beginning on or after 6 April 2008, FRS 8 achieves greater consistency with IAS 24. Related parties identified under FRS 8 will be consistent with those identified under IAS 24 and, while the requirements of FRS 8 are not completely converged with IAS 24 (see further chapter 29 of the Manual of Accounting – UK GAAP), compliance with the amended standard will ensure compliance with the Directive. [FRS 8 App IV para 37].

Disclosure requirements of the Listing Rules and AIM and PLUS-quoted rules

6.111   The Listing Rules, for listed companies, the AIM Rules, for those traded on AIM, and the PLUS trading rules for those traded on the PLUS-quoted market contain further rules and disclosure requirements for substantial property transactions and other transactions with directors that come within following categories:

■   Transactions with related parties (which include directors).

■   Contracts of significance with directors (not AIM or PLUS-quoted companies).

6.112   The UKLA's Listing Rules provide certain safeguards to prevent directors and other related parties from taking advantage of their position. These are based on disclosure, primarily to shareholders, and are set out in chapters 9 and 11 of the Listing Rules – Continuing obligations. They apply to listed companies unless they do not have any equity securities listed. Added to these requirements, disclosure of information regarding contracts of significance with directors must be made in the annual financial report. Related party transactions and contracts of significance under the Listing Rules, the AIM and PLUS-quoted rules are discussed in chapter 29 of the Manual of Accounting – IFRS for the UK, whilst only the AIM Rules are discussed in chapter 29 of the Manual of Accounting – UK GAAP, in the context of related party disclosures in general.

Invalidity of certain transactions involving directors

General rule

6.113　Where a company proposes to enter into a transaction with a director of the company or its holding company, the board of directors will need to ensure that, in doing so, they are not exceeding any limitation on their powers under the company's constitution, that is, its articles of association, any resolution of the company or any agreement between members. If they exceed their powers the transaction is voidable at the option of the company unless it is ratified by the shareholders. [CA06 Sec 41]. This also applies where the party to the transaction includes a person connected with a director (including a company with which he is associated).

Effects of contravention

6.114　Whether or not the transaction is avoided, the director or connected person concerned, and any director who authorised the transaction, is liable to account to the company for any gain and indemnify the company against any loss or damage it suffers as a consequence. Nothing in the rules referred to in this paragraph and in the paragraph above, however, affects any other rule of law under which the transaction may be called into question or under which liability to the company may arise (for instance, if it is an illegal loan). [CA06 Sec 41(1)(3)]. A person other than a director of the company is not liable to account or to indemnify the company if he can show that, at the time the transaction was entered into, he did not know that the directors were exceeding their powers. [CA06 Sec 41(5)].

6.115　The company may treat the transaction as voidable unless one of the following conditions is satisfied:

■　Restitution of the money or other asset which was the subject of the transaction is no longer possible.

■　The company is indemnified for any loss or damage resulting from the transaction.

■　Rights acquired *bona fide* for value and without actual notice of the directors' exceeding their powers by a person who is not a party to the transaction would be affected by the avoidance.

■　The transaction is ratified by the company in general meeting by ordinary or special resolution or otherwise as the case may require.

[CA06 Sec 41(4)].

6.116　However, section 41 of the 2006 Act provides for the situation where the transaction is voidable, but is valid under section 40 of the 2006 Act (power of directors to bind the company free of any limitation under the company's constitution). Where the person dealing with the company (not being a director of the company or its holding company or a person connected with him/her) has acted in good faith, the court may (on the application of that person or the company) make an order either confirming, severing, or setting aside the transaction, on such terms as appears to the court to be just. [CA06 Sec 41(6)].

6.117   Where the company enters into a transaction which is outside the directors' powers and thus voidable under section 41 of the 2006 Act, it may require disclosure under Schedule 1 to SI 2008/410 (refer to para 6.107) as a related party transaction if the transaction has not been concluded under normal market conditions. IFRS reporters complying with IAS 24, 'Related party disclosures' (see Manual of Accounting – IFRS for the UK) will meet equivalent related party disclosures. This was clarified by the ARC in its November 2007 meeting. The position is similar for UK GAAP reporters – see from paragraph 6.110 above and the Manual of Accounting – UK GAAP.

Transactions with directors who are sole members

6.118   There are special requirements for a single member company to document transactions with a director who is also its sole member. Where a limited company with a sole member who is also a director (or shadow director) contracts with that director, it must ensure that the terms of the contract are set out in a written memorandum or are recorded in the minutes of the first meeting of directors of the company following the making of the contract. This requirement does not apply where the contract is in writing or is entered into in the company's ordinary course of business. [CA06 Sec 231].

6.119   Failure to comply with this requirement does not affect the validity of the contract. However, it is a criminal offence and the company and any officer in default is liable to a fine. [CA06 Sec 231(3), (4), (6)].

6.120   A sole director also has a duty to comply with the statutory provisions of section 182 of the 2006 Act which requires him/her to declare at a meeting of the directors the nature of his/her interest in any contract or proposed contract with the company. This was established by *Neptune Vehicle Washing Equipment Ltd v Fitzgerald* [1995] 1 BCLC 352, where the judge said that he was satisfied that for the purpose of section 317 of the 1985 Act there can be a directors meeting in the case of a sole directorship. This case law is still applicable as the requirements of section 317 of the 1985 Act have been replaced without change by section 182 of the 2006 Act (as described in para 6.135).

Money-lending and banking companies

Introduction and definition of a money-lending company

6.121   The 2006 Act defines a 'money-lending company' as *"a company whose ordinary business includes the making of loans or quasi-loans, or the giving of guarantees or provision of security in connection with loans or quasi-loans"*. [CA06 Sec 209(2)]. Money-lending companies are not necessarily banking companies under the 2006 Act, but banking companies fall within the definition of 'money-lending companies' for this purpose.

6.122   A banking company is defined as a person *"who has permission under Part 4 of the Financial Services and Markets Act 2000 (c8) to accept deposits, other than (a) a person who is not a company, and (b) a person who has such permission only for the purpose of carrying on another regulated activity in accordance with permission under that Part"*. [CA06 Sec 1164(2)]. A deposit-taking business is one where money received in the course of business by way of deposit is lent to others or used to finance any other activity of the business. Unless otherwise indicated, the term 'money-lending company' where used below will include a company which is a banking company.

6.123   'Credit institution' is defined in section 1173 of the 2006 Act. This section refers to the definition in Article 4.1(a) of Directive 2006/48/EC of the European Parliament and of the Council relating to the taking up and pursuit of the business of credit institutions. That is to say, an undertaking whose business is to receive deposits or other repayable funds from the public and to grant credits for its own account. A credit institution would, therefore, include an institution, wherever incorporated, carrying on banking-type business.

6.124   A 'banking company' is defined in section 1164 of the 2006 Act (see para 6.122) and refers to the subset of credit institutions incorporated in the UK, which are authorised under Part 4 of the Financial Services and Markets Act 2000 to conduct a deposit-taking business in the UK.

6.125   In addition, a company that is a credit institution is within the definition of a money-lending company as defined in section 209 of the 2006 Act (see para 6.121), because a credit institution makes loans in the ordinary course of its business. However, a money-lending company will not be a credit institution, unless the money-lending company, in addition to making loans, receives deposits or other repayable funds from the general public in the ordinary course of its business.

6.126   The transactions requiring member approval under section 197, 198, 200, 201 and 203 of the 2006 Act and the relevant exceptions to this requirement (see para 6.30 onwards) that apply to companies also apply to money-lending companies.

6.127   Money-lending companies may, however, take advantage of a further exception from the requirement to obtain member approval relating to loans, quasi-loans, guarantees and provision of security of loans and quasi-loans. This exception and the disclosure requirements for money-lending companies (including banking companies) and those specifically for banking companies are considered in the paragraphs that follow.

Exception for money lending companies

Loans on commercial terms

6.128　For transactions entered into on or after 1 October 2007, section 209 of the 2006 Act contains exceptions (subject to certain conditions) for money-lending companies. Consequently, a money-lending company does not require approval for:

- making a loan or quasi-loan to any person (for instance, to a director of the company or its holding company or a person connected with the director); or

- entering into a guarantee or providing security for a loan or quasi-loan.

The exception is only available if the following two conditions are satisfied:

- The money-lending company makes the loan or quasi-loan or enters into the guarantee or provides security in respect of the loan or quasi-loan in the ordinary course of its business. [CA06 Sec 209(1)(a)].

- The amount of the loan or quasi-loan or the amount guaranteed or the amount of security is not greater than, and the terms of that transaction are not more favourable, in the case of the person for whom the transaction is made, than those that the company might reasonably be expected to have offered to, or in respect of, a person of the same financial standing who was unconnected with the company. (In other words, the facility is offered on the money-lending company's normal commercial terms.) [CA06 Sec 209(1)(b)].

Transactions to which the exception from approval is not applicable

6.129　It should be noted, however, that the exception from member approval for money-lending companies in section 209 of the 2006 Act that relates to loans, quasi-loans, guarantees and the provision of security for them (see para 6.128), does not extend to the following types of transaction:

- Credit transactions, or the provision of a guarantee or security in connection with them.

- The assignment of rights or obligations or assumption of liabilities under the above types of transaction.

- Indirect arrangements under the above types of transaction.

These transactions require member approval. Consequently, in these situations, money-lending companies are subject to the same rules as any other company and the provisions set out in sections 201 to 203 of the 2006 Act (as outlined in paras 6.30 and 6.81) apply to them.

6.130   The second condition, that the exception applies only where the loan is made on normal commercial terms (sec 209(1)(b) to the Companies Act 2006), is relaxed where a money-lending company makes a loan to one of its directors or a director of its holding company for the purpose of house purchase or improvement (housing loan). [CA06 Sec 209(3), (4)]. Consequently, a money-lending company (whether a public or private company) is not prevented by that condition from making a loan (but not a quasi-loan or a guarantee) to such a director on *beneficial* terms provided that all the following conditions are satisfied:

■   The loan is to assist the director either to purchase or to improve his only or main residence. This type of loan will also include a loan made by the company in substitution for a loan that another person has made to the director.

■   The company ordinarily makes similar loans of that type available to its employees on no less favourable terms.

[CA06 Sec 209(3), (4)].

Disclosure requirements — money lending companies

6.131   For transactions with directors (and officers that are 'key management') may be caught by the related party disclosure provisions of Schedules 1 and 2 to SI 2008/410 (refer to para 6.107). IFRS reporters complying with IAS 24, 'Related party disclosures' (see Manual of Accounting – IFRS for the UK) will meet the related party disclosure requirements under the 2006 Act. This was clarified by the ARC in its November 2007 meeting. The position is similar for UK GAAP reporters – see from paragraph 6.110 above and the Manual of Accounting – UK GAAP.

6.132   Section 413 of the 2006 Act sets out the disclosure requirements in respect of advances and credits granted by the company, or its subsidiary undertakings, to the company's directors and guarantees of any kind entered into by the company, or its subsidiary undertakings, on behalf of the company's directors.

6.133   Under section 413(8) of the 2006 Act banks and the holding companies of credit institutions need only disclose two items in the financial statements:

■   The amount of an advance or credit.

■   For a guarantee, the amount of the maximum liability that may be incurred by the company (or its subsidiary).

[CA06 Sec 413(8)].

Other matters

Notification to the board

Declaration of interest under sections 177 and 182 of the 2006 Act

6.134   Sections 177 and 182 of the 2006 Act are an indication of the importance in company law of the principle that a company should be protected against a director who has a conflict in interest and duty. It applies to a shadow director and to a sole director (*Neptune Vehicle Washwax Equipment Limited v Fitzgerald [1995]* 1BCLC 352). [CA06 Sec 187]. Where a director is in any way interested in a transaction or arrangement (either proposed or entered into) that involves the company, sections 177 and 182 of the 2006 Act impose a specific duty on the director to declare the nature and extent of the interest in the transaction or arrangement to the other directors. This applies whether the director is either directly or indirectly interested in the transaction or arrangement, or the proposed transaction or arrangement, with the company.

6.135   In declaring an interest in a transaction or arrangement, notice may be given at a meeting of the directors or by written notice or by general notice. [CA06 Secs 177(2), 182(2)]. If notice is given by writing then it must be sent to the other directors by either hard copy or in electronic form. [CA06 Sec 184(3)]. If a declaration of interest proves to be or becomes inaccurate or incomplete, a further declaration must be made. [CA06 Secs 177(3), 182(3)].

6.136   In certain circumstances a general notice will be sufficient. When a director is, for example, a member of another company that might enter into transactions with the company, he/she can give a general notice to the directors that he/she is to be regarded as interested in any future contract with that other company. [CA06 Sec 185].

6.137   Sections 177 and 182 of the 2006 Act do not require declaration of an interest in which the director is not aware or where the director is not aware of the transaction or arrangement in question. However, a director is treated as being aware of matters of which he ought reasonably to be aware. [CA06 Secs 177(5), 182(5), (6)].

6.138   If a director fails to disclose an interest in a transaction or arrangement in accordance with section 182 of the 2006 Act, this will be an offence and the director will be liable to a fine. [CA06 Sec 183].

6.139   The 2006 Act introduces a new provision for companies with only one director. In these circumstances, the director must record in writing the nature and extent of his interest and this declaration is deemed to form part of the proceedings at the next directors meeting. [CA06 Sec 186(1)].

Disclosure required by the articles of association

6.140   To overcome the general rule restricting contracts between directors and their companies, a company's articles of association will generally contain specific requirements for the disclosure to the board by a director of his interest in a contract with the company. If these requirements are not followed, the director risks being accountable to the company for any benefit he derives from the contract. For example, Table A of SI 1985/805, 'Companies (Tables A to F) Regulations 1985', deals, in articles 85 and 86, with directors' material interests in contracts. Note that this part of Table A was not amended by statutory instruments issued under the 2006 Act. The requirements of these articles are as follows:

> *"Subject to the provisions of the Act, and provided that he has disclosed to the directors the nature and extent of any material interest of his, a director notwithstanding his office –*
>
> a   *may be a party to, or otherwise interested in, any transaction or arrangement with the company or in which the company is otherwise interested;*
>
> b   *may be a director or other officer of, or employed by, or a party to any transaction or arrangement with, or otherwise interested in, any body corporate promoted by the company or in which the company is otherwise interested; and*
>
> c   *shall not, by reason of his office, be accountable to the company for any benefit which he derives from any such office or employment or from any such transaction or arrangement or from any interest in any such body corporate and no such transaction or arrangement shall be liable to be avoided on the ground of any such interest or benefit.*
>
> *For the purposes of [the above] regulation 85*
>
> a   *a general notice given to the directors that a director is to be regarded as having an interest of the nature and extent specified in the notice in any transaction or arrangement in which a specified person or class of persons is interested shall be deemed to be a disclosure that the director has an interest in any such transaction of the nature and extent so specified; and*
>
> b   *an interest of which a director has no knowledge and of which it is unreasonable to expect him to have knowledge shall not be treated as an interest of his."* [Table A articles 85, 86].

6037

Annex — Directors loan decision tables

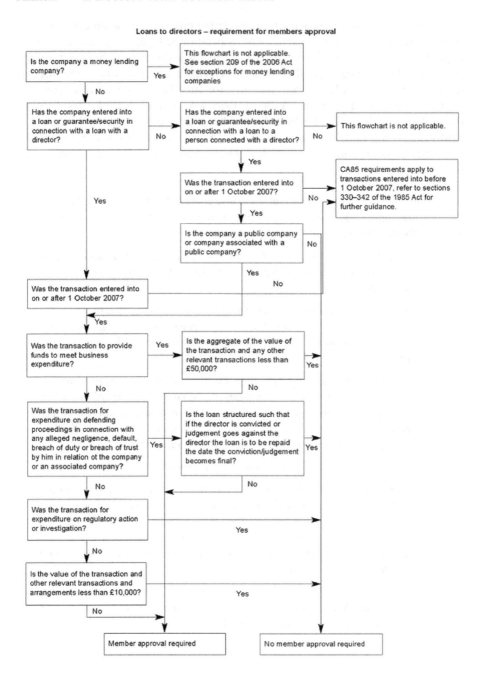

Loans to directors – requirement for members approval

Quasi-loans to directors – requirement for members approval

Is the company a money lending company? — Yes → This flowchart is not applicable. See section 209 of the 2006 Act for exceptions for money lending companies

No ↓

Has the company entered into a quasi-loan or guarantee/security in connection with a quasi-loan with a director or person connected with a director? — No → This flowchart is not applicable.

Yes ↓

Was the transaction entered into on or after 1 October 2007? — No → CA85 requirements apply to transactions entered into before 1 October 2007, refer to sections 330–342 of the 1985 Act for further guidance.

Yes ↓

Is the company a public company or company associated with a public company? — No →

Yes ↓

Was the transaction to provide funds to meet business expenditure? — Yes → Is the aggregate of the value of the transaction and any other relevant transactions less than £50,000? — Yes →

No ↓ (both)

Was the transaction for expenditure on defending proceedings in connection with any alleged negligence, default, breach of duty or breach of trust by him in relation to the company or an associated company? — Yes → Is any liability of the company incurred under the transaction structured such that if the director is convicted or judgement goes against the director the liability is to be repaid the date the conviction/judgement becomes final? — Yes →

No ↓ (both)

Was the transaction for expenditure on regulatory action or investigation? — Yes →

No ↓

Is the value of the transaction and other relevant transactions and arrangements less than £10,000? — Yes →

No ↓

Member approval required

No member approval required

Loans and other transactions involving directors

Credit transactions with directors – requirement for members approval

Has the company entered into a credit transaction or guarantee/security in connection with a credit transaction with a director or person connected with a director?

→ **No** → This flowchart is not applicable.

↓ **Yes**

Was the transaction entered into on or after 1 October 2007?

→ **No** → CA85 requirements apply to transactions entered into before 1 October 2007, refer to sections 330–342 of the 1985 Act for further guidance.

↓ **Yes**

Is the company a public company or company associated with a public company?

→ **No** →

↓ **Yes**

Was the transaction to provide funds to meet business expenditure?

→ **Yes** → Is the aggregate of the value of the transaction and any other relevant transactions less than £50,000?

→ **Yes** →

↓ **No** (from business expenditure)

↓ **No** (from aggregate £50,000)

Was the transaction for expenditure on defending proceedings in connection with any alleged negligence, default, breach of duty or breach of trust by him in relation ot the company or an associated company?

→ **Yes** → Is any liability of the company incurred under the transaction structured such that if the director is convicted or judgement goes against the director the liability is to be repaid the date the conviction/judgement becomes final?

→ **Yes** →

↓ **No** (defending proceedings)

↓ **No** (liability structured)

Was the transaction for expenditure on regulatory action or investigation?

→ **Yes** →

↓ **No**

Is the value of the transaction and other relevant transactions and arrangements less than £15,000?

→ **Yes** →

↓ **No**

Has the transaction been entered into by the company in the ordinary course of the company's business?

→ **Yes** → Is the value of the transaction not greater, and the terms not more favourable than it is reasonable to expect the company to have offered to a person of the same financial standing but unconnected with the company?

→ **Yes** →

↓ **No** (ordinary course)

↓ **No** (value/terms)

Member approval required

No member approval required

Chapter 7

Acquisition of own shares

Acquisition of own shares

Introduction

7.1 The general rule that prevented a company acquiring its own shares was established in 1887 by the case of Trevor v Whitworth on the grounds that such action might amount to 'trafficking' in its own shares or operate as a reduction of capital. The general prohibition, now set out in section 658 of the 2006 Act, is that a limited company cannot acquire its own shares whether by purchase, subscription or otherwise, unless it falls within one of the exceptions specified in Part 18 of the 2006 Act. However, unlimited companies can reduce their capital or purchase their own shares without restriction if the company is authorised to do so by its articles. For limited companies, an acquisition that does not come within the specified exceptions is void and, therefore, has no effect. In addition, there are criminal sanctions available against the company and its officers in such a circumstance. The rules apply also to companies limited by guarantee that have a share capital.

7.2 The only situations where a limited company can acquire its own shares are as follows:

- The shares are purchased under section 690 of the 2006 Act. This includes the purchase of qualifying shares that are subsequently held in treasury. It also includes the purchase of shares out of capital.

- Redeemable shares are redeemed under section 684 of the 2006 Act.

- The acquisition of shares is a reduction of capital duly made. [CA06 Sec 659(2)(a)].

- The purchase of shares is made under a court order. [CA06 Sec 659(2)(b)].

- The shares are forfeited or surrendered as a result of calls on the shares not having been paid. [CA06 Sec 659(2)(c)].

- The shares are acquired without the payment of any consideration (for example, a bequest or a gift). [CA06 Sec 659(1)].

7.3 This chapter deals with the first three exceptions. Consequently, references to 'company' in this chapter are to limited companies. A high level summary of the impact of the first three exceptions is as follows:

Exception	Distributable profits or capital?	Sections of CA06
Purchase of own shares – to cancel	Where there is no fresh issue of shares: must be out of distributable profits, although if a private company has insufficient distributable profits it can purchase the shares out of capital.	690 – 708 709 – 723 733 – 736
Purchase of own shares – to hold in treasury	Must be out of distributable profits.	690 – 708 724 – 732 735 – 736
Redemption of shares	Where there is no fresh issue of shares: must be out of distributable profits, although if a private company has insufficient distributable profits it can redeem the shares out of capital.	684 – 689 709 – 723 733 – 736
Reduction of capital – solvency statement	Out of capital. May increase distributable profits.	641 – 644 654 SI 2008/1915
Reduction of capital – court approval	Out of capital. May increase distributable profits.	641 645 – 654 SI 2008/1915

7.4 This chapter is a practical guide to the company law requirements concerning the purchase and redemption by a limited company of its own shares and the reduction of capital by a company. In setting out the requirements of the law, this guide is not a substitute for taking professional legal advice in light of the specific facts and circumstances of the company wishing to acquire its own shares. This chapter does not deal with the tax implications, which are complex and need to be considered thoroughly before a company embarks on acquiring its own shares.

7.4.1 Most of the requirements in this chapter regarding acquisition of own shares are legal and, consequently, not covered by accounting standards. The accounting implications of the transactions considered in this chapter are dealt with in the Manual of Accounting – IFRS for the UK and the Manual of Accounting – UK GAAP. In particular, it should be noted that a contract that contains an obligation (including contingent obligations) for a company to repurchase or redeem its own shares is subject to the special accounting treatment set out in paragraph 23 of IAS 32 and FRS 25.

Purchase and redemption of own shares — summary of requirements

Why might a company wish to purchase its own shares?

7.5 A company's ability to purchase its own shares can have advantages, particularly for private companies who can for example, remove a dissident shareholder or enable an outside investor to realise an investment.

7.6 The advantages of being able to purchase own shares are, perhaps, less significant for public companies than for private ones, but they can nonetheless be of real benefit. In particular, public companies are able to return surplus funds to shareholders by purchasing and cancelling some of their shares. Structuring a return of capital as a share repurchase rather than as a 'special dividend' can have tax advantages for some shareholders. Some companies have purchased their own shares to boost their net asset value per share or earnings per share. Also, this ability provides public companies with flexibility both in ordering their capital structure and in matching that structure to their needs at any stage of their development. (see for example Table 7.1).

Table 7.1 – Market purchase of own shares

AstraZeneca PLC – Annual Report – 31 December 2008

DIRECTORS' REPORT (extract)

Distributions to shareholders

The Company's stated distribution policy comprises both a regular cash dividend and a share re-purchase component, further details of which are set out in the Financial Review on page 37 and the Financial Statements on page 129.

Pursuant to the shareholders' resolution passed at the 2008 AGM authorising the Company to purchase its own shares, during 2008 the Company re-purchased (and subsequently cancelled) 13.6 million of its own Ordinary Shares with a nominal value of $0.25 each, at an aggregate cost of $610 million, representing 0.9% of the total issued share capital of the Company. The average price paid per share in 2008 was 2397 pence. Shares issued in respect of share schemes totalled 4.1 million. The Board announced in the Third Quarter and Nine Month Results 2008 that no further share re-purchases would take place in 2008 in order to maintain the flexibility to invest in the business. For the same reason, the Board has decided that no share repurchases will take place in 2009.

The Company executed the share re-purchase programme through a combination of discretionary purchases and through irrevocable, non-discretionary instructions. The Company continues to maintain robust controls in respect of all aspects of the share re-purchase programme to ensure compliance with English and other applicable law and the Financial Services Authority's Listing Rules, Disclosure and Transparency Rules and Prospectus Rules. However, in order to maintain flexibility, the Company will seek a renewal of its current permission from shareholders to purchase its own shares at the AGM on 30 April 2009.

Since the Company began its share re-purchase programmes in 1999, a total of 376.3 million Ordinary Shares were re-purchased, and subsequently cancelled, at an average price of 2661 pence per share for a consideration, including expenses, of $18,099 million.

FINANCIAL REVIEW (extract)

CAPITALISATION AND SHAREHOLDER RETURN (extract)

DIVIDEND AND SHARE RE-PURCHASES

In line with the Board's distribution policy and its overall financial strategy to strike a balance between the interests of the business, shareholders and financial creditors, whilst maintaining strong investment grade credit rating, total share re-purchases in 2008 were 13.6 million shares at a total cost of $610 million. This represented 0.9% of the share capital at the start of the year. All shares re-purchased have been cancelled. This brings the total number of shares re-purchased to date since the beginning of the re-purchase schemes in 1999, to 376.3 million shares at a total cost of $18,099 million. The Board has decided that no share re-purchases will take place in 2009 in order to maintain the flexibility to invest in the business.

In the year, 4.1 million shares were issued in consideration of share option exercises for a total of $159 million.

The Board regularly reviews its shareholder returns strategy, and in 2008 reaffirmed the dividend policy, which is to grow dividends in line with reported earnings before restructuring and synergy costs, with an aim to maintain at least two times dividend cover.

[The next paragraph is 7.8.]

Redeemable shares

7.8   Sections 684 to 689 of the 2006 Act set out the requirements in relation to redeemable shares. Redeemable shares are those shares that are to be redeemed, under the terms of their issue, on a particular date, as well as shares that are merely redeemable under the terms of their issue at the option of either the company or the shareholder. [CA06 Sec 684(1)].

7.8.1   Even though redeemable shares will often meet the definition of debt in IAS 32 and FRS 25 and be accounted for as such (see further chapter 6 of the Manual of Accounting – IFRS for the UK and the Manual of Accounting – UK GAAP) they are legally shares and the provisions of the 2006 Act apply to their redemption.

7.9   In order to issue redeemable shares, a public company must be authorised to do so by its articles of association. Article 43(2) of the model articles for public companies states that *"the company may issue shares which are to be redeemed, or are liable to be redeemed at the option of the company or the holder, and the directors may determine the terms, conditions and manner of redemption of any such shares"*. These model articles apply to public companies incorporated on or after 1 October 2009. Table A of SI 1995/805, 'The Companies (Tables A to F) Regulations 1985', remains in force for those companies that adopted it and the latest version contains, in article 3, a similar provision although it specifies that the terms and manner of redemption are to be specified in the articles. Some earlier versions of Table A specified that the terms and manner of redemption were to be determined by special resolution prior to the issue of the shares.

7.9.1   A private company requires no such authorisation in its articles, but the members may exclude or restrict the company's ability to issue redeemable shares by inserting a provision to this effect into the company's articles. Nevertheless, article 22(2) of the model articles for a private company limited by shares, which apply to such companies incorporated on or after 1 October 2009, explicitly permits redeemable shares to be issued.

7.9.2   Redeemable shares cannot be issued by a company unless there are other shares in issue that are not redeemable. [CA06 Sec 684(4)].

7.10   The directors of both public and private companies are able to specify the terms, conditions and manner of redemption (including the amount payable on redemption and the redemption date) if authorised to do so by either the articles or a company resolution. The resolution required in these circumstances is only an ordinary resolution. [CA06 Sec 685(1),(2)]. If the directors are not so authorised then the terms, conditions and manner of redemption must be set out in the articles.

7.10.1   Directors exercising these rights must do so before the shares are allotted and include the terms, conditions and manner of redemption in the statement of capital which must accompany the return of the allotment made to the registrar. [CA06 Sec 685(3); Sec 555].

7.11   In the main, the remaining provisions that apply to the redemption of redeemable shares are the same as those that apply to the acquisition of own shares. Consequently, we set out below some general provisions in relation to the purchase of shares and then discuss the provisions that are common to both purchase and redemption, explaining where there are differences.

Purchase of own shares

7.12   Sections 690 to 708 of the 2006 Act set out the requirements in relation to the purchase of own shares. A public or private company may purchase any of its own shares (including redeemable shares before their date for redemption), provided the company:

- Is not prohibited from doing so by its articles of association, by a shareholders' agreement or by any similar restrictions on the transfer of its shares by members. [CA06 Sec 690(1)]. This will apply particularly to a private company.

- Complies with certain conditions (see paras 7.13 to 7.26).

- Follows the appropriate procedure, which depends on whether it is a *market* (listed companies only) or an *off-market* purchase (see from para 7.63) or the purchase of a right to purchase (a contingent purchase contract – see from para 7.89). [CA06 Secs 693 to 708].

Conditions for purchase or redemption of own shares

7.13 A company must, after the purchase of its own shares, have other non-redeemable shares in issue. Shares held in treasury do not count for this purpose. [CA06 Sec 690(2)]. There is no such requirement for redemption of shares, although a company may not issue redeemable shares unless there are other, non-redeemable, shares in issue. After a purchase of own shares, only one share needs to remain in issue. There appears to be no requirement for a public company to re-register as a private one where, as a result of the repurchase or redemption of its own shares, the nominal value of its allotted share capital has fallen below the authorised minimum of £50,000. This is likely to be because on cancellation of the repurchased shares an equivalent amount is replaced either by a fresh issue of shares or by a transfer to the capital redemption reserve under the capital maintenance provisions.

7.13.1 A company cannot purchase or redeem any of its own shares that are not fully paid. [CA06 Sec 686(1), Sec 691(1)]. For example, it would not be possible to purchase a £1 redeemable preference share issued at a premium of £11, where only £5 has been paid on the share.

Consideration for purchase or redemption of own shares

7.14 The terms of redemption of redeemable shares may provide for the company and the holder of the shares to agree that payment may be made on a later date than the redemption date (for example, by way of a loan), provided that the terms of redemption allowing such later payment are fixed on or after 1 October 2009 (either because the shares were issued on or after that date or because the terms of previously issued shares were altered on or after that date). [CA06 Sec 686(2), (3); SI 2008/2860 2 Sch 73].

7.14.1 Paragraph 6.15A of Tech 01/09, 'Guidance on the determination of realised profits and losses in the context of distributions under the Companies Act 2006', states that *"when payment on redemption is deferred, it is the current value of the redemption promise, at the redemption date, which determines the amount of distributable profits consumed. It is therefore the present value of the amount payable on redemption rather than its absolute amount which must be covered by distributable profits, at the redemption date, for the redemption to be permitted"*.

7.14.2 Shares being purchased, as opposed to redeemed, by the company must be paid for in cash in full on the date of purchase. They cannot, for example, be paid for by instalments. [CA06 Sec 691(2)]. It is also thought unacceptable for, say, the seller of the shares to loan the company a sum of money equivalent to a deferred instalment on the shares being purchased or for the company to exchange a debenture for shares, because the seller has not effectively received payment in cash for the shares.

7.15 It is generally accepted that the term 'purchase' in the context of a company purchasing its own shares, means a purchase of shares for cash. An exchange of shares for other forms of property, such as land, would not be a 'purchase' falling within sections 690 to 737 of the 2006 Act. Such a transaction might be possible, however, in the form of a reduction of capital under section 641 (solvency statement) or under section 645 (requiring court approval) (see further from para 7.93).

Accounting and funding requirements for purchase or redemption of own shares

7.16 The accounting and funding requirements of purchases and redemptions of shares can be complex. A purchase or redemption can only be made out of:

- Distributable profits.

- Proceeds of a fresh issue of shares.

- Share premium (where there is a fresh issue and the shares being purchased/ redeemed were similarly issued at a premium and are now being purchased/ redeemed at a premium).

- Capital (where the company is a private company and the above have been exhausted).

These rules are summarised in the paragraphs that follow and dealt with in detail in the body of the chapter. It should be noted that, in addition to the above, a company could reduce its capital by buying back some shares under a capital reduction even if it has distributable profits (see paras 7.93 to 7.93.4 below).

Purchase or redemption out of distributable profits or proceeds of fresh issue

7.17 Where a company purchases or redeems its own shares other than out of capital (see para 7.19), the shares can only be purchased or redeemed out of distributable profits or out of the proceeds of a fresh issue of shares made for the purposes of the purchase or redemption. [CA06 Sec 687(2), 692(2)(a)]. In addition, any premium payable on the purchase or redemption must be paid out of the company's distributable profits. However, if a premium arose on the original issue of the shares now being acquired/redeemed, the premium payable on their acquisition/redemption may be funded out of a fresh issue of shares made for that purpose, subject to some further conditions (see further para 7.32). [CA06 Sec 687(3)(4), 692(2)(b)(3)]. By virtue of section 687(5) and 692(4) of the 2006 Act, the share premium account is reduced by the amount of premium funded out of the fresh issue. 'Distributable profits' are defined in section 736 of the 2006 Act as those profits out of which the company could lawfully make a distribution equal in value to the payment.

7.18 Certain other payments relating to a purchase of shares can only be made out of distributable profits. For example, payments in consideration for varying a contract for an off-market purchase of a company's own shares (see paras 7.72 and 7.78) or for the release of any obligations under a contract to purchase a company's own shares. [CA06 Sec 705(1)].

Payment out of capital

7.19   Where the total distributable profits and the proceeds of a fresh issue of shares (if any) are not sufficient to meet the purchase or redemption price, a private company may make up the shortfall by a payment from 'capital' (that is, otherwise than out of its distributable profits or the proceeds of a fresh issue of shares). [CA06 Sec 709, 710]. Certain conditions, which are considered from paragraph 7.47, must be met before a payment out of capital can be made, including first using all its distributable profits and proceeds of any fresh issue made for the purpose. As an alternative, a company could instead use the 'reduction of capital' provisions explained from paragraph 7.93 below, which would allow the purchase to be out of capital even if the company has distributable profits.

7.20   If a company redeems or purchases its shares out of capital without having sufficient distributable profits/proceeds of fresh issue or, as a private company, without following the statutory procedure, the acquisition will be void as it would be an unlawful reduction of capital. In such a situation, the shares will remain in issue and are deemed to be held by the shareholders who held them at the time the attempted purchase or redemption was made. If a purchase is made in this way, the company is liable to a fine and, in addition, the directors are liable to a fine and/or imprisonment. [CA06 Sec 658(2)(3)]. Such a payment out of capital may be an illegal distribution and the directors risk being in breach of their fiduciary duty to the company to act in its best interests and, since 1 October 2007, their legal duties to exercise reasonable care, skill and diligence and to promote the success of the company. [CA06 Secs 172, 174].

Summary of basic funding rules

7.21   The basic rules mentioned above are represented in the following diagram. This shows how the purchase or redemption can be funded and is the basis of tables used in each of the examples in this chapter. This assumes that the company is not using the 'reduction of capital' approach described from paragraph 7.93.

PLC		Private company	
Funding of purchase/ redemption:		**Funding of purchase/ redemption:**	
Out of the proceeds of a fresh issue of shares:		Out of the proceeds of a fresh issue of shares:	
1 Nominal value of shares purchased/redeemed restricted to proceeds of fresh issue	X	1 Nominal value of shares purchased/redeemed restricted to proceeds of fresh issue	Y
2 Where there is a premium on the shares being purchased/ redeemed and on their initial issue – the premium on purchase/ redemption restricted to the lower of:		2 Where there is a premium on the shares being purchased/ redeemed and on their initial issue – the premium on purchase/ redemption restricted to the lower of:	
(a) initial premium on issue of shares being purchased/ redeemed		(a) initial premium on issue of shares being purchased/ redeemed	
(b) balance on share premium account including any premium on fresh issue of shares	X	(b) balance on share premium account including any premium on fresh issue of shares	Y
Total not to exceed the proceeds of the fresh issue	X	Total not to exceed the proceeds of the fresh issue	Y
Balance out of distributable profits	X	Out of distributable profits	Y
Total cost of purchase/ redemption	X		
		Balance out of capital	Y
		Total cost of purchase/ redemption	Y

Capital maintenance

7.22   Unless a company is making a reduction of capital (see from para 7.93) or a private company is making an acquisition or redemption of its own shares out of capital (see para 7.19) a company is required to maintain its capital before and after the acquisition/redemption of shares. This generally means that a company has to make a transfer to a capital redemption reserve of an amount equal to the nominal value of the shares that it acquires, redeems, or on cancellation of shares held as treasury shares. [CA06 Sec 733(1)(2)(4)]. But where the acquisition/redemption is funded wholly or partly by a fresh issue of shares, which must be made specifically for the purpose of the purchase/redemption, the amount that is required to be transferred to the capital redemption reserve is the amount by which the proceeds of the fresh issue are less than the nominal value of the shares being purchased/redeemed. [CA06 Sec 733(3)]. In this situation, where the acquisition is funded by a fresh issue, the company's capital is still maintained, although some of the capital may now be represented partly by share premium and partly by an amount transferred to the capital redemption reserve.

Cancellation of shares

7.23   Unless a purchase is a permitted acquisition of 'treasury shares' (see from para 7.111.1 below), a company must treat any shares that it purchases or redeems as being cancelled immediately on acquisition and so the acquisition will reduce the issued (but not, where it still exists, the authorised) share capital by the nominal amount of the shares purchased. [CA06 Sec 688, 706]. An acquisition will generally be complete when the executed stock transfer form and relevant share certificate are delivered to the company, or the transfer formally registered via the CREST system in accordance with the Uncertificated Securities Regulations 2001. The shares acquired must then be cancelled and cannot, therefore, be reissued.

[The next paragraph is 7.25.]

Consent from shareholders having priority rights

7.25   Where the capital of a company includes shares that have priority on a return of capital over the shares that the company proposes to purchase, the company will need to obtain consent to a variation of their rights from the holders of the shares that have the priority right.

Effect of acquisition

7.26   Whenever a company wishes to purchase its own shares and this is not done in proportion to existing shareholdings, the effect of that purchase on the remaining shareholders needs to be considered carefully. For example, the cancellation of the shares purchased will, if no new issue is made, proportionately increase the holdings of the remaining shareholders. This may result in one shareholder or group of shareholders obtaining the power to pass ordinary or special resolutions. Shareholder authority is required for both market and off-market purchases (see para 7.63 below).

Accounting for acquisitions and redemptions of shares

Acquisition/Redemption out of distributable profits

7.27 As explained above, sections 687(2) and 692(2) of the 2006 Act require that the acquisition/redemption of own shares (including any premium paid on the acquisition/redemption) must be made out of the company's distributable profits (or out of the proceeds of a fresh issue). An illustration of the legal position of a company purchasing its own shares out of distributable profits and showing the effect on its balance sheet is given in the example below. The example also illustrates some of the steps a company needs to consider before making such a purchase. The legal procedures for purchasing or redeeming a company's shares are considered from paragraph 7.63 and the disclosure requirements that have to be made in the company's financial statements are dealt with in paragraph 7.41.

7.27.1 For simplicity, the added complexity of the accounting requirements for a contract to purchase own shares under the requirements of paragraph 23 of IAS 32 and FRS 25, 'Financial instruments: Presentation', has been excluded from this illustration.

> **Example – Purchase made out of distributable profits**
>
> Company Z (a private company) is a long established family manufacturing company. Mr Brown (a director of company Z) purchased for £10,000, many years ago, 10,000 of company Z's 100,000 issued ordinary £1 shares. He has now had a major disagreement with his fellow directors about the way in which company Z is run. The directors and the shareholders have agreed that it is in everyone's best interests for Mr Brown to sever his links with the company. He will resign as a director and the company will purchase his shares from him for £24,000 (which is the agreed market value). The company will make the payment out of distributable profits.
>
> At present, company Z's articles of association preclude it from purchasing its own shares. Company Z cannot proceed with the purchase until it alters its articles of association and this will require a special resolution. [CA06 Sec 21].
>
> In addition, company Z can purchase Mr Brown's shares only under a contract with him. Under section 694 of the 2006 Act, the terms of this contract will need to be authorised by a special resolution of the company before the purchase. Either the contract is approved prior to it being entered into; or the contract is entered into but specifies that a purchase may not be made until the terms of the contract have been authorised by special resolution. Mr Brown cannot vote on this special resolution. [CA06 Sec 695]. The company must send a copy of the special resolution to the Registrar of Companies within 15 days of its being passed. [CA06 Sec 29, 30]. Company Z will also need to consider whether the purchase is a 'substantial property transaction' (see chapter 6). The terms of the contract will need to include, amongst other things, a description of, and the number of, the shares to be purchased, the amount of the payment, the date of the purchase and a statement that payment will be made at the time of the purchase. The company can then purchase Mr Brown's shares at any time after the date of the special resolution to authorise the contract or its terms.

If the special resolution is to be effective, company Z will need to make the contract available for inspection both at its registered office during the 15 days immediately preceding the meeting that will consider the special resolution and at the meeting itself, or, in the case of a written resolution, a copy of the contract must be sent to eligible members. [CA06 Sec 696]. Within 28 days of the date on which Mr Brown's shares are delivered to company Z, the company will need to make a return to the Registrar of Companies together with any stamp duty payable. [CA06 Sec 707]. The return must state the following:

- Class of shares.
- The number and the nominal value of the shares purchased.
- The date on which the shares were delivered to the company.
- The stamp duty payable.

Had the company been a public company, it would also have been required to state in the return:

- Aggregate amount paid for the shares.
- Maximum and minimum prices paid in respect of shares of each class purchased.

Under section 708 of the 2006 Act, the company is also required, again, within 28 days of the date on which Mr Brown's shares are delivered to company Z, to give notice of cancellation of the shares to the registrar. This notice must be accompanied by a statement of capital setting out, with respect to the company's capital immediately following the cancellation of shares:

- Total number of shares of the company.
- Aggregate nominal value of those shares.
- For each class of shares: (i) details of voting, dividend, capital and redemption rights attached to the shares; (ii) number of shares; (iii) nominal value of shares.
- Amount paid up and amount unpaid on each share.

Furthermore, company Z will need, under section 702 of the 2006 Act, to keep the contract for the purchase at its registered office (or at an alternative location as permitted by SI 2008/3006) for ten years from the date of purchase. Throughout this time, the contract must be available during business hours for members to inspect. Section 355 requires company Z to keep, for ten years, the minutes of the meeting at which the contract, or its terms, was authorised or, if the authorisation was other than at a general meeting, for example, by written resolution, a copy of the resolution.

In their report attached to the financial statements that relate to the year in which the purchase took place, the directors will have to state the following details in respect of the purchase:

- The number and the nominal value of the shares the company purchased and the percentage of the called-up capital of that description that these shares represent.

■   The aggregate consideration the company paid and the reasons for the purchase.

Company Z must treat Mr Brown's shares as being cancelled on purchase and make the necessary entry in the Register of Members. Because the company made the payment out of distributable profits, company Z will need to transfer £10,000 (that is, the nominal value of the shares purchased) to the capital redemption reserve.

Using the table from paragraph 7.21 above, the purchase is made in the following way:

Funding of purchase:	£'000
Out of the proceeds of a fresh issue of shares	–
Balance out of distributable profits	24
Total cost of purchase	24

The effect on the balance sheet of company Z would be as follows, showing the position both before and after the purchase:

Balance sheet	Before purchase £'000	Purchase of shares £'000	Maintain capital £'000	After purchase £'000
Share capital	100	(10)		90
Capital redemption reserve	–		10	10
Capital	100	(10)	10	100
Distributable reserves	50	(14)	(10)	26
	150	(24)	–	126
Net assets other than cash	125			125
Cash	25	(24)		1
	150	(24)	–	126

The double entry for this transaction is as follows:

	£'000	£'000
Dr Share capital	10	
Dr Distributable profits	14	
Cr Cash		24

To reflect the purchase of 10,000 £1 shares at a premium of £14,000

	£'000	£'000
Dr Distributable profits	10	
Cr Capital redemption reserve		10

To maintain the capital of the company

7.28 It can be seen from the above example that the company's capital has been maintained at £100,000. The company is making the purchase out of distributable profits; the total debited to distributable profits is £24,000 which equals the consideration for the purchase. Some might argue that the double entry should be to credit cash £24,000 and to debit distributable profits £24,000 and to debit share capital with £10,000 and credit the capital redemption reserve with £10,000, which is the way the Act expresses the purchase in section 733. However, for clarity, the double entry throughout this chapter shows each step in the process separately: namely the entries for any issue of fresh capital (there are none in the example above); then the entries for the acquisition of the old capital; followed by the entries needed to maintain the company's capital.

Where to charge the purchase cost

7.29 The requirement in IAS 32 and FRS 25 to account for shares according to the substance of their contractual terms results in some shares (or parts of shares) being presented as liabilities. When such shares are purchased or redeemed the resulting accounting entries have to reflect both the requirements of the relevant accounting standards and the law regarding the preservation of capital. Where a company purchases out of distributable profits some of its shares that had been presented as liabilities, the final result has to show that an amount equal to the purchase/redemption price has been charged against distributable profits, any share premium previously classified within liabilities is added to the share premium account in equity and the nominal value of the shares purchased/redeemed is added to the capital redemption reserve in equity. However, the accounting will also show the elimination of the shares as liabilities, the outflow of cash and the recognition of any gain or loss on elimination of the liabilities.

7.29.1 If the shares meet the definition in IAS 32 and FRS 25 of debt and they are purchased for an amount in excess of their amortised cost carrying amount, the loss on the purchase of the shares should be recognised in arriving at the profit or loss for the period. For companies preparing their financial statements in accordance with EU-adopted IFRS (or in accordance with UK GAAP and applying FRS 26), this is required by paragraph 41 of IAS 39 (or FRS 26). For companies preparing their financial statements in accordance with UK GAAP and not applying FRS 26 (see further chapter 6 of the Manual of Accounting – UK GAAP), this is required by paragraph 32 of FRS 4. Additional accounting entries must be made to ensure that the nominal value of the purchased shares is credited to the capital redemption reserve in equity, that the full purchase price has been charged against distributable profits and any share premium associated with the purchased shares is credited to the share premium account in equity.

7.29.2 If the shares meet the definition of equity in IAS 32 and FRS 25 and are purchased at a premium, the loss on the purchase of the shares should be recognised directly in equity in the profit and loss reserve and shown in the reconciliation of movements in shareholders' funds (required by FRS 3) or the statement of changes in equity (required by IAS 1). It should not be recognised in the statement of total recognised gains and losses (for companies applying UK GAAP) or the statement of comprehensive income (for companies applying EU-adopted IFRS) because the charge represents the capital repaid to shareholders and, therefore, it is not a recognised loss. Additional accounting entries must be made to ensure that the nominal value of the purchased shares is credited to the capital redemption reserve in equity and that the full purchase price has been charged against distributable profits.

Expenses relating to the acquisition

7.30   The expenses directly relating to the acquisition should be treated as part of the overall cost of acquisition and should be treated in the same way as the purchase cost itself (see Table 7.2).

Table 7.2 – Disclosure of expenses relating to an acquisition of own shares

British Sky Broadcasting Group – Annual Report – 30 June 2005

23 Reconciliation of movement in shareholders' funds (extract)

(b) Company

	Share capital £m	Share premium £m	Shares to be issued £m	Capital reserve £m	Special reserve £m	Capital redemption reserve £m	Profit and loss account £m	Total equity shareholders' funds £m
AT 1 JULY 2003	969	2,536	3	844	–	–	(1,121)	3,231
Issue of share capital	2	21	(3)	–	–	–	–	20
Share premium reduction	–	(1,120)	–	–	14	–	1,106	–
Profit for the financial year	–	–	–	–	–	–	456	456
Dividends	–	–	–	–	–	–	(116)	(116)
AT 1 JULY 2004	971	1,437	–	844	14	–	325	3,591
Profit for the financial year	–	–	–	–	–	–	576	576
Dividends	–	–	–	–	–	–	(170)	(170)
Share buy-back	(37)	–	–	–	–	37	(416)	(416)
AT 30 JUNE 2005	934	1,437	–	844	14	37	315	3,581

Share buy-back

On 12 November 2004, the Company's shareholders approved a resolution at the AGM for the Company to purchase up to 97 million Ordinary Shares. During the financial year, the Company purchased, and subsequently cancelled, 74 million Ordinary Shares at an average price of £5.60 per share, with a nominal value of £37 million, for a consideration of £416 million. Consideration included stamp duty and commission of £3 million. This represents 4% of called-up share capital at the beginning of the financial year.

[The next paragraph is 7.32.]

Acquisition/Redemption at a premium out of fresh share issue

7.32 The nominal value of the shares being acquired or redeemed, instead of being funded out of distributable profits, can be funded out of the proceeds of a fresh issue of shares made for the purpose of the acquisition. [CA06 Secs 687(2)(3), 692(2)]. Generally, any premium paid on the shares that the company acquires or redeems has to be made out of distributable profits, but where the shares were initially issued at a premium, the company may fund the premium payable on their acquisition or redemption (or part of that premium) from the proceeds of a fresh issue of shares. The amount of premium that can be funded in this way is equal to the lower of the following two amounts:

- The aggregate of the premiums the company received when it issued the shares it is now purchasing.

- The amount of the company's share premium account after crediting the premium, if any, on the fresh issue of shares it makes to fund the purchase or redemption.

[CA06 Secs 687(4), 692(3)].

7.32.1 A company should be able to identify the amount of premiums it had received on the original issue of the shares it purchases or redeems by using the unique numbers on the share certificates and tracing them back through its register of members that are required to be kept and maintained under section 113 of the 2006 Act. For many companies, and particularly listed companies that have many shareholders and millions of shares in issue, identification of the premiums associated with the purchased shares can be a tedious and time consuming task.

7.33 The example below illustrates a private company that uses the proceeds of a fresh issue as well as distributable profits to fund the purchase of its own shares and the resulting effect on its balance sheet.

Example – Purchase out of a fresh issue of capital

In January 20X0, company Y issued 1,000,000 ordinary shares of £1 each, including 100,000 to Mrs Green, at a premium of 10p per share. After the issue, the balance on company Y's share premium account was £100,000. In January 20X2, company Y utilised the full balance of £100,000 on its share premium account to make a bonus issue of shares to its shareholders.

In July 20X4, company Y made an issue of 75,000 ordinary shares of £1 each at a premium of £1 per share for the purposes of purchasing, at a premium of £1.40 per share, Mrs Green's 100,000 ordinary shares issued in January 20X0. The balance of £90,000 of the purchase price of £240,000 was paid out of the cash resources of company Y.

Using the table in paragraph 7.21 company Y would make the purchase in the way shown below:

Funding of purchase:	£'000	£'000
Out of the proceeds of a fresh issue of shares:		
Nominal value shares purchased		100
Premium on purchase – the lower of:		
(a) Initial premium on issue of the shares being purchased (100,000 at 10p)	10	
(b) Balance on share premium account including premium on fresh issue of shares (see below)	75	
		10
Total not to exceed proceeds of fresh issue		110
Balance out of distributable profits		130
Total cost of purchase (nominal value plus premium = £2.40 × 100,000)		240

The effect on the balance sheet of company Y is as follows:

Balance sheet	Before purchase £'000	Issue of shares £'000	Purchase of shares £'000	Maintain capital £'000	After purchase £'000
Ordinary shares	1,100		(100)		1,000
New ordinary shares	–	75			75
Share premium	–	75	(10)		65
Capital redemption reserve*	–	–	–	–	–
Capital	1,100	150	(110)	–	1,140
Distributable profits	500		(130)	–	370
	1,600	150	(240)	–	1,510
Net assets other than cash	1,350				1,350
Cash	250	150	(240)		160
	1,600	150	(240)	–	1,510

The double entry for this purchase is as follows:

	£'000	£'000
Dr Cash	150	
Cr Share capital		75
Cr Share premium		75

To record the issue of 75,000 £1 shares at a premium of £1 per share.

	£'000	£'000
Dr Share capital	100	
Dr Share premium account	10	
Dr Distributable profits	130	
Cr Cash		240

To recognise the purchase of £100,000 £1 shares at a premium of £1.40 per share.

*There is no transfer to capital redemption reserve because the nominal value of the shares purchased (that is, £100,000) is less than the aggregate proceeds of the new issue (that is £150,000 – see para 7.38) and, as a consequence, the company's capital has been maintained without the need to make such a transfer. The increase in capital of £40,000 comprises the £50,000 additional capital arising from the fresh issue of shares and a reduction in capital of £10,000, which represents the amount by which the share premium account has been reduced. Section 692(4) of the 2006 Act (or, for a redemption, section 687(5)) allows the share premium account to be reduced in the example by £10,000. This is the part of the premium payable on purchase/redemption that is allowed to be funded out of the proceeds of the fresh issue of shares as opposed to being made out of distributable profits. Without it the increase in capital would be £50,000.

7.34   Table 7.3 below shows the redemption by English China Clays plc of 500 preference shares having a nominal value of $0.5million (£0.3million). The purchase is made out of the proceeds of a rights issue and it can be seen from the extract that the payment has been made out of the share capital account, share premium account and distributable reserves. There is no transfer to the capital redemption reserve, because the proceeds of the fresh issue of shares exceeds the nominal value of the shares redeemed. Note that under both EU-adopted IFRS and UK GAAP, many preference shares (and any related share premiums) are presented as debt in the balance sheet. This extract demonstrates the accounting for shares that are recognised as equity.

Table 7.3 – Redemption of preference shares

English China Clays plc – Annual Report & Account – 31 December 1993

Notes to the Accounts (extract)

15 SHARE CAPITAL		£M
(a) Ordinary shares		
(i) Authorised and issued		
Authorised: 360,000,000 ordinary shares of 25p each		**90.0**
Allotted, called up and fully paid:		
At 31st December 1992 267,646,174 ordinary shares		**66.9**
Allotment of 35,243,638 ordinary shares		**8.8**
At 31st December 1993 302,889,812 ordinary shares		**75.5**

	1993	1992
Ordinary shares were issued as follows:		
Rights Issue	**33,497,162**	51,612,153
Scrip dividend elections	**457,457**	425,623
Exercise of share options	**417,055**	323,469
Conversion of 6½% Convertible Bonds Due 2003	**871,964**	241,991
	35,243,638	52,603,236

The shares issued under the Rights Issue, announced on 11th June 1993, were issued at 350p per share and raised approximately **£113.8M** net of expenses. Over 93% of the ordinary shares were taken up and those not taken up were sold on the market. The proceeds of the issue were used to repay US dollar bank borrowings and to redeem the remaining $50M of the US dollar preference shares.

(b) US dollar preference shares

| | Authorised, allotted, called up and fully paid | |
	$M	£M
At 31st December 1992		
500 preference shares		
of US$ 1,000 each	0.5	0.3
Redemption of 500 preference shares	(0.5)	(0.3)
At 31st December 1993	–	–

The Company completed the redemption of the 500 preference shares on 30th July 1993.

16 RESERVES (Extract)

	Group and Company	Group		Company
	Share Premium Account £M	Revaluation Reserve £M	Profit and Loss Account £M	Profit and Loss Account £M
At 31st December 1992				
as previously reported	355.1	98	298.1	180.8
Prior year adjustment	–	–	(2.2)	–
At 31st December 1992 as restated	355.1	98.2	295.9	180.8
Issue of ordinary shares	113.9	–	–	–
Costs in respect of the Rights Issue	(3.5)	–	–	–
Redemption of preference shares	(32.4)	–	(1.1)	(1.1)
Retained profit/(loss) for the year	–	–	0.5	(66.3)
Goodwill arising on acquisition	–	–	(155.5)	–
Transfer	–	(0.3)	0.3	–
Exchange rate movements	0.1	(0.1)	(3.4)	0.3
At 31st December 1993	433.2	97.8	136.7	113.7

[The next paragraph is 7.36.]

Capital maintenance

7.36   Both public and private companies are required by the Act to transfer certain amounts to the capital redemption reserve when they purchase for cancellation, or redeem, any of their own shares, whether these shares are classified as debt or equity in the balance sheet. This is to safeguard creditors by ensuring that the company's legal capital is maintained (except to the extent that a private company purchases its own shares out of capital or where the company undertakes a capital reduction). The capital redemption reserve carries the same restrictions on its use as share capital (so that the ordinary rules regarding the reduction of capital apply to it). One use to which the capital redemption reserve can be put is to pay up unissued shares allotted as fully paid bonus shares (see chapter 23 of the Manual of Accounting – IFRS for the UK and chapter 23 of the Manual of Accounting – UK GAAP).

7.37   The provisions explained below relate to the maintenance of capital where a public or a private company purchases or redeems its own shares. These rules are, however, extended further for private companies purchasing or redeeming shares with a payment that includes a payment out of capital; these additional rules are explained from paragraph 7.55 onwards. The other exception to the capital maintenance rules is when a company undertakes a reduction in capital (see para 7.93).

7.38   A transfer to the capital redemption reserve must be made by a company, whether public or private, in the following circumstances:

■   Where the company has purchased or redeemed its shares wholly out of distributable profits (that is, where no fresh issue of shares is made or no payment is made out of capital or the shares are not held in treasury), it must transfer to the capital redemption reserve an amount equivalent to the nominal value of the shares it purchased/redeemed. [CA06 Sec 733(2)]. It also has to reduce the issued share capital by the nominal value of the shares purchased/redeemed (see example in para 7.27.1). [CA06 Sec 688(b), 706(b)].

■   Where the company cancels shares held as treasury shares, it must transfer to the capital redemption reserve an amount equivalent to the nominal value of the shares cancelled. [CA06 Sec 733(4)]. The company must reduce the amount of its issued share capital by the nominal value of the cancelled shares. [CA06 Sec 729(4)].

■   Where a company has purchased or redeemed its own shares wholly or partly out of the proceeds of a fresh issue (where no payment out of capital is made) and the nominal value of the shares purchased (or redeemed) exceeds the amount of the proceeds, the company must transfer the difference to the capital redemption reserve. [CA06 Sec 733(3)]. This treatment is illustrated in the example that follows:

Example — Nominal value of shares purchased exceeds proceeds of fresh share issue

Company H purchases 100,000 £1 ordinary shares at a premium of £1 (the initial premium on the shares when they were issued was 10p). It has a further 50,000 ordinary shares in issue which were issued for no premium. Company H makes the purchase partly out of the proceeds of a fresh issue of shares and partly out of its distributable profits. Company H issues 30,000 50p 'A' ordinary shares (a different class of share that meets the definition of equity) at a premium of £1.50 (that is, proceeds of £60,000).

The amount that will need to be transferred to the capital redemption reserve is calculated as follows:

	£'000
Nominal value of shares redeemed	100
Proceeds of fresh issue	60
Amount to be transferred to the capital redemption reserve	40

Following the table in paragraph 7.21, company H makes the purchase in the way shown below:

Funding of purchase:	£'000	£'000
Out of the proceeds of the fresh issue:		
(a) Nominal value of shares purchased restricted to proceeds of fresh issue	60	
(b) Share premium account*	–	60
Balance out of distributable profits		140
Total cost of purchase (nominal value plus premium = £2 × 100,000)		200

* Some might argue that part of the purchase can be made out of the share premium account (£10,000 in the example, being the premium on the issue of the shares being purchased, as this is lower than the balance on the share premium account). However, if this argument is pursued, the effect is that the company's capital is reduced by £10,000 and, as a consequence, is not maintained, contrary to the intention of the Act. This approach can also be said to be wrong on the grounds that the proceeds of the fresh issue are £60,000 and this has all been used funding the purchase of the nominal value of the shares being purchased and as a consequence there is nothing else that can come out of the share premium account.

The effect on the balance sheet of company H is as follows:

Balance sheet	Before purchase £'000	Issue of shares £'000	Purchase of shares £'000	Maintain capital £'000	After purchase £'000
Ordinary shares	150		(100)		50
'A' ordinary shares	–	15	–	–	15
Share premium	10	45	–	–	55
Capital redemption reserve	–	–	–	40	40
Capital	160	60	(100)	40	160
Reserves – Distributable profits	150	–	(100)	(40)	10
	310	60	(200)	–	170
Net assets other than cash	150	–	–	–	150
Cash	160	60	(200)	–	20
	310	60	(200)	–	170

The double entry for the purchase would be as follows:

	£'000	£'000
Dr Cash	60	
Cr Share capital		15
Cr Share premium		45

To record the issue of 30,000 50p shares at a premium of £1.50 per share.

	£'000	£'000
Dr Share capital	100	
Dr Distributable profits	100	
Cr Cash		200

To recognise the purchase of £100,000 £1 shares at a premium of £1 per share.

	£'000	£'000
Dr Distributable profits	40	
Cr Capital redemption reserve		40

To maintain the capital of the company.

In total, distributable profits have been reduced by £140,000 being the cost of the repurchase (£200,000) less the amount funded out of the proceeds (£60,000) of the fresh issue for the purpose of the repurchase.

7.39   Table 7.5 below illustrates a purchase out of distributable profits and maintenance of capital by the transfer of an amount equal to the nominal value of the shares redeemed to the capital redemption reserve. In Table 7.5 the company applies IFRS and presents a Statement of changes in equity. Table 7.5.A is another example from a company that applies UK GAAP and presents a Reconciliation of movements in shareholders' funds.

Table 7.5 – Maintenance of capital

CLS Holdings plc – Annual Report & Accounts – 31 December 2009

[Note: Comparatives have not been reproduced in this example, nor have the Directors' report disclosures]

GROUP STATEMENT OF CHANGES IN EQUITY (extract)

for the year ended 31 December 2009

| | Notes | Attributable to the owners of the company | | | | | Minority interest £m | Total £m |
		Share capital £m	Share premium £m	Other reserves £m	Retained earnings £m	Total £m		
At 1 January 2009		16.7	70.5	100.4	152.2	339.8	(1.2)	338.6
Arising in 2009:								
Total comprehensive income/(loss) for the year		–	–	1.2	17.5	18.7	(0.1)	18.6
Purchase of own shares	23	(3.4)	–	3.4	(48.0)	(48.0)	–	(48.0)
Expenses thereof		–	–	–	(0.2)	(0.2)	–	(0.2)
Total changes arising in 2009		(3.4)	–	4.6	(30.7)	(29.5)	(0.1)	(29.6)
At 31 December 2009		13.3	70.5	105.0	121.5	310.3	(1.3)	309.0

26 OTHER RESERVES (extract)

	Capital redemption reserve £m	Cumulative translation reserve £m	Fair value reserve £m	Other reserves £m	Total £m
At 1 January 2009	17.0	59.8	(4.5)	28.1	100.4
Purchase of own shares:					
– cancellation pursuant to tender offer	3.4	–	–	–	3.4
Exchange rate variances	–	(9.5)	–	–	(9.5)
Share of exchange rate variances of associates	–	0.4	–	–	0.4
Available-for-sale financial assets:					
– net fair value gains in the year	–	–	13.5	–	13.5
– deferred tax thereon	–	–	(3.2)	–	(3.2)
At 31 December 2009	20.4	50.7	5.8	28.1	105.0

23 SHARE CAPITAL (extract)

	Number					
	Ordinary shares in circulation thousands	Treasury shares thousands	Total ordinary shares thousands	Ordinary shares in circulation £m	Treasury shares £m	Total ordinary shares £m
At 1 January 2009	**61,745,471**	**5,000,000**	**66,745,471**	**15.4**	**1.3**	**16.7**
Cancelled following tender offer	**(13,721,215)**	**–**	**(13,721,215)**	**(3.4)**	**–**	**(3.4)**
At 31 December 2009	**48,024,256**	**5,000,000**	**53,024,256**	**12.0**	**1.3**	**13.3**

24 TENDER OFFER BUY-BACKS

A tender offer by way of a Circular dated 1 December 2008 for the purchase of 2 in 9 shares at 350 pence per share was completed in January 2009. It returned £48,024,253 to shareholders, equivalent to 77.8 pence per share.

A further tender offer will be put to shareholders in April 2010 for the purchase of 1 in 42 shares at a price of 525 pence per share which, if approved, will return £6.0 million to shareholders, equivalent to 12.5 pence per share.

Table 7.5A – Maintenance of capital

Fidelity European Values PLC – Annual report – 31 December 2009

Directors' Report (extract)

SHARE CAPITAL – SHARE REPURCHASES AND SHARE ISSUES

Pursuant to the authority granted at the 2008 Annual General Meeting 1,727,996 ordinary shares of 25p each were repurchased for cancellation between 1 January 2009 and 18 May 2009. At the Annual General Meeting held on 19 May 2009 the Company's shareholders passed a special resolution which granted the Directors authority to purchase up to 8,061,000 ordinary shares in the market for cancellation. Pursuant to this authority, during the period 19 May 2009 to 31 December 2009 a further 2,070,609 ordinary 25p shares were repurchased for cancellation. In aggregate the total shares repurchased during the year ended 31 December 2009 was 3,798,605 (7.4% of the issued share capital as at 31 December 2009) for a total consideration of £37,913,000 (2008: £51,106,000).

As at 31 December 2009, the total number of shares in issue was 51,116,605 (2008: 54,915,210). The authority to repurchase shares expires on 18 May 2010 and a special resolution to renew the authority in respect of up to 14.99% of the issued share capital as at 5 March 2010 will be put to shareholders for approval at the forthcoming Annual General Meeting.

Since the year end, a further fifteen share repurchases have been made totalling 998,949 ordinary 25p shares. The issued share capital as at 5 March 2010 was 50,117,656. No share issues were made during the year (2008: nil).

Reconciliation of Movements in Shareholders' Funds

for the year ended 31 December 2009

	Notes	called up share capital £000	share premium account £000	Capital redemption reserve £000	capital reserve £000	revenue reserve £000	total equity £000
Opening shareholders' funds: 1 January 2008		14,737	58,615	1,088	767,645	12,560	854,645
Net recognised capital losses for the year		–	–	–	(160,235)	–	(160,235)
Repurchase of ordinary shares		(1,009)	–	1,009	(51,106)	–	(51,106)
Performance fee charged to capital		–	–	–	(7,458)	–	(7,458)
Taxation credited to capital		–	–	–	1,509	–	1,509
Net revenue after taxation for the year		–	–	–	–	20,617	20,617
Dividend paid to shareholders	7	–	–	–	–	(7,991)	(7,991)
Closing shareholders' funds: 31 December 2008		13,728	58,615	2,097	550,355	25,186	649,981
Net recognised capital gains for the year	14	–	–	–	45,099	–	45,099
Repurchase of ordinary shares	14	(949)	–	949	(37,913)	–	(37,913)
Taxation credited to capital	14	–	–	–	506	–	506
Net revenue after taxation for the year	14	–	–	–	–	10,882	10,882
Dividends paid to shareholders	7	–	–	–	–	(19,620)	(19,620)
Closing shareholders' funds: 31 December 2009		12,779	58,615	3,046	558,047	16,448	648,935

1. ACCOUNTING POLICIES (extract 1)

The Company has prepared its financial statements in accordance with United Kingdom Generally Accepted Accounting Practice ("UK GAAP") and the AIC Statement of Recommended Practice ("SORP") for Investment Trusts issued in January 2009.

As a result of technical guidance issued by the Institute of Chartered Accountants in England and Wales in TECH 01/08: "Distributable Profits", changes in the fair value of investments which are readily convertible to cash, without accepting adverse terms at the balance sheet date, can be treated as realised. As a result of the new SORP, capital reserves realised and unrealised are now shown in aggregate as capital reserve in the Reconciliation of Movements in Shareholders' Funds and the Balance Sheet. At the balance sheet date all investments held by the Company were listed on a recognised stock exchange and were considered to be readily convertible to cash.

---

1. ACCOUNTING POLICIES (extract 2)

j) Capital reserve

The following are accounted for in capital reserve:

- gains and losses on the disposal of investments
- changes in fair value of the investments held at the year end
- foreign exchange gains and losses of a capital nature
- performance fee chargeable to capital
- dividends receivable which are capital in nature
- costs of repurchasing ordinary shares

Acquisition at a discount out of fresh share issue

7.40   In certain circumstances, it is possible to make acquisitions of shares at a discount. Where a fresh issue of shares has been made for the purpose of the acquisition, it will still be necessary to maintain the company's capital in accordance with the rules discussed above from paragraph 7.36, by transferring the difference between the amount raised on the fresh issue of shares and the nominal value of the shares being redeemed (if greater) to the capital redemption reserve. [CA06 Sec 733(3)].

> **Example — Acquisition at a discount out of a fresh share issue**
>
> Company A decides to purchase 100,000 of its £1 shares for £90,000, a discount of 10% (the shares were initially issued at a premium of 10p per share). In addition, there are another 100,000 shares in issue which were issued at par. The purchase is made out of the proceeds of a fresh issue of 45,000 £1 redeemable preference shares issued at a premium of £1 (that is, proceeds of £90,000). Under IAS 32 and FRS 25 such redeemable shares and their related premiums will be accounted for as liabilities in the balance sheet. The company has no distributable profits.
>
> Following the table in paragraph 7.21, the company makes the purchase in the following way:

	£'000
Funding of purchase:	
Out of proceeds of fresh share issue:	
(a) Nominal value of shares purchased	90
(b) Share premium	–
	90
Out of distributable profits	–
Total cost of purchase	90

The amount to be transferred to the capital redemption reserve is then calculated as follows:

	£'000
Nominal value of shares purchased	100
Less: Proceeds of fresh issue	90
Amount transferred to the capital redemption reserve	10

The balance sheets before and after are shown below:

Balance sheet	Before purchase £'000	Issue of shares £'000	Purchase of shares £'000	Maintain capital £'000	After purchase £'000
Ordinary shares	200	–	(100)	–	100
Share premium	10	–	–	–	10
Capital redemption reserve	–	–	–	10	10
Capital	210	–	(100)	10	120
Reserves – Distributable profits	–	–	10	(10)	–
	210	–	(90)	–	120
Net assets other than cash and preference shares	210	–	–	–	210
Liabilities (preference shares including related share premium)	–	(90)	–	–	(90)
Cash	–	90	(90)	–	–
	210	–	(90)	–	120

This would appear to show a reduction in capital, despite the transfer to capital redemption reserve. This is because the balance sheets above are for accounting purposes and under the accounting rules the new shares are classified as liabilities, not capital. The balance sheets categorising the shares in accordance with their legal form, showing the maintenance of capital, are as follows:

Balance sheet	Before purchase £'000	Issue of shares £'000	Purchase of shares £'000	Maintain capital £'000	After purchase £'000
Ordinary shares	200	–	(100)	–	100
Preference shares	–	45	–	–	45
Share premium	10	45	–	–	55
Capital redemption reserve	–	–	–	10	10
Capital	210	90	(100)	10	210
Reserves – Distributable profits	–	–	10	(10)	–
	210	90	(90)	–	210
Net assets other than cash and preference shares	210	–	–	–	210
Liabilities excluding preference shares	–	–	–	–	–
Cash	–	90	(90)	–	–
Net assets	210	90	(90)	–	210

The double entry for the purchase would be as follows:

	£'000	£'000
Dr Cash	90	
Cr Liabilities (preference shares including related premium)		90

To show the issue of 45,000 £1 redeemable preference shares at a premium of £1 per share.

	£'000	£'000
Dr Share capital	100	
Cr Distributable reserves		10
Cr Cash		90

To recognise the purchase of £100,000 £1 shares at a discount of 10 per cent.

	£'000	£'000
Dr Distributable reserves	10	
Cr Capital redemption reserve		10

To maintain the capital of the company.

It should be noted that no profit arises on this transaction, although it might appear at first sight that a profit of £10,000 arises on the purchase. This is because no profit is regarded as arising on a transaction with shareholders.

Disclosure requirements

7.41 A company's directors' report and financial statements have to give various information concerning the shares it purchases during the year, the rights of redemption of any redeemable shares and the authority the company has to acquire any of its shares.

Directors' report

7.42   In the year in which a company purchases or redeems its own shares, certain information is required to be included in the directors' report by the Companies Act 2006 and, in the case of listed companies, the FSA's Listing Rules. These requirements are considered in detail in chapter 3.

7.43   In addition, certain disclosures relating to shares are required in the directors' report of a company with any of its securities that carry voting rights admitted to trading on a regulated market (see paras 7.111.2 and 7.111.3 below for regulated securities markets in the UK) at the end of its financial year. These are discussed in detail in chapter 3.

[The next paragraph is 7.46.]

Notes to the financial statements — UK GAAP

7.46   Where any part of a company's allotted share capital consists of redeemable shares the following information is required, by paragraph 47(2) of Schedule 1 to SI 2008/410, 'The Large and Medium-sized Companies and Groups (Accounts and Reports) Regulations 2008', and paragraph 46(2) of Schedule 1 to SI 2008/409, 'The Small Companies and Groups (Accounts and Directors' Report) Regulations 2008', to be given in the notes to financial statements of a company preparing 'UK GAAP financial statements':

■   The earliest and latest dates on which the company has power to redeem the shares.

■   Whether the shares must be redeemed or are redeemable at the option of the company or the shareholder.

■   The premium (if any) payable on redemption.

7.46.1   Paragraphs 47(1) and 48 of Schedule 1 to SI 2008/410 and paragraphs 46(1) and 47 of Schedule 1 to SI 2008/409 require disclosure of other details in respect of a company's shares. These are detailed in the Manual of Accounting – UK GAAP.

Notes to the financial statements — IFRS

7.46.2   IAS 1, 'Presentation of financial statements', requires certain disclosures in respect of capital, to enable users of a company's financial statements to evaluate its objectives, policies and processes for managing capital. These are considered in chapter 23 of the Manual of Accounting — IFRS for the UK.

Acquisitions and redemptions out of capital

7.47 The power to purchase or redeem shares out of 'capital' is available only to private companies as an exception to the rules safeguarding the maintenance of capital designed to protect creditors. Even then the company must comply with the stringent provisions of sections 709 to 723 of the 2006 Act (referred to in paras 7.93 to 7.106.5) before a payment out of 'capital' is made. These provisions apply equally to the redemption of redeemable shares and to the purchase of own shares. There are certain penalties that apply where the Act's provisions are not followed. Paragraphs 7.107 and 7.108 consider the situation where a liability can arise for directors and shareholders where a payment out of capital has been made and the company goes into liquidation within one year of the payment. The other area where the Act's capital maintenance rules are relaxed is under its 'reduction of capital' rules; these apply to private and public companies (although public companies are required to have court approval) and are dealt with from paragraph 7.93.

7.47.1 Pre-authorisation in the articles is not required before making an acquisition or redemption out of capital. However, the members may restrict or prohibit redemptions or purchases out of capital by including a provision to this effect in the articles. [CA06 Sec 709(1), para 1018 of the Explanatory Notes of the 2006 Act].

7.48 For the purposes of payments made out of capital, 'capital' is any payment by a company from a fund other than its distributable profits and the proceeds of a fresh issue. [CA06 Sec 709(1)]. Therefore, a company makes a payment out of capital if it purchases or redeems its shares otherwise than out of distributable profits or the proceeds of a fresh issue of shares. Unrealised profits would be capital for this purpose. Before a payment can be made out of capital, a company must first exhaust its distributable profits and proceeds of any fresh issue.

Permissible capital payment

7.49 The payment that a company may make out of capital when purchasing or redeeming its own shares is restricted to the permissible capital payment. The 'permissible capital payment' (PCP) is equal to the price of the shares being purchased or redeemed less the aggregate of any available profits and the proceeds of a fresh issue made to fund the purchase. [CA06 Sec 710]. The effect of this rule is to require a private company to utilise its available profits and any proceeds arising from a new issue before it makes a payment out of capital. The calculation of the permissible capital payment is represented by the following formula:

PCP = acquisition price – (available profits + proceeds of fresh issue)

Available profits

7.50 The reference to available profits in the calculation of the permissible capital payment is to the company's profits that are available for distribution within the meaning of the 2006 Act. Under section 830 of the 2006 Act, a private company's profits available for distribution are its accumulated realised profits, so far as not previously utilised by distribution or capitalisation, less its accumulated realised losses, so far as not previously written off in a reduction or re-organisation of capital. However, whether the company has any profits to use for the purchase or redemption and for the purposes of calculating the permissible capital payment is affected further by the provisions in section 712 of the 2006 Act.

7.51 Under those provisions the amount of the available profits is determined by reference to the items listed in paragraph 7.52 as they are stated in the relevant accounts. The relevant accounts for determining the permissible capital payment are those accounts drawn up as at any date within the period of three months ending on the date of the directors' statement (made in accordance with section 714 of the 2006 Act) that the directors are required to make regarding the purchase out of capital (see further para 7.95).

7.52 The items that must be considered in determining whether the company has any distributable profits are as follows:

- Profits, losses, assets and liabilities.

- Where the company is preparing IAS individual financial statements, provisions of any kind.

- Where the company is preparing Companies Act individual financial statements (that is, UK GAAP individual financial statements), provisions for depreciation, diminution in value of assets and retentions to meet liabilities (that is, provisions of the kind mentioned in paragraphs 1 and 2 of Schedule 9 to SI 2008/410, 'The Large and Medium-sized Companies and Groups (Accounts and Reports) Regulations 2008', and paragraphs 1 and 2 of Schedule 7 to SI 2008/409, 'The Small Companies and Groups (Accounts and Directors' Report) Regulations 2008').

- Share capital and reserves (including undistributable reserves).

[CA06 Sec 712(2)].

7.53 The relevant accounts, which need not be audited, must enable a reasonable judgment to be made of the amount of any of the items mentioned above. In order to arrive at the permissible capital payment, any of the 'distributions' mentioned below where lawfully made after the date of the relevant accounts and before the date of the directors' statement under section 714 must be deducted from the amount of the company's available profits:

- Financial assistance made out of distributable profits for the purpose of acquiring the company's own shares or its parent company's shares where the assistance comes within sections 677 to 683 of the 2006 Act (see para 7.132.1).

■ Any payment made out of distributable profits in respect of the purchase of any of the company's own shares.

■ Any payment made out of distributable profits in respect of: the company's acquisition of rights to purchase its own shares under a contingent purchase contract; or the variation of an existing contract of purchase; or the release from any obligation relating to a purchase of own shares.

■ Any other distribution or payment lawfully made out of distributable profits, for example, a dividend.

[CA06 Sec 712(3)(4)].

7.54 The example below illustrates the calculation of the permissible payment.

Example — Calculation of permissible capital payment

Company X purchases Mr Smith's shares partly out of the proceeds of a new issue of shares, partly out of distributable profits and partly out of capital. The rules can be illustrated as follows:

In January 20X0, company X issued 100,000 ordinary shares of £1 each to Mr Smith at their nominal value. Subsequently it issued 100,000 ordinary shares of £1 each at a premium of 50p per share. In July 20X5, company X has distributable profits of £60,000 and it issues 50,000 ordinary shares of £1 each at a premium of £1 per share for the purposes of purchasing at a premium of £1 per share Mr Smith's 100,000 ordinary shares issued in January 20X0.

In these circumstances, the permissible capital payment is calculated as follows:

	£'000	£'000
Price of purchase:		
100,000 £1 shares at a premium of £1 per share		200
Less: Proceeds of fresh issue of 50,000 £1 shares at a premium of £1 per share	100	
Distributable profits	60	160
Permissible capital payment		40

Following the table in paragraph 7.21, the purchase would be made in the following way:

Funding of purchase:

	£'000	£'000
Out of the proceeds of the fresh issue:		
(a) Nominal value of shares purchased	100	
(b) Share premium account*	–	100
Out of distributable profits		60
Balance out of capital		40
Total cost of purchase (nominal value plus premium = £2 × 100,000)		200

*No share premium arose on the issue of the shares being purchased, but even if it had the entire proceeds of the fresh issue are already being utilised.

The balance sheets would be as follows:

Balance sheet	Before purchase £'000	Issue of shares £'000	Purchase of shares £'000	After purchase £'000
Share capital	200	50	(100)	150
Share premium	50	50	(40)*	60
Capital	250	100	(140)	210
Reserves – Distributable profits	60	–	(60)	–
	310	100	(200)	210
Net assets other than cash	210	–	–	210
Cash	100	100	(200)	–
	310	100	(200)	210

The double entry for the purchase would be as follows:

	£'000	£'000
Dr Cash	100	
Cr Share capital		50
Cr Share premium		50

To record the issue of 50,000 £1 shares at a premium of £1 per share.

	£'000	£'000
Dr Share capital	100	
Dr Distributable profits	60	
Dr Capital reduction*	40	
Cr Cash		200

To recognise the purchase of £100,000 £1 shares at a premium of £1 per share.

* The permissible capital payment should be deducted from a capital redemption reserve or a share premium account or the fully paid share capital or any unrealised profits of the company (see further para 7.59). In the example it has been deducted from the share premium account.

No available profits due to losses

7.54.1 A company that has cumulative losses will not have any available profits to take into account in determining a permissible capital payment. The law is seemingly silent on whether in such circumstances a purchase out of capital is possible.

7.54.2 Arguably, as the law is silent it might be that such a company could purchase its shares out of its unrealised profits and share capital, ignoring its cumulative losses. However, the directors have to make a statement under the Companies Act 2006 that the company will continue to carry on business as a going concern throughout the year following the permissible capital payment. In doing so, it will be necessary to take into account the company's loss making status and the impact this has on its solvency. Although, the directors may conclude that the company is solvent in the terms demanded by the Act, the auditor when providing his report is required to consider whether he is aware of anything to indicate that the opinion expressed by the directors is not unreasonable in all the circumstances; he may consider the loss making status precludes him from giving such a report. [CA06 Sec 714(6)(c)]. If the required directors' statement and/or the auditor's report cannot be given, then the conditions for the payment out of capital are not met. Before commencing the process for a permissible capital payment, legal advice should be sought to establish the robustness of the legal position. See also para 7.62.1.

Capital maintenance

7.55 The general provisions concerning capital maintenance are explained from paragraph 7.36, but the rules differ for private companies purchasing or redeeming out of capital as explained in the paragraphs that follow.

Transfer to capital redemption reserve

7.56 Where a private company purchases or redeems its shares with a payment that includes a payment out of capital, the following transfers must be made to the company's capital redemption reserve (CRR):

■ If the nominal value of the shares purchased or redeemed *exceeds* the permissible capital payment (where no fresh issue of shares is made), the company must transfer the difference to the capital redemption reserve.

[CA06 Sec 734(2)].

■ If the nominal value of the shares purchased or redeemed *exceeds* the aggregate of the permissible capital payment *and* the proceeds of a fresh issue, the difference must be transferred to the capital redemption reserve.

[CA06 Sec 734(4)].

7.57 This rule can be represented in the following way:

$$\text{Transfer to CRR} =$$
$$\text{nominal value of shares purchased} - (\text{PCP} + \text{proceeds of fresh issue})$$

The position where the permissible capital payment plus the proceeds of a fresh issue of shares exceeds the nominal value of the shares purchased or redeemed is considered in paragraph 7.59.

7.58 The example below illustrates the transfer that is required to be made to the capital redemption reserve.

Example — Transfer to the capital redemption reserve

Companies A, B, C and D (all private companies) each purchase 10,000 of their own shares that were originally issued at their nominal value of £1 per share. In each case, a premium of £1.40 per share is payable on purchase. Company B is issuing 7,000 £1 redeemable preference shares at par and company D is issuing 4,000 £1 redeemable preference shares at par. The preference shares issued by both companies B and D are redeemable at par and are presented as liabilities in the balance sheets of companies B and D respectively in accordance with IAS 32 and FRS 25. The retained profits (all distributable) are company A £50,000, company B £30,000, company C £16,000 and company D £15,000. Following the table in paragraph 7.21, the purchases are thus to be made as follows:

	A £'000	B £'000	C £'000	D £'000
Funding of purchase:				
Out of proceeds of new issue:				
(a) Nominal value of shares purchased restricted to proceeds of fresh issue	–	7	–	4
(b) Share premium	–	–	–	–
	–	7	–	4
Out of distributable profits	24	17	16	15
	24	24	16	19
Balance out of capital	–	–	8	5
	24	24	24	24

In these circumstances, the amount that each company must transfer to its capital redemption reserve is as follows:

	A £'000	B £'000	C £'000	D £'000
Nominal value of shares purchased	10	10	10	10
Less:				
Proceeds of fresh issue	–	7	–	4
Permissible capital payment	–	–	8	5
	–	7	8	9
Transfer to the capital redemption reserve	10	3	2	1

The effect on the summarised balance sheets can be illustrated as follows:

Balance sheets	A £'000	B £'000	C £'000	D £'000
Before purchase				
Share capital	100	100	100	100
Distributable profits	50	30	16	15
	150	130	116	115
Net assets other than cash	125	105	90	80
Cash	25	25	26	35
	150	130	116	115
After purchase				
Ordinary shares	90	90	90	90
Capital redemption reserve	10	3	2	1
	100	93	92	91
Distributable profits	26	13	–	–
	126	106	92	91
Cash	1	8	2	15
Net assets other than cash and preference shares	125	105	90	80
Liabilities (preference shares)	–	(7)	–	(4)
	126	106	92	91

From a legal perspective, the remaining ordinary share capital, capital redemption reserve and preference share capital, after the fresh issue and purchase, are as follows:

Ordinary share capital, capital redemption reserve and preference share capital	100	100	92	95

This shows that the legal capital was maintained for company A and company B and was reduced by the amount of the permissible capital payment (8 and 5) for company C and company D.

The double entry for the purchases is as follows:

Company A	£'000	£'000
Dr Share capital	10	
Dr Distributable profits	14	
Cr Cash		24

To recognise the purchase of £10,000 £1 shares at a premium of £1.40 per share.

Dr Distributable profits	10	
Cr Capital redemption reserve		10

To maintain the capital of the company

Company B		
Dr Cash	7	
Cr Liabilities (preference shares)		7

To recognise 7,000 £1 redeemable preference shares issued at par.

Dr Share capital	10	
Dr Distributable profits	14	
Cr Cash		24

To recognise the purchase of £10,000 £1 shares at a premium of £1.40 per share.

Dr Distributable profits	3	
Cr Capital redemption reserve		3

To maintain the capital of the company (£10,000 less the proceeds of the fresh issue of £7,000)

Company C		
Dr Share capital	10	
Dr Distributable profits	14	
Cr Cash		24

To recognise the purchase of £10,000 £1 shares at a premium of £1.40 per share.

Dr Distributable profits	2	
Cr Capital redemption reserve		2

To maintain the capital of the company as reduced by the PCP (£10,000 and the PCP of £8,000).

Company D		
Dr Cash	4	
Cr Liabilities (preference shares)		4

> To recognise 4,000 £1 redeemable preference shares issued at par.
>
> Dr Share capital   10
> Dr Distributable profits   14
>   Cr Cash   24
>
> To recognise the purchase of £10,000 £1 shares at a premium of £1.40 per share.
>
> Dr Distributable profits   1
>   Cr Capital redemption reserve   1
>
> To maintain the capital of the company as reduced by the PCP (£10,000 less the permissible capital payment of £5,000 and the proceeds of the new issue of £4,000).

Nominal value less than PCP and proceeds of fresh issue

7.59 Where shares are purchased or redeemed with a payment that includes a payment out of capital (but not the proceeds of a new issue of shares) and the permissible capital payment exceeds the nominal value of the shares purchased or redeemed, the company may use the excess to reduce one of the following:

■ The capital redemption reserve.

■ The share premium account.

■ Fully paid share capital.

■ The revaluation reserve.

[CA06 Sec 734(3)].

7.59.1 Surprisingly, section 734(3) does not include the redenomination reserve as a reserve that could be reduced. However, the redenomination reserve could be capitalised into shares prior to a permissible capital payment.

7.60 Furthermore, even where shares are purchased or redeemed out of the proceeds of a new issue, if the aggregate of the permissible capital payment and the proceeds of the new issue exceeds the nominal value of the shares being purchased or redeemed, the company may use the excess to reduce the items listed in paragraph 7.59. [CA06 Sec 734(4)]. This may seem counter intuitive, but the net result is that capital is reduced only by the amount of the permissible capital payment.

7.61 This rule is represented in the following way:

Dr to reduce capital =
PCP + proceeds of fresh issue – nominal value of shares purchased

The position where the permissible capital payment plus the proceeds of a fresh issue of shares is less than the nominal value of the shares purchased is considered in paragraph 7.56.

7.62 The following example illustrates the reduction of the capital redemption reserve and the share premium account to fund the excess.

Example – Nominal value less than permissible capital repayment

Companies E and F (both private companies) purchase 10,000 of their own shares that were originally issued at a premium of 10p per share. The nominal value of the shares in question is £1 per share and, in each case, a premium of £1.40 per share is payable. Company F issues 4,000 £1 preference shares at par (which are redeemable at par) to make the purchase. Company F's new shares will be classified as liabilities in accordance with IAS 32 and FRS 25. Before the purchase both companies have 100,000 £1 ordinary shares in issue and companies E and F have £11,000 and £9,000 distributable profits respectively. Following the table in paragraph 7.21, the purchases are to be made as follows:

	E £'000	F £'000
Funding of purchase:		
Out of proceeds of fresh issue of shares:		
(a) Nominal value of shares purchased restricted to proceeds of fresh issue	–	4
(b) Share premium account	–	–
	–	4
Out of distributable profits	11	9
	11	13
Balance out of capital	13	11
Total cost of purchase (nominal value plus premium = £2.40 × 10,000)	24	24

In the above circumstances, the aggregate amount by which company E and company F may reduce their capital redemption reserve, the share premium account or the fully-paid share capital is as follows:

	E £'000	F £'000
Permissible capital payment	13	11
Proceeds of new issue	–	4
	13	15
Nominal value of shares purchased	10	10
Excess available	3	5

If companies E and F use the available excess solely to reduce the share premium account, the effect on the summarised balance sheets can be illustrated as follows:

Balance sheet

Company E	Before purchase £'000	Issue of shares £'000	Purchase of shares £'000	After purchase £'000
Ordinary shares	100	–	(10)	90
Share premium	10	–	(3)	7
Capital	110	–	(13)	97
Distributable profits	11	–	(11)	–
	121	–	(24)	97
Net assets other than cash	96	–		96
Cash	25	–	(24)	1
	121	–	(24)	97

Balance sheet

Company F	Before purchase £'000	Issue of shares £'000	Purchase of shares £'000	After purchase £'000
Ordinary shares	100	–	(10)	90
Share premium	10	–	(5)	5
Capital	110	–	(15)	95
Distributable profits	9	–	(9)	–
	119	–	(24)	95
Net assets other than cash and preference shares	83	–	–	83
Liabilities (preference shares)	–	(4)	–	(4)
Cash	36	4	(24)	16
	119	–	(24)	95

From a legal perspective, company F's remaining ordinary share capital, share premium account and preference share capital, after the fresh issue and purchase, total £99,000. This shows that the legal capital was reduced only by the amount of the permissible capital payment of £11,000.

The double entry for the purchases is as follows:

Company E	£'000	£'000
Dr Share capital	10	
Dr Distributable profits	11	
Dr Capital (share premium account)	3	
Cr Cash		24

To recognise the purchase of £10,000 £1 shares at a premium of £1.40 per share.

Company F		
Dr Cash	4	
Cr Liabilities (preference shares)		4
To show the issue of 4,000 £1 redeemable preference shares at par.		
Dr Share capital	10	
Dr Distributable profits	9	
Dr Capital (share premium account)	5	
Cr Cash		24

To recognise the purchase of £10,000 £1 shares at a premium of £1.40 per share.

Shares to be purchased/redeemed at a premium in excess of the original premium on issue

7.62.1   The permissible capital payment is defined as the amount, if any, by which the aggregate of the company's available (distributable) profits and proceeds of a fresh issue of shares made for the purpose of the purchase/ redemption is less than the purchase/redemption price of the shares. The normal rules in sections 687 and 692 of the 2006 Act apply in relation to the balance of the purchase/redemption price. A problem arises where the proceeds of the fresh issue of shares (that is, nominal value and share premium) exceeds the nominal value of the shares to be purchased/redeemed. For example, if shares having a nominal value of 100 that were issued for 100 are to be purchased at a premium of 50 (that is for 150) using the proceeds of a fresh issue of 120 (and there are no available profits) the transaction would be unlawful even though the company's overall capital would be reduced only by the amount of the permissible capital payment. This is because, although the permissible capital payment would be 30 (that is, 150 less 120) the remaining premium on purchase of 20 (that is, 120 less 100) would be unlawful under section 692 of the 2006 Act as there are no available (distributable) profits.

Legal procedures for purchase

7.63   The procedures that a company must follow if it wishes to purchase its own shares will depend on whether the purchase is to be an 'off-market' purchase or a 'market' purchase. Certain initial matters to consider are mentioned in paragraph 7.12.

7.63.1 Irrespective of whether a contract for a purchase of own shares is an 'off-market' or a 'market' purchase or is a contingent contract, if it contains an obligation on the company then the accounting treatment specified in paragraph 23 of IAS 32 and FRS 25 must be followed (unless the exceptions in 16A – 16D apply). See chapter 23 of the Manual of Accounting – IFRS for the UK and the Manual of Accounting – UK GAAP.

Definition of 'off-market' and 'market'

7.64 A company's purchase of its own shares is an *off-market* purchase if either of the following apply:

- The shares are not purchased on a recognised investment exchange.

- The shares are purchased on a recognised investment exchange, but are not subject to a marketing arrangement on that investment exchange.

[CA06 Sec 693(2)].

For this purpose, a recognised investment exchange is defined to exclude an overseas exchange. [CA06 Sec 693(5)]. Any other purchase is a market purchase. [CA06 Sec 693(4)].

7.65 Shares are subject to a marketing arrangement where either they are listed on a recognised investment exchange or they can be dealt with on that exchange without prior permission for individual transactions from the authority governing the exchange and without time limit as to when those dealings can take place. [CA06 Sec 693(3)].

7.66 An off-market purchase will, therefore, *exclude* a purchase of shares listed on the London Stock Exchange, the PLUS-listed market, AIM and the PLUS-quoted market.

7.67 A company can make an off-market purchase only where the terms of the proposed contract of purchase have received prior authorisation by the shareholders (see para 7.72) or as a contingent purchase contract, again with the terms having received prior authorisation, under section 694(2),(3) (see para 7.89). The purchase by a private or an unquoted public company of its own shares will normally be an off-market purchase (see paras 7.78.1 and 7.72). A listed company will purchase its own shares either as an off-market purchase or a market purchase depending on the circumstances (see para 7.69).

Purchases by public companies

7.68 As discussed above, the statutory procedure that a public company should follow will depend on whether the purchase will be a market purchase or an off-market purchase.

Authority for market purchase

7.69 A market purchase by a listed public company of its own shares must first be authorised by ordinary resolution of the company in general meeting. The authority may be general or specific to a class or description of shares and may be unconditional or subject to conditions. The authority, however, must:

- Specify the maximum number of shares authorised to be acquired.

- Determine both the maximum and the minimum prices that may be paid for the shares. It may do this by specifying a particular sum or providing a basis or formula for calculating the amount of the price as long as the amount can be calculated without reference to any person's discretion or opinion.

- Specify a date, not more than five years from the date on which the resolution is passed, on which the authority is to expire. The terms of the authority may permit a purchase to be made after its expiry if the contract of purchase was concluded before the authority expired.

[CA06 Secs 701; 281(3)].

7.70 The authority may be varied, revoked or renewed at a company's general meeting by an ordinary resolution, but the company must comply with the conditions in paragraph 7.69 above. [CA06 Sec 701(4)]. A copy of any resolution giving, varying, revoking or renewing an authority to make a market purchase of a company's own shares must be sent to the Registrar of Companies within 15 days of the resolution being passed. [CA06 Secs 701(8), 30].

7.71 Two important differences exist between the authority for a market purchase and the authority for an off-market purchase. With a market purchase, it is the purchase of the shares that requires approval in the form of the authority of the company in general meeting. With an off-market purchase, a specific purchase contract (rather than the shares to be purchased) must be approved by special resolution. The authority for a market purchase need not relate to any particular shares and it need be approved only by an ordinary resolution whereas a special resolution is required for an off-market purchase. However, this less stringent statutory requirement is supplemented for listed companies, first by the Listing Rules and secondly by the insider dealing provisions referred to in paragraph 7.81. Furthermore, the Investments Committee of the Association of British Insurers has made recommendations regarding market purchases (see further para 7.131).

Authority for an off-market purchase

7.72   A company may make an off-market purchase of its own shares only if it does so under a contract the terms of which have received prior authorisation by a special resolution at a general meeting of the company. Either the terms of the contract must be authorised before the contract is entered into or the directors may enter into a contract which provides that shares cannot be purchased until approval of the terms has been obtained. If approval is not obtained the contract will lapse. [CA06 Sec 694(2)]. Where a company wishes to vary the terms of a contract authorised under section 694 of the 2006 Act, the terms of the variation similarly must be authorised by a special resolution in advance. [CA06 Secs 694(4); 697(1),(2)].   In the case of a public company, the special resolution (authorising the contract or the variation) must specify a date not later than five years from the date the resolution is passed, on which the authority is to expire. [CA06 Sec 694(5); 697(4)].

[The next paragraph is 7.74.]

7.74   The special resolution that confers the authority on the company to enter into a contract to purchase its own shares or to authorise the terms of an existing contract (including, in each case, a contingent purchase contract) or to vary or to revoke or renew such authority will not be effective in the two situations described below.

7.75   First, the special resolution will not be effective where a shareholder to whom the resolution relates exercises his voting rights on the shares that are subject to the acquisition in voting on the resolution and the resolution would not have been passed if he had not voted. For this purpose the following will apply:

- a member who holds shares to which the resolution relates is regarded as exercising the voting rights carried by those shares not only if he votes in respect of them on a poll on the question whether the resolution shall be passed, but also if he votes on the resolution otherwise than on a poll;

- notwithstanding anything in the company's articles, any member of the company may demand a poll on that question; and

- a vote and a demand for a poll by a person as proxy for a member are the same respectively as a vote and a demand by the member.

[CA06 Secs 695(1)(3)(4); 698(1)(3)(4)].].

7.76   Secondly, the resolution will not be effective unless a copy of the contract or variation thereof or, if not in writing, a written memorandum of the terms is available for inspection. The contract, variation or memorandum must be available for inspection by members at the company's registered office for not less than 15 days ending on the day of the meeting of the company at which the resolution is to be passed and at the meeting itself. The memorandum must include the names of the members to which the contract/variation relates and the contract/variation must also have annexed to it a memorandum specifying any names that do not appear in the contract/variation itself. [CA06 Secs 696; 699]. Where the resolution proposes a variation to an existing authorised contract, both the original contract, or memorandum of its terms, and the proposed variation, together with any variations previously made to the original contract, must be made available for inspection. [CA06 Sec 699(3)].

7.77 A copy of each special resolution passed by the company must be sent to the Registrar of Companies in the usual manner within 15 days of its being passed. [CA06 Sec 30(1)].

Variation of existing contract

7.78 A payment in consideration of the variation of a contract approved under section 694 of the 2006 Act must be made out of distributable profits. If this is not done, the purchase itself will be unlawful. [CA06 Sec 705].

Purchases by private companies

7.78.1 The above requirements for public companies seeking authority to make an off-market purchase apply equally to private companies except as set out in paragraphs 7.79 and 7.80 below.

7.79 Unlike for public companies, a private company's special resolution giving the necessary authority does not have to specify a date on which the authority expires. In addition, where a private company makes a payment out of capital it must comply with the provisions referred to from paragraph 7.93.

7.80 Where a company uses a written resolution to authorise the purchase, or to vary such a contract or contingent purchase contract, a shareholder whose shares are the subject of the written resolution is not an eligible member thus is not allowed to vote on it. [CA06 Sec 695(2); 698(2)]. Each eligible member must be supplied, no later than the time when the proposed resolution is sent to them, with a copy of the contract or contract together with variation and, where not in the contract/variation, the names of the vendors. [CA06 Sec 696(2); 699(2)(3)].

Insider dealing and market abuse

7.81 The provisions relating to the criminal offence of insider dealing are contained in Part V of the Criminal Justice Act 1993. Since 2001, the FSA is a prosecuting authority for the criminal offence of insider dealing (as defined in the Criminal Justice Act 1993). The provisions prohibit certain dealings in the shares and other securities (such as debt securities) of listed companies. Directors (and others who discharge managerial responsibilities) of such companies should be aware of the provisions of this Act that might affect a company's acquisition of its own shares.

7.81.1 In addition, the FSA's DTR govern the prompt and fair disclosure of relevant information to the markets; set out specific circumstances when an issuer can delay public disclosure of inside information; and contain requirements to ensure that such information is kept confidential in order to protect investors and prevent insider dealing. [DTR chapter 2]. Persons discharging managerial responsibilities (including directors) and their connected persons must notify their company in writing of all transactions conducted on their own account in their company's shares or derivatives or any other financial instruments relating to those shares within four business days of the day on which the transaction occurred. [DTR paras 3.1.2, 3.1.3].

7.81.2   The Financial Services and Markets Act 2000 (FSMA) creates civil penalties for market abuse, which includes insider dealing as one of seven behaviours that can constitute a civil offence. As the level of evidence is lower than in criminal prosecutions, the government hoped that it would be easier to obtain prosecutions for insider dealing. Directors of listed companies are also subject to the Code of Market Conduct issued by the FSA. Criminal offences under the Code of Market Conduct and the FSMA include making a misleading statement and engaging in a misleading course of conduct for the purpose of inducing another person to exercise or refrain from exercising rights in relation to investments. In 2005, two directors of AIT Group Plc received custodial sentences for releasing a misleading trading update statement to the market. This was the first time that the FSA had used its powers to take criminal proceedings under the FSMA.

Returns, notices and contracts

7.82   Following the completion of the purchase of its own shares (including redeemable shares) a company must make certain returns under the Act. No later than 28 days after the delivery of shares to it, the company, whether public or private, must deliver a return to the Registrar of Companies stating, with respect to each class, the number and nominal value of the shares purchased and the date they were delivered to the company. The return must distinguish between shares purchased as treasury shares, sub-dividing these into those that are cancelled and those that are not cancelled, and all other shares purchased. Additionally, a public company must state the aggregate amount paid for the shares and the maximum and minimum prices paid in respect of shares of each class purchased. Failure to file the form is a criminal offence and the directors in default are liable to a fine. [CA06 Sec 707].

7.83   When a company cancels shares it has purchased, it must give notice of the cancellation to the registrar within 28 days of the shares being delivered to it. The notice must be accompanied by a statement of capital setting out the following with respect to the company's share capital immediately following the cancellation:

■   Total number of shares of the company.

■   Aggregate nominal value of those shares.

■   For each class of shares:

- details of voting, dividend, capital and redemption rights attached to the shares;

- number of shares; and

- aggregate nominal value of shares.

- Amount paid up and amount unpaid on each share.

Failure to comply is a criminal offence and the company and directors in default are liable to a fine. [CA06 Sec 708; SI 2009/388 para 2].

7.84   Both private and public companies must keep a copy of each contract, or, if not in writing, a written memorandum setting out its terms, for any off-market purchase, contingent purchase or market purchase they enter into, together with any variations to any such contracts. These documents must be kept at the company's registered office from the date the contracts are concluded until the date which is ten years after the date of the purchase to which they relate (or ten years after some other date specified in the contract). SI 2008/3006 permits companies to specify an alternative inspection location providing certain conditions are met and the company has notified the registrar that the contract is being kept in the alternative location and specifying that location. Companies must make a copy of such a contract available for inspection by any member without charge. A public company must additionally allow the contract to be inspected by any other person, again, without charge. [CA06 Sec 702].

7.85   A company's obligations in relation to making the contracts and memoranda available for inspection by members and non-members are set out in the Companies (Inspection and Copying of Registered Indices and Documents) Regulations 1991 (SI 1991/1998).

7.86   Failure to comply with section 702 of the Act is a criminal offence and the company and directors in default are liable to a fine. [CA06 Sec 703].

Prohibition on assignment of rights

7.87   The rights of a public or private company under a contract to make a market or an off-market purchase of its own shares or a contingent purchase contract cannot be assigned. This prohibition is designed to prevent a company from speculating against its own share price by buying or selling its rights to purchase its own shares. [CA06 Sec 704].

7.88   An agreement by a company to release all or any of its rights under a contract to make an off-market purchase of its own shares or a contingent purchase contract is void unless the terms of the release are approved in advance by a special resolution of the company before the agreement is entered into. In the case of a public company, the special resolution must specify a date not later than five years from the date the resolution is passed, on which the authority is to expire. The procedures referred to in paragraphs 7.74 to 7.77 and 7.78.1 to 7.80 apply to a company when seeking approval for the release as they apply to a proposed variation. [CA06 Sec 700]. A payment made in consideration for the release of the company's obligations must be paid out of distributable profits or the release will be void. [CA06 Sec 705].

Contingent purchase contracts

7.89   Although the 2006 Act does not use the term 'contingent purchase contract', such contracts are nevertheless permitted for off-market transactions. Section 694(3) of the 2006 Act states that the contract (to purchase) 'may be a contract, entered into by the company and relating to shares in the company, that does not amount to a contract to purchase the shares but under which the company may (subject to any conditions) become entitled or obliged to purchase the shares'. For ease, this chapter refers to such contracts as contingent contracts. A contingent contract may give the company an option to purchase shares or give the shareholder the option to require their purchase by the company. Such a purchase contract might arise, for example, where a shareholder is prepared to maintain an investment in a company only if there are arrangements that ensure that he will be able to sell his shares back to the company at any time in the future. In this circumstance, the company may not wish to issue a new class of redeemable shares in order to satisfy the shareholder's wishes. Instead, it may prefer to make a contractual arrangement with the shareholder under which the company may purchase the shares at a later date at the shareholder's option. Similarly, a contingent purchase contract would include, for example, a contract under which a company may be obliged to purchase an employee's shares on his retirement.

7.89.1   Contracts for the repurchase of a company's own shares of the nature discussed in paragraph 7.89 will fall to be accounted for in accordance with paragraph 23 of IAS 32 and FRS 25 (see chapter 23 of the Manual of Accounting – IFRS for the UK and the Manual of Accounting – UK GAAP).

7.90   The use of contingent purchase contracts to buy a company's own shares may be open to abuse unless they are accompanied by certain safeguards for other shareholders. The approach of the Act is to treat contingent purchase contracts in the same way as it treats all other off-market contracts of purchase, thus all the rules and shareholder safeguards that apply to off-market purchase contracts apply to contingent contracts (see from para 7.72).

Legal procedures for redemption

7.91   Many of the legal procedures in respect of redeemable shares are concerned with the issue of the shares as it is upon issue that the terms of redemption are agreed. Such issues are discussed from paragraph 7.8 onwards. Upon redemption the shares are treated as cancelled, the amount of the company's issued share capital is diminished accordingly by the nominal value of the shares redeemed and relevant transfers are made to the capital redemption reserve and/or the procedures for a payment out of capital are adhered to as described above from paragraph 7.47 onwards. The legal procedures to be followed for a payment out of capital are described below from paragraph 7.93.6.

7.92 Within one month of redemption the company must give notice to the Registrar of Companies specifying the shares redeemed. [CA06 Sec 689(1)]. The notice must be accompanied by a statement of capital setting out the following with respect to the company's share capital immediately after redemption:

■ Total number of shares of the company.

■ Aggregate nominal value of those shares.

■ For each class of shares:

  ■ details of voting, dividend, capital and redemption rights attached to the shares;

  ■ number of shares; and

  ■ aggregate nominal value of shares.

■ Amount paid up and amount unpaid on each share.

Failure to comply is a criminal offence and the company and directors in default are liable to a fine. [CA06 Sec 689].

Payments out of capital and capital reductions

Purchase/redemption of own shares out of capital or capital reduction?

7.93 Sections 709 to 723 of the 2006 Act set out rules governing the purchase or redemption of own shares out of capital, with sections 713 to 720 dealing with the legal procedures that must be followed after calculating the amount of the permissible capital payment. These procedures are required as such payments out of capital are an exception to the capital maintenance rule, discussed above, under which companies, once they have issued shares, have to maintain the same level of capital base. The option to purchase or redeem out of capital is only available to private companies.

7.93.1 Until the 2006 Act, purchase or redemption out of capital was the only route available to companies to reduce their capital without going to the courts for approval. Private and public companies could previously apply to the courts to reduce their capital and this remains so under the 2006 Act. However, the 2006 Act introduced an additional procedure, available to only private companies, to reduce their capital without the need to apply to the courts.

7.93.2 A capital reduction (whether or not via the courts) can be used simply to reduce capital without paying anything to shareholders. For example, paid-up share capital could be cancelled to create distributable profits or eliminate a deficit. Equally a capital reduction could involve buying back shares from shareholders for a cash payment or other form of consideration. On the other hand, a payment out of capital will always involve a cash payment.

7.93.3   As seen in paragraph 7.59 above, a permissible capital payment can reduce fully paid share capital, share premium account, capital redemption reserve and revaluation reserve. A capital reduction can be used to reduce the first three as share premium and capital redemption reserves constitute share capital for the purpose of a reduction. In addition, a capital reduction can reduce the redenomination reserve as that also constitutes share capital for the purposes of a capital reduction. [CA06 Sec 628(3)]. However, other types of reserves, such as a revaluation reserve, cannot be reduced by way of a capital reduction, but could be capitalised into shares prior to the reduction.

7.93.4   Paragraphs 7.93.6 to 7.108 below deal with the payments out of capital and capital reductions not involving court approval, while paragraphs 7.108.1 to 7.108.14 deal with court approved capital reductions.

7.93.5   A reduction of capital arising on a redenomination of share capital is dealt with in chapter 23 of the Manual of Accounting – IFRS for the UK and the Manual of Accounting – UK GAAP. The rules that are in this chapter on capital reductions do not apply to a reduction arising on a redenomination. [CA06 Sec 626(6)].

Without court approval

7.93.6   Set out in the following table is a high level comparison of the two methods of purchasing shares out of capital without court approval:

	Payment out of capital	Capital reduction (without court approval)
Available only to private companies (and not to public companies)	✓	✓
Pre-authorisation not required by articles	✓	✓
Permitted provided no restriction or prohibition in articles	✓	✓
Special resolution required	✓	✓
Not permitted if the only shares that would remain are redeemable shares	✓	✓
Solvency statement required by directors	✓	✓
Report required by company's auditor	✓	x
Permitted even if intend to commence winding up the company within twelve months of the date of the solvency statement	x	✓

Permitted only if first use up distributable profits and proceeds of fresh issue made for the purpose	✓	x
Public notice of proposed payment required	✓	x
Creditors can object	✓	x
Payment must be made between five and seven weeks of the special resolution being passed	✓	x
Payment must be in cash	✓	x
Shares must be fully paid up before being bought back or redeemed	✓	x
If payment to buy back shares is less than the capital reduction, it may create distributable profits	x	✓
Could be used to eliminate a deficit or create distributable reserves	x	✓
Various papers	To be available for inspection at registered office or alternative inspection place	To be filed with registrar

Authorisation

7.93.7 Pre-authorisation in a company's articles is not required for either a payment out of capital or a capital reduction. However, the company must be a private company and its articles must neither restrict nor prohibit a payment out of capital or a capital reduction. (The circumstances under which a company may make an acquisition of own shares or redeem shares out of capital are considered from para 7.47.)

7.94 Both the payment out of capital and the capital reduction must be approved by a special resolution of the company in general meeting (see para 7.101). [CA06 Secs 716(1), 641(1)(a), 642(3)]. Alternatively, the company may seek approval by written resolution. [CA06 Secs 717, 642(2)]. However, in that situation, for a proposed payment out of capital, a member holding shares to which the resolution relates is not an eligible member and should not vote on the resolution. [CA06 Sec 717]. Similarly, again for a proposed payment out of capital, the resolution in a general meeting will not be effective where a shareholder holding shares to which the resolution relates exercises his voting rights on those shares and the resolution would not have been passed if he had not voted. [CA06 Sec 717].

Conditions

7.94.1 A private company must, after a capital reduction, have other non-redeemable shares in issue. [CA06 Sec 641(2)]. As private companies cannot hold treasury shares there is no need for the Act to stipulate (as it does in section 690(2) for purchase of own shares generally) that treasury shares do not count for this purpose. After a capital reduction only one share needs to remain in issue. The principle is that a private company cannot reduce its share capital to zero without the sanction of the court.

7.94.2 The equivalent conditions for purchase or redemption of own shares are dealt with from paragraph 7.13 onwards.

Directors' solvency statement

7.95 The directors of a company proposing to make a payment out of capital or a capital reduction must make a statement, in writing, in the prescribed form. [CA06 Secs 714, 641(1)(a), 642, 643; SI 2009/388 para 5; SI 2008/1915 para 2].

7.96 The statement and its content and the procedures required of the directors for a payment out of capital are consistent with, but not identical to, those for a capital reduction. The two statements are contrasted below.

Proposed payment out of capital	*Proposed capital repayment*
■ Having made full inquiry into the affairs and prospects of the company, the directors have formed the opinion:	■ Each of the directors has formed the opinion:
■ As regards its initial situation immediately following the date on which the payment out of capital is proposed to be made, that there will be no grounds on which the company could then be found unable to pay its debts.	■ As regards the company's situation at the date of the statement, that there is no ground on which the company could then be found unable to pay (or otherwise discharge) its debts.
	■ If it is intended to commence the winding up of the company within twelve months of that date, that the company will be able to pay (or otherwise discharge) its debts in full within twelve months of the commencement of the winding up; or
■ As regards its prospects for the year immediately following that date, that having regard to:	■ In any other case (that is, if it is not intended to commence the winding up of the company within twelve

(i) their intentions with respect to the management of the company's business during that year; and

(ii) the amount and character of the financial resources that will in their view be available to the company during that year,

the company will be able to continue to carry on business as a going concern (and will accordingly be able to pay its debts as they fall due) throughout that year.

- The amount of the permissible capital payment for the shares in question.

- Whether the company's business includes that of a banking company or an insurance company.

- Indicate that it is a directors' statement made under section 714 of the 2006 Act.

- It must be signed by every director.

[CA06 Sec 714; SI 2009/388 para 5].

months of that date), that the company will be able to pay (or otherwise discharge) its debts as they fall due during the year immediately following that date.

- The date on which the statement is made.

- The name of each director of the company.

- Indicate that it is a solvency statement for the purposes of section 642 of the 2006 Act.

- It must be signed by every director.

[CA06 Sec 643(1)(3); SI 2008/1915 para 2].

7.97 In forming their opinion on the first of the two sub-bullet points for a payment out of capital (initial situation immediately following proposed payment date) and on all three sub-bullet points for a capital reduction (situation at date of statement and for twelve months following the statement or following winding-up), the Act states that directors *"must take into account all of the company's liabilities (including any contingent or prospective liabilities)"*. [CA06 Sec 714(4); CA06 Sec 643(2)]. Paragraph 961 of the Explanatory Notes to the 2006 Act explains, in the context of the statement for a capital reduction, that a proposed redemption of preference shares treated as liabilities for accounting purposes should be regarded as a contingent or prospective liability. [CA06 Explanatory Notes para 961]. The wording in paragraph 1021 of the Explanatory Notes implies that the point made in paragraph 961 also applies to the statement in respect of a payment out of capital. There is some doubt as to whether 'taking into account' means that the full value of all such liabilities should be included or only the amount of those liabilities that are likely to crystallise immediately and in the following 12 months. This is an area where a company's directors should take legal advice.

7.98 The overall policy of the legislation may be summarised as being to produce a situation where creditors are not going to be prejudiced by the company continuing in business after making a payment out of capital or a capital reduction. Consequently, if directors are in doubt as to whether their company would be able to pay all its debts if all the company's prospective and contingent liabilities were included in assessing its solvency, they should take legal advice before making either statement. If the company becomes insolvent the directors may incur certain penalties. For instance, under section 76 of the Insolvency Act 1986 a director has a liability to contribute to the company's assets if it is wound up within a year of a payment out of capital, unless he can show that he had reasonable grounds for forming the opinion set out in the statement. See further paragraph 7.107.

7.99   It is a criminal offence (punishable by a fine and/or imprisonment) for a director to make a statement without having reasonable grounds for the opinion expressed in it. [CA06 Secs 715, 643(4)(5)]. The directors should, therefore, arrange for financial statements to be prepared to enable, where relevant, the calculation of the permissible capital payment, and arrange for properly worked out cash flow projections to support the opinions required to be expressed in the relevant statement. In addition, the directors should consider whether they need advice when carrying out their creditor review.

Auditor's report to the directors

7.100   The directors' statement in respect of a payment out of capital (but not a capital reduction) must have attached to it a report by the company's auditor addressed to the directors stating that:

■   The auditor has enquired into the company's state of affairs.

■   The amount specified in the statement as the permissible capital payment for the shares in question is, in the auditor's view, properly determined in accordance with sections 710 to 712 of the 2006 Act.

■   The auditor is not aware of anything to indicate that the opinion expressed by the directors in their statement as to any of the matters mentioned in the first two sub-bullet points in paragraph 7.96 (initial situation immediately following the date of the proposed payment and the prospects for the year following that date) is unreasonable in all the circumstances.

[CA06 Sec 714(6)].

Procedure and timing: payment out of capital

7.101   The special resolution for the payment out of capital mentioned in paragraph 7.94 must be passed by the company either on the same day as, or within one week after, the date on which the directors make their statement. The resolution will be ineffective in the following circumstances:

■   If any member holding shares to which the resolution relates exercises the voting rights carried by any of those shares in voting on the resolution and the resolution would not have been passed if he had not done so.

In considering whether a sufficient number of votes have been cast on a show of hands or a poll, section 717(4) of the 2006 Act contains similar provisions to those described in paragraph 7.75 in relation to section 698(4).

■ If the directors' statement and the auditor's report attached to it are not available for inspection by members at the meeting at which the resolution is passed (or were not sent to every eligible member in the event of a written resolution). This means that the directors must liaise with the company's auditor at an early stage, to ensure that they can obtain the auditor's report by the date on which the special resolution is to be passed (or, in the case of a written resolution, by the date on which the resolution is sent to eligible members).

[CA06 Secs 716-718].

7.102   The company must make the payment out of capital between five and seven weeks after the date on which the resolution is passed. This ensures that members and creditors who wish to object have time to apply to the court under 721 of the 2006 Act (see para 7.103). This period cannot be shortened even if all members agree. The accounts required, which are mentioned in the following diagram, are discussed in paragraph 7.51.

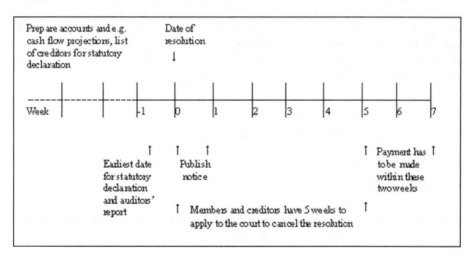

7.103   Where a resolution is passed approving a payment out of capital, any member (other than one who consented to or voted in favour of the resolution) and any creditor may within five weeks of the date on which the resolution is passed apply to the court to cancel the resolution. [CA06 Sec 721(1)(2)]. The court's powers are set out in section 721 of the 2006 Act. The company is obliged to give notice to the Registrar of Companies if an application is made to the court to cancel the resolution and the company must deliver to the registrar a copy of any court order made. Failure to do so renders the company and every officer in default liable to a fine. [CA06 Sec 722(2)(3)(4)].

7.104 Within a week after the date of the resolution for payment out of capital referred to in paragraph 7.94 the company must publish a notice in the London Gazette (for companies registered in England and Wales), the Edinburgh Gazette (for companies registered in Scotland) or in the Belfast Gazette (for companies registered in Northern Ireland) giving the following details:

■ A statement that the company has approved a payment out of capital for the purpose of purchasing and/or redeeming its own shares.

■ The amount of the permissible capital payment.

■ The date of the resolution.

■ A statement specifying where the directors' statement and the auditor's report are available for inspection.

■ A statement that any creditor of the company may, at any time within five weeks after the date of the resolution, apply to the court for an order that prohibits the payment (as discussed in para 7.103).

[CA06 Sec 719(1)].

7.105 The company must also within a week of the date of the resolution either publish a notice containing the same information in an appropriate national newspaper or give notice in writing to each of its creditors to that effect. [CA06 Sec 719(2)]. Furthermore, the company must deliver a copy of the directors' statement and auditor's report to the Registrar of Companies no later than the date on which the earliest of the following occurs:

■ Notice is published in the Gazette.

■ Notice is published in the national newspaper.

■ Notice is given to creditors.

[CA06 Sec 719(4)].

The special resolution must also be filed with the Registrar of Companies within 15 days of it being passed. [CA06 Sec 30].

7.106 The directors' statement and auditor's report must be available for inspection by members and creditors without charge for a period beginning with the latest date on which they could be sent to the Registrar (see para 7.105) and ending with the date that is five weeks after the date of the resolution for the payment out of capital. Failure to do so renders the company and every officer in default liable to a fine and the court can compel an immediate inspection. [CA06 Sec 720]. (See also SI 2007/2612, 'Companies (Fees for Inspection and Copying of Company Records) Regulations 2007', for the obligations of companies in relation to inspection). If the directors' statement and auditor's report are not held at the company's registered office, their location must meet the conditions specified in paragraph 3 of SI 2008/3006 and the company is required to give notice to the Registrar of the place where they are held. [CA06 Secs 720, 1136; SI 2008/3006 para 3].

Procedure and timing: capital reduction

7.106.1 The special resolution for the capital reduction mentioned in paragraph 7.94 must be supported by a solvency statement made not more than 15 days before the date on which the resolution is passed. [CA06 Sec 642(1)(a)]. Within 15 days of the resolution being passed, the company must deliver to the registrar:

- A copy of the solvency statement.

- A statement of capital.

- A copy of the special resolution.

- A statement by the directors confirming that the solvency statement was:

  - not made more than 15 days before the date on which the resolution was passed; and

  - provided to members in accordance with section 642(2) or (3) (made available for inspection by members at the meeting at which the resolution is passed or sent to every eligible member in the event of a written resolution).

[CA06 Sec 644(1), (5); 30].

7.106.2 The Registrar must register the documents in the first two bullet points on receipt at which time the resolution takes effect. [CA06 Sec 644(3),(4)]. The company's special resolution cannot provide for the reduction in capital to take effect at a later date. [CA06 Sec 641(5)].

7.106.3 The statement of capital must state, with respect to the company's share capital as reduced by the resolution:

- Total number of shares of the company.

- Aggregate nominal value of those shares.

- For each class of shares:

  - details of voting, dividend, capital and redemption rights attached to the shares;

  - number of shares; and

  - aggregate nominal value of shares.

- Amount paid up and amount unpaid on each share.

[CA 06 Sec 644(2); SI 2009/388 para 2].

7.106.4 Failure to comply with section 644 (see para 7.106.1 to 7.106.3) is an offence committed by the company and every officer of the company who is in default and each person is liable to a fine. [CA06 Sec 644(8), (9)].

Distributable profits

7.106.5 A company can only purchase its own shares, or redeem them, out of capital if it has first used up all its available distributable profits (see para 7.49 above). There is no such restriction applying to a company wishing to purchase using the capital reduction procedures. In addition, under paragraph 3(2) of SI 2008/1915, 'The Companies (Reduction of Share Capital) Order 2008', any reserve arising from a reduction of capital is to be treated as a realised profit (provided there is not a contrary provision in the company's memorandum or articles). However, if a distribution is contemplated after a reduction of capital, interim accounts of the company are likely to be required showing the company's financial position after the reduction.

Liability on winding up

7.107 Under section 76 of the Insolvency Act 1986, if a company is wound up within a year of making a payment out of capital in respect of a purchase or redemption of its shares and it proves to be insolvent, any shareholder whose shares were purchased or redeemed and the directors who signed the statutory declaration are liable to contribute to the assets of the company. However, a director will be exempt from such a liability if he can show that he had reasonable grounds for forming the opinion stated in the directors' statement.

7.108 The liability of a person whose shares were redeemed or purchased to contribute to the assets of the company is limited to the amount of the payment out of capital he received when the company purchased his shares. Where this applies, the company's directors are jointly and severally liable with the past shareholder for that amount. A shareholder or director who has contributed to the assets of the company under section 76 of the Insolvency Act 1986 has certain rights to claim against any other person who is jointly and severally liable. A shareholder whose shares have been redeemed or purchased with a payment out of capital and who is, therefore, potentially liable to contribute to the assets under section 76, has the right, in order to limit his liability and prevent further loss to the assets, to petition for winding up. The grounds of the petition would be either that the company is unable to pay its debts or that it is just and equitable for the company to be wound up. [Sec 124(3) Insolvency Act 1986].

Court approval

Court approved capital reduction

7.108.1 A limited company, whether public or private, may reduce its share capital by special resolution confirmed by the court. [CA06 Sec 641(1)(b)]. A capital reduction can be used to reduce share capital, share premium account and capital redemption reserves as both share premium and capital redemption reserves constitute share capital for the purpose of a reduction.

Authorisation

7.108.2   Pre-authorisation in a company's articles is not required under the Act, although the company's articles must neither restrict nor prohibit the capital reduction. [CA06 Sec 641(6)].

7.108.3   Before applying to the courts, a company must pass a special resolution authorising the capital reduction. [CA06 Secs 645(1), 641(1)(b))].

Court confirmation procedure

7.108.4   Under this procedure, having passed the special resolution, the company must apply to the court for an order confirming the reduction. If the proposed reduction of capital involves either a diminution of liability in respect of unpaid share capital or the payment to a shareholder of any paid-up share capital (the court can direct otherwise or can determine other instances), every creditor to whom the company owes a debt or claim on a date specified by the court (unless, in special circumstances, the court determines that a class of creditor is omitted) is entitled to object to the reduction of capital if the creditor can show that there is a real likelihood that the reduction would result in the company being unable to discharge its debt or claim when it fell due. For this purpose, the court must draw up a list of creditors entitled to object and may publish notices fixing a day (or days) after which any other creditors will be excluded from the right to object. [CA06 Secs 645(2), (3), 646]. Any officer of the company who intentionally or recklessly conceals the name of a creditor, or who misrepresents a creditor's debt or claim, or who is knowingly concerned in any such concealment or misrepresentation, commits an offence and is liable to a fine. [CA06 Sec 647].

7.108.5   The court may then make an order confirming the reduction of capital on such terms and conditions as it thinks fit. In doing so, the court must be satisfied that every creditor who is entitled to object has either consented to the reduction or its debt or claim has been discharged, has been determined or has been secured. The court may require the company to publish the reasons for the reduction. It may also, if it thinks there are special reasons, require the company to add 'and reduced' to the end of its name for a specified period. [CA06 Sec 648].

7.108.6   The court order must be delivered to the Registrar of Companies. A court approved statement of capital must also be delivered to the Registrar of Companies. This statement of capital must state with respect to the company's share capital as altered by the order:

- Total number of shares of the company.

- Aggregate nominal value of those shares.

- For each class of shares:

- details of voting, dividend, capital and redemption rights attached to the shares;

- number of shares; and

- aggregate nominal value of shares.

- Amount paid up and amount unpaid on each share.

[CA06 Sec 649(1), (2); SI 2009/388 para 2].

7.108.7   A court approved capital reduction takes effect when the court order and statement of capital is *registered* by the Registrar, unless the capital reduction forms part of a compromise or arrangement under Part 26 of the 2006 Act. In the latter case the reduction takes effect at the same time as the other aspects of that compromise or arrangement; that is, on *delivery* of the court order and statement of capital to the Registrar, although the court can order it to take effect on registration rather than delivery. [CA06 Sec 649(3)]. The company's special resolution cannot provide for the reduction in capital to take effect at a later date. [CA06 Sec 641(5)]. The registrar has to certify the registration of the order and statement of capital and the Registrar's certificate is conclusive evidence that the company's share capital is as stated in the statement of capital. [CA 06 Sec 649(5)(6)].

Public companies reducing capital below authorised minimum

7.108.8   Where the court makes an order reducing a public company's capital and this brings the allotted share capital below the authorised minimum (see Manual of Accounting – IFRS for the UK or Manual of Accounting – UK GAAP), the registrar must not register the order unless the court so directs or the company is first re-registered as a private company. [CA06 Sec 650]. Section 651 provides for an expedited procedure, avoiding the need to re-register in the usual way under section 97 of the 2006 Act, if the court so authorises.

Distributable profits

7.108.9   A reserve arising from a court-approved reduction in share capital is a realised profit unless the court has ordered that it is not distributable or the company's memorandum or articles preclude it from being treated as distributable or the company has given an undertaking to the court that it will not distribute the amount until after certain conditions, such as settling creditors, have been met. A reserve might arise if a company applied to the court to reduce its share capital but with no immediate payment to shareholders.

7.108.10   Section 654 of the 2006 Act explicitly states that the reserve is not distributable, but adds that this is subject to any provision being made by an order of the court. SI 2008/1915, 'The Companies (Reduction of Share Capital) Order 2008', is that order and confirms that section 654 does not apply to a reserve arising from a court approved capital reduction and thus such a reserve is a realised profit unless the court has ordered that it is not distributable or the company's memorandum or articles preclude it from being treated as distributable. SI 2008/1886, 'Companies Act 2006 (Commencement No 7, Transitional Provisions and Savings) Order 2008', applies these provisions retrospectively as well as prospectively, that is, they apply to court approved reductions made under the 1985 Act as well as those made under the 2006 Act.

7.108.11   One of the grounds mentioned in section 641 of the Act on which a company may reduce its capital is where capital is lost or is unrepresented by available assets. An example would be where the financial statements showed a deficit on the profit and loss account. The company, in these circumstances, would need to prove to the court that the loss of capital was permanent and not temporary. If the loss was permanent, the court would generally be expected to sanction such applications without opposition on the basis that the reduction would not affect creditors and no members or class of members would be disadvantaged.

7.108.12   Where, however, some or all of the loss of capital could not be shown to be permanent, a cancellation of paid-up share capital might prejudice creditors. An example might be where the application to reduce capital was for an amount greater than the amount required to write off the deficit, or where a company writes off an investment in a loss-making subsidiary, but the loss is not proved to be permanent. In these circumstances the court would need to consider the extent to which the interests of creditors would be safeguarded. Generally the court has no need to impose additional conditions on the basis that the company proposes appropriate mechanisms to protect creditors, for example by way of cash in a "blocked bank account", a bank or parental guarantee or by the provision of an undertaking not to distribute the reserve until various conditions have been met. In the latter case (particularly if the company's creditors are all short-term and it expects to have paid them all within, say, six months) the company may give an undertaking to the court that it will transfer to a special reserve the excess over the amount required to write off the deficit and it will not distribute any of the reserve until after it has settled all the creditors existing at that date or, alternatively, until such time as the company's capital is restored by way of an issue of new shares. Such an undertaking might enable the court to dispense with the need to obtain creditors' consent and sanction the reduction.

7.108.13   In the case where an investment is written off or a provision is released on a subsequent revaluation of assets the company may again undertake to credit the amount to a special reserve. This special reserve would generally be made undistributable for so long as there remains outstanding any liabilities of the company that would be admissible in a winding up beginning on the date of the reduction of capital.

Table 7.6 – Transfer of special reserve

Trafalgar House Public Limited Company – Report & Accounts – 30 September 1994

26 Reserves Company

	Special Reserve £m	Profit and loss account £m	Total £m
As at 1 October 1993	95.0	102.0	197.0
Special Reserve transfer	(95.0)	95.0	–
Transfer to profit and loss account	–	(20.2)	(20.2)
Arising on scrip dividends		7.3	7.3
As at 30 September 1994	–	184.1	184.1

Following the rights issue and placing on 7 January 1994, the balance of the Special Reserve in the accounts of the company became distributable and has accordingly been transferred to the profit and loss account. This is in accordance with the undertaking given to the Court during the year ended 30 September 1991 whereby the amount standing to the credit of the Special Reserve may be reduced by the amount of any increase in its share capital or share premium as a result of any issue of shares paid up by receipt of new consideration.

7.108.14   It is important to note that if a distribution is contemplated after a reduction of capital, interim accounts of the company are likely to be required showing the company's financial position after the reduction.

Court approved versus non-court approved capital reductions

7.108.15   A private company wishing to reduce its share capital may opt for the solvency statement procedure rather than applying to the court for the following reasons:

■   the process will take less time to complete;

■   it is likely to cost less as counsel will not need to represent the company at court; and

■   the company will have more flexibility as to the levels of creditor protection it wishes to put in place and it is likely that these will be less costly than those imposed by the court.

7.108.16   However, there might be certain situations where the court approved procedure will be necessary or advisable because:

■   with the approval of the court it is possible to reduce a company's share capital to zero. In practice this is done as part of a scheme of arrangement where shares are immediately issued in replacement. Under the solvency statement procedure, a company must have at least one shareholder remaining after the proposed reduction holding at least one non-redeemable share;

- the court determines the appropriate level of creditor protection rather than the board. In complex creditor situations or where creditors are unknown, this will provide a greater level of protection for directors from actions for breach of duty; and

- it may not be possible for all directors to sign the solvency statement or there may be directors who refuse to do so.

Failure to acquire shares

7.109   Where a company has agreed to purchase or redeem any of its shares and then fails to do so, the affected shareholder cannot sue the company for damages. However, this does not affect any other right that the shareholder has, except that a court will not order specific performance of the contract if the company shows that it cannot meet the costs of purchasing the shares in question out of distributable profits. [CA06 Sec 735(1)-(3)].

7.110   If a company is liable to purchase or redeem shares, but has failed to do so at a time when it goes into liquidation, the terms of the purchase or redemption can be enforced against it. However, this will only apply if:

- Under their terms, the purchase or redemption was to take place on or before the winding up commenced; and

- The company would have had distributable profits equal to the purchase or redemption price.

[CA06 Sec 735(4)(5)].

7.111   Payments to creditors and to members who have preferred rights, however, will have priority in the winding up. [CA06 Sec 735(6)]. The shares purchased or redeemed must then be cancelled.

Treasury shares

7.111.1   The Act permits companies with *'qualifying shares'* to purchase such shares out of distributable profits and hold them in treasury for resale, transfer or cancellation at a later date. As can be seen from the definition of qualifying shares, private companies are effectively prohibited from holding treasury shares, as are a number of public companies.

7.111.2   'Qualifying shares' are defined as shares that:

- are included in the Official List maintained by the FSA;

- are traded on AIM;

- are officially listed in another EEA State; or

- are traded on a market established in an EEA State, which is a regulated securities market.

[CA06 Sec 724(2)].

7.111.3 In the UK, the regulated securities markets referred to in the last bullet point in paragraph 7.111.2 above, include:

- LIFFE.

- OM London.

- Virt-X.

- Coredeal MTS.

- Jiway.

7.111.4 Where qualifying shares are purchased by a company out of distributable profits (see from paragraph 7.17) in accordance with section 724 of the 2006 Act, the company may:

- hold the shares (or any of them) in treasury; or

- deal with any of them, at any time, as follows:

  - sell the shares (or any of them) for cash consideration (see paragraph 7.111.9);

  - transfer the shares (or any of them) for the purposes of, or pursuant to, an employees' share scheme; or

  - cancel the shares (or any of them) (see paragraph 7.111.12).

[CA06 Secs 724(3), 727(1), 729(1)].

Conditions applying to treasury shares

7.111.5 References to a company holding shares as treasury shares are references to the company holding shares that were (or are treated as having been) purchased by it in circumstances in which section 724 of the 2006 Act applies and have been held by the company continuously since they were so purchased (or treated as purchased). [CA06 Sec 724(5)].

7.111.6 There are no limits on the number of shares that may be held as treasury shares, although a company is precluded from purchasing its own shares (whether for cancellation or to hold as treasury shares) if the purchase would result in there being no shares in issue other than redeemable shares or shares held in treasury. [CA06 Sec 690(2)].

7.111.7 The company may not exercise any rights over the treasury shares it holds, including voting rights. Furthermore, no dividend can be paid, and no other distribution of the company's assets (including any distribution of assets to members on a winding up) can be made, to the company in respect of the treasury shares. However, rights over bonus issues or redemption rights (if the shares are redeemable) do still remain. [CA06 Sec 726].

7.111.8   Where shares are held in treasury, the company must be entered in the register of members as the member holding those shares. [CA06 Sec 724(4)].

Sale or cancellation of treasury shares

7.111.9   As stated in paragraph 7.111.4 above, one of the ways in which a company can deal with its treasury shares is to sell the shares for 'cash consideration', a defined term in the Act. The definition of 'cash consideration' for this purpose is:

- Cash (including foreign currency) received by the company.

- A cheque received by the company in good faith that the directors have no reason for suspecting will not be paid.

- A release of a liability of the company for a liquidated sum.

- An undertaking to pay cash to the company within 90 days of the date on which the company agrees to sell the shares.

- Payment by any other means giving rise to a present or future entitlement (of the company or a person acting on the company's behalf) to a payment, or credit equivalent to payments, in cash (including foreign currency).

[CA06 Sec 727(2)].

7.111.10   The Act includes a provision enabling the Secretary of State to determine that other means of payment are also included within the last bullet point above. This is to provide a mechanism in the event that new methods of settlement are developed or identified. In this regard, paragraph 4(3) of SI 2009/388 provides that a settlement bank's obligation to make a payment in respect of a transfer of a treasury share under the CREST system is to be regarded as a means of payment falling within the last bullet point above.

7.111.11   Where treasury shares are sold, if the proceeds are equal to or less than the purchase price paid by the company for the shares, the proceeds are treated as a realised profit. As the original purchase price was treated as a realised loss (that is, charged against distributable profits) this treatment of the proceeds results in a full or partial restoration of that loss. If the proceeds exceed the purchase price, the excess over the purchase price has to be transferred to the share premium account. The balance is treated as a realised profit, offsetting the original loss caused by the purchase price. The purchase price paid by the company for the shares is determined by the use of a weighted average price method. If the shares were allotted to the company as fully paid bonus shares, the purchase price of them is deemed to be nil. [CA06 Sec 731].

7.111.12   If the company cancels shares held as treasury shares, the company must reduce the amount of its issued share capital by the nominal value of the cancelled shares. [CA06 Sec 729(4)]. However, where the company's memorandum and articles of association impose on it an authorised share capital, the cancellation does not reduce the amount of the company's authorised share capital. The amount by which the company's issued share capital is diminished on cancellation of shares held as treasury shares is required to be transferred to a capital redemption reserve. [CA06 Sec 733(4)].

7.111.13   Where a company cancels shares held as treasury shares it may do so without complying with the Act's provisions relating to reductions of capital. [CA06 Sec 729(5)].

7.111.14   If shares held as treasury shares cease to be 'qualifying shares', other than when shares are suspended from listing or trading, the company is required to cancel them immediately. [CA06 Sec 729(2)(3)].

Delivery of returns

7.111.14.1   Where a company purchases its own shares under the rules for treasury shares set out above, it is required to deliver a return to the Registrar of Companies no later than 28 days after the delivery of shares to it. Details required to be included in the return are set out in 7.82 above. [CA06 Sec 707].

7.111.15   Where a company purchases its own shares under the rules for treasury shares set out above and immediately cancels some or all of these, it is required to give notice to the Registrar, accompanied by a statement of capital, under the general requirements for a purchase of own shares (see para 7.83). [CA06 Sec 708]. Where a company has held shares as treasury shares for some time and subsequently cancels them, it is required by section 730 to deliver a return to the registrar within 28 days of the shares being cancelled. The return must state, with respect to shares of each class cancelled, the number and nominal value of shares and the date on which they were cancelled. The return must be accompanied by a statement of capital, setting out, with respect to the company's share capital immediately following the cancellation:

- The total number of shares of the company.

- The aggregate nominal value of those shares.

- For each class of shares:

    - details of voting, dividend, capital and redemption rights attached to the shares;

    - number of shares; and

    - aggregate nominal value of shares.

- The amount to be paid up and the amount (if any) to be unpaid on each share (whether on account of the share's nominal value or its premium).

[CA06 Sec 730; SI 2009/388 para 2]

7.111.16   Where a company has held shares as treasury shares for some time and the shares have subsequently been sold or transferred for the purposes of, or pursuant to, an employees' share scheme, the company is required to deliver another return to the Registrar of Companies no later than 28 days after the date on which the shares are disposed of. This return is required to state with respect to each class of shares disposed of, the number and nominal value of those shares and the date on which they were disposed of. Failure to comply is a criminal offence and the directors in default are liable to a fine. [CA06 Sec 728].

Failure to comply with the Act

7.111.17   Failure to comply with the Act's provisions on treasury shares is a criminal offence and both the company and the directors in default are liable to a fine. [CA06 Secs 730(6),(7), 732].

Accounting treatment

7.111.18   The accounting treatment for and disclosure of treasury shares is considered in chapter 23 for the Manual of Accounting – IFRS for the UK and the Manual of Accounting – UK GAAP.

Requirements of regulators and other bodies

Listing Rules

7.112   A listed company proposing to purchase its own shares must comply with the relevant conditions set out in chapter 12 of the UKLA's Listing Rules, 'Dealing in own securities and treasury shares'. The rules distinguish between 'equity shares' (which has the same meaning as in the Companies Act and is thus a broader category of shares than 'equity' in IAS 32 and FRS 25) and 'own securities other than equity shares' including securities convertible into or exchangeable for equity shares and warrants or options to subscribe or purchase equity shares.

7.113   The provisions described in paragraphs 7.114 to 7.126 do not apply, however, to transactions entered into in the ordinary course of business by securities dealing businesses or by the company or other group member on behalf of third parties if the listed company has effective 'Chinese walls' between those responsible for the decision-making relating to the transaction and those in possession of inside information relating to the listed company. [LR 12.1.3 R, LR 9.2.7 R].

Buying back shares during prohibited (close) periods

7.114   A listed company (or any member of its group on its behalf) must not purchase or redeem (or make early redemptions of) its own securities during a prohibited period (that is, when a company is in a close period or any period when there exists any matter that constitutes inside information), unless:

- The company has in place a buy back programme where the dates and quantities of securities to be purchased are fixed and have been disclosed in a notification to a Regulatory Information Service (see para 7.118).

- The company has in place a buy back programme managed by an independent third party which makes its trading decisions in relation to the company's securities independently of, and uninfluenced by, the company.

- The company is purchasing or redeeming securities other than shares or securities whose price or value would be likely to be significantly affected by the publication of the information giving rise to the prohibited period.

- The company is redeeming securities (other than equity shares) which, at the time of issue, set out the date of redemption, the number of securities to be redeemed (or formula to determine that number) and the redemption price (or formula).

[LR 12.2.1 R]

7.114.1   The exemption in LR 12.2.1 R(2) (second bullet point in para 7.114) is very useful for those companies that need a full twelve month period in order to complete an announced buy-back programme, although shorter periods are also common, or to gain maximum pricing flexibility while doing so. Listed companies can utilise this permission to buy back shares in their close period by giving the company's broker an authority, prior to the start of a close period, to continue buying shares during the close periods. The purchases should be effected pursuant to the annual buy back authority passed at most companies' AGMs in the usual way and, therefore, no new authority should generally be needed. As companies cannot have control over these independent programmes, directors must be satisfied with the authority they invest in their broker before entering into one of these programmes.

7.114.2   The documents required are relatively straightforward, the main one being an agreement between the company and its broker confirming the broker's authority. The key issues are the parameters around the broker's discretion in the agreement that do not amount to the broker acting as the company's agent. For example, the following may be included:

- Prices to comply with the annual authority (that is, by reference to the trading price five business days preceding the purchase).

- A maximum cap (that is, an absolute number) on the price to be paid per share.

- Limits on the number of shares to be bought back. Practically, as well as to comply with the shareholder authority, these may operate as restrictions on a daily and/or monthly volume basis as well as an aggregate basis.

- Operation of the buy-back programme and in particular whether it should be conducted within the market abuse 'safe harbour' (introduced on 1 July

2005). In essence, this imposes limits by reference to trading volumes and prices and requires additional disclosure.

- ■ Termination rights. Ideally the company may want to provide that the agreement terminates at its absolute discretion or if a material event occurs, such as a profit forecast or major corporate transaction is announced. However, care needs to be exercised, since such termination rights may, in effect, make the broker no more than an agent of the company or even raise market abuse concerns.

Insider trading and market abuse

7.114.3 Companies need to consider insider trading and market abuse legislation (see para 7.81) before entering into independent purchase programmes, as such programmes will be potentially caught by such legislation. Purchase programmes can only be carried out if the relevant individuals at the company are not in possession of inside information. For example, if the agreement is entered into too close to the beginning of the close period, the directors or others who discharge managerial responsibilities (Model Code appended to Listing Rule 9) may be in possession of inside information, thus prohibiting dealing. However, once the contract is entered into any future inside information on the part of the company should not prevent dealing. The broker will need to ensure that its 'Chinese walls' are effective so that its advisory side is not contaminated with inside information from its trading side. Generally, it is not an insider trading offence to take a decision not to trade, so it should be possible to terminate an agreement at any time even if the company is then in possession of inside information. However, there are market abuse issues and legal advice should, therefore, be taken.

Accounting requirements

7.114.4 These agreements with a company's broker are contracts to repurchase own shares. They, therefore, fall to be accounted for as prescribed by paragraph 23 of IAS 32 and FRS 25 (see chapter 23 of the Manual of Accounting – IFRS in the UK and the Manual of Accounting – UK GAAP).

Purchases from related parties

7.115 Where the purchase of own equity securities or preference shares is from a related party (for example, a director, substantial shareholder or person exercising significant influence or associates of these) the requirements of chapter 11 of the UKLA's Listing Rules must be complied with (see further chapter 29 of the Manual of Accounting – IFRS for the UK and the Manual of Accounting – UK GAAP). This is unless a purchase is made by way of a tender offer to all holders of the class of securities or, in the case of a market purchase pursuant to a general authority granted by shareholders, it is made without prior understanding, arrangement or agreement between the company and any related party. [LR 12.3.1 R].

Purchase of own equity shares

7.116   Where a company purchases less than 15 per cent of any class of its equity shares (excluding treasury shares) it may make the purchase through the market in the ordinary way, provided the price paid is not more than the higher of five per cent above the average of the market value of the shares for the five business days before the purchase is made and that stipulated by Article 5(1) of EC Regulations 2273/2003, 'The buy-back and stabilisation regulation'. Otherwise a tender offer has to be made to all shareholders of the class of equity shares to be purchased. [LR 12.4.1 R].

7.117   Where the company proposes to purchase 15 per cent or more of any class of its equity shares (excluding treasury shares), it must make these purchases by way of a tender offer to all shareholders of that class. [LR 12.4.2 R]. Where a series of purchases are made (and shareholders have granted a general authority) that, in aggregate, amount to 15 per cent or more of a class of its equity shares in issue immediately following the grant of that authority, a tender offer need only be made in respect of any purchase that takes the aggregate to, or above, the 15 per cent level. Purchases that have been specifically approved by shareholders should not be taken into account in determining whether the 15 per cent level has been reached. [LR 12.4.3 G].

7.118   The company must notify a Regulatory Information Service immediately when the board decides to submit to the company's shareholders a proposal that the company should be authorised to purchase its own equity shares, although a proposal to renew an existing authority to purchase own equity shares does not require notification. The notification should indicate whether the proposal relates either to specific purchases (giving the names of the persons from whom the purchases are to be made) or to a general authorisation to make purchases [LR 12.4.4 R]. The company should immediately notify a Regulatory Information Service of the outcome of the shareholders' meeting. [LR 12.4.5 R]. However, see paragraph 7.119 as to the timing of the notification of purchase.

7.119   Notification to a Regulatory Information Service of purchases of a company's own equity shares by or on behalf of the company or other group member is required as soon as possible and in any event by 07:30 am on the business day following the day of the purchase. The notification should include:

- The date of purchase.

- The number of shares purchased.

- The purchase price per share for each of the highest and the lowest prices paid, where relevant.

- The number of equity shares purchased for cancellation and the number purchased to be held as treasury shares.

- Where equity shares are purchased to be held as treasury shares, a statement of:

- The total number of treasury shares of each class held by the company following the purchase and non-cancellation of the shares.

- The number of shares of each class that the company has in issue less the total number of treasury shares of each class held by the company following the purchase and non-cancellation of the shares.

[LR 12.4.6 R].

7.120   Where there are in issue convertible securities or warrants or options to subscribe for equity shares of the class proposed to be purchased, the company must hold a separate meeting of the holders. The purpose of the meeting is to obtain the holders' approval by special resolution before the company either enters into any contract to purchase its equity shares of that class or first exercises a general authority to make purchases in the market. However, the company does not require such approval where there are provisions in the relevant trust deed or terms of issue of the securities permitting the company to purchase its own equity shares. [LR 12.4.7 R, LR 12.4.8 R].

7.121   The circular containing the notice of meeting required by the preceding paragraph must comply with the requirements for all circulars. In addition, it must set out clearly the apparent effect, in terms of attributable assets and earnings, on the expectations of the holders on conversion or subscription if the company were to exercise fully the authorisation that it seeks to purchase its own shares at the maximum price allowed. Any adjustments that the company may propose to the holders' rights should also be set out and the information concerning the apparent effect should also be restated on the revised basis. [LR 12.4.9 R].

Purchase of own securities other than equity shares

7.122   Except where the purchases will consist of individual transactions made in accordance with the terms of the issue of the securities, a listed company that intends to purchase any of its equity securities (other than equity shares), for example securities convertible into equity shares, or preference shares, must:

- Ensure that no dealings in the relevant securities are carried out by or on behalf of the company or any member of the group, until the proposal has either been notified to a Regulatory Information Service or abandoned.

- Notify a Regulatory Information Service of its decision to purchase.

[LR 12.5.1 R].

7.123   Purchases, early redemptions or cancellations of the company's own listed equity securities (other than equity shares) or preference shares by or on behalf of the company or any other member of its group must be notified to a Regulatory Information Service when an aggregate of ten per cent of the initial amount of the relevant class of securities has been purchased, redeemed or cancelled and for each five per cent in aggregate of the initial amount of that class acquired thereafter.

[LR 12.5.2 R]. Such notifications must be made as soon as possible and, in any event, no later than 07:30 am on the business day following the calendar day on which the dealing occurred to reach or exceed the relevant threshold. The notification must state the amount of the securities acquired, redeemed or cancelled since the last such notification, the number of that class of the securities remaining outstanding and whether or not the securities acquired are to be cancelled. [LR 12.5.3 R]. In addition, for early redemptions and purchases of shares other than equity shares the notification must include a statement indicating the number of the shares purchased to be held as treasury shares and the number of shares purchased or redeemed early for cancellation. [LR 12.5.4 R].

7.124 In circumstances where the purchase of own securities is not being made pursuant to a tender offer and the purchase causes a relevant threshold to be reached or exceeded, no further purchases may be undertaken until after a notification to a Regulatory Information Service has been made as per the preceding paragraph. [LR 12.5.5 R].

7.125 In the case of securities which are convertible into, exchangeable for, or carrying a right to subscribe for equity shares, unless a tender offer is made to all holders of the class of securities, purchases must not be made at a price more than five per cent above the average of the market values for the securities for the five business days immediately preceding the date of purchase. [LR 12.5.6 R].

7.126 Where, within a period of 12 months, a company purchases warrants or options over its own equity shares which would, on exercise, comprise 15 per cent or more of the company's existing issued shares (excluding treasury shares), the company must send its shareholders a circular containing the following information:

- A statement of the directors' intentions regarding future purchases of the company's warrants and options.

- The number and terms of the warrants or options acquired and to be acquired and the method of acquisition.

- Where warrants or options have been, or are to be, acquired from specific parties, a statement of the names of those parties and all material terms of the acquisition.

- The prices to be paid.

[LR 12.5.7 R]

Treasury shares

7.126.1 Sales for cash, or transfers for the purposes of, or pursuant to, an employees' share scheme, of treasury shares cannot be made during a prohibited period; that is, when a company is in a close period or any period when there exists any matter that constitutes inside information. [LR 12.6.1 R]. However, this prohibition does not apply to:

- Transfers to a savings scheme investing only in the company's securities following either the exercise of an option under a savings related share option scheme or the release of shares from a HMRC approved share incentive plan.

- With the exception of a disposal of securities to a recipient of the shares who is a restricted person (that is one discharging managerial responsibilities), dealings in connection with a HMRC approved employee share scheme, or a scheme on similar terms and conditions, under which participation is extended on similar terms to all or most employees of the participating companies in that scheme.

- The transfers of securities of the company by an independent trustee of an employees' share scheme to a beneficiary who is not a person discharging managerial responsibilities.

- Sales or transfers by the company of treasury shares (other than equity shares) of a class whose price or value would not be likely to be significantly affected by the publication of the information giving rise to the prohibited period.

[LR 12.6.2 R].

7.126.2 If, by virtue of it holding treasury shares, a company is allotted shares as part of a capitalisation issue, the company must notify a Regulatory Information Service as soon as possible (no later than 07:30 am on the following business day). The notification must include:

- The date of the allotment.

- The number of shares allotted.

- A statement as to what number of shares allotted have been cancelled and what number is being held as treasury shares.

- Where shares allotted are being held as treasury shares, a statement of:

  - The total number of treasury shares of each class held by the company following the allotment.

  - The number of shares of each class that the company has in issue less the total number of treasury shares of each class held by the company following the allotment.

[LR 12.6.3 R].

7.126.3 Any sale for cash, transfer for the purposes of or pursuant to an employees' share scheme or cancellation of treasury shares by a listed company must be notified to a Regulatory Information Service as soon as possible and in any event by no later than 07:30 am on the business day following the calendar day on which the sale, transfer or cancellation occurred. The notification must include:

- The date of the sale, transfer or cancellation.

- The number of shares sold, transferred or cancelled.

- The sale or transfer price for each of the highest and lowest prices paid, where relevant.

- A statement of:

- The total number of treasury shares of each class held by the company following the sale, transfer or cancellation.

- The number of shares of each class that the company has in issue less the total number of treasury shares of each class held by the company following the sale, transfer or cancellation.

[LR 12.6.4 R].

[The next paragraph is 7.129.]

Redemption of redeemable shares

7.129   Listed companies must notify a Regulatory Information Service as soon as possible of details of a redemption of listed shares. The particulars to be notified are the number of shares redeemed and the number of shares of that class that remain outstanding following the redemption. [LR 9.6.4 R (3)].

Capital reduction

7.129.1   Listed companies must notify a Regulatory Information Service as soon as possible of details of a proposed change in capital structure. A capital reduction may need to be notified in this way. [LR 9.6.4 R (1)].

Major Shareholding Notification Rules

7.130   It is possible to acquire up to 29.9 per cent of a listed company in one go. The only disclosure rules that apply to acquirers of shares in listed companies are those now contained in the Major Shareholding Notification Rules in the UKLA's DTR. [DTR chapter 5]. The Major Shareholding Notification Rules cover the acquisition of shares and also an 'interest in shares', which may be represented by qualifying financial instruments, such as options, that are held directly or indirectly.

Institutional shareholders

7.131   The interests of large institutional shareholders are represented by investor protection committees that issue guidelines on matters of concern to shareholders. The Investments Committee of the Association of British Insurers has made certain recommendations on the subject of a purchase by a company of its own shares, but no formal guidelines have been published. They request that a special resolution is given for a market purchase, that the authority to purchase shares is renewed annually and that the effect on earnings per share, capital and dividend cover should be considered. They also request that companies undertake in the document that the authority to purchase its own shares will only be exercised if to do so would result in an increase in earnings per share and is in the best interests of shareholders generally.

7.131.1   The institutions are unlikely to object to small purchases (up to five per cent of the issued equity share capital in any one year). Hence, it is common for such approval to be sought at each annual general meeting. Between five and ten per cent, enquiries may be raised as to any special features which might make the proposal undesirable. Above ten per cent, prior consultation should take place or support for the resolution will depend on the circumstance.

7.132   Table 3.18 in chapter 3 includes an example of a special resolution authorising the company to make market purchases. Paragraph 3.140 also details the disclosure required by LR 13.8.8R(1) when matters of special business, such as authority to purchase own shares, are proposed at the AGM.

Financial assistance for acquisition of shares

Definition of financial assistance

7.132.1   Financial assistance is defined in section 677 of the Act. It is widely defined and includes gifts, loans, security and guarantees.

Private companies

7.132.2   Since 1 October 2009, there is no prohibition in the Act on financial assistance being given by private companies for the acquisition of their *own* shares. Nevertheless, directors need to ensure that:

- The transaction is in the best interests of the company, such that they are not in breach of their duty under section 172 of the 2006 Act to promote its success.

- The transaction does not breach the rules on distributions or otherwise constitute an illegal reduction in capital (see further the Manual of Accounting — IFRS for the UK and the Manual of Accounting — UK GAAP).

7.132.3   In practice directors may wish to take steps to demonstrate that they are not in breach of their duties, for example, ensuring that board minutes confirm that the directors have considered the matter carefully and/or are obtaining shareholder approval for the transaction.

7.132.4   Subsidiaries of public companies are prohibited from giving financial assistance for the acquisition of the public companies' own shares. [CA06 Sec 678(1)]. However, section 678 of the 2006 Act gives statutory effect to the decision in *Arab Bank plc vs Mercantile Holdings Ltd* [1994] 2 All ER 74, that the statutory prohibition at the time on a company giving financial assistance for the purpose of acquiring its own shares or shares in its holding company does not apply to the giving of assistance by a subsidiary incorporated in an overseas jurisdiction. Thus, the prohibition on a subsidiary giving financial assistance for the acquisition of the public companies' own shares applies only to subsidiaries governed by the 2006 Act.

Public companies

7.133   A public company is prohibited by section 678(1) of the Act from giving financial assistance for the acquisition of its own shares. This general prohibition on giving financial assistance by a public company is required by the EU 2nd Company Law Directive (77/91/EEC).

7.133.1   The prohibition extends to a public company that is a subsidiary; such a company is not able to give financial assistance for the acquisition of shares in its holding company, whether that holding company is a public or private company. As outlined in 7.132.4 the prohibition applies only to subsidiaries governed by the 2006 Act. [CA06 Secs 678(1); 679(1)].

General rule

7.134   Subject to the exemptions set out below the general rule is that public companies cannot give, either directly or indirectly, financial assistance for the purpose of acquiring their own shares or the shares of their holding company and private companies cannot give, either directly or indirectly, financial assistance for the purpose of acquiring shares of its holding company if that holding company is a public company. This applies to financial assistance given:

■   Both before or at the same time as the acquisition.

■   After the acquisition for the purpose of reducing or discharging a liability incurred by any person for the purpose of the acquisition.

[CA06 Secs 678(1), 679(1), 678(3), 679(3)].

7.134.1   The reference to 'public company' when applying the prohibition on post acquisition assistance, applies to companies that are public companies at the time the assistance is given. For example, a person acquires shares in company X, a private company, and takes out a loan to fund the purchase price. If company X subsequently re-registered as a public company, then neither company X nor its subsidiaries could give assistance in repaying the loan after company X had become a public company, but could have given such assistance prior to that date providing any subsidiary giving assistance was not a public company at the time of giving the assistance.

Exemptions

7.135 The above provisions do not prohibit the following transactions for a public company, provided that it has net assets that are not thereby reduced or the reduction is provided out of distributable profits, or for a private company:

- Lending of money by a company in the ordinary course of its business.

- Provision of financial assistance for an employees' share scheme.

- Provision of financial assistance to enable or facilitate transactions in the company's shares by employees, former employees or their families.

- Loans to employees (who are not directors) to enable them to acquire beneficial ownership of fully paid shares in the company.

[CA 06 Secs 678, 679, 681, 682].

Giving financial assistance by these means would result in a reduction in the company's net assets if provision had to be made in the financial statements for the resultant debt. However, provided this reduction was made out of distributable profits, the financial assistance would be allowed.

7.136 The prohibition in sections 678 and 679 of the 2006 Act does not apply if the company's principal purpose in giving financial assistance is not to give it for the purpose of acquiring shares, or the assistance given for that purpose is an incidental part of some larger purpose of the company and the assistance is given in good faith and in the interests of the company. [CA06 Secs 678(2), 679(2)]. Similarly, for post-acquisition assistance, the prohibition in sections 678 and 679 of the 2006 Act does not apply if the company's principal purpose in giving financial assistance is not to reduce or discharge any liability incurred for the purpose of acquiring shares, or the reduction or discharge is an incidental part of some larger purpose of the company and the assistance is given in good faith and in the company's interests. [CA06 Secs 678(4), 679(4)]. In the case of *Brady v Brady* [1989] AC 755 the House of Lords drew a distinction between the purpose of a transaction and the reason for which it was undertaken. It decided that a larger purpose was not the same as a more important reason and, therefore, even though the financial or commercial advantages of the transaction were possibly the most important reason for providing the assistance, they could not constitute part of the larger purpose. It is thought that the effect of this judgement is to severely reduce the usefulness of these exemptions. Although this case was tried under the 1985 Act, the relevant provisions have been carried forward into the 2006 Act without amendment, so the ruling remains relevant.

7.137 The above provisions do not prohibit the following transactions, even though they may effectively represent financial assistance:

- Distributions made as a lawfully paid dividend or made in the course of winding up.

- Allotment of bonus shares.

- Reduction of capital; either by the solvency statement route or confirmed by court order.

- Redemption or purchase of own shares made in accordance with sections 684 — 708 of the 2006 Act (see above).

- A scheme of arrangement between the company and its members or its creditors under Part 26 of the 2006 Act or an arrangement under section 110 or Part 1 of the Insolvency Act 1986.

[CA06 Sec 681].

7.138   However, in spite of this exemption, it is thought that the source of the money out of which the purchase or redemption is made is important. Thus, if the company makes the payment with borrowed money, there is a risk that it will not be covered by the exemption and the company may be giving financial assistance for the acquisition of its own shares. As a result, where a company is borrowing to fund the purchase and grants security for the borrowing, the giving of security or payment of interest may amount to financial assistance by the company. As there are criminal penalties for giving illegal financial assistance, it is, therefore, advisable for a company to consider the financial assistance provisions and to take legal advice.

Effect of contravention

7.139   Where a company gives financial assistance in contravention of section 678(1),(3) or 679(1),(3), it is liable to a fine and every officer of it who is in default is liable to imprisonment or a fine or both. [CA06 Sec 680]. In addition, the transaction is void so that any property transferred is irrecoverable. The effect of a loan made in contravention of the prohibition from giving financial assistance was considered in *Coulthard v Neville Russell* (a firm) [[1998] 1 BCLC 143]. Although the case was tried under the 1985 Act, the law (insofar as it relates to public companies) is unchanged in this area.

7.140   The facts in the case were that the subsidiary had made a loan to its parent to enable the parent to repay loans which financed the purchase of the subsidiary's shares. The subsidiary subsequently went into insolvent liquidation and the Secretary of State brought proceedings seeking disqualification orders against the directors of the subsidiary. The directors in the meantime brought an action against the subsidiary's auditors alleging that the auditors owed them a duty of care to warn them that the loans were or might be in breach of the 1985 Act, and that, as a consequence of the loans' illegality, the financial statements would not give a true and fair view if they were included as assets. The auditors appealed that the proceedings disclosed no cause of action.

7.141   In the case the Court of Appeal considered the effect of a loan made in breach of the prohibition in the 1985 Act. A loan made for the purpose of giving financial assistance contrary to this prohibition is illegal and unenforceable against the borrower. It follows that the loans made in contravention of the section cannot, properly, be treated as assets of the lending company and that a balance sheet in which such a loan is shown as the company's asset will fail to give a true and fair view of its financial affairs.

7.142 The Court of Appeal dismissed the appeal, without wishing to express any view that the directors' claim would succeed, on the basis that the directors had at least an arguable case against the auditors. The case highlights the importance of identifying potential financial assistance at an early stage by obtaining legal advice.

Chapter 8

Secretarial matters

Chapter 8

Secretarial matters

Introduction

8.1 Company law imposes certain duties and obligations regarding a company's financial management and administration on both the company and its directors. Many of these duties and obligations are of a company secretarial nature and these are considered in this chapter.

8.1.1 In recent years, legislation in this area for GB companies has been contained in the Companies Act 1985 (the 1985 Act). In a similar way, the Northern Ireland Order 1986 applied to NI companies. Although the requirements of the 1985 Act include requirements that are similar to those of the Northern Ireland Order, references to the NI Order are not given in this chapter. The Companies Act 2006 (the 2006 Act) and its supporting regulations replaces all the provisions of the 1985 Act and the Northern Ireland Order and their supporting regulations are covered by this chapter. Implementation of the 2006 Act was staggered and different parts had different commencement dates. Each section of this chapter sets out the principal changes to be introduced by the 2006 Act and states the date of commencement of the relevant section. One consequence of the 2006 Act applying to Northern Ireland will be that it is now correct to refer to UK company law and UK companies.

8.1.2 The main supporting regulations to the 2006 Act that impact on the subject matter of this chapter (in the order they appear in the text) are:

- SI 2009/1581, 'The Companies Act 2006 (Accounts, Reports and Audit) Regulations 2009'.

- SI 2008/409, 'The Small Companies and Groups (Accounts and Directors' Report) Regulations 2008'.

- SI 2008/410, 'The Large and Medium-sized Companies and Groups (Accounts and Reports) Regulations 2008'.

- SI 2008/489, 'The Companies (Disclosure of Auditor Remuneration and Liability Limitation Agreements) Regulations 2008'.

- SI 2008/3007, 'The Companies (fees for Inspection of Company records) Regulations 2009'

- SI 2007/2612, 'Companies (Fees for Inspection and Copying of Company Records) Regulations 2007'.

- SI 2008/3006, 'The Companies (Company Records) Regulations 2008'.

- SI 2008/495, 'The Companies (Trading Disclosures) Regulations 2008'.

- SI 2008/623, 'The Companies (Defective Accounts and Directors' Reports) (Authorised Person) and Supervision of Accounts and Reports (Prescribed Body) Order 2008'.

- SI 2009/1801, 'The Overseas Companies Regulations 2009'.

- SI 2008/569, 'The Partnerships (Accounts) Regulations 2008'.

- SI 2008/497, 'The Companies (Late Filing Penalties) and Limited Liability Partnerships (Filing Periods and Late Filing Penalties) Regulations 2008'.

- SI 2008/373, 'The Companies (Revision of Defective Accounts and Reports) Regulations 2008'.

- SI 2008/374, 'The Companies (Summary Financial Statement) Regulations 2008'.

- SI 2009/1632, 'The Companies (Shareholders' Rights) Regulations 2009'.

8.2   A company's business letters, other documents and web sites must show the correct information regarding the company's name and other details. Furthermore, a company is under an obligation to keep adequate accounting records and statutory books and to retain them for the appropriate period. From such records, the directors have to prepare financial statements for the company for each financial year. When a company's annual financial statements have been prepared in accordance with the 2006 Act's provisions, the company's directors are required to approve, sign and file the financial statements and reports with the Registrar of Companies within prescribed time limits. In addition, the financial statements and reports must be circulated to the members of the company and the other persons entitled to receive them. Private companies have no statutory requirement to lay their financial statements before the members in general meeting.

8.3   This chapter considers the responsibilities of a company's directors for the company's financial statements and the role of its auditors. It discusses the accounting period that a company's financial statements must cover and the rules with which companies have to comply when they publish their financial statements. In addition, the chapter deals with the rules for preparing summary financial statements and for revising defective financial statements (including defective directors' reports and, for public companies, defective directors' remuneration reports). These aspects of company law, together with the formalities regarding meetings and resolutions, including the removal of the requirement for a private company to lay their financial statements before the members at a general meeting, are considered in detail in this chapter.

8.4   In many cases where the company or its directors fail to comply with the Act's provisions they will be guilty of a criminal offence and liable to a fine. In certain situations, the directors can be imprisoned. Breach of other sections of the 2006 Act may result in civil penalties. For example, section 453 of the 2006 Act imposes a civil penalty on companies who breach the rules on the period allowed for filing their financial statements with the Registrar of Companies.

8.5   In the 2006 Act there is no equivalent schedule to schedule 24 to the 1985 Act, which set out the possible penalties for breaching the provisions of the 1985 Act. Instead, penalties have been embedded in the body of the 2006 Act in proximity to the description of the relevant offence.

Accounting records and statutory books

General requirements — accounting records

8.6   A company must ensure that it keeps accounting records sufficient to show the items set out in the 2006 Act (see para 8.9). [CA06 Sec 386(1)(2)]. Part 15 of the 2006 Act sets out the provisions concerning accounting records and company financial statements. A company's directors are under an obligation to present to the company's members, once a year, the following:

■   The company's annual financial statements.

■   The directors' report, including the business review (unless the company is entitled to the small companies' exemption).

■   In the case of a quoted company, the expanded business review and the directors' remuneration report.

■   The auditors' report on those financial statements and directors' report and, in the case of a quoted company, on the auditable part of the directors' remuneration report.

[CA06 Secs 437, 438].

Private companies have no statutory requirement to present the annual accounts and reports to members in general meeting, but they are still required to circulate them to members and others entitled to receive them.

8.7   The company's directors have a duty to prepare annual 'individual accounts' (financial statements) in accordance with the general requirements of the Act and either in accordance with International Accounting Standards (IAS individual accounts) or in accordance with section 395 of the 2006 Act (Companies Act individual accounts). [CA06 Sec 394]. Directors also have a duty to prepare annual 'group accounts' (consolidated financial statements), unless the company falls within the small companies regime or is exempt, in accordance with the general requirements of the Act and in accordance with either International Accounting Standards (IAS group accounts) or in accordance with section 404 of the 2006 Act (Companies Act group accounts). [CA06 Secs 399, 403]. Directors must not approve financial statements unless they are satisfied that they give a true and fair view. [CA06 Sec 393]. International Accounting Standards means those as adopted by the European Union. See further from paragraph 8.25.3.

8.8 There may be other legislation or regulation that specifies the way in which particular companies should keep their accounting records. For example, specific legislation governs charities, registered social landlords, friendly societies, building societies, banks and insurance companies. In addition, a company whose securities are admitted to trading on a regulated market (for example, one listed on the Main Market of the London Stock Exchange (LSE) or on Plus Market's PLUS-listed market) or traded on AIM or on Plus Market's PLUS-quoted market must comply with the UKLA's Listing Rules (LR) and Disclosure and Transparency Rules (DTR) or the AIM or PLUS-quoted Rules respectively.

Adequate accounting records

8.9 The 2006 Act's requirement that every company must keep accounting records in accordance with section 386 of the 2006 Act is summarised below. Counsel has previously advised on the meaning of certain words and phrases used in section 221 of the 1985 Act, which is broadly similar to section 386 of the 2006 Act. This advice is still valid and is shown below. Section 386 of the 2006 Act states that the accounting records must be sufficient to show and explain the company's transactions and, consequently, to:

- Disclose with reasonable accuracy the company's financial position at any time.

- Enable the directors to ensure that any financial statements required to be prepared from the accounting records comply with the Act's requirements (and, where applicable, of Article 4 of the IAS Regulation).

[CA06 Sec 386(2)].

8.10 A company's accounting records should detail the following:

- The sums of money the company received and expended on a day-to-day basis, together with explanations of the amounts it received and expended. [CA06 Sec 386(3)(a)].

- A record of the assets and liabilities of the company.[CA06 Sec 386(3)(b)].

- If the company deals in goods:
    - Statements of stocks the company held at the financial year end, together with supporting statements of stocktakes.
    - Statements of all goods sold and purchased by the company, in sufficient detail to enable the goods and the buyers and sellers to be identified. (This requirement, however, does not apply to companies carrying on retailing).

[CA06 Sec 386(4)].

8.10.1 The 2006 Act restates the requirement to keep accounting records and obliges the company to keep 'adequate accounting records'. 'Adequate accounting records' are defined as those that are sufficient to give the information listed in paragraphs 8.9 and 8.10 above. While it appears that the government did not intend the change in wording to represent a substantive change to the requirements for keeping accounting records, it has sparked a degree of controversy and debate. To obtain clarity on this, the Financial Reporting Council (FRC) adopted a project to assess the implications of the change in wording. The wording of the requirement will, under the 2006 Act, be consistent with the wording of the auditor's obligation to form an opinion as to the adequacy of the company's accounting records (see para 8.31).

Counsel's opinion on section 221 of the 1985 Act

8.11   In March 1992 the Council of the ICAEW issued a guidance statement for members (published in Accountancy April 1992) on the obligation of companies to keep proper accounting records under the Act. This statement was settled in consultation with Counsel. The interpretation of section 221 of the 1985 Act set out below is based on that statement.

8.11.1   The requirements of Part 15 of the 2006 Act are virtually identical and until or unless the project currently underway by the FRC issues new guidance on the obligation under the 2006 Act, it is reasonable to continue to apply the ICAEW guidance issued in 1992. Hence, directors should continue to keep accounting records as they have for the purposes of the 1985 Act so as to meet their obligation under section 386 of the 2006 Act. [CA06 Sec 386(5)].

8.11.2   Equivalent references from the 2006 Act have been inserted into the 1992 guidance for the sake of ease, but this does not imply that Counsel's opinion extends to the 2006 Act.

8.12   Section 386(1)(2) of the 2006 Act obliges companies to keep accounting records. In addition, a parent company must also take reasonable steps to ensure that its subsidiary undertakings (which are not themselves companies) keep such accounting records to enable the parent company's directors to ensure that any financial statements required to be prepared under Part VII of the Act (Part 15 of the 2006 Act) comply with the requirements of the Act and, where applicable, or Article 4 to the IAS Regulation. [CA06 Sec 386(5)].

Duty to keep accounting records

8.13   To fulfil the directors' duty to keep accounting records, they should be made up of an orderly, classified collection of information capable of prompt retrieval, containing details of the company's transactions, assets and liabilities. An unorganised collection of vouchers and documents is not sufficient. The records must enable a trial balance to be constructed from them whatever their physical form. For example, where information is held in a computer database, the software should be capable of retrieving the appropriate data.

8.14   Whether a company is keeping the right kind of accounting records to meet the Act's requirements is a question of fact, which can only be decided on the facts of any particular case. In addition, the prevailing practice of the time in businesses of the type in question would be taken into account in determining whether proper accounting records have been kept. The records must also be sufficient to enable the directors to prepare annual financial statements that satisfy the Act's requirements. [CA06 Sec 386(2)].

8.15   The company's accounting records must be kept in a form that will enable it to comply with the retention period set in the Act. Accounting records must be preserved for six years for public companies or three years for private companies. [CA06 Sec 388(4)]. Furthermore, programmed instructions and supporting documentation in usable form, for example, from a computer database, and any necessary hardware, must be available for the same period.

Disclosure of the financial position at any time

8.16   In the requirement in section 386(2)(b) of the 2006 Act, the words 'at any time' emphasise the obligation to keep accounting records up to date. This does not mean that transactions and events must be recorded instantaneously. It is sufficient if they are recorded within a reasonable time, which will depend upon the nature of the business and other circumstances. What is urgent for, say, a bank, may be less so for another business. In addition, records made to disclose the current financial position (including any stock records or memoranda, such as are referred to in paras 8.19 and 8.20) must be retained for the statutory period.

8.17   The Act requires the accounting records to be sufficient to disclose with reasonable accuracy, at any time, the company's financial position at that time. In doing so the legislation recognises that it is not practicable to keep accounting records in such a way so that financial statements can be prepared, giving a true and fair view, at every moment during the year. In other words, the Act does not expect a company to be able to reconstruct the financial statements as at any past date at random.

8.18   The directors should, at any time, be able to prepare a reasonably accurate statement of the company's financial position from the accounting records. The records should, therefore, contain the primary material on which a set of financial statements would be based. These records need not contain whatever additional items of information it would be necessary to know in order to make those financial statements true and fair. This is because the concept of 'true and fair' is extremely wide and embraces information not necessarily contained within the accounting records themselves. Furthermore, the financial position is not restricted to the cash position, it comprises the assets and liabilities including items such as those referred to in paragraph 8.20 below.

8.19   What constitutes a sufficient record of stocks will depend on the circumstances, for instance, the materiality of stock and stock movements. Continuous stock records can provide adequate information when they are supported by systematic physical checks. Furthermore, the information gathered from those physical checks would generally also be supplemented by accounting entries recording judgements of the stocks' realisable value and times of possible realisation. These entries may need to be in the form of memorandum as indicated in paragraph 8.20 below. Continuous records are not essential if the stock position can be assessed with sufficient reliability from other accounting records, for instance, interim stocktakings.

8.20 Provisions for depreciation, bad debts and other losses are often only made at the end of an accounting year, but section 386(2)(b) of the 2006 Act requires the records to disclose the financial position of the company with reasonable accuracy at any time during the financial year. This requirement can normally be satisfied if the company has a procedure to ensure that an adequate record is made and retained (for example, by way of memorandum), of any expected loss, liability or contingency material to the assessment of the stocks' current position. This type of memorandum would form part of the accounting records.

Sums of money

8.21 Section 386(3)(a) of the 2006 Act states that the accounting records must contain entries from day to day of all sums of money received and expended. The accounting records must, therefore, contain:

- The transaction date.

- The sums received and expended.

- The matters in respect of which the receipt and expenditure took place.

Such entries do not have to be made instantaneously, but must be made within a reasonable time (see para 8.16 above). Where a record of individual receipts is not necessary to explain the transactions (for example, in the daily cash takings of a shop), groups of transactions may be recorded rather than individual ones.

A record of the assets and liabilities

8.22 The accounting records must include details of all the company's assets and liabilities such as debtors, creditors, properties and plant. The records must show the dates of the transactions. Counsel's opinion in 1992 could not have covered 'IAS individual accounts' or 'Companies Act individual accounts', as these were not introduced until 2004 by SI 2004/2947. The following is for information only. For companies preparing 'IAS individual accounts', the IASB's Framework contains definitions of assets and liabilities and rules for their recognition (see chapter 2 of the Manual of Accounting – IFRS for the UK). For companies preparing 'Companies Act individual accounts', the ASB's Statement of principles and FRS 5 contain equivalent definitions and rules (see chapters 2 and 3 of the Manual of Accounting – UK GAAP).

Statements of stock

8.23   Where companies deal in goods, the statements of stock held at the end of each financial year are part of the accounting records. These statements and any statements of stocktakes supporting the year-end stock summary form part of the accounting records. Any continuous stock records or original stock sheets from a physical stocktake also have to be treated as part of the accounting records.

Statements of all goods sold and purchased

8.24   Where the company deals in goods, details of goods sold and purchased and of individual buyers and sellers must be recorded. However, this requirement does not apply to sales made by retailers.

Penalties and disqualification orders

8.25   Failure to comply with the provisions of section 386 of the 2006 Act is an offence. [CA06 Sec 387]. Furthermore, under section 9 of the Company Directors Disqualification Act 1986, the extent of a director's responsibility for the company's failure to comply with section 386 of the 2006 Act is one of the matters the courts must take into account on an application to disqualify the director (see para 8.76).

8.25.1   In an unreported case in March 2000, *R v Anthony Stevens*, the Court of Appeal sentenced a director to three months imprisonment and disqualified him for two years for failing to take all reasonable steps to preserve accounting records of a company under section 222(5) and (6) of the 1985 Act, even though there was no allegation of fraud or dishonesty. The company had gone into liquidation with a deficiency of £376,000. It was accepted that during its trading life accounts had been maintained on a computer system and audited accounts had been prepared for two periods. However, the director had failed to preserve the accounting records and could not hand them over to the liquidator for him to ascertain the full scale of the company's deficiency. Some records were found, but they comprised mainly copies of sales and purchase records and nothing else. Key documents were missing, the sales and purchase ledgers, the cash book, the petty cash book, bank statements, cheque books, paying-in books, VAT returns, correspondence files and records as to assets and liabilities.

Requirements to prepare financial statements

8.25.2   As noted in paragraph 8.6, the directors of every company are required to prepare (and present to members) annual 'individual accounts' (financial statements) and, where applicable, annual 'group accounts' (consolidated financial statements). [CA06 Secs 394, 399].

8.25.3   The Act requires the annual individual accounts (financial statements) to be prepared in accordance with the general requirements of the Act and either International Accounting Standards (IAS individual accounts) or section 396 of the 2006 Act (Companies Act individual accounts). [CA06 Sec 395]. International accounting standards are those accounting standards published by the International Accounting Standards Board as adopted by the EU. These standards are also referred to as International Financial Reporting Standards (IFRS). Section 395 of the 2006 Act requires the Companies Act individual accounts to comply with SI 2008/409, 'The Small Companies and Groups (Accounts and Reports) Regulations (2008)', for companies subject to the small companies regime and SI 2008/410, 'The Large and Medium-sized Companies and Groups (Accounts and Reports) Regulations (2008)', for all other companies.

8.25.3.1 The annual consolidated financial statements must also be prepared in accordance with the general requirements of the Act and either international accounting standards (IAS group accounts) or section 404 of the 2006 Act. Section 404 of the 2006 Act requires Companies Act group accounts to comply with SI 2008/409 for companies subject to the small companies regime (where the directors choose to prepare group accounts) and SI 2008/410 for all other companies.

8.25.3.2 Under the 1985 Act, Companies Act accounts were required to give a true and fair view whereas for IAS accounts the requirement under international accounting standards is to achieve a fair presentation. Section 262(2A) of the 1985 Act attempted to give equal meaning to 'true and fair view' and 'fair presentation'.

8.25.3.3 However, many investor groups were unconvinced and believed 'fair presentation' to be inferior to the 'true and fair' 'gold' standard. To alleviate demands from these investor groups about this and audit quality, the 2006 Act introduced an overarching obligation on directors not to approve financial statements, irrespective of whether they are IAS or Companies Act 'accounts', unless they are satisfied that they give a true and fair view of the assets, liabilities, financial position and profit or loss:

- in the case of the company's individual accounts, of the company;

- in the case of the company's group accounts, of the undertakings included in the consolidation as a whole, so far as concerns members of the company.

[CA06 Sec 393(1)].

This provision reflects the underlying legal duty already expressed in EU law.

8.25.3.4 For companies subject to the UKLA's DTR chapter 4, the directors must also make a statement that the financial statements do, in fact, give a true and fair view.

8.25.3.5 Section 393 of the 2006 Act and the UKLA's DTR reflect the underlying legal duty already expressed in EU law. In 2008 the FRC obtained an opinion from Martin Moore QC on the 'true and fair' concept under the 2006 Act. This, among other things, found that the central conclusions of earlier opinions of Lord Hoffman and Lady Justice Arden on the relationship of accounting standards and the 'true and fair' requirement (see the ASB's 'Foreword to accounting standards') have been endorsed by the courts, which will approach the true and fair requirement in the manner described in those opinions. The 2008 Moore opinion also confirms that the IAS 1 requirement 'to present fairly' is not a different requirement to that of showing a true and fair view, but is a different articulation of the same concept. Furthermore, in June 2005 the FRRP published a legal opinion on the effect of the IAS Regulation on the requirement for financial statements to give a true and fair view in the context of the 1985 Act. The findings in this opinion are still valid under the 2006 Act.

8.25.3.6   The 2006 Act places a requirement on auditors to take this overarching duty to give a true and fair view into consideration when giving an opinion on the financial statements. [CA06 Sec 393(2)].

8.25.4   After the first financial year in which the individual and/or group financial statements are prepared in accordance with IFRS as adopted by the EU (the 'first IAS year'), the individual and/or group financial statements for all subsequent years must also be prepared in accordance with IFRS as adopted by the EU, unless there is a 'relevant change of circumstances'. A relevant change of circumstances occurs if, at any time during or after the first IFRS year:

■   The company becomes a subsidiary undertaking of another undertaking that does not prepare IAS individual financial statements.

■   The company ceases to be a subsidiary undertaking.

■   The company ceases to have securities admitted to trading on a regulated market (that is, it de-lists).

■   A parent undertaking of the company ceases to have securities admitted to trading on a regulated market.

[CA06 Sec 395(3)(4)].

8.25.5   The detailed requirements for the format of financial statements prepared in accordance with EU-adopted IFRS are considered in chapter 4 of the Manual of Accounting – IFRS for the UK, whilst the detailed requirements for the format of financial statements prepared in accordance with section 396 of the 2006 Act are considered in the Manual of Accounting – UK GAAP.

8.25.6   The requirements for preparing consolidated financial statements is considered in the Manual of Accounting – IFRS for the UK and the Manual of Accounting – UK GAAP for consolidated financial statements prepared in accordance with IFRS and UK GAAP respectively.

8.25.7   Details about which companies are required or permitted to apply IFRS or UK GAAP in their individual and consolidated financial statements are considered in of the Manual of Accounting – IFRS for the UK and the Manual of Accounting – UK GAAP.

Directors' duty regarding accounting records

8.26   The 2006 Act codifies the general duties of directors, but does not make any specific reference to their financial and accounting responsibilities. [CA06 Sec 170]. The ICAEW 2009 Members Handbook contains a statement concerning the main duties and responsibilities of a financial or accounting nature and can be obtained from the ICAEW's website.

8.27   The ICAEW's revised statement sets out what, under the 2006 Act, is considered to be best practice rather than what may be acceptable as the legal minimum. It has a section that deals with books of account and other accounting records. The statement gives the following guidance:

> "69. In addition to the statutory requirement to keep adequate accounting records, the directors have an overriding responsibility to ensure that they have adequate information to enable them to discharge their duty to promote the success of the company."

> 70. The duty to promote the success of the company will involve ensuring that adequate control is kept over its records and transactions, for example:

> (a)   cash;

> (b)   debtors and creditors;

> (c)   stock and work in progress;

> (d)   capital expenditure; and

> (e)   major contracts.

> The nature and extent of the accounting and management information needed to exercise this control will depend upon the nature and extent of the company's business.

> 71. To restrict the possibility of actions for wrongful trading, directors will need constantly to be aware of the company's financial position and progress, and the accounting records should be sufficient to enable them to be provided with the information required for drawing conclusions on these matters. The directors should also be satisfied that proper systems to provide them with regular and prompt information are in place."

[ICAEW Members Handbook 2009 Sec 8.1 paras 69-72].

See also paragraph 8.78 below.

8.28   A company's normal books of account include:

- Cash books.

- Sales day book.

- Sales returns book.

- Purchase day book.

- Purchase returns book.

- Creditors ledger.

- Debtors ledger.

- Transfer journal.

- General ledger.

8.29   These books may be retained in book form, or on computer or in any other suitable readable form. Other books of account may be used to assist directors in preparing management accounts. These may include, for example, stock books to record continuous stock records used in a company's costing systems.

Auditors' duties and rights

8.30   In addition to the requirement that a company must keep accounting records, the company has a duty to appoint an auditor, unless it is a company within the small companies regime, which may be exempt from this requirement. Small companies that meet the total exemption requirements set out in section 477 of the 2006 Act are exempt from having their financial statements audited. Under the 1985 Act small companies that were charities were required instead to obtain the report of a reporting accountant. This special provision regarding small charitable companies is not carried forward in the 2006 Act, but reference should be made to the relevant charities legislation for the requirements post April 2008. The 2006 Act introduces a new exemption from audit for public sector companies. These organisations are exempt from an audit under Part 16 if they are not profit making and subject to a public sector audit. [CA06 Secs 482, 483]. In addition, dormant companies that meet the exemption requirements in section 480 of the 2006 Act are exempt from having their financial statements audited.

8.30.1   Apart from the exemptions for small companies and dormant companies, a company's auditors must normally examine the company's financial statements to be sent out to the members or, for a public company, to be laid before the company in its annual general meeting. The auditors must also report to the members on those financial statements. This report must include the auditors' opinion on those financial statements and as referred to in paragraph 8.25.3.3, the 2006 Act places a requirement on auditors to take the directors' overarching duty for their financial statements to give a true and fair view into consideration when giving that opinion. [CA06 Secs 393(2), 495(1)]. In addition, the auditors are required to report on whether the information in the directors' report is consistent with those financial statements. [CA06 Sec 496]. Furthermore, where a directors' remuneration report is prepared by quoted companies, the auditors are required to report to the members on the auditable part of that report. [CA06 Sec 497].

8.31   A company's auditors have a duty, in preparing their report, to carry out investigations that will enable them to form an opinion both on whether the company has kept adequate accounting records and on whether they have received returns adequate for their audit from those branches they did not visit. [CA06 Sec 498(1)(a)]. The 2006 Act generally restates the requirements of the 1985 Act, but refers to 'adequate accounting records' and 'returns adequate for their audit' rather than 'proper accounting records' and 'proper returns adequate for their audit'. The government's intention in restating this requirement was not to change the obligations of either the company or its auditors in respect of accounting records, but to provide consistency in the wording of those obligations; the company must keep 'adequate accounting records' and auditors must investigate whether the company has kept 'adequate accounting records'. However, as indicated in paragraph 8.10.1 there is some concern that the restatement has altered the obligations.

8.31.1   The auditors should also form an opinion on whether the company's financial statements are in agreement with the accounting records. [CA06 Sec 498(1)(b)]. Also, in the case of a quoted company, the auditors should form an opinion on whether the auditable part of the company's directors' remuneration report is in agreement with the accounting records and returns. [CA06 Sec 498(1)(c)]. If the company has not kept accounting records (including returns from UK Establishments), or if the financial statements are not in agreement with those records, or if in the case of a quoted company the auditable part of its directors' remuneration report, is not in agreement with the accounting records and returns, then the auditors must state that fact in their report. [CA06 Sec 498(2)]. However, the auditors need make no reference to these items in the audit report if there are no deficiencies to report.

8.31.2   A new requirement under the 2006 Act applies where the directors have prepared financial statements and reports in accordance with the small companies regime or have taken advantage of the small companies exemption in preparing the directors' report. Here the auditor has to consider whether the directors were entitled to do so and, if in the auditor's opinion they were not, then the auditor has to state this in the audit report. [CA06 Sec 498(5)].

8.31.3   In addition:

- if the disclosure required by Schedule 3 to SI 2008/409 for a company in the small companies regime or Schedule 5 to SI 2008/410 for all other companies of directors' benefits (remuneration, pensions and compensation for loss of office) is not made in the financial statements: or

- in the case of a quoted company, the information forming the auditable part of the directors' remuneration report does not comply with Part 3 of Schedule 8 to SI 2008/410 in that report,

the auditors must include in their report, so far as they are reasonably able to do so, a statement giving the required particulars. [CA06 Sec 498(4)].

8.32   Auditors have a right of access, at all times, to the company's books and accounting records. They also have a right to require such information and explanations from the company's officers or employees, any person holding or accountable for the company's books and accounting records and any person who previously held any of these positions, as they believe they need to perform their duties as auditors. Any such person commits an offence who knowingly or recklessly makes to the company's auditors an oral or written statement that conveys or purports to convey any such information or explanations that are misleading, false or deceptive. Furthermore there is an additional offence if any person fails to comply with the auditors' requests without delay. [CA06 Secs 499, 501].

8.32.1   A parent company's auditors are also entitled to require information and explanations directly from UK incorporated subsidiary undertakings, their officers, employees, auditors, persons holding or accountable for their books and accounting records and any person who previously held any of these positions, as they think necessary for the performance of their duties as auditors. [CA06 Sec 499(1)(b), (2)(c)(d)]. In respect of overseas subsidiary undertakings, the auditors may obtain the necessary information and explanations indirectly by requiring the parent company to get them from those undertakings, their officers, employees, auditors, persons holding or accountable for their books and accounting records and any person who previously held of any of these positions. The parent company must take all such steps as are reasonably open to it to obtain the required information or explanations from the person concerned. For UK subsidiary undertakings and their personnel, they can be held to have committed either offence in a similar manner to the parent company's own personnel (see para 8.32). In the case of an overseas subsidiary undertaking, it is the parent company and all of its officers that commit an offence if the parent company fails to comply with the auditors' request. [CA06 Sec 500, 501].

Senior statutory auditor

8.32.2   Section 503 of the 2006 Act specifies that the audit report must be signed by the senior statutory auditor in their own name on behalf of the audit firm and the name of the senior statutory auditor must be stated in every set of published financial statements. The Act says the audit firm identifies this individual according to standards to be issued by the European Commission on implementation of the EU Statutory Audit Directive (2006/43/EC) or if there are no such standards, according to guidance issued either by the Secretary of State or by a body appointed by him. [CA06 Sec 504(1)]. To be identified as a company's senior statutory auditor, an individual must be eligible himself to be appointed as auditor of the company. [CA06 Sec 504(2)]. The nomination of an individual as senior statutory auditor does not change his exposure to liability. [CA06 Sec 504(3)].

8.32.2.1   In April 2008, the APB issued such guidance in Bulletin 2008/6, 'The "Senior Statutory Auditor" under the United Kingdom Companies Act 2006'. This identifies the engagement partner (as defined in auditing standards) for a company's statutory audit as the 'senior statutory auditor' for the purposes of such an engagement.

8.32.2.2   The 2006 Act makes provision for the name of the senior statutory auditor (and that of the audit firm) to be omitted from the published financial statements and from the copy delivered to the Registrar of Companies, if the company believes that on publication of the name(s) there are reasonable grounds that the auditor (or audit firm) would be subject to violence or intimidation. [CA06 Sec 506]. The company must apply to the Secretary of State to obtain this relief.

Criminal offence for auditors

8.32.3   The 2006 Act makes it a criminal offence to knowingly or recklessly sign an audit report that contains any information that is false, misleading or deceptive. [CA06 Sec 507]. The criminal offence extends to omitting from the audit report a statement required in relation to section 498(2)(b) (statement that the company's financial statements do not agree with accounting records and returns), section 498(3) (statement that necessary information and explanations not obtained) or section 498(5) (statement that directors wrongly took advantage of exemption from the obligation to prepare consolidated financial statements).

Auditors' limitation of liability agreements

8.32.4   Chapter 6 of Part 16 of the 2006 Act makes it possible for auditors to limit their liability by agreement with the company, but the agreement is only effective to the extent that it is fair and reasonable. Section 534 allows a company to enter into a 'liability limitation agreement' with its auditor that purports to limit the liability owed to a company in respect of any negligence, default, breach of duty or trust occurring in the course of the audit of the company's financial statements. Any such agreement must be approved by the company's members as specified in section 536. Such an agreement is not effective if it attempts to limit the liability to an amount that is not deemed to be fair and reasonable in all circumstances.

8.32.4.1   The ICAEW has obtained a legal opinion that confirms that directors can recommend auditor liability limitation agreements to the shareholders without breaching their fiduciary duties. The FRC has issued guidance that sets out factors for directors to consider when assessing the advantages of entering into a limitation of liability agreement and explains which provisions are permitted and the process for obtaining shareholder approval.

8.32.5   A company that has entered into a limitation of liability agreement will have to disclose details of the agreement either in the notes to the financial statements or in the directors' report. [CA06 Sec 538]. The details to be disclosed are contained in SI 2008/489, 'The Companies (Disclosure of Auditor Remuneration and Liability Limitation Agreements) Regulations 2008', and are:

- The principal terms of the agreement.

- The date of the resolution approving the agreement or its principal terms or, in the case of a private company, the date of the resolution waiving the need for such approval.

[SI 2008/489 Reg 8(1)].

8.32.6 The disclosure is required to be made in the notes to the financial statements for the year to which the limitation of liability agreement relates. If the agreement was entered into too late for inclusion in that year's financial statements to be reasonably practicable, then disclosure should be made in the following year's financial statements. [SI 2008/489 Reg 8].

Form of records

8.33 Any register, index, minute book or accounting record that a company is required to keep under the Act may be kept in a bound book or other similar form. If the company maintains any of these items by recording the data otherwise than in a legible form (such as, in the form of a computer record), any duty imposed by the Act to allow the inspection of, or to provide a copy of, that data can be satisfied by reproducing that data in a legible form. But a company must take adequate precautions against falsification of such records. [CA06 Sec 1135-1138].

Statutory books and records and their location

Accounting records

8.34 A company must keep its accounting records either at its registered office or at such other place as the directors think fit. The records have to be available for inspection by the company's officers at all times. [CA06 Sec 388(1)]. For this purpose, an officer includes a director, or a manager, or the company secretary. [CA06 Sec 1121].

8.35 If the accounting records are kept outside the UK, then accounts and returns must be sent to and kept at an appropriate place (for example, the registered office) in the UK, where they should be available for inspection at all times by the company's officers. [CA06 Sec 388(2)]. These accounts and returns should reflect the transactions recorded in the accounting records in order to:

- Disclose the company's financial position at intervals not exceeding six months.

- Enable the directors to ensure that the company's financial statements comply with the Act's requirements and, where applicable, Article 4 of the IAS Regulation.

[CA06 Sec 388(3)].

8.36   The requirements as regards accounts and returns to be sent to the UK pose no problem for most companies that have branches overseas, because their overseas entities will usually return management accounts to the UK at regular intervals (normally, monthly). These management accounts will generally satisfy the requirements of section 388(3) of the 2006 Act.

Statutory books and other records

8.37   The 2006 Act requires a company to keep certain statutory books and records and specify where these should be kept. Companies are permitted to keep statutory books at either their registered office or at a Single Alternative Inspection Location (SAIL). If a SAIL is used it must be situated in the same part of the UK as the company is registered and it must be the same place for all of the registers and records. It is also necessary to notify the Registrar of such a location.

8.38   The company's register of directors and register of secretaries (but see para 8.38.1) must be kept at the registered office or at a SAIL. The register must contain the particulars of the company's directors (including shadow directors) specified by sections 163 and 164 of the 2006 Act and the particulars of the secretaries specified by sections 277 to 279 of the 2006 Act. Unlike the 1985 Act, from 1 October 2009, the 2006 Act does not require shadow directors to be included in the register of directors. [CA06 Explanatory Notes para 289]. Any changes to the particulars of directors and secretaries must also be notified to the Registrar of Companies. The register must be open to inspection by members for no charge and by others on payment of a fee. [CA06 Sec 162(5)]. SI 1991/1998, 'The Companies (Inspection and Copying of Registers, Indices and Documents) Regulations 1991', requires a company to make the register, index or document available for inspection for two hours between 9am and 5pm on business days and to permit the person inspecting it to copy any information by taking notes. The fees that the company is permitted to charge for copying documents are limited by SI 2007/2612, 'Companies (Fees for Inspection and Copying of Company Records) Regulations 2007', and SI 2008/3007, 'The Companies (Fees for Inspection of Company Records) Regulation 2008'.

8.38.1   Private companies are no longer required to have a company secretary, although they may continue to have one if they wish. [CA06 Sec 270]. The 2006 Act states that a director or person authorised by the directors can perform anything required to be done by the secretary in the case of a private company that does not choose to appoint a company secretary. [CA06 Sec 270(3)]. Public companies continue to be required to have a company secretary. [CA06 Sec 271].

8.39   The company's register of charges and copies of all instruments creating such charges must be kept at the registered office or at a SAIL. [CA06 Secs 876, 877].

8.40   The minute books kept at the registered office or at a SAIL, must include minutes of the proceedings of a company's general meetings, decisions of sole members and records of written resolutions of the company. Members are entitled to inspect and request copies of these minutes. [CA06 Secs 355, 358].

8.41   Minutes of meetings of directors must also be entered into minute books, but the Act does not specify a place where these minute books must be kept. [CA06 Sec 248]. The 2006 Act specifies that minutes should be kept for a minimum of ten years.

8.42   The register of members and, where the company has more than 50 members, an index of their names, must be kept at the registered office or at a SAIL. [CA06 Secs 113-115]. Members can inspect the register of members at no cost, but others have to pay a fee. [CA06 Sec 116; SI 2007/2612]. In addition, the company must provide members and others with a copy of the register if so requested.

8.43   If a company keeps a register of debenture holders it must keep this at its registered office or at a SAIL. [CA06 Sec 743]. Debenture holders have the right to inspect and take copies of the register for no charge, but others are required to pay an inspection fee and a fee to copy the register.

8.44   Prior to April 2007, all companies had to maintain a register of directors' interests in shares and debentures of group companies, together with the index. The register and index had to be either kept at the registered office or at the place where the register of members is kept. The Registrar of Companies had to be notified of the place where the register was kept if other than the registered office. The register was open for inspection by members without charge and by others on payment of a fee.

8.44.1   On 6 April 2007, sections 324 to 326 and 328 to 329 of, and parts 2 to 4 of Schedule 13 to, the 1985 Act were repealed under section 1177 of the 2006 Act. This removed the obligation under the Companies Act to keep the register and, also with the repeal of the requirement under Schedule 7 to the 1985 Act, to make the disclosure of directors' interests in the directors' report. However, for companies incorporated in the UK and included on the Official List maintained by the FSA, the UKLA's Listing Rules still require disclosure of directors' beneficial and non-beneficial interests in shares and debentures of group companies. [LR 9.8.6]. In effect, a listed company has to continue to maintain its register of directors' interests and the relief from maintaining such a register lies with unquoted companies.

8.45   Shareholders and holders of certain financial instruments are required by the UKLA's DTR to notify companies included on the Official List maintained by the FSA (that is, those companies listed on the Main Market of the LSE or the Plus Market's PLUS-listed market) and those traded on AIM, Plus Market's PLUS-quoted market or other prescribed markets when such holders have control over the exercise of voting rights attached to the shares equal to or more than three per cent of the total voting rights. [DTR 5.1.2]. Such holders also have to notify the company of acquisitions and disposals of shares and qualifying financial instruments (as defined in DTR 5.3) that take the holder across one per cent thresholds above three per cent (for example, four per cent, five per cent etc. up to 100 per cent). Some voting rights are to be disregarded as set out in DTR 5.1.3, such as those attached to shares held by a custodian or a market maker. The rules apply to direct and indirect holdings. A listed public company has to keep the information it receives in a retrievable form as the UKLA's Listing rules require a statement of such holdings to be made in a listed company's annual financial statements. [LR 9.8.6(2)].

8.45.2   The 2006 Act gives a public company the ability to investigate holdings of its shares by sending a section 793 notice (previously a 1985 Act section 212 notice) to any person who the company believes or has cause to believe may be interested in its shares or have been so in the previous three years. Similarly, a member may require the company to use its power to serve a notice of information. [CA06 Sec 803]. Public companies must maintain a register of interests disclosed under section 793 of the 2006 Act in the manner required by that section together with an index required by section 810. [CA06 Secs 808, 810]. Listed public companies must make a statement of such information collected under Part 22 of the 2006 Act in its annual financial statements. [LR 9.8.6(2)].

8.46   The register required by section 808 of the 2006 Act (and any index) of disclosed interests obtained under section 793 notices must be kept at the registered office or, at a SAIL. [CA06 Sec 809]. The Registrar of Companies must be informed of the location of the register and any change of that location. [CA06 Sec 809(2)]. Any person can inspect the register at no cost, but copies have to be paid for using the scale prescribed in SI 2007/2612, 'Companies (Fees for Inspection and Copying of Company Records) Regulations 2007'. [CA06 Sec 811]. Persons wishing to avail themselves of the rights to inspect the register and/ or obtain copies must apply to the company in the form prescribed in section 811(4) of the 2006 Act.

8.47   A company specifies the intended location of its registered office on incorporation, but it may change its registered office by giving notice on the prescribed form to the Registrar. The change of address will take effect on registration of the notice. Documents held at the registered office must be transferred to the new registered office not more than 14 days after the company gives the notice to the Registrar. [CA06 Sec 87].

Company identification

Company name

8.48   A company's name is important not only for identification purposes, but also as a means of informing the public that it has limited liability status. Consequently, the Companies Act contains several requirements regarding disclosure of company names and other details. Other legislation, such as VAT legislation, may require a company to make additional disclosures, like the VAT registration number to be given on certain company documentation.

8.48.1 Chapter six of Part 5 of the 2006 Act contains the provisions relating to company identification and trading disclosures. The detailed provisions are included in SI 2008/495, 'The Companies (Trading Disclosures) Regulations 2008'.

8.49 A company must state its registered name in characters that can be read with the naked eye on all of its business letters, notices and other official publications, order forms, invoices, cheques, receipts, orders for goods, emails and other forms of business correspondence and other documents specified in regulation 6 of SI 2008/495. In addition, the company must disclose its registered name on its web site.

8.49.1 Failure to give the relevant information renders the company and the signatory liable to a fine. Furthermore, if a director or other officer of the company or a person on its behalf signs or authorises the signing of any of the documents referred to below in which the company's name is not mentioned, he is personally liable for the amount specified unless it is duly paid by the company. The documents are a bill of exchange, promissory note, endorsement, cheque or order for money or goods.

8.49.2 Section 83 of the 2006 Act sets out civil consequences for the company of failure to make the specified trading disclosures required under section 82 of the 2006 Act. The provision for personal civil liability of officers contained in section 349(4) of the 1985 Act has not been carried forward.

8.50 In addition, the following information is required to be stated on all of the company's business letters, order forms and web sites:

- The part of the UK in which the company is registered.

- The company's registered number.

- The address of its registered office.

- For an investment company (as defined in section 833 of the 2006 Act) that it is such a company.

- For a community interest company that is not a public company, the fact that it is a limited company.

- Even if a limited company is exempt under sections 60 and 61 of the 2006 Act from the obligation to use 'limited' as part of its name, or a community interest company that is not a public company, the fact that it is a limited company.

[SI 2008/495 Reg 7].

8.50.1 In the event that a company is being wound up, whether by court or voluntarily – every invoice, order for goods, business letter or order form (whether in hard copy, electronic or any other form) issued by or on behalf of the company, or a liquidator of the company or a receiver or manager of the company's property, being a document on or in which the name of the company appears and all of the company's web sites must contain a statement that the company is being wound up. [Insolvency Act 1986 Sec 188(1)].

8.50.2   If the business letters, order forms or company web site contain any reference to the amount of the company's share capital, the reference must be to its paid up share capital. [CA06 Sec 82].

8.51   Business letters on which the company's name appears should not state the name of any of its directors (otherwise than in the text or as a signatory) unless the letter states the names of *all* of the company's individual or corporate directors. [SI 2008/495 Reg 8]. An equivalent provision is contained in SI 2009/1801, 'The Overseas Companies Regulations 2009', which applies to overseas companies with a UK Establishment.

8.52   A company using the Welsh equivalent of plc or limited (cwmni cyfyngedig cyhoeddus or cyfyngedig) need not state in English that it is a public limited company or a limited company (whichever is appropriate) on all prospectuses, billheads, letter paper, notices and other publications of the company. [Welsh Language Act 1993 Sec 31].

Memorandum and articles of association

8.53   An up to date version of the company's Articles of association must be filed with the Registrar of Companies and the directors must ensure that any alteration to it is filed with the Registrar within 15 days of its coming into force. Any alterations to the Articles of association must be printed.

8.53.1   Under the 2006 Act, the role of the Memorandum of association is reduced. For companies incorporated after October 2008 it is a historical document reflecting simply the company's formation, with all other matters contained within the company's articles. It will not be possible to amend the company's Memorandum after formation. For existing companies, from October 2008 all provisions contained in the memorandum are treated as entrenched provisions of the Articles (see para 8.53.2 below). [CA06 Sec 28].

8.53.2   Section 22 of the 2006 Act allows companies to provide in their articles that certain provisions may only be amended or repealed if specific conditions are met that are more onerous than a special resolution. Such a provision is known as a *'provision for entrenchment'*.

[The next paragraph is 8.55].

Annual return

8.55   An annual return gives general information about a company's directors, secretary (where one is appointed), registered office, shareholders and share capital. Under section 854 of the 2006 Act every company must deliver to the

Registrar at least once in every 12 months an annual return (in the prescribed form) made up to the return date. The return date is a date not later than:

- the anniversary of the company's incorporation; or

- the anniversary of the date of the last return.

8.55.1   A company has 28 days from the return date to deliver its annual return to the Registrar. For filing company documents, reference is made in the rest of this chapter to filing at Companies House or with the Registrar. However, it should be noted that the English and Welsh Registries and the Scottish and Northern Irish Registries are mutually exclusive for this purpose and documents sent to the inappropriate Companies House will be rejected.

[The next paragraph is 8.60.]

8.60   The company's annual return form, must state the date to which it is made up and contain the following information, (required by section 855 of the 2006 Act):

- The name of the company and its company number.

- The address of the company's registered office.

- Particulars of the current directors and secretary (if a private company has elected to have one) including a service address.

- If records are kept at a place other than the company's registered office, the address of that place and the records that are kept there.

- Information relating to the company's type and business activities by reference to certain perscribed classifications available from the Registrar of Companies. These may subsequently be amended if the nature of the company's business alters.

8.60.1   The 2006 Act permits directors to file a service address with Companies House for the public record. Home addresses will still need to be supplied to the Registrar; however, they will generally remain confidential.

8.61   Companies with share capital must also provide a statement of the share capital in the annual return including (as at the date of the return):

- The total number of shares (and if more than one class details of all classes of shares).

- The aggregate nominal value of the shares.

- The total number and voting rights attached to each class of shares.

- The amount paid up and the amount (if any) unpaid on each share – whether on account of the nominal value or by way of premium)

For non-traded companies the following information must be disclosed about shareholders:

- The name of every person who was a member at any time during the return period in alphabetical order or annexed to it an index that is sufficient to enable the name of the person in question to be easily found.

- The number of shares of each class held at the return date by member.

- The number of shares of each class transferred during the return period by or to each member, and the date of registration of the transfer.

For traded companies the following information must be disclosed in the annual return:

- The name and address of every person who held at least five per cent of the issued shares of any class at any time during the return period. The name must be displayed in alphabetical order or annexed to it there must be an index that is sufficient to enable the name of that person to be easily found.

- The number of shares of each class held at the return date for each member who held a least five per cent of the issued shares of any class of share at any time during the period.

- The number of shares of each class transferred during the return period by or to each person who held at least five per cent of the issued shares of any class at any time during that period and the date of registration of the transfer.

8.61.1   A full list of shareholders is required in the first annual return and then only every third year. In other years, a list of changes in membership and holdings suffices. [CA06 Sec 856(5)]. However, companies may provide a full list of shareholders every year.

Members' lists

8.62   The Registrar has specified certain requirements regarding document quality for all documents filed at Companies House. These requirements apply to the lists of shareholders which accompany annual returns as well as to annual financial statements, and are described briefly in paragraph 8.65 below.

Penalties

8.63   A company that does not complete the annual return properly or fails to deliver it to the Registrar within the 28 days of the return date is guilty of a criminal offence. Where the company is guilty of the offence every director and the company secretary will be liable also unless they can show that they took all reasonable steps to avoid committing the offence. [CA06 Sec 858]. Where a public company is late in filing its annual return, it appears that the Registrar may write to its directors at their home address (even if overseas) reminding them of their liability to prosecution.

Information annexed to annual return

8.64   In certain circumstances, a parent company may omit information required by Schedule 2 to SI 2008/409 and Schedule 4 to SI 2008/410 about its subsidiaries, joint ventures and associates if its directors are of the opinion that it would otherwise result in information of excessive length being included its financial statements. [CA06 Sec 410(1)]. Where advantage is taken of this provision, the full information (including that disclosed in the notes to the financial statements and the information excluded from those statements) must be annexed to the company's next annual return. The next annual return is the return delivered to the Registrar after the financial statements in question have been approved under section 414 of the 2006 Act. In addition, the financial statements themselves must contain a statement that the information is given only in respect of the undertakings whose results or financial position, in the opinion of the directors, principally affected the figures shown in the financial statements (including those undertakings excluded from consolidation). [CA06 Sec 410(2)]. The company and any of its officers who fail to comply with these disclosure requirements are liable to a fine.

Document quality

8.65   All documents that companies are obliged by statute to deliver to the Registrar of Companies (for instance, annual financial statements and lists of members accompanying annual returns and allotment forms) must comply with certain document quality and other requirements (see para 8.67.1). Each such document must:

- State in a prominent position the company's registered number. Companies House has requested that the company's registered number is preferably included in bold figures, in the top right hand corner of the document's front page.

- Comply with the requirements specified by the Registrar, including requirements to enable him to copy or read the document.

8.65.1   The Registrar has a duty to make it possible to inspect the information contained in documents delivered to him and for copies to be produced in legible form. As a consequence, the original documents filed must be clear to enable Companies House to scan them to produce an electronic image.

8.66   The Registrar is entitled to reject documents that cannot be reproduced electronically and to require the company to produce documents that do comply within 14 days. If a replacement complying with the relevant section is not delivered within a further 14 days, the original cannot be treated as having been delivered in time. The following briefly sets out the Registrar's requirements as to document quality:

■ Documents should be on A4 size, plain white paper with a matt finish.

■ The text should be black, clear, legible and of uniform density.

Further guidance on print requirements and acceptability of documents is available from Companies House.

8.67 Consequently, as documents should be black on white with a matt finish, glossy annual reports should not be filed at Companies House. Companies House has made it clear that glossy financial statements will be rejected. Companies House considers that a typed version or printer's proof is ideal provided it has been signed, as required, by the company's directors and auditors and, where necessary, by the company secretary.

8.67.1 The Registrar's Rules (the 'Rules') set out the requirements relating to the form, authentication and manner of delivery of documents that companies must submit to Companies House. Companies can deliver documents to the Registrar electronically, *via* a computer software system or the Companies House website, or as paper forms. For companies filing electronically *via* software, the Rules set out the electronic format they must use for each document, how they must authenticate the document to replace the signature and company name and number on paper forms, and how they must send it. For companies delivering paper documents, the Rules provide for the format of paper forms, setting out what the form must look like, how to complete them, who can sign them and where they must be sent.

Retention of accounting and other records

8.68 The Act requires that a private company should keep its accounting records for three years and a public company for six years from the date they are prepared. However, where a company is being wound up, this requirement is subject to any provision with respect to the disposal of records contained in the insolvency rules made under section 411 of the Insolvency Act 1986. [CA06 Sec 388(4)(5)].

8.69 The period for which companies should keep their business documents in general (including their accounting records) is also governed by various other statutes. These include the Limitation Act 1980, the Latent Damage Act 1986, the Taxes Management Act 1970, the Value Added Tax Act 1994 and the Money Laundering Regulations. These may affect the retention of accounting records in the following ways:

■ Limitation Act 1980 (as amended by the Latent Damage Act 1986 and the Consumer Protection Act 1987). This Act limits the time period during which an action can be brought as follows:

- An action on a simple (non-specialty) contract or in tort (other than in respect of personal injuries) — six years from the date when the cause of the action arose, generally the breach.

- An action on a contract under seal (specialty contracts) — 12 years from the date when the cause of the action arose.

- In cases of personal injury, 3 years from:

    (i)   the date the cause of action accrued; or

    (ii)   the date of knowledge (if later) of the person injured.

- In cases of negligence (excluding personal injuries), the time limit for an action for latent damage will be the later of:

    (i)   six years from the date on which the cause of action accrued; and

    (ii)   where the facts are not known at the date the cause of action accrued, three years from the earliest date on which the plaintiff, or any person in whom the cause of action was vested before him, had the knowledge required to bring an action and a right to bring such an action.

- An overriding time limit for actions for negligence (excluding personal injuries) of 15 years is imposed from the date on which there occurred any act or omission:

    (i)   which is alleged to constitute negligence;

    (ii)   to which the damage in respect of which damages are claimed is alleged to be attributable;

- A judgment debt — barred after six years.

- Interest on a judgment debt — not recoverable more than six years after the date on which it accrued due.

- Actions to recover land — 12 years from the date on which the right of action arose.

- Actions to recover trust property, 6 years from the date on which the right of action accrued, save where the claim relates to a fraudulent breach of trust or where the action is to recover trust property from the trustee. In this context, directors are treated as trustees.

- Actions for damages against manufacturers of defective products under Part I of the Consumer Protection Act 1987 — three years from the later of the date of the damage or injury or the date the plaintiff became aware of the cause of the damage or injury (subject to an overall period of ten years from the supply of the product).

- Finance Act 1998, Schedule 18, paragraphs 21, 23 and 27. For corporation tax purposes, a company must keep and preserve its records for a period of six years from the end of the period for which a tax return may be required. Records for these purposes includes records of all receipts and expenses and sales and purchases together with any supporting documents, which includes accounts, books, deeds, contracts, vouchers and receipts. If a company fails to keep and preserve its records, it is liable to a penalty of up to £3,000. HM Revenue & Customs have the power to require a company to produce documents relating to its tax liability.

- Taxes Management Act 1970. HM Revenue & Customs may generally assess within six years of the end of the chargeable period. Where there is fraudulent or negligent conduct, the limit is 20 years. The Taxes Management Act contains two further rules that may be relevant:

  - Production of accounts, books, documents and other information. HM Revenue & Customs may serve notice and require a company to deliver any documents within the company's possession (or power) that contain information relevant to any tax liability.

  - Time limit for recovery of penalties. Recovery of penalties may be commenced at any time within six years after the date on which the penalty was incurred or at any later time within three years of the amount of tax finally being determined on which the penalty is to be ascertained.

- Value Added Tax Act 1994 and VAT regulations. Those companies that are registered for VAT must keep their records and accounts and other related documents for a period of six years unless a shorter period has been agreed with HM Revenue & Customs. These documents must be open to inspection by HM Revenue & Customs at all times. There are special provisions relating to computerised records.

- SI 2003/2682, 'Income Tax (PAYE) Regulations 2003'. For PAYE purposes, employers are under a duty to keep all PAYE records that do not have to be sent to HM Revenue & Customs under the PAYE regulations for not less than three years after the end of the year to which they relate.

- SI 1999/584, 'National Minimum Wage Regulations 1999'. For National Minimum Wage purposes, employers must keep records to establish that an employee is receiving at least the National Minimum Wage. These records must be kept for a minimum period of three years from the end of the pay reference period.

- SI 2000/944, 'Education (Student Loans) (Repayment) Regulations 2000'. For Student Loan purposes, employers must keep a record of all wages sheets, deductions working sheets and other documents and records relating to the calculation and deduction of Student Loan repayments for a period of at least three years after the end of the tax year to which they relate.

- Companies within the scope of the Money Laundering Regulations are required to retain records of the identification of their customers or clients for the duration of the business relationship and for five years after the termination of the business relationship or after an occasional transaction has been completed. Specific transaction records must be retained for five years from the date the transaction was completed, or general transaction records until the business relationship ends.

8.70   Consequently, the period of time for which a company should keep its accounting records depends primarily on the type of document involved. As a general rule, most accounting records should be kept for a period of at least six years. Some types of document may need to be kept for longer. Further guidance is available in the ICAEW's Practice Assurance Standard 2: Help Sheet 20, entitled 'Document retention' (published in 2007).

8.71   To overcome the problems of storing paper accounting records, many companies have historically retained them on microfilm, although electronic storage is now more common. For VAT purposes, HM Revenue & Customs generally accepts records stored on microfilm, microfiche or electronically but the company is required to obtain specific permission prior to destroying original documents.

8.72   In Court proceedings, a Court will normally require the production of the original document. However, where the original document is not available, a court may accept other evidence of the document. A judge has power to admit copies in evidence and to specify the method of authentication. [Civil Evidence Act 1995 Sec 8]. If original company documents are to be copied in hard or electronic format, directors should ascertain that the procedures adopted not only ensure that all records are copied, but also that they are legible, stored safely and capable of being properly authenticated. If accounting records are in a non-legible form any software, etc. necessary to retrieve the information in a usable form should also be retained.

8.73   As a consequence, before a company destroys any documents that it has microfilmed or stored in digital form, it should consider very carefully whether it should retain the original document. It should remember that certain transactions (for example, a property lease) must be evidenced in writing and, therefore, it should not destroy the original document. Also, before a company destroys any accounting records, it should consult its auditors about whether the microfilmed or digitally stored records will provide them with sufficient audit evidence. The auditors will also want to satisfy themselves that the company imposes adequate controls over the microfilming, or digital recording process.

8.73.1   Most accounting records are now stored electronically, all but eliminating this problem. However, it is the company's responsibility to ensure the security of their IT systems and that adequate back-up procedures are in place to prevent records from becoming corrupted or destroyed. Further, it is the company's responsibility to ensure that accounting records are accessible when a company changes its accounting software, for example, it will need to ensure that the old software (and hardware, where necessary) is available to enable the historic records to be accessed.

Penalties

8.74   If a company:

- does not keep adequate accounting records sufficient to show and explain the company's transactions as required by section 386 of the 2006 Act; or

- does not keep its accounting records in the places specified in section 388(1) and (2) of the 2006 Act or does not keep accounts or returns as required by section 388(3) of the 2006 Act;

then, every officer in default will be guilty of an offence unless he can show that he acted honestly and that the default in question was excusable in the circumstances in which the company's business was carried on. [CA06 Secs 389(1)(2), 387]. For this purpose, officer' includes a director, manager or secretary. [CA06 Sec 1173(1)].

8.75   Similarly, where an officer fails to take all reasonable steps to ensure that the company keeps these accounting records for the period specified in section 388(4) of the 2006 Act, (that is three years for private companies and six years for public companies), or intentionally causes any default by the company in observing this obligation, he will be guilty of an offence. [CA06 Sec 389(3)(4)]. Failure to keep accounting records as required by section 386 of the 2006 Act may be attributable to negligence, incompetence or poor administration, but in some cases there may be fraudulent intent. Indeed, a number of alleged fraudsters have been convicted of not keeping proper accounting records even if the prosecution failed to convict them on fraud charges.

8.76   As mentioned in paragraph 8.25, the failure by directors to comply with their obligations to keep accounting records under section 386 of the 2006 Act is one of the matters which a Court is required to take into account when considering disqualifying a director for being unfit to be a director. In *Re Firedart Ltd; Official Receiver v Fairall* [1994] 2 BCLC 340, the company's accounting records were held to be deficient in that the cash book, sales day book, the purchase day book and sales and purchase ledgers had not been written up for a period before the winding up order was issued. In addition, there was a lack of supporting vouchers and explanations for the company's expenditure recorded in the cash book. The judge found that failure to make these relevant entries was a breach of section 221 of the 1985 Act (the equivalent to section 386 of the 2006 Act) and that failure to maintain the evidence sufficient to explain the expenditure was equally a breach of that section.

8.77   The judge also considered that: *"When directors do not maintain accounting records in accordance with the very specific requirements of section 221, they cannot know their company's financial position with accuracy. There is therefore a risk that the situation is much worse than they know and that creditors will suffer in consequence. Directors who permit this situation to arise must expect the conclusion to be drawn in an appropriate case that they are in consequence not fit to be concerned in the management of a company".*

8.78 To guard against the possibility of trading whilst insolvent, directors should ensure that not only are adequate accounting records kept, but that there are appropriate systems in place to provide the board with up-to-date information about the company's financial position on a regular basis. The absence of up-to-date information will be relevant to whether it was reasonable for directors to allow a company to continue trading at a time when it was unable to pay its debts. [*Re Grayan Building Services Ltd: Secretary of State for Trade and Industry v Gray & Anor* [1995] 3 WLR 1]. Directors may be guilty of wrongful trading if their company continues to trade when it is insolvent and may incur personal liability to compensate the company. [Insolvency Act 1986 Sec 214]. The amount which a director may be liable to contribute is likely to be calculated on the amount by which the company's assets can be seen to be depleted by the director's conduct. [*Re Produce Marketing Consortium Ltd (No. 2)* [1989] BCLC 520 at 553].

8.79 Sections 15 to 17 of the Theft Act 1968 impose penalties for obtaining property by deception and false accounting. False accounting includes dishonestly making in an account or record an entry which is misleading, false or deceptive in a material particular or omitting a material particular from such a document. Where a company has committed an offence under section 15, 16 or 17 of that Act with the consent or connivance of any director or other officer, he, as well as the company, will be criminally liable. [Theft Act 1968 Sec 18]. Also, it a criminal offence for any officer of a company to publish, with intent to deceive the company's members or creditors, any written statement or account that he knows is or may be misleading or false on a material point. [Theft Act 1968 Sec 19]. In this connection, any document has to be regarded as a whole. Moreover, even though each part of a statement is strictly true, that statement may be false if it conveys a false impression of the company's position, because material points have been omitted from it.

8.79.1 The Financial Services and Markets Act 2000 (FSMA) creates civil penalties for market abuse, which includes insider dealing as one of seven behaviours that can constitute the civil offence. As the level of evidence is lower than in criminal prosecutions. Directors of listed companies are also subject to the Code of Market Conduct issued by the FSA. Criminal offences under the Code of Market Conduct and the FSMA include making a misleading statement and engaging in a misleading course of conduct for the purpose of inducing another person to exercise or refrain from exercising rights in relation to investments. In 2005, two directors of AIT Group Plc received custodial sentences for releasing a misleading trading update statement to the market. This was the first time that the FSA had used its powers to take criminal proceedings under the FSMA.

Electronic communications with members, others and the Registrar of Companies

Introduction

8.80 The 2006 Act permits a company to take advantage of electronic communications for:

- The electronic transmission of financial statements to members and others entitled to receive them (see para 8.117.1).

- The electronic transmission of summary financial statements to members who have chosen to receive them (see para 8.171).

- The delivery of documents in electronic form to the Registrar (see para 8.82.5).

8.81 In addition, the 2006 Act deals with the use of electronic communications in connection with incorporation, sending notices of meetings (see further para 8.253) and the appointment of proxies. It provides for electronic statements to be delivered to the Registrar as an alternative to statutory declarations in specified instances. The overall effect is that the 2006 Act allows any document or information authorised or required by the Companies Acts to be sent or supplied by, or to, a company to be sent electronically.

8.82 The Institute of Chartered Secretaries and Administrators (ICSA) has produced a booklet, 'ICSA Guidance on Electronic Communications with Shareholders 2007' that provides guidance to companies in the context of the 2006 Act and the FSA rules for companies traded on a regulated market. It sets out 19 points of issues, guidance and recommended best practice. This booklet also deals with the parallel requirements on electronic communications in the UKLA's Disclosure and Transparency Rules (DTR) at DTR 6.1.7 and 6.1.8. Guidance on the interaction between the Companies Act 2006 and the DTR and the transitional provisions for companies with existing electronic communication authorities can be found in the UKLA newsletter, List! 14 (Updated – April 2007).

8.82.1 The 2006 Act also permits companies to communicate with their shareholders *via* their web site, provided that the shareholders have agreed to this method of communication. Agreement can be obtained by passing a resolution allowing the company to communicate electronically and by each member being asked to agree individually. Under the 2006 Act failure to respond to a request to communicate electronically within 28 days can be deemed to be acceptance provided this is made clear to the member in the initial request. Where a member has not agreed to communications in this way, the company may not ask the member again within a period of twelve months. A company must notify its shareholders when it publishes information on its web site, but this notification can be sent by e-mail. Any member of a company or holder of a debenture that has received a document otherwise than in hard copy is entitled to require the company to send a copy of the document in hard copy form. The company may not charge for providing documents in hard copy. [CA06 Secs 1144, 1145, 5 Sch].

8.82.1.1 The 'ICSA Guidance on Electronic Communications with Shareholders 2007' recommends that a company should, where it is aware of the failure in delivery of an electronic communication (and subsequent attempts do not remedy the situation), revert to sending a hard copy of the communication by mail to the recipient's last known postal address. This should be done within 48 hours of the original attempt. The previous version of the guidance also recommended that companies sending their financial statements and reports *via* a web site should, as a precaution, make the documents available on more than one web site through different service providers. This still seems valid advice. The FSA, as the UK Listing Authority, recommends this best practice guide to listed companies.

Meaning of electronic communication

8.82.2 'Electronic communication' is defined as a communication transmitted (whether from one person to another, from one device to another or from a person to a device or *vice versa*):

■ By means of an electronic communications network (within the meaning of the Communications Act 2003). [CA06 Sec 1259].

■ By other means but while in an electronic form.

'Electronic form' is stated in section 1168 of the 2006 Act to be documents or information sent or supplied in electronic form or electronic copy, that is those sent by 'electronic means' or by any other means while in an electronic form (for example, sending an electronic copy (CD) by post). Documents or information sent in electronic form must enable the recipient to read or see them with the naked eye and retain a copy (and ability only to retain a copy in electronic form, such as sending a text message, is sufficient).

A document is sent or supplied by 'electronic means' if it is sent initially and received at its destination by means of electronic equipment for the processing (which expression includes digital compression) or storage of data, and entirely transmitted, conveyed and received by wire, by radio, by optical means or by other electromagnetic means. [CA06 sec 1168].

The glossary to the UKLA's DTR defines 'electronic means' similarly as any means of electronic equipment for the processing (including digital compression), storage and transmission of data, employing wires, radio, optical technology, or any other electromagnetic means.

8.82.3 'Communication' includes a communication comprising sounds or images or both and a communication effecting a payment.

8.82.4 The definitions thus include information provided by the following means:

■ Fax.

■ CD-ROM.

■ E-mail.

■ Text message

■ On a web site.

Delivery of documents generally to the Registrar of Companies using electronic communications

8.82.5   Section 1068(5) of the 2006 Act provides that the Registrar of Companies must secure that electronic communications may be used for the delivery of documents covered by the EU 1st Company Law Directive (68/151/EEC) to the Registrar of Companies. The Registrar of Companies retains the right to reject documents that do not comply with the statutory requirements.

8.82.6   Companies House has established an electronic filing service that enables the electronic submission of statutory documents by e-mail using specialist software. These documents must comply with the structure approved by the Registrar for electronic submission, as documented in the 'Electronic filing technical interface specification' (copies of which are available from Companies House on request).

8.83   All documents received *via* the Electronic Filing Service must be authenticated by (or on behalf of) the company with the company authentication code notified to the company by Companies House by post to the company's registered office. It is also possible to incorporate a company electronically.

Accounting reference periods

Accounting reference date

8.84   The accounting reference date of a company is the last day of the month in which the anniversary of incorporation falls. [CA06 Sec 391(4)]. Its first and subsequent accounting reference periods will, therefore, end on that date, but this date can still be altered in the way permitted by the 2006 Act, which is described from paragraph 8.92.

Financial year

8.85   The directors of a company must prepare financial statements for each financial year of their company. [CA06 Sec 394]. A company's first financial year begins on the date of incorporation (see para 8.88 below) and ends either with:

- the last day of the first accounting reference period; or
- another date determined by the directors that is not more than seven days before or after the end of that period.

[CA06 Sec 390(2)].

8.86   Subsequent financial years begin with the day immediately following the end of the company's previous financial year and end either with:

- the last day of its next accounting reference period; or

- a date determined by the directors not more than seven days before or after the end of that period.

[CA06 Sec 390(3)].

8.86.1   This permits a company to end its financial year on the same day in the week rather than on the same date, if it wishes to. As a result, although a company's accounting reference period cannot exceed a period of 18 months, a financial year (and consequently the financial statements) may cover a slightly longer period. [CA06 Sec 392(5)].

8.87   A parent company's directors should ensure that, except where they consider there are good reasons for it, the financial year of any subsidiary undertakings coincides with the parent company's financial year.[CA06 Sec 390(5)]. The financial year of an undertaking that is not a company formed and registered under the Act refers to any period in respect of which a profit and loss account is required to be drawn up either by its constitution or by the law under which it is established. [CA06 Sec 390(4)].

First and subsequent accounting reference periods

8.88   A company's first accounting reference period starts on the date of incorporation and ends on the accounting reference date (which is determined as set out in para 8.84). This period must not be less than six months (but see para 8.98) and must not exceed 18 months. [CA06 Sec 391(5)].

8.89   Subsequent accounting reference periods will be for successive periods of 12 months. They will start immediately after the end of the previous accounting reference period and will end with its accounting reference date. [CA06 Sec 391(6)]. However, a company may alter its accounting reference date and shorten or lengthen its accounting reference period if it satisfies certain conditions (see para 8.94 below).

8.90   If a company's financial statements are not made up to its accounting reference date, or a date which is not more than seven days before or after this date, they will be rejected by the Registrar of Companies. The period for laying and delivering the financial statements to the Registrar is calculated by reference to the end of the relevant accounting reference period. [CA06 Sec 442]. The date a company chooses for its accounting reference date in the first year after incorporation can alter the accounting requirements considerably. The following three examples illustrate this:

Example 1

Company A is incorporated on 1 April 20X2 and the company *did not* inform the Registrar of Companies of a change in accounting reference date. The company's accounting reference period, therefore, starts on the date of incorporation (that is, 1 April 20X2), and ends 13 months later on 30 April 20X3. [CA06 Sec 391(4)].

Example 2

Company B is incorporated on 1 April 20X2 and the company *did* notify the Registrar of Companies in accordance with section 392 of the 2006 Act of a change in its accounting reference date to 31 December, stating that the accounting reference period is to be shortened. Its first accounting reference period starts on the date of incorporation (that is, 1 April 20X2), and it ends nine months later on 31 December 20X2. It cannot extend the period so that it ends on 31 December 20X3 as this would mean a first accounting reference period of more than 18 months. The next accounting reference period is for 12 months, and it ends on 31 December 20X3. [CA06 Sec 391(5)(6)].

Example 3

Company C is incorporated on 1 April 20X2 and the company *did* notify the Registrar of Companies in accordance with section 392 of the 2006 Act of a change in its accounting reference date to 31 August, stating that the accounting reference period is to be extended. The company's first accounting reference period, therefore, starts on the date of incorporation (that is, 1 April 20X2), and ends 17 months later on 31 August 20X3. If the notice under section 392 of the 2006 Act had stated that the period was to be shortened, it would have ended on 31 August 20X2 (see further para 8.98).

[The next paragraph is 8.92].

Change of accounting reference date by a listed company

8.92   In addition to complying with the requirements of the Companies Act, a company listed in the Official List of the FSA that changes its accounting reference date must notify a Regulated Information Service as soon as possible of any change in its accounting reference date and the new date. [LR 9.6.20R]. If the effect of the change is to extend the accounting reference period to more than 14 months, the company must prepare and publish a second interim or half yearly report. [LR 9.6.21R]. This report must cover either the period up to the old accounting reference date or the period up to a date not more than six months prior to the new accounting reference date. [LR9.6.22G]. The contents of half-yearly or interim reports are dealt with in chapter 31 of the Manual of Accounting – IFRS for the UK.

Change of accounting reference date by an AIM or PLUS-quoted company

8.93   The AIM rules require an AIM company that changes its accounting reference date to notify a Regulatory Information Service without delay. [AIMR 17]. The company is then required to contact AIM to discuss the revised reporting table.

8.93.1   The PLUS-markets rules require a PLUS-quoted company to announce, as soon as possible, any decision to change its accounting reference date. [PLUS-markets rule 49].

Current and previous periods

8.94   A company may give notice to the Registrar that it wishes to alter its accounting reference date in relation to the company's current and subsequent accounting reference periods or its previous accounting reference period and subsequent periods. 'Previous accounting reference period' means the period immediately preceding its current accounting reference period. [CA06 Sec 392(1)]. The period may be shortened or extended, but while it can be shortened any number of times without restriction it cannot be extended more than once in five years unless one of the following applies:

■   The company is a subsidiary or parent of another EEA undertaking and the new accounting reference date coincides with that of the other undertaking or, where that undertaking is not a company, with the last day of its financial year.

■   An administration order is in force under Part II of the Insolvency Act 1986.

■   The Secretary of State directs that a company can extend its accounting reference period more often. He can do this in respect of a notice which has been given or which may be given.

[CA06 Sec 392(3)].

8.94.1   An 'EEA undertaking' means an undertaking established under the law of any part of the UK or the law of another EEA state. [CA06 Sec 392(6)]. An EEA state includes all Member States of the EU and Norway, Iceland and Liechtenstein.

8.95   The company must state on the notice given to the Registrar to alter the current or previous accounting reference date whether the accounting reference period is to be treated as shortened or extended. However, a company cannot extend an accounting reference period to make it exceed 18 months, unless the company is subject to an administration order under Part II of the Insolvency Act 1986. [CA06 Sec 392(5)].

Previous periods

8.96   A notice may not be given to change the accounting reference date in relation to a previous accounting reference period if the period allowed by section 442 of the 2006 Act for laying and delivering financial statements in relation to that period has already expired. [CA06 Sec 392(4)]. The usual period within which a company must deliver is nine months for a private company and six months for a public company, calculated from the end of the accounting reference period.

8.97   The timing of the notice a company gives to the Registrar of a change in its accounting reference date is crucial to the acceptance of that new date, as the notice must reach the Registrar within the period allowed. Consider the following example, which is based on the filing date requirements of the 2006 Act:

Example

A private company's accounting reference date is 31 December. The company last completed and filed its financial statements for the 12 month period ended 31 December 20X1. On 27 September 20X3, the company gives notice to the Registrar that it wishes to change its accounting reference date to 30 June in relation to its previous accounting period ended 31 December 20X2.

The company would then appear to have two choices: it may give notice either to lengthen its accounting reference period and prepare financial statements for the 18 month period to 30 June 20X3 provided the notice is not ineffective under section 392(3) of the 2006 Act (see para 8.94). Alternatively, it may seek to shorten its accounting reference period and prepare financial statements for the six month period to 30 June 20X2. However, if it does the latter, the company will have only three months from the date that the statutory form AA01 is filed with the Registrar to lay the financial statements before the members in general meeting and file them with the Registrar (see para 8.144). [CA06 Sec 442(4)].

If the facts in the example given above remained the same, except that the company gave notice of the change of accounting reference date to the Registrar on 1 October 20X3, then this notice would not take effect. The reason for this is that the period for filing is on the basis of the existing accounting reference date in relation to the previous accounting reference period (that is, 31 December 20X2), would have already expired on 30 September 20X3 (being nine months from the accounting reference date) (see para 8.96 above).

8.98   A company's first accounting reference period cannot be less than six months. [CA06 Sec 391(5)]. However, the company's accounting reference date set at incorporation is one year (see para 8.84.1) and the Act does permit the company to reduce it by giving notice to the Registrar under section 392(1) of the 2006 Act. The procedure is illustrated in the following example, which is based on the filing date requirements under the 2006 Act:

Example

Company D, a private company, is incorporated on 1 April 20X2, and its first accounting period will end on the last calendar day of the month in which the first anniversary of its incorporation falls, that is 30 April 20X3, 13 months later. It then decides that seasonal factors require an accounting reference date of 30 June. The company may, at any time within the period to 1 January 20X4 (that is, the earlier of 21 months from the date of incorporation (see para 8.142) and nine months from the default accounting reference date), give notice to the Registrar that it wishes to alter its current accounting reference date to end on 30 June 20X2, which gives a reference period of three months. The financial statements for 30 June 20X2 would then fall due for filing on either 30 March 20X3 (that is, nine months from the period end) or three months after the filing of statutory form AA01, whichever is the later (see para 8.144).

Preparing and approving financial statements

8.98.1   The directors have a duty to prepare their company's individual financial statements each financial year in accordance with the general requirements of the Companies Act and either in accordance with International Accounting Standards as adopted by the EU (IAS individual accounts) or section 396 of the 2006 Act (Companies Act individual accounts).

8.98.2   The formats and contents for Companies Act individual financial statements are set out in Schedule 1 to SI 2008/409, 'The Small Companies and Groups (Accounts and Reports) Regulations 2008'. Similarly, the format and contents for other companies, banks and insurers are set out in Schedules 1, 2 and 3 respectively to SI 2008/410, 'The Large and Medium-sized Companies and Groups (Accounts and Reports) Regulations 2008'.

8.98.3   'Companies Act individual accounts' (financial statements) must comply with UK accounting standards issued by the ASB. Companies subject to the small companies regime may use instead the Financial Reporting Standard for Smaller Entities (FRSSE) issued by the ASB.

8.99   The form and content of 'IAS individual accounts' (financial statements) must be consistent with IAS 1 as adopted by the EU and comply with the requirements of IFRSs and IASs adopted by that body (see further chapter 2 of the Manual of Accounting – IFRS for the UK).

Company individual financial statements

8.100   In preparing 'IAS individual accounts' (financial statements), the directors must ensure that:

- They comply with the general requirements of the Act, including the requirement that they give a true and fair view of the assets, liabilities, financial position and profit or loss. [CA06 Sec 393]. The general requirements of the Act that continue to apply to companies preparing IAS accounts are set out in 'Guidance for UK companies on accounting and reporting: requirements under the Companies Act 2006 and the application of the IAS Regulation', published by BERR in June 2008. (See further the Manual of Accounting – IFRS for the UK).

- They comply with IFRS and IASs as adopted by the EU.

- The information concerning related undertakings (CA06 section 409), details of off-balance sheet arrangements (CA06 section 410A), particulars of staff (CA06 section 411) and emoluments and other benefits of directors (CA06 section 412) is given in the notes to the financial statements.

8.100.1 In preparing 'Companies Act individual accounts' (financial statements), the directors must also ensure that:

- They comply with the general requirements of the Act, including the requirement that they give a true and fair view of the assets, liabilities, financial position and profit or loss. [CA06 Sec 393]. (See further the Manual of Accounting – UK GAAP).

- The company's individual financial statements comply with Schedules 1, 2 or 3 to SI 2008/410 (as appropriate for companies, banks or insurers respectively) or, for companies in the small companies regime, with Schedule 1 to SI 2008/409 as to the form and content of the balance sheet and profit and loss account and the additional information to be provided by way of notes.

- The information concerning related undertakings (CA06 section 409), details of off-balance sheet arrangements (CA06 section 410A), particulars of staff (CA06 section 411) and emoluments and other benefits of directors (CA06 section 412) is given in the notes to the financial statements. Companies subject to the small companies regime or that qualify as medium-sized company have full or partial exemptions from these disclosures.

- If compliance with the provisions of that Schedule and the other provisions of the Act would not be sufficient to give a true and fair view, the necessary additional information is included in the financial statements or in a note to them. [CA06 Sec 396(4)].

- If, in special circumstances, compliance with any of those provisions is inconsistent with the requirement to give a true and fair view, they must depart from that provision to the extent necessary to give a true and fair view. However, if they do so, the particulars of the departure, the reasons for it and its effect must be given in a note to the financial statements (see further the Manual of Accounting – UK GAAP). [CA06 Sec 396(5)].

[CA06 Sec 396].

The form and content of financial statements are discussed in more detail in chapter 4 of the Manual of Accounting – IFRS for the UK and the Manual of Accounting – UK GAAP.

Company consolidated financial statements

8.101 Where at the end of a financial year a company is a parent company, its directors must prepare consolidated financial statements for the company and its group. Like individual financial statements, these must be prepared in accordance with the general requirements of the Act and either in accordance with International Accounting Standards as adopted by the EU (IAS group accounts) or section 404 of the 2006 Act (Companies Act group accounts). In the latter case, this means complying with the form and content of Schedule 1 and

Part 1 of Schedule 6, or Schedule 2 and Part 2 of Schedule 6, or Schedule 3 and Part 3 of Schedule 6 to SI 2008/410 for companies, banks or insurers. [CA06 Secs 399, 404].

8.101.1   In preparing consolidated financial statements, directors must ensure that they comply, as appropriate, with the matters outlined in paragraphs 8.100 (for IAS group accounts) and 8.100.1 (for Companies Act group accounts).

8.101.2   Directors of companies in the small companies regime have the option to prepare group accounts. [CA06 Sec 398]. Companies Act group accounts must follow the form and content prescribed in Schedule 6 to SI 2008/409. IAS group accounts must be consistent with the requirements of EU-adopted IAS 1.

8.101.3   Directors of medium-sized companies that are parent companies at the end of a financial year must prepare consolidated financial statements for the company and its group. The financial statements must include comparative numbers for the group for the previous financial year, even though consolidated financial statements were not required for that year. For example, the consolidated financial statements for the year ending 31 December 2009 must include comparative consolidated numbers for the year ended 31 December 2008. Companies Act group accounts must follow the form and content prescribed by Schedule 6 to SI 2008/410 as modified by Regulation 4(2) of that SI. [SI 2008/410 6 Sch para 1(1)]. IAS consolidated financial statements must be consistent with the requirements of EU-adopted IAS 1.

8.101.4   The form and content of consolidated financial statements is considered further in chapter 4 of the Manual of Accounting – IFRS for the UK or the Manual of Accounting – UK GAAP. A parent company's individual profit and loss account may be omitted from its published consolidated financial statements in certain situations (see para 8.106 below).

Approval, signing, publishing and filing

8.102   The board of directors must approve the company's financial statements and they must be signed on the board's behalf by a company director signing the company's balance sheet. [CA06 Sec 414(2)]. There is no legal requirement for the consolidated balance sheet to be signed in the same way, but this procedure is regarded as good practice. Every copy of the balance sheet laid before a company in general meeting, or otherwise circulated, published or issued, must state the name of the person who signed the balance sheet on behalf of the board. [CA06 Sec 433(1)].

8.102.1   The copy of the company's balance sheet that is delivered to the Registrar of Companies must state the name of the person who signed it on behalf of the board and must be signed on behalf of the board by a director of the company. [CA06 Secs 444(6), 445(5), 446(3), 447(3)]. These provisions apply irrespective of whether the company is a small company filing abbreviated or shorter-form financial statements. Companies House has stated that a photocopy or faxed signature is not acceptable in any circumstances.

8.102.2   For companies entitled to the small companies exemption in relation to the directors' report, section 444A (inserted by Regulation 6 of SI 2008/393 'The Companies Act 2006 (Amendment)(Accounts and Reports) Regulations 2008') has no requirement for a physical signature on the balance sheet in the copy of the company's annual accounts filed with the Registrar. The copy of the balance sheet must state the name of the person who signed it on behalf of the board. [CA06 Sec 444A(3)].

8.103   In addition to the legal requirements in section 414 of the 2006 Act mentioned above, IAS 10, 'Events after the balance sheet date', and FRS 21, 'Events after the balance sheet date', both require that the financial statements should disclose the date on which the financial statements were authorised for issue and who gave this authorisation. [IAS 10 para 17, FRS 21 para 17]. The date of authorisation will normally be the date on which the board of directors formally approves a set of documents as the financial statements. The date of approval for consolidated financial statements is the date on which the board of directors of the parent company formally approve them.

8.104   The requirements of both the Act and IAS 10 or FRS 21 will be satisfied if the minutes of the board meeting at which the financial statements are considered record the directors' approval of the financial statements. The financial statements would then include, at the foot of the balance sheet, a note along the following lines:

Example

The financial statements on pages X to Y were approved by the board of directors on (date) and are signed on its behalf by:

(Name)

Director

8.105   The pages of the financial statements that are approved would normally include, where applicable, any supplementary accounts or other financial statements (such as a value added statement or current cost information). The reason for this is that the directors should acknowledge their responsibility for all of the financial information that is presented at the meeting.

8.106   Where a parent company prepares consolidated financial statements in accordance with the Act (whether they are 'IAS group accounts' or 'Companies Act group accounts'), it is not required to include its own profit and loss account in the group's published consolidated financial statements. Although not published, the company's individual profit and loss account must be prepared and then approved by the board of directors and signed on behalf of the board by a director of the company in accordance with section 414(1) of the 2006 Act. This should occur at the same time as the rest of the financial statements are approved. Also the financial statements must disclose that the exemption applies. [CA06 Sec 408(4)]. The notes to these financial statements need not contain the information on the parent company's employee numbers and costs. [CA06 Sec 408(2)]. In addition, for Companies Act group accounts, the notes to the consolidated financial statements need not contain the information specified by paragraphs 65 to 69 of Schedule 1 to SI 2008/410 (information supplementing the company's individual profit and loss account). [SI 2008/410 Reg 3(2)].

8.106.1   Omission of the company's individual profit and loss account from a set of published IAS financial statements through use of the publication exemption seemingly causes a tension with the requirements of IAS 1 and the compliance statement required by that standard and also section 406 of the 2006 Act. The EC and BERR have stated that the omission as provided for by European Company Law Directives and UK domestic company law does not breach IAS 1 or the company law requirement. BERR says that the accounting framework that has been used is IAS as adopted by the EU as applied in accordance with the provisions of the 2006 Act.

Liability for approving defective financial statements

8.107   All financial statements (including consolidated financial statements) that are approved by the board must comply with the requirements of the Act and, where applicable, Article 4 of the IAS Regulation (see para 8.98.1 onwards). If the financial statements do not comply with the Act, every director of the company who is party to their approval and who knows that they do not comply, or is reckless as to whether they comply, is guilty of an offence. For this purpose, every director of the company at the time the financial statements are approved is taken to be a party to their approval unless the director shows that he took all reasonable steps to prevent their approval. [CA06 Sec 414(4)(5)].

8.108   There is, however, a statutory procedure (discussed in para 8.214) under which the directors can voluntarily revise any financial statements that they subsequently discover do not comply with the Act. [CA06 Sec 454]. This procedure also applies to a defective directors' report and to a defective directors' remuneration report.

Liability if balance sheet is unsigned

8.109   The company and each of its officers that are in default will be guilty of an offence if either of the following applies:

- A copy of the balance sheet delivered to the Registrar has not been signed by a director as required by section 414 of the 2006 Act (see para 8.102).

- A copy of the balance sheet has been laid before the company in general meeting or is otherwise circulated, published or issued:

- without the balance sheet being signed as required by section 414 of the 2006 Act (see para 8.102); or

- without the required statement of the signatory's name being included (see para 8.102).

[CA06 Sec 433(4)(5)].

8.110   In addition to the liabilities described in the paragraph above, delivering the financial statements to the Registrar of Companies without a signature on the balance sheet is likely to trigger a late filing penalty if the directors cannot rectify the omission before the filing deadline. This is a change to the procedure under the Companies Act 1985 where a 14 day grace period was awarded to rectify such errors.

8.111   The inclusion of a directors' responsibility statement in a company's financial statement was first recommended by the Cadbury Report in 1993 and subsequently included in the Combined Code for listed companies. The Cadbury recommendation to include a directors' responsibility statement has been effectively extended to unlisted companies by ISA (UK & Ireland) 700, 'The auditor's report on financial statements'. This requires the auditors' report to distinguish between the auditors' responsibilities and those of the directors. Where a company's financial statements or directors' report do not include an adequate description of directors' relevant responsibilities, the auditors' report should include a description of those responsibilities. Directors' responsibility statements are dealt with further in chapter 4 of this Manual.

Directors' duties regarding their directors' report

Preparation

8.112   The directors must prepare a directors' report for each financial year. The content of the directors' report is dealt with in chapter 3.

8.113   It is an offence for the directors' report not to comply with the Act's provisions regarding its preparation and content. In this respect, each person who was a director immediately before the end of the period for laying and delivering the financial statements is guilty of an offence, unless he can show that he took all reasonable steps in trying to secure compliance with the Act's provisions. [CA06 Sec 415(4)].

8.113.1   It is also an offence to make a false statement about disclosure to the auditors and every director is liable who knew it was false, or was reckless as to whether it was false and failed to take reasonable steps to prevent the report from being approved. [CA06 Sec 418(5)].

Approval and signing

8.114   The directors' report must be approved by the board of directors and be signed on the board's behalf by a director or by the company secretary (where one is appointed). [CA06 Sec 419]. The approval and signing of directors' reports are considered further in chapter 3.

[The next paragraph is 8.116].

8.116   If the directors' report is either laid before the company (or otherwise circulated, published or issued) without having been signed or without the signatory's name being stated, or delivered to the Registrar without having been signed, the company and every officer who is responsible is guilty of an offence. [CA06 Sec 433(4)]. However, the directors may revise any report they discover to be defective under the procedure for the revision of defective financial statements (see para 8.214).

Directors' duties regarding directors' remuneration report

Preparation

8.116.1   The directors of a quoted company (as defined in section 385 of the 2006 Act) must, for each financial year, prepare a directors' remuneration report. A quoted company does not include companies admitted to trading on the LSE's AIM or Plus Market's PLUS-quoted market. The scope and content of the remuneration report is dealt with in chapter 5.

8.116.5   It is an offence for the directors' remuneration report not to comply with the Act's provisions regarding its preparation and content. In this respect, each person who was a director of the quoted company immediately before the end of the period for laying and delivering the financial statements and reports is guilty of an offence, unless he can show that he took all reasonable steps for securing compliance with the requirements in question. [CA06 Sec 420(2)].

8.116.6   It is the duty of any director of a company, and any person who has at any time in the preceding five years been a director of the company, to give notice to the company of such matters relating to himself as may be necessary for the purposes of Parts 2 and 3 of Schedule 8 to SI 2008/410. A person who does not comply with this requirement, commits an offence and is liable to a fine. [CA06 Sec 421].

Approval and signing

8.116.7   The directors' remuneration report must be approved by the board of directors and be signed on its behalf by a director or by the company secretary. [CA06 Sec 422(1)].

8.116.8   In addition, every copy of the directors' remuneration report that is laid before the company in general meeting, or that is otherwise circulated, published or issued, must state the name of the person who signed it on the board's behalf. The copy of the directors' remuneration report that is delivered to the Registrar must be signed on the board's behalf by a director or the company secretary. [CA06 Secs 433(1)(3), 447(3)].

8.116.9   If the directors' remuneration report is either laid before the company (or otherwise circulated, published or issued) without having been signed or without the signatory's name being stated, or delivered to the Registrar without having been signed, the company and every officer who is responsible is guilty of an offence. [CA06 Sec 433(4)(5)].

Directors' 'safe harbour' provision for directors' reports and remuneration reports

8.116.10   The 2006 Act contains a statutory liability regime for directors in respect of narrative reporting. [CA06 Sec 463]. This effectively incorporates a 'safe harbour' for information in the directors' reports (including the business review) under section 417 of the 2006 Act, the directors' remuneration reports under section 420 of the 2006 Act and any summary financial statement, so far as it is derived from either of these reports. A director is not subject to any liability to a *person other than the company* resulting from reliance, by that person or another, on information in such a report. A director is liable to compensate the company for any loss suffered by it as a result of any untrue or misleading statement in such a report, or the omission from such a report of anything required to be included in it. However, the director is liable only if he knew the statement to be untrue or misleading, or was reckless as to whether it was untrue or misleading, or he knew the omission to be dishonest concealment of a material fact. An explicit statement is not required in the annual report for the 'safe harbour' protection to be invoked.

[The next paragraph is 8.116.12.]

Persons entitled to receive financial statements

8.116.12   Every member of the company, every debenture holder of the company and every person who is entitled to receive notice of general meetings including:

■   any person nominated by a member under a power in its articles of association. [CA06 Sec 145]; or

■   for public companies whose shares are admitted to trading on at least one regulated market, those persons that have been nominated by registered shareholders to enjoy information rights, such as indirect investors whose investments are held through intermediaries. [CA06 Sec 146],

is entitled to receive a copy of each of the following documents for the financial year:

- The company's annual financial statements (which in accordance with section 471 of the 2006 Act comprise the individual financial statements (see para 8.98.1) and, if applicable, consolidated financial statements (see para 8.101)).

- The directors' report.

- In the case of a quoted company, the directors' remuneration report.

- The auditors' report on those financial statements and the directors report and, in the case of a quoted company, on the auditable part of the directors' remuneration report.

[CA06 Sec 423(1)].

8.116.13   For a public company, a copy must be sent to them not less than 21 days before the date of the general meeting at which the financial statements and reports are to be laid. [CA06 Sec 424(3)].

8.116.14   Under the 2006 Act, private companies have no statutory requirement to hold an AGM and lay financial statements before a general meeting. They are required to send out their financial statements and reports to every member, debenture holder and other entitled persons no later than the earlier of the actual date of delivery to the Registrar and the filing deadline. [CA06 Secs 423(1), 424(2)].

8.117   In the case of both public and private companies, copies need not be sent to any person for whom the Company does not have a current address. [CA06 Sec 423(2)].

Financial statements transmitted electronically

8.117.1   Companies are permitted to send copies of the documents listed in paragraph 8.116.12 (referred to as 'financial statements and reports') electronically (instead of sending paper copies) to members, debenture holders and others entitled to receive them (referred to collectively as 'members'). [CA06 Sec 1144(2), 5 Sch 5 Part 3]. Thus a company may either:

- use electronic communications to send a copy of the full financial statements and reports to the address notified to the company by a member for that purpose; or

- make a copy of the full financial statements and reports available to a member on a web site provided:

    - the company and the member have agreed to his having access to the financial statements and reports in question *via* a web site (instead of being sent in paper form); and

    - that member is notified, in the manner agreed with the company of:

- the publication of the financial statements and reports on the web site;

- the address of that web site; and

- where and how on the agreed web site they may be accessed (for example, the format of the documents and the software required to read them).

8.117.1.1 The 2006 Act introduces a new provision to require quoted companies to publish their financial statements on a web site. [CA06 Sec 430]. The financial statements and reports must be made available until the financial statements and reports for the company's next financial year are made available in accordance with this section.

8.117.2 'Address' means any number or address used for the purposes of electronic communications. Electronic communication will include information provided by fax, CD-ROM, e-mail, text message or from a web site (see para 8.82.4 for the definition).

8.117.3 Where a company's financial statements and reports are accessed from a web site, they will only be treated as 'sent' (as required by section 423 of the 2006 Act) if they are published on the web site throughout the period beginning at least 28 days following the notification to members of their availability (see para 8.117.1). However, the proceedings of the meeting will not be invalidated if the financial statements and reports were published in this way for part of the required period and the failure to publish for the remainder of the period is wholly attributable to circumstances that it would not be reasonable to have expected the company to prevent or avoid. [CA06 5 Sch 14].

8.117.3.1 In addition to the right that a member has to be sent a copy of the annual financial statements and reports (as mentioned in para 8.117.1 above), every member and debenture holder of the company is entitled (on demand and without charge) to be given or sent by electronic communication, within seven days, a further copy of the company's last financial statements and reports. [CA06 Secs 431(1)(2), 432(1)(2)]. The electronic communication must be sent to the address the member or debenture holder has notified to the company for that purpose. [CA06 Sec 1144(2), 5 Sch Part 3].

8.117.3.2 Failure to comply with the provisions of sections 423 and 424 of the 2006 Act to send a copy of the financial statements and reports to members will render the company and every officer who is in default guilty of an offence. [CA06 Sec 425]. Failure to supply a member on request with an additional copy of the financial statements and reports within the seven days, will render the company and every officer who is in default guilty of an offence. [CA06 Secs 431(4), 432(4)].

8.117.3.3 Sections 423 and 424 state that a company's financial statements and reports must be published on a web site throughout the period beginning at least 21 days before the company's general meeting and ending with the conclusion of that meeting and members must be notified that they are available on the web site not less than 21 days before the meeting. These sections need to be read in conjunction with the new company communications provisions in sections 1143 to 1148 of, and Schedules 4 and 5 to, the 2006 Act. These sections and schedules make new general provision about communications, including electronic and web site communications for the Companies Acts as a whole, primarily for communications with or from companies, typically with their members but also with debenture holders and others.

8.117.4   A company's ability to use electronic communications to send its financial statements and reports or its summary financial statements is not restricted by a contrary provision in its articles. Electronic communications are discussed further from paragraph 8.80.

Listing, Disclosure and Transparency Rules and electronic communications

8.117.6   The UKLA Listing Rules and Disclosure and Transparency Rules (LR and DTR) also permit issuers to send, circulate or otherwise despatch certain documents to holders of its listed securities electronically. LR 1.4.9 and DTR 6.1.7 and 6.1.8 impose requirements that are similar to the statutory requirements mentioned from paragraph 8.117.1 onwards for sending copies of financial statements and reports to shareholders.

8.117.7   Where an issuer uses electronic communications to communicate with its shareholders, it must also have available for holders of its listed securities a sufficient number of the documents in printed form and free of charge. These must be available during normal business hours at the places mentioned below for a period of not less than 21 days from the date of communication or notification or, if later, the conclusion of any general meeting to which the documents relate. These places are:

- The issuer's registered office in the UK.

- The offices of any UK paying agent that the issuer has.

8.117.8   The FSA has indicated that issuers also have to comply with existing requirements for copies of documents to be submitted to the UK Listing Authority – to be made available at the document viewing facility.

8.118   A copy of all such notices and other communications relating to general meetings must be given to the company's auditors. [CA06 Sec 502]. In addition, the company's bankers may require that they should receive copies of the company's annual financial statements, and, although non-statutory, this requirement could be an enforceable term of either a loan or facility agreement. If all of the members who are entitled to vote at the general meeting are in agreement, the annual financial statements and reports may be sent to members and others less than 21 days before the general meeting. This applies only to public companies under the 2006 Act. [CA06 Sec 424]. If the company is listed on the Main Market of the LSE or Plus Market's PLUS-listed market, the annual financial statements and reports must be sent to the members within four months of the end of the financial period to which they relate. Companies traded on AIM and the PLUS-quoted marked are required to send their annual reports to members within six and five months respectively from the end of the financial period to which they relate. [DTR 4.1.3; AIMR 19; PLUS Rules for issuers 35].

Public companies — presentation of financial statements at general meetings

8.121 The directors of a public company have a duty to present the annual financial statements and reports of the company before the shareholders each year at a general meeting of the company. [CA06 Sec 437]. These financial statements and reports must be laid before the company and filed with the Registrar of Companies before the end of the period allowed for doing so. This period is described in paragraph 8.140.

8.122 The annual financial statements and reports of a public company do not necessarily have to be laid before the shareholders at the AGM; another general meeting will suffice. This is acknowledged in section 437(1) of the 2006 Act and such a meeting is referred to as an 'accounts meeting'. [CA06 Sec 437(3)]. In practice, however, most public companies do lay their annual financial statements and reports before the shareholders at their AGM. The financial statements presented at that meeting should include the directors' report, the auditors' report on the financial statements and, for quoted companies, the directors' remuneration report and the auditors' report on the auditable part of the directors' remuneration report.

Private companies — dispensation from AGMs and laying financial statements

8.123 Under the 2006 Act private companies are no longer required to hold an AGM or lay financial statements before a general meeting. This will have effect unless a company's articles of association specifically require an AGM to be held. This does not remove the requirement to send the financial statements to members under section 423 of the 2006 Act.

8.124 If a company's articles of association require an AGM to be held, but elective resolutions were passed under the 1985 Act, the company need not lay financial statements before a general meeting.

[The next paragraph is 8.132.]

Liability for public companies for not laying financial statements

8.132 The directors of public companies must ensure that they lay copies of the annual financial statements and reports (see para 8.116.13) for each financial year at a general meeting of the company (an accounts meeting) within the period allowed for delivering financial statements to the Registrar of Companies (see section 442 of the 2006 Act and para 8.140 below). If they do not, every person who was a director of the company immediately before the end of that period may be guilty of an offence. [CA06 sec 438]. The penalty applies to those persons who had been directors of the public company immediately before the end of the six month filing period. [CA06 Secs 437, 438].

8.133 It is a defence for a director in this situation to prove that he took all reasonable steps to ensure that the requirements would be complied with before the end of the period allowed. [CA06 Sec 438(2)]. However, it is not a defence that the financial statements and reports had not been prepared. [CA06 Sec 438(3)].

Quoted companies — members' approval of directors' remuneration report

8.133.1 Where a company is a quoted company as defined in section 385 of the 2006 Act immediately before the end of a financial year, it must give notice to members, prior to the general meeting at which financial statements and reports are laid, of an ordinary resolution to approve the directors' remuneration report for the year. [CA06 Sec 439].

8.133.2 No entitlement of a person to remuneration is made conditional on the resolution being passed by reason only of the requirements in section 439 of the 2006 Act. [CA06 Sec 439(5)]. In other words, the success or failure of the resolution to approve the directors' remuneration report does not affect the entitlement of the directors to the remuneration disclosed in the report. This is because remuneration will already be the subject of contracts that cannot be overturned. However, any 'no vote' or significant opposition is likely to indicate that the company has difficulties with its investor relations.

8.133.3 In the event of default in complying with the requirement to give notice of the ordinary resolution to approve the directors' remuneration report, every officer of the company who is in default is liable to a fine. [CA06 Sec 440].

8.133.4 The existing directors must ensure that the resolution is put to the vote at the meeting. 'Existing director' means a person, who immediately before the meeting, is a director of the company. If the resolution is not put to the vote of the meeting, each existing director is guilty of an offence and liable to a fine, although it is a defence for the director to prove he took all reasonable steps for securing that the resolution was put to the vote of the meeting. [CA06 Sec 440(3)].

Delivery to the Registrar of Companies

Filing obligations for quoted and unquoted companies

8.134 In addition to sending out to members and/or laying the annual financial statements and reports before the company in a general meeting, the company's directors also have a duty for each financial year to file a copy of the company's annual financial statements and reports with the Registrar of Companies. [CA06 Sec 441]. Companies that qualify as small (see paras 8.134.2 to 5) or medium-sized (see paras 8.134.6 to 9) may file less than a complete copy of the annual financial statements and reports sent to their members.

The annual financial statements and reports for filing must comprise the following:

- A copy of the company's individual financial statements required by section 395 of the 2006 Act and any consolidated financial statements required by section 399 of the 2006 Act. Where the company's consolidated financial statements are included, the company's individual profit and loss account may be omitted and the notes need not include information on the company's employee numbers and costs provided that the annual financial statements disclose that advantage has been taken of the exemption. [CA06 Sec 408]. This applies irrespective of whether the consolidated financial statements are Companies Act financial statements or IAS financial statements. The balance sheet must state the name of the person who signed it on behalf of the board under section 414 of the 2006 Act and must be signed by a director on behalf of the board. [CA06 Secs 446, 447].

- A copy of the directors' report. It must state the name of the person who signed it on behalf of the board under section 419 of the 2006 Act and must be signed by a director or company secretary (where appointed). [CA06 Secs 446(3), 447(3)].

- In the case of a quoted company, a copy of the directors' remuneration report. It must state the name of the person who signed it on behalf of the board under section 422 of the 2006 Act and it must be signed by a director or the company secretary. [CA06 Sec 447(3)].

- A copy of the auditors' report on those financial statements and that directors' report and, in the case of a quoted company, on the auditable part of the directors' remuneration report. The copy must state the name of the auditor (and where the auditor is a firm) the name of the person who signed it as senior statutory auditor and be signed by the auditor or (where the auditor is a firm) in the name of the firm by a person authorised to sign on its behalf. In circumstances where the auditor's name can be omitted under section 506 of the 2006 Act, it must state that the necessary resolution of the company has been passed and notified to the Secretary of State. [CA06 Sec 447(4)].

[CA06 Secs 446, 447].

8.134.1 Financial statements in a language other than English must be accompanied by a translation certified in the prescribed manner. However, financial statements in Welsh may be filed without an accompanying certified translation by unquoted companies whose registered office is in Wales. [CA06 Sec 1104].

Filing obligations of companies subject to the small companies regime

8.134.2 The directors of a company subject to the small companies regime *must* deliver to the Registrar of Companies for each financial year a copy of the balance sheet and its notes from the annual financial statements sent to its members.

[CA06 Secs 444(1)(a), 472]. The directors must also deliver a copy of the auditors' report on the accounts, unless the company is exempt from audit and the directors have taken advantage of that exemption. [CA06 Sec 444(2)]. The directors *may* also deliver a copy of the company's profit and loss account and/or the directors' report for that year (but see para 8.134.5 below). [CA06 Sec 444(1)(b)(i)(ii)]. They may, of course, deliver a copy of the complete set of the annual financial statements and reports sent to the members.

8.134.2.1   Where the directors of a company subject to the small companies regime choose not to deliver to the Registrar a copy of the company's profit and loss account or a copy of the directors' report, as permitted by section 444(1) of the 2006 Act, the balance sheet must contain a statement in a prominent position that the company's annual accounts and reports have been delivered in accordance with the provisions applicable to companies subject to the small companies regime. [CA06 Sec 444(5)]. This applies irrespective of whether the annual accounts are Companies Act financial statements or IAS accounts.

8.134.3   The copies of the balance sheet and of any directors' report delivered to the Registrar under section 444(6) of the 2006 Act must state the name of the person that signed it on behalf of the board. The balance sheet must be signed on behalf of the board by a director of the company and the directors' report must be signed on behalf of the board by a director or by the company secretary (where appointed). [CA06 Secs 414, 419(1)]. Similarly, the copy of the auditors' report delivered under section 444(2) of the 2006 Act must state the name of the auditors and where the auditors are a firm the name of the person who signed it as senior statutory auditor. The auditors' report should be signed by the auditor and, where the auditors are a firm, should be signed in the name of the firm by a person authorised to sign on its behalf. [CA06 Sec 444(7)]. However, the auditors' names may be omitted if the conditions in section 506 of the 2006 Act are met. In that case there must be a testament that a resolution has been passed and notified to the Secretary of State in accordance with that section. [CA06 Sec 444(7)(b)].

8.134.4   Where the company prepares 'Companies Act accounts' for its members the directors may deliver 'abbreviated accounts' to the Registrar instead of the copy extracts from, or the complete set of, its annual financial statements and reports sent to members described above. These financial statements must consist of a balance sheet, a profit and loss account and notes drawn up in accordance with Regulation 6 of, and Schedule 4 to, SI 2008/409. [CA06 Sec 444(3)]. The copy balance sheet must contain a statement in a prominent position that it has been prepared in accordance with the provisions applicable to the small companies regime companies. [SI 2008/409 4 Sch para 1(2)].

8.134.4.1   Where abbreviated accounts are delivered to the Registrar they must be accompanied by the special auditors' report required by section 449 of the 2006 Act, unless the company is exempt from audit and the directors have taken advantage of that exemption. [CA06 Sec 449(1)(b)]. The special auditors' report must be signed by the auditor (or where the auditor is a firm) by a person authorised to sign on its behalf. [CA06 Sec 449(4)]. In circumstances where the auditor's name can be omitted under section 506 of the 2006 Act it must state that the necessary resolution of the company has been passed and notified to the Secretary of State [CA06 Sec 449(4)]. See also paragraphs 8.160 to 161 below.

8.134.5 A company that qualifies for the small companies regime, or would do so but for being a member of an ineligible group, is entitled to the small companies exemption in relation to the directors' report under section 415A of the 2006 Act. The directors of such a company must deliver to the Registrar of Companies a copy of the company's annual financial statements (that is, the company's individual profit and loss account and balance sheet with supporting notes to both primary statements). [CA06 Secs 444A(1)(a), 471, 472]. Unless the company is exempt from audit and advantage has been taken of that exemption, the directors must also deliver a copy of the auditor's report on those financial statements (and any directors' report). [CA06 Sec 444A(2)]. They may also deliver a copy of the directors' report prepared with the benefit of the exemption in section 415A. [CA06 Sec 444A(1)(b)].

8.134.5.1 The copies of the balance sheet and any directors' report delivered to the Registrar of Companies must state the name of the person who signed it on behalf of the board. [CA06 Sec 444A(3)].

8.134.5.2 The copy of the auditor's report must state the name of the auditor and (where the auditor is a firm) the name of the person who signed it as senior statutory auditor. In circumstances where the auditor's name can be omitted under section 506 of the Act, the report must state that the necessary resolution of the company has been passed and notified to the Secretary of State. [CA06 Sec 444A(5)].

Filing obligations of medium-sized companies

8.134.6 The directors of a medium-sized private company *must* deliver to the Registrar of Companies for each financial year a copy of the annual accounts and reports sent to members. The directors must also deliver a copy of the auditors' report on those accounts and the directors' report. [CA06 Sec 445(1)(2)].

8.134.7 Alternatively, where the company prepares 'Companies Act accounts' the directors may deliver 'abbreviated accounts'. These financial statements must consist of the company's balance sheet as sent to members and a profit and loss account drawn up in accordance with Regulation 4(3) SI 2008/410, 'The Large and Medium-sized Companies and Groups (Reports and Accounts) Regulations 2008'. [CA06 Sec 445(3)]. If abbreviated accounts are delivered to the Registrar they must be accompanied by the special auditors' report required by section 449 of the 2006 Act, unless the company is exempt from audit and the directors have taken advantage of that exemption. [CA06 Sec 449(1)(b)]. See also paragraphs 8.160 to 161 below.

8.134.8   The content of abbreviated accounts is dealt with in chapter 32 of the Manual of Accounting — UK GAAP. Medium-sized companies that prepare IAS financial statements are not permitted to file abbreviated accounts.

8.134.9   The 2006 Act does not grant medium-sized companies that are parent companies any exemption from the requirement to file consolidated financial statements. They may, however, omit the company's individual profit and loss account in the same way as other parent companies may. This applies whether they are preparing Companies Act or IAS financial statements (see further chapter 4 of the Manual of Accounting — IFRS for the UK and the Manual of Accounting — UK GAAP).

Consolidated financial statements not prepared

8.135   Where a company is exempt under sections 400 and 401 of the 2006 Act from preparing consolidated financial statements, a copy of the consolidated financial statements of the ultimate parent undertaking in whose consolidated financial statements the company is included must be appended to the company's financial statements delivered to the Registrar. The exemptions from the requirement to prepare consolidated financial statements are explained further in chapter 24 of the Manual of Accounting – IFRS for the UK and the Manual of Accounting – UK GAAP.

[The next paragraph is 8.139.]

Period allowed for sending out, laying and filing

8.139   As stated above, the directors of all public companies must lay the company's annual financial statements and reports before the company in general meeting and must file them with the Registrar of Companies. These financial statements and reports must be laid and filed before the end of the allowed period. [CA06 Sec 442]. All private companies must circulate copies of the company's annual financial statements and reports to every member, debenture holder and any other person entitled to receive noitice of a general meeting. They must also file a copy with the Registrar of Companies. [CA06 Secs 423, 442]. However, an unlimited company does not have to file its financial statements and reports with the Registrar under certain conditions (see para 8.146 below).

8.140   The 2006 Act sets out the requirements for filing of financial statements and reports. The usual period allowed for filing financial statements and reports with the Registrar is:

■ Nine months after the end of the relevant accounting reference period for a private company.

■ Six months after the end of that period for a public company.

[CA06 Sec 442].

However, this period may be extended or shortened in the situations outlined in the paragraphs that follow.

8.141 If a company's *first* accounting reference period exceeds 12 months, the financial statements and reports must be filed within the later of: nine months for a private company or six months for a public company from the first anniversary of the company's incorporation; or three months from the end of the accounting reference period (see para 8.88 for the meaning of 'accounting reference period'). [CA06 Sec 442(3)].

8.142 The effect of this is that a new private company has to deliver its first financial statements within 21 months of incorporation and that a new public company will normally have 18 months (unless the company shortens its accounting period as set out in para 8.98 above).

Example

A public company is incorporated on 1 August 20X2, and its first accounting reference period ends on 31 December 20X3 (that is, 17 months later). The company must deliver its financial statements to the Registrar by 31 March 20X4. This is because the period allowed is the later of 3 months after the end of the accounting reference period, that is 31 March 20X4, and 6 months from the first anniversary of the inception of the company, that is, 31 January 20X4.

[The next paragraph is 8.144].

8.144 A company may shorten its accounting reference period by notifying the Registrar under section 392 of the 2006 Act (see para 8.94 onwards). Where a company takes advantage of section 392 of the 2006 Act and shortens its accounting reference period, it must file its financial statements for this shorter period before the last to expire of the following:

■ The period applicable under the relevant provision of section 442(2) of the 2006 Act described in paragraphs 8.140 to 8.142 above.

■ Three months after the date on which the notice was given to the Registrar to change the accounting reference date.

[CA06 Sec 442(4)].

8.145 In exceptional circumstances the Secretary of State may extend the time for filing if application is made to Companies House before the expiry of the period allowed for filing the company's financial statements. Any such application will, however, need to give the special reasons why the extension should be granted. [CA06 Sec 442(5)].

Filing exemption for unlimited companies

8.146 The directors of an unlimited company are not required under section 448 of the 2006 Act to file a copy of the company's financial statements with the

Registrar of Companies provided the company was *not*, at any time during the relevant accounting reference period, any one of the following:

- A subsidiary company of a limited undertaking.

- A parent company of a limited undertaking.

- Subject to rights exercisable by or on behalf of two or more limited undertakings which, if exercised by one of them, would have made the company its subsidiary.

- A banking or insurance company or the parent company of a banking or insurance group.

- A qualifying company under SI 2008/569, 'The Partnerships (Accounts) Regulations 2008'. An unlimited company will be a qualifying company if each of its members is a limited company, or is another unlimited company, each of whose members is a limited company or Scottish partnership, each of whose members is a limited company. References to a limited company, another unlimited company, or a Scottish partnership include a comparable undertaking incorporated in or formed under the law of a country or territory outside the UK.

[CA06 Sec 448].

8.147 Where an unlimited company is exempt from filing its financial statements under section 448 of the 2006 Act, its statutory financial statements will be those prepared in accordance with Part 15 of the 2006 Act and approved by the board of directors. If it publishes non-statutory financial statements, those financial statements must include a statement that the company is exempt from the requirement to deliver statutory financial statements. [CA06 Sec 448(4)]. See paragraph 8.155 where the meaning of publishing financial statements is explained.

Exemption for qualifying undertakings

8.147.1 A partnership will be a qualifying partnership if each of its members is a limited company (including a limited company incorporated overseas). The members of a qualifying partnership are required to prepare annual financial statements and have those financial statements audited as if the partnership were a company. Each member is then required to append a copy of these financial statements to its own financial statements delivered to the registrar. Non-UK or EU members of a qualifying partnership will be required to make the partnership's latest financial statements available for inspection at its head office. [SI 2008/569 Reg 5]. However, the members of the qualifying partnership are exempt from these requirements if the partnership is dealt with either by consolidation, proportional consolidation or equity accounting in the consolidated financial statements prepared by:

- a member of the partnership which is established under the law of an EU Member State; or

- a parent undertaking of such a member which is established under the law of an EU Member State.

8.147.2   This exemption is conditional upon:

- The consolidated financial statements being prepared and audited under the law of the Member state concerned in accordance with the provisions of the EU 7th Directive or of International Accounting Standards

- The notes to those financial statements disclosing that advantage has been taken of the exemption.

[SI 2008/569 Reg 7].

Rejection of documents by the Registrar

8.147.3   Companies House is entitled to (and does) reject documents (including financial statements) that fail to comply with the law. Rejected financial statements are treated as unfiled and may result in a company failing to meet its filing deadline (see further para 8.139). The most common reasons for rejection of financial statements are:

- Non-compliance with accounting standards or the Companies Act 2006.

- Incorrect references to the Companies Act 2006.

- Unsigned audit reports (if a signature is required).

- Unsigned balance sheets and directors' reports (if a signature is required).

- Photocopy signatures. These are not acceptable in any circumstances. (The accounts must have manual signatures throughout, that is, at least one director on the balance sheet, the company secretary conventionally on the directors' report (or a director if for a private company no secretary is appointed) and the firm's name signed by the partner on the audit report.)

- Missing pages.

- Figures in the notes failing to agree with the primary statements.

- Typographical errors in figures in the primary statements.

- Casting errors in the primary statements and/or the notes.

- Company number is missing or does not match company name.

- Dormant companies/audit-exempt accounts and directors' statement. Rejection occurs because the required directors' statement has not been made, has not been made correctly or has been placed somewhere other than on the balance sheet.

- Accounting reference periods and dates. A change of accounting reference date requires submission of the necessary forms to the Registrar.

- Duplicate financial statements. These will be returned unless they are meant to replace previously submitted financial statements and comply with the defective accounts provisions.

- Financial statements not capable of being reproduced electronically (see further paras 8.65 to 8.67.1).

Company's liability for late filing

8.148 Where a company does not deliver its annual financial statements and reports to the Registrar within the period allowed, the Registrar has authority to require the company to pay a penalty. The penalties, are set out in SI 2008/497, 'The Companies (Late Filing Penalties) and Limited Liability Partnerships (Filing Periods and Late Filing Penalties) Regulations 2008'. They are based on a sliding scale depending on the length of time between the date permitted by section 442 of the 2006 Act for filing and the actual date of delivery to the Registrar. The penalties are higher for public companies. Under SI 2008/497, if a company files late for a second consecutive year, the fine for that second year is doubled.

8.148.1 The provisions of SI 2008/497 apply to all financial statements and reports that are filed late on or after 1 February 2009, regardless of the company's period end or the Act under which the financial statements are prepared. It should be noted that the fines under SI 2008/497 are considerably higher and the penalty periods shorter than those set out in the 1985 Act.

8.149 The Registrar of Companies applies late filing penalties rigorously and imposes them even if the company is just over the filing deadline. Also, it is the date the financial statements are received by the Registrar of Companies that counts, not the date of posting.

8.149.1 Section 443 of the 2006 Act specifies how the period for filing is to be calculated. This section states that the deadline is the last day of the appropriate month (whether or not that is the corresponding date). Consequently a private company with an accounting reference date of 30 April must file its financial statements with the Registrar of Companies by 31 January the following year, not 30 January as would have been the case under the Companies Act 1985 or *Dodds and Walker [1981] 1 WLR 1441*.

8.150 Where the deadline falls on a weekend or on a bank (public) holiday, the annual financial statements and reports must be posted or be delivered by hand to arrive at Companies House on or before the last working day before the deadline. Companies House advise that financial statements and reports should be delivered at least three days before the deadline.

8.151 The Registrar considers that the late filing penalties extend to the situation where the court has declared that the striking of a company off the register is void and that the company is deemed to continue in existence as if it had never been struck off. The annual financial statements and reports of a company restored to the Register at Companies House may, therefore, be liable to late filing penalties for the period during which the company was dissolved.

Directors' liability for late delivery

8.152 The late filing penalties mentioned above are quite separate from any offence of which the directors may be guilty for not delivering the annual financial statements and reports to the Registrar before the end of the period allowed (see para 8.140). It is a defence for a director to prove that he took all reasonable steps for securing that the requirements to deliver the annual financial statements and reports would be complied with before the end of the period allowed. It is not a defence that the documents were not in fact prepared.

8.153 In addition, if a company has not complied with the filing requirements within the period allowed for laying and filing annual financial statements and reports, any member, or any of the company's creditors, or the Registrar may serve notice on the company requiring it to comply with the filing requirements. If the company's directors fail to make good the default within 14 days after the notice has been served, then the person who served the notice may apply to the court to make an order instructing the directors to comply with the filing requirements within a time the court specifies. The court order may also require the directors to bear the cost of the application. [CA06 Sec 452(1)(2)].

8.154 The Company Directors (Disqualification) Act 1986 provides that if a director is persistently in default in filing any returns, financial statements or other document with the Registrar, he may be disqualified. Default may be conclusively proved if he has been adjudged guilty of three or more defaults in the five years ending with the application date. [The Company Directors (Disqualification) Act 1986 Sec 3(2)].

Exemptions from audit of financial statements

Small companies and groups

8.154.1 Small companies (including dormant companies) may be able to claim an exemption from the obligation to have their financial statements audited if they comply with certain criteria. [CA06 Secs 477, 478]. The audit exemption specifically for dormant companies is discussed in paragraph 8.154.14.

8.154.2 Section 477 of the 2006 Act sets out the conditions for exemption from audit for small companies. A small company may be exempt from the need to have an audit for that financial year if its annual turnover and balance sheet total for the year are not more than £6.5 million and £3.26 million respectively. The 2006 Act does not contain provisions in relation to exemption from audit for small companies that are charities. Charities must comply with the applicable charity law rather than company law to determine whether an audit is required.

8.154.2.1 For a company to qualify as small (or medium-sized) in relation to a financial year if the following qualifying conditions must be met:

■ In the case of the company's first financial year, in that year.

■ In the case of any subsequent financial year:

    ■ in that year and the preceding year;

    ■ in that year and the company qualified as small (or medium sized) in relation to the preceding financial year; or

    ■ were met in the preceding financial year and the company qualified as small (or medium sized) in relation to that year.

[CA06 Secs 382, 465].

In practice, this means that a company is small or is medium-sized if it meets the size tests for two consecutive years and it is not small or medium-sized if it fails the size tests in two consecutive years.

8.154.3 The audit exemption is available to all qualifying small companies, regardless of whether they report in accordance with **UK GAAP or IFRS**.

Small companies ineligible for audit exemption

8.154.4 The circumstances where companies that meet the size exemption criteria but are still prevented from obtaining an audit exemption are set out in section 478 of the 2006 Act. A company will not be entitled to the audit exemption conferred by section 475 of the 2006 Act if at any time during the financial year in question it was one of the following:

■ A public company. (A public company that is dormant may be entitled to the audit exemption for dormant companies (see para 8.154.14).)

■ A small company that is an authorised insurance company, a banking company, an e-money issuer, a MiFiD investment firm or a UCITS management company (as defined by the Financial Services and Markets Act 2000).

■ A company that carried on an insurance market activity.

■ A special register body as defined in section 117(1) of the Trade Union and Labour Relations (Consolidation) Act 1992 or an employers' association as defined in section 122 of that Act or Article 4 of the Industrial Relations (Northern Ireland) Order 1992 (SI 1992/807 (N15)).

■ A group company (that is, a parent company or a subsidiary undertaking) unless:

    ■ throughout the period in the financial year during which it was a subsidiary undertaking, the company was dormant; or

- the company is a parent company or a subsidiary undertaking in a small group that meets the following conditions:

  - the group qualifies as small under section 383 of the 2006 Act for the financial year, (or if all bodies corporate in the group were companies, would so qualify), and the group is not, and was not at any time within that year, an ineligible group within the meaning of section 384(2) of the 2006 Act;

  - the group's aggregate turnover in that year, is not more than £6.5 million net or £7.8 million gross; and

  - the group's aggregate balance sheet total is not more than £3.26 million net or £3.9 million respectively.

  [CA06 Sec 479].

The group in relation to a group company means that company together with all its associated undertakings. For this purpose undertakings are associated if one is a subsidiary undertaking of the other or both are subsidiary undertakings of a third undertaking. [CA06 Sec 479(4)].

8.154.5 Members of a small or dormant company have the right to require the company to obtain an audit of its financial statements and so prevent it from taking advantage of the exemption. Under section 476 of the 2006 Act members holding 10 per cent or more of the company's nominal share capital or ten per cent of a particular class of share may deposit at the company's registered office after the start of the financial year to which it relates and not later than one month before the year end a notice requiring an audit for that year. If the company does not have share capital, the notice must be given by 10 per cent or more of members. If such a notice is deposited, the company will not be entitled to the audit exemption for the year to which the notice relates.

8.154.6 The disclosures listed below are required in order for small and dormant companies to take advantage of the audit exemptions in section 477(1) of the 2006 Act (small companies) and section 480(1) of the 2006 Act (dormant companies) unless its balance sheet includes three statements by the directors to the effect that:

- For the year in question the company was entitled to the exemption under either:

  - section 477 of the 2006 Act in the case of a small company;

  - section 480 of the 2006 Act in the case of a dormant company; or

  - under section 482 of the 2006 Act in the case of a non-profit-making company subject to public sector audit.

- Members have not required the company to obtain an audit of its financial statements for the financial year in question in accordance with section 476 of the 2006 Act (see para 8.154.8 below).

- The directors acknowledge their responsibilities for complying with the requirements of the 2006 Act with respect to accounting records and the preparation of accounts. [CA06 Sec 475(3)].

8.154.7 The required statements must appear above the director's signature on the balance sheet. [CA06 Sec 475(4)]. The unaudited financial statements can be full financial statements, but as the company will be a small company under the 2006 Act, it may, if it prepares 'Companies Act individual accounts' (financial statements) (that is, in accordance with UK GAAP), choose to take advantage of the special provisions of section 444 of the 2006 Act concerning 'abbreviated' or shorter-form financial statements.

8.154.8 The ICAEW has issued Technical Release Audit 02/04, 'Chartered accountants' report on the compilation of financial statements of incorporated entities'. The Technical Release provides guidance to accountants who assist in the compilation of financial statements where a company is not required to have its financial statements audited.

8.154.9 Paragraph 31 of Technical Release Audit 02/04 states that where the financial statements are unaudited, the financial statements should contain a reference to the fact that they are unaudited, either on the front cover or on each page of the financial statements.

8.154.10 Where the directors of a company have taken advantage of the exemption from audit either because it is a qualifying small company (see para 8.154.2) or a dormant company (see para 8.154.14):

- The financial statements sent to those persons entitled to a copy of the company's accounts and reports, in accordance with section 423 of the 2006 Act need not contain an auditors' report.

- No copy of the auditors' report need be sent to the registrar or laid before the company in general meeting.

- Section 837 of the 2006 Act (accounts by reference to which distribution is to be justified) will not apply.

[CA06 Secs 444(2), 445(2)].

A company that qualifies for audit exemption as a small company or a dormant company will also be exempt from the obligation in section 485 of the 2006 Act to appoint auditors. Section 485(1) of the 2006 Act provides that *"An auditor or auditors of a private company must be appointed for each financial year of the company, unless the directors reasonably resolve otherwise on the ground that audited accounts are unlikely to be required".*

8.154.11 Under the 2006 Act only public companies are required to hold general meetings, thus, if under the 2006 Act, a dormant public company ceases to qualify for an audit exemption during the year, the directors may appoint auditors at any time before the next 'accounts meeting' at which financial statements prepared under section 394 of the 2006 Act for the previous financial year are laid. [CA06 Sec 489].

8.154.12 Under the 2006 Act, if a small or dormant private company ceases to qualify for an audit exemption for any reason during the year, the directors shall appoint auditors at any time before the next period for appointing auditors. The period for appointing auditors is no later than 28 days after the period allowed for sending out copies of the company's financial statements for the previous financial year or if earlier the date on which the financial statements for the previous financial year are sent out. [CA06 Sec 485(2)(3)].

8.154.13 If the directors fail to exercise their powers of appointment in either of the above cases, the powers may be exercised by the company's members. [CA06 Secs 485(4), 489(4)]. If a company fails to appoint an auditor or auditors in accordance with section 485 of the 2006 Act (private companies) or section 490 CA06 (public companies), the secretary of state may appoint one or more persons to fill the vacancy.

Dormant companies

8.154.14 A dormant company is exempt from the requirement to have its financial statements audited, irrespective of the accounting framework used to prepare its financial statements, in accordance with section 480 of the 2006 Act, if all the following apply:

■ It has been dormant since its formation or since the end of the previous financial year and both of the following conditions are met:

   ■ It is entitled to prepare individual financial statements for the year in accordance with the small companies regime (sections 381 to 384 of the 2006 Act), or it would be entitled to do so if it but for it having been a public company or a member of an ineligible group (see para 8.154.4).

   ■ It is not required to prepare group financial statements for that year.

8.154.14.1 Section 480 has effect subject to the following sections of the 2006 Act:

■ Section 481 which states that a company is not entitled to the exemption conferred by section 480 (dormant companies) if it was at any time during the financial year in question an authorised insurance company, a banking company, an e-money issuer, a MiFiD ISD investment firm or a UCITS management company (as defined by the Financial Services and Markets Act 2000).

■ Sections 475(2) and 475(3) regarding the requirements as the statements to be contained in the balance sheet (see para 8.154.16 below).

■ Section 476 regarding the rights of members to require an audit.

8.154.15 A company that ceases to be dormant during a year may still be able to take advantage of an audit exemption if it satisfies the size criteria and conditions for the small company exemption (see para 8.154.2 above). If not, it will no longer be exempt from the obligation to appoint auditors (see para 8.154.12).

Effect on financial statements

8.154.16 Where the directors of a dormant company have taken advantage of the exemption from audit in section 480 of the 2006 Act, the following statements are required:

■ A statement required under section 475(2) of the 2006 Act that it is exempt from audit as a dormant company under section 480 of the 2006 Act.

■ A statement required under section 475(3) of the 2006 Act that the members have not required the company to obtain an audit of its accounts for the year in question in accordance with section 476 of the 2006 Act; and that the directors acknowledge their responsibilities for complying with the requirements of this Act with respect to accounting records and the preparation of accounts. [CA06 Sec 480(3)].

8.154.17 The previous year's figures must be shown alongside for comparison, even if there are no items of income or expenditure for the current year. In addition, certain notes to the balance sheet must be included. Companies House has produced model balance sheets and notes for dormant companies in its booklet 'Accounts and accounting reference dates'.

Definition of 'dormant company'

8.154.18 Under section 1169 of the 2006 Act, a company is 'dormant' during any period in which it has no significant accounting transactions. A 'significant accounting transaction' means a transaction that is required by section 386 of the 2006 Act to be entered in the company's accounting records, but excluding the following:

■ Any transaction arising from the taking of shares in the company by a subscriber to the memorandum as a result of his undertaking in connection with the formation of the company.

■ The payment of a fee to the Registrar of Companies on a change of name.

■ The payment of a fee to the Registrar on the re-registration of the company.

■ A penalty under section 453 of the 2006 Act for the failure to deliver financial statements to the Registrar.

■ The payment of a fee to the Registrar for the registration of an annual return.

[CA06 Sec 1169].

Examples of significant accounting transactions

8.154.19   Any transaction by a non-trading company, such as the payment of distributable reserves to its parent, will constitute a significant accounting transaction. Section 386 of the 2006 Act requires, for example, a company's accounting records to contain entries on a daily basis of all money received and expended, a record of its assets and liabilities and a statement of goods sold and purchased. Any such transaction will prevent the company from taking advantage of the dormant company audit exemption. However, if the company qualifies as a small company it may be entitled to the exemption from audit under section 477 of the 2006 Act (see para 8.154.2).

8.154.20   Another difficulty arises when companies, wishing to qualify as dormant and thereby avoid the need to appoint auditors, dispose of assets to other companies in their group in order to facilitate this. Sometimes, particularly where land is concerned, it is only the beneficial interest that is transferred, the company intending to retain only the legal interest or bare legal title. Such transfers are frequently conducted with the minimum of formality and paperwork. However, since 26 September 1989, with regard to land the legal position is that any contract for the sale or other disposition of an interest in land can only be made in writing and only by incorporating, in one document, all the terms which the parties to the transaction have expressly agreed. This document must be signed by or on behalf of each party to the contract. Transfers not complying with these provisions may not be legally effective to transfer land or the beneficial interest in such land. If the 'dormant' company will retain the land and, should that land generate income or incur costs, those will be transactions of the company. Thus, it may not be held to have been dormant during the periods in question.

Additional disclosure to be made by dormant agency company

8.154.21   An additional disclosure requirement applies where the directors of a company are taking advantage of the audit exemption for dormant companies as defined by section 1169 of the 2006 Act and the company has during the financial year acted as an agent for any person. In these circumstances the notes to the financial statements must include a statement that the company has so acted. [SI 2008/409 1 Sch 63; SI 2008/410 1 Sch 71].

Publication of financial statements

Definition of publication

8.155   Section 434 of the 2006 Act sets out the requirements that companies have to comply with when they 'publish' their financial statements. A company will be regarded as 'publishing' financial statements if it publishes, issues or circulates them, or otherwise makes them available for public inspection in a manner calculated to invite members of the public (or any class of members of the public) to read them. [CA06 Sec 436(2)].

8.156 A company may publish the following categories of financial statements:

Statutory financial statements:

- Full financial statements.

- Abbreviated Companies Act accounts for small and medium-sized companies.

- Shorter-form Companies Act accounts for small companies.

- Balance sheet and notes for small companies.

- Financial statements in euros.

- Summary financial statements.

- Non-statutory financial statements.

- Voluntary preliminary statements of annual results (for example, from companies listed on the Main Market of the LSE) complying with the DTR and amended Listing Rules.

- Half-yearly financial reports of quoted companies.

- Interim Management Statements of quoted companies.

The definitions and the rules for publication of these categories of financial statements are discussed in the paragraphs that follow.

Statutory accounts

Full financial statements

8.157 Full financial statements are referred to in section 434 of the 2006 Act as a company's 'statutory accounts'. 'Statutory accounts' in that section means the company's individual financial statements or consolidated financial statements for a financial year, as required to be delivered to the Registrar under section 441 of the 2006 Act. [CA06 Sec 434(3)]. Statutory accounts are referred to in the paragraphs that follow and throughout this book as statutory financial statements.

8.158 A company that publishes any of its statutory financial statements must include:

- The relevant auditors' report under section 495 of the 2006 Act. [CA06 Sec 434(1)].

- Its statutory consolidated financial statements for the same year with its statutory individual financial statements, if it is required to prepare statutory consolidated financial statements by section section 399 of the 2006 Act. [CA06 Sec 434(2)].

8.159 If any of these requirements of section 434 of the 2006 Act are not complied with, the company and any officer of it who is in default will be guilty of an offence. [CA06 Sec 434(4)].

Abbreviated Companies Act accounts

8.160 Abbreviated accounts are not full financial statements; they are a special form of financial statements as defined by legislation. They may be prepared by some small and medium-sized companies that wish to take advantage of the special provisions for such companies for filing financial statements with the Registrar of Companies. [CA06 Secs 444(3), 445(3)]. These provisions permit a company that qualifies as small for a financial year to *file* abbreviated Companies Act individual accounts instead of full or shorter-form individual Companies Act accounts with the Registrar. [CA06 Sec 444(3); SI 2008/409 Reg 6]. Such financial statements must be prepared in accordance with Schedule 4 to SI 2008/409.

8.160.1 A company that qualifies as medium-sized may also file a form of abbreviated Companies Act individual accounts under the provisions for medium-sized companies. [CA06 Sec 445(3); SI 2008/410 Reg 4(3)]. Such financial statements must be prepared in accordance with Schedule 1 to SI 2008/410 as modified by Regulation 4(3) of SI 2008/410.

8.160.2 The directors of a medium-sized company that is a parent company at the end of a financial year must prepare consolidated financial statements. The consolidated financial statements form part of the company's annual accounts (section 471 of the 2006 Act) that the directors must file with the Registrar of Companies (sections 446 of the 2006 Act). However, the annual accounts filed with the Registrar may comprise the company's abbreviated Companies Act individual and group accounts. The abbreviated Companies Act group accounts are prepared in accordance with Schedule 6 to SI 2008/410 as modified by Regulation 4(3) of SI 2008/410. [SI 2008/410 6 Sch para 1(1)].

8.160.3 The intention of these provisions is to provide small and medium-sized companies with a degree of privacy rather than to reduce the burden on them. A small or medium-sized company that files abbreviated accounts must still prepare full financial statements, including consolidated financial statements where required, for its members.

8.161 Abbreviated financial statements in the prescribed form that are filed with the Registrar are the company's 'statutory accounts' for the purposes of section 434(3) of the 2006 Act. In this case the reference in section 435 of the 2006 Act to the auditors' report is to be read as a reference to the special auditors' report referred to in section 449 of the 2006 Act. [CA06 Sec 449(5)]. The provisions relating to abbreviated financial statements are dealt with fully in the Manual of Accounting – UK GAAP.

Shorter-form Companies Act accounts for small companies

8.162 The directors of a company that qualifies as a small company for a financial year are entitled under section 396(3) of the 2006 Act and Regulation 3 of SI 2008/409 to *prepare* its Companies Act individual accounts in one of the two special formats included in Schedule1 of SI 2008/409. Sections 411(1), 416(3) and 417(1) of the 2006 Act permit certain information required by section 411 of and Schedules 5, 6 and 7 to the 2006 Act to be omitted from these financial statements.

8.162.1 If at the end of a financial year a small company is a parent company its directors may also prepare consolidated financial statements under section 398 of the 2006 Act. Where that company's individual accounts are Companies Act accounts and its consolidated financial statements are Companies Act group accounts the latter must be prepared in accordance with Regulation 8 of, and Part 1 of Schedule 6 to, SI 2008/409 for the relevant financial year.

8.163 If the directors prepare shorter-form financial statements for their company under section 396(3) of the 2006 Act and Regulation 3 of SI 2008/ 409, they will be the company's annual financial statements. As a consequence, they must be authorised by the board of directors, sent to members and filed with the Registrar. The company may, however, instead of filing the shorter-form financial statements prepare abbreviated financial statements specifically for filing and file these instead (see paras 8.134.3 and 8.160 above).

8.164 Shorter-form financial statements that are filed with the Registrar are the company's statutory financial statements for the purposes of section 434(3) of the 2006 Act. The formats provided for shorter-form financial statements do not reduce greatly the number of items to be shown compared with full financial statements.

8.165 The accounting requirements concerning shorter-form financial statements are considered in detail in chapter 32 of the Manual of Accounting – UK GAAP.

Balance sheet and notes

8.166 A company subject to the small companies regime may file with the Registrar of Companies just a copy of the balance sheet and notes from the annual financial statements prepared for its members together with, where appropriate, a copy of the auditor's report sent to members. [CA06 Secs 444(1)(a), (2) and 472(2)]. This option is available to all qualifying companies irrespective of whether the financial statements prepared for their members are Companies Act or IAS financial statements. A company that takes this option may also file with its balance sheet and notes, the profit and loss account (and notes) and/or the directors' report sent to its members. [CA06 Secs 444(1)(b), 472(2)].

8.167　The balance sheet and notes (and, where relevant, the profit and loss account and notes) filed with the Registrar are the company's 'statutory accounts' for the purposes of section 434(3) of the 2006 Act.

[The next paragraph is 8.170.]

Summary financial statements

Background

8.170　The 2006 Act permits companies, subject to certain conditions, to send summary financial statements to members in place of full financial statements. [CA06 Secs 426 — 429]. The 2006 Act contains little of the detailed requirements surrounding summary financial statements: instead this is the subject of SI 2008/374, 'The Companies (Summary Financial Statement) Regulations 2008'.

8.171　Companies may send summary financial statements by electronic communication to members. The Act imposes the same conditions for sending summary financial statements to those who wish to receive them electronically, as mentioned in paragraphs 8.117.1 onwards above in connection with the electronic transmission of full financial statements. Sections 1143 to 1148 of, and Schedules 4 and 5 to, the 2006 Act govern a company's sending or supplying documents or information.

8.172　Where summary financial statements are accessible on a web site to persons other than those entitled to receive the full financial statements (entitled persons), the summary financial statements should include the wording required by section 435(1) of the 2006 Act. This is because they are not the company's statutory financial statements and are accessible to a wider audience than the entitled persons (see further para 8.196).

8.173　Section 426(5) of the 2006 Act makes provision for persons nominated to enjoy information rights under section 146 of the 2006 Act (indirect investors). Such persons may be provided with summary financial statements rather than the full accounts and reports.

8.174　Summary financial statements have also been used by building societies, that are allowed to send such summaries to their members under the Building Societies Act 1986.

8.175　Although summary financial statements have been issued by an increasing number of companies, the potential benefits must be set against the extra cost of preparing an additional set of financial statements and reports and their audit. The provisions relating to preparing and issuing summary financial statements are described below.

General conditions

8.176 A company is prohibited from sending summary financial statements to a member instead of full financial statements and reports in the following circumstances:

- Where the company is prohibited from doing so by any provision in its constitution or (where the member is a debenture holder) in any instrument governing the company's debentures. [SI 2008/374 Reg 4(1)].

- Where no auditors' report has been issued on the full financial statements under section 495 of the 2006 Act. [SI 2008/374 Reg 4(2)(a)].

8.176.1 Where the member or other entitled person has indicated a wish to receive full financial statements and reports, they should receive them in addition to the summary financial statement. [CA06 Sec 426(2)].

8.177 In addition, the company must not send summary financial statements for any financial year in place of copies of the full financial statements and reports, unless both the following conditions are satisfied:

- The period allowed for laying and delivering full financial statements and reports under section 442 of the 2006 Act for that year has not expired.

- The summary financial statements have been approved by the board of directors and the original statements have been signed on the board's behalf by a director of the company.

[SI 2008/374 Reg 4(2)].

8.178 Summary financial statements must be derived from the company's annual accounts and reports, and, in the case of a quoted company, the directors' remuneration report (together referred to above and below as 'full financial statements and reports') and comply with the requirements of sections 427 and 428 and the regulations made under those sections. [CA06 Secs 427, 428]. Provided that the summary financial statements sent to members comply with those requirements, the normal rules relating to publishing statutory and non-statutory financial statements in sections 434 and 435 of the 2006 Act do not apply. [CA06 Secs 434(6), 435(7)]. However, where they are accessible from a web site section 435 of the 2006 Act is likely to apply (see para 8.170.2).

8.179 The requirements of sections 426 to 429 of the 2006 Act fall into the following categories:

- The manner in which the wishes of members to receive full financial statements and reports are to be ascertained. These provisions are set out in regulations 5-8 of SI 2008/374.

- The statements to be included in the summary financial statement. [CA06 Secs 427(4), 428(4)].

- The form and content of summary financial statements. [SI 2008/374 Regs 9-11].

Unless these requirements are complied with, a company cannot send out summary financial statements. These requirements are discussed in more detail below.

8.180 In addition to the above information, the UKLA's Listing Rules require companies with securities admitted to trading on a regulated market (that is, the main market of the LSE or Plus Market's PLUS-listed market) to disclose the earnings per share in summary financial statements. [LR 9.8.13].

Ascertaining wishes of members

8.181 A company cannot send summary financial statements to a member in place of its full financial statements and reports, unless it has ascertained that the member does not wish to receive the full financial statements and reports. A company has to ascertain whether a member wishes to receive full financial statements and reports for a financial year (and future years) from one of the following.

- From a relevant notification in writing expressly given to the company by the member as to:
  - whether the member wishes to receive the full financial statements and reports; or
  - whether, instead of full financial statements and reports, the member wishes to receive summary financial statements.

  A notification will be a relevant notification for a financial year if it relates to that year (whether given at the company's invitation or not) and is received by the company not later than 28 days before the first date on which copies of the full financial statements and reports are sent out to members under sections 423(1) and 424(1) to (3) of the 2006 Act.

- Failing any express notification (that is, if a member has not replied to a consultation by notice or has not otherwise informed the company of a wish to receive full financial statements and reports), from a member's failure to respond to an opportunity to elect to receive copies of the full financial statements and reports in response to one of the following:
  - To the company's consultation by notice.
  - As part of a relevant consultation by the company of his wishes.

[SI 2008/374 Reg 5].

Consultation by notice

8.182   This procedure is a simple procedure by which companies may ascertain whether members wish to receive full financial statements and reports or summary financial statements. It enables a company to send to a member by post (or in any other manner authorised by the company's articles or under the company communications provisions of sections 1143 to 1148 of, and schedules 4 and 5 to, the 2006 Act an advance notice that must comply with all the following. The notice must:

- State that for the future the member will be sent summary financial statements for each financial year, unless notification is received by the company in writing of a wish to receive full financial statements and reports.

- State that the summary financial statements will contain a summary of the company's or group's profit and loss account, balance sheet.

- State that the printed card or form accompanying the notice must be returned by the date specified in the notice. This date must be at least 21 days after the notice is sent out and not less than 28 days before the first date on which copies of the full financial statements and reports for the next financial year are to be sent out to members under sections 423(1) and 424(1)–(3) of the 2006 Act.

- Include in a prominent position a statement that a summary financial statement will not contain sufficient information to allow as full an understanding of the results and state of affairs of the company (or group, as applicable) as would be provided by the full financial statements and reports and that members and debenture holders requiring more detailed information have the right to obtain, free of charge, a copy of the company's last full financial statements and reports.

- State that the summary financial statements will contain a statement by the company's auditors as to whether:

    - The summary financial statements are consistent with the annual financial statements and the directors' report (if information derived from that report is included) for the year in question.

    - In the case of a quoted company, the summary financial statements are consistent with the directors' remuneration report.

    - The summary financial statements comply with the requirements of section 427 (for unquoted companies) or section 428 (for quoted companies) and SI 2008/374, 'The Companies (Summary Financial Statement) Regulations 2008'.

    - Their report on the financial statements was unqualified or qualified.

[SI 2008/374 Reg 6; CA06 Secs 427 to 428].

8.183 The printed card or form accompanying the notice (mentioned above) must be worded so as to enable a member, by marking a box and returning the card or form, to notify the company of a wish to receive full financial statements and reports for the next financial year and for all future financial years. Postage for the return of the printed card or form must be borne by the company, unless the member or debenture holder is outside the European Economic Area. [SI 2008/374 Reg 8(2),(4)].

Relevant consultation

8.184 A 'relevant consultation' is an alternative option which companies may use to establish whether a member wishes to receive summary financial statements and also to establish whether any member who has chosen to receive full financial statements and reports would like to change and receive summary financial statements instead. A relevant consultation of the wishes of a member is a notice given to a member by post (or in any other manner authorised by the company's articles or under the company communications provisions of the 2006 Act (sections 1143 to 1148 of, and schedules 4 and 5 to, the 2006 Act) which complies with all the following:

- It states that in future the member will be sent a summary financial statement instead of full financial statements and reports, unless the company is notified in writing that the member wishes to *continue* to receive the full financial statements.

- It accompanies a copy of the full financial statements and reports.

- It accompanies a copy of the summary financial statements for the same financial year and this is identified in the notice as an example of the statement the member will receive in the future, unless the company is notified otherwise.

- It is accompanied by a printed card or form which is worded so as to enable the member, by marking a box and returning the card or form, to notify the company of a wish to receive full financial statements and reports for the next financial year and for all future financial years. Postage on the return of the card or form must be paid by the company unless the member or debenture holder is outside the European Economic Area.

[SI 2008/374 Regs 7, 8(2)(3)].

Statements to be included in all summary financial statements

8.185 All summary financial statements must:

- State that they are only a summary of information in the company's annual financial statements and, in the case of a quoted company, the directors' remuneration report.

- State whether they contain additional information derived from the directors' report and, if so, state that they do not contain the full text of that report or review.

- State how an entitled person can obtain a copy of the full financial statements.

- Contain a statement by the company's auditors as to whether the summary financial statements:

  - Are consistent with the annual financial statements, the directors' remuneration report and, where information derived from the directors' report is included, with that report.

  - Comply with the requirements of section 427 (in the case of unquoted companies) or section 428 (in the case of quoted companies) of the 2006 Act and SI 2008/374.

- State whether the auditors' report on the annual financial statements (and, in the case of a quoted company, the auditable part of the directors' remuneration report) was unqualified or qualified and, if it was qualified, set out the report in full together with any further material required to understand the qualification.

- State whether, in the auditors' report on the annual financial statements the auditors' statement under section 496 of the 2006 Act (whether the directors' report is consistent with accounts) was qualified or unqualified. If it was qualified, the qualified statement should be set out in full, together with any additional information needed to understand the qualification.

- State whether the auditors' report contained a statement concerning proper accounting records or inadequate returns under section 498(2) of the 2006 Act, or failure to obtain certain necessary information and explanations under section 498(3) of the 2006 Act. If so, the statement will have to be set out in full.

[CA06 Secs 427(4), 428(4)].

- State the name of the director who signed them on behalf of the board.

- Include, where the company is required to prepare consolidated financial statements, a statement in a prominent position that the summary financial statements do not contain sufficient information to allow as full an understanding of the results of the group and state of affairs of the company or of the group and of their policies and arrangements concerning directors' remuneration as would be provided by the full financial statements and reports; and that members and debenture holders requiring more detailed information have the right to obtain, free of charge, a copy of the company's last full financial statements and reports.

- Where a company is not required to prepare consolidated financial statements, a similar statement appropriately amended to refer solely to the company must be included in the summary financial statements.

■   Contain a clear, conspicuous statement of how members and debenture holders:

   ■   can obtain, free of charge, a copy of the company's last full financial statements and reports; and

   ■   may elect in writing to receive full financial statements and reports in place of summary financial statements for all future financial years.

[SI 2008/374 Reg 9].

[The next paragraph is 8.185.2.]

8.185.2   As noted above, the summary financial statements must state whether the auditors' report on the annual financial statements (and, in the case of a quoted company, the auditable part of the directors' remuneration report) was unqualified or qualified and, if it was qualified, must set out the report in full together with any further material required to understand the qualification. APB Bulletin 2008/3, 'The auditors' statement on the summary financial statement' states that, if the auditors' report on the full annual financial statements includes an 'emphasis of matter' paragraph that includes a reference to a note to the financial statements, unless that note is included in the summary financial statements, the information contained in it should be reproduced in the auditors' statement.

Form and content of summary financial statement

8.186   Schedules 1 and 4 to SI 2008/374 specify the forms for summary financial statements prepared by companies and groups respectively that prepare their annual financial statements in accordance with UK GAAP. Schedules 7 and 8 of those regulations apply to companies and groups respectively that prepare their annual financial statements in accordance with EU-adopted IFRS. The remaining schedules apply to banking and insurance companies and groups.

8.187   The paragraphs that follow outline the form and content of summary financial statements that are applicable to companies that prepare consolidated financial statements in accordance with UK GAAP or EU-adopted IFRS (except banking, and insurance, companies and groups to which different rules apply).

8.188   Summary financial statements must contain the information prescribed by the relevant schedule (see para 8.186) to the regulations in such order and under such headings as the directors consider appropriate. In addition, any other information necessary to ensure that the summary financial statements are consistent with the full financial statements and reports for the financial year in question must be given.

Summary directors' emoluments and remuneration report information

8.189   The summary financial statements must include:

- The whole or a summary of the notes to the financial statements for the year in question that sets out the information on the aggregate amount of directors' emoluments and other disclosures required by paragraph 1 of Schedule 3 to SI 2008/409, 'The Small Companies (Accounts and Directors' Report) Regulations 2008', or paragraph 1 of Schedule 5 to SI 2008/410, 'The Large and Medium-sized Companies (Accounts and Reports) Regulations 2008', as the case may be.

- To the extent that the company is required to produce a directors' remuneration report, those portions of the report for the year in question that set out the statement of the company's policy on directors' remuneration (paragraph 3 of Schedule 8 to SI 2008/410) and the performance graph (paragraph 4 of Schedule 8 to SI 2008/410).

- Where, at the end of the year, the company has securities carrying voting rights admitted to trading on a regulated market (for example, the main market of the LSE or the Plus Market's PLUS-listed market), the information required by paragraphs 13 and 14 of Schedule 7 to SI 2008/410 to be included in the directors' report that derives from the EU Takeovers Directive. (This may be sent together with the summary financial statements, rather than included within them.) These requirements are considered further in chapter 3.

[SI 2008/384 Regs 9, 10].

Summary profit and loss account

8.190 The format of the summary consolidated profit and loss account will depend the format the company has adopted in its full financial statements.

8.191 For companies or groups preparing their annual financial statements in accordance with UK GAAP, the summary profit and loss account is required to contain the following line items:

- Turnover.
- Income from interests in associated undertakings.
- The net of other interest receivable and similar income and interest payable and similar charges.
- Profit or loss on ordinary activities before tax.
- Tax on the profit or loss on ordinary activities.
- Profit or loss on ordinary activities after tax.
- Extraordinary items (although these have been all but eliminated by FRS 3).
- Profit or loss for the financial year.
- Earnings per share (for listed companies).

[SI 2008/374 Sch 1 para 1; LR 9.8.13].

8.191.1 For companies or groups preparing their annual financial statements in accordance with EU-adopted IFRS, the summary profit and loss account (which is shown in the illustration below) is required to include each of the headings and sub-totals included in the full profit and loss account, although aggregation of such headings and sub-totals is permitted where they are similar in nature and the directors consider it appropriate. In addition, as mentioned in paragraph 8.180, listed companies must disclose of earnings per share. As illustrated, the summary profit and loss account will not add up from top to bottom.

Summary consolidated profit and loss account	
Turnover	X
Operating profit	X
Other interest receivable and similar income and interest payable and similar charges	X
Share of post tax income from associates	X
Profit or loss on ordinary activities before tax	X
Tax on profit or loss on ordinary activities	X
Profit or loss on ordinary activities after tax	X
Profit or loss attributable to minority interest	X
Profit or loss attributable to equity shareholders	X
Earnings per share	
– basic	X
– diluted	X

Summary balance sheet

8.191.2 Summary financial statements must include a summary balance sheet.

8.192 For companies or groups preparing their annual financial statements in accordance with UK GAAP, the summary balance sheet is required to show, under such headings as the directors consider appropriate, a single amount for each heading to which letters are assigned in the format used for the full balance sheet in the order set out in that balance sheet. Balance sheet formats are discussed in chapter 4 of the Manual of Accounting – UK GAAP.

8.192.1 For groups preparing their annual financial statements in accordance with EU-adopted IFRS, the summary balance sheet is required to show each of the headings and sub-totals included in the full balance sheet, although such headings and sub-totals may be combined where they are similar in nature and the directors consider it appropriate. An illustrative summary balance sheet is shown below.

Summary consolidated balance sheet

Fixed assets		
Tangible fixed assets		X
Intangible fixed assets		X
Current assets	X	
Current liabilities	(X)	
Net current assets/(liabilities)		X
Total assets less current liabilities		X
Long-term liabilities		(X)
		X
Capital and reserves		X
Minority interests		X
		X

8.193 Whether a group prepares UK GAAP or IFRS financial statements, the order of the line items included in the summary balance sheet must be consistent with the order of the line items included in the annual financial statements.

Dividends

8.193.1 The summary financial statements are also required to contain the information concerning recognised and proposed dividends that is included in the notes to the annual financial statements. [SI 2008/374 Sch 1 para 2, Sch 7 para 1(2), Sch 8 para 1(2)].

Comparative information

8.193.2 For both the summary profit and loss account and the summary balance sheet. Comparative information must be disclosed for the immediately preceding financial year. This information must be prepared on the same basis as the comparative information included in the group's annual financial statements.

Penalties

8.194 Default in complying with sections 426 to 428 of the 2006 Act or SI 2008/374 renders the company and every officer of it who is in default, guilty of an offence and liable to a fine. [CA06 Sec 429].

Non-statutory accounts

8.195 Non-statutory accounts are not full financial statements. A company must comply with the provisions of section 435(1),(2) of the 2006 Act when it *publishes* non-statutory accounts. 'Non-statutory accounts' means any balance sheet or profit and loss account of the company or the group that either relates to, or purports to deal with, a company's or group's full financial year, otherwise than as part of the company's statutory financial statements. [CA06 Sec 435(3)]. This means that where a full year's figures and a narrative explanation of those figures are recognisable as either a balance sheet or a profit and loss account of the company or the group, the rules that relate to non-statutory accounts are likely to apply. 'Publication' and 'statutory accounts' are discussed in paragraphs 8.155 and 8.157.

8.196 Where a company publishes non-statutory accounts, those accounts must be accompanied by a statement indicating:

- That the accounts are not the company's statutory accounts.

- Whether or not the statutory accounts have been delivered to the Registrar for the same year.

- Whether or not the auditors have reported under section 495 of the 2006 Act on the statutory accounts for that year.

- Whether or not the auditors' report was qualified or unqualified or contained a statement:

  - Drawing attention by way of emphasis to any matters without qualifying the report.

  - Under section 498(2) of the 2006 Act, where accounting records or returns have been inadequate, or the financial statements have not agreed with the records or returns.

  - Under section 498(3) of the 2006 Act, where necessary information and explanations have not been received.

[CA06 Sec 435(1)].

8.197 Where a company publishes non-statutory accounts dealing with one financial year and the company's full financial statements are subject to audit, a statement along the lines of one or other of the following examples (as appropriate) should be included in the non-statutory accounts. (See para 8.199 for the statement where there is comparative information.)

Example 1

The figures and financial information for the year 20XX do not constitute the statutory financial statements for that year. Those financial statements have been delivered to the Registrar and included the auditors' report which was unqualified and neither drew attention to any matters by way of emphasis nor contained a statement under either section 498(2) of the 2006 Act (accounting records or returns inadequate or accounts not agreeing with records and returns), or section 498(3) of the 2006 Act (failure to obtain necessary information and explanations).

Example 2

The figures and financial information for the year 20XX do not constitute the statutory financial statements for that year. Those financial statements have not yet been delivered to the Registrar, nor have the auditors yet reported on them.

[The next paragraph is 8.199.]

8.199   Where published non-statutory accounts deal with more than one year (for example, voluntary preliminary statements of the annual results of listed companies that must include comparative figures for the previous year), the one document may contain two sets of non-statutory accounts. Where this applies, the wording of the appropriate statement in paragraph 8.197 should be adapted to cover both sets of accounts. An example is Table 8.1. In this example reference is made to the prior year figures (prepared under the 1985 Act) and the 2010 figures (prepared under the 2006 Act).

Table 8.1 – Statement under section 435(1) CA 2006 in respect of non-statutory accounts

Invensys PLC – Preliminary announcement – 31 March 2010

18 Financial information

This preliminary announcement ('statement') was approved by a duly appointed and authorised committee of the Board of Directors on 23 May 2010. This statement does not comprise the statutory accounts of the Group, as defined in section 434 of the Companies Act 2006. The financial information for the year ended 31 March 2010 has been extracted from statutory accounts on which an unqualified audit report has been issued which does not include references to any matters to which the auditors draw attention by way of emphasis without qualifying their report and does not contain a statement under section 498(2) or (3) of the Companies Act 2006. Those accounts are yet to be delivered to the Registrar of Companies.

The statutory accounts of Invensys plc for the year ended 31 March 2009 have been delivered to the Registrar of Companies. The auditors, Ernst & Young LLP, reported on those accounts in accordance with section 235 of the Companies Act 1985 and their report was unqualified, did not include a reference to any matters to which the auditors drew attention by way of emphasis without qualifying the report and did not contain a statement under section 237(2) or (3) of the Companies Act 1985.

8.200   A company that does not comply with the requirements for the publication of non-statutory accounts outlined above and any officer who is in default will be guilty of an offence. [CA06 435(5)].

8.201   Published non-statutory accounts must not include the auditors' report made in connection with the company's annual financial statements in accordance with section 495 of the 2006 Act. [CA06 Sec 435(2)].

Additional rules for listed companies

Preliminary announcements

8.202   Preliminary statements of annual results of companies admitted to trading on a regulated market (for example, the main market of the LSE or Plus Market's PLUS-listed market) are no longer required under the UKLA's Listing Rules and, thus, *voluntary*. However, if a listed company issues a voluntary preliminary statement of annual results it must comply with LR 9.7A.1 and be published as soon as possible after it has been approved by the board. Despite the rule change, market trends indicate that preliminary announcements are still being produced as they are generally considered to play a key part in the annual financial reporting cycle as they are the first public communication of companies' results for the whole year. Preliminary announcements of listed companies (including those traded on AIM and the PLUS-quoted market) are considered in more detail in the Manual of Accounting – IFRS for the UK.

Annual financial report

8.203   Companies admitted to trading on a regulated market must, within four months of the period end, make public their annual financial report under DTR 4. Further details on the content and publication requirements are dealt with in the Manual of Accounting – IFRS for the UK.

Half-yearly financial reports

8.204   Issuers of any shares and debt (denominated in units of less than 50,000 euros) admitted to trading on a regulated market (for example, the main market of the LSE and Plus Market's PLUS-listed market) must publish half yearly reports within two months of the period end. [DTR 4.2.2] Further details on the content and publication requirements are dealt with in the Manual of Accounting – IFRS for the UK.

Interim management statements

8.205   The FSA's DTR require companies with listed shares that do not already report quarterly (either voluntarily or to meet regulatory requirements) to prepare interim management statements (IMS). See further the Manual of Accounting – IFRS for the UK.

[The next paragraph is 8.207].

AIM Companies

8.207   The AIM Rules provide that AIM companies must prepare a half-yearly report and issue it within three months of the end of the relevant period. The half-yearly report should cover the six month period from the date of the financial information disclosed in the admission document and at least every subsequent six months thereafter (apart from the final period of six months preceding its accounting reference date for its annual audited financial statements). [AIMR 18]. The guidance notes to the Rules state that the LSE will suspend AIM companies that are late in publishing their half-yearly report or annual financial statements. The content of interim reports for AIM companies is dealt with the chapter 31 of the Manual of Accounting – IFRS for the UK.

PLUS-quoted Companies

8.207.1   The PLUS Markets Rules provide that PLUS-quoted companies must prepare an interim report for the first half of each financial period and issue it as soon as possible, but no later than three months after the end of the relevant period. The interim report should contain a statement by the Board, the profit and loss account and a statement of whether or not the information has been reviewed by the company's auditor. [PLUS markets Rules 30-31]. Final results must be issued within five months of the period end and, in addition to the information contained in the interim report must contain a balance sheet, a statement of earnings per share, dividend details and comparatives.

Status of half yearly reports, annual financial reports, preliminary announcements and other statements

8.208   Half yearly reports are considered to be non-statutory accounts, because they contain comparative financial information for the last full financial year. Consequently, the provisions of the Companies Act 2006 that relate to non-statutory accounts (mentioned in para 8.195 above) apply. Half yearly reporting (interim reporting) is dealt with more fully in the Manual of Accounting – IFRS for the UK.

[The next paragraph is 8.210.]

8.210   Preliminary statements of annual results that listed companies may issue are *prima facie* considered to be non-statutory accounts. This is because the preliminary results either relate to, or purport to deal with, a company's full financial year. Furthermore, the information that paragraph 9.7A of the UKLA's Listing Rules (for voluntary preliminary announcements) require companies to give on a preliminary basis is capable of being recognised as a balance sheet or a profit and loss account. Consequently, where a listed company publishes a preliminary statement of annual results, the rules in the Companies Act 2006 that relate to non-statutory accounts apply. The ASB's statement, 'Preliminary Announcements', states that the preliminary announcement should contain a statement that satisfies the provision of section 435 of the 2006 Act regarding the publication of non-statutory accounts. [PA para 50]. The requirements for preliminary announcements are discussed more fully in the Manual of Accounting – IFRS for the UK.

8.210.1 Where a company publishes annual financial reports preliminary statements of annual results or half-yearly reports they must comply with the rules for non-statutory financial statements and include the appropriate wording referred to in paragraphs 8.197 and 8.198 above.

8.211 Another possible example of non-statutory accounts is the special reports that some companies prepare for employees. Much depends on whether the report either relates to, or purports to deal with, the company's activities during a full financial year, and also on whether it takes the form of a recognisable balance sheet or a profit and loss account. Where the report meets the non-statutory accounts criteria, the rules for such accounts must be followed and the appropriate wording used.

8.212 The five year or ten year summaries of financial information provided by listed companies are not considered to be non-statutory accounts. The reason for this is that the purpose of such a summary is not to deal with a company's activities for any particular year. Rather its purpose is to put the company's current position in a larger perspective and to provide pointers for the future.

Compensation for false statements in reports and financial statements

8.213.1 With effect from 8 November 2006, the 2006 Act inserted specific provisions into the Financial Services and Markets Act 2000 (FSMA) concerning liability of listed companies for false and misleading statements in their annual financial reports, half yearly reports or interim management statements required under the EU Transparency Obligations Directive (2004/109/EC), as implemented in the UK through the UKLA's DTR. [FSMA Sec 90A(1)(a); CA06 Sec 1270]. The provisions also extend to any preliminary statement of results that may be given voluntarily under Listing Rule 9.7A. [FSMA Sec 90A(1)(b)]. Listed company in this respect generally means a UK incorporated public company that has any of its securities traded on a regulated market situated or operating in, or outside, the UK. [FSMA Sec 90A(2)].

8.213.2 The listed company is liable to pay compensation to a person who has acquired any of its securities and has suffered a loss in respect of them as a result of any untrue or misleading statement in the publications referred to in paragraph 8.213.1, or as a result of an omission of a matter required to be included in the relevant publication. A loss is not regarded as having been suffered as a result of the statement or omission in the relevant publication, unless the person suffering the loss acquired the relevant securities in reliance on the information in the publication, and at the time when, and in circumstances in which, it was reasonable for him to rely on that information. Furthermore, the listed company is liable only if a person discharging managerial responsibilities (for example, a director) within the company responsible for the relevant publication knew the statement to be untrue or misleading, or was reckless as to whether it was untrue or misleading, or knew the omission to be dishonest concealment of a material fact. A person other than the listed company (for example, a director) is not subject to any liability, other than to the listed company, in respect of such loss.

Revision of defective financial statements

8.214   The Companies Act 2006 contains provisions that:

- Permit directors to prepare revised financial statements, a revised directors' report or a revised directors' remuneration report where it appears to them that the annual financial statements, the directors' report or the directors' remuneration report did not comply with the Act or, where applicable, Article 4 of the IAS Regulation ('voluntary revision'). [CA06 Sec 454].

- Permit the Secretary of State (in the absence of a satisfactory explanation from the company's directors as to the question of whether the annual financial statements comply with the Act), to apply to the court for an order that revised financial statements, directors' report or directors' remuneration report should be prepared. Such an application can only be made by the Secretary of State or a person authorised by the Secretary of State ('compulsory revision'). [CA06 Secs 455, 456, 457]. The FRRP is authorised for this purpose. By agreement with BIS, the normal ambit of the FRRP is public and large private companies, BIS dealing with all other cases.

8.214.1   Chapter 11 of Part 15 of the 2006 applies to revisions of financial statements or reports for accounting periods commencing on or after 6 April 2008. The 2006 Act states the broad principles allowing revision of financial statements, but the detail is found in SI 2008/373, 'The Companies (Revision of Defective Accounts and Reports) Regulations 2008'.

Voluntary revision

8.215   The detailed regulations governing preparing, auditing and issuing revised financial statements and directors' reports, where the revision is voluntary, are contained in SI 2008/373, 'The Companies (Revision of Defective Accounts and Reports) Regulations 2008'. The content of the regulations are described below.

8.216   If it appears to the company's directors that the financial statements, the directors' report or the directors' remuneration report did not comply with the requirements of the Companies Act 2006 or where applicable Article 4 of the IAS Regulation, they may prepare revised financial statements or a revised report or review. [CA06 Sec 454(1)]. Where copies of the previous financial statements or report have been laid before the company in general meeting or delivered to the Registrar, the revisions are required to be confined to:

- Correcting those aspects in which the previous financial statements did not comply with the requirements of the Act or, where applicable, Article 4 of the IAS regulation.

■ Making any necessary consequential alterations.

[CA06 Sec 454(2)].

It appears, therefore, that if the directors wish to revise the financial statements, directors' report or directors' remuneration report after the financial statements are sent out to members, but before they are laid before the company in general meeting, the revisions do not have to be confined to the matters listed above.

8.217 Revision of the financial statements, directors' report or directors' remuneration report may be made either by preparing replacement financial statements or directors' reports or by preparing a supplementary note indicating the corrections to be made to the original documents.

8.218 Where a decision has been made to replace the original financial statements or directors' report or directors' remuneration report, they should be prepared in the normal way in accordance with the Act's provisions that were in force at the date on which the original financial statements and directors' report were approved. (And not, as might have been expected, the provisions in force at the company's year end date.) There could, therefore, be additional consequential amendments to be made as a result of changes in the Companies Act 2006 between the company's year end and the date of approval of the original financial statements.

8.219 The regulations state that the Act's provisions relating to the matters to be included in a company's annual financial statements shall apply to the revised financial statements (whether prepared in accordance with UK GAAP or IFRS) as if the revised financial statements were prepared and approved by the directors as at the date of approval of the original financial statements.[SI 2008/373 Reg 3(1)]. Similar provisions for directors' reports and directors' remuneration reports are contained in regulation 3(4) of SI 2008/373. The purpose of this is to exclude from consideration events that occur between the date of approval of the original financial statements and the date of approval of the revised financial statements, directors' report or directors' remuneration report.

Approving and signing revised financial statements

8.220 The regulations provide that the revised financial statements must be approved by the board and signed by a director on the board's behalf. In the case of revision by supplementary note the signature should appear on the supplementary note.

8.221 Where the original financial statements have been sent to members, laid before the company in general meeting, or delivered to the Registrar, all the following must be stated in the financial statements that are revised by replacement.

■ That the revised financial statements replace the original financial statements for the financial year (specifying it).

- That they are now the company's statutory financial statements for that financial year.

- That they have been prepared as at the date of the original annual financial statements (that is, the date on which the original financial statements were approved) and not as at the date of revision (that is, the date of approval of the revised financial statements) and, accordingly, do not deal with events between those dates.

- The respects in which the original financial statements did not comply with the Act's requirements.

- Any significant amendments made as a consequence of remedying the defects.

[SI 2008/373 Reg 4(2)(a)].

8.222 Where the financial statements are revised by supplementary note the following statements must be made in the note:

- That the note revises in certain respects the company's original annual financial statements and is to be treated as forming part of those financial statements.

- That the annual financial statements have been revised as at the date of the original financial statements and not as at the date of revision (see point three in para 8.221) and, accordingly, do not deal with events between those dates.

[SI 2008/373 Reg 4(2)(b)].

8.223 The date of approval of the revised financial statements must be given in those financial statements. In the case of revision by supplementary note, the date should be given in the note itself. [SI 2008/373 Reg 4(2)].

Approving and signing revised directors' report or directors' remuneration report

8.224 Similar considerations apply to a revised directors' report or revised directors' remuneration report. The revised report must be approved by the board and signed on its behalf by a director or, or in the case of a revised directors' report, by a director or the company secretary. In the case of revision by supplementary note the note must be signed. Where the original directors' report or original directors' remuneration report has been sent to members, laid before the company in general meeting, or delivered to the Registrar of Companies, all the following must be stated in the report that is revised by replacement:

- That the revised report replaces the original report for the financial year (specifying the year).

- That it has been prepared as at the date of approval of the original directors' report or original directors' remuneration report and not as at the date of approval of the revision and, accordingly, does not deal with any events between those dates.

■ The respects in which the original directors' report or original directors' remuneration report did not comply with the Act's requirements.

■ Any significant amendments made as a consequence of remedying the defects.

[SI 2008/373 Regs 5(2)(a), 6(2)(a)].

8.225 Where the report is revised by supplementary note the note must state the following:

■ That the note revises in certain respects the original directors' report or directors' remuneration report of the company and is to be treated as forming part of that report.

■ That the directors' report or directors' remuneration report has been revised as at the date of approval of the original report and not as at the date of approval of the revision and, accordingly, does not deal with events between those dates.

[SI 2008/373 Regs 5(2)(b), 6(2)(b)].

8.226 The date of approval of the revised report must be given in the revised report (or in the supplementary note, if revision is made by supplementary note). [SI 2008/373 Regs 5(2), 6(2)].

8.226.1 An example of a report and financial statements that have been revised by replacement is given in Table 8.2. In this example the directors' report is referred to as the annual report on the affairs of the Group. The date of approval of the revised report and financial statements is given in th directors' report and on the balance sheet as 16 March 2010.

Table 8.2 – Statement on revision of directors' report and financial statements

Psion plc – Annual report – 31 December 2010

Revision of Annual Report and Financial Statements

This revised annual report and the revised financial statements replace the original annual report and the original financial statements for the year ended 31 December 2009 which were approved by the Board of Directors and authorised for issue on 4 March 2010. They are now the annual report and the statutory financial statements of the company for that financial year. In accordance with the Companies Act 2006 ('the Act'), the annual report and the financial statements have been revised as at the date of the original financial statements and not as at the date of this revision. Accordingly they do not deal with events between 4 March 2010 and 16 March 2010.

The revision relates to the misclassification of £3.1m of expenses between cost of sales and operating expenses. As a result, gross profit has increased from £60.6m to £63.7m, distribution costs have decreased from £40.0m to £36.3m, and administrative expenses have increased from £18.2m to £25.0m. Certain consequential revisions have been made in the Operational Review.

There is no change to reported operating loss, adjusted operating profit, or net assets. All other line items in the primary statements and notes to the financial statements remain unchanged.

The Act requires that where revised financial statements and annual report are issued, a revised auditors' report is issued and this is on page 50.

DIRECTORS' REPORT (extract)

The directors present their annual report on the affairs of the Group, together with the financial statements and auditors' report for the year ended 31 December 2009. The Report on Corporate Governance set out on pages 34 to 38 forms part of this report.

Auditors' report

8.227　The report on the revised financial statements should be made by the company's current auditors. If, however, there has been a change of auditors between the date of the original financial statements and the date of the revised financial statements the directors of the company may resolve that the report will be made by the former auditors. In this case, the former auditors will have to agree to do so and be qualified for appointment as the company's auditors. [SI 2008/373 Regs 7(1), 7(2)].

8.228　Whether the auditors' report as present or former auditors, the contents of the report must be the same. It must deal with all of the following matters:

- Whether in the auditors' opinion the revised financial statements have been properly prepared in accordance with the Companies Act 2006 (and, where applicable, those of article 4 of the IAS regulation) as they have effect under the regulations.

- Whether in their opinion a true and fair view, seen as at the date when the original financial statements were approved, is given by the revised financial statements of the state of the company's affairs at the end of the financial year, and of the profit or loss of the company for the financial year (or, in the case of consolidated financial statements, of the state of affairs of the company and the group at the end of the financial year and of the profit or loss of the group for the financial year).

- Whether in the auditors' opinion the original annual financial statements failed to comply with the Act's requirements (and, where applicable, those of article 4 to the IAS regulation) in the respect identified by the directors:

  - in the situation where the revision is made by replacement, in the statement the directors are required to make in the revised financial statements (see the fourth point in para 8.221 above); and

  - in the situation where the revision is made by supplementary note, in the supplementary note.

[SI 2008/373 Reg 7(3)].

8.229   The auditors must also state whether the information in the original directors' report or, if this has been revised, the revised report, is consistent with the revised financial statements. [SI 2008/373 Reg 7(4)].

8.230   Where the financial statements are not being revised, but the directors' report or directors' remuneration report is, the present or former auditors (as the directors decide) are not required to report on the financial statements. They must, however, report on the revised report and state the period covered by the financial statements with which it is consistent.

8.231   Where the directors' remuneration report has been revised, the auditors' report must state whether, in the auditors' opinion, any auditable part of that revised report has been properly prepared. [SI 2008/373 Reg 9(4)].

[The next paragraph is 8.234.]

Effects of revision

8.234   As soon as the revised financial statements, revised directors' report or revised directors' remuneration report are approved by the directors, they become the annual financial statements, directors' report or directors' remuneration report of the company in place of the original financial statements or report for all Companies Act purposes. For instance, regarding publishing statutory financial statements, the provisions in section 434(3) of the 2006 Act (see para 8.157 above) will then apply to the revised financial statements.

8.235   If the original financial statements, directors' report and (where applicable) directors' remuneration report have already been sent to members and others entitled to receive copies, the directors must send copies of the revised financial statements and report(s) review together with the auditors' report, to those persons. The revised copy has to be sent not more than 28 days from the date of the directors' approval of the revised financial statements and report. Where, however, the revision has been made by supplementary note the directors need only send the supplementary note and the auditors' report on the revised financial statements (or, as the case may be, on the revised report). The directors must also send a copy of the revised financial statements or report, together with the audit report within 28 days of approval of the revision to each person who, at the date on which the revised financial statements or report are approved, is:

■   A member of the company.

■   A holder of the company's debentures.

■   A person who is entitled to receive notice of general meetings.

[SI 2008/373 Reg 12(3)].

Some of these people will not have been entitled to receive the financial statements at the time the original financial statements were sent out.

8.236 Where the original financial statements, directors' report and, where appropriate, directors' remuneration report have already been laid before members, the company will have to lay the revised financial statements, report(s) and (where applicable) review, together with the auditors' report, before the next general meeting at which annual financial statements are laid, unless they choose to lay them before an earlier general meeting. [SI 2008/373 Reg 13].

8.237 Where the original financial statements, directors' report and, where appropriate, directors' remuneration report have already been delivered to the Registrar of Companies, the directors must deliver the revised financial statements and report(s), together with the auditors' report to the Registrar within 28 days of the date of their approval of the revised financial statements and report. Where the revision has been by supplementary note, only that note and the auditors' report on the revised financial statements (or as the case may be on the revised report) need be delivered. [SI 2008/373 Reg 14].

Abbreviated financial statements

8.238 The regulations provide for the revision of abbreviated financial statements where these are affected by the revision of a company's full financial statements. In this case *either* the revised abbreviated financial statements should be delivered to the Registrar of Companies within 28 days with a statement as to the effect of the revisions made *or* the company must deliver a copy of the revised financial statements and directors' report together with the auditors' report. The latter alternative must be adopted, if, as a result of the revision, the company is no longer entitled to file abbreviated financial statements. Where abbreviated financial statements are not affected by the revision to the full financial statements, a note stating that the full financial statements have been revised in a respect that has no bearing on the abbreviated financial statements, together with a copy of the auditors' report on the revised financial statements, must be delivered to the Registrar. [SI 2008/373 Reg 15]. Regulation 16 of SI 2008/373 provides for the revision of abbreviated accounts which do not comply with the Act for reasons other than the revision of the full financial statements.

Companies exempted from audit

8.239 A small or dormant company that is exempt from audit by virtue of section 477 and 480 of the 2006 Act can apply the regulations as if they omitted any reference to an auditors' report. [SI 2008/373 Reg 18].

8.240 Under the 2006 Act, where, as a result of revisions to its financial statements, a company is no longer entitled to exemption from audit, an auditors' report on the revised financial statements must be prepared and delivered to the registrar within 28 days of the date of the revision. [SI 2008/373 Reg 8].

Summary financial statements

8.241 Where a company has sent summary financial statements to members, the company is permitted to prepare revised summary financial statements, or a supplementary note indicating the corrections required, if one of the following applies:

■ The summary financial statements did not comply with the requirements of the Act or supporting regulations (see para 8.170).

■ The contents of the summary financial statements are affected by the revision of the annual financial statements, such that they no longer comply with the requirements of the Act or supporting regulations.

[SI 2008/373 Reg 17(2)].

8.241.1 Where the company prepares a supplementary note, that note is required to state that it revises the summary financial statements and is to be treated as part of those statements. [SI 2008/373 Reg 17(5)].

8.241.2 The company must send the revised summary financial statements or the supplementary note to all those who received the original summary financial statements and to any person to whom the company is entitled, as at the date of the revised summary financial statements, to send summary financial statements for the current year. [SI 2008/373 Reg 17(2)].

8.242 If the revision by the company of the annual financial statements or directors' report, directors' remuneration report does not affect the summary financial statements, the company must send a note stating that the annual financial statements, directors' report or directors' remuneration report for the year have been revised in a respect that has no bearing on the summary financial statement for that year. This note should be sent to the same persons as mentioned in paragraph 8.241.2 above. If the auditors' report on the revised financial statements, directors' report or directors' remuneration report has been qualified, a copy of that report must also be sent attached to the note. [SI 2008/373 Reg 17(6)].

8.243 The revised summary financial statement or note must be sent within 28 days of the date of approval of the revised financial statements or directors' report.

Compulsory revision

8.244 Responsibility in connection with the compulsory revision of defective financial statements is shared between the FRRP and BIS. The FRRP's ambit is in respect of the financial statements of public and large private companies. BIS remains responsible for all other companies. The FRRP operates under the aegis of the FRC. Its role is to examine the directors' report (including the business review) and annual accounts of unquoted and quoted public, and large private, companies to determine departures from the accounting requirements of the Companies Act. The FRRP also has remit over the half yearly reports of listed companies, but not the Interim Management Statements required by paragraph 4.3 of the UKLA's DTR. In respect of quoted companies, the FRRP derives part of its authority from the FSA.

8.244.1 Within this framework, the FRRP's main concern is stated to be material departures from accounting standards (UK and EU-adopted IFRS) where such a departure results in the financial statements in question not giving a true and fair view as required by the 2006 Act. In practice, the FRRP concerns itself with a variety of matters within the framework. Where a company's financial statements are defective the Panel will endeavour to secure their revision by *voluntary* means, but if this approach fails it has the power to make an application to the court under section 456 of the 2006 Act for an order compelling a revision.

8.244.2 The FRRP's role does not extend to considering whether the business review complies with the non-mandatory, but best-practice, ASB 'Reporting statement: Operating and financial review'. However, where a company states that it has voluntarily complied with the statement, the Panel will take this into account in its review.

8.245 Since its inception in 1991 to the end of 2008, the FRRP has issued public statements in respect of its findings on over 100 companies. To date no court application has been pursued as the companies concerned have all agreed to make revisions on a 'voluntary' basis in line with the FRRP's opinion. Although such revisions are 'voluntary' in the terms of the 1985 and 2006 Acts, in practice some of the 100-plus companies went along with the FRRP's wishes very reluctantly, on the basis that doing so is preferable to being taken to court. The operations of the FRRP are discussed further in the Manual of Accounting – IFRS for the UK and the Manual of Accounting – UK GAAP.

8.246 There are no regulations governing preparing, auditing and issuing financial statements and directors' reports that are compulsorily revised, as the court is empowered to give directions as to these and other matters as it thinks fit.

Meetings and resolutions

Directors' meetings

8.247 The board of directors will generally have power to manage the company's business. The Companies Act 2006, Model Articles (the '2006 Model Articles') provide, *"Subject to the provisions of the articles, the directors are responsible for the management of the company's business"*. One of the factors in deciding how often the board should meet would be the nature of the company's business. Any of the company's directors can call a board meeting and the company secretary, if one is appointed, also has to call such meetings if he is requested to do so by a director. The company's articles usually specify the number of directors required to constitute a quorum at such meetings. The 2006 Model Articles provide for a quorum of two directors.

8.248   No specific notice period is necessary to call a board meeting provided the notice period is, in the circumstances in question, a reasonable one and the notice has been given to all directors. If some directors do not receive proper notice of a board meeting, the decisions taken at it will be invalid. A board meeting can be held informally, but a casual meeting will not be sufficient if all parties do not agree to treat it as a meeting.

8.249   The question sometimes arises as to whether the directors can hold a board meeting by telephone or other electronic means. The issue as to whether a meeting will be properly constituted if it is held by means of a conference call or video conferencing has not been tested in the English courts. It is, however, thought that provided there is a carefully worded provision permitting telephone meetings in the articles and the meeting is duly convened, the meeting would be valid. The articles of association of many companies incorporate powers to permit telephone board meetings to occur or meetings to be held by electronic means. The 2006 Model Articles make it clear that directors do not have to be in the same place nor have to communicate using the same means of communication for directors to participate in a directors' meeting.

General meetings

8.250   A public company can hold the following types of shareholder meetings: AGMs; general meetings; and class meetings. One of a public company's general meetings each year must be an 'accounts meeting' at which it lays its annual accounts and reports (see para 8.122). This will generally be its AGM. There is no requirement for private companies to hold an AGM. All shareholder meetings of private companies are now termed general meetings. These meetings are regulated partly by statute and partly by a company's articles. The directors may call general meetings (as permitted by section 302 of the 2006 Act). If the directors are required to do so by the company's members in accordance with the Act, they must call a general meeting within 21 days of the request and that meeting must be held no later than 28 days after the date of the notice convening the meeting. [CA06 Sec 304]. For a company that has only one member, the quorum required to be present at the meeting, subject to any provision in the Articles, is one qualifying person. In other cases two qualifying persons are generally a quorum. A qualifying person is a member of the company, a person authorised under section 323 of the 2006 Act (representation of corporations at meetings) or a person appointed as proxy of a member. [CA06 Sec 318].

8.250.1   The directors must call a general meeting once the company has received requests from the required percentage of members. The required percentage is five per cent of paid up capital having voting rights. For this purpose, any of the company's paid up capital held as treasury shares should be disregarded. The requisition by the members for such a meeting must state the general nature of the business to be dealt with at the meeting and may include the text of the resolution intended to be moved at the meeting. [CA06 Sec 303(4)]. If the directors do not call a meeting within 21 days (to be held not more than 28 days thereafter) the requisitionists may do so themselves within three months and claim expenses of holding the meeting from the company. [CA06 Sec 305].

Annual general meetings

8.251 Public companies must hold an AGM within six months of the year end. [CA06 Sec 336(1)]. Private companies that are traded must hold an AGM within nine months of the year end. A public company or a private company that is traded must specify that the meeting is an AGM in the notice calling it. A public company's annual financial statements, including the directors' report, auditors' report and for listed public companies, the directors' remuneration report, are usually, but do not have to be, laid before the company at its AGM. However, if this is not the case the annual financial statements and reports must be laid at a general meeting designated as an 'accounts meeting' (see para 8.122 above).

8.252 It is the directors who usually convene the AGM. [CA06 Sec 302]. If the company fails to hold an AGM, the company and every director who is in default will be guilty of an offence. [CA06 Sec 336(4)].

8.252.1 Section 527 of the 2006 Act introduced a new right for shareholders of quoted companies from April 2008. The members may require the company to publish on its web site a statement setting out any matter relating to the audit of the company's financial statements that are to be laid before the company in the next accounts meeting, or circumstances in relation to the auditor ceasing to hold office since the last accounts meeting. [CA06 Sec 527]. A company is required to comply once requests have been received from members holding five per cent of the voting rights or when 100 members each holding shares on which an average of £100 has been paid up. There is no requirement to include any of the matters raised in the agenda for the accounts meeting. If the directors choose to respond to the matters raised, they may wish to consult with the auditors prior to doing so.

Notice

8.253 The directors are required to give at least 21 days notice in writing to call an AGM. [CA06 Sec 307(2)]. Notice of general meetings can be given in hard copy, in electronic form or *via* a web site. [CA06 Sec 308]. This is covered by the company communications provisions found in sections 1143 to 1148 of, and Schedules 4 and 5 to, the 2006 Act. For company meetings other than AGMs (including all private company general meetings 14 days notice in writing is required, subject to any provisions in a company's articles of association. Traded companies must provide at least 21 clear days' notice unless shareholder approval to the shorter 14 day period has been obtained and the facility to vote by electronic means is available to all members. [CA06 Sec 307A]. It is possible to call company meetings on shorter notice if in the case of a public company AGM all members who are entitled to attend and vote at the meeting agree to the short notice. In the case of a general meeting of a private company 90% of the members having a right to attend and vote at the meeting must consent and in the case of a general meeting of a public company 95% of the members having a right to attend and vote at the meeting must consent. [CA06 Secs 307(4), 337(2)]. The notice should state the time, place and date of the meeting and the general nature of the business to be transacted. For public companies' AGMs the notice must specify that it is an AGM. [CA06 Secs 311, 337(1)]. Traded companies must also include details of: the web site at which further information about the company is available; the voting record date; voting procedures; proxy appointments; electronic voting procedures; and the right to ask questions. [SI2009/1632]. Business ordinarily conducted at AGMs comprises: receiving or adopting the financial statements; declaring a dividend; appointing and reappointing directors; and reappointing auditors and fixing their remuneration.

8.254   More detailed information should be given in the notice of the proposals to be considered at the meeting if business other than ordinary business is to be placed before shareholders. In relation to the notice convening the AGM of a listed company, if business other than ordinary business (see para 8.253) is included, an explanatory circular must accompany the notice. The explanation may be included in the directors' report if it is to be considered at the AGM. Any circular should comply with content requirements of the UKLA's Listing Rule 13.3.1. [LR 13.8.9G].

8.255   The notice periods required to be given for meeting often cause confusion in practice. The notice periods for shareholders' meetings must be 'clear' days. This means that it is necessary to disregard both:

■   the date on which the notice is served or deemed to be served. Companies must consult their articles of association, but the notice period is usually 24 or 48 hours after posting; and

■   the date of the meeting itself.

8.256   The notice period rules work in the way illustrated in the table below.

	'24 hour' articles Day	'48 hour' articles Day
Notices despatched	1st	1st
Notices deemed to be received	2nd	3rd
First day of the notice period	3rd	4th
Twenty-first day of the notice period	23rd	24th
AGM can take place on or after	24th	25th

8.257   The Combined Code (2008) and the UK Corporate Governance Code recommend that AGM notices should be sent to shareholders at least 20 working days before the meeting. [CC 2006 D.2.4]. Refer to chapter 4 of this Manual for further details.

[The next paragraph is 8.259.]

Single member companies

8.259   Companies with only one member should comply with the usual formalities relating to meetings with the necessary modifications for a single member company. For instance, when the single member takes a decision, which is of the nature that may be taken by a company in general meeting, that member must provide the company with a written record of that decision. [CA06 Sec 357]. If the decision is taken by way of a written resolution, the resolution must be recorded in the same way as minutes of the proceedings of a general meeting (see para 8.275). [CA06 Sec 356].

[The next paragraph is 8.262.]

Class meetings

8.262   Where a company's share capital is divided into different classes of shares, meetings of the different classes have to be held where required by the Act, the company's articles or the shares' terms of issue. Class meetings are most frequently required when it is proposed to vary the rights attached to a particular class of shares. [CA06 Sec 334].

Resolutions

8.263   Resolutions of a private company may be passed as a written resolution or in a general meeting of the members. Resolutions of public companies must be passed in a meeting of the members. [CA06 Sec 281(1)(2)]. Section 281 of the 2006 Act states that where, the members or the articles of association do not specify the type of resolution required, an ordinary resolution is required. The 2006 Model Articles provide that a resolution is to be decided on a show of hands, unless a poll is demanded on or before the result of the show of hands is declared. The articles may not require the number of members required to demand a poll to be greater than five members entitled to vote at the meeting. [CA06 Sec 321]. The procedure for a poll is usually set out in the articles. [CA06 Sec 321]. On a poll, every member shall have one vote for each share he holds. [CA06 Sec 284].

8.263.1   Under section 341 of the 2006 Act, quoted companies have to disclose the results of all polls taken during a general meeting on their web site. The company must ensure that the following information is available on the web site: the date of the meeting; the text of the resolution or the subject matter of the poll; and the number of votes cast for and against the resolution. Traded companies must also state the percentage of the issued share capital represented by the votes for and against each resolution as well as the number of abstentions received.

8.263.2   In addition to the information set out in 8.263.1, traded companies must disclose the number of votes validly cast; the proportion of the issued share capital represented by those votes and the proportion of the issued share capital represented by the votes for and against a resolution.

8.264 Companies' articles of association frequently make it easier for shareholders to demand a poll by reducing the number of members or the proportion of shares below the maximum set out in section 321 of the 2006 Act. Also the articles must be consulted to see whether they specify such matters as:

- Format of proxy cards.

- Adjournment of meetings.

- The chairman's right to demand a poll.

- Provisions concerning where and when any validly demanded poll can be conducted and the results announced.

8.264.1 It should be noted that the Combined Code on corporate governance contains additional recommendations regarding proxy voting and proxy forms (see further chapter 4).

8.265 There are often circumstances where it would be advisable for companies to appoint independent scrutineers, for example, if a close result is expected or where perhaps the resolution is particularly contentious. In certain situations a scrutineers' report is required, for example, at meetings held at the request of a court. The scrutineers need not be the company's auditors, unless the company's articles say they should be, which is rare.

8.265.1 The 2006 Act gives members of a quoted company the right to require an independent report of any poll taken or to be taken at a general meeting. The minimum threshold for the demand is five per cent of the voting rights or 100 members each holding shares on which an average of £100 has been paid up. [CA06 Sec 342(2)]. The members request must be made within one week of the meeting at which the poll was taken. [CA06 Sec 343(2)].

8.265.2 The directors must appoint a person who meets the independence requirements set out in section 344 of the 2006 Act and has no other role in relation to the poll on which he is to report.

Ordinary resolutions

8.266 An ordinary resolution is defined in the 2006 Act as a resolution that is passed by a simple majority of the votes cast by those entitled to vote. [CA06 Sec 282(1)]. An ordinary resolution is passed as a written resolution, or in a meeting on a poll, if it is passed by members representing a simple majority of the total voting rights. It is passed on a show of hands if passed by a simple majority of members entitled to vote. The Act requires an ordinary resolution, for example, for the removal of a director from office (section 168 of the 2006 Act with special notice); to approve directors' service contracts for over two years (section 188(2) of the 2006 Act); to approve loans, quasi-loans and credit arrangements for directors and their connected persons (sections 197 to 203) and to approve substantial property transactions that the company enters into with its directors (section 190(1) of the 2006 Act).

[The next paragraph is 8.268.]

Special resolutions

8.268 A special resolution is required by the Act for certain important transactions, for instance, alteration of a company's objects or articles (section 21 of the 2006 Act), reduction of share capital (section 641(1) of the 2006 Act), and off-market purchase of its own shares (section 694(2) of the 2006 Act). A special resolution requires a majority of not less than three quarters of votes cast by those members entitled to vote. The notice period for a special resolution is the same as an ordinary resolution. A resolution is not passed as a special resolution unless the notice states that the proposed resolution is a special resolution. [CA06 Sec 283(3)(6)]. The intention to propose a resolution as a special resolution and the resolution itself must be given in the notice of the meeting. A copy of every special resolution must be sent to the Registrar of Companies within 15 days after it is passed. [CA06 Sec 30]. A copy of all such resolutions must also be attached to every copy of the articles subsequently issued.

[The next paragraph is 8.271.]

Written resolutions

8.271 Section 288 of the 2006 Act sets out a procedure whereby a private company may pass a written resolution in place of an ordinary or special resolution. A written resolution may be passed with the same majority as if it were an ordinary or special resolution proposed in a general meeting, that is, a simple majority for an ordinary resolution and by 75 per cent of the members entitled to vote for a special resolution. The effective date of the resolution is when the resolution is signed by or on behalf of the required majority of eligible members. [CA06 Sec 296(4)].

8.272 Under the 2006 Act written resolutions no longer have to be notified to the company's auditors, although the company's auditors are entitled to receive all communications relating to a written resolution as are required to be supplied to the members of a company. An appropriate record book of written resolutions (including the signatures) must be kept in the same way as minutes of general meetings. [CA06 Sec 355].

8.272.1 A copy of the proposed written resolution must be sent to every member eligible to vote on the resolution. The copy must be accompanied by a statement explaining how to signify approval and the date by which the resolution must be passed if it is not to lapse.

8.273 A written resolution may be proposed by either the directors or members of a company. A company is required to circulate a resolution from the members, within 21 days of the request, if the request is received from members representing at least 5 per cent of the voting rights. [CA06 Secs 292, 293.] The expenses of the circulation are to be met by the members who requested the resolution. [CA06 Sec 294]. A member signifies agreement to a proposed written resolution when the company receives an authenticated document identifying the resolution to which it relates and indicating agreement to the resolution. A proposed written resolution will lapse if it is not passed within the period specified for this purpose in the Articles or if none is specified a period of 28 days beginning with the circulation date. [CA06 Sec 297].

8.274 There are two situations where written resolutions cannot be used: to remove a director before the expiration of his period of office; and to remove an auditor before the expiration of his term of office. [CA06 Sec 288(2)].

Records of meetings

8.275 The Act requires companies to keep records comprising copies of all resolutions passed otherwise than at a general meeting, minutes of all proceedings of a company's general meetings, meetings of its directors and managers to be entered into books kept for that purpose and provides for penalties on default. [CA06 Secs 248, 355]. The 2006 Act states that these records should be kept for a minimum of ten years. Where minutes have been kept and have been signed by the chairman of the meeting or the next succeeding meeting they are evidence of those proceedings. Once those minutes have been signed, if any mistakes are found in them they should be rectified only by a further minute passed at a subsequent meeting.

8.276 The books containing the records of resolutions passed otherwise than at a general meeting and minutes of the proceedings of general meeting must be open to inspection by members at the registered office or at the SAIL (see para 8.37). A company must make such resolutions available for inspection on a day which has been specified by the person wishing to inspect the records so long as that day is a working day and the required notice has been given. The records of a private company will then be available for inspection for a period of at least two hours from the start of the period requested by the inspector. A public company must make its company records available for inspection for at least two hours between 9am and 5pm on each working day (S1 2008/3006 'The Companies (Company Records) Regulations 2008'). A member is entitled on payment of the prescribed fee to be provided with a copy of any such minutes within fourteen days of his request. Failure to do so by the company and any officer is an offence. In addition, the Court may compel immediate inspection. [CA06 Sec 358]. The place where minute books can be kept is dealt with in more detail in paragraph 8.37 above.

Index

Locators are:

  paragraph numbers: 11.149, for Chapter 11, paragraph 149

Entries are in word-by-word alphabetical order, where a group of letters followed by a space is filed before the same group of letters followed by a letter, eg 'capital structure and treasury policy' will appear before 'capitalisation'. In determining alphabetical arrangement, initial articles, conjunctions and small prepositions are ignored.

Index

Index

Index

Index

capital redemption, and, 7.106.1—7.106.4
capital reduction, and, 7.129.1
checklists, 7.Annex
closed periods, during, 7.114—7.114.2
conditions, 7.13—7.13.1
consent of priority shareholders, 7.25
consideration, 7.14—7.15
contingent purchase contracts, 7.89—7.90
contracts, 7.83—7.85
contravention, 7.139—7.142
directors' report, and
  generally, 3.75—3.76
  introduction, 7.42—7.43
  listed companies, 3.77—3.78
disclosure requirements
  directors' reports, 7.42—7.43
  introduction, 7.41
  Listing Rules, under, 7.129
  notes to financial statements, 7.46—7.46.2
discount from proceeds of new issue, at
  accounting requirements, 7.40
  generally, 7.17—7.18
distributable profits, from
  accounting requirements, 7.27—7.30
  charging purchase cost, 7.29—7.29.2
  expenses of acquisition, 7.30
  generally, 7.17—7.18
effect, 7.26
failure to acquire, 7.109—7.111
financial assistance for
  definition, 7.132.1
  effect of contravention, 7.141—7.144
  private companies, by, 7.132.2—7.132.4
  public companies, by, 7.133—7.138
funding requirements
  assignment of rights, 7.87—7.88
  capital maintenance, 7.22
  distributable profits, 7.17—7.18
  introduction, 7.16
  payment out of capital, 7.19—7.20
  proceeds of new issue, 7.17—7.18
  summary, 7.21
initial considerations, 7.12
insider dealing
  generally, 7.81—7.81.2
  legal procedures, 7.114.3
institutional shareholders, and, 7.131—7.132
introduction, 7.1—7.4.1
legal procedures
  acquisitions from capital, 7.93—7.106
  assignment of rights, 7.87—7.88
  contingent purchase contracts, 7.89—7.90
  contracts, 7.83—7.85
  definition of off-market', 7.64—7.67
  insider dealing, 7.81—7.81.2
  introduction, 7.63—7.63.1
  notices, 7.82—7.86
  off-market', 7.64—7.67
  private company purchases, 7.78.1—7.80
  public company purchases, 7.68—7.78
  returns, 7.82—7.86
legal procedures for public company purchase
  authority for market purchase, 7.69—7.71
  authority for off-market purchase, 7.72—7.77
  introduction, 7.68
  variation of existing contract, 7.78
Listing Rules, under
  accounting requirements, 7.114.4
  closed periods, during, 7.114—7.114.2
  insider trading, 7.114.3
  introduction, 7.112—7.113

market abuse, 7.114.3
prohibited periods, during, 7.114—7.114.2
purchase from related parties, 7.115
purchase of equity shares, 7.116—7.121
purchase of non-equity shares, 7.122—7.126
redemption of redeemable shares, 7.129
Treasury shares, 7.126.1—7.126.3
Major Shareholding Notification Rules, 7.130
market abuse, 7.114.3
notes to financial statements
  IFRS, 7.46.2
  UK GAAP, 7.46—7.46.1
payment out of capital, by
  accounting requirements, 7.47—7.62
  available profits, 7.50—7.54
  capital maintenance, 7.55—7.62
  generally, 7.19—7.20
  legal procedures, 7.93—7.106
  liability on winding up, 7.107—7.108
  no available profits, 7.54.1—7.54.2
  nominal value less than PCP and proceeds of fresh
    issue, 7.59—7.62
  permissible capital payment, 7.49—7.54.2
  shares to be purchased at a premium in excess of
    the original premium, 7.62.1
  transfer to capital redemption reserve, 7.56—7.58
premium from proceeds of new issue, at
  accounting requirements, 7.32—7.34
  generally, 7.17—7.18
private company purchases, 7.78.1—7.80
prohibited periods, during, 7.114—7.114.2
public company purchases, 7.68—7.78
purchase from related parties, 7.115
purchase of equity shares, 7.116—7.121
purchase of non-equity shares, 7.122—7.126
redeemable shares, 7.8—7.11
redemption of redeemable shares
  generally, 7.129
  legal procedures, 7.91—7.92
reduction of share capital, by
  accounting requirements, 7.47—7.62
  available profits, 7.50—7.54
  capital maintenance, 7.55—7.62
  generally, 7.19—7.20
  legal procedures, 7.93—7.106
  liability on winding up, 7.107—7.108
  no available profits, 7.54.1—7.54.2
  nominal value less than PCP and proceeds of fresh
    issue, 7.59—7.62
  permissible capital payment, 7.49—7.54.2
  shares to be purchased at a premium in excess of
    the original premium, 7.62.1
  transfer to capital redemption reserve, 7.56—7.58
regulatory requirements
  institutional shareholders, of, 7.131—7.132
  Listing Rules, under, 7.112—7.129
  Major Shareholding Notification Rules, 7.130
requirements
  accounting requirements, 7.16—7.20
  cancellation of shares, 7.23
  conditions, 7.13—7.13.1
  consent of priority shareholders, 7.25
  consideration, 7.14—7.15
  funding requirements, 7.16—7.22
  initial considerations, 7.12
  introduction, 7.5—7.6
  redeemable shares, 7.8—7.11
returns, 7.82—7.86
Treasury shares
  accounting treatment, 7.111.18
  cancellation, 7.111.12—7.111.14

Index

Index